Woodlot
and
Ballot Box

Woodlot
and
Ballot Box

*Marathon County in
the Twentieth Century*

Howard R. Klueter
James J. Lorence

Printed by
Worzalla Publishing Company
Stevens Point, Wisconsin

TABLE OF CONTENTS

Preface and Acknowledgements

This study attempts to fill a notable void in the literature of central Wisconsin history. Since the pioneering work of Judge Louis Marchetti in 1912, there has been no serious effort to record the historical development of the region's most populous heartland county. Hence, it was natural that, in the nation's Bicentennial year, Marathon County citizens should turn to a reexamination of their historical roots. The present volume is the result of their efforts.

The project originated in the Heritage Subcommittee of the larger Marathon County Bicentennial Committee. Conceived as a part of an extensive "Marathon County Heritage Program," this book represents the combined labor of many citizens, groups, and institutions. As in any such undertaking, our debts are many. We here acknowledge the contributions of some of those whose aid has been most valuable.

Our financial obligations are numerous: to the Marathon County Board of Supervisors for the generous appropriation that gave us our start; to Employers Insurance of Wausau for its continuing support from the project's earliest stages; to the American Revolution Bicentennial Administration and the Wisconsin American Revolution Bicentennial Commission for a grant that financed early research; to the University of Wisconsin Center System for providing one of the authors precious time for his work; to the Thomas H. Jacob Foundation, Inc., Alexander Properties, Inc., Murco Foundation, J. C. Sturtevant Foundation, Hagge Foundation. and D. C. Everest Foundation for their institutional support; to Mrs. George Foster, Mr. & Mrs. D. Dunbar Schuetz, Mr. & Mrs. Ronald Westgate, the Kiwanis Club of Wausau, and the *Daily Herald* for their contributions; and to the University of Wisconsin Center-Marathon County and the Marathon County Historical Society for physical facilities and helpful cooperation at all stages of the program.

Vital to our work was the assistance of the staffs at the libraries used in our research, including the Wisconsin Historical Society in Madison, University of Wisconsin Center-Marathon County, Marathon

County Historical Society, Marathon County Public Library, Milwaukee County Historical Society, Legislative Reference Bureau and Forest Products Library, both in Madison; Steenbock Memorial Library, Geology Library and Memorial Library, all at the University of Wisconsin-Madison; and the Area Research Center at the University of Wisconsin-Stevens Point. Particularly helpful were: John Schmitt, Judy Strebig, Gary Gisselman, Beth Drees, Debra Grasso, and Jean Swenson. Others who provided research assistance included: John Cline of Wausau, Adrienne Dabroski of the Marathon County Health Department, Scotty Walters of the Wisconsin Statistical Reporting Service in Madison, and the personnel at the Wausau Area Chamber of Commerce and the Marathon County Highway and Park Departments. Grateful acknowledgement is due Tom Topinka for his original photographic work in "The Journey."

We are also indebted to the historians James McHale of Lily, Stanley Mallach of Milwaukee, and Steven Karges at the University of Wisconsin-Madison for sharing their professional expertise with us at various stages of our work; equally valuable advice was given by George Johnson, William Smiley, III, and Ann Stevens, who commented on portions of earlier drafts. In addition, technical and clerical assistance was provided by Debra Sommi, Ann Landes, Catherine Weitzman, Sally Paul, and Shirley Niemeyer, whose competence made the mechanical aspects of our task less burdensome.

A special note of thanks is due Edward Schoenberger, Gerald Viste, Raymond Ott, and William R. Peters, whose enthusiastic support was vital to the completion of the project. Their encouragement aided in the solution of the problems encountered early in our work.

Especially dedicated to the effort was Linda Thornburg of the Marathon County Historical Society. Always an energetic and capable research assistant, her work with primary sources contributed significantly to the task of gathering the necessary information for large portions of the book. Equally valuable was her role in organizing the material for an early draft of Chapter IV. Her many talents are reflected in various phases of our study.

Perhaps the single most important contributor to the volume in its final form was our project editor, Associate Prof. Linda Ware of the University of Wisconsin Center-Marathon County. Prof. Ware's sensitive criticism has brought the study an order and structure absent in our early work. Our professional interaction, not always harmonious but invariably lively, has resulted in needed alterations; it is a tribute to her wit and candor that change has been so painless.

And finally, we acknowledge our greatest debt: to Donna, wife and friend, whose patience and support have sustained us from the beginning.

H. R. K.

J. J. L.

February, 1977

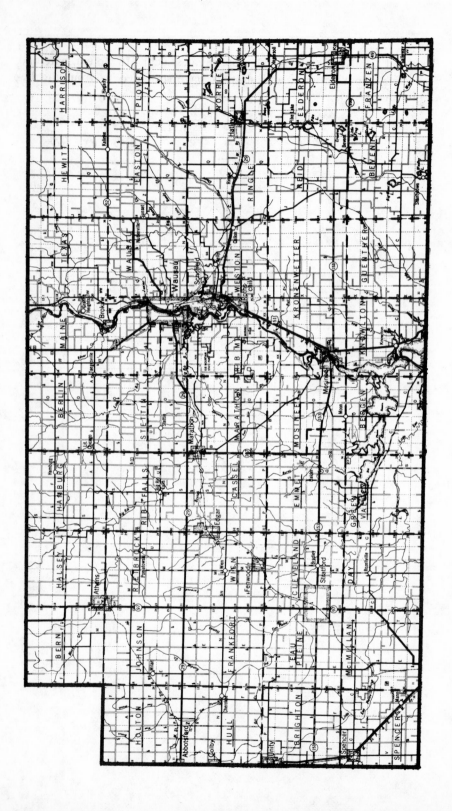

The Journey

The journey says as much about the county as the destination. It begins in the quiet residential neighborhoods of the county's largest city, Wausau. The homes, neatly spaced, are neither exceptionally large nor particularly small: they provide examples of both past and contemporary architectural design. Unlike many of the more recent enclaves known as suburbia, a sense of the past, of historical roots in both the literal and figurative sense, is pervasive. The neighborhoods, carved out of hardwood stands of aspen, birch, maple, and elm, have a pleasing aesthetic appeal and remind the traveler of this region's forest heritage. The tree-lined streets are simply numbered, or named for the founding fathers of both the country and county. Another feature of the landscape serves to differentiate these neighborhoods from newer suburban communities. Just beyond the wooded hills, the equivalent of only a few city blocks away, one can find horse ranches and dairy farms—parallel reminders of agriculture's contribution to the county's economic coming of age in the twentieth century.

One particular building and street stand out as one nears the city's downtown business district. Occupying one whole block, surrounded by comfortable shaded residences, is the red brick building which has housed the city's first, and until 1970, its only public high school since just before the turn of the century.[1] A frequent recipient of state-wide and even national recognition for both academic and athletic achievements during its seventy-eight years, this institution represents more than any other structure in the county the attempt of its people to grow, and improve, and thus ensure the vitality of the 1,586 square miles in north-central Wisconsin known as Marathon County. Traveling only one block south from the high school, one comes to perhaps the most significant street in the county's twentieth century industrial development: McIndoe Street, named for Walter D. McIndoe, the pioneer lumberman who more than any other man could be termed the father of the county.[2] Turning right and traveling west toward the central business district, one passes by the homes which once belonged to the county's twentieth century industrial entrepreneurs, men such as Ross, Yawkey, Winton, Woodson, and Everest, whose foresight and business ventures led to the area's successful transition into the post-lumber era of Wisconsin economic history, men whose stories will be told in subsequent chapters of this book.

Writing at the turn of the century, a local chronicler said of Wausau:

> The city enjoys a splendid retail trade, and this ac-
> counts for the finely furnished and well-stocked stores.
> . . . The average volume of local trade is much larger
> than in most cities of equal or even greater size. This
> is in a measure accounted for by the fact that a large
> area of rich agricultural country is exclusively tri-
> butary to the market and because trade is attracted
> from a considerable distance . . . The promises are
> that Wausau will in time become the greatest trade
> center in Northwestern Wisconsin.[3]

More than seventy years later, these observations have held up and the enthusiastic prediction largely borne out. By 1972, the "far away" city housed 98 wholesale establishments and 477 retail establishments, with sales totaling $119,647,000.[4] The essential character of that central business district, however, has undergone substantial change since that earlier portrait was sketched; for better or worse, depending on one's point of view, downtown Wausau has kept up with the times. The observer, approaching the downtown area, sees stores which are often local branches of large national retail chains. Yet enough locally owned and controlled small businesses remain to call the imagination back to the city's formative years, when there was still relatively little of the business phenomenon known as 'the diffusion of decision-making power.'[5] Traveling down the main street of the city's central business district, one can see graphic evidence of an easy blending of America's economic past and present. Within a mere four blocks of each other on Third Street, standing like opposite poles of the county's economic history, are Wausau's oldest currently operating manufacturer, Murray Machinery,[6] and its newest commercial enterprise, The First American National Bank complex which opened on December 29, 1975, owned by a syndicate of nationally known sports and show business personalities.[7]

The reminders of this area's heritage do not end as one leaves the city's downtown, however. Where the Wisconsin River is crossed by the Scott Street bridge, three landmarks compete for attention. The intersection of Scott and Washington Streets overlooks the former site of the once mighty water power known as Big Bull Falls, now dammed for electric power for the city. Just a few yards south of that intersection stands a small granite monument, encircled by shrubbery, marking the location where, in 1839, pioneer lumberman George Stevens established the first "permanent white settlement" in the county. Then, with a glance directed only a little further south, one can see the former Chicago and Northwestern Railroad depot—the little railroad station which has been witness to a major share of this county's twentieth century history ever since its construction in 1899: the travels of thousands of residents and visitors alike, the several departures of this region's famed military unit Company G, and the arrival on August 15, 1928, of an incumbent U.S. President. Since it was chosen in 1954 to serve as part of the trademark of a local insurance company in its national advertising, this station has done more than any other single institution or individual to identify this area in the national mind.[8]

The nostalgia created by these two landmarks of the region's historical tradition is pleasant but short-lived, however; once on the west side of the river, it is again apparent just how far this city has come into the twentieth century. The economic forces that have been at work on urban landscapes throughout the country since the end of World War II have not passed Wausau by. The factories, which in earlier decades confronted the west side streets "as candidly as the underwear hanging from the clothesline," (to use the phrase of a past Wausau historian) have largely given way to structures representative of more recent national economic trends. To take the most prominent example: at the corner of Stewart Avenue (formerly Clinton Street) and First Avenue on the west bank of the Wisconsin River for 82 years stood a showcase of the city's thriving wood products industry, the Curtis & Yale Company's Plant No. 1. Since 1963, a shopping center, perhaps the pre-eminent symbol of postwar American life, has resided there. If one were to detour several blocks north on First Avenue to see the Pied Piper Shoe Company building—a familiar feature of Wausau's industrial landscape since 1916—one would now find a wholesale air conditioning distributorship and a thrift shop.

But historical continuity and change can and do blend in these neighborhoods. Continuing west on the avenue named for lumberman-entrepreneur-politician Alexander Stewart (whose contributions to the growth of the county spanned portions of two centuries), one comes upon the site of the former County Normal School building. Constructed in 1902, the structure stood for more than forty years as a symbol of the county's commitment to education for its rural youth.

In 1976, although the building itself has long since disappeared, the same spirit that prompted its construction lives on: the location is now the home of the first of the two-year campuses of the University of Wisconsin. When one arrives only four blocks further at the newest of the city's two middle schools, one senses that this region's commitment to learning, symbolized by these two educational institutions, stands as solidly as the adjacent seventy-eight acres of pine in Marathon Park.

Having finally reached the western outskirts of the city, one's final images of Wausau while traveling west on Highway 29 are two symbols of protection, one the result of strictly human ingenuity, the other owing its existence to the earliest plans of nature. To the north stands the gleaming white complex which has housed Employers Insurance of Wausau since its construction in the mid-1960's—a company which has been an important partner in this area's twentieth century business growth, and which, for that matter, has had an impact on economies beyond the borders of Marathon County and the state. To the southwest, resembling a long, rising wall of uptilted wilderness, stands one of the state's highest elevations, Rib Mountain. Rising 1,940 feet above sea level and looming some 800 feet above the Wisconsin River along its eastern edge, the wooded slopes of quartzite rock have contrasted stolidly with the human efforts beneath them to bring stability and permanence out of the surrounding countryside.

Once outside the city limits on the west side of Wausau, one sees that business and industry—represented by the firms which have located in this 150 acre tract designated for industry—are still the predominant features of the landscape. Several farm implement dealerships are the only real hint of the approaching rural heartland. Yet, in this border zone between urban and rural regions is a remnant of a past gone well before even the early years of the twentieth century. Barely two miles west of the 160,000 square foot packaging plant which in 1968 chose to build in the newly created industrial park is a preserve where a herd of buffalo move and graze. This juxtaposition of American present and past in the countryside reinforces the impression that balance and diversity have indeed characterized Marathon County's history.

Continuing west on Highway 29 through a series of wooded hills, as if on a blacktop rollercoaster, one sees cleared fields and barns emerge from the far hills to the south and along the roadside to the north. Yet, a glance in the direction of the south at Highway 107 reveals not only an agricultural landscape, but also the hillside com-

The First American Center

Marathon City

munity of Marathon City, highlighted by the twin steeples of the red brick St. Mary's Catholic Church, a geographic and spiritual center of the village since 1875. It is not until one crosses the Rib River, approximately ten and one-half miles from Wausau, that the agricultural character of the county becomes predominant. Barns and silos and farm land spread around isolated stands of forest in the distant background. The power poles lining the left hand side of the road and the telephone poles on the right are the closest signs of the technology which has come to farm life here over the course of the twentieth century. But the county trunk highway which runs north to Rib Falls brings the forest stands again up to the roadside, and then suddenly forest and farm land alternate on the immediate landscape, as they did in the transitions of early twentieth century economic history. After several miles of this contrasting scenery one reaches the durable rural institution, the tavern, where a right turn leads to the journey's ultimate destination.

Traveling north along the now-gravel road through the township named for lumberman, colonizer, and lawyer Frederick Rietbrock,[9] the paramount position occupied by this county in Wisconsin agriculture for much of the twentieth century can for perhaps the first time be fully understood. Farms stretch to the horizon on all sides. However, the diversity of this journey soon surfaces again. Almost before realizing that the town road has given way to a paved county trunk highway, one suddenly finds himself entering a hamlet named in 1880 for the Polish prince and military hero of the late eighteenth and early nineteenth centuries, Joseph Poniatowski. Even a quick survey of its main street yields an awareness of the currents of history quietly reflected in this region. The red brick church to the east with the faded Polish script at the base of its steeple speaks of the importance of religion to the county immigrants and their descendants as they struggled throughout the twentieth century to find sustenance in the soil. The Gesicki general store re-creates those earlier days when the residents purchased at one location, often after a long and exhausting trip, the basic necessities and few affordable luxuries of life. The old gasoline pumps in front recall the first automobiles in the county and the changes they brought to economic, social, and even political life.

These impressions remain upon stopping at the intersection which forms Poniatowski's southern boundary, where a turn to the left is made on the county trunk. After continuing west for a half mile through more farm land, another right turn and only a quarter of a

"The Center"

mile north, one arrives at the final destination of this twenty mile journey through Marathon County. A few yards back from the road stands a geological marker. Flanked on either side by neatly trimmed shrubbery, with a forest grove to its left and an open field beyond, the rectangular wood marker on two thick wooden posts announces,

> THIS SPOT IN SECTION 14, IN THE TOWN OF RIETBROCK, MARATHON COUNTY, IS THE EXACT CENTER OF THE NORTHERN HALF OF THE WESTERN HEMISPHERE. IT IS HERE THAT THE 90TH MERIDIAN OF LONGITUDE BISECTS THE 45TH PARALLEL OF LATITUDE, MEANING IT IS EXACTLY HALF WAY BETWEEN THE NORTH POLE AND THE EQUATOR, AND IS A QUARTER OF THE WAY AROUND THE EARTH FROM GREENWICH, ENGLAND.[10]

While no cosmic significance emerges from this geographic fact, it is nevertheless satisfying to find this particular spot here in Marathon County, Wisconsin. The journey has showed this to be an area with a sense of past roots underlying the present beginnings—a diversity and a balance good to find in a region with such an idiosyncratic geographic location. It is a region that throughout the twentieth century has been at the center of things, at least for its inhabitants. It is a county whose

8

activities, whether economic, social, or political, have occasionally had impact beyond its boundaries. Conversely, it has not been immune to twentieth century trends and influences outside its borders, whether state-wide or national in scope and character. This, then, is the tale that will be told in the following pages: in short, the story of the people of this American county in north-central Wisconsin during the course of the twentieth century, and the story of the social, economic and political growth they made possible in their time.

FOOTNOTES

[1] The early history of the high school building gives ample testimony to the region's substantial twentieth century growth. When the original unit was erected in 1898 at a cost of $65,000 with a subsequent enrollment of 183, there was criticism that it was much larger than would ever be needed; even the structure's advocates forecast 1950 as the year when a sufficiently large attendance would justify its then present size. The extreme overcrowding brought about by a more than quadrupling of the enrollment in just thirty years, however, clearly exposed the wishful thinking of both sides. When the addition of a two-room barracks in the fall of 1921, and the removal of freshmen to the Central School Junior High School in 1924 failed to provide sufficient relief, a new plant was finally constructed in 1936 at a cost of $265,000. Even this soon proved inadequate, however, and the subsequent decades saw mounting agitation for further expansions, and eventually for new additional high schools. See *Wausau Daily Record-Herald, Wausau Golden Anniversary Edition,* August 9, 1922, Section 3, p. 6. *Wausau Daily Record-Herald, Centennial Edition,* March 13, 1939, Historical Section, p. 60.

[2] After his election to the Wisconsin Assembly as a Whig in 1849, McIndoe introduced and secured passage of a bill to detach territory from Portage County and create a new county which he subsequently named "Marathon." By provision of the enacted legislation, the new county was organized in the spring of 1850. For a glowing tribute to McIndoe and his activities, see Louis Marchetti, *History Of Marathon County And Representative Citizens* (Chicago: Richmond-Arnold Publishing Co., 1913), pp. 78-81, 582-588. See also *Wausau Pilot,* February 11, 1926, p. 3.

[3] George Alfred Martin (comp.), "Wausau in 1900," Illustrated Holiday Supplement to *Central Wisconsin; Wausau Herald; Wausau Pilot,* December 25, 1900, p. 5.

[4] When Schofield and Rothschild are included, the figures climb to 561 establishments with sales of $135,800,000. Marathon County as a whole by 1972 housed 999 retail establishments with sales totaling $194,974,000. Of the Wisconsin cities that could be classified as potential trade centers for "Northwestern Wisconsin," only Eau Claire as of 1972 had a greater number of retail establishments and a higher dollar volume of sales. In fact, of the twenty-three northern Wisconsin counties, besides Marathon, which Arlan Helgeson classifies as the Wisconsin Cutover region, the city of Wausau alone had a greater number of retail establishments than seventeen: Bayfield, Ashland, Iron, Vilas, Forest, Florence, Oconto, Clark, Polk, Burnett, Washburn, Sawyer, Price, Taylor, Lincoln, and Langlade; and equalled the number within two others: Shawano and Barron. Only four of the Cutover counties: Douglas, Marinette, Chippewa, and Oneida had more retail establishments than Wausau; the latter, however, had a higher retail dollar sales volume than all twenty-three counties. Marathon County, as a whole, led all the Cutover counties by a wide margin in terms of both the number of retail establishments and the dollar volume of retail sales, Chippewa County coming closest in the former with 571 and Ashland County in the latter with $91,241,000. See U.S. Bureau of the Census, *Census of Retail Trade, 1972, Area Statistics, Wisconsin,* RC 72-A-50. pp. 64-70.

In terms of wholesale trade, of the potential "Northwestern Wisconsin" trade centers, again, only Eau Claire as of 1972 had a greater number of establishments than did Wausau, while the latter possessed a greater number of wholesale business concerns than did all twenty-three other Cutover counties. Unfortunately, no similar comparison of sales is possible since the figures for the city of Wausau, and Burnett and Florence Counties were withheld to avoid disclosure; however, Marathon County as a whole, with its 208 wholesale establishments reporting sales of $169,128,000, led twenty of the twenty-one reporting Cutover counties in that category with only Douglas County having a higher dollar sales volume. See U.S. Bureau of the Census, *Census of Wholesale Trade, 1972, Area Statistics, Wisconsin,* WC 72-A-50, pp. 17-19.

[5] In 1900 fully one-third of the manufactured products in the United States were made by partnerships and individual proprietorships. See Frederick Lewis Allen, *The Big Change, American Transforms Itself 1900-1950.* (New York: Harper & Row, Perennial Library, 1969), p. 62.

[6] The D. J. Murray Manufacturing Company was already nineteen years old as the twentieth century dawned in Marathon County, and at that time was described thus: "The D. J. Murray Manufacturing Company enjoys the proud distinction of being the largest foundry and machine shop in the Northwest, and also . . . makes every piece or part of machinery used about a saw mill. . . ." See Martin, pp. 32-33. The story of the firm's subsequent response to the changing economic realities taking place in northern Wisconsin will be detailed in a later chapter.

[7] The site on which the new First American Center is located — on the corner of Third and Scott Streets — is one of the most historic in the city. When the Marathon County Bank building was constructed on the site in 1892, it marked the first solid brick structure to be built in Wausau; the bank's location was henceforth known as "Store No. 1, Opera Block." That building also served as one of the first home offices of the newly organized Employers Mutuals Insurance Company in 1911-1912. Much fanfare accompanied the construction and opening of the new more than half million dollar First American National Bank building on the corner on March 28, 1926. Housing, in addition, the offices of lawyers, doctors, dentists, insurance agencies, and business consultants, the eight-story structure served as a focal point on the Wausau skyline for the next half century, finally being razed in early 1976 to make room for the First American Center — a model financial institution of the 1970's, occupying the entire city block bounded by Third, Scott, Fourth, and McClellan Streets. See *Wausau Pilot,* May 27, 1926, pp. 1, 12. *Wausau-Merrill Daily Herald,* January 7, 1976, p. 3.

[8] The station depicted in the advertisements of Employers Insurance is, in reality, a composite of Wausau's two railway stations: the skyline behind the Northwestern depot and the Milwaukee Road station located on Grant Street on the city's east side. The former was converted in 1965 into a popular Oriental restaurant; the latter as of 1976 serves its parent railroad as an office building.

[9] Frederick Rietbrock's sizable contributions to the advancement of agriculture in northwestern Marathon County in the first years of the twentieth century will be detailed in a later chapter.

[10] The .14 acre of land on which the marker stands, constituting the smallest park in Marathon County, was donated to the county at a cost of one dollar by Mr. and Mrs. Ervin Wisnewski on July 15, 1968. This tiny piece of land in the Town of Rietbrock is only one of several distinctive features of the county's geography and geology. A study of the rock formations below the surface of the earth revealed that the site of the city of Wausau was part of the first dry land ever to appear, and that the district around the city roughly outlined by Brokaw, Nutterville, Kelly, Mosinee, Hardwood Hill, and Taegeville contains the next oldest rocks in geological history. This land, according to state geologist, W. O. Hotchkiss, dates back approximately 160 million years.

Moreover, Wausau and the region south of the city escaped the glaciers that came down from Canada, depositing millions of tons of glacial drift in Wisconsin and gouging out thousands of lake bottoms. The rest of the county was not as fortunate, however. Geologists have discovered terminal moraines of the first, second, and third glacial drifts in many sections of the county. The third ice sheet came as far south as Granite Heights and within a mile of Wausau on the west side of the city. Its moraine runs west as far as Rib Falls where it meets the eastern edge of the first glacial drift which runs almost directly south to Wisconsin Rapids. Traveling east from Wausau on Highway 29, the edge of the second glacial drift can be seen running north and south just beyond Ringle. See *Wausau Daily Record-Herald, Centennial Edition*, June 30, 1972, p. 35.

PART I
Out of the Woods

CHAPTER ONE

Lumbering In Marathon County: A King Dethroned

Nothing in nature has been more intimately associated with the history of Wisconsin than the tree. The story of the state's economic development could in large measure be told by the story of the use of its forests. Although timber originally covered six-sevenths of its land area, the true forest area of Wisconsin lay approximately in the northern three-fifths of the state. A huge virgin forest dominated by pine lay north of a line drawn roughly southwest from Manitowoc to Portage and then northwest to the fall line of the St. Croix River. A seemingly insatiable demand for pine lumber from the prairies of Illinois and westward tempted the early lumbermen of the nineteenth century north into this region, where nine great river systems penetrated forests of nearly 130 billion feet of pine.[1] The largest of them, draining an area which contained close to one-fourth of all the pine in the state, was the Wisconsin River; and at the heart of this plentiful forest was the land area that became Marathon County. Here along the banks of the Wisconsin and its tributaries stood the monarch of this forest kingdom, the white pine. Then, stretching back more than a mile from these river banks, were a variety of hardwoods: ash, basswood, birch, elm, maple, oak; along with hemlock and more pine: now Norway and jackpine as well as white. This admixture created a forest cover so dense that it was claimed that there were some areas where the rays of the sun never pierced through the branches. If Wisconsin was indeed once an "empire in pine," to use the phrase of Robert Fries, then certainly the area which would come to be known as Marathon County had to be one of the showcases of that empire.

The rich potential afforded by this standing timber, the adjacent rivers, and the growing western markets was not long in finding exploiters. Five years after Daniel Whitney openly constructed the first sawmill on the Wisconsin River near Point Baussee (Nekoosa) in 1832,[2] an adventurous lumberman from the state of New York, Robert Wakely, came into this portion of the river valley to learn where the Wisconsin River headed. In the course of his excursion northward, after leaving Shaw Rapids (Stevens Point), Wakely first encountered the thick timbered country alluded to earlier. He continued north, past Big Bull Falls (Wausau) for an additional twenty-four miles until he reached Grandfather Bull Falls. Observing the region's abundant water powers, Wakely became excited about the profitable opportunities this area offered someone with enterprise and sufficient financial backing. With this optimism, he set off for the center of the American lumber industry, St. Louis, to find a receptive ear for his story of the marvelous economic possibilities of north-central Wisconsin.

Robert Wakely would not be disappointed. The curious paradox of promise and despair so often present in economic affairs was by the late 1830's firmly entrenched in the American lumber industry. Clear pine lumber was bringing forty dollars to fifty dollars a thousand feet. Moreover, the timber barons had by this time thoroughly exhausted most of the standing timber along the Mississippi River. Thus, the lumbermen gathered in St. Louis listened intently to Wakely's description of the dense forests and great water powers he had encountered in his travels up the Wisconsin. One, in particular, listened with keen interest. A native of Almond, New York, George Stevens was a familiar figure in St. Louis lumber circles. For many years he had rafted his lumber down the Alleghany and Ohio Rivers to St. Louis. However, by the conclusion of his most recent trip to that city in 1838, George Stevens was a broken and despondent man. Several business reverses had put his personal financial situation in serious straits; his physical health had also suffered a series of setbacks. Already in a pessimistic frame of mind, Stevens was at first frankly skeptical of his fellow New Yorker's enthusiastic claims. Yet, he reasoned, a trip to northern Wisconsin might at least help his health, if not retrieve his financial condition. Accordingly, this man 'of giant frame and middle age, tired of society and eager for adventure and exploration'[3] agreed to serve as the advance agent of the St. Louis timber interests. That same year he set off alone to explore the upper reaches of the Wisconsin River valley.[4]

The details of George Stevens' travels before reaching Marathon County have been ably recounted elsewhere[5] and need not concern us here. When he arrived at the region that had so impressed Robert Wakely, he saw that his friend's enthusiastic description of the mixed pine and hardwood forests and convenient water powers had been no exaggeration. In fact, he felt Wakely had not done the primitive country justice. After an investigation of the territory around Big Bull Falls, the pioneer returned to his home in New York and secured a claim to two lots of land on the east and west sides of the Wisconsin totaling roughly seventy acres.[6] He then turned this choice property over to the three St. Louis entrepreneurs who had financed his expedition, thereby satisfying whatever claim they may have had on him.

Having begun to free himself from both financial obligation and ill health, Stevens resolved to return to the forests of northern Wisconsin and build a sawmill at Big Bull Falls. He moved his family to Belvidere, Illinois, hired a young millwright from that city as an assistant, and, with two ox teams and a teamster, set off in 1839 on a second arduous journey into the heart of the Wisconsin River pinery. After moving provisions and equipment from Portage to Shaw Rapids and finally to Big Bull Falls, Stevens and his crew began to construct the planned mill and the supplemental series of dams and the guardlock needed to harness the area's water powers.

This was no easy task, however. As in all newly opened forests, old windfalls, swamps, and pot holes made internal travel extremely difficult. Moreover, Stevens was plagued by various personnel problems. In a letter to one of his St. Louis financial backers, the harried explorer complained of the shortage of available labor despite a relatively high wage: "Hands are very scarce and wages $25.00 per month and impossible to get half as many as we need at that. . . . I hope you have sent me . . . a carpenter. . . . Kline might have worked for me at $3.00 per day but I could not get him."[7] Those workers that he did have were not always satisfactory: ". . . my millwrights disappointing me is worse than all the rest."[8]

Nonetheless, Stevens and his crew eventually completed work on the dams, the guardlock, a bridge, and the sawmill. Looking out over all he had built on the river by the fall of 1839 and over the surrounding timber, Stevens was optimistic. He wrote on September 28, 1839:

> It is decidedly the best mill site I ever saw or heard
> of in the union, and being the head of navigation and
> the timber much better above than below, and thirty
> miles of handsome river to float logs down, and the
> timber in many places standing on the bank, can be
> felled and rolled in without a team. A lumberman
> who went some sixteen miles above, exploring the
> pinery, about two weeks ago, declared he could stock
> a double mill for three years without any team at all.[9]

George Stevens had no doubts about the rich potential of this region and the prominent role it would come to play in the future of the Wisconsin lumber industry.

While the initial output of the Stevens mill was not large, its construction symbolized the major trend taking place in the Wisconsin economy at that time. In the years following the Panic of 1837, although business throughout the country was severely depressed, the upper Wisconsin region enjoyed a substantial boom due to both its pine resources and its accessibility to older, established settlements. So swift was the exodus to the Wisconsin River forests that only one year after George Stevens began his lumbering operation at Big Bull Falls, almost every suitable millsite on the upper river had been taken, totaling twenty-four in all, running forty-five saws by 1847. With this activity in the Wisconsin River pinery leading the way, the lumber trade finally superseded the fur trade and lead mining as the chief commercial enterprise in the territory. A business depression in the Eastern pineries after 1850, along with the gradual exhaustion of the timber in the older lumbering areas, provided yet another movement of capital and manpower westward, and for the next several decades the sights and sounds of logging typified the economic adventure unfolding in the forests of Marathon County and the rest of northern Wisconsin.[10]

There were great opportunities to be found in the woods in the early logging days. Yet, despite the romanticism which came to surround the life of the logger and lumberman, making a living in the forests of northern Wisconsin was often a hard and hazardous existence. Transportation, for instance, was one of the major problems facing the first county lumbermen. Until 1845, no roads were laid out in that section of the pinery. Foodstuffs and machinery often had to be brought over treacherous ground, and provisioning by waterway, with frequent portages and other hazards, could be equally arduous.[11] Once the initial difficulties had been overcome and the mill was established, the job of transporting the hewn timber first to the millsite, and then to the marketing and distribution center, had problems all its own, involving both legal and navigational obstacles.

The first legal tangle was that rivers and streams had to be declared navigable in order to prevent mill owners and farmers from blocking them with dams and other obstructions. In Wisconsin the courts were usually helpful in this respect, ruling that a waterway which could float timber was a 'public highway.' Saw logs, therefore, had just as much right to be on the rivers as barges, rafts, or steamboats. On the other hand, just as navigable streams could not be blocked by such artificial constructions as bridges, piers, fences, or duck ponds, lumbermen could not build storage or flooding dams without the special permission of the state legislature. This was not a simple process, as the lawmakers did not always cooperate; in fact, the lumbermen never succeeded in getting a general act passed. But individual permits were more readily obtainable. Between 1840 and 1900 the Wisconsin legislature granted nearly 350 franchises for the construction of logging dams, although securing these charters frequently involved delay and expense.

Even the apparent solution to a tough technical problem could result in troublesome legal issues. When a tangled mass of logs came down the river into the milltown, the jumble had to be halted, sorted, and then delivered to the various mills.[12] To accomplish this task, a contraption known as a boom stretched across the river; it was designed to stop the logs and through sorting gaps place them in separate pockets. Since a boom constituted a hindrance to navigation, permission to construct one had to be secured from the state legislature. Few individuals had the necessary political clout to persuade the Wisconsin body to grant a monopoly which could stop navigation on a particular waterway. Thus, the lumbermen found it necessary to combine to overcome the lawmakers' reluctance.

Some of the earliest organizational efforts of this kind occurred along the Wisconsin River. The Little Bull Falls Boom Company was formed in 1852, and four years later the Wisconsin River Boom Company was organized. By 1879 Big Bull Falls, which had been renamed Wausau, had large enough booms to hold safely 30 million board feet.[13] The very next year the young community was petitioned to take ten thousand dollars worth of stock in the boom company so that the capacity could be enlarged. Newly formed boom companies in the industry often combined with driving companies to obtain both political influence and the heavy investment required for boom construction. This trend was also witnessed in the upper Wisconsin valley: in 1882 a meeting in Wausau resulted in the creation of a driving association for the Wisconsin River and its tributaries.

The boom and driving companies soon became tempting targets for litigation. Farmers came to view these logging associations as giant corporations possessing a river monopoly that damaged their fields and meadows. Log jams and splash dams occasionally backed water over farm land, and enthusiastic log drivers trampled upon sprouting grain. Seeing the 'Boom' as rich and powerful, the aggrieved farmer had little hesitation about suing the offending company. Throughout much of the nineteenth century lumbering period, damage suits against boom and driving companies added color to the pages of rural newspapers, provided lawyers with tidy fees, and presented politicians with appealing platform planks.[14]

Working the Wisconsin

The Rank and File, Knowlton Log Drivers

The more strictly navigational problems of early lumber transportation centered around both the material and the transporting medium itself. As noted earlier, sizable stands of pine predominated along the banks of the Wisconsin River in Marathon County. Fortunately for the pioneer loggers, the buoyance of pine gave it excellent floatability, and it could therefore be shipped by water to mill or market with relative ease. Such was not the case with the abundant hardwood and hemlock further inland. The hardwoods, being typically denser than pine and thus more easily waterlogged, often got stuck in shallow water and were then harder to refloat. And unpeeled hemlock often sank after being in the water only a short time.[15]

From the earliest days of the lumbering industry the practice of rafting logs downstream instead of merely driving them loose had been fairly common. In 1840 forty thousand square feet of cut timber were rafted south from the Wisconsin River, and for the next three and a half decades the river raft was the principal means of moving Marathon County lumber to Mississippi River markets. So important did the raft become to the economic health of the area, that rafting pins known as "grubs" were considered an acceptable form of legal tender for either private or public transactions. An observer recalled that they were, in fact, '. . . an even better medium of exchange than gold coin. A settler coming into town with a load of grubs on his ox sled commanded the immediate attention and respect of every business man, as all were anxious to secure his very valuable article of commerce.'[16]

Whatever method of transportation was utilized, disadvantages existed. The log migration began as soon as possible in the spring after the winter's ice had broken up and moved out. On the Wisconsin River within Marathon County the cut lumber had to travel over a succession of rapids and eddies that surged over uneven and rocky bottoms. The responsibility for keeping the logs steadily in motion belonged to the "river pigs," also known as "catty men." Recruited from among the most courageous and skilled of the lumberjacks, they were expected in the course of a drive to perform such duties as breaking impeding river ice, rolling logs stranded on shore back into the current, and breaking up the almost inevitable log jam. Despite their ability, they sometimes fell victim to the dangerous waters. A resident of the eastern section of the county recalled his first days in the occupation with little nostalgia:

> The sun was going down when three of us got to a half dozen logs on the bank. They were frozen to the ground. Two men got on one side of the logs and I got on the other side with my back to the river, hooked my pieve on and started to pull. The hold gave out and I tumbled backwards into twelve feet of water. My partners held out a pole and pulled me out, soaking wet and no dry clothes to change into and all the kidding about the nice bath I had. It was five miles to camp. When we got there my clothes were frozen stiff. . . . I was wondering what was going to happen to me. I had had a bad cold. It scared me so I went to bed with the wet clothes, put more blankets on and went to sleep.[17]

The young man was lucky: he did recover, to the surprise of his fellow crew men.

Rafting, although offering some advantages in terms of economy and security, had its own difficulties. The rafts had to be taken apart at various points along the river and the individual cribs floated over the rapids to be reassembled below. This time-consuming chore was only a slight inconvenience, however, compared to the physical danger of navigating the turbulent waters. Much loggers' lore revolved around the hazards connected with guiding the lumber rafts down the river. In this respect the tales of rafting in Marathon County matched those of any lumbering area in the state of Wisconsin, since that portion of the Wisconsin River running through the county presented some of the most perilous problems a raftsman would ever encounter.

The first hint of potential trouble ahead was sensed when the roar of Big Bull Falls could be heard in the distance. More rafts were smashed running over this spot, so it was claimed, than any other place on the Wisconsin. If the raft were safely guided through, it then moved into Sturgeon Eddy and after traveling some fifteen miles reached what many rivermen considered the most dangerous point on the entire run, Little Bull Falls, with the adjoining Kelly and Shoemaker's rocks. Here the river narrowed and the raft would plunge down over a series of falls into a gorge thirty feet deep. Entering a powerful whirlpool, the raft, with the tremendous force of a cargo weighing as much as 350,000 pounds, was often submerged for the next half mile in a seething mass of foam and waves. According to legend, one hundred rivermen lost their lives negotiating these falls during the rafting era of Wisconsin lumbering. Years later, area residents were vividly reminded of the danger when Marathon Paper Mills executive Charles S. Gilbert told an Exchange Club audience in Wausau about the drowning of his father at Little Bull in the spring of 1872. For those raftsmen with skill and luck, the bank a half mile below the falls was a welcome haven. Those who were fortunate enough to reach this refuge knew that probably the most dangerous stretch of the Wisconsin River had been passed.[18]

It would be difficult to overstate the impact that the introduction of railroads into the pine forests of northern Wisconsin had on the lumber industry of the county and state. Prior to 1865, most Wisconsin lumbermen were content with the raft as their primary vehicle of log transportation. After the Civil War, however, a rapidly expanding market led to the consensus that the heavy dependence on the convenient waterways was retarding the industry's potential. The state lumber business was moving toward consolidation by the early 1870's, and the millowners began looking at railroads as a way to save money and thereby enhance the profits of their more settled operations.

The advantages looked appealing. By this time desirable timber close to a driving stream was growing scarce, and the lumbermen saw the railroad as the means to exploit large inland tracts previously considered worthless. Although hauling by rail was more expensive on a ton-mile basis than driving by river, the former was less affected by variations in the weather and could also extend the logging season beyond the winter months. Moreover, railroads eliminated the distinction between pine and hardwood logging; the only difference in expense proved to be a small and arbitrary change of rate charged by the railroad. The railroad thus made it economically feasible to cut an entire tract of timber in a single operation. Additional savings could be realized due to the simple fact that the construction of rail lines within the pineries meant that the lumbermen could supply their armies of lumberjacks and animals at a much lower cost than previously.

With these considerations in mind, lumbermen throughout the state began taking an active interest in railroad building. This concern was manifested in a number of ways: by their personally investing in railroad companies; by selling them such needed items as ties, bridge timbers and lumber at bargain prices; by being generous with such privileges as right-of-way, and finally, by exercising political pressure in both the state legislature and Congress. In this last respect, Wausau lumberman Walter McIndoe was one of the leaders. He had become one of the major lumbermen in the area through his purchase in 1848 of the Stevens mill at Big Bull Falls. Two years after his election to Congress in 1862, McIndoe spearheaded the successful effort to secure a generous land grant for the Wisconsin Central Railroad; this included within Marathon County all the odd sections in the subsequent townships of Spencer, Brighton, Hull, and Holton, within ten miles on either side of the right-of-way. With such encouragement from the lumber interests, railroad building in Wisconsin underwent a much needed period of expansion, with an average of two hundred miles of track per year being built in the twelve years following 1871.[19]

Once the community of interest between the lumber industry and railroading was firmly established, a whole new technological era in logging began. A series of creative innovations began to appear in the Wisconsin River pinery as railroad lumbering started to come into its own. Land-locked mills, finding their distance-cost from the forest greatly reduced, increased in number. Mills were now brought to the timber and established on a temporary basis wherever there was a promising tract. This procedure was particularly attractive in the latter years of the nineteenth century, as timberland rose in value and surviving tracts became more inaccessible. Little logging, for instance, was done in the Town of Norrie until the Chicago & Northwestern passed through in 1880 on its way to Wausau. Several sawmills were subsequently established in the area, producing a considerable amount of lumber before closing around the turn of the century. When such mainlines penetrated the northern forests, logs were also hauled directly from the woods to established milltowns, a practice facilitated by milling-in-transit rates.

The consequences of this later innovation had probably the most far-reaching significance, not only in terms of specific benefits to the lumber industry itself, but also for the broader development of the forested areas. As the railroads stretched deeper into the pineries, new lumbertowns sprang up along the lines. In Marathon County this pattern of organized settlement was repeated again and again, with the leading player being the most important lumber road of the era, the Wisconsin Central Railroad.

Through the efforts of Congressman McIndoe, the final legislation authorizing the Wisconsin Central's land grant was amended to specify that the road had to pass through his home county. Thus, by the time the Milwaukee to Ashland line was completed in 1877, it traveled through Marathon County for twenty-four miles adjacent to its western border. Although the railroad did not traverse a great distance, no fewer than five mill settlements sprang up in the wake of its construction: Mannville, Spencer, and Unity, within the white pine belt; and Colby and Abbotsford only a little farther north in the hardwood and hemlock forests.

The arrival of another road, The Milwaukee, Lake Shore & Western in 1891, brought still more communities into existence with the assistance of area lumbermen. The village of Fenwood was platted by the railroad's own attorney, and soon thereafter Wausau's C. S. Curtis built a sawmill at the site. The village of Edgar was platted by the same attorney, and a mill was erected by S. M. Quaw and George Gumaer near the station. To the southwest, when it became a certainty that the railroad would lay an extension from Wausau to Marshfield and build a station in the Town of Eau Pleine, another young lumberman was quick to take advantage of the opportunity. Seeking to expand the operations of his newly incorporated R. Connor Company beyond Wood County, W. D. Connor built a new band sawmill at the station site and named the little community platted by the railroad after his Canadian birthplace, Stratford.

Once railroad logging started to become an established practice, many temporary spurs were built to help log isolated tracts. Such a line was constructed in the early 1870's from the McMillan Brothers mill in the larger Town of Spencer to Mannville on the Wisconsin Central line. Wishing to end its dependence on pine and cedar log drives down the Little Eau Pleine River, the R. Connor Company built the Marathon County Railway eastward to Halder in the Town of

Emmet. Once the line was connected with the Chicago & North-western, the firm's goal of shipping hardwoods was realized. These spurs also led to the founding of pockets of settlement in the timbered wilderness. The little village of Milan in the Town of Johnson began as a railroad station on the Abbotsford - Northeastern spur running between Black Creek Falls, later renamed Athens, and Abbotsford. By the early twentieth century it had evolved into a community that possessed a saw and planing mill with a company store, a blacksmith shop, a hardware store, and a meat market.[20]

By far the most impressive development in which lumber commerce was playing an important role was taking place, however, in Wausau. The community that had grown out of George Stevens' primitive sash-style mill had early on become the key to the Wisconsin River industry, due largely to its strategic location at an especially steep rapids near the junction of two of the river's larger tributaries, the Rib and Eau Claire Rivers. Flowing south from Lac Vieux Desert on the Wisconsin-Michigan border, the Wisconsin River passed through valuable timberland to Wausau and then continued across the state until it joined the Mississippi at Prairie du Chien. Its drainage basin totaled 12,280 square miles—about twenty-one per cent of the state—and included not only Marathon County, but all or part of Vilas, Oneida, Lincoln, Langlade, Price, and Taylor Counties. By the early part of the twentieth century Wausau lumbermen had extensive holdings in the first five counties. The timber output of this drainage basin proved to be enormous. As the new century began, it had yielded just over 30 billion board feet of pine, a figure that amounted to slightly more than twenty-three per cent of the state's entire output.[21]

Given its advantageous geographic position, it is not surprising that Wausau became a focal point of lumbering activity not only in Marathon County, but in most of northern Wisconsin. A host of ambitious lumbermen soon followed George Stevens into this region of the pinery. Along with Walter McIndoe, John C. Clarke, B. G. Plumer, and other pioneers came to Wausau, commenced mill operations, and helped supply the increasing amounts of lumber needed in the rapidly expanding West. In the process they also assisted in the early growth of the organized community that was developing in that "far away place" on the upper Wisconsin.[22]

The arrival of the railroad in the newly incorporated city in 1874 brought both greater growth opportunities and the not always desirable characteristics of a prospering urban settlement in the early stages of development. Congressman McIndoe had assumed that his amendment to the 1864 land grant act would be sufficient to secure rail service for Wausau. The Wisconsin Central, however, bypassed the village in favor of the greater amount of government land in the less settled western portion of the county. After years of legal and political maneuvering the Wisconsin Valley Railroad, which would eventually become a part of the Chicago, Milwaukee, St. Paul & Pacific system, finally agreed to extend its line from Tomah and Grand Rapids (now know as Wisconsin Rapids) to Wausau. The arrival of the first railroad cars in the young city led to a celebration which would not be equaled again in the community until the end of World War I some forty years later. Then, in 1880, three years before the final lumber raft was dispatched down the Wisconsin, the Milwaukee, Lake Shore & Western, with no special inducement and little publicity, came to Wausau to prepare to extend its line westward through the county to Marshfield.[23]

With railroad transportation firmly established, Wausau became the departure point for the upper Wisconsin pinery, and consequently, the northmost settlement of importance in the Wisconsin valley. Various contractors and logging firms, as well as the railroad companies, made the city their place of wage payment. Woodsmen, construction gangs, and settlers needing supplies congregated within its boundaries to such a degree that the floating population often numbered close to one thousand. In fact, for a while the city took on some of the aspects of a thriving frontier town, complete with shady characters and ladies of the evening on the streets. More important, the significance of the railroad's arrival was reflected in the expansion of the community's permanent residential base. After an initial thirty-year period of progressive but relatively unspectacular growth, Wausau's population enjoyed a marked upsurge in the 1870's that continued right up to the beginning of the new century: from 1,349 in 1870 to 4,277 in 1880; 9,253 in 1890; and 12,354 in 1900.[24]

This increase in urbanization also did no harm to the city's expanding lumber trade. Lumber production quadrupled, from 6 million board feet coming from seven mills in 1874 to 25.7 million board feet out of six mills in 1875, to 31 million board feet from six mills in 1876. The value of shipments rose to $14,000 a day. The disastrous effects of the nation-wide depression of the 1870's did halt the upward trend for a time, although the shock was experienced in this area much later than in many sections of the country. Then, the selling price of lumber fleets in Mississippi River markets dropped to as little as ten dollars. But the railroad was still too new to provide any relief.

With many small lumber dealers going bankrupt and men working in the woods for five dollars a month and board, the output of the city's seven mills in 1877 plummeted to just over 18 million board feet.[25] By 1880, however, the worst had passed, and just three years later both the number of mills in the city and their lumber production were at an all time high: a total of eleven mills turning out 120 million board feet.[26]

Although the city's total cut in subsequent years was subject to fluctuation, especially when the effects of another national depression were experienced in the mid-nineties, the final three years of the old century saw another dramatic increase in Wausau's lumber production. Indeed, by 1900 its busy sawmills had established the city as the leading production center on the upper Wisconsin, and had earned for it the designation as "one of the capitals of American lumberdom."[27] A number of mills were responsible for the attainment of this reputation in national lumbering circles. A historical sketch of the two largest, the Alexander Stewart and Jacob Mortenson Lumber Companies, can, however, serve both to illustrate the rich diversity that marked the Wausau lumbering scene at the turn of the century and to introduce some of the people who would play a major role in the evolution that this area's lumber business would undergo in later years.

In Alexander Stewart the county had a representative of one of the leading traditions in the Wisconsin lumber industry. Like many of the state's legendary timber barons—Philetus Sawyer, Isaac Stephenson, the Doughty brothers, and Orrin Ingram—Stewart had initially studied the business in the Eastern pine regions, learning logging and log driving while still in his teens in the Canadian province of New Brunswick. Coming to the United States in 1849, at age twenty, he first settled in Blackberry, Illinois. His stay there was relatively brief, for he soon grew nostalgic for the pine forests of his earlier years. Accordingly, he moved northward to seek his fortune in the reputedly rich pine wilderness surrounding Big Bull Falls.[28]

Once in the mills and lumber camps of the Wisconsin pinery, the young woodsman insisted on receiving his pay in the form of lumber and shingles. After accumulating a sizable amount, he undertook to raft his "wages" down the Wisconsin and Mississippi Rivers, to be sold in St. Louis. With the patronage of a sympathetic banker, Henry Corwith, young Stewart saw the size of his rafts grow year by year, and consequently began to amass a fortune that would eventually amount to many millions of dollars. In time, his success led him to join his brother John in forming the J. & A. Stewart firm. By 1872 the business had so grown that the already prominent valley lumber-man expanded his operations by purchasing the most famous mill on the upper Wisconsin: the pioneer George Stevens-Walter McIndoe mill.

The growing business of the young Stewart operation soon necessi-tated another move which was to have far-reaching significance for not only the future success of that particular firm, but for the future development of county industry as a whole. Finding it impossible to attend personally to all the details of management, Alexander Stewart decided to take on a partner. His choice was another am-bitious young lumberman who had only recently settled permanently in Wausau, Walter Alexander.

Like Stewart, Walter Alexander was of Scotch ancestry, having been born in Glasgow the year before Marathon County was formally or-ganized. At age nine, his family emigrated to America, settling on a farm in Portage County. Unlike his father, however, young Alexander chose the forests rather than the soil as the source of his livelihood, for most of his boyhood days were spent in the company of his ma-ternal uncle, the seemingly omnipresent Walter McIndoe. The example provided by McIndoe's activist personality along with his vision of the potential of the county in the maturing lumber industry must have made a deep impression on the youngster. Before completing his second year of college at Ripon, he decided to abandon his formal education, returning instead to Wausau to learn the intricacies of the lumber trade under the watchful eye of his famous uncle. The young man proved an apt pupil. In a relatively short time he assumed much responsibility over McIndoe's extensive interests. Upon the latter's death in 1872, Alexander, at age twenty-three, took complete charge of the business. His management skill did not fail to impress Alexander Stewart. Thus, after absorbing the Stevens-McIndoe mill, one of his first decisions was to bring in Walter Alexander as a full partner, in the expanded firm, which was subsequently renamed the Alexander Stewart Lumber Company.

The new partnership proved to be a fruitful one. With the historic mill serving as the nucleus, and Walter Alexander assuming an in-creasing share of management responsibility under his official title of secretary-treasurer—especially during Alexander Stewart's absence while serving in Congress from 1896 through 1900—the company con-tinued to grow and prosper. The old mill was rebuilt several times, until its capacity had increased from 10,000 feet a day to more than 100,000 feet every ten hours. Indeed, by 1900 the firm's physical plant was equipped with all the necessary modern machinery, including both band and circular saws, and a newly constructed planing mill. Its major source of supply was a large tract of uncut timber in the Wisconsin valley, with most of the stock, in keeping with the new order of log transportation, coming to the mill by rail.

The Alexander Stewart operation, however, was by no means limited to Marathon County. The firm itself, or its two top executives, owned stock in several lumber companies in Wisconsin and Michigan, and numerous lumber yards in Nebraska, Iowa, Illinois, and Indiana. In addition, the company owned a timber tract valued at several hundred thousand dollars and a sawmill in Arkansas. The heart of the operation, nonetheless, rested in Wausau. In both the last year of the old century and the first year of the new, the company's lumber cut exceeded 30 million feet of pine, thereby making it the runaway leader in terms of output in both the city and the county. In short, in the Alexander Stewart Lumber Company, Marathon County possessed one of the model organizations in the entire American lumber industry.[29]

A slightly larger cast of characters was instrumental in the early development of the Jacob Mortenson Lumber Company. Jacob Mortenson, Charles Edgar, Charles J. Winton, and Fowler P. Stone came from different backgrounds and points of origin, yet they brought to their new venture a series of prior interlocking business relationships. Jacob Mortenson emigrated from Denmark to this country at age seventeen in 1866. He began work in his new land as a common laborer in the woods near Manistee, Michigan. By the time he arrived in Wausau some seventeen years later, his position in the world had risen considerably. He came to the city as the manager of the shipping department of the McDonald Lumber Company of Kansas City—a concern in which he had recently purchased an interest. Once established in the community, Mortenson formed in the late 1880's a number of new business associations which would in time constitute the nucleus of the lumber company that would bear his name. With Charles J. Winton he formed the Winton Lumber Company, a firm that dealt in timberlands and logs. Winton, a native of Addison, New York, had come to Wausau in roughly the same period as his partner, with a solid background in lumber manufacturing, his father having operated a sash and door factory in the Empire state. In 1888 Mortenson teamed with veteran lumberman Charles Edgar to form Mortenson & Edgar, a retail lumbering firm at Galesburg, Illinois.[30] Edgar brought to this and to their future enterprise both a rare managerial ability and a complete knowledge of conditions in the pine regions. Finally, in 1889 Mortenson joined with Fowler P. Stone in establishing the lumber firm of Mortenson & Stone.[31] Stone, who had come to north-central Wisconsin a year before his senior partner, was bred from a background that had instilled in him both religious discipline and business acumen. After completing his public school education in Camden, New York, he attended Cazenovia seminary near Utica. He also brought to the relationship an expert knowledge of the lumber business through his sixteen-year association with the Curtis sash and door operation in both Clinton, Iowa, and Wausau.

This group constituted the brain trust which in 1893 purchased the ten-year old Leahy and Beebe mill as the center of operations for the newly organized Jacob Mortenson Lumber Company. By the turn of the century the mill was equipped with all the essential machinery, including both a band saw and resaws, had a capacity of approximately 75,000 feet of lumber per ten hours, and was connected with a modern planing mill. Like the Stewart firm it received most of its log sup-ply by rail—with one crucial difference. The railroad track ran be-side the river, and the logs, upon reaching the mills, were dumped into a section enclosed by a tight board fence. This artificial pond was heated by steam to prevent freezing, thus enabling sawing to take place even in the coldest months of winter. Such ingenuity combined with the managerial experience of its directors to make the Jacob Mortenson Lumber Company the second most productive lumber concern in both Wausau and the county at the turn of the century, with a cut of 30 million feet of pine.[32]

These two firms were clearly the giants of pine lumbering in the city of Wausau as the twentieth century began. Other firms, to be sure, did make a contribution to lumbering's pre-eminent position in the city's economy.[33] None, however, either individually or in com-bination could approach the Stewart and Mortenson companies, which together accounted for 96.5 per cent of Wausau's pine timber cut in 1900. And with these two firms leading the way, Wausau was just as clearly the dominant force in Marathon County's lumber industry with its mill accounting for just under half of the county's entire pine lumber cut.[34]

While Wausau's leading position within the county lumbering com-munity was undeniable, to suggest that the activity in the remainder of the county was inconsequential would be an injustice. After all, more than fifty per cent of Marathon County's 1900 pine timber out-put did originate outside of that city. Three miles south of the county seat in Schofield, for example, the Brooks & Ross Lumber Company mill was not only responsible for a healthy pine cut of 20 million feet—third largest in the county—but provided, in addition, a testing ground for some of the leaders whose experience would prove invaluable to county industry in the years ahead.

The millsite itself and the surrounding area was developed largely through the initiative of Dr. William Scholfield. Arriving in this region in 1851, he intended at first to stay only long enough to purchase fence lumber for his new Mineral Point farm. An examination of the countryside, especially its water powers, led the physician to change his mind. Optimistic about the prospects for successful lumbering operations, Scholfield purchased instead the entire Martin waterpower sawmill on the Eau Claire River. He immediately set out to put the mill and dam in good working condition, and then laid out the village that would come to bear his name: erecting homes and establishing stores, warehouses, and other facilities.[35] Following the doctor's death in 1863, the operation was run for the next twenty years by his widow and her brother, Charles P. Haseltine. They, in turn, disposed of the mill and its property in 1883 by selling it to one of Chicago's most prominent lumbermen, E. Wellington Brooks and his protege, John D. Ross.

The Brooks-Ross relationship had begun in Michigan some sixteen years earlier, at the Ford River Lumber Company where E. Wellington Brooks held the offices of secretary and general manager. In 1867, a twenty-four year old Canadian from Lancaster, Ontario, John D. Ross, was hired by the concern as a bookkeeper. Like so many of the men who would play an important role in the development of the Marathon County lumber industry, young Ross did not take long to see his abilities rewarded. After only two years with the firm, he became at age twenty-six a stockholder in the corporation and was named manager of operations. In 1882, Ross left Ford River to join his mentor in Chicago, where they organized the E. W. Brooks & Co. distributing yard. Wishing to expand the scope of this enterprise, the pair entered the manufacturing field the following year through their purchase of the Haseltine mill at Schofield. Although he planned to devote his full attention to the manufacturing end of the business, Ross still felt he needed a capable manager to oversee the entire Schofield project. To fill the post he called on his former understudy at Ford River, Walter H. Bissell.

Perhaps more than any of the other famous figures in Marathon County lumbering history, Walter Bissell seemed destined for the role he would come to play. The Bissells were considered one of the oldest and most prominent lumbering families in the United States. Harmon Bissell, Walter's grandfather, had operated a sawmill in Litchfield County, Connecticut for many years before moving his family to Fond du Lac in the early 1840's. There he and his son Leonard bought, repaired, and ran the first sawmill—one of the old fashioned gate variety— ever constructed in that Wisconsin county. Soon thereafter, in an attempt to introduce more modern technological methods, the pair built the first steam mill in that part of the state.

Coming from such a proud lumbering tradition, it is not surprising that Leonard Bissell's second son, Walter Henry, decided to learn the business first hand at an early age, even if it meant forsaking his formal education. In January, 1872 at age thirteen he left school to enter the employ of one of his home city's leading lumber firms, U. D. Mihills & Co. His family background notwithstanding, Bissell began at the bottom, as an errand boy, learning his first lessons in lumbering on his feet. More than fifty years later, after achieving numerous business successes, this elder statesman of Wisconsin lumber would remark about his first job, 'and to this day I can't forget how I used to run my legs off.'[36] The work was often tedious, but the young office boy kept busy. His studious intensity quickly attracted the attention of his superiors, and within six months he was promoted to the book-keeper's desk. There he remained for the next five years, absorbing knowledge about the business while preparing himself for bigger things to come.

The evolution of Walter Bissell's connection with John Ross began during his later years of employment with the Mihills firm. In the course of his duties the ambitious bookkeeper had frequent contact with John S. McDonald of Fond du Lac, president of the Ford River Lumber Company. Highly impressed with the youth's character and personality, McDonald persuaded him to come to Michigan and accept a similar position with his company. Upon reaching Ford River in 1877, its new bookkeeper was placed under the supervision of its man-ager—the rising star of that organization—John D. Ross. Before long Walter Bissell himself rose in the organization, becoming Ross's right hand man; thus was formed an association that would result several years later in Bissell's acceptance of Ross's invitation to resign his post at Ford River and take complete charge at Schofield. Under the stewardship of Walter H. Bissell and John D. Ross, the Brooks & Ross Lumber Company would reach a peak capacity of 35 million feet annually, specializing in the shipment of lumber to New England markets.[37]

Meanwhile, to the southwest, a prosperous lumbering operation was in full swing near that treacherous point on the Wisconsin River known as Little Bull Falls. The prime mover behind the successful Mosinee venture was another legendary name in the annals of county lumbering, Joseph Dessert. Born and raised in the Maskenougee area of Quebec, Dessert had first earned his living in Canadian lumber camps. His initial visit to the States was in a different capacity; in 1840, at age twenty-one, he came to the Lake Superior region of Minnesota as a fur buyer for the American Fur Company, a position he would hold for the next several years. His major accomplishments were to lie in another direction, however, for by this time the story of the Wakely - Stevens discovery had spread. Hearing about the north-central section of the Wisconsin Rivery pinery in the course of a fur buying trip to an isolated post, the young Canadian decided a change of scenery and career plans was in order.

Confident of success if he acted quickly, Dessert, after a brief visit home, set off on much the same journey that fellow Canadian Alexander Stewart had made some years earlier, finally reaching Little Bull Falls on foot in the late fall of 1844. In these new surroundings, his first employment was that of a common laborer in the old style "slash saw" mill that John L. Moore had constructed only two years earlier. Like his contemporaries at Big Bull Falls, he soon experienced the hardships of living in what was still considered an uninhabitable wilderness.[38] Despite the privations, Dessert stayed on, gaining experience and acquiring knowledge of the timber resources and local lumbering conditions. He was determined to head an operation of his own, and the opportunity was not long in coming. In 1849 he, along with three partners, purchased the little mill that had been his sole source of employment since coming to the pinery. Gradually he bought out the interest of the others, until by 1859 he was sole owner of both the mill and the water power at Little Bull Falls, which had been renamed Mosinee at his suggestion.

The next forty years witnessed an unceasing effort by Joseph Dessert to keep his enterprise up-to-date in terms of both methods of operation and logging technology. In the early years logs were floated down area rivers to the company's sawmill, with the unfinished lumber then rafted to Iowa and Missouri river ports.[39] With the advent of the railroad in the Wisconsin River valley, the company built and later remodeled its own planing mill, which enabled finished lumber to be shipped out of Mosinee on railroad cars. The sawing process was also modernized over the years. The old "slash saw" was replaced by a rotary in 1862, and when the mill was rebuilt following the disastrous floods of the early 1880's, a band saw was installed. For a long period of time the sawmill's power supply was furnished by two water wheels; by 1898 steam power had been entirely substituted, with the exception of a single small wheel which ran a dynamo for electric lights.

By the turn of the century Joseph Dessert could take pride in the knowledge that his was the most productive county lumbering concern outside the Wausau-Schofield area. At the company's main camp, located in section 26 of the Town of Kronenwetter, timber felled in Kronenwetter, Guenther, and Reid was loaded on the company's own standard-gauge logging trains and shipped to Mosinee. With as many as fifty cars being employed daily, the 1900 pine cut of the Joseph Dessert Lumber Company reached 28,372,000 feet—a nineteen per cent increase over the previous logging season.[40]

The success story would be incomplete if special acknowledgment were not made of the Dessert firm's importance to the overall development of Mosinee. From the beginning, the economy of the community revolved around the fortunes of the Dessert operation. As many as one hundred sixty men were employed at the company mill, with another fifty usually able to find work at each of the four logging camps. The firm, moreover, came to own up to twenty houses in the area that were rented to the employees for five to eight dollars a month. Despite the opportunity for abuse inherent in such economic dominance, there seemed to exist a genuine spirit of cooperation between the parent company and the dependent community. The Dessert company, unlike, for example, the leading lumber concern in Stratford, never paid its workers in scrip which could be used only in a company store. Joseph Dessert himself took an active interest in enriching the quality of his employees' lives. In 1898 he supervised the construction of the Joseph Dessert Public Library. Upon its completion, instead of turning it over for the village to support, Dessert appointed a governing board of trustees and personally bore the expense of new books and maintenance for the next several years.

This spirit was returned in kind. During the national hard times of the 1890's, when many mills were forced to close, the Dessert operation was able to remain open, due to the workers' voluntary agreement not to expect full pay until business conditions improved. The community took obvious pride in its major industry. When the Wausau press once categorized the Dessert organization as one of the lesser manufacturers in the county, the *Mosinee Times* responded with righteous indignation, paying tribute in the process to the enterprise which

Joseph Dessert had nurtured:

> The Dessert Lumber company and all its vast in-
> terests have not been set apart from Marathon county;
> neither have they diminished in point of weath, popu-
> larity or influence. In fact the Dessert Lumber company
> own and control one of the leading industries of
> Marathon county and have a supply of lumber on
> hand equal to any company in the Wisconsin River
> valley. We simply mention this, because in a recent
> issue of one of the Wausau papers, the attempt was evi-
> dently made to classify the Dessert Lumber company
> with the smaller manufacturers who manufacture less
> than a million or two a year, by making no mention
> of the company in a classified statement of the amount
> of lumber manufactured and amount on hand at the
> leading mills throughout the county. A company that
> is employing from 375 to 400 hands and 80 to 90
> teams and is running night and day, is certainly worthy
> of being classified with the leading manufacturers of
> the county. Probably the publisher had a motive to
> the value of about $25 in publishing his little article on
> "the leading lumber manufacturers of Marathon coun-
> ty" and omitting the name of one of the leading com-
> panies.[41]

With the goodwill of the host village and a thoroughly modern plant supplied by 25,000 acres of county forest land, the immediate future looked bright. As the new century began it was confidently predicted that "a second crop of splendid pine" would "keep its mills busy for many years" to come.[42]

The history of lumbering activity taking place in the northwestern portion of Marathon County at this particular time was, again, largely the story of the ambition and determination of a single individual, Frederick Rietbrock. Born in Kenosha County on April 6, 1839, Rietbrock's formative years were spent on the family farm. Although farming would play an important part in his later life, the young man first chose to study the law. After receiving his law degree from the University of Michigan in 1865, the fledgling attorney decided to return to Wisconsin. Settling in Milwaukee, he opened his own office and subsequently formed a partnership with D. H. Johnson and fellow Ann Arbor classmate L. W. Halsey. In a relatively short period of time, Rietbrock became prominent in the legal and political circles of the city, serving one term as Milwaukee County district attorney and act- ing as chairman of the county Democratic committee for a number of years.

That the pioneer spirit existed within Frederick Rietbrock is hardly surprising. His immigrant father had been one of the pioneer settlers of Kenosha County in the late 1830's. Moreover, by the 1870's Milwaukee was in the midst of an economic slump. Thus, while attending to a lawsuit in Wausau, Rietbrock's eye was caught by an advertisement of the Wisconsin Valley Railroad, whose land agent had located in that prospering lumbertown. Making an exploratory journey west to the sawmill community of Rib Falls, he found the timbered country much to his liking. Accordingly, Rietbrock began land purchases in the middle of the decade which would continue for the next several years. In time he interested his law partners in his lumbering and colonization plans, and eventually their enterprise came to encompass the major part of three county townships and control nearly 50,000 acres of heavily timbered land.

This portion of Marathon County had but slight experience with the woodsman's ax as Rietbrock began his purchases. As was typical throughout the pinery, only the white pine in close proximity to the streams had been felled. When the federal government undertook a thorough survey of the region in 1853, it was noted that the highlands contained dense growths of pine, hemlock, and a variety of hardwoods. The area's lowlands, in turn, were covered with hemlock, birch, balsam, and ash. The surveyor's notes also indicated that many of the trees had reached a considerable size. Pine, hemlock, and birch from twenty to thirty inches in diameter were noted, while numerous hardwoods had reached diameters of from fifteen to eighteen inches.

The center of lumbering operations in this territory had been chosen and purchased by Rietbrock in 1879 on a spot along Black Creek. Envisioning a village on the location, he named it Black Creek Falls and hired a crew from Grafton in Ozaukee County to build the first sawmill there.[43] Like the pioneer Stevens mill, it was originally driven by water power and employed a "Muley" upright saw. At a later time, a steam operated mill with a circular saw and newer technological devices came into use. This same crew also undertook the construction of needed supplemental facilities. A "Company House" was built to serve as a station for new settlers involved in the agricultural colonization aspect of the Rietbrock enterprise. Moreover, a road was cut west to Dorchester on the Wisconsin Central line.[44]

Unlike many of his fellow county lumber kings, Frederick Rietbrock chose not to live near his operation, but to remain in Milwaukee, close to his law practice. Nevertheless, in the Black Creek Falls area there was no doubt as to who was in charge. When the supply road to

Dorchester proved inadequate, Rietbrock decided that his village needed a railroad connection. The Wisconsin Central, however, proved reluctant to build the line, so Rietbrock determined to do the job himself.
Financed chiefly by Milwaukee capital, the Abbotsford and Northeastern Railway was incorporated in April, 1889, and chartered to build
a spur from Abbotsford to Wausau by way of Black Creek Falls.[45]
Virtually no detail of the enterprise escaped Rietbrock's attention. An
unexpected crisis at the mill, such as the destruction of a dam by
spring flooding, would cause him to leave Milwaukee in great haste,
arriving at Athens[46] on horseback from the Dorchester railway station.
Personnel problems also received his very personal attention. On a
particularly cold week during the winter logging season when the
thermometer plunged to twenty below zero, the loggers decided it was
too cold to work. Their work stoppage was abruptly halted when
Rietbrock appeared on the scene, announced that the crew was going
to work, and promptly broke the camp thermometer to prevent any
future complaining.[47] With such scrutiny to detail, the success enjoyed by Rietbrock's enterprise by the turn of the century was not
difficult to understand. In 1900 the lumber firm of Rietbrock &
Halsey[48] was the leading pine lumbering operation in the Athens area,
with a cut of 1,500,000 feet, which ranked it fifth in the entire county.

While Rietbrock's dominating influence in the village was undeniable—nearly one-third of the Athens population was in his direct employ—the community was not a one-man town, at least as far as lumbering was concerned. As in Mosinee, there was no company store
subjecting residents to a feudal credit system. Furthermore, a number
of other logging operations did make a contribution to the total Athens
pine timber output. M. Braun & Sons[49] recorded a cut of one million
feet; the Athens Manufacturing Company, presided over by Joseph
Chesak of Poniatowski, cut 150,000 feet; and the Big Rib Lumber
Company cut 50,000 feet. In Athens the Rietbrock company was king,
but not strictly sovereign.[50]

Indeed, as the new century began, it was possible to find lumbering
concerns sprinkled throughout virtually every section of the county.
Among the most prominent in terms of longevity of operation or output of pine lumber were: the Sellin sawmill on the boundary between
the townships of Hamburg and Berlin, the McIntosh mill in the Town
of Wausau, Baesmann Brothers of Rib Falls, Herman & Menzner of
Marathon, Fritz and Fry of Unity, and the Colby Lumber Company.[51]
Thus, Marathon County was an integral part of a vigorous Wisconsin
lumber industry which, at the beginning of the twentieth century, had

achieved a pre-eminent position in both the state and the nation as a whole. By 1900 the state lumber industry employed 21,701 wage earners, or 15.3 per cent of the total number of Wisconsin workers, making it the largest employer among state manufacturing industries. In addition, by that time, Wisconsin had surpassed Michigan as the leading lumbering state in the country, in terms of the value of its lumber and timber products.

In fact, as the nation entered the new century, the entire American lumber industry had reason to feel a sense of satisfaction in reflecting upon what it had accomplished in the century just passed. The *American Lumberman* in a retrospective editorial pointed with pride to the "birth, growth and apparent maturity of the lumber industry of the United States" that had taken place in the nineteenth century. Not only had that period witnessed numerous advances in sawmill technology,[52] but "all branches of the business" had undergone "the same degree of improvement." The planing mill, for example, had not existed when the 1880's began. "The logging railroad and the application of machinery to logging [were] practically all a matter of

Greetings from the Edgar Logging Camp, 1894

38

Airing out the Cook Shanty, Rietbrock Company Lumber Camp, North of Athens, 1910

the last thirty years." The future could be just as bright. While there were some who might "imagine that lumber will go out of use . . . this will never be the case as long as trees grow." Wood, the trade journal confidently asserted, "will continue to contribute to the necessities and the arts and the luxuries of human existence."[53]

The total picture insofar as Wisconsin was concerned was not quite so simple, however. The outward display of optimism and the positive indicators notwithstanding, by 1900 there was reason for genuine apprehension within the state lumber industry. Looked at in a relative context, the statistics told a different story. Both the number of establishments and the number of wage earners engaged in the lumbering sector of Wisconsin manufacturing had undergone a significant decrease during the previous decade. The value of Wisconsin's lumber and timber products, although first in the nation, had likewise suffered a relative decline over the same period: the 1900 figure being 5.5 per cent below that of ten years earlier.[54]

The source of difficulty within the "empire" was plain enough. Its life blood, the pine forests, had been treated as a one-time resource and was, as a consequence, seriously depleted at the beginning of the twentieth century. A report prepared by the Commissioner of Industrial Statistics noted that, although Wisconsin led all the lumber-producing states in output of white pine lumber, its production had dropped fifteen per cent between 1889 and 1899. This decline was traced directly to the exhaustion of the state's timber stands. The commissioner concluded with the sobering observation that most lumbering counties had long since seen their years of maximum cut.[55]

This state of affairs could not be blamed on simple ignorance of the problem. In 1873 the state press had published an estimate, originating from Pennsylvania, that the supply of pine in Wisconsin would be gone in another thirty years. After that, predictions were made almost annually of the imminent disappearance of the state's pine resources. These warnings were finally given official sanction shortly before the arrival of the new century. In 1897, forestry expert Filbert Roth made a three-months' study of northern Wisconsin forest conditions, at the direction of the U.S. Department of Agriculture in consultation with the newly created Wisconsin State Forestry Commission.[56] His findings, published early the following year, presented a startling view of the actual state of Wisconsin's supposedly inexhaustible forests. Of an original stand of approximately 130 billion feet of pine, only slightly more than 17 billion feet remained. Although precise estimates were difficult, that supply of pine could last no more than another ten or twenty years. The report detailed the enormous waste that had taken place in the pineries. Since 1840, 27 billion feet of white pine alone had been wasted. More than sixty per cent of that figure was due to fire, with the balance resulting from storms, old age, and wasteful cutting practices.

In Marathon County, in particular, the assessment was mixed. Along with Chippewa, Clark, and Wood Counties, it continued to furnish large quantities of pine logs in all sizes. Due to the extensive cutting, however, the average size of the logs was half of what it had been twenty years ago. A considerable number of fires during the dry season of 1894 had taken their toll as well. Thus, according to Roth, by 1898 only the southwestern portion of the county—the area roughly comprising present day Bevent, Guenther, Reid, and the western part of Kronenwetter—contained considerable merchantable pine timber. The culled condition of the forests made supply estimates difficult, but, as was the case in every county he visited, Roth heard the view expressed in Marathon County that the man whose pine supply was

almost gone and who was finding it hard to buy more, believed everyone else shared his problem.[57] The subsequent report of the Commissioner of Industrial Statistics confirmed this impression and supported the rest of Roth's observations.

The reasons for this serious state were manifold. Careless lumbering practices resulted in much waste. The continued use of "Muley"
and circular saws was a prime example. A later study revealed that had
band saws been used exclusively after 1872, production figures could
have been increased by one billion board feet by 1905. Much young
timber was also destroyed by falling trees and as a result of road
building. The destruction of valuable material in slab burners as refuse and frequently uneconomical methods of cutting were additional
factors. By far, however, the greatest waste was caused by fire. At
most, only forty per cent of the original Wisconsin forest cover ever
reached the saw mills; the rest literally went up in flames. Wasteful
cutting practices were mostly to blame. Loggers often took only the
choicest parts of the hewn trees; what remained was left in the forest
to dry and become fuel for a future conflagration. Potentially useful
windfalls and partly decayed trees were also left behind, ultimately
to serve the same purpose. Given such laxity, it is hardly surprising
that tragedy struck. In 1885, an eighty-mile strip of the Wisconsin
River valley was practically all ablaze. As noted earlier, Marathon
County was especially hard hit in 1894, prompting Filbert Roth specifically to recommend the need for preventive organization. Despite
this and similar warnings, in 1908, fires occurred in nearly every
one of the thirty-two counties of northern Wisconsin.[58]

Also at fault was a certain sense of inevitability, a feeling of being
caught up in an economic process about which little could be done.
Ironically, as improved methods of logging were adopted and the
effectiveness of the logging process increased, the pace of deforestation
accelerated. To suggestions that he curtail his production, the lumberman could reasonably reply: 'this is lumber country and we have
no other employment. Men must eat to live and must work to
eat. . . .'[59] A similar economic rationale could even be found in the
waste factor. Inefficient methods of logging continued because it was
cheap lumber that was in demand, and extravagant logging methods
contributed in large measure to its cheapness. And that, after all, was
of primary importance in expansion-oriented nineteenth century
America. In the end, the lumbermen were simply giving the public
what it wanted: more jobs, the opportunity to create private fortunes,
and new communities. The often ruthless destruction of Wisconsin's

forests did not undermine community standards. Rather, the record indicates that on the whole, the dominant societal values actively supported or, at best, acquiesced in the exploitation of the state's priceless resource.[60]

The reception given Filbert Roth's findings is a case in point. The publication of the report caused only a small ripple of interest in the state press. The *Milwaukee Sentinel* gave the study front page coverage complete with banner headlines; but, for the most part, there was no serious public discussion of Roth's research. Such was apparently the case in Marathon County. No evidence has been found in the available county press that the release of the report was announced or that its conclusions and admonitions were discussed editorially—this in spite of the significance of the report for the future of the county's leading industry. Other signs, however, soon appeared that pointed to the rapid destruction of the pine forests and the resulting inevitable decline of lumbering. An article in the *Wausau Pilot* projected that in Wisconsin and Minnesota "the best grades of pine . . . have been pretty well cut off, and the days of the big sawmills in this section are pretty well numbered. From three to five years will close most of them as far as the making of famous white pine lumber is concerned." This was especially true for the Wisconsin River valley where "the big mills have about three years ahead of them in white pine."[61] If there was any complacency within the county concerning the article's message, it was undoubtedly shattered when the Joseph Dessert Company mill closed for good in 1904, the firm's final large pine harvest having been completed two years earlier.[62]

Other indications of the end of an era were more symbolic. As early as 1900 the sight of two immense pine logs being hauled down Wausau's main street from the Town of Wausau could attract several hundred onlookers. During a 1903 visit to Wausau, Edward Herman of the Herman & Menzner concern in Marathon City reported the marketing of a monster pine tree at his mill. Cut near Rib Falls, this "schoolma'am" tree produced thirteen marketable logs scaling 5,000 feet.[63] That this single pine came to be publicized in a national lumber journal was a significant comment on the state of the county's once teeming pine forests. In fact, by 1910 pine timber had become such a rarity, that a particularly good cut by the Menzner mill was "viewed as almost a curiosity," and considered worthy of an inspection trip to the mill yard.[64] In the summer of 1911, the Falls City House barn, a familiar landmark of the pinery days around Little Bull Falls, was demolished. The dismantling of the structure which had sheltered lumbermen's teams for nearly three-quarters of a century served as a further reminder that "king pine" was in the process of abdication.[65]

Most lumbermen were well aware of what was going on around them—that, given the rate of the annual cut, the virgin pine stands would eventually disappear. In fact, long before the real squeeze came, changes were instituted that reflected the imminence of exhaustion. Lower grades of timber came to be used, and there was a greater concentration of timberland ownership. One of the most noticeable changes was the growing inclination to cut the hemlock and hardwoods that had been spurned by older lumbermen. Hardwood logging had begun to assume importance as far back as the early 1870's and had been aided immeasurably by the penetration of the railroad into the forests. Acceptance of hemlock was slower, but by the mid-nineties a growing demand for hemlock bark provided a helpful additional market. In this new phase of logging, the Town of Easton was a major scene of activity. The hemlock logs were peeled in May and June with the cords of bark then transported by sleigh or rail to area tanneries. Accordingly, the public prejudice against hemlock was gradually overcome, and by 1902 the hemlock cut of Wisconsin and Michigan was equivalent to approximately twenty-two per cent of the pine lumber product of Wisconsin, Michigan, and Minnesota combined. By 1906, in fact, the total hemlock and hardwood cut in the Badger state topped one billion board feet and exceeded the pine cut for the first time.[66]

Marathon County was in a favorable position to take advantage of this trend in state lumbering. The Roth report placed the county in a belt of mixed forests, with over five million feet of hardwood and hemlock per acre of stocked area. Although these forests had already been heavily cut into for more than a decade, Marathon County's supply of standing hemlock timber exceeded that of eighteen of the Cutover counties; its amount of standing hardwood surpassed that of all but one of the other twenty-two counties in that region.[67]

In this new lumbering era, additional county firms and personalities came to the forefront. The Barker & Stewart Lumber Company of Wausau under the leadership of W. C. Landon was one prominent example. Organized in 1887 through the purchase of the Clark, Johnson & Company mill on McIndoe Island, this relative newcomer on the Wausau lumbering scene by the turn of the century became the undisputed leader in the county in hemlock production, with a cut of eleven million feet. In contrast, its pine cut that same year amounted to a meager 800,000 feet. The dominant product of the firm did not change over the years. By 1910 its total output of 45 million feet consisted of seventy-five per cent hemlock, twenty per cent hardwoods, and only five per cent pine.

The success achieved by the Barker & Stewart operation was due in large part to the efforts of its energetic top executive, W. C. Landon. His rise to prominence within the Marathon County lumbering community followed a pattern similar to that of the other notables discussed thus far. His family was not native to the north-central Wisconsin area. Born at Algonac, Michigan, in 1872, he, like Frederick Rietbrock, spent his youth working on the family farm. His formal education was minimal, being limited to short winter school terms. His migration to Wisconsin at age twenty-two was occasioned by his cousin H. C. Stewart's invitation to come to Wausau and join his lumber firm. Landon accepted and began learning the business as a member of "the perspiring shirt-sleeve yard crew." Like most of the other county lumber kings, his progress was steady. After a two-year period of piling lumber, he was taken into the office and within three years was made office manager. Upon the firm's incorporation in 1904, he assumed the vice-presidency; and finally on January 1, 1908, following the death of C. C. Barker, he was elected president, thus completing his rise to the top in fourteen years. Under Landon's stewardship, despite a reputation for pursuing a basically conservative timber policy, the Barker & Stewart Lumber Company was noted for making some of the largest real estate transactions in the area. In 1909, for example, the concern purchased within a two-week period 9,768 acres of mixed hardwood and hemlock timber in the Towns of Hewitt and Harrison, involving a total consideration of $67,426. Landon's abilities did not go unrecognized by his associates in the industry; in 1910 he was elected president of the prestigious Northern Hemlock and Hardwood Manufacturers' Association.[68]

As had been the case with pine, the activity in hardwood and hemlock lumbering was by no means limited to Wausau firms. For the first six years of its existence, McMillan & Brother of southwestern Marathon County had cut pine exclusively. By 1900, however, it ranked second in the entire county in hemlock output with a cut of five million feet. The head of the organization, B. Frank McMillan, was another respected figure in the highest councils of the industry. He was especially appreciative of the fact that 'Lumber used to be bought, now it must be sold.'[69] The early pine lumberman had to only be concerned with the production of lumber. The members of the "second generation," involved with hardwood and hemlock, had, in addition, to create a market for their product. To this end, McMillan was an enthusiastic advocate of activist trade associations. Speaking before the 1903 conference of the Northwestern Hemlock Manufacturers' Association, he insisted:

> Now, Mr. Chairman, if we are going to have an association we have got to have one that will do some good and one that we can be proud of, or I am going out of business. I am not going to spend my time in attending associations where they don't do something. It is a waste of time. This association has made me thousands of dollars and it is a good thing, or was once, and can be made a good thing again. We have all got to take hold and to help the others in their efforts. No one man can do it alone and no one man is to blame for our present lassitude. Here we meet only once a year when we ought to meet three or four times.[70]

Any association worthy of existence had to be aggressive and effective. Accordingly, McMillan was called upon by the association's president to attend the initial convention of the newly organized National Association of Manufacturers in St. Louis to look after the group's interests. This was important because "... there [were] many

The B. F. McMillan Sawmill

things that . . . a local association [could not] cope with."[71] McMillan executed his assignment admirably. An original rule of the national organization proved that only associations exclusively made up of manufacturers could join. Such a requirement would have effectively barred the hemlock group. At McMillan's insistence, the stipulation was relaxed to permit eligibility for membership to any association that had at least seventy-five per cent of its members engaged in manufacturing.[72]

In the final years of the ninteenth century and the first years of the twentieth, additional hardwood and hemlock operations proliferated throughout Marathon County. The R. Connor Company, taking profitable advantage of the national depression in the early nineties, had by 1897 purchased an enormous amount of hardwood timber. The 1899 cut of the John Manser mill at Kelly reached approximately six million feet, with the hemlock and hardwood accounting for seventy-five per cent of the total. By 1900 the output of mills at the Dells of the Eau Claire River and at Kelly had earned for Lamar Sexmith, a protege of John D. Ross, the designation as one of the largest hemlock producers in Wisconsin. With Stevens Point and Grand Rapids firms leading the way, the Knowlton area anticipated a 1902 cut of seven million feet of mixed timber. By 1903 the Wausau Lumber Company was stocking not only its own mill at Edgar, but also the Italian mill in Cassel, the Hamann mill in Frankfort, and the Barney mill in Hamburg.[73] Indeed, it appeared that things had never been better. The *American Lumberman* informed its readers in early 1903 that all Marathon County mills were reporting "wonderful stocks," and made the prediction that the coming winter cut would most likely be a record breaker. The heavy freight traffic on the two railroads passing through Wausau was indicative of the bustling activity. The stress was so great that "the shipper who manages to secure an empty car considers himself in great luck."[74]

Yet, in reality, the increased attention devoted to hemlock and hardwood would prove only a short term palliative. Wasteful logging practices haunted this branch of the industry as well. A retiring president of the Hardwood Manufacturers' Association declared that the early history of hardwood lumbering was "pathetic and lamentable," marked by wanton destruction, with the choicest trees being cut into badly manufactured lumber and then put on the market unseasoned and unfit for use. In the Town of Easton, at a time when pine was still chiefly sought, hewn logs of maple, oak, and elm were simply placed on piles and burned. Similar habits continued on into the twentieth century. In the Town of Hewitt, logs which could not be cut into twelve-foot lengths were cut instead into a single sixteen-foot length, with the remainder left in the forest to rot. The *American Lumberman* complained that in Wisconsin, hemlock was felled for either the lumber or the bark, but the two operations were rarely combined. A visit to almost any hemlock mill would reveal bark being treated as an unusable byproduct. Conversely, there were whole townships where the ground was littered with rotting timber cut solely for the bark.[75]

It was only a matter of time before the consequences of such extravagance, plus the normal workings of active demand, would be felt. County residents were given a preview of things to come when the B. F. McMillan Company mill was forced to close in early 1911 for a want of timber. Causing considerably more alarm in Wausau was the later shutdown of the Barker & Stewart mill. The sawing of the last log there in the fall of 1915—a ceremony which, according to the *Record-Herald*, "resembled a funeral" with "the blowing whistles [sounding] a requiem"—left several hundred men with neither jobs nor prospects of future employment. Added to the industry's woes was the breakout of full-scale war in Europe, which caused a drop in exports and a resulting decrease in business. Fewer than fifteen years into the new century, the county was witnessing the closing of some of its leading hemlock and hardwood concerns, as pressures on the Wisconsin lumber industry intensified.[76]

Another course of action for those lumbermen with sufficient capital was to keep moving to new sources of supply, no matter how far from the original base of operations. Wausau lumbermen were among the major followers of this trend. In 1901 six of the most influential—Alexander Stewart, Walter Alexander, Walter Bissell, John Ross, Charles Winton, and Cyrus Yawkey—began to hold regular informal meetings to discuss the common problems that arose from the deteriorating situation in the Wisconsin forests. The members of this Wausau Group, as they came to be known throughout the American lumber industry,[77] reached the conclusion that in spite of their freewheeling, independent tradition, concerted action was necessary if they hoped to survive financially. Having made up their minds, they began to look beyond the state's borders to other, less exploited, timberlands as sources of both new supply and investment.

One region that seemed to offer great promise was the southern United States. The South had begun to attract lumbermen after the repeal of the Southern Homestead Act in 1876 opened the way to unrestricted cutting. Wisconsin lumbermen, in particular, began to move south after 1880 when Southern yellow pine, with its advantageous stumpage and labor costs, began to undersell native white pine in their own state. To meet this challenge, they first organized their own industry as much as possible to cut down competition, and then, as added insurance, began investing in Southern timberlands themselves. Although the pace was slowed somewhat by the protests of public-spirited southerners who believed that too much of their timber resources were falling into northern hands, the economic hard times following the Panic of 1893 caused a substantial increase in new acquisitions. The Wausau Group entered the picture at the end of this period. Its first purchase was made in 1901 and consisted of 150,000 acres in the Arkansas soft pine belt near Malvern. The year after, a mill with an annual capacity of 50 million feet was constructed, and the Wisconsin-Arkansas Lumber Company was incorporated.[78]

The major figure involved in the Wausau Group's first southern venture was Cyrus C. Yawkey. Like his business associate and close personal friend, Walter Bissell, Yawkey seemed preordained to pursue a career in lumbering; the name of Yawkey was one of the oldest and most notable in the history of the American lumber business, with long-established roots in Ohio and Michigan. Although Cyrus Yawkey obtained more formal schooling than most of his colleagues in the Wausau lumbering community, the business knowledge he also absorbed through growing up in a lumber-oriented atmosphere would be more valuable in determining his future. Unlike his peers, he began at the top. After a brief interim in the Michigan hardware business, upon reaching the age of twenty-one, Yawkey organized his own firm, Yawkey & Corbyn, in 1883. He remained there only five years, however; in 1888 he joined his uncle, William C. Yawkey, a prosperous midwestern and southern lumberman,[79] in moving to northern Wisconsin. After buying sizable tracts in western Oneida County, the pair formed their own company, with the nephew supervising the construction of the company mill at Hazelhurst.

The transition to this tiny hamlet would be a profitable one for Cyrus Yawkey. He quickly became the biggest logger in the district south of Tomahawk Lake between the region's rail lines. Moreover, by virtue of his locating there, he became a neighbor of Walter Bissell, headquartered at Arbor Vitae only a few miles north.[80] Their paths eventually crossed and they became intimate friends, thereby establishing an important link in the formation of the original Wausau Group. The connection, in fact, led to the second big move by the Group into the southern lumber industry. Large tracts of longleaf pine were purchased in Mississippi's Jones and Wayne Counties in 1902, and the Wausau Southern Lumber Company was organized. The mutual recognition by Yawkey and Bissell that their joint operations in Hazelhurst and Arbor Vitae[81] were nearing an end led to the creation some years later of definite plans for exploitation of these southern holdings. Consequently, in 1911, the Wausau Southern Lumber Company entered the manufacturing field with the construction of a large sawmill at Laurel, Mississippi. Two years later another enterprise was begun at Laurel with the organization of the Marathon Lumber Company. A second mill was constructed which was supplied by timber acreage in Smith and Jasper Counties.[82]

The gaze of area lumbermen also came to focus on the Pacific Northwest. As early as 1885, that region's Douglas fir and redwood had captured the interest of Wisconsin lumbermen. Promotional tours conducted by Pacific coast railroads aided the migration. By the turn of the century numerous Wisconsin operators had been logging the territory for several years, while retaining their interests in the Badger state. Reports sent back to the state described the available timber as "simply immense." In a 1902 evaluation of future lumber markets, the *Wausau Pilot* declared in a gush of enthusiasm: "The West coast is now the lumber supply section of the United States, and . . . will be able to meet the demand for a hundred years."[83]

Such praise notwithstanding, the Wausau Group did not choose to become involved in the Pacific region until a much later date. Even then, the involvement was not so heavy as in the South. Through the consolidation of two Douglas fir and western hemlock properties in Oregon's Willamette Valley, the Silver Falls Timber Company was finally formed in 1912, headquartered in Silverton, Oregon. With a large modern plant and supplemental facilities, the company began to ship by rail three years later to retailers all over the country. The top executives in this successful operation included Cyrus Yawkey, his son-in-law A. P. Woodson, Fowler P. Stone, and brothers Walter and S. B. Bissell.

A subsequent northwestern undertaking demonstrated that the Wausau Group was not infallible in selecting their investment opportunities. The formation and management of the B. C. Spruce Mills (Ltd.) was one of the Group's few but most glaring failures in the lumber business. The firm began with the interest of Group associate B. F. Wilson in British Columbian timber. In 1919 he convinced his colleagues to build a mill at Lumberton, British Columbia. Wilson had an impressive record of achievement in earlier lumbering ventures around Star Lake and in a variety of other Wausau businesses. His good fortune, however, would not carry over into Canada. The B. C. Spruce firm ran into problems almost immediately. A series of difficulties, including changes in design and construction mistakes, delayed the opening of the mill while costs mounted. Once operations finally began, expensive logging methods growing out of the rugged terrain and the great distance from markets created additional financial strain. An oversupplied lumber market and a period of declining prices complicated the situation even further. As the company continued to eat up capital and fall farther behind, the local investors persisted in believing that the application of only a little more money and time would insure success. Finally, by the mid 1930's, the company's stock was worthless, and Cyrus Yawkey and the other Wausau owners ended the fiasco by selling the stock to themselves so they could claim a tax loss. Not everything touched by the Wausau Group turned to gold.[84]

But, with the notable exception of the B. C. Spruce experience, these ventures helped to change Wausau's position of importance in lumbering circles. Although it remained a significant production center for some years to come, the city's primary importance changed to that of a managerial center for various lumbering enterprises throughout northern Wisconsin and the rest of the country. As the twentieth century progressed, Wausau increasingly became the home office location of companies with mills and land holdings far from Marathon County. Yet, the major managerial decisions were made in Wausau, and most important to this area, the profits accumulated in the county seat.

Lumbering operations did continue in Wausau and in other county communities, but their character had undergone some significant changes by the 1920's. New personalities, for instance, were in control of Wausau's most productive and historic lumber plant. On March 2, 1912 the mills of the Alexander Stewart Lumber Company were purchased by an Antigo area corporation, the B. Heinemann Lumber Company. Its founder, Benjamin Heinemann, was no stranger to local business circles, having earlier run a general mercantile business in the city, and later getting his initiation in the lumber business with the George E. Foster lumber firm. News of the transaction's completion generated much excitement in the community. The Heinemann company possessed the largest remaining timber holdings in the area, located on the headwaters of the Trappe, Pine, and Eau Claire Rivers.

To cut this timber, the mill complex would be overhauled and a payroll of at least $75,000 to $100,000 would be provided. Antigo had offered stiff competition in trying to retain the establishment, but the combined efforts of the Wausau Street Railroad Company, the Alexander Stewart firm, and local land agent G. D. Jones had snatched the prize, and thereby given the city's lumber industry a much needed shot in the arm. By 1922, three years after the elder Heinemann's death, the operation was still strong. This heir to the Stevens legacy continued to lead the way in production, with the greatest portion of its annual output of 35 million feet being shipped to the Atlantic seaboard. Not only did the company possess one of the largest mill complexes in the state, but it also claimed to hold the world's records for the biggest carlot shipments. With the company owning 35,000 acres of timber in Wisconsin and Michigan, the *Record-Herald* optimistically forecast that it had sufficient sources of supply "to keep its mills running for at least another quarter of a century." Management reins were still firmly in Heinemann family hands, with two of the founder's sons and his son-in-law occupying the highest executive offices.[85]

Jacob Mortenson Sawmill

The city's second largest lumber concern at the turn of the century, the Jacob Mortenson Company, had also seen several changes by this time. The company had survived the fire of 1904, and had subsequently constructed a new mill. New blood had come into the organization three years earlier, when employees J. H. Johannes, R. H. Genrich, and Peter Larson became stockholders. Charles Edgar, however, left the firm in 1916.[86] Six years later, although Jacob Mortenson and Fowler Stone continued to hold the leadership positions, the principal product of the company had changed considerably, in keeping with the altered conditions in Wisconsin's forests. After 1901, hemlock received the most attention until 1916, after which most of the cut consisted of various Wisconsin hardwoods. Business, however, had fallen off considerably. In an examination of the company's health, the *Record-Herald* lamented that the mill's output was far below 18 million feet, owning to generally depressed industrial conditions and the decreased harvest of pine and hemlock.[87]

Outside Wausau, the larger operations also had a different look about them. In Schofield, the Brooks & Ross Company had weathered a 1910 mill fire and the 1917 death of John D. Ross and continued to operate "one of the model plants of the State." Its mill had a capacity of at least 25 million feet and was supplied by company-owned tracts in Shawano, Iron, and Vilas Counties, and in Michigan's Upper Peninsula. The success enjoyed by Brooks & Ross was due largely to the efforts of John F. Ross and M. P. McCullough. The elder Ross's only son was prepared to assume the leadership role, having obtained a thorough education in every aspect of lumber manufacturing during the early 1890's. After a brief career in the insurance business in Chicago, young Ross returned to the family business, took control of its forest operations, and later served as vice-president until his father's death. Following his promotion to the presidency, he specialized in supervising the logging operations carried on within the company's extensive holdings. Taking charge of the mill was his brother-in-law, M. P. McCullough.

Although marrying the boss' daughter certainly didn't hurt Matthew McCullough's standing in the Ross organization, his knowledge and experience made him an invaluable asset to the new president. Born at Elkton, Maryland, he was first employed in the general office of a railroad company in Chicago. He moved to Schofield just prior to the start of the twentieth century and began working at Brooks & Ross, removing lumber from a planer. After a year and a half of various jobs around the plant, he began his upward climb in the organization by being sent to the firm's Chicago office for six months. Following an additional eighteen months of service in the home office, he was assigned to Arbor Vitae in 1902 as assistant sales manager for the Ross Lumber Company. Finally, in 1904, the same year as his marriage to John D.'s daughter, Louise, the well-traveled bridegroom was called back to Schofield to become general manager of the Brooks & Ross interests; by 1922 he had added the titles of vice-president and secretary.[88]

Accompanying the changes in personnel were important shifts in product emphasis. The third leading pine producer in the county as of 1900, Brooks & Ross by 1922 was cutting fifty per cent hardwood, thirty-five per cent hemlock, and only ten per cent pine. Five years later, the figures had changed to eighty per cent hardwood, ten per cent hemlock, and ten per cent pine; the former was marketed among industrial consumers and the latter two among retail yards.[89]

Lumbering did not disappear entirely from the Mosinee scene following the 1904 closing of the Dessert mill. That same year a successor organization, the Mosinee Land, Log & Timber Company, was formed. Heading the new concern was Joseph Dessert's nephew. Like his uncle, Louis Dessert had worked around lumbering operations as a boy and had come to Marathon County from his native Canada as a young man. After a suitable period of apprenticeship in his uncle's company, he obtained a quarter interest in the firm in 1880 and played an active executive role during the remaining years of the Dessert mill's existence. At its end, with both Joseph Dessert and his chief associate, son-in-law Henry M. Thompson retiring to Milwaukee, it fell to the nephew to try to keep this integral part of Mosinee's economy alive. The continued presence of the Dessert name in the new company must have been a source of reassurance to the community. That familiar personalities from the old firm—Thomas Davis and Frank McReynolds—held executive posts also conveyed a sense of continuity. The purpose of the new concern, moreover, was broader in scope: to engage in lumbering, in the purchasing and selling of real estate, and, unlike the Joseph Dessert Company, in exclusively marketing retail lumber.[90]

The company made a valiant effort. It quickly acquired the competing Gardner Brothers mill on Four Mile Creek and set up a planing mill at Flanner, three miles north of the village.[91] Some four years later it triumphed over the R. Connor Company in acquiring the entire remaining land holdings of the Joseph Dessert Company located west of the Wisconsin River. The purchase of this valuable 34,345 acre tract of mixed timber in the townships of Mosinee, Bergen, and Emmet was hailed at the time as one of the most important land transfers in the county. For a while the mill was able to turn out as much as three million board feet a year. The glory days were not to be recaptured, however. By 1920, with the large timber stands of the past only a memory, the company's city-based sawmill closed permanently. Demand from farmers for custom sawing kept the firm technically alive, but operations were conducted on a greatly reduced scale with a small sawmill installed in the planing mill building.[92]

Change was also inevitable in the western county lumbering scene. The paternalism that had characterized the relationship between the Rietbrock Company and the Athens community remained to some degree following Frederick Rietbrock's death in 1906, when the leadership reins were placed in the hands of his son-in-law, William Erbach. The differences in the character of the industry were more striking, however. In the first place, the area sawmills were no longer turning out lumber for construction purposes. Instead, the product of the Rietbrock and Braun mills was going to furniture and box companies, representative of the maturing wood products industry. Moreover, the farmers, who had long been important timber suppliers for the local mills, began to be more selective in what they sold, saving pine and hemlock for their own building purposes. Finally, an important change in logging transportation was also taking place near the end of the twenties. The growing unprofitability of clearing land by rail and sleigh caused Athens lumbermen to add motor trucks to their transportation fleets. This was also the case in the Marathon area, where since 1925 the Menzner Company had been forced to purchase timber tracts with or without the land, to keep its mill running. The introduction of the truck made it economically easier to keep moving farther from home base in search of stock, as traditional sources of supply continued to dry up.[93]

As with most empires throughout history, the decline of the lumber industry in Wisconsin and Marathon County was a gradual process, with no single event signaling the end. It has been estimated that the state lumber industry had entered its final phase by 1906. However, at least two new sawmills commenced operations in the Town of Berlin in the 1920's, and the number of lumber concerns in Wausau had increased to a maximum of thirty-three by 1925.[94] The eventual growth of a responsible conservation policy for state forests was another encouraging twentieth century trend. In this respect, the creation in 1907 of the Wausau-based Wisconsin Valley Improvement Company and the later activities of Wausau-reared lumberman John Mylrea were of major significance.[95]

In spite of these developments, there was unassailable statistical evidence that the industry's health was deteriorating as the century progressed. The total state lumber cut recorded in 1925 was sixty per cent below the figure tabulated a quarter century earlier; the number of operating state sawmills decreased by more than seventy-seven per cent during the same period. Not surprisingly, Wisconsin's relative importance in national lumbering suffered a simultaneous and dramatic decline. After being the leading lumber producer in the United States at the turn of the century, the state had fallen to eighth place by 1909, and ranked fourteenth by 1923, amidst projections that large-scale logging operations within its border would cease within another twelve years.[96]

The general business malaise occasioned by the Great Depression added yet another strain. Caught in a three-way crossfire of declining production, bloated stocks on hand, and no evidence of increasing demand, the state lumber industry entered into a contract with the state government to regulate production and attempt to keep employment evenly distributed. This joint effort, according to Governor Phillip La Follette, would 'stop the complete shutting down of plants,' and '. . . apply to the lumber industry in Wisconsin some of the principles upon which the co-operative societies in other economic fields operate.' Supervising the implementation of the agreement was a committee of five representing the state and a committee of seven representing the lumber industry, with the latter group having decidedly more power in the arrangement.[97] It is interesting to note that four of the seven members of the lumberman's committee—John D. Mylrea, W. W. Gamble,[98] W. D. Connor, and Matthew P. McCullough—had ties to Marathon County.[99]

The government-business partnership, no matter how well intentioned, could not cure the industry's basic illness. Gloomy forecasts continued to be issued throughout the Depression years. A bulletin released in 1930 by the Wisconsin College of Agriculture predicted that it was doubtful that more than one-fourth of the operating state mills had an assured log supply beyond the next decade.[100] Two years later, at Governor La Follette's request, the Committee on Land Use and Forestry—of which John Mylrea was a member—issued a detailed report "on the economic conditions that have followed in the wake of the removal of the timber wealth." Its supplemental data was no more encouraging. White pine had almost entirely disappeared from

Wisconsin forests, the last sizable commercial stands having been cut and sawed in 1930. Northern hardwoods, which had increasingly borne the brunt of forest exploitation since 1895, were also rapidly diminishing in terms of both acreage and volume. In fact, the total state lumber output for 1930, including lath and shingles, was at the lowest level ever recorded in history by the Wisconsin lumber industry. In 1900 Marathon County alone had four sawmills with an annual cut of more than 25 million feet; by 1929 there were only six in the whole state. Despite a recent and heavy importation of lumber, Wisconsin's forest resources were being depleted faster than they could be replaced through growth. Sawtimber was being removed sixteen times as fast as new timber was growing to merchantable size.[101]

Given the steady advance of the depletion process, it was only a matter of time before its logical conclusion, foreshadowed by the Dessert, McMillan, and Barker & Stewart closings, would be felt in Marathon County. One by one, familiar fixtures in the county lumbering fraternity began to disappear. Even before the debilitating effects of the Great Depression, the pioneer Sellin mill, which had provided employment for residents of Berlin, Hamburg, Maine, and Stettin, closed in 1927 and was dismantled three years later. The larger concerns were soon to follow. The end of manufacturing operations for Wausau's B. Heinemann Lumber Company came in 1935; the following year its landmark mill complex, a symbol through generations of the contributions made by George Stevens, Walter McIndoe, Alexander Stewart, Walter Alexander, and finally Benjamin Heinemann, to the economic growth of the Wausau community, was razed by WPA workers, providing an ironic reminder of the supremacy of economic necessity. A closing of equal symbolic significance for the Athens area occurred in the fall of 1937, when the Rietbrock mill completed its final cut. The *Athens Record* composed something of an epitaph in noting the event "which, like a shadow, had been for a long time creeping forward slowly: Now, its work accomplished, the mill stands like a quiet landmark of the past. No longer do we hear the rip of its saws nor the blast of its exhaust. The mill is silent forever!" Sawmills did continue to operate in the village for some years thereafter.[102] However, the subsequent destruction of the Rietbrock mill by fire effectively ended the lumbering era of Athens' economic development.[103]

The Brooks & Ross mill proved slightly more successful in withstanding the hostile business climate. Its prospects had looked shaky during the early 1930's, due to irregular periods of operation. The end finally appeared at hand in 1935 when the Brooks and Ross Company sawed its last log, and many of the employees began to apply for relief jobs in the expectation that the mill would be permanently closed. A reprieve of sorts was granted to Schofield later in the year when the mill and other company properties were purchased by a newly organized Wausau Group enterprise, the Yawkey-Alexander Lumber Company. Under the new management the mill had a relatively fruitful run for the next several years, sawing logs obtained from a tract of hemlock and hardwood timber located in Lincoln County.[104] The inevitable could only be postponed for a time, however, and on September 1, 1942, the company was forced to halt its sawmill operations because of war-related difficulties.[105] President and General Manager Harold C. Collins[106] personally announced the end with a mixture of finality and regret:

> We meet here on a sorrowful and historic occasion. Sorrowful, because many of you have been employed in this mill for the greater part of your lifetime. Historic, because the mill has operated in this village for many years and because the fine white ash log which we just sawed is probably the last one to go through this mill in the village of Schofield. You, of course, all realize our own timber is now depleted.[107]

With its dismantling by the Connor interests,[108] the last of the large capacity sawmills that had once dominated Marathon County's industrial landscape had joined the realm of historical memory.

There were, to be sure, survivors in the postwar era, but their condition plainly indicated how far lumbering had fallen in the industrial hierarchy of the county by the mid-twentieth century. In Wausau the familiar Mortenson name remained,[109] although the company had gone through considerable changes. During the early Depression years, its base of operations was moved west, away from the Wisconsin River bank, and the firm's emphasis changed to retail sales of lumber, roofing, and other building materials. In terms of leadership, this period also witnessed the deaths of Fowler P. Stone and J. H. Johannes; nonetheless, some links with the past were maintained through the later assumption of management responsibilities by R. H. Genrich and descendants of the deceased.[110] In Mosinee, the legacy of Joseph Dessert was carried on by the small sawmill operation of the Mosinee Land, Log & Timber Company;[111] at no time, however, did its annual cut exceed half a million feet. Four years after the death of Louis Dessert's son, Howard, in 1969, his daughter Margaret decided to liquidate the company and devote her full attention to running a more profitable subsidiary, a wholesale craft shop.[112] Thus, by the mid-1970's, there existed outside of Wausau only two lumbering concerns with roots going back to the nineteenth century. In Marathon City, a third generation of the Menzner family was keeping that area's historic mill operation alive, while in the Town of Brighton a fourth generation of Andersons had inherited the family mill that had been a fixture in the Spencer area for more than seven decades. Both had survived destructive fires and the economic forces fatal to so many others, to remain as symbols of a prosperous lumbering past.[113]

The question remains: did the county and state lumber industry have to come to such an inauspicious end? The question admittedly suggests some condemnation of the lumbermen. It would be tempting and easy to conclude simply by excoriating them for their haste and carelessness in the woods. And to a large extent it would be justifiable. Waste continued long after the Roth report warned of the serious consequences such ravishment entailed for the future survival of the Wisconsin lumber industry.[114] The first loyalty of many lumbermen was to their balance sheets, not to the land that gave them their wealth. When times became difficult, those who were able joined the rush south and west to fresh sources of supply, leaving the Cutover as an undistinguished monument to Wisconsin's lumber heritage. However, to pronounce a guilty verdict on the lumber kings and then end the discussion would not be fair. Their activities, after all, contributed much to the organized settlement of county communities in the forested wilderness. Moreover, compelling economic influences over which the lumbermen had imperfect control continued to chip away at their industry as the twentieth century progressed. The conditions imposed by available technology formed one major example. Not until the truck was introduced into the logging process did small operations become economically feasible. In the heyday of the heavy logging railroads, with big camps and massive equipment in the woods, the lumbermen saw only one way to make their investments pay off—take every marketable log in sight. Another economic force which operated to the detriment of the industry and about which the lumbermen could do little was the law of demand. As the twentieth century unfolded, a decrease in demand helped weaken an already shaky lumber industry. The per capita consumption of lumber products dropped from 458 board feet in 1899 to approximately 280 board feet by 1928. This situation was brought about by three factors: the growing timber shortage, disproportionate population increases, and an unmistakable drop in demand for lumber products. The great fear expressed among the hemlock and hardwood lumbermen at their 1915 convention—the growing competitive threat of lumber substitutes—continued to haunt their business in the years ahead. Indeed, by 1939, a group of congressional investigators was being told by a leading Wisconsin lumberman that since the beginning of the century a seventy-five per cent decline in the use of wood had taken place.[115]

Finally, it is essential to point out once again that the lumbermen did not have to subvert contemporary community standards to cut down the forests as they saw fit. To repeat a point made earlier: there was no discernible discussion of the Roth report in the county press. Moreover, before 1927 the logger could and did reasonably argue that the "cut out and get out" philosophy was actually being encouraged by a government taxation policy that served to eat up profits if limited cutting was undertaken.[116] In short, many environmental crises later, it seems that timber was merely the first of our precious natural resources to be taken for granted by virtually everyone in the pursuit of economic expansion. In any case, those in the county most directly affected by the decline of the lumber industry had little interest in apportioning blame for the deteriorating situation. Nor did they have the time. A recent student of the process has determined that all of the Marathon County lumbertowns in his study—Wausau, Athens, Schofield, Mosinee, Spencer, and Unity—had entered their period of continuing decline by the end of the first decade of the twentieth century.[117] Early in the new century, decisions had to be made that would determine the future economic health of the county. The exact magnitude of that decline could not, of course, have been foreseen at that time, but storm clouds were clearly visible on the horizon.

FOOTNOTES

[1] Since its most commercially valuable stands were white and Norway pine, this forest area was commonly referred to as the pinery, though, in fact, there were sizable tracts of mixed conifers and hardwoods which were not dominated by pine. Wisconsin's pine forests were part of a great forest belt which stretched from New England through the Great Lakes, with Lake Erie marking its southernmost fringe. This tremendous forest dominated both the Michigan peninsulas and the northern three-fifths of Wisconsin, and then extended northward through eastern and northern Minnesota into Canada. When Jean Nicolet became the first white man to explore this Lake States region in 1634, he found an area which contained 122.7 million acres of land, of which 103.7 million acres were forest. The total stand of timber in Wisconsin's roughly 30 million acres of original forests, while it can only be approximated, easily exceeded 200 billion board feet. See Robert C. Nesbit, *Wisconsin, A History* (Madison: The University of Wisconsin Press, 1973), pp. 296-297; J. H. Alexander, "A Short Industrial History of Wisconsin," *The*

Wisconsin Blue Book, 1929 (Madison: Democrat Printing Company, 1929), p. 42; John Newhouse, "Logging On The Upper Wisconsin," History of Wausau, (manuscript in the Archives of the State Historical Society of Wisconsin, 1939), p. 1; Maurice L. Branch, "The Paper Industry In the Lake States, 1834-1947," (Ph.D. dissertation, University of Wisconsin, 1947), pp. 90-91; State of Wisconsin, *Forest Land Use In Wisconsin*, Report of the Committee On Land Use And Forestry (Madison: Executive Office, 1932), p. 12.

[2] Lumbering operations had been undertaken in the region prior to the building of Whitney's mill in 1832. However, as they were covertly conducted on Indian territory, and federal law forbade white men to log on Indian lands without special permission, it constituted trespassing and was therefore illegal. At least one instance was recorded of such intruders being evicted upon being discovered by United States soldiers. Whitney's mill was the first officially sanctioned private timber cutting operation on the Wisconsin River. See Newhouse, "Logging," pp. 1-2.

[3] This description of George Stevens is taken from Judge George W. Cate's history of Stevens Point, quoted in the *Wausau Pilot*, March 18, 1926, p. 6.

[4] The timing of Stevens' journey was also most opportune. As pressure steadily mounted from western settlers for more lumber at a cheaper price for construction purposes, the federal government's earlier reluctance to encroach upon Indian lands disappeared. In 1837 General Henry Dodge concluded a treaty with the Menominee Indians which ceded a forty-mile strip of land extending three miles wide on each side of the Wisconsin River from Point Baussee to Big Bull Falls. It was this territory that Stevens was sent out to investigate. See Newhouse, "Logging," p. 2; E. B. Thayer, "Observations on the History of Marathon County," (manuscript in the Marathon County Historical Society, 1939), pp. 1-2; *Wausau Pilot*, March 18, 1926, p. 6.

[5] See Marchetti, *Marathon County*, p. 60; E. B. Thayer, "A Tale Before The Daughters American Revolution, March 8, 1929," (manuscript in the Marathon County Historical Society, 1929), p. 2.

[6] "The volume of the land was on the west side of the river. It took in the river from about the Barker & Stewart Island and extended south, taking in the islands below the falls." *Wausau Pilot*, March 18, 1926, p. 6.

[7] *Wausau Pilot*, April 1, 1926, p. 3.

[8] *Ibid.*

[9] *Ibid.*

[10] Thayer, "A Tale," p. 3.

Robert F. Fries, *Empire In Pine, The Story of Lumbering in Wisconsin, 1830-1900* (Madison: The State Historical Society of Wisconsin, 1951), pp. 8, 12, 16-17.

William G. Rector, *Log Transportation in the Lake States Lumber Industry* (Glendale: The Arthur H. Clark Company, 1953), p. 150.

[11] In a letter dated December 7, 1838, Stevens said of his return trip from Big Bull Falls to Almond, New York: "I arrived safe home, although we had one of the most tremendous gales ever experienced on Lake Huron and on Lake Erie; the boat got on fire, but was extinguished without any material damage." *Wausau Pilot*, March 25, 1926, p. 7.

[12] Most of the rivers had several lumbermen logging on the banks, all of whom expected to use the same "natural highway" simultaneously. Since keeping the logs separated was an impossibility, each owner marked his logs by stamping his brand on the ends. A second mark was often axed into the bark to determine ownership when the logs lay in the water.

[13] The Wausau Boom Company was organized in 1871 under the guiding hand of Walter McIndoe. The company's six-mile long system of booms came to extend as far north as Brokaw and cost an estimated $30,000. The system had storage space for 30 million feet of logs and facilities for handling 100 million feet annually; by 1895 it had a capacity of 150 million feet. See "Minute Book, Wausau Boom Company, 1871 - 1905," Marathon County Historical Society; Newhouse, "Logging," p. 20.

[14] Fries, *Empire*, pp. 48-50.

Rector, *Log Transportation*, pp. 91-146.

William G. Rector. "From Woods to Sawmill, Transportation Problems in Logging," *Southern Lumberman*, July 15, 1949, pp. 54, 56, 60.

[15] Sinking was not the only cause for the 'shrinkage' in the number of logs which finally reached the booms. Timber floating over the valley floor during high water would be stranded when the river eased back into the channel. A wet log exposed to the sun's rays often rotted. Worms and insects were quick to attack. Finally, so long as the logs were placed in the water, lumber thievery was a factor. See Rector, "From Woods to Sawmill," p. 62.

[16] The "grubs" were made from small trees, dug up with the roots attached to them. They had to be four feet in length and large enough after being dressed to fill a hole two inches in diameter, with a head left on the root end approximately three inches in diameter to keep them from pulling through the grub plank. See Wausau Pilot, June 3, 1926, p. 6; Rector, Log Transportation, p. 150.

[17] "Otto Schoepke's Autobiography," (manuscript in the Marathon County Historical Society), p. 6.

Pneumonia was not the only disease the lumberjacks had to fear. A logger from the Town of Easton remembered that diphtheria would occasionally strike the lumber camps. See Elsie Thorpe, comp., "History Of The Township Of Easton," (manuscript in the Marathon County Historical Society), p. 34.

See also Wausau Pilot, June 3, 1926, p. 6; Newhouse, "Logging," pp. 15-18.

[18] "Exchange Club Told Of Lumber Rafting In Early Days," undated newspaper clipping in Charles Dodge Collection, Lumber Business Box, State Historical Society.

Wausau Pilot, June 3, 1926, p. 6.

Wausau Daily Record-Herald, Centennial Edition, March 13, 1939, Historical Section, p. 45; Industrial Section, pp. 93, 95. "Daring Loggers," Special Wausau Number Wisconsin Magazine, 1952, p. 43.

[19] Nesbit, Wisconsin, pp. 299, 302-303.

Fries, Empire, pp. 84-86.

James Bruce Smith, "Lumbertowns in the Cutover: A Comparative Study of the Stage Hypothesis of Urban Growth," (Ph.D. dissertation, University of Wisconsin, 1973), pp. 33-34.

Harold Miner, "Economic Development," History of Wausau, (manuscript in the Archives of the State Historical Society of Wisconsin, 1939), pp. 12-13.

See also Marchetti, Marathon County, pp. 67, 142.

[20] Smith, "Lumbertowns," pp. 33-34.

Miner, "Economic Development," pp. 12-13.

Fries, Empire, pp. 86-87.

Etta Burnett et al., Spencer, Wisconsin, 1874 - 1974, p. 18.

Colby, Wisconsin Centennial, 1873 - 1973, p. 4.

100 Years — Abbotsford, Wisconsin, p. 15.

Mary Roddis Connor, A Century With Connor Timber, Connor Forest Industries, 1872 - 1972 (Stevens Point: Worzalla Publishing Company, 1972), pp. 12, 16.

Arlan C. Helgeson, "Athens, Wisconsin, A Study Of The Economic Development Of A Northern Village," (Master's dissertation, University of Wisconsin, 1948), pp. 28-29.

Alfred Schmidt, "History of Milan," from packet of material on the history of Milan contributed by Mr. Alfred Schmidt, Box 335, Milan, Wisconsin 54453.

See also Marchetti, Marathon County, pp. 137-138, 502, 507, 517, 523, 527, 562, 568.

[21] The Wisconsin River pinery ranked third among the state's river systems in this respect. Its 23.1 percentage yield placed it far ahead of the third ranking St. Croix pinery, which had yielded 9.7 per cent of the state total. Only the Chippewa - Red Cedar pinery, dominated by the Weyerhauser interests and Knapp, Stout and Company yielded more: 43 billion board feet, or 33.2 percent of the total Wisconsin output. See Filbert Roth, Forestry Conditions of Northern Wisconsin, Wisconsin Geological and Natural History Survey, Bulletin No. 1, Economic Series No. 1 (Madison: State of Wisconsin, 1898), p. 16.

[22] For a complete account of the activities of the pioneer Wausau lumbermen, see Marchetti, Marathon County, pp. 67-72. For a fairly complete listing of the earliest upper Wisconsin valley mills and their respective lumber products, see Wausau Daily Record, June 24, 1906, p. 5.

[23] Miner, "Economic Development," pp. 12-16. For a more detailed account of the legal and political infighting which took place over the effort to secure rail service for Wausau, see Marchetti, Marathon County, pp. 154-160.

[24] Harold Miner, "General History," History of Wausau, (manuscript in the Archives of the State Historical Society of Wisconsin, 1939), pp. 30-31.

[25] The available data shows that other county lumbertowns were not as seriously affected by the national hard times: the lumber cut from 1876 to 1877 fell only slightly in Mosinee, and actually rose in Spencer and Unity.

[26] Smith, "Lumbertowns," pp. 59-66.
Miner, "Economic Development," pp. 18-19.

[27] "Builders of Great Industries — Being a Story of the Wausau Group and the Men Who Made It," American Lumberman, July 9, 1927, p. 1.

[28] Stewart made the balance of his trip, from Milwaukee to Wausau, on foot. At that time, the "road" from Stevens Point to Wausau was little more than an Indian trail. For Stewart's description of his journey, see Wausau Pilot, February 4, 1926, p. 6.

[29] Martin, "Wausau in 1900," pp. 129-130.
"Builders of Great Industries," p. 57.
Wausau Pilot, May 28, 1912, p. 4; February 4, 1926, p. 6; March 11, 1926, pp. 1, 8; January 30, 1900, p. 1; January 29, 1901, p. 1.
Wausau Daily Record-Herald, May 24, 1912, pp. 1-2; March 8, 1926, pp. 1, 4.

[30] Mortenson and Edgar would also form a connection with Walter Alexander. The following year the Alexander & Edgar Lumber Company was organized with Jacob Mortenson serving as secretary.

[31] The pair would also be associated in the Garth Lumber Company of Wisconsin and Michigan: Stone as secretary and treasurer, Mortenson as a principal stockholder.

[32] Martin, "Wausau in 1900," p. 103.
"Builders of Great Industries," p. 57.
Wausau Daily Record-Herald, Golden Anniversary Edition, August 9, 1922, Section 4, p. 3.
Wausau Daily Record-Herald, May 26, 1924, p. 1; January 18, 1934, p. 1; June 29, 1933, p. 1.
Wausau Pilot, May 29, 1924, p. 1; January 18, 1934, p. 1; June 29, 1933, p. 1; January 29, 1901, p. 1.

[33] Besides the Stewart and Mortenson firms, the American Lumberman listed the following concerns as having contributed to Wausau's pine cut in 1900:
Arntsen & Hirsch — 115,000 feet
Barker & Stewart — 800,000 feet
Curtis & Yale Co. — 1,000,000 feet
Lystul & Erickson — 150,000 feet
J. Slimmer & Co. — 125,000 feet

[34] Wausau Pilot, January 29, 1901, p. 1.

[35] Initially, the community was known as the village of Eau Claire.

[36] "Builders of Great Industries," p. 56.

[37] "Builders of Great Industries," pp. 56-57.
Wausau Daily Record-Herald, May 27, 1926, p. 8; December 12, 1933, p. 1.
Although Bissell's tenure at the Brooks & Ross Company was for only five years, he was in the years ahead to continue as the chief supervisor of important projects undertaken by the Ross interests. In 1888, following the company's purchase of a large tract of timberlands along the Prairie River in neighboring Lincoln County, he organized and managed the mills of the Ross-financed Wisconsin Valley Lumber Company at Harrison. When that region's timber supply had been exhausted some five years later, a large acquisition of white pine timber was made tributary to Arbor Vitae, and Bissell was again called upon to set up and head the mill of the newly formed Ross Lumber Company located in that Vilas County community.

[38] Delays in provisioning due to the primitive transportation routes and the great distances that had to be covered was, again, a major problem. On one occasion supplies became so low at Little Bull Falls that the workers' sole diet for days consisted of salt pork and black strap molasses. 'We could not do much work on food such as that,' Joseph Dessert later recalled, 'but there was no help for it until supplies arrived once more, so we made the best of it and performed such work as we were able.'

[39] Although in this period the immediate area around Mosinee was logged, many

pine logs were also floated down the Rib and Wisconsin Rivers from Dessert logging projects along the Rib in Marathon County and near its headwaters in Taylor County.

[40] The *American Lumberman* also listed the Gardner Brothers firm as having contributed to Mosinee's 1900 pine lumber output, with a cut of 100,000 feet.

[41] *Mosinee Times*, February 4, 1898, p. 8.

[42] Martin, "Wausau in 1900," pp. 69-70.
Mosinee Times, August 8, 1957, p. 8.
Wausau Pilot, February 29, 1926, p. 3; January 29, 1901, p. 1.

[43] Among this twenty-five to thirty man work team was Andrew Kreutzer, who would choose to make Black Creek Falls his home and would subsequently become one of the major figures in the county's political history.

[44] Dorchester, just within Clark County, was twelve miles closer to the new settlement than Wausau. In addition, the Wisconsin Central route from Milwaukee to Dorchester was more direct than the competing Wisconsin Valley line, connecting Wausau to Tomah.

[45] Rietbrock's dedication and resolve was evidenced by the fact that he mortgaged more than 10,000 acres of his personal holdings to help finance the railroad project. Over the years the company utilized other methods of log transportation in addition to the rail route. Although Black Creek was too small for actual log drives, some pine logs were floated down the tiny stream to the Rib River, then to the Wisconsin, and finally to the Dessert mill at Mosinee. To bring logs to the parent mill, a forerunner of the tractor known as a steam hauler was used. This was a locomotive equipped with caterpillar treads and bobsled runners in front. The "Black Horse" was an object of widespread interest in the Athens area. The iced trails on which it ran could be seen in the Towns of Halsey, Johnson, and Bern. The steam hauler was not the safest device to operate. The pilot in charge of steering had to sit in front and was completely unsheltered from the worst winter weather. Frank Writz, Sr., who piloted the Rietbrock locomotive during the company's entire twentieth century life span, as a protective measure began to grow a beard every August; it was claimed that by Thanksgiving only his eyes could be seen through the mass of hair. Tragedy struck the R. Connor firm on May 19, 1911 when its steam hauler, "Rosie," crashed through a weakened bridge during a giant hailstorm, killing its crew. The disaster ended steam hauler use in the Stratford area. See Connor, *Connor Timber*, p: 89.

[46] The name change, which apparently occurred in the early 1890's, was precipitated by the local merchants, who were constantly finding their shipments confused with those intended for Black River Falls in Jackson County. Accordingly, they called on the village school teacher, F. A. Strupp, to come up with a new name. Applying his book learning, Strupp concluded that the logical name for what would someday be the leading community in a county named Marathon, had to be Athens.

[47] As was typical throughout the north woods, conditions endured by the Rietbrock crews were far from the idyllic picture portrayed by much logging legend. In the course of a rigorous winter, food provided for the men often froze. The average wages in the early 1880's amounted to a dollar a day plus board, with the Rietbrock Company assuming fifty cents a day per capita for the latter. It was not unusual, however, for the men to have to wait two months or more to get their pay.

[48] Rietbrock's law partners displayed less interest in the ventures as the years went by, and dropped from the organization altogether by 1901, the firm name then being changed to the Rietbrock Land and Lumber Company.

[49] The firm, later re-named Braun Brothers & Company, over the years conducted only limited logging operations of its own, according to a former resident of the area; instead, it mostly purchased timber and then sawed it. What logging the company actually did itself was conducted in the Town of Rietbrock. The Brauns, being related to the old German stock in and around Poniatowski, did a large amount of their business with their in-laws in that region.

[50] Helgeson, "Athens, Wisconsin," pp. 15-19, 24-26, 28-29, 36-37.
American Lumberman, January 20, 1900, p. 21.
Wausau Daily Record, July 23, 1906, p. 5.
Wausau Pilot, January 29, 1901, p. 1.

Interview with former Athens area resident, April, 1976.

[51] Alma Fromm, "Sellin Sawmill Was Thriving Pioneer Enterprise," *Wausau Daily Record-Herald*, November 25, 1967, p. 14.

Wausau Pilot, January 29, 1901, p. 1.

DuWayne Zamzow, ed., *Berlin's Memories In 1976*, p. 23.

Ruth Prahl, "History of the Town of Wausau," (manuscript in the Marathon County Historical Society, 1976), p. 2.

A. G. Straub, *The History of Marathon, Wis. 1857 To 1957* (Marathon: Marathon Times, 1957), p. 49.

The *American Lumberman* included the following additional concerns as having contributed to the county's 1900 pine timber cut:

R. B. Salter & Co., Colby
McMillan & Bro., McMillan
G. H. Rohrback, Rozellville
John Gardner, Spencer
J. H. Harding, Spencer
Wausau Lumber Co., Edgar
Carl Schield, Nutterville
John Loy & Co., Stettin
J. Loye & Co., Stettin
Quaw Lumber Co., Edgar
G. H. Altenburg, Dancy

[52] According to the *American Lumberman*, the "shot gun" steam feed, which moved the log carriage to the saw, was "the greatest single improvement tending to increase the capacity of the saw mill. . . ." In Marathon County the Rietbrock company installed such a device when its steam operated mill was constructed.

[53] *American Lumberman*, January 5, 1901, pp. 15-16.

Robert F. Fries, "A History Of The Lumber Industry In Wisconsin," (Ph.D. dissertation, University of Wisconsin, 1939), p. 352.

U.S. Department of Commerce, Bureau of the Census, *Twelfth Census of the United States: 1900*, vol. 8, *Manufacturers*, pt. 2, Wisconsin, p. 953.

Further technological improvements in lumbering were forecast. A prominent Wisconsin valley lumberman predicted that the first decade of the new century would see more of a revolution in methods of sawmill operation than the previous ten had witnessed in log transportation. In less than ten years' time practically every mill in the valley figured to be operated by electricity instead of by steam. See *Wausau Daily Record*, January 29, 1900, p. 3.

[54] *Twelfth Census*, vol. 8, pt. 2, p. 953.

[55] Fries, "A History," p. 410.

[56] Enlisting the aid of railroad land agents, timber cruisers, and county officials, Roth included in his study area most of the territory from Jackson and Wood Counties north to the state boundary: twenty-seven counties with a total land area of about 18.5 million acres or approximately fifty-three per cent of the entire state.

[57] Roth, *Forestry Conditions*, pp. 1-78 passim.

Milwaukee Sentinel, February 8, 1898, pp. 1, 10.

Vernon Carstensen, *Farms or Forests, Evolution of a State Land Policy for Northern Wisconsin 1850 - 1932* (Madison: University of Wisconsin Press, 1958), pp. 27-28.

According to the Roth report, Marathon County's supply of standing pine timber — 200 million board feet — was exceeded by fourteen of the counties in the Wisconsin Cutover region, and was equaled by another. Thus, only four Cutover counties had less standing pine timber than did Marathon County at the close of the nineteenth century. See Roth, *Forestry Conditions*, p. 9.

[58] Fries, "A History," pp. 418-420.

Fire in the woods was not the only peril county lumbermen had to face. The mills themselves could be inviting targets for fiery destruction. In the summer of 1906 the Brehmer sawmill in the Town of Flieth burned to the ground. Acknowledged as "one of the best equipped little mills in the country, having its own electric light plant and all of its machinery up to date," the $12,000 operation was unluckily only lightly insured. Similarly, in the spring of 1915, the Menzner mill at Marathon City was reduced in two hours "to a pile of ashes and debris." The flames made no discrimination as to the size of the operation. In the summer of 1904, at a time when the pages of the *Wausau Pilot* were filled with stories of monstrous blazes throughout the United States, the mill of the Jacob Mortenson Lumber Company was completely destroyed due to a delay in turning in a fire alarm. See *Wausau Daily Record,* July 27, 1906, p. 5; *Marathon Times,* April 6, 1915, p. 1; *Wausau Pilot,* July 26, 1904, p. 5.

[59] *Northwestern Lumberman,* September 28, 1878, quoted in Charles E. Twining, "Plunder And Progress: The Lumbering Industry In Perspective," *Wisconsin Magazine of History* 47 (Winter 1963 - 1964): 123.

[60] Twining, "Plunder And Progress," pp. 122-123.

Nesbit, *Wisconsin,* p. 310.

[61] *Wausau Pilot,* November 11, 1902, p. 1.

[62] *Mosinee Times,* August 8, 1957, p. 8.

Joseph Dessert subsequently moved to Milwaukee where he was to spend the remaining seven years of his life in retirement.

[63] *Wausau Daily Record,* February 15, 1900, p. 3.

American Lumberman, January 24, 1903, p. 51.

[64] *Marathon Times,* January 14, 1910, p. 1.

[65] *Wausau Pilot,* June 20, 1911, p. 5.

[66] Fries, "A History," p. 411.

Rector, *Log Transportation,* pp. 287-288.

"Schoepke's Autobiography," p. 3.

Thorpe, "Easton," pp. 40, 49.

American Lumberman, January 18, 1902, p. 12.

Smith, "Lumbertowns," pp. 23-24.

[67] Roth, *Forestry Conditions,* pp. 9, 61-62.

[68] Interview with George C. Landon, June 30, 1976.

American Lumberman, November 12, 1910, p. 1.

Central Wisconsin, August 28, 1909, p. 5.

Wausau Daily Record-Herald, August 28, 1909, p. 5.

A number of other county lumbermen held important office in this trade association. At the organization's 1915 annual meeting, M. P. McCullough, a Ross lieutenant at Brooks & Ross, was re-elected chairman of the Advertising Committee (re-named Bureau of Promotion). This was a major responsibility, considering the association members' often expressed concern about the high powered advertising campaigns being conducted on behalf of lumber substitutes. He was later elected president. See Northern Hemlock & Hardwood Manufacturers' Association, *Some Lumber Problems, Minutes of the Sixth Annual Meeting* (Wausau, Wis.: Secretary's Office, 1915), pp. 43-54, 98-100, 102. The presidency was later held by Walter Bissell's eldest son, F. K. Bissell, in the late 1920's, and by Harold C. Collins in the early 1940's. See "Builders Of Great Industries," pp. 60-61: *Wausau Daily Record-Herald,* September 2, 1942, p. 1.

[69] Northern Hemlock & Hardwood Manufacturers' Association, *Some Lumber Problems,* p. 52.

[70] *American Lumberman,* February 14, 1903, p. 24.

[71] *Ibid.,* p. 25.

[72] *Ibid.*

[73] Connor, *Connor Timber,* pp. 16, 19, 26.

Wausau Pilot, October 10, 1899, p. 1; December 31, 1901, p. 1.

American Lumberman, January 27, 1900, p. 24; March 28, 1903, p. 32.

[74] *American Lumberman,* February 7, 1903, pp. 32-33.

[75] *American Lumberman,* January 20, 1906, p. 37; January 18, 1902, p. 12.

Thorpe, "Easton," pp. 23, 32.

[76] *Wausau Pilot,* February 28, 1911, p. 1.

Wausau Daily Record-Herald, September 22, 1914, p. 1.

George C. Landon Interview.

[77] In a retrospective look at the activities of the Wausau Group, the *American Lumberman* declared it "one of the great lumber institutions of the Nation, an institution that . . . is the product not of cold business scheming nor ruthless financial manipulation, but the direct result of life-long friendships . . . between

a distinguished group of remarkable men and families." Nonetheless, the Group was made up of no-nonsense lumbermen whose actions were determined by definite preferences. One anecdote is illustrative. A close friend believed he had a profitable lumber deal in the works that the Wausau Group would want to get in on. Accordingly, the Group was convened, and the hopeful prospective partner made a lengthy sales pitch covering every imaginable detail about the available timber stand, with one omission. When he had finished, he was asked a single question by one member of the Group: "Charley, what kind of pine is this? Is it white pine or red pine?" With some surprise, he replied, "This is hemlock." With that, the presiding officer of the Group slammed his hand on the table and said, "The meeting is adjourned; we're *pine* men." Interview with John Forester, August 20, 1975, Marathon County Public Library Oral History Collection. This inflexibility would soften in time, however, reflecting the changing realities within Wisconsin's forests. See C. C. Yawkey to J. D. Mylrea, November 11, 1925, John D. Mylrea Journals, vol. 9, Marathon County Historical Society.

[78] Fries, *Empire*, p. 82.

"Builders of Great Industries," pp. 56, 58.

Steven Burton Karges, "David Clark Everest And Marathon Paper Mill Company: A Study Of A Wisconsin Entrepreneur—1909-1931," (Ph.D. dissertation, University of Wisconsin, 1968), pp. 49-50, 54-56.

Ralph Hidy, Frank Hill, and Allan Nevins, *Timber and Men: The Weyerhaeuser Story* (New York: The Macmillan Company, 1963), pp. 207-208.

The principal stockholders in the Wausau-Arkansas Lumber Company were Cyrus C. Yawkey; his son, William H. Yawkey; his uncle, William C. Yawkey; Walter Alexander; Alexander Stewart; and several other area lumbermen.

[79] William C. Yawkey had joined the first rush of northern lumbermen to southern timberlands, purchasing in the late 1880's large tracts in Alabama, Florida, and Louisiana.

[80] See ftn. 37.

[81] Yawkey and Bissell jointed forces in 1906, forming the Yawkey - Bissel Lumber Company to log a sizable area of timberland purchased from Frederick Weyerhaeuser.

[82] "Builders of Great Industries," pp. 59-60.

Karges, "David Clark Everest," p. 56.

[83] *Wausau Pilot*, November 11, 1902, p. 1; June 26, 1900, p. 1.

[84] "Builders of Great Industries," pp. 61-62.

Karges, "David Clark Everest," pp. 227-228.

Wausau Daily Record-Herald, June 23, 1934, p. 1.

Notation in John D. Mylrea Journals, vol. 8, Marathon County Historical Society.

[85] *Wausau Daily Record-Herald*, March 5, 1912, p. 1; *Golden Anniversary Edition*, August 9, 1922, Section 4, p. 10.

Wausau Pilot, June 3, 1919, p. 7; March 5, 1912, p. 6.

[86] Edgar went on to become a figure of national importance in the lumber industry. During the world war, he served as chairman of the lumber committee of the Council of National Defense, and later as director of lumber, War Industries Board. In recognition of his service, the U.S. Government awarded him a distinguished service medal in 1923, a year after his death.

[87] *Wausau Daily Record-Herald, Golden Anniversary Edition*, August 9, 1922, Section 4, p. 3.

"Builders Of Great Industries," p. 57.

[88] Another Ross son-in-law, A. T. Evans, served the company as treasurer out of Chicago.

[89] "Builders Of Great Industries," p. 61.

Wausau Daily Record-Herald, Golden Anniversary Edition, August 9, 1922, Section 4, p. 8; March 24, 1936, p. 1; July 15, 1971, p. 6.

Wausau Pilot, June 18, 1927, p. 4.

[90] The Joseph Dessert Lumber Company had been primarily a wholesale establishment. After the closing of its mill, the company remained active in the selling of real estate.

[91] In 1911 the company relocated its saw and planing mills back to Mosinee.

[92] *Mosinee Times*, August 8, 1957, p. 8.

Wausau Pilot, November 2, 1909, p. 5.

Interview with Margaret Dessert, June 21, 1976.

[93] *Wausau Daily Record,* July 23, 1906, p. 5.

Helgeson, "Athens, Wisconsin," pp. 60-61.

Straub, *Marathon, Wisconsin,* p. 49.

[94] Fries, Empire, p. 240.

Zamzow, *Berlin's Memories,* pp. 24-25.

Wausau Daily Record-Herald, Centennial Edition, March 13, 1939, Industrial Section, p. 82.

[95] Among several steps taken by the state in 1907 to strengthen its forest policy, the Wisconsin Valley Improvement Company was authorized to build dams and storage reservoirs along sections of the Wisconsin River in order to help achieve a more uniform stream flow. Walter Alexander and G. D. Jones were among the company representatives who lobbied in the state legislature for that authorization. See Fries, *Empire,* p. 25; Wisconsin Valley Improvement Company, *The Wisconsin River — Namesake Of A State* (Wausau: privately published), p. 1; *Wausau Pilot,* February 26, 1907, p. 1.

In his lumbering career John D. Mylrea combined an expert knowledge of hemlock and hardwood logging and a devotion to forest conservation, which had been instilled in his formative years at the Biltmore Forest School in North Carolina. In 1925 Mylrea initiated a campaign to persuade the U.S. Forest Service to create a national forest out of northern Wisconsin Cutover land. After five years of intense lobbying among lumbermen and politicians alike, the Wausau native saw his dream realized. In 1930 the Forest Service purchased nearly 4,000 acres of Cutover land from his Rhinelander-based Thunder Lake Lumber Company to create the Nicolet National Forest Reserve. See "Biography of John D. Mylrea," (manuscript in the Marathon County Historical Society), pp. 1-2.

[96] Alexander, "Short Industrial History," p. 42.

U.S. Department of Commerce, Bureau of the Census, *Thirteenth Census of the United States: 1910,* vol. 9, *Manufactures,* Wisconsin, p. 1346.

Wisconsin State Journal, April 8, 1926, p. 2.

Milwaukee Journal, December 31, 1939, p. 12.

[97] If a majority of the lumber industry group determined that a greater demand for mill products was taking place or that other conditions were having the effect of curtailing proper competition, the committee was authorized to either increase production rates or even abrogate the agreement entirely.

[98] W. W. Gamble was closely identified with the Bissell interests and served as general manager of the Wausau Group lumbering operation at White Lake. See "Builders of Great Industries," p. 60.

[99] *Milwaukee Journal,* October 4, 1931, pp. 1, 3. A copy of the contract can be found in the Legislative Reference Bureau, State Capitol, Madison, Wisconsin.

[100] *Wisconsin State Journal,* September 26, 1930, p. 2.

[101] *Forest Land Use,* pp. 1, 14, 38, 51, 120.

[102] As of 1948, the Braun mill was turning out approximately a half million feet of lumber annually: only about twenty per cent of their output during the twenties. President Albert Braun estimated that ninety-two per cent of his business involved retail sales.

[103] Zamzow, *Berlin's Memories,* pp. 23-24.

Fromm, "Sellin Sawmill," p. 14.

Undated Newspaper clippings in Charles Dodge Collection, Lumber Business Box.

Athens Record, September 9, 1937, p. 1.

Helgeson, "Athens, Wisconsin," pp. 65, 78.

[104] The Schofield firm staged something of a last hurrah for the entire Wisconsin lumber industry when in late 1937 it felled on its holdings north of Gleason what was believed to have been the largest white pine left standing in the state. Experts from the Forest Products Laboratory fixed 1511 as the approximate natal year of the tree. A ticket for the dinner held to commemorate the event can be found in the Charles Dodge Collection, Lumber Business Box. See also "A White Pine Monarch," *Wisconsin Magazine of History* 22 (September, 1938): 44-45.

[105] A shortage of labor in the woods severely limited the available log supply.

Moreover, the size of the mill meant that logs had to be shipped on an extremely high freight rate while OPA policy established price ceilings that did not give the company the required advantage of its location. In short, had the necessary timber been available, the firm would have had to pay a high inbound log freight without receiving the advantage of location on its outgoing lumber shipments. See *Wausau Pilot*, May 16, 1935, p. 1; November 7, 1935, p. 1; *Wausau Daily Record-Herald*, September 2, 1942, pp. 1, 14.

[106] Harold Collins, who had spent much of his career on the Rhinelander lumbering scene, served as something of a midwife-in-reverse in this particular period of Marathon County lumbering history. Earlier, he had assumed the responsibility of liquidating the B. Heinemann Lumber Company.

[107] *Wausau Daily Record-Herald*, September 2, 1942, p. 14.

[108] The dismantling process was accomplished under the joint ownership of the Roddis Lumber & Veneer Company and the Connor Lumber Company. Picture with historical background caption in Charles Dodge Collection, Lumber Business Box.

[109] In 1960 the firm's name was changed to Mortenson and Stone Lumber Company, reflecting the dominant position of the Stone family in the company presidency since 1939.

[110] *Wausau Pilot*, June 29, 1933, p. 1; January 10, 1935, p. 2.

Wausau Daily Record-Herald, Centennial Edition, June 30, 1972, p. 5.

[111] The Joseph Dessert Lumber Company was formally merged with the Mosinee Land, Log & Timber Company in 1964.

[112] Margaret Dessert Interview.

[113] *Wausau Daily Record-Herald*, January 25, 1964, p. 3.

Burnett et al., *Spencer, Wisconsin*, p. 39.

The 1975 Manufacturers & Processors Directory Of Marathon County listed a total of five lumbering firms in the county. Although precise employment figures for each were unavailable, together, their total maximum possible employment was eighty-one workers.

[114] In the period between publication of the Roth report and completion of the study undertaken by the Committee on Land Use and Forestry, an additional four billion feet was wasted. See *Forest Land Use*, p. 13.

[115] *Forest Land Use*, p. 48.

Milwaukee Journal, December 31, 1939, p. 12.

[116] The Forest Crop Law enacted in 1927 permitted owners of timberland to defer paying taxes on their timber until cutting had been completed.

[117] Smith, "Lumbertowns," pp. 63-66.

CHAPTER TWO

Diversity Out of Adversity: The Emergence of a Post-Lumber Industrial Economy

Noting the deteriorating conditions of Wisconsin's forests and, consequently, its lumber industry, the State Forestry Commission reported that as of 1898, inhabitants of dozens of cities and villages had begun speculating on the future. 'Everyone,' stated the commission, 'has seen settlements very prosperous ten years ago which are now abandoned by almost all their former inhabitants.'[1] In the heart of the Wisconsin River valley, a sense of passage from the familiar certainties represented by the dominant lumber industry was indeed present. For many community leaders, however, the response to this transition was not one of fear or alarm. Rather, there was a decided enthusiasm for the new horizons that would create opportunities for innovation, personal success, and material prosperity. A scholar of the psychological variable in history has linked this process, in a slightly different context, with the American postwar generation of the 1920's.[2] Yet a similar anticipation of change was present in northern Wisconsin better than two decades earlier, as evidence of the decline of the lumber industry began to accumulate. Symptomatic of this spirit was the formation in late 1899 of the Wisconsin Valley

Advancement Association. Owing largely to regional newspaper agitation on the subject, leading businessmen, bankers, and lawyers from the major cities along the Wisconsin River gathered in Tomahawk's Mitchell Hotel on December 12 to organize an association dedicated to "the advancement and up-building of the Wisconsin River Valley."[3] Marathon County was well represented at this initial meeting, and its delegates immediately assumed roles of major responsibility in the organizational hierarchy. Representing Wausau, Lester A. Rose was elected secretary, while Neal Brown and W. H. Mylrea were appointed to the three-man committee on by-laws. Named to the governing board of directors were Wausau's A. L. Kreutzer and D. L. Plumer, and Mosinee's Charles Gardner and H. M. Thompson.[4] Before adjournment, the conference was also addressed by four Wausauites: Brown, Mylrea, M. A. Hurley, and E. T. Wheelock. Thus, from the outset, Marathon County personalities exercised a sizable influence in shaping the destiny of the infant organization.[5]

The scope of the association was broadly defined, for that historical period. It would take in all six of the counties along the upper Wisconsin River, from Vilas in the north to Wood in the south. The premise underlying its formation was basic. The Wisconsin River valley had the potential to outrank any other section of the state in economic development. The region's abundant resources needed only to be "touched by the magic hand of enterprise" to achieve that potential. All that was required to release the cornucopia of prosperity was the application of sufficient capital and labor. This would be the aim and objective of the Wisconsin Valley Advancement Association: to bring in both ingredients and, in the process, become the vehicle to lead its six member counties into a multi-faceted, post-lumber economy that would be the showcase of the entire country.[6]

As a first step in reaching this lofty goal, the association's board of directors undertook over the next several weeks a series of moves designed to institutionalize their fledgling organization. Specialized committees were created to cover a variety of economic concerns, with appointments based on membership expertise.[7] In a further attempt to fashion a working infrastructure, a decision was made to appoint a three-member advisory board in each town in the valley. Substance had to be given to the association program. Accordingly, an ambitious industrial project was unveiled: the construction of a 150-mile electric railroad connecting the cities, villages and towns of the valley from Port Edwards north to Eagle River. The railway could be of inestimable value to Marathon County. Power was needed to exploit fully its sizeable granite resources. The building of a power supply to run the railroad would provide the electricity for mining, manufacturing, and transportation. "Vast quarries" could be opened at once. Moreover, according to D. L. Plumer, enough light and heat would be generated 'for a community of a million souls.'[8] In preparation, association president W. H. Bradley journeyed to New York to seek financial support from prominent Eastern capitalists, and a hydraulic engineer was hired to make a survey and measurement of the water powers of the Wisconsin River and its tributaries.[9] Finally, an aggressive public relations campaign was mounted to give both the valley and the association visibility throughout and beyond the state. Heading the drive was the association's secretary, Lester Rose.

Though the nominal head of the association was Tomahawk's founder and leading lumberman, William H. Bradley, Lester Rose was unquestionably the organization's chief spokesman and promoter during the first months of its existence. He was a relative newcomer to the area, having settled in Wausau in 1898 to assist Edgar Wheelock in publication of the *Daily Record*.[10] Yet he brought to his new duties with the association the attributes of "a hard worker and a vigorous and forcible writer,"[11] and did not take long to display his talents. Brimming with all the enthusiasm of a recent convert to the cause, Rose delivered an official birth announcement for the Valley Advancement Association in the *Milwaukee Sentinel*, shortly into the new century. The full page article, although lengthy, deserves some examination, since it casts clear light on the mind-set of one of the most energetic promoters of a new economic order for Marathon County and the rest of the upper Wisconsin River valley. Moreover, it clearly illustrates the psychological reaction to changing circumstances discussed earlier.

Throughout Rose's discourse one finds the twin themes of death and rebirth. The striking introductory headline itself—"A King Dethroned"—which was then paraphrased in the first line of the body, alerted readers to the former. Rose opened by paying homage to the prominent lumbermen of Marathon County and the upper Wisconsin, men who had become wealthy through a subservient alliance with "King Pine." His home city of Wausau had likewise worshipped and prospered at the throne of this monarch. All that, however, was now history, for "The king [was] dead! Long live the king!" After a biographical tribute to W. H. Bradley,[12] Rose explained that indications of a more diversified industrial base were already apparent in such localities as Wausau and Merrill. Thus, a new era of economic development was at hand in the Wisconsin River valley, which he likened to a revolution in which not a shot had been fired. Now it was the mission of the Wisconsin Valley Advancement Association to lead the way. The organization would, in fulfillment of this mission, "bring before the world of manufacture and commerce" the valley's resources, which made it "the natural location for paper mills, wood pulp mills, sulphite mills, tanneries and hardwood manufacturers." On either side of the river between Wausau and Merrill lay "mountains of granite" for building and art purposes. No Wisconsin granite held higher favor in the building world than the Marathon County red product. In Rib Hill, about two miles from Wausau's city limits, there was enough quartzite "to make sand paper to supply the world." Most important of all were the region's giant water powers. Even such an astute entrepreneur as D. L. Plumer did not fully comprehend that in the heart of Wausau, for instance, there was a water power that could be developed at small cost that would add 10,000 to the population of the city, and there were numerous resources from which manufacturing institutions could gather their supplies. Perhaps carried away by his own rhetoric, Rose issued a challenge to the *Sentinel* readers:

> Just you think of it, you Milwaukeeans who have been used to coming up here and living in an odor of saw dust and pine lumber and hearing nothing else but lumber talked, can now find this valley and find such men as D. L. Plumer, Walter Alexander, Col. Kreutzer, M. A. Hurley, Judge Ryan, ex-Att. Gen. Mylrea, Judge Silverthorn, August Kickbush, John Ringle, C. S. Curtis, J. M. Smith, E. A. Foster, Neal Brown, Charles and David Winton, C. F. Dunbar, H. E. McEachron, . . . Yawkee [sic] . . . Dessert and Thompson of Mosinee, . . . and hundreds of others boasting of the great water powers, the hard wood industries, the granite quarries, the new electric railway . . . and every mother's son of them ready to take off their [sic] hat and hurrah for the Wisconsin valley.[13]

Every possible obstacle, Rose concluded, had been overcome, and prosperity was ready to continue its march through the entire stretch of territory traversed by the Wisconsin River.

Verbal excesses aside, the Rose article had a significant impact. The *Sentinel* ran a favorable editorial comment on the story and added several complimentary words of its own for the Wisconsin valley. The piece also attracted the attention of the Chicago newspapers, some of which printed summary editorials. Locally, the article was reprinted

in full in both the *Daily Record* and *Pilot*, with the latter predicting
that the valley "will beat all records during the next ten years."[14]
The pen of Lester Rose had indeed helped place the Wisconsin River
valley and the Advancement Association in the light of public scrutiny.
This was but one aspect of Rose's publicity campaign, however, for
he simultaneously undertook a concerted effort to woo the state press.
His vehicle towards this end was the annual convention of Wisconsin's
newspaper editors, held the first week in February at Green Bay.
Appearing before the Badger editors, Rose invited 600 members of
the State Press Association and their wives to spend their summer
vacation in the valley as guests of the Advancement Association. After
thanking the editors on behalf of the association for their help thus
far, the secretary painted an epicurean picture of what lay in store
for them on their summer outing. It would begin at the Dells and
end at Eagle River with Marathon County stops at Mosinee and
Wausau. "Just say you will come and leave the details to us," he
assured the editors. Rose concluded his pitch by revealing that his
fellow officers had instructed him to make it plain to the editors that
they were invited to a novel treat: " 'Tell them', said Col. Kreutzer
and Walter Alexander, 'that they will be up against the real thing
when they strike the Wisconsin valley.' "[15] Two steps were then taken
to crystallize the arrangements. A representative of the St. Paul Railway Company followed Rose to the rostrum and offered the use of his
company's road for the excursion. After the convention adjourned,
Rose buttonholed every member of the editor's executive committee
and extracted a promise from each that he would attend the summer
outing. Upon returning to Wausau, Lester Rose was well satisfied
with what he had accomplished at Green Bay. He had successfully
set in motion a plan to further impress the newspaper elite of Wisconsin with the potential of the Wisconsin River valley and thereby
enlist them as unofficial press agents for both the valley and the
Advancement Association.[16] Rose unabashedly admitted his purpose
in the pages of the *Daily Record*. He had not issued the invitation
"purely as a public benefactor." Instead he "had mercenary motives,
an ax to grind."

> I am placing myself in the light of an agent for a
> stretch of country that needs especial attention from
> the gentlemen of the press. . . . When the Wisconsin
> State Press association was invited, it was expected that
> the members of it would go home and say nice things
> about us, not little social courtesies, biographies or
> obituaries of our prominent citizens. . . . We expect

of the editors that are to be our guests a return for
our hospitality. We expect them to do their level
best and the greater the inspiration we give to them
while they are our guests, the better their missives will
be, consequently, the greater results to the Wisconsin
Valley in the future. When you touch a man's stomach
you are in conference with his soul, feed a man well
and you make of him a friend for life, entertain him
royally and your memory will ever be kept fresh and
green in his mind. . . . It will be bread cast upon the
waters that will return after many days.[17]

Wausau, in turn, immediately began preparations to help insure that
the editors' trip was an entertaining one. Plans were formulated to
hold a flower carnival with a circus at the Opera House during their
stopover in the city.[18]

The Wisconsin Valley Advancement Association had gotten off to a
promising start in the first months of its existence. Its early record
of achievement was impressive on three levels. First, a functioning
internal organization with roots extending down to the valley communities had been fashioned. Wausau was a particular center of
activity in this respect. A citizens' meeting held in late January to
form a local auxiliary was enthusiastic to "a degree which bordered
on the hysterical," with an interminable number of rousing speeches
being delivered and A. L. Kreutzer singing a hymn. The other cities
in the valley, admonished W. H. Mylrea, had better 'look out for
Wausau.' "All were looking at this city and it should be a matter
of pride with Wausau people to hustle earnestly for the whole valley."[19]
Amidst the hoopla serious business was transacted. A permanent
three-man advisory committee consisting of Walter Alexander, Joseph
H. Reiser,[20] and W. H. Mylrea was appointed, and a membership of
thirty was enrolled. The self-proclaimed "love feast" ended with the
announcement of a plan to hold a larger revival meeting in the Opera
House to foster the "Wausau Spirit" and better inform the public of
the valley's resources and capabilities. Such enthusiasm seemed in-
fectious. The following month, 116 new memberships were received
from other valley communities, and Langlade County petitioned the
association for membership status.[21] Secondly, an impressive industrial project had been initiated. W. H. Bradley had returned optimistic from his New York visit and planned a second trip to conclude
the financial arrangements. Financing the railway scheme, he assured
the director, was 'no longer a question.'[22] Finally, a promotional alliance with the state press was being forged, which would result in

the valley's resources becoming better known abroad. With these accomplishments to build on, the future of the association looked as bright as that of its client region.

As it turned out, however, the editorial seduction at Green Bay would be the high point of the organization's life. Difficulties soon befell the corporation, and its early momentum slowed. One major problem centered around the much heralded summer trip taken by the State Press Association. The first rendezvous in the courtship turned out to be a disaster. To begin with, when the editors reached their north woods campsite, they found glaring discrepancies between reality and what had been promised in the invitation at Green Bay. To quiet the grumbling, Lester Rose delivered a speech that evening at dinner promising that any faults would be remedied: "they Were," he reassured them. "The Guests Of The Wisconsin Valley Association and that Association did not do things by halves but would see that everything was provided at once to make them comfortable."[23] The editors were shortly to receive another, even more unpleasant surprise. Upon breaking camp they learned that everything furnished for their entertainment had been charged to them, not to the host Advancement Association. One of the directors subsequently explained that their secretary had issued the invitation to the Press Association without the organization's knowledge or consent, and only after its acceptance had he sought the board of directors' approval. The directors had refused to ratify the plan, and then had failed to notify the editors that the association would have nothing to do with the excursion. Whether Rose had exceeded his authority or was, in fact, being made the scapegoat cannot be determined, although the circumstantial evidence indicates the latter. Local newspaper accounts of the postconvention Advancement Association meeting give no hint of any disapproval of Rose's actions. The secretary, moreover, assured the directors that "the editors would be on hand and take their summer vacation in the valley."[24] In any case, considering the length of time between the invitation and the excursion, it does seem curious that the association directors made no move to rectify any possible misunderstanding until the bills came due. The *Pilot* thought it impossible that Rose had acted without authorization and termed the association's plea "at this late date . . . pretty thin."[25] Whatever his degree of culpability, Rose's credibility had been seriously damaged, and at the next board of directors' meeting he tendered his resignation, the ostensible reason being a more lucrative position elsewhere. The association gave its secretary "a flowery vote of thanks" for his services and made no further comment on the affair.[26] In one motion the organization had lost perhaps its most enthusiastic and capable advocate, and its carefully cultivated relationship with the state press had been dealt a severe blow.

The Press Association fiasco seemed to open a Pandora's box of problems for the Advancement Association. Access to money for financing industrial projects should have been a simple matter: association members represented more than $75 million of local capital. And in the early part of the year generous financial contributions had been common. Yet the necessary funds to keep the corporation running quickly grew scarce. It was reported at the end of the association's first year of operation that only 65 members out of 300 had paid their dues. The sparse treasury made it impossible to hire a new permanent secretary and carry on effective work. An estimated $5,000 was needed to put the association in working order. As a partial remedy, A. L. Kreutzer recommended that the directors solicit contributions from their home counties and local associations. By the next meeting favorable responses had been received from Marathon, Wood, and Portage Counties, each appropriating $250. Other donations brought the expense fund to $1,775, but this was still far short of the required amount. Poor attendance also began to plague the organization. Small attendance at many board of directors' meetings meant that transaction of important business had to be postponed. On more than one occasion the lack of even a quorum resulted in entire meetings being rescheduled. By the end of 1901 the *Pilot* was adding to its announcement of a forthcoming association convocation the following: "At least it is hoped that the attendance will warrant the calling of the meeting to order."[27] Given this indifference, it is hardly surprising that inertia began to affect other associational activities. The electric railway project continued to be discussed at length and optimistic predictions continued to be issued, but no concrete actions to begin construction were undertaken. Finally, by early 1902 the situation had become critical. After several successive meetings without the presence of a quorum, President Bradley announced in disgust that no further meetings would be held until sufficient interest was displayed to warrant their calling. The *Central Wisconsin,* noting the lethargic state of the corporation, began to ask "Shall the Association Die?"[28] The question was not only rhetorical. The death of W. H. Bradley in early 1903 was also a symbolic one for the organization he had headed.[29]

How then can the Wisconsin Valley Advancement Association be evaluated? A clear distinction has to be drawn, based on the association's own defined goals. In a propagandistic sense, there is no doubt that the organization had a definite record of accomplishment. Primarily due to the enthusiastic efforts of Lester Rose, it had alerted the public to and awakened interest in the great economic potential that existed in the Wisconsin River valley in the post-lumbering era. It is equally clear, however, that as an active agent of industrial expansion in the region, the organization was basically a failure. The group's first major industrial project—the electric railway—rather than unlocking other doors of industrial development, never got out of the talking stage. Not until the birth and maturation of the Wisconsin Valley Improvement Company later in the century would its ambitious industrial program for the entire valley begin to be realized. In short, as an early effort at regional planning, the Wisconsin Valley Advancement Association never lived up to its promise.

One explanation of the association's demise was that capital and attention were increasingly being focused on more localized pursuits. Community self-interest was a powerful prejudice, firmly entrenched even during the salad days of the Valley Advancement Association. Nowhere was this more true than in Marathon County's leading city. In his address to the earlier mentioned citizens' meeting, W. H. Mylrea, after exhorting the people of Wausau to work for the common good of the entire Wisconsin valley without regard to locality or city, added the cautionary proviso: "but at the same time the interests of Wausau should be looked after."[30] If local pride did contribute to the demise of this early experiment in regional planning, it was also an important motivator for those sawmilling centers that hoped to escape the fate described by the State Forestry Commission. Long before the report was issued, however, at a time when the local lumber industry was still in relatively good health, elements in Wausau had begun to campaign for a more diversified industrial base. As early as 1881, an organization known as the Wausau Board of Trade issued a circular calling attention to the city's advantages as a source of capital investment in both manufacturing and merchandising. The pamphlet confidently asserted 'We have more inhabitants, more business, finer residences and more and better business blocks than any other city in Central and Northern Wisconsin,' clearly implying that other firms would do well to locate in this commercial paradise.[31] By 1886 the *Central Wisconsin* had begun to warn of the precarious position of a one-industry town; three years later its journalistic competitor, the *Torch of Liberty,* issued a similar caveat. Municipal government soon joined the press in recognizing the potential problem. Assuming the most vigorous leadership role was Mayor Robert E. Parcher during the early 1890's. "More factories" became the battle cry of his administration. In a notable departure from the doctrine of strict free enterprise, he offered municipal aid as an inducement for new business to locate in the city. Committing further heresy, the mayor persuaded a reluctant city council to purchase seventy-seven acres of land for sites for prospective industrial establishments, a move which foreshadowed the industrial parks concept of the post-World War II era.[32] Lavish newspaper publicity was also utilized. In 1895 the *Milwaukee Sentinel* ran a better than full page illustrated article on "The Progress Of Wausau," detailing the story of "A Timber City Which Has Grown Into One of the Most Prominent Business Centers of the State." The anonymously authored piece, which promoted the city as "A Local Center Where . . . Property Is Cheap" and "Home Life . . . Is Incomparable" was, like the earlier Board of Trade circular, clearly an invitation to restless businessmen searching for new investment opportunities.[33]

This promotion continued in the early years of the twentieth century, as lumber production figures dropped and other signs began to point towards a steady decline of the state's leading industry. A pamphlet put out by the Wausau Industrial Association asked "Looking for a Factory Site? Looking for Water Power? Want to organize some great Industrial Enterprise?" The supplied answer, naturally, was "See Wausau"; the city whose "watchwords are Energy, Enterprise, Push."[34] The verbal bouquets were matched with visual displays as the city made a special effort to impress visiting dignitaries. While in town to attend the opening of the new opera house in early 1900, T. J. Cunningham, editor of the *Chippewa Falls Independent,* was shown numerous examples of Wausau's "progress and 'increasing vitality.' " Highly impressed, the former Wisconsin Secretary of State subsequently printed a complimentary article in his paper that Lester Rose himself could have authored. Later that same year the city pulled out all stops to entertain a visiting delegation of the Milwaukee Merchants and Manufacturers' Association.[35] The community was also given advice on how it could help build up its industry. Speaking before local merchants, W. H. Mylrea enumerated a number of suggestions for advancing industrial expansion in Wausau: the creation of a freight bureau, the promotion of steam and interurban railways, the financial and personal encouragement of prospective factories, the compilation and publication of data showing the city's growth, industries and attractions, and the creation of a news bureau to advertise the city abroad. The carrying out of these basic proposals, concluded the former state attorney general, could make Wausau a city of 50,000 people.[36]

The logical offshoot of this promotional activity was a desire on the part of Wausau businessmen for a more organized promotion and protection of their interests. Although early attempts at forming an advancement association were unsuccessful, local businessmen displayed an ability to band together when their welfare appeared to be threatened. In 1905 the American Merchants' Protective Agency opened a branch office in Wausau with virtually every businessman in the city as a member. The agency's service was to rate every Wausau resident as to his promptness in paying bills. Monthly lists of delinquents would be compiled, printed, and issued to each member. In case anyone might get the mistaken impression that this rating system was some kind of blacklist, the *Daily Record* patiently explained that "This list is not sent out as a dead beat or black list, but is issued as a report of the business of a corporation to its stockholders." Moreover, information would also be provided on parties who were punctual in settling their debts. Nonetheless, this perfectly innocent stockholders' report would be of great benefit, for "Hereafter in Wausau it will be impossible for dead beats to work their graft . . ."[37]

Perceived as an even greater threat than the "dead beat" menace was the re-election of Governor Robert La Follette in 1904. Specifically, the danger was his apparent advocacy of abolishing the commodity tariff for rail transportation and substituting a distance tariff used in neighboring Iowa. In the final weeks before election day, the pages of the *Daily Record* were filled with interviews of local industrial leaders, attempting to show the economic havoc that would reign in the city if the La Follette distance tariff were imposed. The conclusion in each case was the same: the particular factory would either have to drastically reduce the size of its operation, shut down entirely, or move out of Wausau. Summary articles also appeared demonstrating the measure's overall debilitating effect on the local economy. According to the businessmen's calculations, the distance tariff would cause Wausau to lose $995,000 in industrial capital, $4,272,500 in annual product, $502,900 in annual wages, and 1,486 jobs. The distance tariff was, in short, "Wausau's Danger;" a vote for La Follette would be a vote against Wausau.[38] When the votes were tabulated, La Follette's plurality in the city had dropped 465 from the previous election, from 529 in 1902 to 64 in 1904.[39] While it is impossible to ascribe this dramatic decline solely to the scare tactics of the Wausau businessmen, it is reasonable to conclude that their intense pre-election campaign must have played some part. Although technically unorganized, the Wausau business and industrial elite was capable at an early date of concerted action in defense of its common interests.

The desire for a formal support organization continued, however, and gained new momentum at the beginning of the twentieth century's second decade. The most noticeable feature of the crystallizing interest was an effort to enlighten both the general public and any apathetic businessmen as to what was at stake. M. C. Ewing,[40] general manager of the Wausau Street Railway Company, minced no words in a pamphlet entitled "Commercial Opportunities." Every successful commercial city had four requisites for prosperity: raw materials, transportation, power, and constructive men. Wausau had an abundance of the first three factors and a sufficient number of the fourth.[41] Individual effort was not enough, however, to achieve the desired amount of commercial growth. An occasional 'Boosters' Banquet, although well intentioned, was a waste of time. What was needed was a "live energetic commercial club." This movement should be non-political, representative of every interest and class of citizen that made up "this old shingle town," and have as its sole aim commercial growth. Such a club, he concluded, should be active within sixty days, and the repository of all knowledge and reports of new industrial institutions.[42] Ewing's call was given added force on March 2, 1912 when Wausau secured the prized B. Heinemann Lumber Company. The successful seduction, intoned the Record-Herald, was "only more evidence of the need in this city for a live Commercial club, for there are many other industries which can be had if well directed efforts are made to get them."[43] In agreement for once with its rival, the Pilot added ". . . we understand, from reliable information, that there are several other factories which are contemplating coming to Wausau and with an organization formed with a paid secretary we ought to be able to nail some of them."[44] Within four days a notice was distributed throughout the city under the signature of M. C. Ewing and several other community leaders, publicizing a meeting to be held at the Marathon County Court House on the evening of March 11 to "assist in organizing a Commercial Club" for "the promotion by organized effort of the commercial interests of Wausau."[45] The Record-Herald, urging every citizen interested in the city's welfare to attend, could not overestimate the importance of the gathering:

Third Street, Wausau, Early 20th Century

> Wausau has reached what may well be called a
> critical point in its career. It is up to the people to
> decide whether it shall be a lumber town—declining
> and growing sleepier and of less importance as the
> lumber industry becomes exhausted—or whether it
> shall proceed to utilize its advantages and grow into
> a large and progressive manufacturing center.
>
> This problem will be decided by the people of Wau-
> sau and nobody else. In this age of keen competition
> in town building, when centers of population all over
> the country are shouting their advantages from the
> house tops, the place that sits back and expects nature
> and the good sense of investors to fight its battle is
> doomed to disappointment.
>
> . . . Therefore, come out Monday night. Talk the
> matter over freely. Let the meeting be the beginning
> of a campaign which will give Wausau a leading place
> among the manufacturing and commercial centers
> of the state.[46]

The message hit home. By the time the meeting was gaveled to
order, more than 500 had jammed into the circuit court chambers.
The business transacted during the next two hours closely paralleled
that of the early organizational meetings of the Wisconsin Valley
Advancement Association; the name, in fact, chosen for the club was
the Wausau Advancement Association. Temporary officers and directors were elected, by-laws were promulgated, and numerous speeches
were delivered praising both the city and the new association. Out of
the routine and boosterism typical of such gatherings, two revealing
insights into Wausau's personality emerged. In one sense the leadership of the organization, contrary to Mark Ewing's rhetoric, did not
represent every class of citizen in the community. Without exception,
they were members of the city's business and professional elite. Laboring men were conspicuous by their absence. While a relatively broad
spectrum of commercial interests was included, one class of the city's
population dominated the association's leadership.[47]

A second noteworthy feature of the meeting was the speech of
Marvin Rosenberry. In his brief address, the Wausau attorney emphasized a heretofore unmentioned advantage of the newly created
association. Every year the Wausau school system was turning out
young graduates with the skill, training, and ambition to head industrial enterprises. Yet these future entrepreneurs were being forced
to move away from their birthplace in order to have the chance to
utilize their talents. By bringing in new enterprises and thereby enlarging the local field of opportunity, the association would help keep

these young men at home. Rosenberry's admission of a "brain drain" in Wausau is interesting in itself. Even more fascinating, however, is the suggestion of parochialism inherent in his analysis. By keeping those born and raised in Wausau in the upper echelon of the job market at home after their formal schooling, control of the city's economy would be kept in strictly local hands.

The meeting by any standard was a success. "The tone of the meeting," declared the *Record-Herald,* "was excellent." A consensus had been reached that it was time for Wausau to take this step, and the initial organizational work had been undertaken in a spirit of harmony. "With a long, strong pull . . . the new Wausau Advancement Association would be of great benefit."[48] The next several years saw many efforts to strengthen the organization and integrate it into the business life of the community. The organization's first secretary, R. S. Kellogg, had been able to devote only part of his time to the job. A full time secretary, A. C. Schmidt, was hired in 1913 and served in that capacity for the next five years. In 1918 the association was able to broaden its base by merging with the Wausau Merchants and Manufacturers' Association.[49] A new name was adopted—the Wausau Chamber of Commerce—with William R. Chellis becoming the secretary of the larger organization. A more visible identity for the Chamber was also established by moving out of city hall into its own suite of offices in the Borowitz Building on the 200 block of Jefferson Street. When Chellis resigned his post in 1921 to accept an appointment as United States Marshall for the Western District of Wisconsin, D. A. Caldwell, the secretary of the Marshfield Chamber of Commerce, was imported to fill the vacancy. The next year a young graduate of the Wausau Business Institute, Walter Roehl, took a job with the Chamber as a stenographer, beginning a relationship that would span the next four decades.[50] In contrast to its predecessors and the Wisconsin Valley Advancement Association, the Wausau Chamber of Commerce would survive and become a partner to the city's twentieth century economic growth.

The role that evolved for the Wausau Chamber would, however, have a slightly different emphasis from its founders' intentions. Although it enjoyed some success in luring industrial establishments to the Wausau area,[51] its major contribution consisted of promoting and publicizing projects which helped create a favorable business climate within the city.[52] This more conservative posture resulted from the fact that by the time the advancement association was finally organized, Wausau's industrial landscape had already undergone some significant changes from the nineteenth century era of sawmill dominance.[53] Indeed, by 1912, much of northern Wisconsin had practically completed the transformation of its industrial profile, a reshaping based primarily on the rising importance of manufacturing concerns which used wood as their chief raw material. By the end of the twentieth century's first decade, Wisconsin claimed twenty-one separate wood products industries. Almost every community in the state that survived the passing of the old lumber industry did so by building up a successful economy around one or more wood-using industries which utilized those varieties of timber still in relatively plentiful supply.[54]

In Marathon County, Wausau led this movement. The various calls in the late nineteenth century for new industries had not gone unheard. Aided by the proximity of abundant hardwood stands, the lumber capital of the upper Wisconsin valley became a natural focal point for a variety of wood products industries. As early as 1904 woodworking enterprises accounted, according to one index, for 42 per cent of the city's capital investment, 43 per cent of its industrial product, 53 per cent of its wage payments, and 56.6 per cent of its industrial labor force.[55] By 1927 Robert Fries estimates that between 60 and 80 per cent of all the city's wage earners were hired by wood-using factories.[56]

The first such operation to appear in Wausau was probably the modest sash, door, and blind factory started by George Werheim in the early 1870's. Overcoming both the destruction of his plant by fire and the subsequent withdrawal of his financial partner, the determined German-born carpenter had by the turn of the century built his business into a leading specialist in interior finish, which was in considerable demand from Iowa, Illinois, and Michigan.[57] In 1912 the Werheim plant was taken over by the newly organized J. M. Kuebler Company, which undertook numerous renovations and began producing a variety of millwork products, including doors, windows, mouldings, and hardwood flooring, as well as interior finish.[58]

The next major enterprise of this type to be established in the city was also due largely to the efforts of a single individual. The origins of the Curtis & Yale story go back to the late 1860's. At age eighteen Cornelius S. Curtis had made up his mind: he would leave the family farm near Rochelle, Illinois and join his two older brothers in Clinton, Iowa, there to begin a career in their recently established sash and door factory. After learning the practical end of the business,[59] he was assigned to represent the firm on the road. In the course of his travels through sixteen states and territories, he stopped on at least one occasion in Wausau, a visit which would be significant for both his

and the city's future. Impressed by the various signs of urban development he saw going on around him, he urged his brothers to build
a similar factory in the burgeoning lumbertown. His advice was
eventually taken, for in 1881, Curtis Bros. & Co. decided to build a
branch plant in the heart of the Wisconsin River pinery. Cornelius
Curtis returned to Wausau in the summer of that year to assume
management of the operation, which was incorporated in early 1893 as
the Curtis & Yale Company. Under his supervision, the firm undertook
a policy of expansion in the last decade of the old century which
would rival that of Wausau itself. The purchase of a Minneapolis
jobbing house, Carpenter Bros., was followed by the opening of an additional warehouse and salesroom in Milwaukee. The most extensive
expansion of the Curtis complex was the purchase of the abandoned
chair factory of the Wausau Furniture Company, one of the unsuccessful municipal aid projects of the Parcher administration. This single
acquisition nearly doubled Curtis & Yale's productive capacity, enabling it to claim the distinction of being Wausau's largest manufacturing institution by the turn of the century. Thus, upon the death of
Cornelius Curtis in January, 1916, his youngest son Walter inherited
control of a manufactory which symbolized one of the city's first giant
steps into a new period of economic transition.[60]

A third such operation was initiated in the twentieth century by
another familiar figure in the local sash and door industry, George
Silbernagel, who had spent a lifetime preparing for that opportunity.
He began to learn the rudiments of his future career while in his teens
under the tutelage of his father, a partner in the Madison sash and door
firm of Silbernagel and Dean. The son undoubtedly could have stayed
in Madison and eventually taken his father's place, but he desired
more independence. Accordingly, he moved to Wausau in 1899 and
found work with the expanding Curtis & Yale Company as an esti-
mator. He rose to the top of both that department and the sales department. After thirteen years with Curtis, however, Silbernagel believed the time had come for further advancement. In 1912 he and
another ambitious Curtis supervisor, John Kuebler, left to form their
own company: the previously mentioned J. M. Kuebler Company.
Here he would spend the next thirteen years as company secretary and
treasurer. Finally, in 1925, Silbernagel was to fulfill his ultimate ambition. In the summer of that year he severed his connection with
Kuebler to build a factory on Lemke Street. Construction was completed in the spring of the following year, and in April, 1926, the
plant of Silbernagel & Sons began operations with an employment

roster of seventy men. Having realized his dream, George Silbernagel was determined that his company would not be known merely as Wausau's "other sash and door factory." Acknowledged as an "inventive genius," he put into practice his own concept of a fully electric factory utilizing high speed machines for greater output. Most of the plant's revolutionary machinery was, in fact, designed by the founder himself. In addition, Silbernagel made sure that his influence would be felt in more than just technical innovation, and thus insure that his creation would survive him. These goals were accomplished by bringing his three sons—George Jr., Edward, and Bernard—into the organization and giving them various management responsibilities at the outset. To a degree surpassing even the Curtis Company, the Silbernagel concern was destined to be a family project.[61]

The sash and door factories may have been first on the scene, but they were not the only type of wood products operation to be successfully established in Marathon County's leading city. Box factories, for example, came to be another familiar sight in Wausau by the early twentieth century. The oldest venture of this kind was also the result of a brotherly interest in expanding a mutual field of investment. In the late 1880's three Chicago brothers—James, David, and Clarence Goodwillie—purchased the J. Smith planing mill and immediately converted the structure into a box shook factory. The company's physical plant was subsequently expanded until it covered a full five acres and provided regular employment for over one hundred workers. By the early 1920's its manufacturing capacity was said to be sufficient to lay a two-foot boardwalk from Wausau to New York City. A corresponding increase in the product line also took place until the company was capable of producing anything in the box line from soap boxes to piano crates.[62]

The success enjoyed by the Goodwillie brothers insured that they would not long have the local field to themselves. A formidable competitor was established in 1892 when the Quaw planing mill was bought, overhauled, and filled with box-making machinery. The executive leadership of the newly incorporated Wausau Box and Lumber Company constituted an imposing array of success stories in area business and professional circles. For Charles V. Bardeen, assumption of the company presidency complemented an already distinguished legal career, which would be capped in 1898 by his appointment to the State Supreme Court.[63] The firm's treasurer, Charles E. Turner, brought to the office a substantial and colorful amount of experience gained in a variety of county business enterprises. His first employment in Marathon County had been as a skillful, if not totally unscathed, bee-raiser in Dancy. In two years his pet industry had grown to four hundred colonies. After concluding that the often severe county winters were not conducive to long-term success in that enterprise, he took on the responsibility of managing both the sawmill and company store in that community. The four years immediately preceding his plunge into the box business had been spent in Wausau managing the sawmill jointly owned by Robert Parcher and the Stewart brothers. The name of stockholder S. M. Quaw was synonymous with lumbering in the Edgar area. Finally, in its secretary, W. B. Scholfield, the box operation had within its executive ranks the heir to one of the most famous family traditions in county industrial development. Scholfield brought more than just his name to the operation, however. His previous business background was perhaps not as thorough as his father's, or for that matter even Charles Turner's, but he was far from a neophyte. After serving the typical period of apprenticeship as bookkeeper in his uncle Charles P. Haseltine's lumber company, William Bowie Scholfield decided to strike out on his own. He first entered the mercantile business in Wausau, and after moving to Merrill, combined that undertaking with running a planing mill. The greatest challenge and opportunity were yet to come. When Bardeen, Quaw, and a fifth incorporator, J. D. Coleman, retired from the firm in 1898, Turner and Scholfield bought up their interests. With the former becoming president and the latter adding on the duties of treasurer, the pair assumed the major share of responsibility for the Wausau Box Company's continued prosperity.

At first glance such a goal may have seemed elusive, considering that the men were of different political persuasions. William Scholfield firmly subscribed to the principles of the Republican party, while Charles Turner was an equally ardent Democrat. Yet, by the end of 1920 the Wausau Box Company was a model of what a bipartisan spirit of cooperation—or perhaps a shared dislike of Robert La Follette— could accomplish. In the twenty-eight year period since incorporation the company's work force climbed from ten men to 150; its yearly payroll rose from $8,000 to $117,000; and its annual business increased from $30,000 to nearly $500,000. Not that there weren't obstacles that had to be overcome. The death of Charles Turner in December, 1919, represented a major loss of management expertise.[64] While Turner's only son, Wells, remained in the executive hierarchy for a time as secretary, it was the Scholfield family that moved quickly to fill any potential leadership vacuum. The elevation of W. B. Scholfield to company president was an immediate stabilizing influence. When the new president's two sons, William R. and Harvey H. Scholfield, returned to Wausau from Iowa in January to purchase the Turner interests, an additional guarantee of continuity was provided. Another hardship that had to be dealt with was that familiar nemesis for those economically involved with wood—fire. The first such catastrophe to strike was the 1907 burning of the original company plant.[65] Total disaster was averted in this case only when the Dessert planing mill was purchased and physically moved from Mosinee to Wausau. An even more significant blaze, however, destroyed the plant in 1927. In the aftermath of this disaster, the Scholfield family chose the survival route of merger rather than a second rebuilding process. An agreement was reached in early June which united the Wausau Box Company and the Goodwillie-Green Box Company into a new concern, the Marathon Box Company, which would carry on the local interests of each. Capitalized at $200,000, the joint enterprise planned to utilize the enlarged Goodwillie-Green facility for production, with an anticipated increase in output.[66]

This combination did not leave the city with a monopoly in the box product line, however, for by this time a third enterprise, the Wisconsin Box Company, was in its twenty-seventh year of operation. The firm had been organized in June, 1900, by a group of local lumbering personalities: Edwin Latshaw, John Hildensperger, E. A. Gooding, and Ben Heinemann. Although in future years John Hildensperger continued on the board of directors, and the Heinemann name remained in the organization, the real power came to reside with the family headed by Edward August Gooding.[67] This vital dynasty began in May, 1913 when the elder Gooding took the final step up the corporate executive ladder to the presidency. For the next forty-eight years he, followed by his two sons, Guy and Donald, would head the operation. The signs of company growth and progress evident by the early 1920's indicated that the Gooding stewardship was a beneficial one. Expansion from a single department in 1900 to three necessitated an increase in capitalization from $15,000 to $210,000. The dollar value of the firm's annual business multiplied more than tenfold over the same period. In 1921 machinery was installed that enabled the company to become one of only three factories in the state able to produce wire-bound boxes. With the Gooding sons managing separate departments, preparations were well along for an eventual smooth transition of power.

Nonetheless, the end of the decade would also be a time of trial for the newest of the Wausau box companies. A devastating fire in late April, 1929, completely leveled the plant, with the power house and office the only structures to survive. The $160,000 loss left the company's future very much in doubt. It was, recalled Guy Gooding some ten years later, 'a very trying time for our company.' The onset of the Depression did not make the situation any more promising. The directors eventually decided to rebuild, however, and in the latter part of the year a new $100,000 factory was completed and ready for business. The contrasting symbolism of death and continuity was intensified when E. A. Gooding finally succumbed to a lengthy illness in late December, and Guy K. Gooding began what would be his twenty-three year tenure as company president. Like its cross-town competitor, the Wisconsin Box Company had survived losses of leadership and facility, and was ready to face the ordeal of unprecedented national hard times.[68]

The Wausau industrial roster included a variety of other concerns involved in manufacturing wood derived products. In January, 1893, the Wausau Novelty Company began turning out an assortment of wood novelties, including toys and toy furniture. By the 1920's the company's best known and most popular product was its line of kindergarten chairs, made in roughly half a dozen models of selected hardwood. Heading the operation were two of the original directors, E. A. Gooding's brother-in-law, Frank Kelly, and O. G. Schilling.[69] E. A. Gooding also exercised some direct influence by serving as company secretary and sitting on the board of directors.

The year 1893 also marked the opening of Wausau's only veneer factory, when the Underwood Veneer Company moved from Appleton and began operations on the city's southwest side. The initial intention of founder J. A. Underwood had been to manufacture only veneer, but a growing demand by the furniture industry for three and five ply panels induced the New York native to add a panel department in 1898. Both the firm's late nineteenth and early twentieth century history were highlighted by regular increases in capacity, capitalization, and employment.[70] This impressive record of growth was attributed in large part to J. A. Underwood's "untiring energy" and "wise business foresight." His death in the summer of 1910, however, necessitated a change in leadership. The selection of company treasurer and general manager Otto C. Lemke as successor brought to the forefront yet another dominating figure in the city's twentieth century industrial development. The new president was unique among the local entrepreneurs discussed thus far. He was, first of all, a native of

Marathon County, born and raised on the family farm in the Town of Berlin. He didn't come to the job with experience in just the world of business. Prior to joining the Underwood firm as a bookkeeper in 1902, he had taught for several years in the county's schools. Yet, if there were any doubts about his ability to take command, they were soon dispelled. The policies initiated during the Underwood regime were preserved under Lemke's supervision. An early signal was the complete rebuilding of the firm's plant facilities on Cleveland Avenue and Thomas Street in 1912, which led to a several-fold increase in capacity. Employment continued to rise as well. By 1923, the company had a labor force of four hundred men, a better than two-hundred per cent increase in just under twenty years. The acquisition of timberlands, a practice begun in 1907, was stepped up to guarantee a minimum twelve-year supply of northern hardwoods. In addition, virtually every continent on the globe was tapped for the wood used in making the company's rare veneers. Firmly in control of all this activity was the former Berlin schoolteacher, who not only held the title of president, but retained the responsibilities of treasurer and general manager.[71]

Wausau could also claim two excelsior mills by the turn of the century. The Wausau Excelsior Company began in 1892 and before long was turning out twelve tons of its product every twelve hours. Five years later William Keogh—a Chicago wholesaler of upholstering material—called on Ole Billier[72] and gave him *carte blanche* to build and manage a new excelsior mill in the city, with the stipulation only that it be capable of turning out the finest quality product. Billier eagerly accepted the offer and set about building a factory that corresponded to his own standards of proper machinery and interior arrangements. With the site of the defunct Marathon County Excelsior Company serving as the primary base of operations, the Chicago Excelsior Company commenced cutting in the spring of 1898. The factory fell victim to fire in July, 1899, but Billier's determination and expertise coupled with Keogh's financing enabled a new plant equipped with a sprinkler system to open within ninety days.

No listing of Wausau's leading woodworking firms would be complete without mention of the Wausau Manufacturing Company. Organized in 1917 by Russell Lyon, George E. Foster, and H. E. Smith, the concern incorporated to manufacture both cement products and wood novelties, the most novel of which was toothpicks. Its toothpick factory at 1101 Cherry Street was one of seven in the entire country and the only one of its kind in the state of Wisconsin. Using stocks of white birch secured within a radius of one hundred miles from the city, the plant was capable by the early 1920's of turning out 5,770,000,000 toothpicks in a three-hundred-day period, enough to supply fifty-two to every man, woman, and child in the United States. With its product shipments going to Canada, Cuba, and even Hong Kong at least one member of the Wausau wood products fraternity was doing its small part in the inter-war years to make the world a closer place.[73]

As these sketches indicate, Wausau increasingly became a major location site for new kinds of manufacturing institutions which, utilizing wood as their chief raw material, naturally gravitated towards the old lumbering centers. Indeed, local lumbering personalities in many cases provided either the facilities for these enterprises or exercised sooner or later a significant degree of control over their affairs. One need only recall the names of Ben Heinemann, Charles Turner, S. M. Quaw, and E. A. Gooding. Cyrus Yawkey formed an affiliation with the Wisconsin Box Company early in the twentieth century, becoming vice-president; A. P. Woodson and Harold Collins also eventually occupied seats on that firm's board of directors. Outside of Wausau, in the remainder of Marathon County, this pattern of development was much less pronounced with respect to the types of wood products firms already discussed. In Athens the Chesak Saw and Planing Mill constructed in 1891 later incorporated under the name of the Athens Manufacturing Company, to reflect its shift towards the production of wood products. The only truly new industrial starts occurred in Edgar where an excelsior mill was built in 1910 by Justine Means. Two years later an alliance of Edgar businessmen and farmers formulated plans to begin a veneer factory which would take advantage of the abundant stands of hardwood near the village. The project was aborted, however, when shortly before completion of the plant the Earney brothers purchased the facility and converted it into a basket factory.

Thus, in terms of its industrial character, much of Marathon County still remained firmly tied to a dying lumber industry.[74] It would take the emergence of another wood products industry, papermaking, early in the twentieth century to break this one-sided pattern and breathe new life into a potentially stagnating county industrial economy.

The growth of the paper industry in Marathon County had its origins in nineteenth century technical changes in the paper production process that served both to enlarge the scope of the industry within Wisconsin and to alter the location of the state's important production centers. Since the introduction of the art of papermaking to the American

Edgar Veneer Factory, 1912

colonies in 1690, and until the latter part of the nineteenth century, rags were the only practical raw material available for paper manufacturing. This fact was reflected in the pioneer stage of the Wisconsin industry. The state's first paper mill was built around 1847 in Milwaukee, a population center that could provide the necessary quantity of rags. The early mills on the lower Fox River valley, the state's first real center of paper production, also used rags as their chief source of fiber until about 1890. This commodity, however, had traditionally been in short supply, and with the development and refinement of paper machines the scarcity problem became even more acute. While substitutes such as straw were adopted with mixed results, the solution to the fiber shortage lay in the use of woodpulp. The discovery and implementation of practical means for extracting fiber from wood signaled the beginning of the modern paper industry. And as woodpulp increasingly gained acceptance as the primary raw material for papermaking, a new axis of the Wisconsin industry began to form along the upper Wisconsin River valley, where both necessary ingredients, wood and water power, were accessible.[75]

Of course, this maturing branch of the Wisconsin paper industry owed its eventual twentieth century stature to more than just machines, trees, and the Wisconsin River. It needed entrepreneurs with the capital, ambition, and skill to harness the region's technical, human, and natural resources. In the upper Wisconsin valley, this role was filled principally by the area's lumbermen, who were in search of new avenues of investment for their tremendous accumulations of surplus capital. Specifically, within Marathon County the lead was taken by that talented and influential congregation known as the Wausau Group. Motivated by both the lure of profit and the desire to remain in the city in which they already exercised the dominant economic, civic, and social influence, its members began near the turn of the century to focus their creative energies on the development and management of paper companies located near their home base.

The first such enterprise with Wausau Group involvement was the organization of the Wausau Paper Mills Company just before the close of the nineteenth century. In this case, however, the initial exploration which preceded the creation of the second major paper company on the Wisconsin River was done by prominent representatives of outside paper interests: Norman H. Brokaw of Kaukauna and W. L. Edmonds of Appleton. Reminiscent of the pioneer lumbermen Wakely and Stevens, the two paper magnates had been attracted to the Wausau area in the spring of 1889 by the region's reputed "splendid water powers" and the contiguous "great forests of hemlock, spruce, and balsam." After a thorough examination of three possible locations along the river, land north of Wausau at the "five mile dam" was selected for the millsite, and on July 12 ground was broken. Eight months later the $400,000 Wausau Paper Mills complex was completed, and on March 31, 1900, a special edition of the *Central Wisconsin,* made from the plant's first product, heralded the arrival of the newest member of Marathon County's industrial family, which was dubbed "the rainbow of promise."

The concern was not long in living up to the optimistic nickname. Two machines had been installed when the wooden plant facility began operations; in 1902 two more were added. Accordingly, by 1905 the plant's total daily capacity had increased from eighteen tons to fifty-five tons of groundwood pulp, and from thirty tons to fifty tons of paper. Flood waters in 1911 and 1912, followed by a wood room fire in 1914 dimmed but did not extinguish the light of the Brokaw rainbow. By the early 1920's, the practically rebuilt brick facility was doing an annual business of three million dollars. Employment in roughly the first twenty years of the company's life had climbed from 150 to more than 300 men.

Wausau Group influence, to be sure, had been present in the early stages of the operation's development. Alexander Stewart and Walter Alexander were listed among the company's original stockholders. Stewart, moreover, was selected as the company's first vice-president; upon his death in 1912, he was succeeded by Cyrus Yawkey. Nonetheless, the early leadership of Marathon County's first paper mill had a distinct non-Wausau tinge about it. The firm's financial backers included Norman Brokaw, W. L. Edmonds, his brother E. A. Edmonds, and A. C. Merriman of Marinette. The executive offices were also divided between Wausauites and outsiders. E. A. Edmonds held the position of treasurer, while his brother had the dual responsibilities of secretary and general manager. Norman Brokaw was the formal head of the organization as president. Veterans of the Kaukauna and Appleton paper enterprises were also prominent in the lower supervisory positions. However, with a firm foothold established, Wausau Group domination was only a matter of time. The naming of Walter Alexander as the company's second president tipped the balance. When death in 1926 ended his lengthy tenure in that office, control remained in both the nuclear and extended family, as Ben Alexander was tapped to take his father's place. Thus, early in the twentieth century the first link had been forged in the paper chain of industrial diversification for both Marathon County and the Wausau Group.[76]

The Wausau Paper Mills operation was an impressive beginning for the nascent county industry. As the *Central Wisconsin* took pains to emphasize, however, that mill had been built on the smallest water power on the Wisconsin River. The county's full potential in this respect was still waiting to be exploited:

Downtown Brokaw, Early 20th Century

On this river within the county are six other water
powers, each of which in the course of time will turn
the wheels of as large or even larger institutions On
the tributaries of the Wisconsin also within the county
are sixteen other water powers ranging from 250 to
1600 horse power. The aggregate of the whole is 70,500
horse power, only about 15 per cent of which is developed.[77]

The subsequent promotional campaign of the Wisconsin Valley Advancement Association made much the same point: there remained
great opportunities for further paper mill development along the great
river in general and, in particular, on the water powers within the
borders of Marathon County.

Yet, almost a full decade passed before a second major project was
undertaken by the Wausau Group. In the first years of the new century, it will be remembered, their main attention was focused on penetrating the southern United States pine belt when the realization set
in that their lumbering days in northern Wisconsin were numbered.
Once they had established a firm presence in the southern lumber industry, their interest again turned towards the creation of new diversified enterprises closer to home. Their re-entry into the paper manufacturing field was signaled by the founding in 1910 of the Wausau
Sulphate Fibre Company. The foundation for the project had been
laid in February, 1908, when Louis Dessert concluded six weeks of
negotiations by selling the idle water power of the Joseph Dessert
Lumber Company to another Wausau Group venture, the Wausau
Street Railway Company, for an estimated $50,000.[78] All that remained
was a suitable opportunity for development.

That occasion arrived when news reached Wausau that Olai Bache-
Wiig had successfully introduced the sulphate pulpmaking process to
the North American continent at the Brompton Pulp and Paper Company in East Angus, Quebec. Seizing the initiative, Wausau Group
representatives persuaded Bache-Wiig to come to Wausau for a conference. The outcome of the February 26, 1910, meeting was a decision
to promote and incorporate a company to manufacture sulphate pulp
in the county and to install a paper machine for the production of kraft
paper, thus creating the first complete sulphate operation in the United
States. Once the preliminary financial arrangements had been completed, the first organizational meeting of the newly incorporated
Wausau Sulphate Fibre Company was held in the city on March 10,
1910. Chosen to head the concern was another multi-talented Wausau
Group associate, Karl Mathie, who had recently returned from man-

aging another paper company in which the Group had an interest—
the Watab Pulp and Paper Company of Sartell, Minnesota.[79] The
remaining executive and director positions were filled primarily by
local lumbering figures, including W. C. Landon, Fowler P. Stone,
B. F. McMillan, and Louis Dessert. Soon thereafter, decisions were
also reached to locate the plant at Mosinee and purchase the Little
Bull Falls water power from the Wausau Street Railway Company.

News of the transaction, accompanied by a report that construction
of an "immense plant" would begin at once, generated much excitement in the Mosinee area. And there was good reason for the enthusiasm. The community had been languishing ever since the closing
of the Dessert mill in 1904. Securing the new pulp and paper operation
would provide a badly needed economic shot in the arm. The job of
erecting the complex alone gave an immediate boost to local employment. Noted the *Mosinee Times* on June 24, 1910: "The first pay day
of the Wausau Sulphate Fibre Company occurred last Friday and the
men employed on the works showed a very pleasing countenance indeed as they wended their way home with their pay in their pocket."
The progress of plant construction was followed closely and duly reported by the paper. The completion of each step in the process was
cause for community self-congratulations, and, sometimes, for even a
little jab at its neighbor to the north:

> Up at Wausau they make a great what-to-do about
> their Lake Wausau, but we are in shape to go 'em one
> better with a puddle that is really worthwhile.
>
> Lake Mosinee is now on the map. The dam is
> finished, the coffer dam on the old mill dam removed
> and on Wednesday afternoon at 3 o'clock the big gates
> at the guard lock were closed down to allow the pond
> to fill up.
>
> The present dam will carry about three feet more
> head than did the old Dessert dam, so it will be seen
> that quite a respectable lake will be the result.

Indeed, the securing and completion of this second county paper mill
was unabashedly portrayed as nothing less than "the turning point in
the history of Mosinee."[80]

The *Mosinee Times* may well have been correct in its appraisal of
the company's importance to the community. The existence of the
Wausau Sulphate Fibre operation halted and then dramatically reversed the serious decline in the village population that had coincided
with the six-year period following the closing of the Dessert sawmill.
From 1900 to 1910 the village population had dropped 25.9 per cent

Wausau Sulphate Fibre Company In Construction, Mosinee, 1910

from 657 to 482. At the end of 1920, however, the population had shot up to 1,161, a 140 per cent increase over the 1910 figure. By way of contrast, Wausau's population increased only about 13 per cent over the same period. The next decade witnessed a less spectacular but still consequential population increase of 5 per cent. This growth was reflected in a building boom which had the effect of increasing the urban character of the community. A town hall complete with jail, fire hall, public rest rooms, and council rooms was built in 1921. That same year a new high school was erected with facilities for over four hundred students. Improvements were also instituted in the downtown area. The village's main street was paved in 1922, and the following year street lights were added to the business section. Mosinee's only theater was built in 1923 and two hotels, the Swanee and Mosinee, opened in 1928. Recreation was not ignored: a ball park was built in 1922 and a swimming pool was added the next year. Accompanying both the population growth and the resulting internal improvements was a movement to upgrade the village's standing to city status. Outside of the natural desire to obtain some sort of official recognition of its impressive development, such a move would also increase the community's representation on the county board. A referendum on the change was defeated in the early 1920's, but agitation on the subject continued throughout the remainder of the decade. Even the Wausau press took note of the campaign, and in the process pointed to the tremendous progress that had taken place in the community since the arrival of the Wausau Sulphate Fibre Company:

> The village of Mosinee at present is in the throes of the usual growing pains most progressive communities experience when prosperity and community development have progressed to a certain state. There is a movement on foot just now to cast off the prosaic habiliments of a village and assume the more glamorous garb of a city. Few communities in this section of the state have profited from the incentive of industry to the extent that Mosinee has. Coupled with this has been a constructive policy in the administration of civic and municipal affairs that has given to the community advantages not enjoyed by many aggressive cities of larger population. Whether or not the more munificent title of city will bring added prestige is problematical. Nevertheless our neighbors to the south are to be complimented upon their aggressive attempt to throw off the swaddling clothes of their enterprising village, which some of the more optimistic are convinced have been outgrown for some time.[81]

The movement finally achieved success in 1931, when the city council by a two-thirds vote officially changed Mosinee's urban standing to city ranking, and Dr. E. F. Butler was named the first mayor of Marathon County's third city.[82]

During this period the expansion of the Wausau Sulphate Fibre Company more than equalled the improvements the operation sparked within the host village. In addition to the installation of new machinery and an increase in plant size, a subsidiary operation was added in late 1928, when the mill purchased the controlling interests of the Bay West Paper Company at Green Bay. Earlier that year, indirect recognition of the community of interest that existed between company and village was made when the company's official name was changed to Mosinee Paper Mills Company, in order to connect the mill with the trade name of its product. Despite this move, the major share of control over the firm's destiny continued to reside not in Mosinee, but in Wausau. By 1922, Fowler P. Stone had risen to the company presidency, with Karl Mathie holding the title of chairman of the board. In addition, G. D. Jones and A. L. Kreutzer occupied the respective offices of secretary and treasurer, while Mark Ewing and John F. Ross made up two-thirds of the remaining board of directors membership. Mosinee interests were represented in the firm's leadership ranks by Louis Dessert, who continued to occupy a vice-presidency. Former village resident H. M. Thompson also sat on the board. But there was no escaping the fact that the balance of power tipped towards the home base of the Wausau Group. That control tightened even more when a second generation member of the Group, Aytchmonde P. Woodson, assumed the presidential office prior to the death of Fowler Stone in the early 1930's.[83]

The ultimate Wausau Group venture in the county paper industry had its origin in another water power acquisition. On March 31, 1893, the Wisconsin Legislature authorized John D. Ross and his attorney, W. C. Silverthorn, 'to build and maintain a dam across the Wisconsin River on any lands that they may own or control' at Rothschild. That right was transferred in 1903 to Ross, Charles Winton, and E. W. Brooks, with the crucial stipulation that any surplus water power not necessary for logging or the improvement of navigation could be used for 'carrying on any manufacturing and electric lighting business. . . .' Ironically, perhaps the key stimulus for the eventual creation of the paper mill came from Robert La Follette. One of the major reforms advocated by La Follette during his gubernatorial campaign was regulation of public utilities. Accordingly, in 1905, his allies in the legislature enacted a law requiring that all previously granted franchises for the building and maintaining of dams on navigable streams 'which have not been exercised . . . within four years from the date of passage . . . of this act shall be forfeited and terminated.' The intent of the act was to prevent multiple franchise holders such as the Wausau Group from indefinitely monopolizing the electric power situation in one area. The immediate consequence of the law was that Ross, Winton, and Brooks had to do something with their waterpower site by 1909 or turn it over to the state.

A partial solution came on April 27, 1906 when Neal Brown, G. D. Jones and Charles Gilbert incorporated the Rothschild Water Power Company, and four days later acquired the Ross-Winton-Brooks franchise. Wausau Group members managed the company and owned most of its stock. The owners had initially planned to build either a sawmill or a public utility on the site. But by late 1908, with the termination date nearing, Neal Brown came up with the idea that the Group should build its own paper mill on the Rothschild location.

With the assistance of Cyrus Yawkey, Walter Alexander, and Charles Gilbert, plans were initiated to transfer most of the stock of the Rothschild Water Power Company to a new firm, the Marathon Paper Mills Company.

On January 19, 1909 the plan was announced to the general public. The front page of that day's *Wausau Daily Record-Herald* carried the banner headline: "Wausau Will Have A New Paper Mill." The accompanying article detailed the formation of a $750,000 corporation that would employ an estimated 350 men. The list of men interested in the concern was dominated by the original members of the Wausau Group and their associates.[84] In case the populace failed to comprehend the total significance of the new enterprise, it was spelled out in the paper the following day by one of the organizers. The project would result in an increase of Wausau's population to 20,000 within five years. The construction of a 450 foot dam across the river at Rothschild would create a beautiful lake which, in turn, would "make Wausau one of the most attractive summer resorts in the state." The mill, in short, would "put Wausau on the map as nothing else has done for years."[85]

The company's stockholders held their first official meeting in B. F. Wilson's office on February 13, 1909. The main order of business was the election of officers, and the only suspense involved in the selection process was which Wausau Group member would be elected to which office. The results were as follows: C. C. Yawkey was chosen as president; C. J. Winton, vice-president; B. F. Wilson, secretary; and Walter Alexander, treasurer. The corporation's board of directors consisted of the aforementioned officers, Walter H. Bissell, Neal Brown, and G. D. Jones. Brown was also retained as company counsel. The only other major items of business were the selection of firms to design the dam and corporation's plant facilities, and the hiring of a general manager to oversee the entire operation. In retrospect, this last decision was probably the most important one ever made by the Wausau Group with regard to their enterprises. The appointment that day of David Clark Everest as Marathon general manager would have far reaching consequences not only for the future of the Marathon Paper Mills Company, but also for the subsequent development of Marathon County's industrial economy.

D. C. Everest was born on October 13, 1883 in Pine Grove, Michigan, roughly fifteen miles northwest of Kalamazoo. The son of a moderately successful manufacturer, Everest had enjoyed a comfortable childhood. In his youth he achieved the reputation of being a skillful orator, to the extent of giving speeches with William Jennings Bryan on the "Commoner's" campaign swing through Michigan in the 1896 presidential campaign.[86] A double tragedy in his family three years later marked the first turning point in Everest's life. First, his father's uninsured plant burned to the ground; then, in a frantic effort to rebuild, the father contracted typhoid fever and died. Thus, to support his mother and younger sister, Everest abandoned his dream of enrolling at the University of Michigan. Instead, on January 6, 1900, he secured the job of office boy with the Bryant Paper Company of Kalamazoo. His salary was twenty-six dollars a month; the hours were from seven in the morning until whenever the work was done.

At Bryant, young Everest first displayed his talent for recognizing an opportunity and taking profitable advantage of it. One of his assigned tasks involved weighing bales of paper stock. While rummaging through the bales, Everest discovered many historic books and letters, some bearing the signatures of George Washington and Thomas Jefferson. Realizing he had stumbled onto a gold mine, the eager office boy used his first month's salary to purchase several of the bales. Back at his rooming house he removed all the valuable autographed letters and historic books and sold them to supplement his salary and to purchase even more piles of this scrap paper. Recalling this side venture years later, Everest remarked that these sales netted him many times his salary and were '. . . really a lifesaver for me and my family.'

D. C. Everest did not concentrate his efforts on sorting scrap paper, however, for by 1902 he had risen to full-time bookkeeper. Combining the jobs of bookkeeper and accountant, he studied all phases of the Bryant operation and was soon in a position to advise the plant's general manager, Frank Milham, on management decisions. When Milham became an officer of the newly organized Munising Paper Company, he gave high recommendation to Everest, who was consequently hired as the firm's assistant manager at age nineteen. More experience was gained in his five-year stint at Munising and a subsequent fifteen-month tenure as manager of the Williams-Gray paper machinery firm of Chicago. With his reputation established throughout the industry by 1909, it is not surprising that on the day news of the Marathon project was released to the public, Everest received a visit from Neal Brown to discuss the position of general manager. Impressed with his knowledge of the entire papermaking process, Brown invited Everest to come to Wausau before the end of the month to meet the other Wausau Group members.

At that conference, Everest's qualifications, a recommendation from a Munising's associate, and Neal Brown's enthusiasm were all factors in his favor. But given all that, he may have owed his appointment as much to his only physical oddity as to his first job in the industry. His almost total baldness hid the fact that he was only twenty-five years old. Nonetheless, looking over the much older men interviewing him, Everest waited for the fateful question about his age, and finally the matter was brought up while discussing his qualifications. Before he could reply, however, another director interrupted with a question about how he had gotten his start in the paper business. The mention of his office boy experience greatly appealed to that particular director, who explained, 'By golly, that's good. That's the way I started.' 'From there on,' Everest recalled, 'he carried the ball for me.' The age question was forgotten as the discussion proceeded to other topics. D. C. Everest's head would serve him well many times in his Marathon County business career, but never in quite the same way.[87]

The decision to hire Everest as general manager did not automatically guarantee a trouble-free future for the Marathon enterprise. Construction difficulties, management and production problems, labor shortages, and a series of destructive floods all plagued the company's early life. Marathon did not truly overcome its initial problems until 1913. During this shaky period, Everest was given a relatively free hand to deal with the various crises as he saw fit. One of the traits of the Wausau Group was its ability to pick capable lieutenants to oversee their enterprises, delegate to them far-reaching authority, and absorb them ultimately into their power structure. Everest also displayed this talent over the course of his forty-six year involvement with Marathon County industry. Even before being officially hired, he had begun to recruit his management team at Marathon. The most significant selection was probably a Munising associate, Alton Van Douser, who was brought into the organization as an auditor. Van Douser's tenure at Marathon, where he rose to the position of director, would surpass Everest's. By the time he left the organization in 1955, the protege was almost as famous as Everest in state paper and business circles.

Marathon's general manager was not entirely infallible in his selection of underlings, however. In the aftermath of one of the floods which damaged the company's facilities, Everest was having difficulty finding an experienced dynamiter to blast out some defective concrete on the apron of the dam. One day a stranger walked into Everest's office, announced that he went by the name of "Dynamite Bill," and was just the man Everest was looking for. Delighted, Everest interviewed the applicant and then hired him. Everything proceeded normally the first day. Then, late in the evening Everest was practically rocked out of his bed by the sound of a tremendous explosion. Running to the mill, he asked an employee on the scene what had happened. 'It's Bill,' the shaken worker replied. 'He's blown up the place.' A subsequent investigation revealed that instead of using the customary half-pound sticks of dynamite in fifty holes, Bill had tried to complete the job with one-pound sticks in one hundred holes. The result of this extra effort was a pulverized concrete apron, broken windows, debris inside the mill, and a terrified work force. Bill, by one means or another, had disappeared. There the matter rested until another caller visited Everest's office one week later and asked if he knew the whereabouts of someone who matched Bill's description. When Everest asked for an explanation, his visitor identified himself as an officer of the state mental asylum. It seemed that a fellow who liked to call himself "Dynamite Bill" had recently escaped from the institution.

Despite this somewhat rocky beginning, the mill operations eventually began to show signs of progress, due largely to Everest's 'hard work and long anxious hours. . . .' Once the initial stumbling blocks were cleared, Everest began to apply the tenets of his business philosophy to the Marathon enterprise. His belief that the key to success lay in concentration on specialty products where there was less competition led to Marathon's growing emphasis on the manufacture of new products between 1913 and 1919. Primary attention was focused on paper food packaging products such as waxable paper and bleached line board. Everest and other Marathon officials anticipated correctly a trend towards more attractive and efficient means of food packaging. An associate remembers that Everest was fond of making the observation that this specialization guaranteed the company's existence, since "people are never going to stop eating."[88]

With the drive for specialization showing results by 1920,[89] Everest turned next towards implementing another of his basic business beliefs—the necessity of both backward and forward vertical integration of Marathon's operations. He had, in fact, begun the first half of the process in 1919 with a timberland purchase program, an event which also signaled his emergence over Cyrus Yawkey as the dominant figure in the Marathon organization.[90] The recession affecting the entire paper industry in the early 1920's was an added inducement to move in the other direction of the integration process. In particular, Everest desired the absorption of Marathon's largest single customer, the

The Risk-Takers: Left to Right, C. C. Yawkey, J. F. Ross, George S. Gaylord, C. J. Winton, Walter Alexander, Walter Bissell, D. C. Everest, Brown Katzenbach, Judd S. Alexander, 1922

Menasha Printing and Carton Company. Seven years of negotiations were climaxed in June, 1927, by the Marathon directors' decision to purchase the entire Menasha operation, in exchange for their firm's stocks and bonds. The merger elevated Marathon from the status of a mere paper mill to a vertically integrated concern with even more power and prestige in the state and national paper industry.

While this first step of forward integration brought numerous advantages to the Marathon Paper Mills Company, it also created a serious internal conflict within the enlarged organization. For, in buying the Menasha firm, Marathon had also acquired its owner and general manager, George Gaylord. Over the years Gaylord had exercised power at Menasha comparable to that at Marathon by Everest. Moreover, the success enjoyed by the firm under his leadership convinced him that his business philosophy and methods were the correct ones to follow. Unfortunately for the smooth functioning of the combined enterprises, these principles were in direct conflict with those adhered to by Everest. Gaylord's preferred policies were the embodiment of the old ideas of free enterprise and "rugged individualism." He favored the aggressive pursuit of all available business even if it meant underselling and thus antagonizing his competitors. Everest, on the other hand, was more in tune with the prevailing American business philosophy of the post-war era: cooperation should replace ruthless competition in order to achieve stability of both prices and markets.[91] Abhorrence of price cutting had always been a cornerstone of his business philosophy. Like many industrialists, he had gone to Washington after the American entry into World War I, and had participated in the close government-business partnership that had existed in the home front war effort. This experience had solidified his earlier predispositions. While he had deviated on occasion from the policy of cooperation with competitors if it furthered his or Marathon's interest,[92] Everest was a staunch advocate of trade associations and was willing informally to allocate markets with the competition.[93] These convictions had served Everest well at Marathon and, accordingly, he was convinced that they should be continued by the new organization.

Given such diametrically opposed philosophies, Gaylord's unwillingness to recognize Everest's position as general manager of the entire company, and the sizable egos of both men, friction was inevitable within the organization. A showdown was avoided for over a year while Everest studied the rudiments of the converting business. In 1929, as he began to take a more active role in all phases of the Marathon operation, tensions also started to escalate. The die was cast when the pair openly disagreed over the proper response to a sharp break in pail and carton prices, a conflict which arose from their differing basic philosophies. Everest had hoped that Gaylord's recognized talents could be utilized in the company's activities, but he was determined that his policy decisions should be final. Thus, at a June conference of the company's executives and directors, the general manager openly asserted his claim to supremacy and was overwhelmingly supported. To the day he finally left the organization, George Gaylord never completely accepted that reality. But, with that exception, by the end of the 1920's David Clark Everest was the leader of the Marathon Paper Mills Company. With this secure and powerful base, he was ready to assume an even larger role in Marathon County's economic affairs in the years ahead.[94]

In summation, it would be difficult to overstate the importance of the paper industry to Marathon County's development in the twentieth century. A better appreciation of its significance can be gained, however, by examining instances in which the development of the county paper industry helped to preserve and create county institutions. The D. J. Murray Manufacturing Company, incorporated in August, 1883, was another of Wausau's pioneer industrial establishments.[95] The original purpose of the company had been to manufacture and service sawmill machinery for northern Wisconsin and upper Michigan lumbering interests. Thus its fate was linked with that of the state lumber industry, and by the early 1920's the practically non-existent market for sawmill machinery left the firm's future in doubt. A change in ownership and product emphasis proved to be the company's salvation, however. In early 1921, D. J. Murray decided to sell his interests. The makeup of the new directorship contained familiar names in the movement for local industrial diversification: W. L. Edmonds, Walter Alexander, Mark Ewing, John F. Ross, and D. C. Everest. And with this leadership, it is not surprising that a decision was made to shift production to specialization in pulp and paper mill machinery. Before long, the Murray designers and engineers had come up with a number of labor and timesaving devices which were eagerly adopted by the paper industry.[96] A mutually profitable relationship was thus established, and a piece of Wausau's nineteenth century industrial history remained on the scene.[97]

Machine Shop, D. J. Murray Mfg. Co., Late 19th Century

The paper industry was capable not only of preserving an old county business establishment, but of creating a new county community. Originally, the founders of Marathon Paper Mills had no intention of starting a village in Rothschild. The workers would reside either in Wausau or Schofield. But with keen local competition for labor, the desirability of residential development within walking distance of the mill soon became apparent. Therefore, in September, 1909, the company recorded a fifteen-block plat for the village of Rothschild at the office of county clerk John King. The firm then proceeded to transform Rothschild into a modern company town. First, a Chicago landscape artist was hired to design the village. The construction contracts specified that fifty-two homes, no more than five of which could be of the same design, were to be equipped with electric lights and plumbing. Besides providing the water supply and fire protection, the concern erected a store, a large boarding house, a community hall and a school. Once construction was under way, the Wausau Group's street railway extended its line into the village. By 1912, this community, on a hillside overlooking the plant from across the railroad tracks and road, contained nearly one hundred structures. And by 1920, the Marathon operation could take direct credit for having founded a county village with a population of 413, which would climb to just under 500 by 1930.[98]

Such development did not come free to the county as a whole, however. The economic and community growth made possible by the paper mills, was achieved at a distinct social cost. Both the mills and the communities they created, or in the case of Mosinee, urbanized, dumped their raw sewage into the Wisconsin River. The report of a joint study undertaken in the mid-1920's by the Wisconsin Conservation Commission and the State Board of Health detailed the stream pollution problem on that stretch of the Wisconsin River within Marathon County:

> From Brokaw to Mosinee the stream receives pollution at Brokaw, Wausau, Schofield and Rothschild, the population contributing domestic sewage being estimated at 21,876 and the population equivalent of the industrial wastes principally from pulp and paper mills is 262,800. The stream is colored and turbid during low flow and fibrous and sewage sludges were noted, particularly below Wausau, Rothschild and above the dam at Mosinee. The dissolved oxygen in the stream decreased to below that critical for fish life below Brokaw and was frequently zero above the dam

at Mosinee, during low stream flow and high tempera-
ture. Even following flood conditions in the latter
part of the investigation an appreciable decrease in the
dissolved oxygen was noted. Other chemical deter-
minations emphasized the polluted conditions of the
river. Critical conditions for fish and other aquatic
life existed in this portion of the stream during low
stream flow and high temperatures.[99]

Little comfort could be derived from examining the corresponding
figures for Mosinee. There, the sewage from a resident population of
1,461 and the industrial wastes from the pulp and paper mills, with an
estimated population equivalent of 80,900, entered the river. From
Mosinee to Stevens Point, "the oxygen [was] entirely depleted during
extremely low flows."[100] Moreover, the paper mills also had a detri-
mental effect on the more aesthetic aspect of the quality of life.
Around the turn of the century, a local author eulogized the atmosphere: "Marathon County air is a tonic more potent than lotions or
elixirs compounded of drugs. It brings roses to the pale cheek and
invigorates and restores the debilitated."[101] Once the paper mills
were established, residents of the host communities and the surrounding countryside soon discovered that the pungent odor caused by the
cooking phase of the papermaking process made even the semblance of
this exaggerated claim disappear.

If the Wausau Group had become involved only in the creation of
paper mills, its contribution to Marathon County's industrial diversification would have been monumental. However, the investment interests of its members extended to still other manufacturing and
business enterprises. The Group entered the electrical products field
on April 23, 1914, with the organization of the Marathon Electric
Manufacturing Company.[102] Heading this concern were two second
generation members of the Group: Walter Alexander's second son,
Judd, was named president, while A. P. Woodson was selected vice
president.[103] Both maintained lengthy connections with the firm;
Alexander for thirty-four years, Woodson for forty-four years. Each
would hold the position of chairman of the board at the time of his
death. Mineral products were added to the Group's sphere of influence when a connection was formed with the Wausau Abrasives
Company, an operation which utilized the pure silica quartz from Rib
Mountain to manufacture sandpaper.[104]

The Group's willingness to finance industrial research resulted in
the invention of a new product and the creation of an eventual multi-
million dollar industry. On April 22, 1924, William Mason, a research

associate of Thomas Edison and an employee of the Wausau Southern Lumber Company, sent the following telegram to Walter Alexander:

HAVE NEW METHOD FOR DISPOSING OF SAW-
MILL WASTE FROM ANY WOOD AT A PROFIT
WANT TO MEET YOU AND EVEREST AND POS-
SIBLY OTHERS TO GET YOUR ADVICE ON THIS
PROPOSITION WIRE WHEN IT WILL BE CON-
VENIENT FOR YOU TO SEE ME IN WAUSAU

The previous month Mason had designed and built a device to reduce waste wood chips to fiber. These fibers could then be made into a structural insulating board. He needed more money, however, to carry on his work—thus, the telegram to Alexander. In response, the Wausau Group provided him with a modest initial investment of $10,000 as well as permission to conduct further research at the Rothschild paper mill. This additional experimentation at Marathon resulted in the invention of a new hardboard now known world-wide as Masonite.[105] On August 24, 1925, D. C. Everest presided over the first meeting of the founders of the Mason Fibre Company in Walter Alexander's office. A million dollar corporation was formed, with the principal stockholders including both the old and newer members of the Group. The enterprise began producing both insulating board and hardboard in mid-1926 at its newly constructed plant in Laurel, Mississippi. There were some early manufacturing difficulties, but by January, 1929, the company had grown so rapidly that a managerial reorganization was required. Brown Katzenbach, a local certified public accountant and another long-time Group associate, was named general manager, and an executive committee of D. C. Everest, Ben Alexander, and Matthew McCullough was appointed to provide additional direction. The renamed Masonite Corporation continued to show a profit throughout most of the Depression and turned into one of the Group's most successful ventures.[106]

The safety hazards associated with an expanding industrial economy created a demand for insurance protection. Here, too, Wausau Group members quickly assumed a dominant role in providing this service. Their first attempt received official sanction in early May, 1909, when the Great Northern Life Insurance Company was granted a business license by the state insurance department, allowing the firm to deliver $250,000 worth of already written policies. A subsequent stockholders' meeting selected Neal Brown as the company's first president. Chosen as vice-president and general manager was another local resident with a state-wide reputation, Dr. William A. Fricke, who had served as Wisconsin Insurance Commissioner from 1895 through October, 1898. The elected board of directors included the entire original membership of the Wausau Group, along with numerous other local business and professional notables. With such leadership, the *Portage Democrat* predicted that ". . . the company is surely destined to become one of the largest and most prosperous life insurance institutions of the county."[167] By 1922, the concern's assets had increased more than seven fold, and the insurance departments of Wisconsin and Illinois were reporting that the firm's financial statement showed 'a growing and prosperous condition.'[168]

As in the paper industry, the Group's most ambitious project in the insurance field was prompted by another progressive reform. In this case it was the enactment by the Wisconsin Legislature on May 3, 1911, of what would be the first constitutional workmen's compensation law in America. Adopting the principle that an employer was automatically liable for injuries suffered by his employees in the course of their employment, the legislation signaled an end to one of the biggest scandals of the Wisconsin industrialization movement: the treatment accorded injured industrial workers by their employers.[169] The bill would also provide the Wausau Group with its greatest opportunity to expand its sphere of economic influence in the twentieth century.

Shortly before the new law was to go into effect, the Group, along with several other Wisconsin valley business leaders, met in Wausau on July 18 to determine how best to accommodate their interests to the revolutionary concept embodied in the legislation. While their precise attitude towards the legislature's action is difficult to determine,[110] every industrialist in attendance recognized that workmen's compensation would be a business fact of life in fewer than two months. The most advantageous means of protecting both their companies and their employees under the new law had to be found. The solution agreed upon that day, though not entirely novel, was every bit as revolutionary as the law that spawned it. They decided to share one another's liabilities by forming a mutual insurance company.[111] Thus, on August 25, 1911, the first meeting of the Employers Mutual Liability Insurance Company was held. The location belied the importance of the event, for it was above an old cigar store in the Marathon County Bank building offices of the Great Northern Life Insurance Company. Nonetheless, the necessary organizational business was transacted: by-laws and articles of incorporation were approved, executive officers and directors were elected. Port Edwards paper manufacturer George F. Steele was selected as the company's first president. The presence of Neal Brown, B. F. Wilson, Cyrus Yawkey, Walter Alexander, and several of their allies on the board of directors indicated that the Wausau Group would exercise the controlling influence over the new company's affairs. That dominance was soon given symbolic recognition. On September 1, 1911, the same day the Wisconsin Workmen's Compensation Act went into effect, the first policy of Employers Mutual was issued to the Wausau Sulphate Fibre Company.[112]

The Group soon discovered that pioneering in the field of industrial insurance was the most difficult bit of economic trailblazing they had ever attempted. 'None of us who are engaged in the management of this company,' wrote Neal Brown, 'have been insurance sharps or experts.'[113] Unlike their earlier lumbering and paper ventures, there were no precedents to help them make this novel type of enterprise successful. The magazine *Insurance World* doubted not only the workability of the mutual approach, but the whole Wisconsin concept of workmen's compensation:

> "The plan embodies a large undertaking and we fail to note a man on the committee competent to cope with the situation. The insurance scheme involved is the most intricate of any now written. . . . The State of Wisconsin is undertaking a gigantic venture (workmen's compensation) and we would imagine that its non-feasibility will be quickly demonstrated unless started along safe lines."[114]

Moreover, since the compensation law was a voluntary or elective arrangement in its first two years, in order to avoid constitutional problems, the salesmen of the young firm had actively to recruit business.[115] Businessmen had to be convinced both to accept the new legislation and then to carry their insurance through the mutual liability approach.

This persuasion was not easy in the face of the open hostility of the rival stock insurance companies. The private casualty concerns had emerged from the hearings of the Industrial Insurance Committee as one of the chief villains of the precompensation era. Fearing the loss of profitable business, they were also one of the chief opponents of the Workmen's Compensation Act. Matthew McCullough recalled that '. . . the stock companies that had carried our liability insurance told us it would cost us almost triple the present insurance rate if we recognized the new law.'[110] Once the legislation was a reality, their enmity shifted to their new competitor, the mutual insurance firm in Wausau. Before the end of 1911, a rumor was circulated that the young company "had fallen through." The source of the falsity was suspected to be the private insurance companies.[117] Then the stock companies attempted to portray the Wausau operation as the advance agent of Socialism or Bolshevism in the United States. The following analysis presented by an insurance agent in a letter to one of Employers' policyholders was typical:

> Bolshevism is rampant throughout the country. The I.W.W.'s and the Reds are inciting trouble wherever possible. In our own state we have new organizations such as the Equity League and the Non-Partisan League as well as Victor L. Berger and a hotbed of Socialists. It seems to me that we have enough agitation against corporation profits without business men lending a voice to it.[118]

The culmination of this bitter propaganda campaign was the wide dissemination of a little booklet, in which the head of a Minneapolis stock company displayed in no uncertain terms his contempt for the Wausau firm, referring to it as "the Wausau Mutuals." Ironically, this tactic resulted only in a flood of mail addressed to "Wausau Mutuals" from curious businessmen desiring more information about the company's plan and method of operation, 'much to the delight, naturally,' of the Employers' executives.

Probably most harmful, however, was a rate-cutting war initiated by the private casualty companies. Responding to this tactic seriously depleted the Wausau firm's financial reserves, and had the directors seriously contemplating the possibility of liquidating the company by early 1914. The question of an adequate rate level also precipitated a conflict within the organization, the outcome of which would have major significance for the company's future. The protagonists were the firm's prestigious vice-president and general manager, Dr. William A. Fricke, and a young assistant secretary, Hans J. Hagge, who had left a successful Chicago court reporting business to join the Employers organization about five weeks after it opened for business. Hagge firmly believed that the company was going to develop a substantial deficit unless it raised its rate level. Fricke just as firmly disagreed, and the result was "some rather bitter arguments" and "considerable ill feeling" between the two. Finally, the matter was brought before the board of directors in January, 1914, who concurred with their young executive's assessment. For a few moments, however, the victory appeared to be a hollow one, as one of the directors declared that the Wausau Group had never had a failure and that to avoid one now perhaps the company should be dissolved. Hagge appealed for an opportunity to turn the operation's fortunes around. After outlining his plans to raise rates and reduce expenses, he received something less than a resounding vote of confidence. But it represented a chance, and that was all he needed. For the next thirty-eight years, first as general manager, then as president, Hans Hagge would be the dominant personality in the Employers Mutual operation. Many years later Hagge recalled the dark period in the company's early history with some bitterness:

> You know what a hopeless little peckerwood opera-
> tion ours was back in the days of Doctor Fricke who,
> in addition to all of his other accomplishments, was
> quite a juggler of figures. He thought he could make
> them mean something that they weren't. He wasn't
> fooling anyone but himself and then when we found
> ourselves in a hellish mess, he resigned because the di-
> rectors raised a lot of hell with him and concluded to
> dissolve the company. Thanks to Charlie Crownhart
> and Neal Brown, the directors finally reluctantly gave
> me an opportunity to see what I could make out of the
> wreck and, believe me, since then (1913) I have been
> working like a crazy fool but — thank the Lord and my
> many fine able assistants, we have made quite an insti-
> tution out of the wreck.[119]

Economy was the initial keynote of the Hagge regime, and his policies eventually began to show results. Dividends were paid to Employers' customers for the first time in 1915. By 1919 the company's assets had reached one million dollars. As its financial situation began to stabilize, the firm began to establish its reputation for innovation in the American insurance industry. This was especially evident in the area of advancing industrial safety. A motion picture, "The Awakening," was produced in 1919 to promote Employers' accident prevention program. Carrying this regard for worker safety one step further, the company in 1928 became the first in the workmen's compensation field to establish an industrial nursing program. Another first during the 1920's was the establishment of a rehabilitation workshop for injured workers, an innovation that turned into a highly effective piece of advertising for both Employers and its customers. Physical expansion was another hallmark of this period. The company entered Michigan in 1918, Minnesota the next year, and in 1921 started businesses in Illinois and Iowa. A separate company, the Employers Mutual Indemnity Corporation, was organized in 1923 to handle policyholders' needs for auto, public liability, and other lines of casualty insurance. Thus, by 1931, when Hans Hagge replaced Matthew McCullough as company president, Employers Mutual had grown into the leading writer of workmen's compensation in Wisconsin. It was also well on the way to becoming the Wausau Group's most successful, and Marathon County's best-known, business institution.[120]

This, then, was the Wausau Group's ultimate contribution to the industrial diversification movement in Marathon County, as well as, perhaps, other areas of the country. Originally drawn together only for the purpose of preserving their investments in the lumber industry, the Group had played the leading role in transforming the character of Marathon County's industrial economy. That the image of Wausau, in particular, changed from the lumbering capital of the Wisconsin valley to the leading business and commercial center of northern Wisconsin by the end of the twentieth century's third decade was in large part the story of these men and their activities. It is not surprising that due to their numerous successes in first lumbering, then wood processing, public utilities, and insurance, a certain aura has grown around these industrialists. Before concluding this discussion of Marathon County's industrial diversification, a few final observations might be made about the Wausau Group, to put the legend in better perspective.

As was the case in the lumber industry, a decision by the Wausau Group to enter other industrial fields was not an automatic guarantee of success for the particular venture involved. The experience of the Ontonagon Fibre Company, organized in 1923, was one notable example. The financial backing and supervision provided by the Group never did succeed in turning the Michigan firm from a 'lemon into lemonade,' to use D. C. Everest's phrase. Closer to home, it should be remembered that Employers Mutual was on the brink of disaster until the Chicago court reporter, Hans Hagge, was given a chance to make the operation profitable. Marathon Electric had, at best, an uneven record of financial success during its first sixteen years of existence. Not until a General Electric salesman, James J. Wall, was brought into the organization in 1930 did the company begin consistently to live up to the founders' expectations.[121] Finally, in this respect, the Group "never made a dime" from the Wausau Abrasives Company.

The Wausau Group members have also received deserved praise as community builders. Certainly in the case of Wausau they demonstrated their commitment to active participation in the life of the city.

These men were not only giants of industry, but, through their membership in various local clubs and organizations, were the civic and social leaders of the community. Moreover, the Group's pulp and paper projects were instrumental to the founding of Brokaw and Rothschild, and the virtual re-birth of Mosinee. Nevertheless, this dedication to community development was not universal; it did not extend to at least one northern Wisconsin sawmill town touched by a Wausau Group enterprise. The residents of Arbor Vitae had high hopes for the future when the Yawkey-Bissell Lumber Company came into the community in 1906. These expectations mounted when the company sponsored the establishment of a local church and a recreation center. However, "neither Cyrus Yawkey nor the Bissells were interested in staying to build up new industries after the logging was over." Most of the homes and buildings were, in fact, taken apart and shipped south in the form of used lumber to the Group's new factory project in Laurel, Mississippi.[122]

The Wausau Group members have often been portrayed as freewheeling enterpreneurs and risk-takers. A Yawkey-Woodson family member has remarked that the way the Group organized and financed their ventures would make the hair of a modern-day broker "turn white and then fall out. They enjoyed the fun of taking risks and turning these risks into success." As with most any legend, this part has some truth to it. But to leave the assertion unqualified would be misleading. In the first place, the Group's accountability to banks was not a major worry. By 1911 its members were capable of exercising a high degree of interlocking control over the local money market. Walter Alexander, for instance, was an officer in five of Wausau's seven general financial institutions. A number of his associates sat on several bank boards of directors. During his years with the Wausau Group, A. P. Woodson was a director of the Marshall & Ilsley Bank of Milwaukee. Moreover, if a particular enterprise wasn't successful, there was an added cushion against financial hardship. On more than one occasion, Group members used the stock of a failed company to reduce their income taxes. Such was the case with B. C. Spruce Mills, Ontonagon, and the heretofore unmentioned Peshtigo Paper Company.

While many of the Group's procedures were informal, its investments could be undertaken with caution. A former president of Masonite, John Coates, recalled that the Group, having financed unsuccessful turpentine extraction projects, 'was skeptical at first' when William Mason approached them, and consequently 'underwrote a small insulation board plant. . . .'[123] Sometimes this caution translated into an unfortunate rigidity. An insistence on receiving cash rather than stock in "any fly-by-night enterprise" from St. Paul kept the Group from establishing a foothold in Minnesota Mining and Manufacturing when the latter purchased the Wausau Abrasives Company in 1929. When an increase in the capitalization of Marathon Paper Mills was required in late 1911, the stockholders authorized what proved to be a lucrative stock issue. Six thousand shares of preferred stock (at one hundred dollars per share) were offered for sale with a six per cent annual dividend; in addition, this stock participated equally in all dividends declared on Marathon's common stock. The fact that the Marathon directors purchased a large amount of the issue themselves indicated that the Wausau Group members were ready to seize a suitable opportunity to enhance their own financial positions. It also evidenced a theme that has surfaced before: a desire by the Wausau elite to keep control of local industry in local hands, or more specifically, in the hands of the leading Wausau families. Outsiders were thus excluded, but in the process the potential entrance of fresh blood, new ideas, and innovative approaches was also minimized.[124]

This last observation should not be taken to mean that only the Wausau Group and its projects were responsible for the county's industrial metamorphosis. The region's less publicized granite industry was in its early stage of development long before the appearance of the first pulp and paper mill. Granite Heights, approximately seven miles north of Wausau in the Town of Texas, was the site of the first openings made in the bluffs east of the Wisconsin River. The initial quarry was opened by Adam Groth and Hugo Peters in the early 1880's. Unfortunately, the two pioneers limited their operation to the production of paving blocks for the Chicago market. The demand for that commodity was by then already on the decline, and thus the firm ceased business operations after only a couple of years. Their place was soon taken by the Cohn & Robertson Manufacturing Company, which utilized the stone for monument construction. In 1897, Fred Devoe purchased Cohn & Robertson's Granite Heights quarry and began to develop the property on an unprecedented scale. After building up his Granite Heights operation over several years, Devoe induced Robert Parcher, D. J. Murray, D. L. Plumer, and Walter Alexander to join him in incorporating the Marathon County Granite Company, the expanded works moving to Wausau in the fall of 1901.

The modest proliferation of similar enterprises was reminiscent of the earlier growth of the county lumber industry. Anderson Brothers & Johnson opened its Ruby red quarry in the Town of Maine across the river from Granite Heights in 1895; in 1913 this firm also re-located in Wausau. August Kickbusch & Son started another quarry at Granite Heights around 1909. Henry Zillman, Chris Bloom and Alex Archie organized the Lake Wausau Granite Company in July, 1914. Their first quarry, located in the Town of Stettin, yielded green granite. Shortly, a second quarry was opened in the Town of Maine to produce red granite; following several subsequent moves, operations were fixed in 1939 along the northeast edge of the Town of Texas. The Rib Mountain Granite Company was founded in 1925 by one of the leading personalities in the county Republican party, Arthur W. Prehn. Considering his political affiliation, the manner in which Prehn secured his labor force was, to say the least, ironic. The decision of the Marathon Granite Company to have an open shop in 1925 resulted in the discharge of twenty unionized employees. After working their own quarry in the Town of Maine for eight months, the men received offers from both Merrill and Wausau to help start a granite plant. Their choice of the latter resulted in the formation of the Prehn operation, which later added a second quarry in the Town of Texas.[125] Another name which would become well-known in the county's twentieth century political history established a final major granite concern, when the Kannenberg family began operations in the Town of Texas in 1927.[126]

A variety of other personalities, business establishments, and products were prominent features of the local industrial scene by the end of the 1920's. The Heinzen brothers organized the Wausau Iron Works in 1908 to manufacture a new kind of snowplow. The plant of the Marathon Rubber Products Company was constructed in 1914. The Gilbert Shoe Company, founded in 1913, was re-organized the following year by a group of local businessmen, including Charles and Will Dodge, C. H. and C. J. Hooker, Otto Muenchow, and Hans J. Hagge. Production facilities were originally located in the abandoned Longfellow School building on Seymour Street. As of 1922, the firm operated two plants. A modern Factory No. 1 was located on North First Avenue, and Factory No. 2 in the old abandoned City Hall building on West Washington Street. C. W. Parsons incorporated the Wausau Concrete Company in 1919; with the assistance of I. J. Westerveld and A. J. Miller, the company began turning out concrete stave silos and concrete culvert and sewer pipe. In 1923 Edgar James McEachron was persuaded by a former University of Wisconsin classmate, Walter H. Thom, to leave Madison for Wausau, and start a business that would take advantage of a craze that was sweeping the country—radio.[127] The result was the establishment of the Marathon Battery Company in the Mathie-Ruder Brewing Company building, a move made possible by Prohibition. McEachron's favorite hobby was fishing. Thus, it was no surprise that when "Mac" wished to compensate for slack periods of battery production, he bought out the interests of the Bass Hound Bait Company at Stevens Point in 1929 and established the Marathon Bait Company as a separate division of his battery firm. Most of the operation was eventually moved to Wausau, with a fly-tying branch retained in Stevens Point. Another man's favorite leisure time activity was instrumental in creating a different major local industry. In 1923, a local Ford dealer, T. H. Jacob, started a plant to produce tools used in the manufacture and maintenance of Ford automobiles; this hobby in time developed into the Hammer Blow Tool Company. The polishing and surfacing machines used by the Wausau granite concerns were built by the Marathon Foundry & Machine Company, organized in June, 1925, by O. C. Lemke and Edward C. Helmke. Appropriately, the final sketch in this collection of diversified industrial enterprises involves a firm organized by a familiar figure in the county's lumbering past. W. C. Landon returned to his former home town in the early 1920's, after building lumber mills in Pelican Bay, Oregon and Sylacauga, Alabama, to help found the Wausau Motor Parts Company in October, 1923. Along with W. R. Scholfield, Karl Mathie, E. K. Schuetz, W. E. Curtis, Dr. Joseph Smith, and E. H. Viele, he purchased the two-year old Menominee Piston Ring Company and transported its machinery and inventory from Michigan to Wausau.[128]

The broad-based and sustained enthusiasm for industrial growth in Wausau was in marked contrast to the experience of another of the Marathon County sawmilling centers facing its own period of transition—Athens. Many changes were apparent in the little village in the early 1900's, each of them tending to increase the self-awareness of the community, and in the process laying groundwork for the eventual breakup of the paternalistic system founded by Frederick Rietbrock. One such occurrence was the founding of the *Athens Record* in 1902. Owned by Rietbrock, the paper often reflected his views. Yet it also came to share the aspirations and enthusiasms of the growing village. In particular, the *Record* took pride in pointing to the development of the new enterprises that had been established with local capital by 1904. This expanded industrial roster featured the Athens Brick and Tile Factory, the Athens Electric Light and Power Company, the Athens Telephone Company, the Bank of Athens, and the Athens Printing Company. By the *Record's* own admission, the parochial policy of favoring local rather than outside investment was certainly not a Wausau phenomenon. The result of this enlightened insularity, claimed the paper, was that "the recently incorporated village could boast of more corporations for its size than any other town in Wisconsin."[129]

The creation of new businesses was matched by a corresponding increase in population. By 1910 Athens had become the largest village in Marathon County, with a residential population exceeding nine hundred.[130] To satisfy the wants of the growing community, a variety of retail establishments also began to emerge. Included were department stores, hardware and furniture stores, clothing stores, ice cream parlors, and eight saloons. This embryonic mercantile class soon displayed signs of urban thinking. A clamor for a chamber of commerce resulted in the formation of the Athens Advancement Association in 1905, and a Business Men's Club in 1923.[131] A meeting of village merchants in 1907 resulted in a decision to close their stores daily at 6:30 P.M. except Wednesday and Saturday. Such a move, it was proudly declared, was "in line with the best business methods practiced in all the larger cities."[132]

These developments did not mean that Frederick Rietbrock's substantial influence over village affairs had lessened to any significant degree. One of the first actions of the local advancement association was to petition Rietbrock for a combination coach and baggage car for the Abbotsford and Northeastern, inasmuch as visitors to the village were unenthusiastic about arriving in the caboose.[133] Although the *Athens Record* contended that there were no 'Rockerfellers [sic] in Athens,' it conveniently ignored the fact that the Rietbrock family either owned outright or controlled all of the new companies listed earlier. Even before Rietbrock's death, son-in-law William Erbach began to assume the mantle of paterfamilias, determining both the character and amount of further economic expansion in the community. When the village was beset by a series of mildly disruptive strikes in 1901, Erbach apparently concluded that too large a labor force might pose a threat to community stability, and therefore to the dominance enjoyed by the Rietbrock family. Accordingly, he instituted what many saw as a firm policy of discouraging additional industrial development in the village.[134] In 1905 the Advancement Association appointed a committee of Erbach, George Kreutzer, and E. E. Schlegel to meet with the management of a corporation that was considering Athens as a possible location site. When negotiations stalled and nothing developed, despite association enthusiasm for securing the enterprise,[135] Erbach was thought to be the chief obstacle. In 1907 a Merrill firm became interested in placing either a box or excelsior factory in Athens. These negotiations, likewise, fell through when the company's representatives were told that the village lacked the necessary raw materials, an idea later disputed by several Athens businessmen.[136] When the idle plant of the Athens Brick and Tile Company became the object of bidding by outside corporations, Erbach refused to sell, even though he expressed no intention of opening the factory again. While these incidents may have been simply manifestations of the traditional preference for local financing, many observers again saw in Erbach's actions a conscious policy of promoting industrial stagnation.[137] Whatever the motivation, these decisions had the effect of keeping the Athens industrial base essentially lumber dominated. In the first three decades of the twentieth century, the percentage of total capital invested in non-lumber industrial projects in Athens never rose above twenty per cent; by 1930 it had, in fact, fallen to eight per cent.[138] Under the direction of the Rietbrock interests, the dominant pattern of Athens' adjustment to the decline of the lumber industry would take a different shape.

Nonetheless, there was no denying that industrial diversification and the benefits derived from it had taken hold in Marathon County by the 1920's. Wausau, of course, had taken the lead. The percentage of its total manufacturing capital invested in non-lumber enterprises had risen from twenty-two per cent at the turn of the century to thirty per cent in 1910, and to forty per cent by 1920. Notwithstanding this record of accomplishment, the desire for even more progress along this line was strong. The *Wausau Pilot* was calling in 1922 for the compilation of an inventory of the city's raw materials and products for the purpose "of determining what new industrial projects might succeed."[139] The spirit generated by the "Work For Wausau" and "Prosperity Day" campaigns of the previous decade was still lively.[140] Along with the industrial growth came an increase in the city's pride and assertiveness. Shortly after the state capitol building in Madison was destroyed by fire in 1904, the *Daily Record* claimed that Wausau's location and commercial importance made it the logical site for the new capital. This suggestion was repeated the following year with the endorsement of the *La Crosse Chronicle*.[141] Even so, six years later, the *Pilot* was complaining that the city fathers were not doing all that could be done to make Wausau befit its rank as a city: "It is time that we cast aside all our village ways and notions and take our place as one of the large cities of the state."[142]

But, as we have seen, Wausau was not the whole story. New paper mills and adjoining communities were created in Brokaw and Rothschild. Mosinee claimed the only completely kraft paper mill in the United States; that mill also spawned a population and building boom in the village that culminated in the adoption of city status. Signs of modernization were evident in Athens. Stratford was showing a similar restlessness to move ahead. Voter approval of a $40,000 village waterworks and sewerage system on September 30, 1919, was only one step in a concerted effort to build an "up-to-date community" able "to attract new business from abroad."[143] The two-story Chrouser building now stood where there had once been an "objectionable frog pond." The Stratford State Bank had outgrown its capacity and was under reconstruction; the refurbishing would add $20,000 to the value of the structure. The increasing number of automobiles, trucks, and tractors in the area had resulted in construction of The Auto Sales Company building, to keep the "powerful and practical machines in repair." All these improvements demonstrated that Stratford was also moving "to the front."[144] With these examples of an impressive beginning and the assistance of a booming national economy, the potential of Marathon County's new industrial order appeared capable of surpassing the expectations of even the most optimistic in the nearly forgotten Wisconsin Valley Advancement Association.

FOOTNOTES

[1] Fries, *History*, p. 414.

[2] See Doris Kearns, *Lyndon Johnson and the American Dream* (New York: Harper & Row, Publishers, 1976), p. 60.

[3] *Wausau Pilot*, December 19, 1899, p. 1.

[4] C. C. Yawkey, still headquartered in Hazelhurst at that time, was also appointed to the board. Walter Alexander was in attendance at later directors' meetings.

[5] For biographical information on the Marathon County participants, see Marchetti, *Marathon County*, pp. 621-623; 633; 630-631; 609-610; 613; 235; 884-886, 889; Martin, "Wausau in 1900," p. 28.

[6] *Wausau Pilot*, December 19, 1899, p. 1.

[7] The six permanent committees included Finance with C. C. Yawkey appointed to membership; Printing, Advertising, Statistics and Information with A. L. Kreutzer serving as chairman; Hydraulics and Manufactures with D. L. Plumer appointed to membership; Electricity, Railways and Transportation; Timber and Mineral Resources with H. M. Thompson appointed to membership; and Agriculture, Highways and Immigration with Charles Gardner appointed to membership.

[8] *Central Wisconsin*, January 20, 1900, p. 8.

[9] *Wausau Pilot*, December 26, 1899, p. 1; January 30, 1900, p. 1; February 20, 1900, p. 1.
Central Wisconsin, January 20, 1900, pp. 4, 8.
Wausau Daily Record, January 29, 1900, p. 3.

Bradley's Fifth Avenue hotel room was a beehive of activity during his stay. Numerous private conferences were held with prominent electric railway financiers, including representatives of Andrew Carnegie. The secrecy in which the negotiations were held along with the class of conferees involved created wide interest in the valley and led to speculation that "one of the biggest electric railway deals . . . in the west" was in the works.

[10] Not a great deal is known about Lester Rose's life before he arrived in Wausau. Born in Oneida County, New York on June 1, 1847, he had by his own account worked as a locomotive engineer, painter, newspaper reporter, advertising agent, and Ottawa, Illinois newspaper publisher before coming to north-central Wisconsin. See *Wausau Daily Record*, September 13, 1900, p. 3.

[11] *Wausau Pilot*, September 17, 1900, p. 5.

[12] Rose revealed that Bradley had first tried around 1888 to join the Wausau business establishment, upon moving to Wisconsin from his native Michigan. He speculates that the Wausau capitalists, fearing Bradley, turned him away, thereby necessitating his move forty-five miles north. This parochial reluctance of Wausau business leaders to admit outsiders to their ranks is a theme that will reappear later.

[13] *Milwaukee Sentinel*, January 28, 1900, p. 5.

Rose did not entirely ignore the lumber industry. He was, despite references to "King Pine" abdicating his throne and other like remarks, reluctant to admit that the valley's pine forests were in any peril. After conceding their imminent extinction for the sake of argument, the ever optimistic journalist pointed toward the rising importance of hardwood, which he rated as a more valuable and equally important product.

[14] *Wausau Pilot*, January 30, 1900, p. 4.

[15] *Wausau Daily Record*, February 10, 1900, p. 5.
Wausau Pilot, February 13, 1900, p. 1.

[16] An earlier proposal with the same goal involved admitting members of the press who resided in the valley to honorary membership in the association. See *Wausau Pilot*, January 30, 1900, p. 1.

[17] *Wausau Daily Record*, June 9, 1900, p. 5.

[18] *Wausau Daily Record*, February 10, 1900, p. 5; February 13, 1900, pp. 2, 3.
Wausau Pilot, February 13, 1900, p. 1.

In addition to leading the high-powered campaign, Lester Rose on at least one occasion served as an intermediary for a manufacturer planning to locate a factory in Wausau. See *Wausau Pilot*, May 29, 1900, p. 1; *Wausau Daily Record*, June 9, 1900, p. 1.

[19] *Central Wisconsin*, January 20, 1900, p. 1

[20] For biographical information, see Marchetti, *Marathon County*, pp. 317-318.

[21] *Wausau Daily Record*, February 16, 1900, p. 3.

[22] *Ibid.*

Moreover, reported Bradley, 'I discovered one thing, the Wisconsin valley is known all along the line from here to New York and Boston, and everywhere it is looked up to as the one section from which great things are expected.'

[23] *Wausau Pilot*, August 14, 1900, p. 5.

[24] *Wausau Pilot*, February 20, 1900, p. 1.

[25] *Wausau Pilot*, August 14, 1900, p. 5.

[26] *Wausau Daily Record*, August 17, 1900, p. 3.
Wausau Pilot, August 21, 1900, p. 7.

Rose died in Milwaukee the following month from heart trouble. See *Wausau Daily Record*, September 13, 1900, p. 3; *Wausau Pilot*, September 17, 1900, p. 5.

[27] *Wausau Pilot*, December 31, 1901, p. 1.

[28] *Central Wisconsin*, February 22, 1902, p. 4.

[29] *Wausau Pilot*, December 26, 1899, p. 1; December 25, 1900, p. 5; January 22, 1901, p. 1; December 31, 1901, p. 1; March 5, 1901, p. 1.
Central Wisconsin, February 22, 1902, p. 4.

[30] *Central Wisconsin*, January 20, 1900, p. 1.

[31] The officers of the board were: president, Judson M Smith; vice-president, W. C. Silverthorn; secretary, T. C. Ryan; treasurer, D. L. Plumer; directors, William H. Knox, August Kickbusch, V. A. Alderson, R. P. Pratt, John Ringle, and Alexander Stewart. See John G. Gregory, ed., *West Central Wisconsin: A History*, vol. 2

122

(Indianapolis: S. J. Clarke Publishing Company, Ind., 1933), pp. 638-639.

[32] Parcher's actions are particularly noteworthy considering his life-long career in business. See Marchetti, *Marathon County*, pp. 308-309; Miner, "Economic Development," p. 25; *Wausau Pilot*, December 10, 1907, p. 5; November 21, 1911, p. 1; January 21, 1926, p. 3.

[33] *Milwaukee Sentinel*, August 11, 1895, pp. 17, 18.

[34] Wausau Industrial Association pamphlet cover, Charles Dodge Collection, General Box.

[35] *Wausau Daily Record*, January 20, 1900, p. 8; August 22, 1900, p. 3.

[36] *Wausau Pilot*, February 7, 1911, p. 4.

[37] *Wausau Daily Record*, February 3, 1905, p. 3.

[38] *Wausau Daily Record*, October 28, 1904, p. 2; October 29, 1904, p. 5; October 31, 1904, p. 5; November 2, 1904, pp. 2, 5; November 3, 1904, p. 5.

[39] *Wisconsin Blue Book*, 1905, pp. 334-335.

[40] Mark Clayton Ewing was one of Wausau's more colorful industrialists. A native of Ohio, he had come to Wausau in 1893 as tobacco salesman bearing the nickname "Climax," the name of one of his favorite tobaccos. Ewing quickly alerted the city that it had an unusual new resident. According to legend, on his first day in town he rode a wild bronco the length of main street. Starting in business as a laundry owner, he would, by the time of his death in 1922, become synonymous with the Wausau public utility industry. See "Lights and Trolleys," *Special Wausau Number*, pp. 59-60; *Wausau Daily Record-Herald*, August 11, 1922, p. 1.

[41] Ewing hardly endeared himself to neighboring Mosinee when he declared "There is no particular reason why Wausau should be at Big Bull Falls instead of Mosinee, except that the men who came here were better town builders than those who came to Mosinee."

[42] M. C. Ewing, "Commercial Opportunities," undated pamphlet in Charles Dodge Collection, General Box.

[43] *Wausau Daily Record-Herald*, March 5, 1912, p. 1.

[44] *Wausau Pilot*, March 5, 1912, p. 6.

[45] "For a Greater Wausau," March 6, 1912, Charles Dodge Collection, General Box.

[46] *Wausau Daily Record-Herald*, March 9, 1912, p. 4.

[47] Ewing was appropriately elected temporary president and one of the temporary directors. The temporary secretary was an investment bond and insurance broker. The remainder of the temporary directorship consisted of the operator of a general store, a brewery executive, a bank vice-president, a land company executive, a prominent attorney, a jewelry company executive, and the presidents of two industrial firms. See *Wausau Daily Record-Herald*, March 12, 1912, pp. 1-2; June 14, 1945, p. 8; January 10, 1973, p. 12; *Wausau Pilot*, December 23, 1919, p. 1; Marchetti, *Marathon County*, pp. 625-627; 747; 760; 763; 834-835; 868; 871; 882-883; 898-899; 936-937.

[48] *Wausau Daily Record-Herald*, March 12, 1912, p. 4.

[49] The Merchants and Manufacturers' Association had been formed in 1913-1914 with W. C. Landon as president.

[50] *Wausau Daily Record-Herald*, *Golden Anniversary Edition*, August 9, 1922, Section 3, p. 1.

Wausau Area Chamber of Commerce, *50th Annual Report*, March 28, 1962, pp. 1, 5, 7, 8.

[51] The Wausau Advancement Association also took credit for securing the Edgar Basket Factory which located in the village in 1912. See *50th Annual Report*, p. 1.

[52] This trend was particularly evident during the period Waupaca transplant Lee I. Yorkson served as chamber secretary from 1921 through 1934. In a retrospective assessment of his eleven years in office, the *Record-Herald* listed as the highlights of his term numerous betterment projects, but included not a single case of the acquisition of a major new industry. See *Wausau Daily Record-Herald*, *Centennial Edition*, March 13, 1939, Commercial Section, p. 27.

[53] The *Record-Herald* had explicitly recognized this situation when the Wausau Advancement Association was born. Speculating on the possible benefits the organization could provide for the city, the paper conceded that "If it does nothing else than to keep the institutions we now have here and to see that they are treated fairly, it will be worth while." See *Wausau Daily Record-Herald*, March 12, 1912, p. 4.

[54] Fries, "History," p. 418.

[55] The index used is the *Wausau Daily Record's* listing of principal Wausau industries published during the 1904 campaign against the distance tariff. See *Wausau Daily Record,* November 2, 1904, p. 2.

[56] Fries, "History," p. 432.

[57] There is evidently some difference of opinion concerning the firm's origins. Marchetti states that Werheim started in business with F. W. Kickbusch in 1872, the relationship continuing until 1880. After the dissolution of the partnership, he contends that Werheim built a similar factory on Third Street. According to George Alfred Martin, Werheim began his business in 1873, with H. S. Hazeltine as his original partner. After their plant was destroyed by fire and Hazeltine refused to re-invest, Werheim rebuilt the factory on a larger scale, which, in turn, became the Werheim Manufacturing Company. See Marchetti, *Marathon County,* p. 234; Martin, "Wausau in 1900," p. 109. Still other sources list 1879 as the year of the company's founding. See Miner, "Economic Development," p. 37; *Wausau Daily Record-Herald, Centennial Edition,* March 13, 1939, Industrial Section, p. 89.

[58] *Wausau Daily Record-Herald, Centennial Edition,* March 13, 1939, Industrial Section, p. 89.

[59] One biographical account indicates that young Curtis apparently soon became dissatisfied with his progress in the organization. After less than a year with the company, he quit his position as head of the sash department and entered the grocery and general merchandising business. His departure was not a permanent one, as he rejoined the family firm in January, 1873. See *Wausau Pilot,* January 11, 1916, p. 1.

[60] *Wausau Pilot,* January 11, 1916, p. 1.

The Live Wire, High School Journalism Supplement to the *Wausau Pilot,* May 22, 1924, pp. 1, 3.

Wausau Daily Record-Herald, January 6, 1916, p. 1; *Centennial Edition,* March 13, 1939, Industrial Section, p. 94.

Undated *Wausau Daily Record-Herald* clipping, Charles Dodge Collection, General Box.

Martin, "Wausau in 1900," pp. 124, 126.

Miner, "Economic Development," pp. 19, 26.

Like Fowler Stone, John M. Kuebler also had a lengthy association with the Curtis firm, serving as a plant superintendent for twenty-six years.

[61] *Wausau Pilot,* May 14, 1936, pp. 1, 5.

Wausau Daily Record-Herald, May 8, 1936, p. 1; *Centennial Edition,* March 13, 1939, Industrial Section, p. 92.

[62] *Wausau Daily Record-Herald, Golden Anniversary Edition,* August 9, 1922, Section 2, p. 11.

[63] Although Charles V. Bardeen has not received the acclaim given Marvin Rosenberry or even Louis Marchetti in other historical accounts, he was truly one of Marathon County's most eminent attorneys and jurists. His law partnerships included associations with State Senator John A. Kellogg and Attorney General W. H. Mylrea. A year after the formation of the latter partnership, Louis Marchetti was admitted to membership in the firm, this being the first such alliance in his career. In 1891 Bardeen was elected the first judge of the Sixteenth Judicial Circuit, a position he held until January, 1898 when he was appointed to the State Supreme Court by Governor Edward Schofield, filling the vacancy created by the death of Associate Justice Alfred W. Newman. Wausau's first member of the state high court served until his own death on March 20, 1903. It is interesting to note that despite Bardeen's rise to the top of the state legal profession, he is given only the barest mention by his former associate Louis Marchetti in the *History of Marathon County,* and even then is presented in a not totally flattering light. See Marchetti, *Marathon County,* pp. 418-419. See also *Wausau Pilot,* March 24, 1903, p. 5; *Wisconsin Blue Book,* 1921, pp. 318-319.

[64] In 1906 Turner served as president of the National Association of Box Manufacturers of the United States and Canada, an organization which numbered among its members most of the leading box manufacturers in North America.

[65] Turner and Scholfield seemed to have especially bad luck with fire that year. On February 15, 1907 another of their jointly run enterprises, the Eau Claire Box

and Lumber Company plant, was entirely destroyed by fire, involving a loss of $25,000 to $30,000. See *Wausau Pilot*, February 19, 1907, p. 1.

[66] *Wausau Daily Record-Herald, Golden Anniversary Edition*, August 9, 1922, Section 2, p. 11; *Centennial Edition*, March 13, 1939, Historical Section, p. 62.

Wausau Pilot, First Annual Industrial and Historical Edition, January 27, 1921, p. 4; December 23, 1919, p. 1; June 9, 1927, p. 1; April 22, 1937, p. 1.

Martin, "Wausau in 1900," pp. 18-19.

[67] E. A. Gooding's twenty-nine year tenure with the Wisconsin Box Company was quite an accomplishment, considering his previous business background, which made him one of Wausau's most extensively traveled executives. The Lockport, Illinois, native had gained most of his early experience working in the commission offices of the Chicago firm, Rumsey Bros., and in a Breckenridge, Colorado, banking house. Before finally settling in Wausau to focus his energies on the box business, Gooding had consecutively managed the Parcher sawmill in Wausau in the early 1880's, moved to Minneapolis in 1887 to join his uncle Charles P. Haseltine in the brick manufacturing business, returned to Wausau in 1889 to subsequently .help organize the German American Savings Bank, and moved back to Illinois in 1892 to enter the oatmeal manufacturing business with brother-in-law W. G. Norton.

[68] *Wausau Pilot, First Annual Industrial and Historical Edition*, January 27, 1921, p. 4; January 2, 1930, p. 1.

Wausau Daily Record-Herald, Golden Anniversary Edition, August 9, 1922, p. 12; *Centennial Edition*, March 13, 1939, Industrial Section, p. 89; December 28, 1929, p. 1; October 19, 1963, p. 9.

[69] For biographical background, see Marchetti, *Marathon County*, pp. 771, 878-879.

[70] Marchetti notes that even during the economically depressed years from 1894 to 1896, the factory ran continuously with the only loss of operating time resulting from occasional breakdowns.

[71] *Wausau Daily Record-Herald*, July 27, 1910, p. 1; *Golden Anniversary Edition*, August 9, 1922, Section 2, p. 5; *Centennial Edition*, March 13, 1939, Industrial Section, p. 92; August 18, 1947, p. 1.

Wausau Pilot, August 2, 1910, p. 1.

The Live Wire, High School Journalism Supplement to the *Wausau Pilot*, May 22, 1924, p. 3.

Marchetti, *Marathon County*, p. 382.

The Underwood firm also boasted some of the best athletic talent in local industry. Under the direction of sales manager, George Vehlow, the company teams dominated the Wausau Indoor League in the early 1920's.

[72] Ole Billier was one of the novel figures in the Wausau industrial establishment. Being of Norwegian descent, he was a rarity in German-dominated Wausau. The Norwegian nationality made up only three per cent of the county's total number of foreign born in 1900. After emigrating to America in 1880, he first settled in Neenah, where he followed his trade as millwright. He allegedly set fifty per cent of the water wheels in the Fox River Valley, a distinction which earned him the nickname "Water Wheel Ole." Moving to Wausau in 1892, he became involved in municipal politics representing his ward on the common council and was praised as "one of the hustlers of the city."

[73] Marchetti, *Marathon County*, pp. 385-386.

Martin, "Wausau in 1900," p. 83.

Miner, "Economic Development," pp. 26, 30.

Wausau Daily Record-Herald, Golden Anniversary Edition, August 9, 1922, Section 2, p. 3; *Centennial Edition*, March 13, 1939, Historical Section, p. 75.

The Berst-Foster-Dixfield Company of New York purchased the interests of the Wausau Manufacturing Company in 1929, and later changed its name to the General Woodenware Corporation.

[74] *Wausau Daily Record-Herald, Centennial Edition*, March 13, 1939, Industrial Section, p. 89.

Marchetti, *Marathon County*, pp. 502-503, 512.

Helgeson, "Athens, Wisconsin," p. 47.

James Bruce Smith calculated that as of 1900 Schofield and Mosinee still had one hundred per cent of their local manufacturing capital invested in lumbering; Spencer and Unity, ninety-eight per cent.

[75] For a detailed account of the evolution of the Wisconsin paper industry, see Karges, "David Clark Everest," pp. 1-27; Francis Bowman, *Paper In Wisconsin, Ninety-Two Years Industrial Progress,* (Rothschild, Wis.: By the author for the Marathon Paper Mills Company and the Menasha Products Company, 1940), pp. 10-15. See also Branch, "The Paper Industry," pp. 47-50.

[76] Karges, "David Clark Everest," pp. 25, 61.
Martin, "Wausau in 1900," p. 75.
"Fire, Flood, and Age," *Special Wausau Number,* pp. 35-38.
Wausau Pilot, First Annual Industrial and Historical Edition, January 27, 1921, p. 27.
Central Wisconsin, Special Paper Mills Edition, March 31, 1900, pp. 1, 8.
Wausau Daily Record-Herald, July 6, 1944, p. 1; March 7, 1964, p. 3.

[77] *Central Wisconsin, Special Paper Mills Edition,* March 31, 1900, pp. 1, 8.

[78] The formation of the Wausau Street Railway Company marked the Wausau Group's second major move into public utilities. It also brought to the forefront of the Group another important figure: the multi-talented lawyer, poet, and politician Neal Brown. In response to citizen complaints that Wausau had become the largest city in Wisconsin without a street railway, Brown, in August, 1906, led G. D. Jones, V. A. Alderson, and Mark Ewing in the organization of the Wausau Street Railway Company. The election of officers resulted in Brown being named president; C. C. Yawkey, vice-president; and Ewing, manager. The first trolley wire was strung on April 16, and the first street cars were run to Schofield on May 25. The supervision of the railway system, which eventually ran not only to Schofield, but also to Rothschild Park and northern Wausau, was only one facet of the company's subsequent activities. The purchase of the Dessert water power was one of the first steps in a major effort towards expansion of its corporate realm. On March 7, 1908, the railway company acquired the Wausau Electric Light Company; reflecting the change in emphasis, the name of the new combination was changed in 1915 to the Wisconsin Valley Electric Company. With its directors sensing the possibility of creating a uniform utility service for the Wisconsin valley, the next thirteen years witnessed company utility purchases in Merrill, Mosinee, Stevens Point, Tomahawk, Antigo, Rhinelander, Waupaca, Brokaw, Otter Rapids, Eagle River, and Minocqua. The culmination of this consolidation process occurred on June 3, 1933, when Wausau's Wisconsin Valley Electric Company merged the Waupaca Electric Service and Railway Company, the Valley Transit Company, the Wisconsin Valley Power Company, and a second Wisconsin Valley Electric Company, with all properties combined under the last name. The public barely had time to digest the news of that combination when two days later a second merger was announced, involving the enlarged Wisconsin Valley Electric Company and another public utility giant, the Wisconsin Public Service Corporation of Oshkosh. By 1939 this public utility colossus was serving twenty-two counties in northern and central Wisconsin, and upper Michigan, containing a population of 420,000. See "Lights and Trolleys," *Special Wausau Number,* pp. 59-60; *Wausau Daily Record-Herald,* August 11, 1922, p. 1; *Centennial Edition,* March 13, 1939, Historical Section, p. 44. For biographical information on the remarkable Neal Brown, see *Wausau Pilot,* Sept. 25, 1917, p. 4; *Wausau Daily Record-Herald,* September 19, 1917, pp. 1-2.

[79] During his previous residence in Wausau, Mathie had been a leader in local educational circles, serving as principal of Wausau Senior High School, and city superintendent of schools. In 1901 he was elected president of the Wisconsin State Teachers' Association, and the following year he was the Democratic candidate for state superintendent of public instruction. Mathie's father had founded the city's first brewery in 1869, and money from that enterprise "enabled him to live well while Superintendent of Schools." However, alleged embarrassment over this source of income induced him to ask G. D. Jones to secure for him the position at Watab. See Phoebe Jones Kline to Hester Jones, Granville D. Jones Papers, State Historical Society, Madison. See also *Wausau Pilot,* December 31, 1901, p. 1; December 15, 1938, pp. 1, 4; *Wausau Daily Record-Herald,* December 9, 1938, p. 1.

[80] *Mosinee Times,* August 8, 1957, p. 10.

[81] *Wausau Daily Record-Herald,* March 18, 1926, p. 4.

[82] Colby had incorporated as a city in 1891.

[83] *Mosinee Times*, August 8, 1957, p. 10.

Wausau Daily Record-Herald, Centennial Edition, March 13, 1939, Industrial Section, p. 80.

"Daring Loggers; 'First' in Production Achieved in Early Days of Mosinee Paper Mill," *Special Wausau Number*, pp. 43-46.

Karges, "David Clark Everest," p. 62.

[84] *Wausau Daily Record-Herald*, January 19, 1909, p. 1.

That domination was further reflected in the composition of the original list of stockholders. The owners of the Rothschild Water Power Company held 5,900 shares out of a total of 7,500. Alexander Stewart, Walter Alexander, and Charles Winton were the largest subscribers with 650 shares apiece.

[85] *Wausau Daily Record-Herald*, January 20, 1909, p. 1.

The project was also beneficial to those owners of Marathon Paper Mills with timber holdings. The unidentified organizer added that the mill meant "a market for thousands of cords of hemlock and spruce wood, not only for the farmers of this vicinity, but for timber owners all over the northern part of the state." Not coincidentally, those interested in the new company controlled nearly 500 million feet of hemlock and spruce in the region tributary to Wausau.

[86] During his formative years, Everest was an ardent Democrat. His entry into the business world occasioned his becoming an equally staunch Republican.

[87] Everest was always thankful that the age question had been forgotten. The directors, in fact, never learned his true age until much later. One of Everest's favorite stories involved an incident that occurred shortly after he was hired as Marathon's general manager. Everest had hired a thirty-four year old mechanical engineering graduate from the University of Wisconsin as an assistant. Discussing the appointment with one of the directors, he was advised, 'Don't ever leave that "boy" in charge of the mill when you're away.'

[88] Interview with Glenn Stevens, August 20, 1975, Marathon County Public Library Oral History Collection.

[89] By 1920 Marathon Paper Mills was the state's leading producer of paper specialties; by 1927 it, along with two other firms, was turning out seventy to eighty per cent of the paper pails and cartons manufactured in the United States.

[90] While Everest had always been permitted free reign, Yawkey had exercised a close supervision. By 1919, however, with many other business commitments demanding his attention, Yawkey turned over to his general manager control of everything at Marathon but the company's financial matters.

[91] For a brief but incisive discussion of this change in the attitude towards competition by American businessmen, see Eric F. Goldman, *Rendezvous With Destiny* (New York: Random House, Vintage Books, 1955), pp. 236-239.

[92] Everest had little hesitation about raiding other paper companies to obtain his managerial staff. A similar ambivalence was evidenced in his attitude towards labor unrest. Until it became inevitable, Everest was openly hostile to any form of labor union activity, and thus abhorred strikes. Yet, when a wave of strikes hit Fox River valley and Michigan paper mills, Everest took profitable advantage of the competition's labor troubles by selling large amounts of pulp to plants whose normal sources of supply were closed by the strikes.

[93] The culmination of this enthusiasm for minimizing harmful competition was his advocacy of creating a Food Container Corporation of America. The enterprise would combine Marathon with several other giants in the industry, and be in a position to dominate prices in the entire food packaging field. Any potential confrontation between Everest and the Antitrust Division of the Justice Department was averted by the 1929 stock market crash, which forced him to abandon his plan.

[94] "The Marathon Story," *Special Wausau Number*, pp. 21-26.

Wausau Daily Record-Herald, October 23, 1955, pp. 1, 11.

Milwaukee Sentinel, October 30, 1955, p. 11.

Wausau-Merrill Daily Herald, March 5, 1976, pp. 1, 4.

Karges, "David Clark Everest," chaps. 2-7 passim.

[95] Long-time city residents claimed that "Old man Murray" had his plant and foundry running several years before 1883. Their contention was apparently substantiated by the little red school house which stood for many years on the company site and was used for storage. That structure and the Humboldt School

annex, known as the "foundry school," were built in 1880, according to the records.

[96] These included huge barking drums, chip crushers, slashers, agitators, vibrating chip screens, and roll heading and roll wrapping machines.

[97] " 'Old Man Murray' Tackled Anything," *Special Wausau Number*, pp. 39-40. *Milwaukee Sentinel*, February 17, 1957, p. 13.

Wausau Daily Record-Herald, Golden Anniversary Edition, August 9, 1922, Section 3, p. 2.

[98] Karges, "David Clark Everest," pp. 85-87, 112.

Wisconsin Blue Book, 1921, p. 466; 1931, p. 612.

Due to the danger posed by intoxication on the job to both worker and company, Rothschild, like Brokaw, was made a "dry" community.

[99] Wisconsin State Board of Health, *Stream Pollution In Wisconsin*, A Joint Report of the Conservation Commission and State Board of Health of Wisconsin Concerning Activities in the Control of Stream Pollution, From July 1, 1925, to December 31, 1926 (Madison: State of Wisconsin, 1927), p. 130.

[100] *Ibid.*

[101] Martin, "Wausau in 1900," p. 27.

[102] Included among the organizers were Cyrus Yawkey, Neal Brown, Judd Alexander, Aytchmonde Woodson, D. C. Everest, Karl Mathie, Louis Dessert, Marvin Rosenberry, and Olai Bache-Wiig.

[103] Aytchmonde P. Woodson would become the leading activist within the Wausau Group after the death of his father-in-law, Cyrus Yawkey. Upon his death in 1958, he held executive office in at least twenty-four different firms both within Marathon County and throughout the county, including the presidency of the Wausau Cemetery Association. Recalling these numerous business associations, plus Woodson's interest in local hospitals, a former employee remarked: "He had you coming and going. He had you when you were born; he had you when you worked; and he had you when you died." *Wausau Daily Record-Herald*, October 8, 1958, pp. 1, 4. Interview with Don Streeter, 1976, Marathon County Public Library Oral History Collection.

[104] *Wausau Daily Record-Herald, Centennial Edition*, March 13, 1939, Industrial Section, p. 84; Commercial Section, p. 37; *Golden Anniversary Edition*, August 9, 1922, Section 3, p. 2.

John E. Forester Interview.

[105] The discovery of this first wood fiber hardboard came about by accident. At an early stage of the experimentation process at Rothschild, D. C. Everest wanted to show a sample of Mason's product to a potential customer. Accordingly, an employee placed a piece of the wet lap in a steam press to dry it more quickly. Upon returning from lunch he discovered that the overheated sample had turned into a hard, dense, and perfectly dry board. As a result of this accident, the Mason Fibre plant was redesigned to manufacture this hardboard as well as insulation board.

[106] "Exploded Wood," *Special Wausau Number*, pp. 47-49.

Karges, "David Clark Everest," pp. 243-245.

John E. Forester Interview.

[107] Reprinted in *Wausau Pilot*, November 30, 1909, p. 1.

[108] *Wausau Daily Record-Herald, Golden Anniversary Edition*, August 9, 1922, Section 4, p. 10. See also *Wausau Daily Record Herald*, May 7, 1909, p. 1; May 8, 1909, p. 1; *Wausau Pilot*, May 11, 1909, p. 5; May 21, 1912, p. 5. For details of Dr. William A. Fricke's distinguished career in the Wisconsin insurance industry before joining Great Northern, see Marchetti, *Marathon County*, pp. 650-651.

[109] The precompensation era had not been kind to those Wisconsin laborers injured on the job. State courts had created nearly insurmountable common law barriers favoring the employers. A study revealed that early in the twentieth century, sixty-four per cent of the accident suits filed in Wisconsin courts had been thrown out of court on the basis of such defense as contributory negligence, assumption of risk, and the fellow-servant rule.

[110] From Republican Cyrus Yawkey to Jeffersonian Democrat Neal Brown, the members of the Wausau Group shared a conservative economic philosophy; as such they were generally opposed to so-called "progressive reforms." The concept of workmen's compensation may have been an exception. Ashland State Senator

A. W. Sanborn, chairman of the special Industrial Insurance Committee charged with investigating a workmen's compensation bill, noted that 'The second reason for having a compensation is to utilize for injured employees a large portion of the great amount of money wasted under the present system. Under the present system only from 29 percent in 1904 to 50 percent in 1908 of the amount paid by employers to casualty or employers liability companies to indemnify them against the liability created under the present system reached the injured employees or their dependents and the latter's attorneys.' Long-time Employers Mutuals executive Benno Kuechle notes that the elimination of such waste made possible by the compensation law was in line with conservative business principles. Indeed, a number of the Wausau company's early executives retrospectively claimed to have been in sympathy with the concept of workmen's compensation from almost the beginning. See Interview with Benno E. Kuechle, August 21, 1975, Marathon County Public Library Oral History Collection; Michael Salsieder, Employers Insurance — Meeting the Needs of the Policyholders, company history in Archives of Employers Insurance of Wausau, pp. 2-3; 50th Anniversary Of Workmen's Compensation In America, 50th Anniversary Of Employers Mutuals of Wausau, booklet in Archives of Employers Insurance of Wausau, pp. 2-4. See also Robert Asher, "The 1911 Workmen's Compensation Law: A Study in Conservative Labor Reform," *Wisconsin Magazine of History* 57 (Winter, 1973-1974).

[111] The concept of an employers' mutual insurance company had been proposed by Dr. Fricke to the Industrial Insurance Committee in 1910. A similar recommendation was contained in Section 26 of the committee's report.

[112] The second workmen's compensation policy written by Employers Mutual was for director W. C. Landon's Barker & Stewart Lumber Company. Landon served as the company's second president from 1914 to June, 1915. See *Good People*, Employers Insurance of Wausau monthly newspaper, February, 1976, p. 3; "Employers Mutuals Are 'Wausau's Own,'" *Special Wausau Number*, p. 31; Salsieder, Employers Insurance, p. 1.

[113] *Good People*, March, 1976, p. 3.

[114] 50th Anniversary, p. 6.

[115] The witty sales pitch employed by Neal Brown should be noted in this respect. See *Good People*, March, 1976, p. 3; "The Wausau Philosopher," Neal Brown Papers, Area Research Center, University of Wisconsin-Stevens Point.

[116] *Good People*, April, 1976, p. 6.

[117] J. D. Beck to Hon. William A. Fricke, December 7, 1911, Employers Mutuals Papers, Area Research Center, University of Wisconsin-Stevens Point.

[118] Earl E. Fisk to Mitchell Joannes, December 16, 1919, Employers Mutuals Papers, Area Research Center, University of Wisconsin-Stevens Point. See also Clyde F. Schlueter, *The Wausau Story of Employers Insurance of Wausau* (New York: The Newcomen Society in North America, 1974), p. 13.

[119] H. J. Hagge to Chief Justice Marvin B. Rosenberry, December 30, 1946, Marvin B. Rosenberry Papers, Archives of the State Historical Society, Madison.

[120] Salsieder, Employers Insurance, pp. 4-17.
50th Anniversary, pp. 6-7.
Benno E. Kuechle Interview.
Schlueter, *The Wausau Story*, pp. 12-14.
"Employers Mutuals," *Special Wausau Number*, p. 32.
Good People, April, 1976, p. 6; May, 1976, p. 3.

[121] James Wall took the office of general manager seriously. At the start he not only operated the plant, but designed motors, and went out on the road as a salesman. See *Wausau Daily Record-Herald*, February 26, 1960, pp. 1, 10.

[122] *Lakeland Times*, May 22, 1958 in John D. Mylrea Journals, vol. 3.
Wausau Daily Record, July 28, 1906, p. 2.

[123] *Wausau-Merrill Daily Herald*, October 30, 1975, p. 3.

[124] Karges, "David Clark Everest," pp. 54, 57, 99-100, 226-241.
Miner, "Economic Development," p. 39.
Wausau Daily Record-Herald, October 9, 1958, p. 4.
John Forester Interview.

[125] The Prehn family also organized the Wausau, Wisconsin Granite Company. Besides operating a quarry at Amberg in Marinette County, the firm initiated a

new quarry in the Town of Texas around 1934.

[126] "Granite Industry Inspired by Wausau Ledges," *Special Wausau Number*, p. 65.

Miner, "Economic Development," pp. 30, 35-36.

Marchetti, *Marathon County*, pp. 395-397.

Wausau Daily Record-Herald, Centennial Edition, March 13, 1939, Industrial Section, pp. 84, 88; March 13, 1963, p. 3; February 22, 1964, p. 9.

Uncited newspaper clipping in Charles Dodge Collection, Business Box.

These quarries turned out a variety of building stones, each with a distinctive shade name. Most were red: Marathon Ruby Red, Dark Red, Wausau Red, Marathon Red, Wisconsin River Red, Rose Red, and after the founding of the Kannenberg Granite Company, Mystic Red. In addition, there was Marathon Grey and two green stones: Wausau Green and Parcher.

[127] Another version credits off-hand conversations McEachron had with Justice Marvin Rosenberry at Rotary Club meetings as being the crucial factor in his decision to start the battery firm.

[128] *Wausau Daily Record-Herald, Golden Anniversary Edition*, August 9, 1922, Section 3, p. 10; Section 4, p. 10; *Centennial Edition*, March 13, 1939, Historical Section, pp. 62, 63; Industrial Section, pp. 84, 88; May 4, 1961, p. 4; March 2, 1963, p. 3; April 13, 1963, p. 5; May 25, 1963, p. 9; December 14, 1963, p. 3; January 11, 1964, p. 5; April 18, 1964, p. 5.

"Your Car Motor Has Wausau-Made Parts; 33-Year-Old Concrete Manufacturing Firm Has Kept Pace," *Special Wausau Number*, pp. 51, 71

Miner, "Economic Development," p. 37.

George C. Landon Interview.

Charles Dodge notations on Marathon Shoe Company, Charles Dodge Collection, Business Box.

[129] Helgeson, "Athens, Wisconsin," p. 47.

[130] *Wisconsin Blue Book*, 1921, p. 467.

[131] The two organizations merged in 1923, with the stipulation that the board of directors would be composed of a merchant, a farmer, a manufacturer, a professional man, and a laborer. See *Athens Record*, July 12, 1923, p. 1.

[132] *Athens Record*, July 10, 1907, p. 1.

The Athens merchants quickly discovered that the competition from mail order houses posed a serious threat to their survival. The *Athens Record* proved a helpful ally, however, printing suggestions on how to fight "the mail order evil," and denouncing those who patronized such establishments. See *Athens Record*, March 16, 1905, p. 1; March 23, 1905, p. 4. Wausau merchants were also ready to vigorously defend their interests when threatened. A 1911 city council order prohibiting signs over sidewalks "brought a howl from the merchants," who contended that it was as necessary for a mercantile establishment to have a sign as it was "for a cow to have a tail in fly time." See *Wausau Pilot*, November 21, 1911, p. 1.

[133] *Athens Record*, February 9, 1905, p. 1.

[134] Helgeson, "Athens, Wisconsin," p. 58.

[135] *Athens Record*, February 9, 1905, p. 1.

[136] *Athens Record*, April 11, 1907, p. 4.

[137] Helgeson, "Athens, Wisconsin," p. 57.

[138] Smith, "Lumbertowns," p. 118.

[139] In making this suggestion, the *Pilot* sounded a familiar theme: "We cannot let Wausau stand still. If we do our young men and women, educated at great expense to the community, will leave, to contribute their energies and abilities to the upbuilding of other places." See *Wausau Pilot*, May 18, 1922, p. 2.

[140] *Wausau Pilot*, June 2, 1914, p. 5.

Wausau Daily Record-Herald, February 15, 1916, p. 1; February 29, 1916, p. 1.

[141] *Wausau Daily Record*, February 11, 1905, p. 5.

[142] *Wausau Pilot*, April 18, 1911, p. 1.

[143] *Stratford Journal*, September 19, 1919, p. 1. See also *Stratford Journal*, September 26, 1919, p. 1; October 3, 1919, p. 1.

A waterworks and sewer system was finally approved by the Athens village board and residents in 1923 after seventeen years of opposition from the Rietbrock family. See Helgeson, "Athens, Wisconsin," pp. 58-59.

[144] *Stratford Journal*, October 31, 1919, p. 1.

CHAPTER THREE

Agricultural Growth:
A New Coronation

The agricultural colonization of Wisconsin began in the 1830's. The first section of the state to be so developed was southern Wisconsin. Characterized by rolling prairies and oak openings, the agricultural potential of that region had been propagandized by soldiers returning from the Black Hawk war. The arriving settlers discovered, however, that the land was not a trouble-free paradise. Tough root-matted sod, red-root, and hazel brush made breaking the prairie a difficult chore. Shortages of wood and even water forced many of the farm makers to move to the oak openings. Yet, while much trial and error still lay ahead, it was clear by the 1850's that the territory was good farm land. The construction of plank roads and railroads to the lake ports provided additional certainty that prosperous farming was possible in southern Wisconsin.[1]

By contrast, Marathon County, and the rest of that section of Wisconsin designated as the New North, had initially an unfavorable reputation with respect to potential agricultural development. Eastern lumbermen, it will be remembered, were the region's first white settlers. Confining their logging operations to the country on either side of the Wisconsin River, they found great quantities of white pine growing on a relatively light, sandy soil. Thus, the lumbering pioneers added to their glowing reports of the region's timber resources the caveat that the pine soils also made the area totally unfit for agriculture.

As with most stereotypes, this labeling was unwarranted. All but the northeastern tip, the extreme eastern edge, and the southeastern part of Marathon County lay in what was later to be classified as the Central Dairy Region, a section characterized by long, gentle slopes with a growing season of from 120 to 130 days. A soil known as Colby silt loam predominated in practically the entire western half of the county and in a belt running along approximately its northern border.[2] Permeated with rich decaying vegetable matter from the hardwood and hemlock forests, this heavy, productive soil was excellent for growing both grasses and grains. A similar soil composition would be found in the best agricultural regions of southern Iowa, northern Missouri, and northeastern Kansas.[3] Not every report on northern Wisconsin, to be sure, was negative. As early as 1852, Albert G. Ellis was confident that the section would be not only agriculturally self-sufficient, but also capable of exporting a surplus of farm products:

> "A general notion seems to prevail, that the lands
> of these pineries are only valuable for their timber,
> that it never can become an agricultural district. But
> the facts are otherwise. Whoever recollects western
> New York, as it was forty years ago, may have a good
> idea of northern Wisconsin as it is now; and who-
> ever sees Wisconsin forty years hence, may behold its
> prototype in western New York at this moment."[4]

Five years later, Ellis specifically recommended the lands of Marathon County for this type of development.[5] Nevertheless, the Eastern prejudice against pine soils created a great deal of skepticism.[6] The fertility of Marathon County's soil and thus its suitability for agricultural endeavors would have to be proved by actual demonstration.

This challenge soon found willing takers. If the hardwood regions of Marathon County had little to attract native settlers, they were quite appealing to the foreign-born. Romance may cling to the exploits of the Yankee lumberman, but Marathon County owes its development just as much, if not more, to the variety of European nationalities who cleared and farmed the wilderness over the course of two centuries. German immigrants were the first to arrive in sizable numbers. The advance guard of this colonization came primarily from Hesse-Darmstadt and settled in the towns of Maine and Berlin around 1855. By 1890, however, the largest group—from 1,500 to 2,000 families—had emigrated from Pomerania. Many came also from West

Prussia and about 150 families from Brandenburg. This German community congregated chiefly in the northern and central townships: Marathon, Cassel, Maine, Berlin, Wien, Wausau, Stettin, Rib Falls, and Hamburg. Scattered settlements could also be found in several of the eastern towns: Harrison, Easton, Norrie, Pike Lake, and Elderon. A late nineteenth century study of German immigration to Wisconsin stated that seventy-five per cent of the county's population was of German parentage, and that mainly North German in origin.[7] Later research indicated that shortly after the turn of the century, Marathon County's settlement pattern was possibly even more German dominated. By 1905, an estimated thirty-six of the present forty-one county townships were predominantly populated by those of German descent.[8]

This heavy concentration of German settlers was not accidental. The region's climate, soil, and vegetation were comparable to that section of Germany bordering on the North Sea. A liberal state land policy meant that much of the northern Wisconsin territory could be purchased for $1.25 per acre. Other more general state policies also had a favorable impact. When admitted to statehood in 1848, Wisconsin had no public debts arising from large-scale internal improvements. The immigrant, therefore, had no reason to fear the burden of taxation. Finally, the state constitution was generous to foreigners with respect to the franchise, requiring only one year of residence for the right to vote. All of these facts were duly reported by the early county settlers to friends and relatives back home in Germany.[9]

Private organizations also tried to stimulate interest in county lands for farming purposes. The often crowded conditions and scarce employment opportunities experienced by the German immigrants in the larger American cities created a receptive market for these promotional efforts. In 1856 disgruntled Pittsburgh factory hands and day laborers organized a homesteaders' society and sent representatives west to find a suitable location for establishing a small village with adjoining farm lands. The eventual choice was 3,000 acres of land eleven miles west of Wausau, purchased from a Stevens Point law firm. In one of the all too common cases of misrepresentation, a tempting picture was presented of an already laid-out village with an adjacent steamboat landing and passable roads. When the first eager contingent arrived in 1857, however, the steamboat took the members no farther than Mosinee, where they were forced to cut a path through fifteen miles of wilderness to their tract. This, they discovered, was also in the midst of an immense forest, waiting to be developed. The main body arrived in 1858, also to find none of the expected signs of civilization. Many were understandably disillusioned, and those with enough money returned to Pittsburgh. But most, having no other recourse, remained to clear the land. In time their exertions resulted in the creation of the farming community of Marathon City, described just before the turn of the century as "an exceedingly quiet town, slow but prosperous."[10] Beginning in 1879, Frederick Rietbrock sent Andrew Kreutzer on frequent trips to New York City to secure German immigrants for the acreage he in turn had purchased in the northwestern part of the county.[11]

The railroads were another agency important in promoting agricultural settlements in the area. The Wisconsin Valley Railroad, owners of 200,000 acres in both Marathon and Lincoln counties, distributed pamphlets and maps throughout Wisconsin and Germany, and even employed an agent to travel in the targeted country. In addition, by 1886, the prospective farmer was offered free transportation to Marathon County from any point in the state if he purchased eighty acres of railroad land, half-fare for a forty acre purchase. The Wisconsin Central used similar tactics, with one major difference. At the request of Wisconsin Central president Charles Colby, agent Kent K. Kennan was dispatched to Basle, Switzerland, in 1880 to serve also as the agent for the state board of immigration. Having its representative's activities clothed in official garb proved a significant advantage for the railway. Nearly 5,000 immigrants, mostly from the forest lands of Bavaria, were secured and dispersed along the Wisconsin Central line from Stevens Point to Ashland.

Even the clergy became involved. In 1883, a Reverend W. Koch wrote an enthusiastic pamphlet from Black Creek Falls for friends in Basle and Aargau, entitled "Wo find ich eine Heimath in der Fremde?" (Where shall I find a German homeland abroad?). Interested in establishing an evangelical community, Koch extolled the agricultural virtues of north-central Wisconsin. This region might not be a "Promised Land," but its soil was good enough to raise crops for two years simply by harrowing. Moreover, the forests furnished an abundance of fuel and building materials. Equally optimistic were articles appearing in *Der Ansiedler in Wisconsin,* a Milwaukee newspaper devoted to furthering northern Wisconsin settlement, and in an 1881 pamphlet written by K. Ludloff describing a trip through the north-central area. As alluded to earlier, the efforts of these different groups and individuals brought results by the beginning of the twentieth century. The 1900 census indicated that the German-born population of Marathon County had more than tripled since 1870, comprising 69.8 per cent of the county's total number of foreign-born.[12]

Other ethnic enclaves were evident by this time. After Prussia's victory over France in 1871 dimmed hopes for an independent Poland, large numbers of Poles began to enter the United States. In Wisconsin an especially large settlement sprang up around Milwaukee, where its members tried to improve their economic lot by working in the city's factories or on its docks. With depressed industrial conditions increasing unemployment in urban areas, however, many responded to the Wisconsin Valley Railroad ads and purchased land in Marathon County. Around 1875 the first group of Polish emigrants arrived in Cassel. By 1886 at least thirty families had settled in the central part of the present-day township. Frederick Rietbrock had begun his colonization efforts before the project to resettle Germans. In 1878 a group of forty jobless Polish families, previously employed at Bay View Grist Mills in Milwaukee, settled on the eastern edge of his purchase. Such was the origin of the community of Poniatowski. Later advertisements of his Marathon County holdings emphasized that 'numerous polanders' had been placed 'on these lands at very reasonable terms.' By 1895 Marathon County was one of only four

Early Mechanization, Threshing, Town of Emmet, 1895

Wisconsin counties outside the Fox Valley to have more than one hundred Polish immigrants.[13] In addition, a significant Norwegian element had congregated mainly in the southeastern corner of the county and would in time localize in the Town of Elderon.[14] The "Irish Settlement," which came to include practically all of the Town of Emmet, part of the Town of Mosinee, and a small section of the Town of Cleveland, began forming in the late 1850's. Similar to the German experience at Marathon City, the Irish pioneers discovered that the founding of a home in the forested wilderness was no simple matter. Supplies had to be carried on their backs from Mosinee or Stevens Point. They also were forced to find various means of supplementing their incomes while farming operations were still in the primitive stages. Many men worked part of the year harvesting the fields in the older agricultural sections of southern Wisconsin. Entire families were often engaged in digging the valuable rafting "grubs." In the spring maple syrup and sugar were made. The settlement began to lose its solely Irish identity between 1875 and 1880, when several Bohemian families moved into Emmet.[15]

A larger Bohemian colony was in the making in the Rocky Ridge area near Mosinee during the 1890's. Three land promoters of Czech extraction ran advertisements in Czech language papers and circulated an attractive booklet in the Czech language. The ads unabashedly depicted Rocky Ridge as a "semi-paradise" where fertile soil produced grain crops with unheard-of yields, and good hunting and fishing were available from the front doorstep. The Czech families lured by these enticing portraits came from widely separated locations: some migrated from Iowa, other from Kansas and Nebraska. By early in the twentieth century their chosen section of Rocky Ridge was known alternately in Mosinee as the "Black Hills" or the "Bohemian Settlement."[16] A separate Bohemian community was established in the northwestern part of the county during the same period. Between thirty and forty families from Chicago, Iowa, and Nebraska settled in the Town of Johnson, mainly in the vicinity of Corinth and Wuertzburg. When the Panic of 1893 led to the closing of the Bessemer iron mines on Michigan's northern peninsula, a number of the unemployed workers of Bohemian extraction pulled up stakes and moved their families to the northern part of the Town of Holton to take up farming.[17] Once again, Marathon County's agricultural lands served as a safety valve for victims of industrial depression.

With the assistance of these various components, the county had made great strides in its agricultural development by the turn of the century. In 1860, ten years after the county's formal organization, only 156 farms were in operation. By 1880 the number had climbed to 1,705, and in the next twenty years the farm count increased to 4,276. Farm acreage showed an equally impressive growth rate. In 1860, 20,366 acres had been devoted to farming; in 1880, 183,827 acres; and by 1900, 442,878 acres. This translated into an increase in the percentage of county land area in farms from only 2 per cent in 1860 to 18.2 per cent in 1880, and to 43.9 per cent by 1900.[18]

Farm life, however, still had many qualities of a frontier existence. Farm houses in more than one township were visited by bands of

Plowing, Town of Cassel, 1925

Indians and caravans of gypsies. By all accounts the Indians were friendly, often trading woven baskets for salt pork. The white settlers, by contrast, were not adverse to taking advantage of them; farmers sometimes stole from each other and then blamed the thefts on the Indians. The gypsies had a less favorable reputation. A Town of Johnson resident remembered that chickens had to be watched closely when gypsies were nearby, since gypsy women would squat over the birds with their full skirts and make off with them. One story circulated in the northeastern part of the county claimed that the gypsies threw out fishing lines baited with corn to catch and steal chickens before the owners would miss them. Disease was another danger. A smallpox epidemic struck the Town of Wausau around the turn of the century, with watchmen having to be hired to guard the infected homes. Finally, a variety of wild animals stalked the wooded areas. Long-time residents of Cassel and Frankfort recall bears as the most troublesome.[19]

Nonetheless, as the twentieth century unfolded, numerous promotional efforts were undertaken to insure that the favorable population and acreage trends continued. A flattering write-up of Marathon County's "utopian conditions" appeared in a 1903 issue of the *Wisconsin Agriculturalist*. The author advised farmers from southern Wisconsin, Illinois, Iowa, and Minnesota to "take . . . a little vacation" in north-central Wisconsin and view the progress for themselves: "It does one's heart good to drive in a field where the crops are so thick that you wonder where it all grew." The article included promotional pitches from established farmers in Fenwood, Granite Heights, Knowlton, Hamburg, and Bevent. All praised their localities as containing excellent farming country. The advice offered by Jacob Dix of Fenwood was typical: "There is good wild land yet to be had in Marathon County, and I advise any reader of the *Agriculturalist* who intends to buy to do so as soon as possible. . . ."[20]

The advertisements were not strictly limited to emphasizing the advantages of Marathon County. Local land promoters faced serious competition from Canadian lands in the first years of the twentieth century. An increased flow of northern Wisconsin residents to the western provinces during 1901 and 1902 was greeted with particular alarm. This enthusiasm was at least temporarily dampened, however, by the comments of a party of Easton farmer-emigrants who visited Alberta in the spring of 1903. Their report, which was widely publicized in newspapers throughout the state, was a nearly unbroken tale of disillusionment: impossible roads, rough country, undrinkable well water, along with over-priced breakfasts and rude treatment in a Canadian town, were all prominently mentioned. "To go from Marathon county to Canada," they concluded, "is like going out of a nice feather bed to sleep in a horse blanket." The story drew a vigorous protest from the Canadian land agent in Wausau, who complained further that he was denied space for an exhibit at the Wausau fair.[21]

Publicity of a more positive nature was forthcoming. With the Canadian problem very much in mind, northern Wisconsin landholders met in Eau Claire in the spring of 1903 to discuss the possibility of creating some sort of promotional organization. Their deliberations resulted in a number of landholders contributing one hundred dollars each to form the Wisconsin Development Association. By July several thousand dollars had been raised to buy space in Wisconsin newspapers and those of adjoining states for the purpose of advertising north-central Wisconsin lands. Marathon County personalities were deeply involved in the association's activities. Frederick Rietbrock headed the organization with typical enthusiasm. He personally authored an article on farming advantages in northern Wisconsin which was published in several newspapers. The group's secretary, L. K. Wright of Wausau, had already published a pamphlet in 1902 on the *Resources of Northern Wisconsin*. During the association's short life, he was credited with contributing much of its promotional material. Apparently, however, no attempt was made to keep the organization alive after its original contributions had been expended; and by 1912 the *Marathon Times* was still lamenting the exodus of settlers to Canada.[22]

Nonetheless, as with industrial development, gains in agricultural settlement would continue despite the demise of an early support organization. In March, 1905, the Mosinee Business Men's Association announced that the Holway Land Company was considering the purchase of nearly 20,000 acres in the Town of Kronenwetter. To help open these "rich lands" to settlement, a new highway would be constructed almost directly north from Mosinee, one mile north of the Knowlton town line, to Bevent. Thus, the project would have the added benefit of giving the Town of Pike Lake access to Mosinee and the advantage of a market on the St. Paul road. Gone would be the inconvenience of driving twenty-eight miles to the Stevens Point market. The new road would mean only a twelve or fourteen mile trip to Mosinee instead. "The importance of the project to the county "can scarcely be overestimated," declared the *Wausau Daily Record*:

> If the land is sold in eighty acre tracts it will mean
> two hundred and fifty new families and probably 1,250
> new residents for the county. Besides this the ma-
> terial wealth of the county will be added to as the
> farms are developed and residences and farms are
> built, and there will be a considerable increase in
> the amount of taxes paid to the county.[23]

This particular "development scheme" was destined to have a major impact on the county's ethnic composition. The first step in the process occurred in early 1912 when the Holway firm sold its 20,000 acres to the Worzalla brothers of Stevens Point. From the beginning there was no secret that a particular nationality group was targeted for the next purchase of this tract. Already a large section of Marathon County near Mosinee was populated by Poles,[24] and this transaction anticipated a substantial increase in their numbers. An immediate influx of five hundred families that spring was forecast, with another 3,000 expected to follow. "This big sale of northern Wisconsin land," announced the *Marathon Times,* was "merely the beginning of a big plan by Polish farmers in Ohio, Pennsylvania and New York, who have realized that northern Wisconsin is rich in agricultural possibilities."[25]

Anton, John, and Steve Worzalla wasted little time in trying to make these projections a reality, even if they had to distort another reality to do so. They placed ads in Polish language newspapers and distributed pamphlets in the Polish language depicting the independent life a farmer could enjoy in this section of Marathon County. Their literature contained pictures of model farms and idealized produce, thereby creating the mistaken impression that the area was already in a highly advanced stage of development. The pamphlets also emphasized the establishment of a Polish community named Pelplin (later renamed Peplin), serviced by a post office, railroads, and factories.

Their appeals had the desired effect on the land-hungry Poles. But contrary to the original expectation, they apparently generated the most response in the urban Polish enclaves of Chicago, Cleveland, Pittsburgh, and the eastern Pennsylvania coal mining districts. As could be expected, these latest victims of overenthusiastic salesmanship were shocked to find their dream colony still little more than a wilderness dominated by brush, stones, and stumps. The few who could afford to leave, returned to the cities; the majority, having invested all their money in their individual tracts, remained to clear away the obstacles. The summer months were spent trying to eke out the best living possible on the land. During the winter the men left their families to find additional employment. Many found work either in the Worzalla sawmill or in the local paper mill; others had to travel a much greater distance. Some went to the industrial cities of Illinois. At least one had to go as far as the West Virginia coal mines. By 1919 some progress was evident in the Peplin farming community. Dozens of small homes with a few acres of clearing dotted the countryside.[26] Yet existence was still far from the idyllic picture appearing in the Worzalla literature. A settler who arrived at the end of this colonization period recalled that as late as 1920:

> There were no roads, the trails that joined these clearings called by many "the little farms" were at times impossible to get through, even the main highway was no better. Many a time these settlers had to carry their groceries five miles or more. Since there were no bridges on the creeks folks many times had to swim in the icy water in spring to get to Mosinee Paper Mills to work or get to store for shopping. In winter the snow drifts put the end of all traveling. There were no snow plows, no tractors, no cars, only one team of horses in the whole community of thirty families.[27]

Life wasn't easy, but there were concerned individuals who provided invaluable assistance. Ed Emmerich, a country store owner of German descent, gave virtually unlimited credit to the Polish settlers. Their mutual trust became so great, in fact, that whenever one of the residents was preparing to leave the settlement, the Poles would forewarn Emmerich in the event the individual owed him money.[28]

Education was another necessity in a community where only three residents were American citizens by 1920. In this instance, the leadership role was assumed by Casimir Orzechowski. After teaching as many as ninety children during the week, he would spend his Sunday afternoons voluntarily teaching their parents how to become citizens. Sunday evenings were spent helping them fill out naturalization papers. At his suggestion the examiner came to Mosinee to conduct tests, thereby saving his adult students a trip to Wausau. His contributions to improving rural education spanned thirty-two years, helping to earn him the nickname of "The Voice of Peplin."[29]

Meanwhile, to the northeast, those of Dutch descent were forming their own colony. In October, 1902, several Dutch residents of Mil-

"Allemande Left" — Hatley Square Dance, 1904

waukee sent representatives to the towns of Plover and Easton to investigate the prospects for farming and settlement. Their favorable report induced their pastor, the Reverend P. Vanderkam, to conduct his own investigation. His subsequent purchase of eighty acres in section 31 of Plover provided the final endorsement. The first five Milwaukee buyers were soon followed by an additional five from Milwaukee, Cedar Grove, and Sheboygan in the winter of 1902-1903. From this modest beginning, the colony began to expand rapidly. Inquiries were received from other Dutch settlements in the United States, with requests that Vanderkam lecture to them. As a result, "week after week a stream of Holland landseekers came to Wausau and . . . bought land." Many were quite poor and could pay very little at first for their tracts. Some of the poorest, knowing next to nothing about clearing land, had to be helped in almost every conceivable way.[30] Ads in Dutch newspapers attracted more settlers to the Ringle area during the next decade. Again, many had no previous experience in farming, so clearing the land "took a lot of doing." Several years passed before there was enough pasture to begin feeding dairy cattle. A later group of Hollanders from Sheboygan County, however, got off to a faster start by bringing along their own dairy cows and settling on the more cleared western banks of the Eau Claire River.[31]

Thus, by the end of the twentieth century's second decade, Marathon County continued to show gains in rural settlement. Over 1,700 farms had been added since 1900. Total farm acreage had increased by slightly more than 208,000 acres during the same period; 64.5 per cent of the county's land area was now in farms. The rural population had increased by more than fifty per cent to 46,598.[32] These gains were partly reflected in the organization of additional townships. Franzen and Ringle were established in 1901, Bern in 1902, Flieth in 1905,[33] Green Valley in 1914, Reid in 1917, and Guenther in 1920. Of the older townships, Kronenwetter registered the most impressive population growth, with an increase of 1,558 since 1900. Mosinee was next with 651. Johnson and Knowlton also recorded relatively large population gains with increases of 509 and 405 respectively.[34]

With only twenty per cent of the county's land under actual cultivation, the promotional fever did not die during the 1920's. Enthusiasm for more settlers was evident despite the onset of a general agricultural depression and the danger posed to farm prices by overproduction. Perhaps the most zealous advocate was the Madison-based National Land Colonizing Company. Founded in 1920, the organization was formed "to give publicity to Upper Wisconsin" and "to locate farmers on rich virgin lands in this state. . . ."[35] Owning large tracts a few miles from the village of Mosinee, the company singled out Marathon County for special advertising attention. One of their brochures urged prospective buyers to take a day or two off, catch the Chicago, Milwaukee & St. Paul to Mosinee, and visit its field office on the second floor of the Mosinee State Bank building. The trip would be a revelation for those wasting their lives on rented farms or living in virtual slavery in the city:

> If you come to Mosinee, you will find men in the
> office, ready to take care of you and show you around
> the country. As you leave Mosinee in an automobile,
> you will be surprised at the big well developed farms
> that you see, with their splendid dairy herds. When
> you see the fine buildings and the big fields, you
> will hardly be able to believe that these valuable
> farms are owned by men who came to this country
> only five to ten years ago.[36]

All of these farms, it was claimed, were on "the richest soil, with no sand or hills." And the company's holdings contained the same rich clay loam soil. A first clearing with a brush scythe would yield at least ten acres of crops in a year. The company was offering nothing less than the best land it could find in Upper Wisconsin; one could travel for days and not find a higher grade of farm land. These admittedly strong statements were backed up by a guarantee to pay the visitor's traveling expenses if he found a single misrepresentation in the company's literature or pictures.[37]

The claims of the land agents had changed little over the years. However, in one very important respect, the company did distinguish itself from the older land promoters. The romantic, back-to-the-soil tone of its rhetoric notwithstanding, it recognized that the pioneer spirit was a thing of the past. Thus, it not only advertised the advantages of its tracts, but offered attractive services designed to help the settler get started in his new life. Reimbursing the customer's railroad fare was only the beginning. The company would go so far as to put up a set of new buildings for the farmer and loan him a dairy cow. Furthermore, each time five acres were brushed and two plowed, another loan would be granted for an additional cow. Added to these inducements were invitations from various county officials in such publications as the *Marathon County Farm Journal*. The rhetoric was less flamboyant, but the message was the same. Marathon County offered unbounded opportunities for the new settler with courage and initiative. And he would be warmly welcomed.[38]

Despite the postwar slump in farm prices, the appeals did not go entirely unanswered. The total number of county farms increased through 1925 by 10.8 per cent to 6,717. Farm acreage also rose during the first half of the decade, but by only 2.6 per cent to 668,333 acres. As a result, the average size of a county farm had decreased to 99.5 acres—the lowest figure since 1890. The percentage of county land area in farms, meanwhile, climbed to just over 66 per cent. By 1930, although the number of farms had dropped to 6,359, acreage was up 6.8 per cent to 713,796 acres. Accordingly, the percentage of land area in farms measured slightly over seventy per cent, and the average size of a Marathon County farm rose to 111.2 acres—the highest figure in fifty years.[39]

The intense colonization campaign of the early twentieth century left its mark in one other important respect. While the population of twenty-six townships could still be classified as predominantly German in ethnic composition by the 1930's, other nationality groups had made significant inroads. Distinct Norwegian and Dutch settlements were located east of the Wisconsin River; Irish and Bohemian communities, west. The Poles had made the most impressive gains, however. They had extended their numerical dominance from Bevent, Reid, Cassel,[40] and Rietbrock to include Franzen, Guenther, Knowlton, Kronenwetter, and Mosinee. Only four townships—Rib Mountain, Spencer, Brighton, and Hull—were considered not to have a dominant nationality group.[41] In a much broader sense than agricultural development the county's rural ethnics had enriched the land. Their presence had introduced a diverse array of tradition, customs, and even ways of looking at life that made Marathon County, at the very least, a more interesting place to live.

The variety of agricultural products raised in the county matched the diverse origins of its rural population. Crops of hay, potatoes, peas, oats, rye, barley, and wheat began with the earliest German pioneer settlements.[42] Clover and timothy grew upon county logging roads as soon as they were opened, with pigeons suspected as the source of seed dispersal. Corn did not grow well at first, due to the cold late springs brought about, in turn, by the forest conditions. But as increased land clearing reduced shade, it too became an established crop.[43] Apples were another early failure that were later grown successfully. In 1896, in fact, the Wisconsin State Horticultural Society

Digging Potatoes, Town of Elderon, Early 20th Century

selected the Ed Single farm in the Town of Maine as the site for its experimental orchard. Excellent crops of apples, as well as plums and cherries, were soon being harvested on the ten-acre spread, causing society secretary Frederic Cranefield to comment in 1907: "If there are farmers near Wausau who have planted and replanted fruit trees ending in failure, and their honest belief is that fruit trees cannot be grown in Marathon county, such persons should visit the . . . society's orchard and take a look at the ten year old trees there."[44] Any lingering doubts were removed three years later when the orchard's apple exhibit captured top honors at the society's convention in Milwaukee. Undeveloped land lying near the orchard, available at ten to twenty-five dollars an acre, was praised as being equal or superior to western land selling for twenty times the price.[45] Apples, plums, blackberries, and strawberries were also proving especially successful in the Athens vicinity shortly after the turn of the century.[46]

Some interesting possibilities were experimented with, but never did catch on. Grapes were tried in Stettin, but failed to ripen properly. Sugar cane proved to be a failure in present-day Kronenwetter in 1876, but later enjoyed limited success in Stettin, making a good quality of sorghum. Tobacco growing was practiced in several sections: the Colby, Unity, and Athens areas, Berlin, Stettin, Kronenwetter, and Easton. Although a total harvest of 664 pounds was reported in 1883, this type of farming never advanced beyond the hobby stage. Moreover, the quality of the plant remained untested in those areas where it could be found growing early in the twentieth century. An interest in sugar beets developed throughout northern Wisconsin during the late nineteenth century. One Stettin resident claimed around 1903 that his farm was producing beets of "prodigious proportions" and was yielding thirty-four tons per acre. In general, however, this potential new cash crop never lived up to expectations, and enthusiasm eventually waned.[47]

A few new crops began to receive increased attention early in the twentieth century. Alfalfa, for example, was first successfully grown by Anthony Vetter in the Town of Marathon in 1910. The next several years witnessed planting by growing numbers of farmers. To sustain this trend, a large bundle of the hay with four-foot stalks was exhibited in Wausau in 1914. Nonetheless, some resistance to raising alfalfa persisted, as doubts were expressed about the texture of county soil. In response, the *Marathon County Farm Journal* singled out in 1923 the Gust Norbohm farm in the Town of Elderon as proof that the crop could be successfully grown. By 1929 the county was producing almost 3,000 tons of this quick-growing dairy feed on 1,280 acres, the acreage figure having more than doubled since 1924.[48] Marathon County members of the Wisconsin Experimental Association were experimenting with soybean planting around 1915. Touted as a particularly beneficial substitute when other crops had failed—both as a source of rich protein feed and as a means of increasing field fertility— the legume rapidly came into favor. In 1923 farmers from the towns of Texas, Elderon, and Weston, and the villages of Edgar, Athens, Mosinee, and Stratford were reporting splendid yields to the *Marathon County Farm Journal*.[49]

By far the most novel of the newly cultivated crops was ginseng. Long valued in the Orient for its supposed medicinal properties, the plant was discovered growing wild in the Marathon County woods around 1877. Heavy demand eventually depleted the natural wild growth, however. Thus, shortly after the turn of the century, Reinhold Dietsch in the Town of Hamburg, and the Volhards, Hornungs, and Buchbergers in the Town of Marathon started their own "shang" gardens. Cultivating the herb was no simple matter. A forest-like

Penetrating the China Market, Fromm Brothers Ginsing Garden, 1930

environment had to be recreated, including the simulation of fresh breezes and sunlight peeking through trees. Blight was a constant hazard once the plant was domesticated. Besides care, a great deal of patience was required. Growers had to wait at least five years before harvesting their crops. Plenty of land was also needed inasmuch as the crop refused to grow a second time on the same acreage. A second generation ginseng farmer remembers that many of the early growers 'didn't know how to take care of the seed,' which had no oil in its makeup and was therefore more susceptible to damage. Some help was provided by Wausau's J. H. Koehler. After extensive study of the plant, he edited and printed the "Ginseng and Golden Seal Growers' Handbook." The work may have been hard, but the potential financial rewards seemed to justify the effort. Reinhold Dietsch claimed he could make $20,000 per acre.

This projection proved especially enticing to four brothers in the Town of Hamburg. As of 1904, Walter, Edward, John, and Henry Fromm were still searching for a way to finance their ambition to raise silver foxes. An off-hand remark by their father about Dietsch's alleged gold mine aroused their curiosity. Checking the market reports in a monthly trade journal, *Hunter-Trader-Trapper,* they discovered that their fellow townsman was not making an idle boast. Dried ginseng root from the north-central states was selling at six dollars a pound. No further incentive was needed. After carefully scanning the woods to observe the plant's habits, the brothers began the laborious and expensive task of transplanting the wild ginseng in specially constructed arbors. The venture was conducted on a trial and error basis for several years. Each new problem that arose was also a learning experience. The first returns from the plant were somewhat disappointing, but finally, in 1919, fifteen years after they had taken the first 150 plants from the forest, their perseverance was rewarded. That year Fromm Brothers made a sixty-nine barrel shipment to Boehmer & Co. of New York valued at $45,000. Over the years the Fromms developed machines and techniques for making seed beds, perfected methods for treating seeds and plants for disease, and found improved ways of digging and preparing the root for market. Many of their innovations became standard procedure for other ginseng growers.

With the Fromm brothers leading the way, Marathon County became the leading center of ginseng cultivation in the country. Even before they entered the picture, county growers had formed a mutual aid association affiliated with the National Cultivated Wild Ginseng

Growers' Association. Many traditional farmers scoffed at this species of "freak farming," but it remained a lucrative crop. In announcing the formation of the Chellis & Sampson Ginseng Company in late 1909, the *Pilot* noted that "ginseng raising has proven a profitable business for those who have engaged in it extensively."[50] Fifteen years later, J. H. Koehler indicated that half an acre could easily bring a grower $6,000 to $7,000 if he knew how to get results. Timber no longer represented the only potential source of wealth to come out of Marathon County forests.[51]

This assortment of crops constituted only part of the county's agricultural productivity. Livestock was another major component. Chickens were imported from southern Wisconsin early in the settlement period. Their eggs could be traded for credit at the nearest country store; later they could be exchanged directly for cash, as merchants sought to meet the competition of mail order houses. Early in the twentieth century George Kreutzer was handling a large volume of eggs each season at his general store in Athens. Other signs of poultry's growing importance were in evidence. In the Town of Hamburg, Henry E. Voight was publishing the only German poultry magazine in the United States, *Gefluegel Zuechter*. Voight claimed that his journal had extensive circulation in neighboring states. Several breeders of pure bred flocks could also be found in the county by 1903. In 1911, L. H. Cook organized a county poultry breeders' association. The organization's goals were basic: "promote improvement of the breeds of poultry in [Marathon] county, work up enthusiasm in the business and . . . arrange poultry exhibits each winter."[52] The first such show was held the following year, thereby enabling local poultry raisers to exchange ideas and exhibit, buy, and sell the best strains of pure bred fowl. By 1929 Marathon County had 334,800 chickens on its farms, producing more than 32 million eggs.[53]

As of 1860, there were only three horses in the entire county west of Wausau. Their numbers began to increase, however, as horses gradually replaced oxen for use in clearing and cultivating land. Shortly after the turn of the century it was reported that horses were better represented than most other breeds of county livestock; most of the horses were the direct offspring of the heavy breeds of draft horses brought in by the lumbermen. By 1920, in fact, Marathon County ranked third in the state in the number of horses and mules. This four-legged source of power carried a value of slightly more than 2 million dollars. The number would steadily decline in the years ahead, however, as automobiles and tractors became the major suppliers of horse power in farm work. Nonetheless, as of January 1, 1953, Marathon County had more horses and mules than any other Wisconsin county, although the 5,700 head was litle more than a third of the figure recorded a decade earlier.[54]

Sheep raising followed a similar pattern in its early stages. Only half a dozen sheep were counted in all of Marathon County in 1860. But a decade later the number had soared to 1,482, the animals being used by settlers for both wool and mutton. Less spectacular but significant gains were recorded over the next three decades, until by the turn of the century the country's total of 33,218 sheep ranked it twentieth in the state. Additional growth seemed probable after 1900, when a concerted publicity campaign sought to transform the entire Wisconsin Cutover into a major sheep producing area. Early credibility was provided when Colonel W. W. Burch, editor of the *American Sheep Breeder,* decided around the turn of the century to start a sheep ranch in the region. His choice of location was editorially hailed as "the harbinger of a new era for the stump lands."[55]

Favorable comments and advice on sheep raising in northern Wisconsin continued to grace the pages of industry periodicals well into the twentieth century's second decade. The region's grasses were praised as particularly nutritious for both lambs and ewes. Moreover, it was emphasized that sheep fed on growth that was harmful to the farm. An owner of cutover hardwood land in central Wisconsin was advised in the *Breeder's Gazette* to get a flock of sheep to clear the brush from his section. The animals profitability was repeatedly stressed. Declared a veteran sheep man in the *County Gentleman*: 'Sheep are better than cattle as an investment. The returns from sheep are two to one over cattle, on an area suitable for both.' The war-time devastation of Europe's livestock industry was viewed as a bonanza. With surplus Argentine and Australian mutton likely to be diverted from the United States to Europe, America would be forced to produce all that was needed for home consumption. The *American Sheep Breeder* carried the promotional process one step further. Claiming unusual interest among its readers in the Wisconsin Cutover's "exceptional opportunities," the journal established an information bureau to answer all inquiries about the region and furnish names of "reliable owners."[56] Hints on sheep raising also appeared in the *Marathon County Farm Journal.* Frank Kleinheinz, long-time sheep expert at the College of Agriculture, paid a visit to the county in the summer of 1919 to conduct sheep meetings in interested townships.

The blandishments notwithstanding, the anticipated boom never materialized. Although Marathon County's relative rank in the number of sheep improved to thirteenth place by 1910, its sheep population had actually declined by almost 9,000 since 1900. A twenty-five per cent gain from 1917 to 1919 was not sustained. Some prospective breeders were undoubtedly discouraged by warnings from other experts that sheep could not thrive in a wilderness of brush. Local farmers also offered excuses, such as the threat of wolves, prowling cur dogs, and trouble with neighbors over constructing "sheep tight" fences. The region's long, cold winters were another severe handicap. Finally, a general post-war depression in the sheep industry accelerated the downward trend. By 1920, the county's sheep total had fallen to 10,860. Following 1924, the industry in the West and Midwest recovered from the sub-normal conditions, and a renewed token effort was undertaken to revive interest in sheep raising. H. A. Woodward, associate editor of the *Marathon County Farm Journal,* employed all the familiar arguments concerning profitability and practicality in a 1925 article entitled "Why Not Sheep?"[57] The county sheep total enjoyed a brief upsurge in 1926 and 1927, but then resumed its downward course to a figure of 10,200 by 1930. Marathon County, like the rest of the Cutover, was not destined to become one large sheep pasture.[58]

Even less successful was an Angora goat craze that briefly swept the Cutover early in the twentieth century. The prime instigator of the movement was Bayfield newspaper editor Currie E. Bell. After purchasing one hundred goats in Iowa for his newly organized Bayfield Angora Goat Company, Bell prematurely claimed that the animals could simultaneously clear brush from Cutover land and enrich the soil. Newspaper dissemination of his boast sparked an Angora fad throughout northern Wisconsin—even Marathon County was not immune. Several flocks were found within its borders by 1903. John Seubert of Marathon City was singled out for special mention in the *Pilot,* having secured a flock of three hundred to clear wild land of brush. However, the goat fancy soon lost its momentum for a variety of reasons. Unlike sheep, few claims were ever made that goats were profitable, either in terms of mohair or meat. Farmers quickly discovered that high fences were required to get Angoras to clear the right land. Angora kids, moreover, could not withstand cold, damp spring weather. Finally, contrary to popular assumption, the goats could not survive on brush, but needed good grass pasture. Goat raising fever thus dissipated even more rapidly than did the enthusiasm for sheep.[59]

One additional factor helps to explain the declining prominence of sheep and goats in the county agricultural scheme. By the turn of the century another breed of livestock, the dairy cow, was already claiming a dominant position on county pastures. Unlike the older agricultural regions of Wisconsin, Marathon County did not go through a dominant wheat growing period. The wheat industry had already moved largely to the West when settlers entered the region in any number.[60] Dairying, as part of a more diversified type of farming, began in the wake of lumbering, as permanent pastures and hay fields were established on newly cleared land. The area's cool summer nights, plentiful supply of pure water, fertile soil, luxuriant grasses, and abundance of feed crops made it especially suitable for this very specialized type of agricultural enterprise. With advocates such as William Dempster Hoard urging state farmers in general to abandon wheat in favor of dairying, it did not take long for these advantages to be perceived and acted upon. Quoting the apt summation of Eric Lampard: "From the outset [in Marathon County], grass and especially clover seemed the best crop and where clover grew soon followed the cow."[61]

Signs of dairying's growing importance were apparent well before the end of the nineteenth century. As of 1885, hay, oats, wheat, potatoes, beef, and pork were still the leading county farm products, but 232,450 pounds of butter and 4,317 pounds of cheese were also produced that same year. The initial preference of Marathon County's dairy pioneers for butter production was not difficult to understand. Butter making was a much simpler process than cheese making, and could be done in the farm kitchen. A home churn took up considerably less space than the large heating vats required in cheese making. However, this simplicity often resulted in a product of, at best, uneven quality. A local agricultural expert made the following unflattering assessment in 1903:

> The home farm dairy is not a success if one is to judge the quality of the product offered for sale in the towns. . . . Education in the correct method of making butter is sadly needed in the homes of the country. Cleanliness needs to be taught. The butter brought in by the farmers to the grocers is generally of a very poor quality. It is salvy, streaked, dirty, and has a bad flavor and odor.[62]

Creameries began to make their appearance in the county around 1895. Eleven were counted by 1901, seventeen by 1905. While the quality of the creamery product was usually far superior, here too there was some lack of uniformity. Those county creameries operated by graduates of the University of Wisconsin Dairy School were judged to be turning out a "very creditable product." Other creameries, however, were run by incompetents with limited experience, gained while working previously in some other creamery for only a few months.[63] Yet, the greater reliability of the creamery article was fully recognized by the merchant. Shortly after the turn of the century, creamery butter was selling for thirty cents a pound, while the farm-made variety was selling for fifteen to eighteen cents per pound. By 1913, the Athens Creamery was conducting a $55,000 a year business. Nevertheless, butter making remained very much a household project; it would take many years before creameries reduced domestic manufacturing to relative insignificance. In 1905, domestic production of butter accounted for sixty-two per cent of the county's output. Four years later it still made up forty-four per cent of the total butter production. Farm-made butter continued to decline in importance, but by 1919, it still represented a relatively significant 28.6 per cent proportion of the county's total output. The number of county creameries, meanwhile, reached a peak of twenty-nine in 1910, but then declined to fourteen by 1920.[64]

Cheese making proved a better alternative for Marathon County farmers. Cheese kept better than butter and could be shipped farther. In addition, the county's cool climate made it an advantageous location for cheese production. On the other hand, the time, care, and skill involved placed the process beyond the ability of most householders. The haphazard methods of kitchen handicraft produced, as was the case with butter, a product of unpredictable quality. The quantity of cheese manufactured in the county in 1885 was one-fourteenth the amount of butter produced; the value of that cheese, by contrast, was one-thirtieth the value of the butter. The fact that more milk was required to produce a pound of butter than a pound of cheese only partly explained the disparity. The poor quality of the cheese was also responsible. It would take the importation of the factory system pioneered in New York state to transform cheese making into a significant agricultural activity in both the state of Wisconsin and Marathon County.[65]

Steadily the new system took hold. Cheese factories began to appear in the region northeast of Athens as early as 1891. These early industrial anomalies in the countryside operated only a few months of each year, from the time the grass turned green in spring until the

pasture disappeared in the fall. Typically modest, family-run enterprises, they handled only three to four hundred pounds of milk a day
and paid approximately fifty cents per hundred pounds. By 1898,
however, enough interest had been generated among local farmers to
keep the Athens area factories open all winter. Rural acceptance of
industrial discipline was also reflected in the increasing number of
county factories; from ten in 1895 to thirty-three in 1905. At the end
of the century, in fact, Marathon County, with twenty-one factories,
had the only sizable cheese industry in all northern Wisconsin.[66]
Dominance of the factory in cheese manufacturing was undisputed.
Domestic production measured a mere .7 per cent of total county output as of 1905; by 1909, the figure had dropped to less than .08 per
cent.[67] As the number of factories continued to grow—114 by 1915,
143 by 1919—while the timber continued to fall, a new economic order
was taking shape in Marathon County. Its outline could be discerned
in the changing freight of the Abbotsford and Northeastern Railroad.
In the winter of 1911-1912, five hundred cars a month were being
shipped from Athens on this new part of the Wisconsin Central system.[68] The principal cargo was timber products: lumber, cordwood,
and pulpwood. But increasingly, space had to be reserved for dairy
products. By 1924, the nearly 2,400,000 pounds of cheese produced by
the sixteen factories operating within a six and one-half mile radius
of Athens required more than one hundred cars a year.[69]

Another indication of dairying's rising status could be seen on the
farm itself. County farmers were rapidly losing interest in the "dual
purpose" cow suitable for milk or beef. Many farmers initially believed that increased feeding alone would dramatically multiply a
cow's milk production, a fallacy vigorously fought into the 1890's by
William Dempster Hoard and other founding fathers of Wisconsin
dairying. The shift in opinion towards specialized dairy cattle was
signaled by the formation of breeding associations. These groups could
purchase and maintain a pedigreed sire that few individuals could
afford; thus, many farmers could have the use of an animal that was
otherwise beyond their financial means. The size of Marathon County,
however, presented a problem for organizers. A solution was found
when a former county agent, F. G. Swoboda, conceived the idea of
organizing local breed clubs around trading centers, each having a
definite work program. By the early 1920's, the County Holstein Association, with a membership of approximately 350 and neighborhood
breed clubs in Unity, Wausau, Colby, Elderon, Stratford, Athens,
Edgar, Spencer, and Plover, was the strongest breeding organization.

The County Guernsey Association was a close second, with a membership of nearly 250 and clubs in Unity, Wausau, Colby, Elderon, Stratford, Athens, Edgar, and Hatley. The Brown Swiss breeders had their own flourishing group: the North Central Brown Swiss Association, while Unity hosted the first county Ayrshire club in the state. In all, it was estimated that more than 1,200 pure bred sires were being used by Marathon County dairy farmers, with Holsteins, Guernseys, and Brown Swiss the most numerous.[70]

A second cooperative effort aimed at herd improvement was the cow testing association. In exchange for a nominal fee, the member-farmer could obtain the service of a specialist who would test and report on the butter fat production of his herd. This would enable him to select the best milkers for breeding and eliminate those "boarder" cows producing less than the cost of feed and labor. By 1915, there were thirty-nine such associations in the state testing 19,000 cows. The boom in Marathon County cow testing came somewhat later in 1919. By 1922, programs were organized in Spencer, Cherokee, Dorchester, Wausau, Edgar, Stratford, and Plover; several were also in the process of organization at Athens, Elderon, Unity, and Marathon City. Six associations were listed as fully active: Wausau-Marathon, Edgar-Marathon, Cherokee-Colby, Tri-County, Stratford, and McMillan-Marshfield, with another four being reorganized. Cow testing had become so popular, in fact, that applications for membership in the Wausau-Marathon organization had become too numerous for a single tester. Accordingly, a second branch of the association was formed the following year by farmers in the Wausau district. Besides the earlier mentioned services, the first county organizations served a valuable publicity function, publishing reports of good production and sending them to local publications and state farm magazines. As a result, farming communities outside the state learned that the county possessed a surplus of good dairy cattle, and they, in turn, sent buyers to the region. In August, 1922, the *Marathon County Farm Journal* reported that during the previous six months, thirty carloads of surplus stock had been shipped to other states, with tested cows bringing a price of twenty to thirty dollars more per head.[71]

The attention to herd improvement was but one illustration of dairying's dominant position in twentieth century Marathon County agriculture. A variety of statistics provided confirmation. Between 1925 and 1930, milk cows and heifers accounted for over two-thirds of all cattle in the county. Milk alone represented sixty-one per cent of gross farm income by 1927, and remained above fifty per cent by 1936. That Marathon County had become one of the leading dairy centers of Wisconsin was evident at an earlier date. By 1920, its 54,284 head of dairy cattle ranked third behind Dane and Dodge counties, while the value of its dairy products, $7,185,167, having tripled since the previous decade, ranked sixth. The dairy cow had now replaced the white pine as the pre-eminent symbol of the county's economic importance to the outside world.[72]

State-wide recognition of this changing state of affairs came early in the twentieth century. The Wisconsin Dairymen's Association, the second oldest organization of its kind in the United States, elected to hold its thirty-third convention in Wausau in February, 1905. The avowed purpose of the event was to bring together state dairying experts to discuss problems of special interest to northern Wisconsin farmers. To this end, papers and addresses were presented on topics ranging from the improvement of dairy herds to the proper care of milk on the farm. Exhibits of dairy machinery and products as well as farm produce were also prominently displayed. The affair was, in short, designed to provide Marathon County farmers with "an exceptional opportunity for an expert education right at home."[73]

County farm women were not ignored in the convention program. Adda F. Howie of Elm Grove urged the farm mother to teach her daughter that "it is the heaven born mission of a woman to be a home-maker." The natural order must not be tampered with.

> From the time as a wee toddling girlie she hugs her dollies and plays at house keeping with bits of broken china, the homemaking trait is strong within her and if we succeed in diverting her natural instincts we will have blotted out the sweetest, most lovable and noblest characteristic God has given to woman. . . . Let us teach her that there is art and science in cookery, dishwashing, and scrubbing.[74]

Future farm wives were also advised on how to catch and hold onto a good husband. Similar to a farmer capturing a colt, the girl should put her "oats"—good cooking, tidy housekeeping, and skillful darning and mending—in a pan and shake them while standing in her father's doorway. And once the right man came along, the wise woman should never complain, find fault, or nag if she hoped to keep his love and respect.

Most of the convention oratory, however, was designed to foster continued enthusiasm for dairying in the host county. This was done, in part, by praising the area's soil, water, and other natural advantages for dairy farming. Former Wisconsin Governor William Dempster Hoard related how he had come to Marathon County twenty-five years earlier to investigate its agricultural prospects and had subsequently counseled readers of *Hoard's Dairyman* to come there, in preference to the Dakotas and other western states. The region's dairy products were likewise extolled. Its butter was credited with being as good as that made in the southern part of the state; its cheese was conceded to be even better than the southern product. Warnings were also issued to drive home the intended message. Former association president C. P. Goodrich pointed to the case of Jefferson County, where farmers had learned the hard way that "the man who sold hay instead of feeding it to stock was on the high way to ruin." The pioneer farmers had believed that all they had to do was plow the ground, sow their grain, gather the crops, and repeat the process year after year. Such a course had been followed from 1840 to about 1870. The inevitable result had been the depletion of the soil and the impoverishment of the practitioners. Turning to dairying had meant their salvation. Jefferson County dairymen were now earning two million dollars annually. Moreover, their crops were larger and the fertility of their farms had been restored. The moral was simple: Marathon County farmers should not repeat the earlier mistake of their southern Wisconsin brethren; they should concentrate increasingly on dairying as opposed to general farming. The dairy farmer was portrayed as more prosperous than any other class of farmer. His income varied little from year to year. Unlike the regular farmer, he did not live on credit but paid as he went. The specters of rising debt and a mortgage were unknown. The potential for successful dairying was there, and a promising start had been made. Yet more progress was possible. While Marathon County was raising more than two and one-half times the amount of clover and timothy grown in Jefferson County, it had fewer than half as many cows.[75]

Notwithstanding the care that went into preparing the convention agenda and the lively discussions that followed many of the speeches, the event was not as successful as its sponsors had hoped. The problem was not that the exhortations and advice fell on deaf ears, but that they fell on fewer than had been anticipated. At least one local dignitary and newspaper apologetically noted the absence of large numbers of county farmers at the sessions, blaming both the winter harvest season and the unfavorable weather for the disappointing attendance.[76] Some suspicion of "book farmers" and their scientific

Milk Bound for Market, Town of Wien, 1923

approach to agriculture was also undoubtedly involved. In the beginning even the revolutionary Babcock test had been opposed by some county residents who regarded it as unwarranted 'meddling.'[77] Nevertheless, expert-oriented farm education had gained a foothold by the early twentieth century.

An initial and immediate success were the farmers' institutes, inaugurated in 1886 with a $5,000 appropriation from the state legislature. In October of the following year, Marathon County farmers were invited to a Stevens Point institute to hear talks by 'talented and successful farmers and men of experience' on crops, cultivation, stock, and dairying. Those who attended must have been impressed, for agitation quickly developed, demanding similar gatherings in Marathon County. As a result, the first institute was convened in Wausau in 1889, and thereafter, the affairs—usually running two days each—were periodically held throughout the county. In addition to lectures, some of these meetings also featured musical and literary programs and the awarding of prizes for the best samples of farm produce. At a January, 1915, institute in Marathon City, the contests were expanded to include a box of cigars for the best bologna sausage, three dollars in trade for the heaviest married couple, and a subscription to the *Marathon Times* for the man with the largest foot.[78]

A less transient center for educating the county's rural youth was established in Wausau when the Marathon County School of Agriculture and Domestic Economy was organized under Act 288, passed by the 1901 state legislature. The concept of an agricultural school originated with State School Superintendent Lorenzo D. Harvey. After investigating the project's feasibility, Harvey sought and obtained the help of University College of Agriculture Dean William A. Henry and Marathon County School Superintendent John F. Lamont in selling his idea. Wausau State Senator A. L. Kreutzer proved a helpful ally in the legislature. The new school, claimed to be the first of its kind in the country, opened in October, 1902, housed in a newly constructed building adjacent to the county fairgrounds. Its curriculum, at least for the boys, was designed to instill modern principles of farming that would place the industry on a rational scientific basis.[79] Ignorant and antiquated methods would be replaced by those based on successful research and experimentation. Moreover, only those subjects bearing on local conditions were taught. The school and its objectives received the endorsement of William Dempster Hoard at the 1905 dairymen's convention. Lamenting the "cheap view" many farmers had of themselves, the state's foremost advocate of scientific agriculture saw the institution as both enlarging the farmer's outlook and giving him more confidence in his own worth.[80]

The agricultural school shared its facilities with another institution that symbolized a new commitment towards improving rural education. The objective of the Marathon County Normal School was slightly different but no less important: the training of rural teachers. During the nineteenth century scant attention had been paid to the qualifications of those desiring to teach in rural areas. Frequently an individual's ability to answer a list of questions prepared by the county superintendent with reasonable proficiency was enough to obtain a teaching certificate. All too often the applicant's physical prowess was valued as much as his intellectual capabilities, since the task of keeping the older unruly pupils in line was part of the job. After years of neglect, state educational leaders and the legislature moved to insure some standards of competency in providing rural education. Legislation introduced by Senator Kreutzer was enacted in 1899, authorizing the creation of two county training schools for teachers. The Marathon County Board quickly responded. That summer it perfected plans for establishing the first normal school in the state. Classrooms were obtained in the Humboldt School until the new Wausau high school was completed. A curriculum was fashioned by a board composed of H. J. Blanchard, Andrew Kreutzer, and John Lamont. Oliver E. Wells, a former state school superintendent, was hired as the first principal at a salary of $1,800; his assistant, Rosalia Bohrer, was retained for $1,300.[81] On opening day, September 11, 1899, thirty-four students were enrolled, with the number increasing to fifty-six during the first year. The 1902 construction of its own building signaled the end of the normal school's trial period. Upon the dissolution of the co-occupant agricultural school, a demonstration school was added, and students from outlying districts were admitted. Although the Marathon County Normal School was no longer a unique institution by 1922, its supporters claimed that its "spectacular growth" over the previous three years had made it the largest center of rural teacher training in Wisconsin.[82]

Education for rural women in the early twentieth century was not disregarded, but it followed closely the precepts laid down by Adda Howie. The girls' specialized course of study at the agricultural school was designed to place the female student nowhere after graduation except in the home. It ranged from cooking and sewing to the more intellectually taxing subjects of jelly making and pickling.[83] The school's superintendent, R. B. Johns, explained to the state dairymen in 1905 that his teachers were not preparing girls to become hotel cooks or professional seamstresses, although "qualifications for these may come incidentally. . . ." No, the intent was much broader in scope. Female graduates obtained increased power to solve the perplexing problems involved in managing a home.

> Girls who take the course can calculate the cost of a dinner, and can select the articles with an intelligent appreciation of their food value and are therefore more competent to provide for the table of the home than those not so accomplished.[84]

The work of the county's home demonstration agent had much the same purpose. Marathon County had its first experience with the office during the First World War. An extension worker, Mary Brady, traveled throughout the region teaching economy measures, particularly how to make the most efficient use of the available food supply. She was so useful that at the end of the war she was re-hired on a permanent basis by the county board, with the state and federal governments assuming part of the expense. During her four and one-half years of service, Brady expanded her mission of improving the farm home by starting a county seat short course for girls and organizing clubs. By the time of her departure for the Milwaukee County Agricultural School, several of the twenty-seven women's clubs active in the county were participating in community service projects.[84] The boys' and girls' clubs she organized did meritorious work in sewing, canning, gardening, and poultry and calf raising.

Her successor, Vangel Russell, more than kept up the level of activity. Additional homemakers' clubs were formed, girls' 4-H clubs grew in number, a county federation was created, and the county seat short course for women became a regular feature of the agent's yearly work. During what was claimed to be a typical month, the energetic agent delivered 28 lectures; gave 22 demonstrations; made 52 home visits; established 15 projects with local leaders for each; and distributed 1,031 bulletins. Traveling 1,283 miles, she came in direct contact with over 1,700 county residents. In her spare time she received 94 office calls and 90 phone calls, held 94 conferences, and wrote 186 personal letters in response to inquiries. Moreover, her Wausau office sent out 528 circular letters and 41 articles for newspapers and magazines. A touching, if slightly macabre, indication of her popularity occurred when a farmer entered her office one day requesting that she accompany him to the train depot. His wife's coffin was waiting there about to be taken home for burial. Explained the man, hat in hand, " 'She thought a heap of you, and I knew it would comfort her to have you look at her before she goes.' " When this remarkable lady moved to Montana, the office was occupied for short periods by first, Jean Feeney, and then by her sister, Ruth Feeney. After both left to pursue extension work in Massachusetts, Edith Bangham continued the efficient tradition of her predecessors. Their efforts earned a national reputation for Marathon County in the home demonstration field. Nellie Kedzie Jones,[86] the State Leader for the University of Wisconsin's Home Economics Extension, noted in 1933 that the U. S. Agriculture Department was watching the work of the county office with 'much approval,' and 'often [cited] its achievements as an example for other states.' Others may have worked diligently on behalf of women's suffrage or in promoting the "New Woman" of the 1920's, but for the overworked farm woman of this period, the home demonstration agent was, in her own way, a valued advocate of her interests.[87]

The Wausau location of the three preceding institutions directs attention to another aspect of Marathon County's agricultural growth: the supportive role played by its major urban center. The interdependence of village and countryside had been established early. Products raised by the county's first farmers brought a higher price in local markets—principally lumber camps and boarding houses— than could be obtained in southern Wisconsin. Yet they were also less expensive than those imported from other agricultural regions.[88] As the county seat began to expand commercially, the farming communities took on added importance. Wausau attorney Marvin Rosenberry bluntly spelled out the relationship in a 1900 open letter to the *Daily Record*:

> At the present little if any county trade comes here from south of Mosinee. Tens of thousands of dollars go every year to the farmers of Eldron, Pike Lake, Knowlton and Bergen and but a very small percentage of it is spent in this city. It goes to Appleton, Oshkosh and Stevens Point. This territory every inch of it belongs legitimately to Wausau and Wausau ought to get it. Many thousands of dollars go to Merrill from the towns of Berlin, Hamburg, Maine and Texas that would come here with proper encouragement and a little enterprise.[89]

The "rich territory" west of Fenwood in Day, Cleveland, Eau Pleine, McMillan, Spencer, Frankfort, Hull, Holton, and Johnson was another lucrative source of trade that Wausau should court more actively.

Despite the critical tone of Rosenberry's observation, Wausau business leaders had long shown an interest in the agricultural development going on around them. Storekeeper August Kickbusch was an early prominent example. His confidence in the young county's agricultural potential had been displayed three years before he chose to make Wausau his permanent home. During his first visit to the region in 1857, he purchased 364 acres of farmland in the Town of Hamburg before returning to Milwaukee. More ambitious demonstrations of faith would follow. In the spring of 1867, Kickbusch returned to his native Pomerania and persuaded 70 peasants and day laborers from Greifenberg and Regenwalde to emigrate to Wisconsin. Although only a portion of this group settled in Marathon County, he and his brother Frederick ultimately would be instrumental in colonizing much of the country west of Wausau. The Kichbusch store on First and Washington streets would be a valued source of provisions and advice for the German pioneers.[90]

August Kickbusch would not be alone in attempting to make Wausau an active partner in Marathon County's agricultural growth. He was joined by other Wausau businessmen in reorganizing the Marathon County Agricultural Society in December, 1866, after more than nine years of relative inactivity.[91] On January 26, 1867, Kickbusch and B. G. Plumer presented to the revitalized association a deed for eighty acres on the village's southwestern limits. The only stipulation with the gift was that the land be used as a site for a fairgrounds. The society's annual fair was initiated on the property in October of the following year and became a showcase for both the county's agricultural products and the latest advances in farm machinery.[92] Individuals from other parts of the county became prominent members of the society in time, but Wausau personalities continued to form a major component of the organization's leadership and to serve as sponsors of its principal event. When many of the fairgrounds' original structures were razed in the early 1920's in conjunction with the transfer of the society's land holdings to the county, the construction of new buildings was made possible in part by the personal contributions of Cyrus Yawkey, D. L. Plumer, and Walter Alexander.[93] Louis Wright, the body's energetic secretary from 1896 to 1906, worked not only to make the fair "second to none," but also to generate publicity for the county's infant dairy industry. The decision by the state dairymen and buttermakers to hold conventions in Wausau came about largely through his efforts. When such conferences were held in the city, convention planners could count on the participation of Wausau business and professional luminaries. At the previously discussed 1905 dairymen's convention, speeches were delivered by W. C. Silverthorn, G. D. Jones, and Neal Brown; and papers on the history of the Clover Belt were presented by John Lamont and Marvin Rosenberry, the latter standing in for the ailing author, John C. Clarke.[94]

Bad weather and the winter harvest season notwithstanding, the disappointing attendance of county farmers at this convention indicated that the city-county alliance was still evolving by the turn of the century. Weak links existed in the chain of interdependence. Marvin Rosenberry tartly noted two soft spots in deploring the small amount of country trade coming to Wausau from certain townships. Many farmers were simply unaware that the county seat had anything to offer them. Indeed, half the residents of the western part of the county "[didn't] know where Wausau was on the map." The blame lay not with the farmers but with Wausau; the city was not adequately advertising its advantages to the rural population. Most important, however, in Rosenberry's view, was the need for "good roads in every direction" to facilitate travel between the rural heartland and the central city. Wausau was not going to grow if the county was "stuck in the mud six months in the year."[59]

The attorney's admonitions were not ignored. Initiatives aimed at increasing rural awareness of Wausau and establishing an improved system of county roads began the twentieth century interaction between the city and its hinterlands. The means employed to achieve the first objective were frequently indirect. Flattery continued to be utilized: addressing the 1911 banquet of the Wausau Merchants' Association, W. H. Mylrea paid "a glowing tribute to the boy from the farm." The agricultural districts, Mylrea emphasized, produced the great men of the nation, individuals who didn't know the meaning of failure.[96] Probably more productive were efforts to have Wausau institutions help the farmer to obtain useful information; thus a reservoir of goodwill for the city and its business establishments was created. For example, the Wausau Advancement Association joined the already crowded fraternity of organizations promoting agricultural settlement. Based on the Rosenberry premise that "Wausau cannot grow unless the country grows along with it," the organization published around 1915 the booster booklet, *Farming in Marathon County, Wisconsin.* After reciting the familiar list of county agricultural assets and presenting testimonials from prosperous farmers in the towns of Texas and Easton, the agent of Wausau business added the clincher: "No resident of Marathon County has ever been lost in a blizzard."[97]

In the summer of 1919, a new publication, *The Marathon County Farm Bureau Journal,* made its debut. Published in cooperation with the Wausau Chamber of Commerce and the Marathon County Bankers' Association,[98] the monthly was devoted to county farm news and expert advice on modernizing farm operations. Yet for twenty-five cents a year the rural subscriber was exposed to much more. Paging through his copy, he could not fail to notice the liberal number of advertisements, many of them full-page, for Wausau business firms. Thus, besides educating the farmer on the desirability of pure bred stock and silos, the magazine also informed him of the latest bargains at Winkleman's Department Store or of the new line of farm machinery at Silverthorn Brothers. With an estimated 4,000 subscribers by early 1920, the *Farm Bureau Journal* (*Bureau* being dropped from the title by the February, 1921 issue) gave Wausau merchants an effective medium of communication to rural consumers. Moreover, as editor Franklin Gritzmacher pointed out, the businessmen's patronage was instrumental in keeping the subscription price low.[99] Local advertisers in the *Wausau Daily Record-Herald* undoubtedly received a similar publicity boost when the paper sought to increase its appeal to the county audience by establishing a special farm section in 1923. Under the supervision of Edward E. Payne, the section had the same explicit purposes as the *Farm Journal*: disseminating county agricultural news and promoting better farming methods. And these aims were competently pursued. On the occasion of the section's tenth anniversary, county and state officials alike praised the *Record-Herald* for its farm coverage.[100] Nonetheless, an increased county readership resulting from the page also meant more potential dollars for those Wausau businesses advertising in the paper. Once again community service and self-interest dovetailed.

But first, the county's farmers had to get to Wausau. And that required adequate transportation, particularly in the form of roads. The organized movement for better roads in Marathon County began to gather momentum in August, 1899, when Wausau businessmen made preparations for hosting the Harvest Home Good Roads Convention. A sense of urgency was introduced at the Court House meeting; B. F. McMillan, warned that Stevens Point was far ahead of Wausau in road building. The Portage County community was presently constructing a macadam road into the southeast corner of Marathon County to tap the trade from Pike Lake. Following pep talks from Neal Brown, R. E. Parcher, and M. A. Hurley, an executive committee was chosen to oversee arrangements for the October affair. Wausauites dominated the group's membership: assisting chairman C. F. Dunbar were R. E. Parcher, John Ringle, Neal Brown, and J. M. Smith. B. F. McMillan and Maine town chairman Ernst Koch were added to provide some measure of county participation.[101]

A carnival atmosphere surrounded the late fall festivities, which featured a road building demonstration on Grand Avenue, from the railroad bridge south. This alone, declared the *Pilot,* "should induce the presence of every farmer in the county."[102] Members of the Wausau business community remained highly visible participants. When it became apparent that there weren't enough men to complete the excavation, supervisors S. M. Quaw, W. B. Scholfield, Frank Kelly, and August Marquardt removed their coats and joined the work crew. By evening sixty-five rods of high quality road had been constructed on the avenue. Concluding the day-long program was the creation of an organization to sustain the enthusiasm generated by the convention. Unanimously chosen to lead the good roads committee were B. F. McMillan, president; R. E. Parcher, vice president; John Ringle, secretary; and Walter Alexander, treasurer. In an attempt to create county-wide commitment for the cause, an additional vice president was elected from each township and incorporated community. Assessing the convention's impact, the *Pilot* contended that even though rainy weather had held down attendance, the event would "go down in history as marking the epoch of good road building in Marathon county."[103] More sobering was Marvin Rosenberry's later comment that progress required something besides "one or two spasms" or "loud talking at road conventions."[104]

Concrete gains would be forthcoming, however, as government became infected with the good roads enthusiasm. The first important step was the enactment by the 1907 state legislature of a pair of county aid highway laws enabling townships to receive matching financial assistance for highway improvement from the county. The lawmakers also began to form a specialized bureaucracy by establishing a highway division in the Wisconsin Geological and Natural History Survey. The department's role was limited to conducting research and giving advice to local officials upon request. Any further state help required a constitutional amendment, since Article VIII, Section 10 of the Wisconsin Constitution forbade state aid for internal improvements. Accordingly, the 1905 and 1907 legislatures passed a joint resolution allowing the state to appropriate money and levy taxes for "the construction or improvement of public highways." The measure was overwhelmingly approved in the 1908 general election,[105] thereby clearing the way for passage of the landmark State Aid Law of 1911. As a capstone for the state program, the 1911 legislature created a State Highway Commission with supervisory powers and authority over all state financed highway construction. On June 27, 1911, Governor Francis McGovern appointed the first such commission, choosing John H. Van Doren of Birnamwood for the sole six-year term.[106]

Marathon County was not oblivious to these developments. State Senator Edward E. Browne, a member of the Good Roads Association, lectured the Men's Club of the Wausau Universalist Church in 1909 on the importance of good road building in the area and on the pending state highway legislation.[107] The availability of state financial aid touched off a flurry of local activity to take advantage of the new law. Townships set about raising their share of money for highway and bridge projects. The county board also displayed increased interest in road building and maintenance. Road machinery was purchased, a plan for a county highway system was drawn up, and a separate highway fund was created. The ultimate expression of this new commitment was the election of R. H. Brown as the county's first highway commissioner.[108]

During the remainder of the decade the revived concern about good roads was especially strong in the Town of Hull. Recognizing that their town had 'the worst roads in the county' as of 1914, the townspeople "got busy" and instituted a plan of systematic road dragging. They approved plans to purchase and build the necessary machinery, and voted to replace the town's fourteen road districts with eight road dragging districts. The price tag on this ambitious program amounted to more than $2,300 in 1918. By 1919, a large tractor and grader had been added to a fleet of fifty steel and wooden drags. Town Chairman Robert Hamilton boasted that "every mile of road" in the town would be graded before the end of the year. A June, 1919 road building demonstration at Cherokee, attended by nearly five hundred county residents, publicized Hull's progress over the previous five years.

In fact, significant strides had been made throughout the county. In a 1923 review of county farm conditions, the *Farm Journal* noted that over 2,200 miles of hard surfaced roads had been "made possible in the last few years by the county board of Marathon County through its tax payers." This system included eight county trunk lines and six state trunk highways. A permanent concrete highway program was also underway, with more than seven miles of concrete laid on the heaviest traveled roads.[109] Much more than "loud talking" had been generated by the good roads movement since the turn of the century.

Not that county taxpayers were always cooperative. The defeat of the 1919 Good Roads Bond Issue represented a striking example of rural independence and a temporary but stunning setback for better roads advocates. Faced with the necessity of raising more money in order to receive increased federal highway aid,[110] the county board unanimously voted in November, 1919, to submit a $4,000,000 bond referendum to the electorate at the end of December. The proposition was intended to help finance construction of 140½ miles of concrete and 125 miles of gravel roads embracing all the major market highways.

A high-powered campaign was quickly launched to sell the plan. At the urging of County Board Chairman Frank Gaetzman and the board's roads and bridges committee, a mass meeting was held at the county court house in late November to elect an organization to direct the publicity blitz. The Marathon County Good Roads Association was subsequently formed, chaired by Wausau investment bond dealer Alfred Zimmerman. Armed with the slogan "Help Pull Marathon County Out of the Mud," the group ran a series of educational ads in the Wausau newspapers, the *Marathon Times,* the *Athens Record,* the *Stratford Journal,* and the *Marathon County Farm Bureau Journal.*[111] The latter two publications conducted spirited campaigns of their own in support of the bond issue. Both were aimed at the county's farmers. The *Farm Bureau Journal's* effort featured published endorsements from leading county citizens and favorable articles from Judge A. H. Reid and State Senator C. B. Bird. Editor Franklin Gritzmacher accompanied Frank Gaetzman and J. D. Christie of Schofield on a "boosting trip" across the county, designed to 'give the [bond] matter all the publicity possible. . . .' In a more subtle vein the magazine noted that "the poor condition of the roads" had prevented many village bankers from attending the recent annual meeting of the county bankers' association in Wausau. The story went on to report the bankers' promise of assistance to the good roads movement in the upcoming election. The Stratford paper editorialized on what passage of the bond issue would mean for the farmer. The resulting system of hard surfaced roads would be a manifold blessing. It would increase the efficiency of his operation, keep his children on the farm, and increase the value of his land.[112]

Virtually no appeal or approach went unused. The good roads association argued that since most farmers owned automobiles, the savings on tires alone would pay for the new cement roads. Meanwhile, the *Stratford Journal* printed test results that showed a team of horses wasted energy hauling on a poor road. Improved roads gave the farmer more time for work and more time for leisure. Even if he didn't live on a road scheduled to be paved, he would benefit: the connecting system of gravel roads made the concrete lines more readily available.[113] The *Record-Herald* even called a temporary truce in its battle against the socialist menace. In the spirit of tripartisanship, the paper printed a pro-bond open letter from the city's new Socialist Assemblyman Herman Marth. The scourge of the Wausau elite now appeared in its principal organ to counsel that "no farmer or laborer in Marathon County should hesitate for a moment to vote for the Good Roads Bond Issue." The modernized roads would "shorten the distance from the farm to the kitchen door." Moreover, fifty-five per cent of the project's cost would "go into the pockets of labor used in constructing the highways."[114] Overall, one theme was constantly stressed to the rural audience. The issuance of bonds represented an economy measure. A vote against the bonding plan was a vote for bad roads and, thus, a heavier tax burden in the long run.

All the arguments were to no avail. The bond issue went down to defeat by slightly more than 1,000 votes. As expected, the measure carried in Wausau with a light turnout blamed for the margin of only 319 votes. However, in a bad omen for Herman Marth, the sixth, seventh, eighth, and ninth "socialist wards" did not follow the lead of their assemblyman, a fact emphasized by the *Athens Record*.[115] In Colby the proposition was supported by a unanimous twenty to nothing vote. Ten of the county's fifteen villages also backed the measure.[116]

But it was a far different story in the townships. There, the bond proposal, to use the *Pilot's* phrase, "remain[ed] fast in the mud." The pro-bond campaign had badly missed the mark with respect to its major target, the county's farmers. The *Stratford Journal's* proselytizing had been effective in the village, where bonding had been approved 128 to 39; in the surrounding Town of Cleveland, however, the plan had been soundly rejected 106 to 7. Only four townships—Day, Elderon, Green Valley, and Ringle—voted in favor of the bond issue, earning praise from the *Record-Herald* for their "commendable public spirit."[117] The Hull vote finished in a tie, reflecting an ambivalence born of local self-reliance. The remaining thirty-seven towns formed a solid wall of opposition. The old dissenters of 1908 were in their familiar places: Berlin (147-4), Easton (94-20), Hamburg (103-8), Maine (103-28), Stettin (110-12), Wausau (88-22), Cassel (55-28), and Rietbrock (84-18). Yet with the exception of Flieth and Spencer, nowhere had the margin of defeat been close. Strong supporters of highway funding in 1908 had now deserted the cause with a passion: Emmet (102-5), Holton (84-9), Texas (108-17).[118]

Election post-mortems were at a loss to explain the defection. The *Record-Herald* registered surprise that towns "which would receive immediate great benefit" from the new highway system "voted almost solidly against the measure. . . ." The *Pilot* thought it "hardly possible that the farmers of Marathon county [were] so set against good roads as to have deliberately voted against the bond issue." The *Athens Record* expressed disappointment, but offered no analysis. Anyone solely dependent on the *Farm Bureau Journal* for news wouldn't even have known the outcome of the election.[119] There were some general observations. The Wausau press blamed the setback on a general low turnout resulting from indifference, and on an insufficient amount of time to educate the public. In any case, concluded the *Record-Herald,* "it is certain that in some localities matters entirely foreign to the issue were allowed to influence a considerable number of voters."[120]

There was more to it than that. Having been recently pressured into conformity with superpatriotism, those of German descent were unwilling to have anything else supported by the county power structure forced upon them. The normally outspoken editor of the *Marathon Times,* Frank Leuschen, had remained editorially silent on the bond issue—a reliable barometer of that resistance. A war-related fatigue characterized much of the rural community. County farmers had a healthy suspicion of Wausau-inspired indebtedness dating back to the Wisconsin Central bonds dispute of the early 1870's.[121] The immediate postwar period was not a propitious time to try to overcome that reluctance. A general weariness with financial sacrifices had undoubtedly set in. Inundated by war bond drives, they were in no mood to give again.

The road bond defeat also may have been an indication that farmers were beginning to feel uneasy about their financial well-being. From a 1919 peak their gross income would drop more than a third within the next few years.[122] The *Farm Bureau Journal* was reporting in the late summer of 1920 that "Not in years has there prevailed among the farmers of Marathon county such a feeling of discouragement over the dairy situation as at the present time." This sentiment was echoed by County Agent Swoboda before the Marathon County Bankers' Association. The disparity between dairy prices and high feed, labor, and equipment costs had even the best farmers talking of selling off or substantially reducing their herds. By November, the situation had so deteriorated that a planned pep talk at the Wausau Grain Show from an incurable optimist like Dean Harry L. Russell of the University College of Agriculture featured a call for belt tightening and avoidance of "unnecessary expenditure."[123] A $3,000,000 bond issue was approved by county voters later in the 1920's,[124] but the lesson of 1919 was clear. Despite Wausau's commercial importance, agriculture alone was capable of dictating the speed and scope of the region's development.

If further confirmation of agriculture's standing in the county economy was required, it came from the lumber industry itself. The county's pioneer lumbermen had, of course, initially believed the region to be unfit for farming. But as their need for provisions grew, they began to encourage the practice. Some even started their own limited agricultural operations. James Moore grew potatoes on the islands of the Wisconsin River in 1845, while John LeMessurier made a primitive start at dairying by bringing three cows from Portage to Wausau. Abraham Brawley cleared a farm at Cemetery Hill in 1847. Benjamin Single did the same in 1848 on the eventual site of the State Trial Orchard. Joel Briggs followed suit across the river from Brokaw; this land was still under cultivation at the turn of the century. Joseph Dessert purchased a farm near Marathon City in 1850. It was a group of sawmill mechanics and millwrights that made the first attempt at starting a farming community in the county. Established along a hardwood ridge extending from Wausau seven miles northeast to Nutterville, the "Mechanics' Ridge" settlement proved short-lived. The farming was difficult, and most of the inhabitants had sold their plots by the mid-1850's, when the first trickle of German immigration caused land values to rise. Nonetheless, the community foreshadowed the close bond that would form between lumberman and farmer.[125]

As permanent agricultural settlements were established during the latter half of the nineteenth century, the immigrant farmer found an important source of financial support in the expanding lumber industry. The camps provided a ready market for his produce and gave him winter work. Timber cleared from the farm also became a marketable resource, particularly after the arrival of the railroads. This wood was in demand for a variety of items: railroad ties, tan bark, shingles, posts, staves and heading, spoke and hub timber, and fuel. Cordwood, bark, logs, and maple sugar could be bartered in the lumbertowns. In fact, it was not unusual for the farmer's woodlot to bring in more income than his crops and livestock. With almost every log worth some compensation, the farmer was, in effect, rewarded for clearing his property. As a result, clearings grew in size, and agriculture advanced accordingly. This profitable arrangement continued in the new century. Progress reports in the *American Lumberman* typically noted the significant contributions made by neighboring farmers to a mill's supply of hemlock and hardwood. The Wausau Advancement Association and the *Farm Journal* emphasized the woodlot's value to prospective and established farmers alike. By the early 1920's, mixed wood was worth between eleven and twelve dollars a cord on the open market at Wausau. Farm-manufactured maple syrup sold from $2.50 a gallon upwards in Wausau and nearly all the villages. During the Great Depression, rural residents with wood for sale had an important economic safety valve.[126]

The relationship reached its ultimate expression, however, in the personal involvement of many lumbermen in agricultural pursuits. What emerged was a class of gentlemen farmers: businessmen who encouraged the adoption of scientific agricultural practices through the example of their model farms. Notwithstanding earlier cases of lumbering interest in farming, the true pioneer in this field was Robert Parcher. From the time of his arrival in Marathon County in the late 1850's, Parcher was involved in the interaction between farm and forest. His general store in Wausau rivaled the Kickbusch establishment in popularity with the German settlers. Hay, peas, barley, and wheat were taken in exchange for groceries and flour and then resold to the local lumber camps. The mercantile years were an educational experience for the Vermont native. Listening to the immigrants' tales of hardship, he gained an appreciation of the need for new and improved farming methods, something the conservative German farmers approached with hesitation. Thus, when Parcher added farm management to his numerous business interests, he was receptive to the principles of scientific agriculture. Crop cultivation, in particular, fascinated him. Raising his own corn seed, he had a better than twenty-year record of success with the crop. By 1902, he was devoting at least twelve acres to the flint and yellow dent varieties. At the 1893 Chicago Columbian Exposition, Parcher may have upstaged "Little Egypt" temporarily by receiving awards for his exhibits of peas and Japanese buckwheat. By the time of his death in 1907, his two farms in the northern part of the city were praised as "the best stocked in the county" in terms of farm machinery.[127]

In one major area Parcher was not an advocate of innovation; for unexplained reasons, he never became interested in the raising of "fancy stock." That distinction would fall to others. B. G. Plumer made one of the first attempts at cattle improvement by importing a Durham bull in 1860. Samuel Quaw started to upgrade sheep in 1873. By the turn of the century a concerted effort was under way to improve the quality of county farm animals. Farmer-lumbermen were among the leaders of the movement. Having spared no expense in equipping their barns or in bettering their herds, they presented their livestock as models to be imitated. Exhibits at the county fair were designed to instill envy in the "farmer boy," thereby generating a commitment to improve his own livestock. The potential sources of that envy were numerous. As of 1903, Walter Alexander owned the only herd of Aberdeen Angus cattle in Marathon County. Robert Freeman of

Emmet made an impressive entry into the field of Shorthorn breeding by purchasing a bull and two imported heifers at a total cost of $950. The 1909 Lincoln County Fair included exhibits of Angus and Guernsey cattle raised by B. F. Wilson and one of Shorthorn cattle from Samuel Quaw. The most popular breed of cattle, however, was the Red Poll variety. Jacob Slimmer had the greatest number of registered animals in the county. C. S. Curtis kept the heaviest bull on his farm at Taegesville. After buying Jacob Slimmer's aging bull, John Manser began raising a herd at Kelly. Adding diversity to the lumbermen's stock breeding were Jacob Slimmer's Berkshire pigs, Samuel Quaw's and B. F. Wilson's Shropshire sheep, and C. S. Curtis's draft stallion. B. F. McMillan raised horses as well as cattle on the two hundred-acre farm surrounding his home.[128]

Yet the undisputed leader of this group had to be Frederick Rietbrock. A part of the lawyer-turned-lumberman had never really left the Kenosha County family farm. He had enjoyed his share of professional success in Milwaukee, he averred late in his life, but his experiences on the farm had been the most spiritually satisfying. But farming was far more than a hobby for the Athens patriarch. After turning over direction of the lumber business to his son-in-law in 1896, Rietbrock devoted the remaining years of his life to becoming the leading agriculturalist in the four surrounding townships. Agriculturalist, not farmer: the distinction was important in Rietbrock's mind. 'The difference,' he was fond of explaining, '. . . is that the farmer takes money out of the land and the agriculturalist puts it in.'[129] The description would have been at best ironic for almost any other lumberman, but not for him. Securing immigrant settlers was only the beginning of Rietbrock's interest in developing agriculture in northwestern Marathon County. His ego, if not his conscience, would not permit it to be otherwise.[130]

The remark also had more figurative truth to it than he perhaps intended. Among his contributions, Rietbrock gave the farmers of his region "an object lesson in the use and care of manure." Because the rich soil in the western part of the county had initially needed little fertilizer, proper care of the soil had been lax. Some farmers even built their barns close to streams to facilitate the disposal of animal wastes. Those who did use this resource upon their fields failed to do so to maximum advantage. The farmer-lumbermen, for their part, generally considered the droppings in their stables a nuisance. Such was not the case in Athens, where Rietbrock built a track and carrier to transport the manure from his stables to a special

Gesicki Saloon and Store, Poniatowski, 1924

shed with a cement floor. There it was stored until needed. In what would be a long effort to encourage the use of fertilizers in Marathon County, Frederick Rietbrock was among the first.[131]

The founder of Athens was equally dedicated to livestock productivity. Shorthorn cattle, Shropshire sheep, and Berkshire pigs were all bred on his forty-acre Helendale Farm (named after his wife). But the breeding of dairy cattle was his special pride and joy. Through his association with Wisconsin dairying leaders like William Dempster Hoard, Charles L. Hill, and A. J. Phillips, Rietbrock made Helendale Farm the home of one of the best Guernsey herds in the state.[132] His great herd bull, Guydette, was reputed to be "one of the finest Guernsey bulls in the west." It was the crowning achievement of his final years that his prize cow, Yeksa Sunbeam, brought nationwide attention to Marathon County in 1905 by breaking the world's record for the production of butterfat.[133]

Important as these contributions were, Rietbrock aspired to an even higher place in the agricultural history of northern Wisconsin. That same combination of genuine concern and sense of self-importance could no more be satisfied with being remembered only as an exemplary agriculturalist than as a land settlement promoter. Consistent with his paternalistic nature, he sought to structure the region's agricultural growth. This desire meant displays of personal generosity.

His purebred Guernsey bulls were loaned to farmers wishing to improve their own herds. It also meant serving as a teacher, either personally, or through the institutions led by him and his family. Visitors at cattle shows often saw the stocky man with a long white beard pointing out the good and bad features of an animal with his imported European cane. At the 1905 state dairymen's convention, Rietbrock was always ready to offer his views on dairy farming in the Cutover. At his direction Helendale Farm became an educational center for the surrounding farming community; years after his death it was attracting dairy enthusiasts from all over the nation. From the outset the *Athens Record* devoted a sizable amount of space to solving farm problems. Included among its eight pages were summaries of bulletins issued by the University of Wisconsin College of Agriculture.[134]

Finally, this ambition meant the creation of new institutions. At its inaugural meeting the Athens Advancement Association adopted a proposal to hold monthly village market days. The event's immediate success precipitated the establishment of an annual fair designed to attract the rural population from a radius of thirty miles. By the early 1920's, the three-day festival had become a fixture of farm life in western Marathon County. And the farm dollars drawn to both the market days and the fair made Athens a gadfly competitor of Wausau for the coveted farm trade west of Fenwood. A second association action taken under the leadership of the Rietbrock family had even greater significance for long-term agricultural progress. In July, 1905, a young graduate of the Wisconsin College of Agriculture, D. O. Thompson, was hired to conduct a community milk testing program. Originally designed to spur the breeding of better dairy cattle, the itinerant "cow meetings" came to include lectures on crop raising, the feeding of dairy stock, and other farm improvement topics. With infusions of financial aid and moral support, the Rietbrock family was responsible, in the opinion of many agricultural historians, for launching the forerunner of county agent work in the United States.[135] Part of the Rietbrock legacy thus extended farther than even the man himself might have imagined.

That legacy also symbolized the county's passage into a new economic era of diversification, both industrial and agricultural. The possibility of that transformation, particularly the agricultural aspect, had seemed remote to many Wisconsin pulse-takers as late as 1890. Inhabitants of the southern part of the state had traditionally regarded northern Wisconsin as a forested frontier region, one in which scat-

Farm Homestead, South of Milan, 1912

tered lumber camps and mill towns were the only signs of civilization. But a variety of determined promotional groups and immigrant settlers had labored to give the country an agricultural character, as timber supplies dwindled. After examining the Fourteenth Census, the *Wisconsin Magazine of History* editorialized in the early 1920's that their efforts were bearing fruit. As of 1920, the twenty-nine counties of the New North had more inhabitants than either of the Dakotas or any of the Rocky Mountain states except Colorado. Its rural population had grown by more than 140,000 in twenty years, while that of southern Wisconsin had remained relatively constant. An agricultural colonization movement had unfolded in the pineries rivaling the earlier migrations to the western prairies.[136]

That assessment was overly generous. Other statistics, particularly the percentage of improved or cultivated land, indicated a less enviable record for promoters of agricultural settlement in northern Wisconsin. Twenty of the Cutover counties had less than fifty per cent of their land in farms by 1920. Only on the southern fringe— in Polk, Barron, Chippewa, Clark, Marathon, and Shawano counties— had significant progress been made in agricultural development. And among that group, Marathon County was a decisive leader, in both the number of farms and crop land acreage. The latter had grown from 41,315 acres in 1880 to 242,357 acres by 1920. Moreover, Marathon County was acclaimed as having the largest rural population of any county in the state. A successful transition from lumbering to agriculture had been accomplished, aided, in part, by the lumbermen themselves.[137] Anyone doubting the prevailing trend had only to view the 240 acre farm owned by the Brooks & Ross Lumber Company adjacent to its plant. But there was little time for smugness or self-congratulation. The sharp decline in agricultural prices that had accompanied the beginning of the decade had to be contended with. Recovery for all of northern Wisconsin agriculture would be "slow, uneven, and incomplete."[138] And, as the county was destined to discover, economic diversity was not an absolute guarantee of stability.

FOOTNOTES

[1] Carstensen, *Farms or Forests*, p. 5.

David Katcher, "The Rural Region," *History of Wausau* (Wausau: Centennial Project, 1939), p, 76.

[2] Colby silt loam occupied three-quarters of the towns of Berlin, Bern, Brighton, Easton, Eau Pleine, Frankfort, Halsey, Hamburg, Hewitt, Holton, Hull, Johnson, McMillan, Rietbrock, Spencer, Texas, Wausau, and Wien. This soil type covered forty-seven per cent of the county's total area.

[3] Helgeson, "Athens, Wisconsin," pp. 9, 17.

Katcher, "The Rural Region," pp. 74-75.

Wisconsin State Department of Agriculture, *Marathon County Agriculture*, Wisconsin Crop Reporting Service Bulletin (Madison: State of Wisconsin, 1946), pp. 15-16.

Wausau Daily Record-Herald, August 28, 1909, p. 5.

[4] Carstensen, *Farms or Forests*, p. 6.

[5] Gregory, *West Central Wisconsin*, vol. 2, p. 500.

[6] Marathon County aside, this skepticism turned out not to be totally unfounded. Forty-six years after Ellis's observation, Filbert Roth estimated that nearly forty per cent of the land in his study area was "either not at all suited to farming or only doubtfully so and should by all means be left to forest." See Roth, *Forestry Conditions*, p. 5. Albert Ellis was perhaps the first of many to be overly optimistic about the agricultural potential of all of northern Wisconsin. See Arlan Helgeson, *Farms In The Cutover, Agricultural Settlement in Northern Wisconsin* (Madison: The State Historical Society of Wisconsin, 1962).

[7] *Wausau Pilot*, August 26, 1926, p. 3.

Kate Everest Levi, "Geographical Origins of German Immigration to Wisconsin," *Collections Of The State Historical Society of Wisconsin*, vol. 14, (Madison: Democrat Printing Company, 1898), pp. 358-359.

[8] D. G. Marshall, "Cultural Background of Wisconsin People (Nationality Background)," (maps located in the Archives of the State Historical Society).

[9] *Wausau Pilot*, August 26, 1926, p. 3.

Levi, "Geographical Origins," p. 359.

Helgesen, "Athens, Wisconsin," pp. 22 23.

Albert Bernhardt Faust, *The German Element in the United States*, vol. 1 (New York: The Steuben Society of America, 1927), pp. 473-480.

[10] Levi, Geographical Origins," pp. 392-393.

Katcher, "The Rural Region," pp. 78-79.

Wausau Pilot, August 26, 1926, pp. 3, 8.

Straub, *Marathon, Wisconsin,* pp. 9-10.

[11] Levi, "Geographical Origins," p. 360.

Helgeson, "Athens, Wisconsin," p. 21.

The Rietbrock lands also attracted a large number of Germans from the southern Wisconsin counties around Milwaukee, usually the sons of immigrant farmers.

[12] Kate Asaphine Everest, "How Wisconsin Came By Its Large German Element," *Collections Of The State Historical Society Of Wisconsin,* vol. 12 (Madison: Democrat Printing Company, 1892), pp. 329-333.

Levi, "Geographical Origins," pp. 359-360.

Faust, *The German Element,* vol. 1, pp. 473-480.

Katcher, "The Rural Region," p. 88.

Helgeson, "Athens, Wisconsin," pp. 21-22.

Census data obtained from the Legislative Reference Bureau, Madison.

These figures should be placed in perspective. According to the 1870 United States Census, eighty-two per cent of the county's foreign-born residents were German. This figure dropped to seventy-three per cent in 1880, and then rose slightly to seventy-four per cent in 1890. The 1905 Wisconsin Census revealed that sixty-seven per cent of the county's foreign-born were of German origin. By that year all of the foreign-born constituted only twenty-five per cent of the county's total population. See *Marathon County Agriculture,* p. 2.

[13] The other three were Milwaukee, Shawano, and Portage counties.

Edmund G. Olszyk, *The Polish Press In America* (Milwaukee: Marquette University Press, 1940), pp. 1-3.

Dolores Marzynski, "Cassel," pp. 2-3 (manuscripts in Marathon County Historical Society).

Helgeson, "Athens, Wisconsin," pp. 18-19.

Katcher, "The Rural Region," p. 85.

Charles N. Glaab, Lawrence H. Larsen, *Factories in the Valley, Neenah-Menasha, 1870-1915* (Madison: The State Historical Society of Wisconsin, 1969), p. 202.

[14] Marshall, "Cultural Background."

"Two Centuries," Special Bicentennial Section of the Milwaukee *Journal,* July 4, 1976, pp. 33-34.

Another Norwegian enclave would surface in the northeastern section of the county: roughly in the area comprising the southeast corner of Hewitt, the northeast corner of Easton, the northwest corner of Plover, and the southwest corner of Harrison.

[15] *Wausau Pilot,* July 28, 1927, p. 3.

"History of the Town of Emmet," (manuscript in the Marathon County Historical Society).

[16] *Mosinee Times,* August 8, 1957, p. 9.

[17] "Ethnic Groups, Bohemians," (written observations by Loddie Loskot in the Marathon County Historical Society).

Interview with Clarence Rankl, August 4, 1975.

[18] Wisconsin State Department of Agriculture, *Marathon County Agriculture,* Wisconsin Crop Reporting Service Bulletin (Madison: State of Wisconsin, 1954), pp. 13, 20.

Seventy-one per cent of Marathon County's population was listed as rural in 1900.

[19] Thorpe, "Easton," pp. 19, 23, 25, 35, 49-50, 53.

"Schoepke's Autobiography," pp. 1-3.

"The William Roder Family of S. Milan," Milan packet, p. 1.

Prahl, "Town of Wausau," p. 1.

Interview with Mrs. Louis Karlen, August 20, 1975, Marathon County Public Library Oral History Collection.

"Rings In The Woods, A History of Township of Frankfort," (manuscript in the Marathon County Historical Society), pp. 8-9.

[20] *Wausau Pilot,* August 18, 1903, p. 1.

[21] *Wausau Pilot,* May 19, 1903, p. 1.

Helgeson, *Farms,* p. 70.

[22] Helgeson, *Farms,* p. 71.

Marathon Times, March 8, 1912, p. 1.

[23] *Wausau Daily Record*, March 15, 1905, p. 3.

[24] *Marshfield Herald*, January 13, 1912, p. 1.

Marathon County agricultural lands (specifically those owned by B. F. McMillan) had received an important endorsement in July, 1904 from Frank J. Grutza, secretary of the Polish National Alliance. After inspecting Marathon, Taylor, and Price counties, Grutza reported that "the land in Marathon county is as good for farming purposes as any in the state. While the Marathon land is the most expensive, I was better pleased with it than that of the other counties." Grutza added that he had received more than one hundred letters from prospective immigrants and expected to locate fifty settlers in the county within the next two months. See *Wausau Pilot*, July 26, 1904, p. 1.

[25] *Marathon Times*, February 9, 1912, p. 1.

[26] Casimir Orzechowski, "Short History of Peplin," Casimir Orzechowski Collection, Marathon County Historical Society.
Mosinee Times, August 8, 1957, p. 3B.
Interview with Mrs. Conrad Sitko, August 15, 1975.

[27] Casimir Orzechowski, "Autobiography," p. 9, Casimir Orzechowski Collection.

[28] Mrs. Conrad Sitko Interview.

[29] Casimir Orzechowski was one of the most energetic rural personalities in Marathon County's twentieth century history. In addition to his other teaching responsibilities, he organized the Pioneer 4-H Club in 1921 with the aid of Walter von Berg and Wakelin McNeil to teach area children better farming methods. This club, the first in Marathon County and the second in Wisconsin, went on to receive national recognition, with Orzechowski serving as its leader for thirty years. An avid student as well as teacher, he held the county record for taking the greatest number of correspondence courses. Education was only one of his many avocations. He helped form the Peplin Co-operative Association in 1922, and led the organization until its dissolution in 1947. He was also a licensed chiropractor and ran unsuccessfully for the state assembly six times. At the time of his death in 1975, at age eighty-three, he was serving as honorary chairman of the Mosinee Area Bicentennial Committee. Shortly after his death, he was eulogized in a letter to the *Mosinee Times* by Jan Boharewicz, the president of the Polish-American Association of Wisconsin: "He was beloved in the Mosinee district and far away. He was called with affection 'The Teacher', and he was a great teacher, teaching loyalty to his country and devotion to the Polish Heritage." For more information on this remarkable individual, see the Casimir Orzechowski Collection, Marathon County Historical Society; *Wausau-Merrill Daily Herald*, May 30, 1975, Focus Section, p. 10; *Mosinee Times*, August 14, 1975, p. 14.

[30] *Wausau Pilot*, July 19, 1904, p. 4.

[31] Interview with Wilhelmina Geurink, May 14, 1975, Marathon County Public Library Oral History Collection.

[32] The county's urban population (restricted by definition to that of Wausau) showed a slightly greater increase of fifty-one per cent. Several of the county's villages were also incorporated during this period: Athens in 1901, Spencer in 1902, Brokaw and Unity in 1903, Schofield and Fenwood in 1904, Stratford in 1910, Hatley in 1912, and Rothschild in 1917.

[33] The new town was authorized by a twenty-seven to sixteen vote of the county board on January 6, 1905. Comprising the twenty-eight sections of Weston lying west of the Wisconsin River, it was originally named after Weston Town Chairman George Erickson, who had introduced the resolution dividing the township. According to the *Daily Record*, the board's action "was not secured without a struggle." District Attorney F. E. Bump filed an opinion at the time that the new town couldn't legally be set off. The board's action was allowed to stand, but the town's name was subsequently changed to Flieth. In 1930 it was given its present name of Rib Mountain. See *Wausau Daily Record*, January 6, 1905, p. 3; Della Bopf, *Rib Mountaineer, The Mountain and a Township*, p. 19.

[34] *Marathon County Agriculture*, 1954, pp. 20, 13.
Wisconsin Historical Records Survey Project, *Inventory Of The County Archives of Wisconsin*, no. 37, Marathon County (Madison: Wisconsin Historical Records Survey Project, 1940), pp. 14-15.

Wisconsin Blue Book, 1921, pp. 466-467.

[35] National Land Colonizing Company, *How You Can Get A Wisconsin Farm,* Bulletin 1 (Madison, n.d.), p. 2.

This publication listed nine faculty members of the University of Wisconsin College of Agriculture and State School Superintendent John Callahan as being among the company's sponsors.

[36] National Land Colonizing Company, *Marathon County, Wisconsin, Home of Ready-To-Start Farms,* Bulletin 4 (Madison, n.d.), p. 3.

[37] *Ibid.,* pp. 3, 6.

[38] *Marathon County Farm Journal,* August, 1922, pp. 5, 19; 8-9.

[39] *Marathon County Agriculture,* 1954, p. 20.

Due in part to the Depression's adverse influence on urban employment, the number of county farms reached a record high of 7,039 by 1935. Kronenwetter had the most with 297; followed by Holton with 243. Guenther, with 75, had the fewest. Farm acreage was up 69,403 acres, increasing the county's percentage of land area in farms to 70.7 per cent. In general, those townships in the north-central part of the county had the largest acreage, those on the south-central border, the smallest. Wausau, Hull, and Easton had the highest percentage of land acreage in farms, while Green Valley, Bergen, and Guenther had the lowest. In terms of the average dollar value per farm, Hamburg and Brighton ranked highest, Guenther and Harrison lowest. See Wisconsin State Department of Agriculture, *Marathon County Agriculture,* Wisconsin Crop Reporting Service Bulletin No. 202 (Madison: State of Wisconsin, 1940), pp. 9-11.

[40] According to Marshall's calculations, the Germans and Poles shared dominance in Cassel as of 1905.

[41] Marshall, "Cultural Background."

"Two Centuries," pp. 33-35.

[42] Acreage trends were as follows for crops of:

	Tame Hay	Oats	Barley	Potatoes	Rye	Wheat
1860	1,075	265	4	233	65	330
1870	2,787	2,549	166	228	86	2,760
1880	9,821	7,554	581	1,255	662	7,623
1890	34,619	18,553	912	2,426	2,177	6,851
1900	51,726	31,166	4,797	5,004	6,182	8,125
1910	72,606	38,085	12,244	6,856	3,985	1,878
1920	97,820	55,350	9,980	8,920	6,800	3,865
1930	116,080	66,040	16,630	9,100	2,250	1,540

Marathon County Agriculture, 1954, p. 30.

[43] Corn Acreage was as follows:

1860	98
1870	4
1880	517
1890	709
1900	2,671
1910	3,742
1920	16,410
1930	23,560

Marathon County Agriculture, 1954, p. 30.

[44] *Wausau Pilot,* May 14, 1907, p. 1; August 25, 1903, p. 4; May 7, 1907, p. 1.

Katcher, "The Rural Region," p. 94.

[45] *Marathon Times,* February 4, 1910, p. 1.

[46] *Wausau Pilot,* August 25, 1903, p. 4.

[47] *Wausau Pilot,* August 18, 1903, p. 4; August 25, 1903, pp. 1, 4.

Katcher, "The Rural Region," p. 94.

Helgeson, *Farms,* pp. 69-70.

A few acres of tobacco were harvested in 1930. Only ten acres were devoted to sugar beets in 1935. See *Marathon County Agriculture,* 1940, p. 29a.

[48] Clover and timothy still accounted for most of the county's hay acreage. A record harvest of 131,100 acres was estimated for 1929. By the drought year of 1934, however, clover and timothy acreage had dropped to 25,520 acres. A subsequent

replacement of acreage resulted in an estimated harvest of 117,130 acres in 1937. Alfalfa acreage reached a record total of 7,620 acres that same year.

Marathon County Agriculture, 1940, p. 34.

Katcher, "The Rural Region," p. 102.

Marathon County Farm Journal, July, 1923, p. 16.

[49] Katcher, "The Rural Region," pp. 102-103.

Marathon County Farm Journal, September, 1923, p. 10.

[50] *Wausau Pilot*, November 9, 1909, p. 1.

The Chellis & Sampson operation was located on a three-acre tract on the Wausau city-Town of Flieth dividing line, between Cleveland and Third avenues.

[51] Straub, *Marathon*, p. 54.

Wausau Daily Record-Herald, November 3, 1972, Focus Section, pp. 1-3; October 9, 1965, p. 9; August 31, 1963, p. 1.

The Live Wire, High School Journalism Supplement to the *Wausau Pilot*, May 22, 1924, p. 8.

Marchetti, *Marathon County*, p. 393.

Katherine Pinkerton, *Bright With Silver* (New York: William Sloane Associates, 1953), pp. 12-31, 34, 49, 72-74, 98-99, 104-106, 120-123, 126, 127, 136.

Marathon Times, November 21, 1919, p. 1.

The ginseng market was disrupted first by the Sino-Japanese War and then by World War II. The re-establishment of communication with the Far East reopened the ginseng trade, although the new Communist government in China discouraged its use. By the mid-1960's there were an estimated thirty-six ginseng growers in Marathon County, who were growing around eighty-five per cent of the nation's supply. All but ten per cent of this figure was shipped to the Orient. Fromm Brothers continued to head the list with one hundred acres devoted to the plant. Total American ginseng exports for 1974 were valued at 11.1 million dollars. See *Wall Street Journal*, September 9, 1975, p. 10.

[52] *Wausau Pilot*, March 21, 1911, p. 1.

[53] Katcher, "The Rural Region," p. 80.

Helgeson, "Athens, Wisconsin," pp. 50-51.

Wausau Pilot, August 25, 1903, p. 4.

Marathon Times, January 21, 1916, p. 1.

Marathon County Agriculture, 1940, p. 39.

[54] *Wausau Pilot*, August 18, 1903, p. 1; August 25, 1903, p. 1.

Katcher, "The Rural Region," p. 90.

Marathon County Farm Journal, August, 1922, p. 5.

Marathon County Agriculture, 1946, p. 50; 1954, p. 47.

[55] Helgeson, *Farms*, p. 67.

Marathon County Agriculture, 1954, p. 47.

Wisconsin Blue Book, 1903, p. 253.

[56] *American Sheep Breeder*, August, 1916, pp. 485-486.

Country Gentleman, April 20, 1918, p. 20; April 13, 1918, p. 10.

Breeder's Gazette, January 20, 1916, p. 130.

Marathon County Farm Journal, June, 1919, p. 13; July, 1919, p. 4.

[57] *Marathon County Farm Journal*, March, 1925, p. 4.

[58] *American Sheep Breeder*, April, 1917, p. 213.

Helgeson, *Farms*, p. 68.

Reuel B. Frost, "The Geography Of The Distribution Of Sheep In Wisconsin," (Master's Dissertation, University of Wisconsin, 1928), pp. 1, 17, 40.

Wisconsin Blue Book, 1915, p. 112.

Marathon County Agriculture, 1954, p. 47; 1940, p. 37.

[59] Helgeson, *Farms*, p. 69.

Wausau Pilot, August 25, 1903, p. 1.

Swine, by contrast, was a more consistently popular item. County hog numbers increased from 295 in 1860 to 16,524 in 1900; to 18,079 in 1910; and to 29,600 by 1920. In 1923, the *Marathon County Farm Journal* was reporting that although "market fluctuations cause an increase and decrease in the number of hogs kept on the farm each year . . . the man who is sticking to pork production as an important side line of dairying . . . is making good returns." This was because "the pig next to the dairy cow is the most economical producer of human food." The county's splendid crops of barley and corn also made hog raising a profitable enterprise. See *Marathon County Farm Journal*, September, 1923, p. 12; *Marathon County Agriculture*, 1954, p. 47.

[60] Several factors discouraged wheat farming in Wisconsin. One source of dissatisfaction was the discovery that successive years of planting the crop caused increasing soil depletion. Moreover, the soft winter wheat preferred by millers proved susceptible to winter kill in the severe climate. The appearance of pests, such as the cinch bug, and the plant diseases of smut and rust added a final contribution to declining yields. See Nesbit, *Wisconsin*, pp. 280-283.

[61] Early county settlers also commonly grew rutabagas for cow feed.

Eric E. Lampard, "The Rise Of The Dairy Industry In Wisconsin: A Study of Agricultural Change in the Midwest, 1820-1920," (Ph.D. Dissertation, University of Wisconsin, 1955), p. 180.

Marathon County Agriculture, 1954, p. 5.

Wausau Pilot, August 25, 1903, p. 4.

Katcher, "The Rural Region," pp. 90-91.

Helgeson, "Athens, Wisconsin," p. 62.

[62] *Wausau Pilot*, August 25, 1903, p. 1.

[63] *Ibid.*, p. 4.

[64] Katcher, "The Rural Region," pp. 92-93, 100, 107.

Lampard, "The Rise Of The Dairy Industry," p. 399.

Wausau Pilot, August 25, 1903, p. 1.

Helgeson, "Athens, Wisconsin," p. 49.

Eric E. Lampard, *The Rise Of The Dairy Industry In Wisconsin: A Study in Agricultural Change, 1820-1920* (Madison: The State Historical Society Of Wisconsin, 1963), p. 272.

Creamery butter production increased gradually from 232,450 pounds in 1885 to 1,234,000 pounds in 1909; it then decreased to a low of 406,000 pounds by 1921, followed by a sharp increase to approximately 2,349,000 pounds in 1925. See *Marathon County*, 1940, p. 41.

[65] The factory system of cheese production was inaugurated by a Rome, New York cheesemaker, Jesse Williams, in the spring of 1851.

[66] In 1895 the butter output of the county's five creameries still surpassed the production of its ten cheese factories: 718,075 pounds versus 51,114 pounds. By 1905, the situation had been reversed: cheese factory output measured 1,123,708 pounds while butter creamery production totaled 733,103 pounds. By the 1930's, twelve per cent of the county's farmers, located primarily around Wausau and along the Wisconsin River, were selling their milk to creameries. Cheese factories, by contrast, were taking milk from approximately sixty-four per cent of the county's farms, with the heaviest concentration of producers located in the western part of the county. As the county's cheese production continued to rise, so did its ranking among Wisconsin's other factory cheese counties. Marathon County was not included among the top twelve in 1905; by 1915, its output of 10,580,000 pounds placed it sixth behind Dodge, Sheboygan, Manitowoc, Green, and Clark counties. Four years later, Marathon County's output of 17,811,000 pounds moved it into third place behind only Dodge and Sheboygan counties. See Lampard, "The Rise Of The Dairy Industry," pp. 376, 397, 399; *Marathon County Agriculture*, 1940, p. 13.

[67] Home manufacture of cheese underwent a slight increase during the twentieth century's second decade. Yet, as of 1919, it still represented the negligible quantity of 14,455 pounds. See Katcher, "The Rural Region," p. 107.

[68] The Abbotsford and Northeastern was made a part of the Wisconsin Central system in 1910.

[69] The milk from at least 3,348 cows was required to manufacture this amount of cheese, which was being shipped to all parts of the country and abroad. See *Athens Record*, March 13, 1924, p. 1; Helgeson, "Athens, Wisconsin," pp. 48-49, 62; Katcher, "The Rural Region," p. 100.

[70] By the 1930's, forty per cent of the county's farms were reporting Holsteins; thirty-one per cent, Guernseys; and roughly four per cent, Jerseys, Brown Swiss, and Ayrshires.

Katcher, "The Rural Region," pp. 97-98.

Lampard, *The Rise Of The Dairy Industry,* pp. 170-171.

Marathon County Farm Journal, August, 1922, p. 5.

Marathon County Agriculture, 1940, p. 13.

[71] Katcher, "The Rural Region," pp. 106-107, 109.

Lampard, *The Rise Of The Dairy Industry,* pp. 183-184.

Wausau Daily Record-Herald, Golden Anniversary Edition, August 9, 1922, Section 3, p. 1.

Marathon County Farm Journal, August, 1922, pp. 24-25, 5; August, 1923, p. 14; September, 1923, p. 22.

The cooperative movement touched numerous components of rural economic life. At the turn of the century, half of the county creameries were cooperatives. The Stratford Co-operative Creamery was considered a model of success by 1919 with over sixty patrons. The Athens Cooperative Produce Company evolved from an Equity feed store in 1912. Three years later six Town of Hull farmers purchased carloads of feed for resale. Their Cherokee operation was the forerunner of the Harmony Co-operative Produce Company at Colby. A third such produce association was formed in Elderon. The Farmers Cooperative Packing Company of Wausau was organized in January, 1916. Renamed the Wisconsin Packing Company three years later for public relations purposes, it was by the early 1920's the only successful cooperative packing concern in the United States. Five hundred of the firm's 1,800 farmer-owners were from Marathon County. Cooperative cheese marketing was advocated by the Wisconsin Cheese Producers' Federation to enable the farmer to store and sell his own cheese as market conditions dictated. Locally the organization's goals were explained and promoted by federation field man F. G. Swoboda. The plan received the endorsement of another cooperative booster, the Marathon County Union of the American Society of Equity, at its September, 1921 quarterly convention at Hatley. Thirty-five county cheese factories were marketing their product through the federation by 1923. Forty local Equity societies and twelve stock shipping associations were also operational by this time. In October, 1929 the first state-wide conference to exclusively discuss cooperative marketing and organization was convened in Marshfield. F. G. Swoboda, by then field manager of the National Cheese Producers' Federation, presided over the meeting. See Katcher, "The Rural Region," p. 96; *Stratford Journal,* August 8, 1919, p. 1; Helgeson, "Athens, Wisconsin," pp. 59-60; *Colby,* p. 97; *Marathon County Farm Journal,* November, 1921, pp. 3, 7; September, 1923, p. 1; *Wausau Daily Record-Herald, Golden Anniversary Edition,* August 9, 1922, Section 3, p. 10; *Wausau Pilot,* September 15, 1921, p. 1; October 24, 1929, p. 8. Not every cooperative venture was an unqualified success, however. The Consolidated Farm Company's 2,000 acre cooperative farm in the Town of Spencer qualified as a notable example. In the spring of 1910 a majority of the farm's immigrant stockholders stormed the company's office and severely beat one of its agents, claiming they had been "fleeced" and demanding their money back. See *Wausau Pilot,* May 10, 1910, p. 1.

[72] *Marathon County Agriculture,* 1940, pp. 37, 13.

Katcher, "The Rural Region," pp. 108-109.

Marathon County Farm Journal, August, 1922, p. 5.

[73] *Wausau Daily Record,* October 18, 1904, p. 2; February 8, 1905, p. 5; February 10, 1905, p. 5.

[74] *Wausau Daily Record,* February 9, 1905, p. 5.

[75] *Wausau Daily Record,* February 9, 1905, p. 5.

At the turn of the century Marathon County had only one cow for every three people, while Jefferson County had more than one cow for each person in the county.

[76] *Wausau Daily Record,* February 10, 1905, p. 5.

[77] Katcher, "The Rural Region," p. 95.

In the spring of 1890, Stephen M. Babcock, a staff member of the University of Wisconsin College of Agriculture, developed a simple and inexpensive method of measuring the butterfat content of milk, thereby solving one of dairying's most vexing problems. The innovation provided the dairy industry with an improved method of payment for milk based on quality rather than weight, thus eliminating the profitability of watering milk prior to delivery. Declared one factoryman, 'the

Babcock Test can beat the Bible in making a man honest.' The United States Department of Agriculture estimated in 1900 that the test was saving Wisconsin producers $800,000 annually. See Nesbit, *Wisconsin,* p. 290; Lampard, *The Rise Of The Dairy Industry,* pp. 197-203.

[78] Nesbit, *Wisconsin,* p. 293.

Katcher, "The Rural Region," p. 91.

Marathon Times, January 21, 1916, p. 1; January 8, 1915, p. 1; January 1, 1915, p. 1.

[79] The 1909 course listing for boys included agricultural botany, farm crops, soils, manures and fertilizers, gardening and fruit growing (an orchard was laid out on the school grounds north of Stewart Avenue), breeds of livestock, stock judging, farm poultry, stock feeding, principles of breeding and dairying (milk, butter, cheese). Two lines of shop work—blacksmithing and carpentry—were originally offered. By 1909 freehand and mechanical drawing, rural architecture, and rural engineering had been added.

[80] *Wausau Pilot,* August 25, 1903, p. 4; September 28, 1909, p. 1.

Wausau Daily Record, February 11, 1905, p. 5; February 8, 1905, p. 5.

[81] Wells was succeeded in 1914 by Randall Johnson. D. A. Swartz served as the normal school's third principal from 1921 until his death in August, 1930, after which M. C. Palmer assumed the position.

[82] By the late 1930's, the normal school's enrollment contained students from every high school in Marathon County, as well as several students from neighboring counties.

Wausau Daily Record-Herald, Centennial Edition, March 13, 1939, Commercial Section, p. 34.

Wausau Pilot, September 12, 1899, p. 1.

Marathon County Farm Journal, October, 1922, p. 11.

[83] Some variety was added to the girls' curriculum by instruction in nursing, general architecture, and general drawing. Both boys and girls were offered courses in English composition and literature, arithmetic, bookkeeping, chemistry, history, parliamentary law, elements of vocal music, and literary society.

[84] *Wausau Daily Record,* February 11, 1905, p. 5.

Wausau Pilot, September 28, 1909, p. 1.

[85] For several years the Corinth Women's Club provided the material for school hot lunches. When the school board appropriated money for the program, the club acquired playground equipment for the school. The Marathon Women's Club assisted in the construction of a camping site in the Town Hall Park. Playground equipment and bath houses were later added. The Mosinee organization furnished a rest room in the town hall, and played a major role in securing and equipping a camping site in their community. The group also financed a yearly flower garden and hobby show for the local boys' and girls' club.

[86] Nellie Kedzie Jones was no stranger to Marathon County. From 1911 until 1918 she and her husband (Congregational minister and history professor, Howard Murray Jones) lived on Smoky Hill Farm in the Town of Green Valley. There, from 1912 to 1916, this pioneer in the field of home economics wrote an advice page in *The Country Gentleman* read by farm women all across the country. See Jeanne Hunnicutt Delgado, ed., "Nellie Kedzie Jones's Advice to Farm Women: Letters from Wisconsin, 1912-1916," *Wisconsin Magazine of History* 57 (Autumn, 1973): 3-27.

[87] *Marathon County Farm Journal,* July, 1919, p. 26; August, 1924, p. 15; August, 1922, p. 12.

Wausau Daily Record-Herald, Golden Anniversary Edition, August 9, 1922, Section 3, p. 1; February 14, 1933, p. 8.

[88] The proximity of farms to the new city could be a nuisance, however, In his inaugural address of April 16, 1872, Wausau's first mayor, August Kickbusch, urged the city council to speedily enact ordinances to prevent horses, cattle, and hogs "from running at large in the city limits."

Katcher, "The Rural Region," p. 81.

Wausau Daily Record-Herald, Golden Anniversary Edition, August 9, 1922, Section 2, p. 1.

[89] *Wausau Daily Record,* January 27, 1900, p. 3.

184

[90] August Kickbusch's son, Robert, later claimed that his father's success in securing emigrants caused a furious Bismarck to order him to leave the region and never return. See *Wausau Daily Record-Herald, Golden Anniversary Edition,* August 9, 1922, Section 2, p. 3. See also *Wausau Pilot,* August 18, 1903, p. 4; August 6, 1926, pp. 3, 8; Levi, "Geographical Origins," p. 359. When German farmers were misled by their clergymen about the objectives of the Bennett Law (see Chapter VI), Kickbusch allayed their fears by explaining the legislation's actual intent. See *Milwaukee Sentinel,* January 20, 1890, p. 4.

[91] The Marathon County Agricultural Society was originally founded at Big Bull Falls in 1857. On August 1, thirty-four influential community residents attended a meeting at the Forest House called by Thomas Hinton for the purpose of forming such an association. The local newspaper accounts of the session indicated that all the necessary organizational details were enthusiastically consumated and plans were made to publicly display 'fruits of the soil' exhibits to increase public awareness of the county's agricultural resources. Despite an apparently promising start, research conducted during the 1939 Wausau Centennial turned up no further press records of society activities until the December, 1866 reorganization. See *Wausau Daily Record-Herald, Centennial Edition,* March 13, 1939, Historical Section, p. 2.

[92] The exposition's progress could be measured by the increased premiums. The county board appropriated two hundred dollars for that purpose for the first fair, with a total of $243.50 eventually being spent. By 1929, the premium expenditure had grown to nearly $16,000 before retrenchment had to be undertaken.

[93] A majority of the Marathon County Board initially balked at the transfer arrangement in 1920, fearing that the increased taxes required to carry out the renovations would be too burdensome for rural residents.
Marathon County Farm Journal, May, 1920, p. 26.
Katcher, "The Rural Region," p. 82.
Wausau Daily Record-Herald, Centennial Edition, March 13, 1939, Historical Section, p. 2; *Golden Anniversary Edition,* August 9, 1922, Section 3, p. 1.

[94] Neal Brown, along with A. L. Kreutzer, also addressed the Wisconsin State Horticultural Society when it held its 1900 annual meeting in Wausau. Kreutzer at that time owned the county farm on which the state trial orchard was located.
Wausau Pilot, June 5, 1900, p. 1; June 26, 1900, p. 5; November 2, 1909, p. 5.
Wausau Daily Record, February 8, 1905, p. 5; February 10, 1905, p. 5; February 11, 1905, p. 5.

[95] *Wausau Daily Record,* January 27, 1900, p. 3.

[96] *Wausau Pilot,* February 7, 1911, p. 4.

[97] Wausau Advancement Association, *Farming in Marathon County, Wisconsin.* Th snow storms of north-central Wisconsin could, nevertheless, paralyze the county. See *Marathon Times,* February 2, 1917, p. 1. The association's further contention that grasshoppers never destroy Marathon County crops would be demolished in the early 1930's (see Chapter IV).

[98] Since its founding in 1914, the bankers' association had made county agricultural progress an area of special interest. The group lobbied successfully before the county board for the appointment of a county field man. When county corn crops failed in 1915, an association committee purchased seed corn and arranged for its distribution to farmers. At the body's 1915 annual meeting, president Walter W. Oby of Stratford emphatically endorsed diversified farming, crop rotation, and other scientific farming techniques. See *Wausau Daily Record-Herald,* December 16, 1915, pp. 1, 3.

[99] *Marathon County Farm Bureau Journal,* June, 1919, p. 1; February, 1920, p. 3; September, 1919, p. 3.

[100] *Wausau Daily Record-Herald,* February 14, 1933, p. 8.

[101] *Wausau Pilot,* August 8, 1899, p. 1.

[102] *Wausau Pilot,* October 3, 1899, p. 5.

[103] *Wausau Pilot,* October 17, 1899, p. 5.
An ironic but timely reminder of the convention's purpose was provided when a scheduled bicycle parade had to be cancelled due to the muddy condition of the city's roads.

[104] *Wausau Daily Record,* January 27, 1900, p. 3.

[105] The amendment was adopted statewide 116,407 to 46,762, with only a few of the eastern and southeastern counties voting against it. In Marathon County the resolution carried by a mere 323 votes out of 4,491 cast. The Wausau vote was decisive: eight of the city's nine wards voted for the amendment providing a plurality of 435 votes. Outside the county seat nineteen of the thirty-nine townships opposed the change. Traditional German frugality was reflected in the sizable "no" vote in such towns as Berlin (83-17), Easton (108-20), Hamburg (61-41), Maine (70-42), Stettin (87-16), and Wausau (86-30). Townships with a large Polish element were also notable for the strength of their opposition: Cassel defeated the amendment by 121 to 6; Rietbrock by 107 to 9. *Wisconsin Blue Book*, 1909, p. 558; Certified Copy of Statement of Board of Canvassers, County of Marathon, 1908 General Election, Constitutional Amendments, (located in the State Historical Society of Wisconsin).

[106] M. W. Torkelson, "Wisconsin Highways," *Wisconsin Blue Book*, 1931, pp. 9-11.

M. G. Davis, comp., *A History of Wisconsin Highway Development 1835-1945* (Madison: State Highway Commission, 1947), pp. 20-25.

[107] *Wausau Pilot*, October 12, 1909, p. 1. The *Pilot* encouraged the use of disintegrated granite, rather than macadam, for road construction in the countryside. See *Wausau Pilot*, May 19, 1914, p. 5.

The *Mosinee Times* joined the mounting good roads agitation in 1911 by urging immediate construction of a new highway from the Marathon City road west of Mosinee to Wausau. Such a route would give farmers in Emmet, Mosinee, Bergen and Day a "more direct outlet" to the county seat. See *Wausau Pilot*, February 28, 1911, p. 1.

[108] Calvin Cook, comp., "Summary of Marathon County Board Proceedings, November 14, 1911-April 24, 1912," (located in the Marathon County Historical Society.)

[109] *Marathon County Farm Bureau Journal*, July, 1919, pp. 4, 26.
Marathon County Farm Journal, September, 1923, p. 10.

[110] See Torkelson, "Wisconsin Highways," pp. 12-14.

[111] *Marathon Times*, November 21, 1919, p. 1; December 19, 1919, p. 8; December 25, 1919, p. 8.
Marchetti, *Marathon County*, p. 936.
Wausau Pilot, December 30, 1919, pp. 1, 4.
Athens Record, December 18, 1919, p. 10; December 25, 1919, p. 4.
Marathon County Farm Bureau Journal, December, 1919, p. 27; January, 1920, pp. 9, 27-29.

[112] *Marathon County Farm Bureau Journal*, December, 1919, pp. 3, 31; January, 1920, pp. 3, 22.
Marathon Times, November 28, 1919, p. 1.
Stratford Journal, December 5, 1919, p. 1.

[113] *Marathon Times*, December 25, 1919, p. 8.
Stratford Journal, December 12, 1919, p. 1.

[114] *Wausau Daily Record-Herald*, December 26, 1919, p. 3.

[115] *Wausau Pilot*, January 6, 1920, p. 4.
Athens Record, January 1, 1920, p. 1.
For a detailed account of the rise and fall of socialism in Marathon County, see Chapter VI.

[116] Abbotsford, Athens, Brokaw, Edgar, Elderon, Marathon City, McMillan, Mosinee, Rothschild and Stratford voted in favor of bonds; Fenwood, Hatley, Spencer, Schofield, and Unity opposed the measure. The Schofield result was attributed to the village already having paid for concrete roads put in by the county. *Athens Record*, January 1, 1920, p. 1.

[117] *Wausau Daily Record-Herald*, December 31, 1919, p. 1.

[118] *Wausau Pilot*, January 6, 1920, p. 4.
Wausau Daily Record-Herald, January 3, 1920, p. 1.

[119] *Wausau Daily-Record-Herald*, December 31, 1919, p. 1.
Wausau Pilot, January 6, 1920, p. 4.
Athens Record, January 1, 1920, p. 1.

[120] *Wausau Daily Record-Herald*, December 31, 1919, p. 1.

186

[121] See Marchetti, *Marathon County*, pp. 154-156.
[122] Katcher, "The Rural Region," p. 105.
[123] *Marathon County Farm Bureau Journal*, September, 1920, p. 3; November, 1920, p. 7; December, 1920, pp. 5, 31-32.
[124] Davis, *Wisconsin Highway Development*, p. 132.
[125] *Wausau Pilot*, August 18, 1903, p. 4.
Thayer, "Observations," p. 9.
Katcher, "The Rural Region," pp. 77-78.
Marchetti, *Marathon County*, pp. 94-95.
Wausau Daily Record-Herald, April 20, 1959, p. 2.
[126] *Marathon County Agriculture*, 1954, p. 5.
Katcher, "The Rural Region," pp. 87, 89.
Helgeson, "Athens, Wisconsin," pp. 35-36.
Thorpe, "Easton," pp. 37, 40, 49.
"Schoepke's Autobiography," p. 3.
American Lumberman, January 20, 1900, p. 21; January 10, 1903, p. 38; January 13, 1906, p. 49.
Wausau Advancement Association, *Farming*, pp. 25, 27.
Marathon County Farm Bureau Journal, November, 1919, p. 12; March, 1920, p. 3.
Marathon County Farm Journal, September, 1923, p. 14.
Interview with Clarence Mielke, August 22, 1975, Marathon County Public Library Oral History Collection.
Farmer and lumberman also faced the common danger of forest fire. In the spring of 1915, a severe blaze swept through the towns of Marathon, Mosinee, and Flieth, destroying not only the lumber camps of the John Weeks Lumber Company, but also twenty-five head of cattle recently purchased by Fred Prehn. *Marathon Times*, April 30, 1915, p. 1. Fires later threatened agricultural operations in the Town of Green Valley. See Howard Murray Jones to Brothers and Sisters, October 10, 1920, Howard Murray Jones Papers, State Historical Society.
[127] Besides machinery in general use, Parcher owned a threshing machine, engine, and hay press. His farms were situated on both sides of the Wisconsin River. The partially cleared eastern location was sold in late 1906 to be used as the site for St. Mary's Hospital. The completely cleared western spread, which at one time included a fish pond, was disposed of the summer before his death.
Wausau Pilot, August 18, 1903, p. 4; December 10, 1907, p. 5.
Katcher, "The Rural Region," p. 95.
[128] Katcher, "The Rural Region," pp. 81-82.
Wausau Pilot, August 25, 1903, p. 1.
Central Wisconsin, August 28, 1909, p. 5.
Marshfield Herald, January 20, 1912, p. 1.
In addition to using his oratorical skills on behalf of hemlock lumbering and good roads, B. F. McMillan served as a zealous missionary for the agricultural potential of northern Wisconsin. Speaking extemporaneously before the 1912 Chicago Land Show, the retired lumberman conceded that he owned land in Louisiana, California, British Columbia, and Saskatchewan. Moreover, all were good investments. However, he then went on to deliver an enthusiastic pitch for settlement in upper Wisconsin. See *Marshfield Herald*, January 20, 1912, p. 1.
[129] Helgeson, "Athens, Wisconsin," p. 38.
Wausau Daily Record, February 8, 1905, p. 5.
[130] A manifestation of the Rietbrock ego was the picture of himself that hung in many a settler's cabin. The portrait was a gift bestowed with each land contract.
[131] *Wausau Pilot*, August 25, 1903, p. 1.
Helgeson, "Athens, Wisconsin," pp. 38, 44, 70.
Katcher, "The Rural Region," p. 103.
The habit of taking the soil's fertility for granted, once implanted, proved difficult to break. After conducting his own investigation, a local expert concluded that as of 1903 not one pound of commercial fertilizer had ever been used in Marathon County. Education was deemed the solution, Thus, the new county agricultural school began what was believed to be a pioneering program of experimentation with commercial fertilizers in its gardens. The University of Wis-

consin Extension Service, the county agent's office, and the *Farm Journal* later joined the propaganda campaign for proper fertilization. Yet as late as 1928, records of the Athens Cooperative Produce Company indicated that it was difficult to dispose of a single carload of fertilizer.

[132] A. J. Phillips sold Rietbrock his first Guernseys. William Dempster Hoard would deliver one of the eulogies at Rietbrock's funeral; Charles H. Hill would serve as an honorary pallbearer.

[133] *Wausau Pilot,* August 25, 1903, p. 1.

Helgeson, "Athens, Wisconsin," p. 39.

Helgeson, *Farms,* pp. 7-8.

Athens Record, August 2, 1906, p. 1.

Wausau Daily Record, July 23, 1906, p. 5.

[134] Rietbrock, like most devoted teachers, was also an avid student, intently gathering information at meetings of the University of Wisconsin Short Course on agriculture.

[135] Helgeson, "Athens, Wisconsin," pp. 39-40, 51-54.

Wausau Daily Record, February 8, 1905, p. 5; February 10, 1905, p. 5.

Athens Record, February 9, 1905, p. 1.

Helgeson, *Farms,* p. 7.

Rietbrock's presence at early demonstration meetings was an important factor in selling the novel program to the settlers. D. O. Thompson went on to become editor of the *Athens Record* in 1906, and subsequently expanded the newspaper's role as a source of information for farmers.

[136] *Wisconsin Magazine of History,* 6 (1922-1923): 104-106.

[137] Area lumbermen also became involved in the organization and management of agriculture-related industries. The Rietbrock family controlled the Ceres Roller (flour) Mills, incorporated in 1892, and the Athens (pea) Canning Company, organized in 1923. The former operation was acquired by the Athens Cooperative Produce Company in 1920. The Wausau Canning Company was incorporated around 1902 by Fowler P. Stone and Robert E. Parcher. Walter Alexander and E. A. Gooding also served on the board of directors. See Helgeson, "Athens, Wisconsin," pp. 27, 30, 59-60; Fred A. Stare, *The Story Of Wisconsin's Great Canning Industry* (Madison: The Wisconsin Canner Association, 1949), pp. 325-326, 599.

[138] Carstensen, *Farms or Forests,* pp. 91, 130.

Forest Land Use, p. 20.

Helgeson, *Farms,* pp. 112-113.

Wisconsin Magazine of History, 6 (1922-1923): 106.

Wausau Daily Record-Herald, Golden Anniversary Edition, August 9, 1922, Section 4, p. 10.

CHAPTER FOUR

Ruled By Reverses:
The Depression In Marathon
County

Marathon County, like the rest of the country, was preoccupied in the 1930's with the Great Depression. The longest and most severe economic crisis in the nation's history would test the resiliency of the county's economy and challenge the abilities of its people to an extent which surpassed the lumber industry's demise and the birth-pangs of the agricultural sector. It took time, however, for this reality to sink into the public consciousness. No sense of impending doom could be detected in either the country or the county after the first shock wave—the stock market crash of October, 1929. In Wausau, editorial comment was far from pessimistic. There was no suggestion that the events on Wall Street were finally exposing fundamental weaknesses in the prosperous economy of the twenties—industrial over-expansion, a maldistribution of income, a weak banking structure, and an overdependence on consumer durable goods.[1] The *Record-Herald* admitted that "certain nervous persons" were "predicting a nationwide panic because of the present excitement. . . ," but it went on to endorse the view expressed by President Hoover that business condi-tions were generally sound. In fact, the newspaper, like most of the nation's financial community, saw the crash as even having a salutary effect, since it would drive the "amateurs," the "crazy speculators," out of the market "to attend to their own jobs or business or profession 'back home'." Some "rigid economy" might be necessary for a time, but the losses would be slight compared to the gains in sobriety and good sense.[2]

Locally, at least, the optimism seemed justified. A newcomer to Wausau in 1929 would have seen signs of an energetic community, characterized by robust industrial growth. Since July of that year, the D. J. Murray Manufacturing Company had added thirty-five new employees, expected to hire more, and planned to expand its physical plant. It had grossed $600,000 the previous year and had paid $250,000 to employees. In 1929, it was filling orders for businesses nationwide, producing an ingeniously designed radiator that eliminated the need for pipes, a new saw for cutting rocks in quarries, machinery for power dams, and a device to remove steam and cooking odors from household stoves.

Manager E. M. Bassier was optimistic about his company's future development. In an interview with the *Pilot,* he proudly claimed that residents of cities larger than Wausau expressed surprise at the ability of the Murray plant to compete with factories located closer to their market. What they neglected to consider, he said, was the accessibility of iron mines and raw materials to the Wausau area.[3]

The *Record-Herald* applauded the resourcefulness of the Murray Company and urged Wausau citizens to become familiar with the sixty-odd manufacturers that supported Wausau's economy. The Wausau Common Council allocated $15,000 for a survey of the region's industrial advantages, and received prompt commendation from the local press. The *Pilot* recommended that the city exploit its local ingenuity. It pointed out that real industrial development usually came from companies which started within the community, and rarely from established companies or branch plants which moved into the area. Fresh ideas and new products were what the city needed.[4]

A healthy desire for expansion seemed to have taken hold. In 1930, H. L. Geisse, General Manager of the Wisconsin Valley Electric Company, announced plans for the construction of rural electric lines, for an extension to the existing streetcar facilities, and for the rebuilding of distribution systems within the Wausau area. The company anticipated spending $215,000 in Wausau alone, and planned similar projects for Merrill, Stevens Point, Tomahawk, Minocqua and Eagle River, Rhinelander, Antigo, and Waupaca. The *Pilot* saw the proposed construction as part of a national trend which was bringing new vigor to American enterprise. "Uneasiness caused by the recent stock market orgy seems to have vanished as the dew before the sun," it said. Wausau and Marathon County had other construction plans for 1930: a new high school, an isolation hospital, and a post office. The county would move "along the lines of steady, wholesome and permanent progress" on the road President Hoover had charted.[5]

But a harbinger of the approaching penury and misery appeared in a December issue of the *Pilot*. The neediest charity cases in the area suffered far more than in earlier years. One man was trying to support his pregnant wife and five children on $16.80 a week. They lived in a house which hardly kept out the cold, with barely enough fuel, blankets, or linens; and the children, including one who had tuberculosis, lacked shoes and winter clothing. Another man was making only $20.75 a week, a small amount to support a tubercular wife and six children. In each case, the family had heavy debts and was unable to borrow more money to buy household necessities. It was only a matter of time before the gloom of economic hardship would fully penetrate the county's borders and make a much larger share of the population aware of its presence.[6]

The first signs of unprecedented poverty were just beginning to reach the local consciousness. During "Thrift Week" of January, 1930, the *Pilot* found it necessary to print a creed reminding citizens of their financial responsibilities:

work and earn	own your own home
make a budget	make a will
record expenditures	invest in safe securities
have a bank account	pay bills promptly
carry life insurance	share with others

Otto Muenchow ran for mayor on a ticket which exemplified this Franklinesque thrift. His victory signified city residents' growing awareness of the need to halt the economy's continued plunge. Moreover, it indicated continued faith that traditional remedies would be sufficient. The *Pilot* urged Muenchow to economize, to obtain fire insurance rate reductions for the city, and to adopt a "pay as you go policy." It also thought the new mayor should promote home industry and not permit "unsuccessful plants and jobless, homeless men to clutter the gutters of Wausau."[7]

In December of 1929, industry had begun laying off employees, and within four months Wausau streets were accommodating some of the jobless. By 1931, unemployment had become a serious problem. But the belief that depression conditions would disappear as suddenly as they had arisen was still popular in some quarters. Mayor Muenchow stated his emphatic belief in local governments' abilities to "work out their own salvation." He was convinced that, while one's heart might sympathize with unfortunates throughout the country, the federal government had more urgent obligations than the care of the poor. Muenchow believed that relief of the "temporary depression" could be most efficiently achieved by state and local government. His position was supported by the *Pilot*, which also thought the city should give jobs to some of those who were getting relief money.[8]

But the local community was losing its power to help. In December of 1931, John D. Mylrea received an increasingly typical letter from his friend Andrew L. Kreutzer, president of the Wisconsin Valley Trust Company. Kreutzer advised Mylrea that the auditors had refused to "pass" a loan for which Mylrea had given shares of Thunder Lake Lumber Company as collateral. The auditors had a peculiar dislike for paper mill and lumber stock. Mylrea later remarked that letters like Kreutzer's "sent shivers up one's back, not only on your own account but knowing the writers of such letters were up against it and just had to have payments on loans to serve their institutions. In few cases, could we sell anything, at even below cost, to help relieve their situation."[9]

The troublesome auditors and a run on the banks in 1933 resulted in a bank closing that year, the first in Wausau's history. On January 30th, Mayor Muenchow declared a holiday for the four local banks. While the terms of Muenchow's proclamation provided for a months' respite, the actual closing lasted only one day. On Monday an almost continuous conference of bank directors came up with a plan that would allow an immediate partial resumption of business. The following day, January 31, the banks reopened, but transacted new business exclusively. The money deposited before January 30 was locked in the banks' vaults, where checks and withdrawal slips could not retrieve it; but funds deposited after the 30th were freely circulated.

Bank patrons did not panic. Businessmen were worried about how they would manage during the month, but individual depositors voiced witticisms appropriate to the event. "At last we have a democracy with all of us on the same level," quipped one man. Another facetiously tried to trade his fountain pen and car for a loaf of bread and a few bushels of potatoes.

The *Pilot* admitted that a "serious business situation" existed, but assumed that "depositors here, while they may be subject to necessary hardships and unavoidable delay, will be paid eventually the full amount of their deposits." Both local papers urged depositors to be calm and to subscribe to a waiver proposal drafted by local financiers that deferred immediate payment of money. The "stabilization plan," as it was termed, guaranteed full payment of deposits over a five-year period. Partial withdrawals of five, ten, and fifteen per cent could be made at six month intervals.

D. C. Everest and Andrew Kreutzer appealed to citizens to save homes, businesses, churches, and schools by signing waivers. Invoking patriotism and the pioneer spirit Kreutzer cited the need for "courage to face hardships so that what they [the pioneers] built will not crumble. Nobody will lose anything if we can only cooperate, and we will see this thing through."

His plea was effective. By the end of the declared holiday, the banks had obtained sufficient waivers to continue business on a normal basis. But in March, they closed again when President Roosevelt declared a national bank holiday. Waiver agreements were once more circulated throughout the city. By the end of the second holiday, the First American State Bank had taken over the interests of the American National and First National Banks. It agreed to pay seventy per cent on the original waiver plan; the other thirty per cent was to remain in the bank as a trust fund.

February of 1934 brought a happy, if temporary, end to the uncertainty. The First American State and Citizens' State Banks released $2 million in deferred certificates of deposits, made possible by the sale of $300,000 in debentures to the Reconstruction Finance Corporation. The banks also received the endorsement of the Federal Deposit Insurance Corporation, which guaranteed deposits of up to $2,500. Demonstrating their good faith, Wausau citizens transferred approximately seventy-eight per cent of their funds from savings to checking accounts. They might have withdrawn the money.[10]

Nevertheless, the specter of depression was threatening the tax structure of the county itself. In January of 1934, Marathon County was forced to levy a 5.7 per cent increase over the 1932 taxes. This gave the county the unwelcome distinction of having the highest percentage of tax increase of any county in the state that year. A $157,000 increase in annual payments to purchase delinquent tax certificates, in addition to the bank closing, made the tax hike necessary.[11]

County farmers were perhaps more accustomed to austerity in their daily lives. Nonetheless, during the 1930's, even they experienced an unprecedented degree of economic difficulty. One Easton farmer was forced to sell three of his best cows at fifteen dollars a head to pay his taxes. The price went as low as a penny a pound. Eggs, meanwhile, were selling for nine cents a dozen. Clothing had to be made out of feed and flour sacks. The added deprivations made the rural population understandably restless.

In 1933, patrons of the Athens Creamery withheld milk, dumped butter, and picketed the plant to protest the low prices they were getting for their milk. Farmers Union members in Halsey disapproved of Athens merchants' use of coal and threatened to boycott merchants who would not buy wood from their woodlots. Good will was not entirely absent, however. An Athens priest reportedly saved the Bank of Athens by persuading his parishioners to leave their money in the bank during a time of panic. Because of his efforts, the Athens bank did not close. It eventually took over the bank of Milan, which apparently lacked equally inspired spiritual guidance.[12]

By the time the first phase of the New Deal had been enacted, Marathon County officials no longer desired sole responsibility for relief measures: they welcomed the Civil Works Administration's interference. The first CWA projects, thirty in all, employed about 900 county residents, who were put to work repairing and redecorating government buildings, and improving government grounds. In Mosinee, CWA workers relocated the ball park and built tennis courts; in Marathon, they built a park and a swimming pool; in Hatley, they resurfaced the street; and in Stratford, they repaired a village hall. By December of 1933, the number of men employed on county projects had jumped to 1,600 and the number of projects to 168. White collar workers were busy assessing residential properties for tax assessors, Rib Mountain crews were building toboggan slides and an observation tower, and unemployed teachers were now making $15.00 a week assisting at public schools. The farmer, however, had a hard time of it. If he owned one cow, the possession of which meant his being defined as employed, he was ineligible for CWA work.

The manna that had descended so suddenly was not inexhaustible: the county rapidly exceeded its alloted quota of CWA workers. In early January of 1934, between 6,000 and 7,000 county men were working for the Civil Works Administration. Two weeks later the number had been reduced by over 4,000, eliminating alleged "chiselers" and leaving only the indigent on the payroll. County supervisors were so alarmed by the cut-back that they sent a memo to Harry Hopkins, federal CWA administrator, asking for an indefinite extension of CWA money and permission to rotate men on the projects.[13]

Joseph Reis, chairman of the Town of Johnson during the Depression, recalled that the competition for CWA work brought out the less noble side of human nature in both the applicants and himself:

> Everybody wanted to work, even those who were fairly well to do, and some that had money on interest. The spirit of the CWA was a relief measure and I had followed the spirit of the rulings as close as I could, which created a lot of enemies. The applications for poor relief in the Town of Johnson were something terrible. There was [sic] a lot of men who did not try to help themselves but tried to get aid, and here is where I got hard boiled, and believe me, they were not so anxious to see me for the second time.[14]

Yet not everyone shared that recollection. One Wausau observer may have been sentimentalizing when she reminisced about the Depression era, but her comments provide another side of the story:

> There wasn't greed then as there is now. Everyone tried to make a go of it, but there was no race or anything; no one wanted to lay around in them [sic] days—everyone wanted to work . . . People were better and more respectable [sic] of each other and helped each other more. Everyone was in the same boat and you didn't try to cheat anyone; just like you didn't want anyone to cheat you. We had a Model T and we used it only on Sundays. We didn't think we were better than those who had less than we did.[15]

The level of affluence was reflected, in part, in the fluctuation of relief statistics. CWA work quotas varied between 3,500 men in December of 1933 and 603 men in March of 1934. There were problems with checks arriving late, and the title and name of the local project administrator changed almost as frequently as the quotas. When the FERA programs replaced the CWA projects, county relief director Louis Pauls was able to smooth out some of the administrative wrinkles. Although quotas still varied from one month to the next, they fluctuated less than during the CWA phase of relief. The fact that the county supplied almost thirty per cent of the FERA relief funds may have contributed to the more efficient operation of the relief office.[16]

Of all the New Deal projects that influenced Marathon County during the Depression period, few were as successful as the Civilian Conservation Corps camp established in the Town of Rib Mountain in 1935.[17] Few, moreover, were so popular with virtually every segment of the county population. Even the traditional local critics of Franklin Roosevelt's economic policies were enthusiastic about this particular part of the New Deal program. The Wausau Chamber of Commerce was credited with having played a leading part in securing the facility. The *Record-Herald,* in a notable editorial departure, hailed the camp as "good news for both Wausau and Marathon County."[18]

The endorsements from these bastions of economic conservatism represented no ideological conversion, however. The explanation for the broad-based support lay in the major mission assigned to the camp and to the 250 young men employed there: the improvement of Rib Mountain State Park. At the park's official dedication ceremonies in September of the previous year, Governor Albert Schmedeman had remarked:

> When we return to normalcy economically, we of the state of Wisconsin may expect to see the tourist industry again become one of the most important the state has.
>
> Foresightedness would compel us to prepare for the good days to come again . . . The improvement of our tourist facilities logically then becomes one of the forward steps which we may make in marking time until the rest of the country again sends us ever increasing numbers of visitors.[19]

The chance to improve the county's share of the tourist trade was a more powerful motivator than the economic philosophy providing that opportunity. The *Record-Herald,* in announcing the camp's creation, noted that the CCC work would increase Rib Mountain's attractiveness for tourists. "It is one of the most interesting and beautiful spots in the state, which has been insufficiently publicized in past years. The . . . improvements planned will place Wisconsin's only mountain very much in the spotlight."[20] With the community solidly behind the project, the work accomplished by the CCC camp was surely one of the New Deal's best moments in Marathon County. Not only did its recruits help renovate Rib Mountain State Park by widening road beds, laying out paths, and sodding much of the area, but they were also scheduled to assist on several other county park improvement projects.[21]

If the financial troubles of the early 1930's weren't sufficient to humble the community, nature inflicted its own torments. Voracious grasshoppers ate their way through crops and seed in 1932 and 1933, causing fear and disgust among county farmers. During the first invasion, the pests even got as far as downtown Wausau. On the morning of July 13, city residents were shocked to discover hordes of hoppers on Third and Scott streets, as well as inside many office buildings and stores. Hundred of thousands were killed in a single weekend. After the second extermination, two hundred fifty of them were found dead on an average square foot of ground. An effective campaign was almost impossible to wage because no one had money to spend for the molasses, bran, and arsenic that constituted the poison mash. County Agent W. J. Rogan distributed $800 in state aid, and begged Wausau organizations for more money, warning that unless the mash was applied immediately, it would be too late to save the crops. Apathetic businessmen failed to respond, although they, too, would be hurt by a crop failure. The Chamber of Commerce thought the county should provide the funds. The Kiwanis Club agreed to raise forty per cent of the needed amount if other service organizations would do their part; but it was alone in responding to Rogan's challenge. Ultimately, Rogan extracted an additional $450 from the county coffers.[22]

The county's belief in its ability to rid itself of the Depression had proven naive. The spirit of boosterism, apparent in the nation as well as the county in the early 1930's, seems simplistic in retrospect. Yet, sometimes the county put its sense of community-mindedness, its self-confidence, and its visions of plenty to good use. On February 1, 1934 the George Silbernagel & Sons Company was almost entirely destroyed by a fire. The resulting $70,000 worth of damages and the closing of a plant which had employed seventy men added to the city's growing financial despair. Since 1925, the sash and door factory had seen a steady increase in production and profit, and previous to the fire, Silbernagel had anticipated another year of economic growth. That early immunity to the effects of the depression induced several cities in Wisconsin, immediately after the fire, to court the Silbernagel firm. They offered exemption from taxation—even free land and buildings. The Wausau City Council and Chamber of Commerce, fearing the removal of a major industry by some rapacious sister city, offered an alternate solution to the Silbernagel problem. In a short time, the factory resumed operations on an enlarged scale in the old Wausau Novelty Works building. The city had purchased the land, machinery, and plant of the novelty company and presented them to George Silbernagel, with an agreement for repayment over a period of several years.

Because the city responded quickly to the disastrous fire, and because the Silbernagel family possessed determination and business sense, the firm continued to prosper. Employment figures jumped from sixteen men in 1925 to one hundred sixty-two in the latter part of 1934; and by the end of 1939 the company employed three hundred sixty-nine men. Profits and payroll figures increased proportionately.[23]

But Marathon Rubber, which also faced dissolution during the Depression, did not fare so well. The story began with the closing of the plant in late May of 1933. A Milwaukee bank, which had carried a loan for the company, could no longer afford to extend credit to businesses outside of Milwaukee. Faced with payment of a $22,000 loan or liquidation of its assets, Marathon Rubber unsuccessfully sought money from the Federal Reserve, the Reconstruction Finance Corporation, and local banks. With a mixture of ingenuity and desperation, the rubber company was eventually able to obtain subscriptions for $9,000 worth of stock from its eighty-five jobless employees. A campaign to solicit another $50,000 in stocks from local citizens was started, and a petition to the Common Council, signed by five hundred people, asked additional aid.

Employees of Marathon Rubber wrote letters to the editor of the *Record-Herald* pleading for community support. They stressed the stable financial condition of the business, the amount paid the city in taxes, electric bills, and salaries, and the power of the company to draw additional capital to Wausau, as good reasons to buy stock. One writer compared the situation to the log-jams early lumbermen had faced on the Wisconsin River, hoping that the "bank-jam" could be broken by stock purchases. "We are willing to work," he said. "We do not want charity. Our city has enough to take care of . . . Give us a chance to feed and clothe our children and keep our factories going, thus helping the city as well as helping to feed and clothe their children. All we ask is unlock the jam in our banks and let the golden stream turn the wheels of our industry again as in past years."

The Wausau Common Council was sympathetic but could not provide any hard cash. The city could not even obtain a loan to bolster its own finances. The school treasury was $18,000 in the red at the time, and owed teachers, janitors, and clerks back salaries. But a committee to support the drive for stock subscription was duly appointed, and the burden of financing Marathon Rubber was dumped on the shoulders of private citizens.

By June 15, Marathon Rubber had reopened on a part-time basis with a limited crew; and the drive for support was still going on. The company was optimistic: businessmen had purchased stock with money they might have used to invest in their own businesses. By August of

1933, twenty more people had been reemployed, and the payroll had increased by six hundred dollars. But the valiant efforts of company and community were far from sufficient. The firm was finally forced to close. In June of 1934, the Common Council, having regained its solvency, purchased the plant and machinery of Marathon Rubber for $35,000, a figure which represented complete liquidation of company assets. The Council then signed an agreement with Joseph J. Usow of Milwaukee, who reopened the plant under new management. Usow received the business on the conditions that he pay annual property taxes not to exceed $1,000 and that after two years he begin paying on the city's loan to him. The city was to keep the property deed until Usow had made payments of $25,000, free from interest, or until he had expended $500,000 in wages. Aubrey Burnett, former president of the company, remained with the firm, although Usow had complete management control and moved to Wausau to oversee the operation. Had Usow foreseen the labor problems he was soon to encounter, he might have had second thoughts about undertaking such a venture.[24]

Labor-management tensions accounted for a good many of the headaches Marathon County endured in the later Depression years. Although the unions had gained a slight foothold in the twenties, it wasn't until the county began to feel the pinch of unemployment that unions obtained substantial power. Yet by 1937, A.F. of L. affiliates were walking out of businesses ranging from trucking outfits to box companies, usually a short time after the unions had organized. In 1936, the *Pilot* smugly claimed that an A.F. of L. representative couldn't organize its shop because working conditions were too good. The paper probably represented the view of most local businesses when it stated that "the employment of good craftsmen, the payment of fair wages, the conscientious adjustment of hours, the provision of desirable working conditions and a full compliance with Wisconsin and federal social security measures" were adequate labor provisions. Unions were superfluous. But by June of 1937, the headline *"Pilot Signs Agreement With A.F. of L. Affiliate"* appeared on the paper's front page. The official union seal had become indispensable.[25]

The "need" for labor's endorsement was something most companies had to be convinced of. A good many of the strikes occurred partly because of union desire for, and management unwillingness to grant, a closed shop. April of 1937 ushered in a period of bitter conflict, which began with the cessation of business at five local trucking firms. Truck owners were called out of a conference with union officials to find that a strike was in progress. Not surprisingly, the conference failed to bring a satisfactory settlement, and was adjourned when one owner walked out of the meeting. The issue that was to cost both drivers and owners the most money was the demand for a closed shop. Before the one-hundred strikers returned to work four days later, a million pounds of merchandise lay undelivered in Wausau and nearby cities, and the truckers had done everything possible to prevent retrieval by purchasers or contract carriers. Settlement finally brought the truckers the coveted closed shop, higher wages, and shorter hours; but management retained its right to hire the men it wanted, with a three-month probationary period before union membership was required.[26]

The ability of unions to protect individual members was one of the advantages of a closed shop. Robert King, president of the local teamstems' union, tested this when he called a strike at the Steffke Freight Company in 1938. Thirty-two men struck for twenty-three days in protest of the dismissal of two men whose insurance had been cancelled due to bad driving records. In desperation, W. A. Steffke offered to rehire the careless drivers for office work, to submit the question of dismissal to a vote of employees, or to abide by the decision of a labor relations board. But King would not call off the strike. He wanted the company to sanction uninsured drivers. The final agreement, reached with the aid of national and state labor relations board members and Mayor August Poltzer, called for payment of the dismissed men's salaries for about a month. King had achieved his actual goal: demonstration of the union's ability to command management's attention.[27]

Marathon Electric could testify to that power. While the truckers were out in 1937, the company was in the midst of an even greater crisis. Trouble had begun back in January of the previous year, when the National Labor Relations Board filed a complaint against the firm, alleging discrimination against certain employees because of union sympathies and affiliations. Marathon Electric, which had dismissed several men, denied knowledge of the workers' union affiliation. The complaint brought a series of court appeals, as management unsuccessfully sought a restraining injunction against a NLRB investigation of the plant. Shortly thereafter, in April, 1937, the United Electrical and Radio Workers of America, a C.I.O. affiliate, further complicated matters by organizing the first C.I.O. union in Wausau. Marathon Electric reportedly signed a closed shop contract and recognized the Electrical Workers as sole bargaining agent, after an employee vote revealed that over two-thirds of the workers favored the union.

A.F. of L. members, enraged at alleged discrimination against federation members (and at the rapid support the C.I.O. was gaining at the plant) called a strike, claiming that they were going to be fired unless they joined the C.I.O. union immediately. It was never clear to the press exactly how many of the plant's three-hundred sixty-nine employees had walked off the job. The A.F. of L., however, claimed to have one hundred strike supporters.

As tension between members of the rival unions increased, Mayor George W. Borowitz shut down the plant, fearing violence. J. J. Wall, general plant manager, promptly demanded that the mayor reopen the factory. Denying that A.F. of L. people had been threatened with dismissal, he cited an agreement with Milwaukee's J. E. Hayes, a regional A.F. of L. representative, to postpone labor discussions until the original charges against the company and the counter-injunction had been decided upon. Wall also claimed that Hayes had agreed to abide by the results of an employee election between A.F. of L. and C.I.O. factions.

Negotiations to settle the strike resulted in a seven-point agreement assuring A.F. of L. members that they would not be discriminated against nor lose their jobs if they refused to join the C.I.O. Both Kenneth Conklin, head of the C.I.O. union at Marathon Electric, and J. E. Hayes still claimed a majority of workers' support. But an election, supervised by the Labor Board a month and a half later, revealed that 208 workers favored the C.I.O. while only 101 voted for the A.F. of L.

The election brought another strike when the C.I.O. was designated the official bargaining agent. Tempers flared. A.F. of L. members claimed a C.I.O. man drove a car over a woman in an attempt to break a picket line. C.I.O. members countered with a charge that federationists attempted to push the car into the river. A Steffke Motor Company trucker said federation members had prevented him from delivering Marathon Electric products to Ripon by establishing a picket line at Plainfield. And General Manager James Wall claimed that Eldon Melvin, president of the Wausau Central Labor Body, had threatened to surround the plant with three to four thousand A.F. of L. men. Finally, a permanent injunction against the picketers put an end to the strike.[28]

Badly shaken by the C.I.O. victory at Marathon Electric, the A.F. of L. felt a need to flex its muscles. On June 17, three thousand members marched in a parade which culminated in a demonstration outside a building where C.I.O. members were meeting. Labor Day of 1938 brought another display of power, with four thousand federation workers parading through downtown Wausau. On this occasion, I. F. Goldberg, Milwaukee counsel for the A.F. of L., spoke out against "selfish and self-advancement seeking leaders of the C.I.O.," while Walter Graunke, Central Labor Union counselor, urged moderation and "reasonable and sane action from the side of labor."[29]

In the last half of 1937, "sane action" meant strikes that occurred with the regularity of falling dominoes. Underwood Veneer Company workers wanted a forty-hour week, a fifteen-cent raise, and a closed shop. Minnesota Mining and Manufacturing men settled for an open shop and a three and one-half cent hourly increase, after management reportedly gave bed and board to strike breakers inside the plant. Before the settlement was reached, one worker nearly killed himslf while cutting a 2,800 volt cable connected to the building. Wisconsin Box Company employees and garage workers and mechanics struck for higher wages and more money for overtime; and one-hundred Marathon Rubber laborers walked off the job to protest dismissal of a woman worker.[30]

Marathon Rubber was to confront the A.F. of L. again in 1940, when a strike was called August 31st. A new contract was due to be negotiated and the union was determined to see a closed shop, but management was opposed. In the midst of the production of 1,000 raincoats a day for army and navy personnel, the company was forced to shut it doors to five hundred employees. The problem was intensified by the approaching deadline for bids on more raincoat contracts. The U. S. War Department sent a representative to urge both company and strikers to settle their differences while they worked, as the army desperately needed the coats. When that measure failed, an army-navy liaison officer and nationally known strike mediator came to help smooth the way toward renewed production. But the union wouldn't budge. Walter Graunke alluded to the recent jurisdictional dispute as good reason for a closed shop. He denied any lack of patriotism in a union refusal to be "stampeded back into a factory because army orders [were] on file."

Two dissenting employees of Marathon Rubber indignantly took management's side of the question in a letter to the editor of the *Record-Herald*. Claiming that the strike had been called by about fifteen union members, the writers accused the union of driving business out of Wausau, losing orders for coats, and holding up vital government contracts. They also claimed that Usow had received, in the spring of the year, pledges from all employees not to strike, as a large government order was pending. On assurance of continued support, he had then accepted the contract, increased employment by about one hundred per cent, and opened a second plant to accommodate the extra work load. Now the plant was paralyzed and long-time employees who refused to join the union were being blamed for the strike's duration. The "so-called union" was denying management its right to operate and non-union members their right to obtain "happiness and safety" in the way they saw fit.

After six exhausting weeks of negotiations, the strike was settled. The new contract, good through December 31, 1941, prohibited strikes, lockouts, and shut downs. Current union members were subject to dismissal if they left the union. Old employees had forty-five days to join the union or lose all seniority rights.[31]

Ultimately, the Wausau Central Labor Body became a force which neither management nor management supporters could afford to ignore. Its influence culminated in the establishment of arbitration boards that had the power to make legally enforcible decisions. The boards were composed of a Central Labor Body representative, a management representative, and one other person acceptable to both sides. In an emotionally charged atmosphere, these bodies added elements of objectivity and compromise. For workers they could insure the degree of economic self-sufficiency that came with employment. Such was the case of Elsie Hoeft, who was discharged from Marathon Rubber for her attempts to create dissatisfaction among plant workers. In a two to one decision, the board ruled that the reasons for Mrs. Hoeft's dismissal were "frivolous;" that not only was she to be rehired, but she was to receive back salary, minus her unemployment compensation, for the eight months during which she had been without work. The strikes that had ended labor peace in Marathon County after 1937 had dramatically demonstrated the workers' plight. Backed by federal government labor legislation the heightened militancy also resulted in a begrudging respect for laborers' rights and interests.[32]

Yet, amidst the turmoil and confusion, there was time to reflect on how far the county and its people had come in the twentieth century. In January, 1933, for example, the fiftieth anniversary of the founding of the Deutcher Arbeiter Unterstuetzungs Verein (D.A.U.V.) was celebrated in Wausau. The observances honoring the five remaining charter members of this local relief and social organization for persons of German extraction served a valuable dual purpose. They provided a needed reminder of how much the county owed to those of German descent for its development. More important perhaps, they brought to mind the fact that times hadn't always been easy in Marathon County, but that with a measure of cooperation, survival was possible.[33]

More extensive and elaborate arrangements accompanied the celebration of Wausau's centennial in 1939. The city spent several years preparing for the event, which lasted a full eight days, from June 27 to July 4. Highlighting each of those evenings was the staging of a pageant, "Highlights of a Century," one scene of which recreated the arrival of George Stevens one hundred years before. While the observances were Wausau-oriented, the county as a whole was not ignored. Among the honored visitors returning to the city for the occasion was Amy Creed, who sixty-seven years earlier had journeyed with her husband to the western part of the county and helped found the settlement of Unity. Even in this celebration of the past, the realities of the present played a prominent part. One of the first steps of the local centennial association had been to secure a WPA appropriation to conduct historical research. Subsequently, both WPA and NYA groups began to compile data connected with the organization and growth of the city.[34]

Time was also taken for charting the future. The Wausau Chamber of Commerce engaged Francis F. Bowman to prepare a survey on the capabilities and potential of the Wausau Industrial Area.[35] After studying the various components of development, Bowman submitted a detailed analysis of the area's industrial situation to chamber president Allan Abrams in August, 1939. Its principal assets were enumerated: an ample labor supply; available industrial sites; advantageous sources of raw materials (especially dairy products, relative to Midwestern markets); the lowest taxation rate of any central or northern Wisconsin community with the exception of Clintonville;[36] and a strong sense of community pride.[37] Liabilities were also listed, including a shortage of immediately available factory space and homes, higher shipping costs to the Chicago and eastern markets compared to other sections of the state, and higher coal transportation costs than other Wisconsin centers due to its inland location. Bowman concluded his report with numerous recommendations for further industrial development of the area. Suggestions were made as to both the kinds of industries which should be given encouragement, and the appropriate civic action to achieve those ends.[38] The Bowman report was solid evidence that local business leaders were confident that general prosperity would inevitably return, and that they would be ready to resume the area's industrial advancement. The feeling of helplessness was evaporating. Nevertheless, more sacrifice would be required before a normal economic climate could be restored. Another preoccupation, another source of insecurity involving much more than economic survival, was in the process of forming across two oceans, in Europe and in Asia.

FOOTNOTES

[1] For a brief, insightful analysis, see William E. Leuchtenberg, *The Perils of Prosperity, 1914-1932* (Chicago: The University of Chicago Press, 1958), pp. 241-248.

[2] *Wausau Daily Record-Herald*, October 30, 1929, p. 8; October 28, 1929, p. 8; November 1, 1929, p. 8.

[3] *Wausau Pilot*, October 24, 1929, p. 1; *Wausau Daily Record-Herald*, November 21, 1929, p. 17.

[4] *Wausau Daily Record-Herald*, November 29, 1929, p. 10; *Wausau Pilot*, November 7, 1929, pp. 1, 4; October 24, 1929, p. 4.

[5] *Wausau Daily Record-Herald*, November 27, 1929, p. 1; *Wausau Pilot*, November 29, 1929, p. 10.

[6] *Wausau Pilot*, December 19, 1929, p. 1.

[7] *Wausau Pilot*, April 3, 1930, p. 1; David Bernhardt, "A Wausau Area Viewpoint: Early Depression Years in 1929-1932," research paper, University of Wisconsin Center—Marathon, May 2, 1973, in hands of author, p. 13.

[8] *Wausau Pilot*, May 29, 1930, p. 4; November 5, 1931, p. 4; January 1, 1931, p. 2. The percentage decline in employment in manufacturing industries for Wausau between September 1929 and September 1931 was approximately 35.5 per cent, which placed the Wausau area unemployment rate sixth highest among Wisconsin's thirty largest cities in that period. The percentage decline in payroll in the same period was a sharp 52.1 per cent. Finally, by September of 1931, Wausau area employment had plummeted to an index of 73.3 based upon a base year figure of 100 representing average employment in the years 1925-1927. By comparison, Stevens Point found itself at 90.6, Wisconsin Rapids at 112.3, Green Bay at 89.3, Rhinelander at 82.8, Appleton at 85.8, and Eau Claire at 94.5. These figures indicate that compared with surrounding communities and others with similar industrial bases, Wausau was relatively hard hit in the early years of the depression. John R. Commons, *An Economic Survey of Wisconsin* (Madison: Prepared at the Request of Governor Philip F. LaFollette, December, 1931), Charts 9, 9a, 95.

[9] A. L. Kreutzer to J. D. Mylrea, December 30, 1931, John D. Mylrea Journals, vol. 6.

[10] *Wausau Pilot*, February 2, 1933, pp. 1, 4; February 9, 1933, p. 1; February 23, 1933, p. 1; January 4, 1934, p. 1; February 8, 1934, p. 1.

[11] *Wausau Pilot*, February 1, 1934, p. 1.

[12] Thorpe, "Easton," pp. 24, 28, 30.
Helgeson, "Athens, Wisconsin," pp. 71-73.

[13] Money paid yearly in wages in manufacturing industries of Wausau dropped by over $1,400,000 between 1929 and 1934, and by over $2,830,000 in the county as a whole during the same years. In August of 1933, in Wausau alone, there were 1,860 people over eighteen years old out of work. Dept. of Commerce, Bureau of the Census, *Biennial Census of Manufacturers: 1933*, Wisconsin, pp. 3, 6.

[14] Helgeson, "Athens, Wisconsin," p. 72.

[15] Thomas Mesalk, Depression Interview, December, 1975, in possession of author.
Moreover, not everyone suffered. One of A. P. Woodson's daughters recalled that her family, for example, was not much affected by the Depression. See Alice Forester Interview, August 20, 1975, Marathon County Public Library Oral History Collection.

[16] *Wausau Pilot*, September 28, 1933, p. 1; November 30, 1933, pp. 1, 5; December 21, 1933, pp. 1, 6; December 14, 1933, p. 1; January 4, 1934, p. 1; December 7, 1933, p. 1; February 8, 1934, p. 1; January 11, 1934, p. 1; January 18, 1934, p. 1.

[17] The camp was located on the west bank of the Wisconsin River opposite the Marathon Paper Mills plant.

[18] *Wausau Daily Record-Herald*, April 10, 1935, p. 10.

[19] *Wausau Pilot*, September 13, 1934, p. 1.

[20] *Wausau Daily Record-Herald*, April 10, 1935, p. 10.

[21] The proposals included improvements in Eau Claire Dells Park, Elderon Park, Athens Park, and Cherokee Park. See *Wausau Pilot*, April 18, 1935, p. 2; October 31, 1935, p. 1.

[22] *Wausau Pilot*, June 30, 1932, p. 4; July 7, 1932, p. 1; July 14, 1932, p. 4; July 6, 1933, pp. 1, 2; June 15, 1933, p. 1; June 22, 1933, p. 1; June 29, 1933, p. 3. *Wausau Daily Record-Herald*, July 2, 1932, p. 1; July 5, 1932, p. 3.

[23] *Wausau Daily Record-Herald*, February 1, 1934, p. 1; February 7, 1934, p. 1; Charles Dodge Collection, Lumber Business Box.

[24] *Wausau Pilot*, June 8, 1933, p. 1; June 1, 1933, pp. 1, 4; June 15, 1933, p. 1; August 10, 1933, p. 1; May 31, 1934, p. 1; June 28, 1934, p. 1; *Wausau Daily Record-Herald*, May 27, 1933, p. 1; Marathon Rubber Clippings File, Marathon County Historical Society.

[25] *Wausau Pilot*, August 27, 1936, p. 4.

[26] *Wausau Daily Record-Herald*, April 29, 1937, p. 1; April 26, 1937, p. 1; April 28, 1937, p. 1.

[27] *Wausau Pilot*, September 8, 1938, p. 4; September 15, 1938, p. 2.
The union could be tough with its own membership. At a 1937 union meeting the truckers instituted a three-dollar fine for any member missing a Labor Day parade unless excused by the president. When a dispute arose with a Wausau department store the following year, a motion was passed requiring a fifteen dollar fine for any member caught entering the establishment. The penalty would also be imposed if any member of his family patronized the store. See "International Brotherhood Of Teamsters, Local 446 Minute Book, March 16, 1937 - October 4, 1939," Area Research Center, University of Wisconsin-Stevens Point.

[28] *Wausau Pilot*, January 16, 1936, p. 1; February 23, 1936, p. 2; March 11, 1937, p. 1; April 8, 1937, p. 1; May 6, 1937, p. 2; June 17, 1937, pp. 4, 1; June 24, 1937, p. 1; *Wausau Daily Record-Herald*, January 12, 1937, p. 1; April 28, 1937, p. 1; April 29, 1937, p. 1; April 30, 1937, p. 1; May 1, 1937, p. 1.

[29] *Wausau Pilot*, June 17, 1937, p. 8; September 8, 1938, p. 1.

[30] *Wausau Pilot*, September 9, 1937, p. 1; October 7, 1937, p. 1; September 30, 1937, p. 4; October 14, 1937, p. 1; October 21, 1937, p. 4; October 28, 1937, p. 8; September 9, 1937, p. 1; September 16, 1937, p. 1.

[31] *Wausau Daily Record-Herald*, September 11, 1940, p. 1; September 13, 1940, p. 4; September 16, 1940, p. 1; October 8, 1940, p. 8; October 15, 1940, p. 1; September 17, 1940, pp. 1, 4.

[32] *Wausau Daily Record-Herald*, September 5, 1942, pp. 1, 2; See also *Wausau Daily Record-Herald, Centennial Edition*, March 13, 1939, Commercial Section, p. 37.

[33] *Wausau Daily Record-Herald*, January 6, 1933, p. 4; January 12, 1933, pp. 1, 12.

[34] *Wisconsin Magazine of History* 23 (September, 1939): 121-122; *Wausau Daily Record-Herald, Centennial Edition*, March 13, 1939, Commercial Section, p. 26.

[35] Bowman incorporated the cities of Wausau and Mosinee, and the villages of Brokaw, Schofield, and Rothschild into one economic unit, which he termed the Wausau Industrial Area.

[36] By 1938, of the thirty-nine Wisconsin cities classed as industrial in character, eighteen had a lower tax rate than Wausau, two were equivalent, and nineteen were higher. With the exception of Clintonville, all of the cities with a lower tax rate were in the southeastern part of the state. Wausau's full value rate of 27.0 mills and Mosinee's 20.6 compared favorably to Stevens Point's 39.8, Superior's 34.5, Merrill's 33.0, Chippewa Fall's 32.4, Wisconsin Rapids's 31.6, Marshfield's 30.7, Eau Claire's 29.3, and the state's average of 29.9.

[37] Bowman was particularly impressed with "the sustained interest that Wausau business leaders have taken in their community. Through all the changes from a one industry lumber town to the diversified stage of industrial development

today these men have continued to invest the working capital of their companies in Wausau and in the development of new products."

[38] Francis F. Bowman, Jr. to Allen Abrams, August 20, 1939; Francis F. Bowman, Jr., "An Analysis of the Wausau Industrial Area" (letter and report in Wausau Area Chamber of Commerce).

CHAPTER FIVE

Recent Economic Highlights: Diffusion

As the international situation darkened, new sunlight brightened the county's industrial landscape. Two announcements, one from Washington, D.C., and one from Wausau in the early fall of 1940, illustrated the contrast. On September 16, at 2:08 p.m. Wausau time, President Roosevelt signed the nation's first peacetime conscription bill, ordering 16½ million young Americans to register for possible service in a "great new citizen army." The following day, over nine hundred miles to the west, Marathon Electric's president, James Wall, announced his company's intention to build a new $200,000 plant on Wausau's west side. Positive side effects of the project were evident by spring: construction at the Randolph and East Cherry Street site had sparked a building and real estate boom in the upper sixth ward. Meanwhile, the company had expended more than $100,000 in the city for building materials, electrical energy, and transportation. And there was one further benefit. According to Wall, the new facility would ease the recent demand on the company for small motors needed for national defense.[1] The new preoccupation was at hand.

Once America formally entered its second twentieth century war, Marathon County settled into the routine of homefront sacrifice, symbolized by ration schedules; paper, scrap metal, and war bond drives;

and casualty reports. More encouraging was the stimulus given to local industry by war-related production.[2] From mid-1940 through the beginning of 1944, the U.S. military awarded county manufacturers slightly more than fifteen million dollars in war contracts, the most for any county in north-central Wisconsin.[3] The infusion meant the end of the Depression for the industrial sector of the county economy. As of 1943, the Wausau Industrial Area's principal employers were showing a 39.8 per cent increase in employment over 1940; their total payroll had nearly doubled during the same period.[4]

Long before the conflict ended, the business community was anticipating the return of a peacetime economy. Specifically, the Wausau Chamber of Commerce intensified the commitment to economic planning first evidenced by the Bowman report. In April, 1943, D. C. Everest was appointed chairman of a new chamber committee charged with undertaking a comprehensive postwar planning project. After a six-month study of previous efforts in the field, the group began its own program by surveying local industries for postwar employment projections. The results revealed the challenge that lay ahead. The total 1946 employment estimate, although thirteen per cent below the wartime peak, would still be twenty-one per cent higher than the 1940 figure. If postwar prosperity was to be achieved, jobs would have to be found for this additional capacity once the war products outlet was closed.

That necessity made the next phase of the committee's program vital. In April, 1944, a committee sub-group under the supervision of the state chamber of commerce conducted a survey of Wausau and rural Marathon County consumer buying preferences for the immediate postwar period. The data obtained through personal interviews and mailed questionnaires would be a guide for "deciding on lines of commodities which should first be manufactured for civilian use." The post-war labor force could thus be channeled into the most profitable avenues of peacetime production. Moreover, since the industrial survey had indicated a higher wage average for 1946,[5] such a study would enable retailers and wholesalers to run their businesses to maximum advantage. Finally, this type of market research promoted "public faith in the future." This was perhaps the most important contribution. Public confidence was a crucial prerequisite for the consumer purchasing needed to avert a new economic collapse. And the survey did indeed forecast a healthy buying trend for durable and semi-durable goods in the first postwar year. A potential expenditure of $15,751,000 was projected for Wausau, with new housing accounting for over fifty per cent of that figure. While an automobile was the item first desired after the war, the greatest number of respondents expressed an intention to buy home furnishings and appliances; home repairs and remodeling finished a close second in this respect. In the rural region, where a potential demand of $17,695,000 was predicted, the preferences were slightly different. There the greatest amount of money would be spent on automobiles and trucks. However, farm machinery and equipment were the most popular products, with the tractor given an especially high priority.[6] Overall, a positive blueprint for postwar expansion had been charted. Towards this end, planning continued to be the favorite topic of discussion among Wausau area businessmen throughout 1944.[7] When U. S. Commerce Secretary Jesse Jones leveled the general criticism that there was "entirely too much planning and talking about the post-war world" when the war hadn't yet been won, the *Record-Herald* bluntly replied "You're Wrong, Mr. Jones." Winning the war had to receive top priority, of course, but "the titanic task of reconversion" necessitated practical planning well in advance; to do otherwise would invite the return of economic chaos.[8] Wausau area business leaders were determined to be prepared.

The concern paid dividends. Marathon County's industrial sector continued to show impressive growth during the postwar decades. Employment reached record high levels in 1956 and 1964; by the early 1960's, Wausau area firms were employing more than one-third of the workers in the nine-county central Wisconsin region. Industrial payrolls expanded in kind. Between 1950 and 1966, they failed to register an annual increase only in 1958. Postwar records in this category were achieved in first 1964, then in 1966. The number of firms surveyed by the chamber reached an all time high of seventy-two in 1964.[9]

The pattern of this development had fairly well crystallized by the mid-1960's. Expansion of old enterprises, as opposed to the importation of new types, was responsible for nearly eighty-five per cent of the region's industrial expansion. The paper industry remained a strong heir to the legacy of lumbering; the county's manufacturers led the state industry in new investment by a wide margin.

Not surprisingly, the leadership of D. C. Everest was a major factor. Everest had presided over substantial growth in the Marathon Paper Mills operation in the twenty years since 1930. While the Depression had not left Marathon unscathed, the company had operated at a financial loss only during 1932. Its success was reflected in the 1944 corporate name change to Marathon Corporation; 'paper mills no longer properly reflect [ed] the scope of our activities,' according to Everest. By the war's end Marathon had a sizable chest of war profits, a backlog of deferred projects, and a host of new ideas spawned by the war.

By comparison, at Wausau Paper Mills the situation was bleak. Business had never fully recovered from the Depression. The prolonged slump had been blamed on the managerial decisions of the Edmonds faction, which allegedly paid out several million dollars in dividends at the expense of keeping the mill in good condition. Compounding the problem, no doubt, was the 1941 flood, which had caused $800,000 in damages. By far the worst natural disaster in the company's history, it "practically tore the heart out of the organization." An Everest-led syndicate came to the rescue, however, by purchasing the ailing Brokaw operation in 1948.[10] After personally nursing the company back to health for two years, Everest turned the presidency over to Merrill paper executive and former Marathon employee David B. Smith. The succession would be the ultimate example of Everest's knack for recruiting talented subordinates. Under Smith's direction, a modernization and expansion program was instituted that marked the turning point in the company's revival. The culmination of Smith's program was a $4,250,000 expansion completed in 1961. Besides nearly doubling the plant's output, the project gave a boost to the general area economy. The addition of 174 production workers spread an average monthly payroll of $50,000 throughout local communities. And the resulting increased demand for hardwood was a financial windfall for approximately a thousand owners of small and large woodlots within a 150-mile radius of the village. Thanks to Everest's "magic hand," the rainbow was showing new promise.[11]

But the hand was getting old. Age, in fact, was catching up with much of Marathon Corporation's management team. Rigidity in method and managerial structure had set in. The firm's size was also becoming a handicap. Its extremely rapid growth, almost to the point of over-expansion, intensified that inflexibility and strained its finances. An era for the company, the paper industry, and the county ended in 1950, when Everest resigned as Marathon's president and general manager to become chairman of the board. However, the failure of his fabled recruiting ability brought him back reluctantly the following year. His hand-picked replacement, William L. Keady, an outsider inexperienced at running a firm of Marathon's size, proved unequal to the task and resigned. Everest returned to his old posts, but age, poor health, and his own inability to find suitable remedies, soon had him hunting for a new successor. This time his choice was John Stevens, Jr., a thirty-year veteran of the Marathon organization and head of its Canadian subsidiary. In April, 1952, Everest relinquished control of his company for good, devoting his final years to the hobby nurtured at Bryant, the study of history.[12] Death and history claimed him on October 28, 1955.

With or without Everest, Marathon's days as an independent entity were numbered. The company increasingly found itself unable to compete with the giant combinations being formed in a new age of corporate mergers. Accordingly, on December 3, 1957, the stockholders voted overwhelmingly to merge with American Can Company. Major shifts were undertaken by the new owners, and a $10 million expansion of the Rothschild mill in 1967 increased the firm's standing as a major area employer. But American Can's subsequent decision to withdraw from the fine paper business resulted in the plant's sale in 1973 to the Weyerhaeuser Company, an ironic fate for the creation of the independent-minded Wausau Group.[13]

The smoothest transition appears to have taken place at Mosinee. With the price of kraft dropping from $240 a ton in 1920 to $55 a ton by 1931, the Depression took its toll on the city's paper mill. Cutbacks in wages and employment had to be made. By 1939, however, conditions had improved to the point where the company initiated the practice of giving Christmas gifts to employees. The highlight of the war years was the 1944 purchase of 52,000 forested acres in Douglas County for development "into a perpetual source of timber for the Mosinee mill by modern methods of cutting for sustained yield and reforestation."[14] The charter promulgated for the management of this "industrial forest" was hailed as a historic act of "capitalistic statesmanship" by the *Record-Herald*.[15] Five years later, the Mosinee Industrial Forest had grown to 68,500 acres, with the planting of over two million seedlings; by 1960, it had expanded to 85,000 acres. A $5 million modernization project was begun after the war, which included the enlargement of the pulp mill and the rebuilding of the firm's three paper machines. The fourth and largest was added in 1964 to manufacture machine-glazed specialty papers. The Mosinee company's own drive towards vertical integration was then resumed. A Converted Products Division was started at Columbus, Wisconsin in 1966; the Calwis and Green Bay Plastics companies became wholly-owned subsidiaries of the parent operation two years later.[16] By 1970, a divisional reorganization became necessary: the company's name was changed to Mosinee Paper Corporation, with the Pulp and Paper

Division and general headquarters residing in Mosinee. Throughout, the mill remained the primary guarantor of community development. A forestry program for Mosinee's public schools was launched in 1943 with the purchase of seventy-five acres of timber in the Town of Mosinee. When a newsprint shortage occurred after the war, the *Mosinee Times* used the company's brown kraft paper for its print medium. The 579 workers on the mill's 1952 payroll represented more than one-third of the city's population; its local taxes for the year made up over sixty per cent of the tax budget.[17]

Much the same could be said for the paper industry's contribution to the county's industrial economy. As of 1962, the local concerns as a group were the leading employer in the Wausau area and the largest source of wages. They provided approximately thirty per cent of the jobs and nearly thirty-five per cent of the industrial payroll dollars. And over $5 million was spent to secure pulpwood from northern Wisconsin woodlot owners. These distinctions would no longer hold true by the mid-1970's; yet at the start of the decade the Mosinee and Brokaw firms and the American Can divisions in Rothschild and Wausau were still ranked among the county's top eight manufacturing employers. Paper might no longer be the region's "economic backbone," as the *Record-Herald* had claimed in 1963, but that forest product remained a necessary ingredient for its economic health.[18]

For the remainder of the wood-related industries, the post-war record was more ambiguous. Some, such as the Wisconsin Box and Marathon Box companies, faced heavy post-war competition from substitute materials but still met the challenge while retaining their old identities. Marathon Box, in fact, opened a Wausau-based subsidiary, the Stevens Container Corporation, in 1962, to produce corrugated paper boxes. Others, however, underwent a change in ownership as the price of survival. The postwar demand for housing induced Joseph Usow to purchase the J. M. Kuebler Company in 1946 and rename it Marathon Millwork. That same year a large Chicago building company, Harris Brothers, took over the Silbernagel family business; six years later the firm's name was changed to The Silcrest Company. In 1951, the Connor interests returned to Marathon County[19] by acquiring the Underwood Veneer plant along with its Michigan timber holdings; the company's sales offices were moved from Marshfield to Wausau several years later.

New management often resulted in a change in production. The Silbernagel concern had already made one such shift during the war, from sash and door making to the manufacture of shell boxes. Sash and door production was subsequently resumed, but with significant differences. In line with the developing trend towards specialization in the nation's building industry, the firm's millwork line was reduced in order to concentrate on the most popular items. This drive reached its logical conclusion in 1958, when specification millwork was discontinued, and production was focused solely on the Crestline brand of products first introduced in 1954. Unlike most of its competitors, the company began to use aluminum in its millwork. A readjustment of the market area also took place. Nationwide selling was ended in favor of a fifteen-state area from the Dakotas to the East coast and south to Missouri and North Carolina. Finishing the reorganization was a second name change in 1958 to the Crestline Company.[20] At the Connor company's new Underwood Division, a changeover was made in 1963 to the manufacture of wood kitchen cabinets, since its veneer and plywood were having difficulty competing with less expensive foreign imports.

Along with a "new look" frequently came renovations or expansions beneficial to local prosperity. When Joseph Usow took over the Kuebler operation, he found dilapidated plant buildings with dirt floors and horses being used for transporting lumber. Under the direction first of Usow, then of his sister and nephew, flooring was laid, remodeling done, and the literal form of horsepower phased out by 1950. The firm's employment and payroll were increased by more than tenfold between 1946 and 1963. At Crestline a ten-year expansion program was initiated in 1960, which, upon completion, made it the nation's second largest producer of windows.[21] The local showcase of the project was an 85,000 square-foot addition to the Cleveland Avenue facility, dedicated in the summer of 1971. Nearby, the Connors were busy deepening their business roots in Wausau. The 1964 construction of a 34,000 square-foot factory building doubled employment at the Thomas Street site, thus making Connor the largest kitchen cabinet maker in the state. And, two years after the 1968 acquisition of a Minneapolis toy manufacturer, that subsidiary's plant facilities were moved to Wausau on North First Avenue.[22]

These two final instances of expansion represented a badly needed comeback for the Wausau area woodworking industry. Between 1952 and 1962, employment in that industrial grouping had been cut in half. One event was primarily responsible: the demise of the venerable Curtis plant in the spring of 1962. Few announcements in Marathon County history have been more momentous than the one issued from Clinton, Iowa, that final Monday in April by Curtis Companies President Acton Chalu: 'Due to a serious drop in fixture sales and disappointing, uneconomical production results in kitchen cabinets, our Wausau factory must be closed effective today.'[23] In one stroke nearly three hundred workers were left jobless, and a ninety-one year era in the county's wood products industry had come to a sudden, unexpected end.

Moreover, few events have been as traumatic. News of the closing was greeted with 'stunned silence' throughout the company. Outward signs had been optimistic. A half-million dollars worth of new machinery for mass production of kitchen cabinets had only recently been installed. The labor force had been working at full capacity until the mysterious weekend notification of a 'layoff.' As the shock wore off, bitter post-mortems were voiced by plant veterans. The consensus was that the shutdown was 'a useless waste,' brought about by 'alleged mismanagement' dating back to 1958. Aloof foremen, chaotic hiring practices, and a generally poor system of internal communication resulting in 'sub-standard work' were all blamed. Some saw the 1955 decision to switch production from sashes, doors, windows, and stairwells to kitchen cabinets and store fixtures as the underlying cause. Others cited a lost Montgomery Ward's account for display cases as the precipitating factor. It was immaterial, of course. Whoever or whatever was at fault, most of the newly unemployed foresaw an uncertain future at best. Only eleven per cent of the Curtis workers were eligible for a company pension, a disappointing commentary on a firm that prided itself on devotion to "industrial democracy." Day after day, as demolition operations went on, groups of sad-eyed men gathered at the plant site. More than nostalgia was involved. A piece of their lives was being torn down.[24]

The closing of other familiar industrial institutions further signaled the passage of old growth patterns. Foreign imports, changing consumer preferences and "two near disastrous fires" at its Aetro-Liter Division had left Marathon Battery vulnerable by the mid-1960's. When Donald Moen replaced E. D. McEachron as president in late 1965, the denouement had begun. Glowing projections were made periodically, following a financial reorganization and successive takeovers by firms in St. Paul, Minnesota and Houston, Texas. Temporary revivals were noted. But when the latter company announced construction of a new factory in Waco, Texas, the Wausau plant's fate was sealed. In August, 1971, the Henrietta Street facility was closed, with operations and equipment moved to Waco. The local work force did not fare as well. Out of more than two hundred employees, only five or six supervisory personnel were scheduled to be transferred to Texas.[25]

The peak-and-valley history of the Pied Piper Shoe Company[26] reached a similar low point in early February, 1967, when a "temporary shutdown" laid off 150 workers. This time, however, the new valley would be the company's ultimate grave. After two sales of the plant site to developers, the building was razed in March, 1973.[27]

Another Charles Dodge operation, the Cereal Mills Company,[28] succumbed in the early summer of 1968. Modernization on several fronts had caught up with the firm whose origins traced back to 1845. Traffic patterns and new zoning regulations had effectively foreclosed the possibility of physical expansion. The encroachment of houses further and further into the countryside and the increasing size of farms also undermined the company's usefulness.[29]

A 106 year era in the region's economic and social history ended in late 1966, when the county's last operating brewery, the Marathon City Brewing Company (named Marathon Brewery, Inc. since March 10, 1965), followed its Wausau rivals, the Mathie-Ruder and Wausau Brewing companies, into oblivion.[30]

New establishments did appear on the scene. But there was a fundamental difference about these postwar industrial starts compared to those of the earlier diversification period. The addition of new firms now seemed a more formal, institutionalized process than in the freewheeling days of the Wausau Group. The main reason was the leading role being played by the Wausau Chamber of Commerce. Innovation was still possible, however. The scarcity of industrial-site property within Wausau's city limits led the chamber to adopt a supposedly novel approach towards industrial development: the area concept. Chamber business recruiters would offer prospective industries the best sites available, regardless of municipal boundaries. The framework of Wausau's industrial growth would be thus expanded to include adjacent villages and townships.[31]

The area concept's first practical application came in 1946. That year the chamber acquired a 47-acre tract on the former location of the Brooks & Ross Lumber Company for $22,000. The Schofield Industrial Area was born, the first industrial site of its type in Wisconsin. The selection of Schofield for the pilot program had not been a hasty decision. A comparative study had convinced chamber officials that the village could provide essentials such as railroad trackage, fire protection, and sewer and water systems at the most reasonable cost. Cooperation of village officials was deemed excellent from the outset.

Nonetheless, the project got off to an inauspicious beginning. Much criticism was leveled at the chamber's action, since any plants built in Schofield would be outside Wausau's tax base; indeed, that complaint had not died some nineteen years later. Any prior skepticism was heightened when the first firm to locate on the chamber purchase, an aluminum oil tank manufacturing concern, folded.

But perseverance began to pay dividends. Edward A. Drott decided in 1948 to bring his construction machinery manufacturing business from Milwaukee back to the Wausau area. His return represented a prize catch for the Schofield site. Beginning with five employees in the Brooks & Ross engine room, the Drott firm had become one of the county's eight largest industrial employers by 1970.[32] The Schofield Industrial District had been judged a success at an earlier date. Only five companies had been operating there in 1952; that number had grown to eleven a decade later. Employment had increased nearly five times during the same period, the total payroll more than seven times. In fact, virtually all the original acreage had been occupied by 1958, prompting the chamber to purchase fifty additional acres northeast of the site. Invited to address the 1965 Governor's Conference on Industrial Development, Wausau chamber representatives especially emphasized Schofield's industrial progress over the past twenty years. Their industries were employing more than seven hundred people and paying out annual wages in excess of $5 million.

Metalworking operations were responsible for the bulk of this growth. Indeed, since the end of the war, they had shown the most impressive development of any industrial grouping in the entire Wausau area. The number of such firms had risen steadily from eleven in 1949 to twenty-four by 1964. Metalworking employment had increased by about twenty-five per cent between 1952 and 1962, placing it a close second to the paper industry by the latter date. The following year metalworking surpassed paper as the leading industrial employer in Marathon County, with the lead lengthening in 1964.[33] The largest growth in payrolls was also occurring in that category. By 1973, the county metal products industry had taken a slight lead over paper in payroll expenditures, a wide one by 1974.

The Schofield industrial boom helped spark a familiar phenomenon: a growing urban sense in the village's image of itself. Sentiment for changing Schofield's corporate status to that of city had become strong by 1950. The process was completed the following year, with village president Isidor Schultz elected the first mayor of Marathon County's fourth city. Institutions befitting the new status subsequently appeared. A new high school, named for D. C. Everest, opened in the fall of 1953. A Schofield Businessmen's Association was organized in 1957; by the early 1960's, it included approximately seventy members, representing between seventy-five and eighty per cent of the local businesses. Substantial gains in population and assessed valuation, evident by the early 1960's, were cited as additional symbols of progress.[34]

The success of the Schofield experiment spawned imitation. Rothschild, Spencer, and Abbotsford later established industrial areas or parks; the Town of Weston had set aside two such sites by 1974. Stettin provided the ultimate model for township hospitality, however. A sizable tract of its land was acquired by the D. J. Murray Company in the mid-1950's. Forty acres were used in 1964 for construction of a new foundry. The plant would serve the dual purpose of increasing production and relieving congestion at Murray's Wausau facility.[35] The company's expansion program was heartily endorsed by Stettin Town Chairman Ray Ott, who promised the "full cooperation of the

The Early "Wausau Story" — Employers Mutuals

Town Board." An even more striking example of that cooperation came on the day of the Murray groundbreaking. Employers Mutuals announced on May 15 that it had purchased 191 acres in Stettin for the location of all the firm's Wausau operations; moreover, that property would be annexed to the City of Wausau to guarantee the availability of municipal services. Completed by 1967, the multi-million dollar complex replaced the Grant Street structure, which had served as Employers' home office since June, 1941. That building, appropriately enough, would next be utilized as Wausau's new city hall.[36] The township lost still more territory to the city in 1968 when 150 acres were annexed for creation of the Wausau West Industrial Park. And the part played in that transfer by a Wausau chamber subsidiary, the Wausau Area Development Corporation, indicated that the process of industrial development had reached a new plateau of structured formality.[37]

Yet in what seemed an era of growth through committee action, individual initiative could still have an impact. Anton Hoffer bought a "stone mill" machine in 1943 and started a Wausau paint manufacturing business. Approximately two years later Hoffer and Bernard Greenheck opened a plant for the manufacture of steel glass block ventilators; by the early 1960's, the Marmet Corporation had evolved into a leading producer of aluminum curtain wall. The Palesch Machine Shop began in 1947 as a hobby for a millwright at the Silbernagel company. And polio victim Glenn Straub organized the Wausau Metals Corporation in 1956.[38]

But it was the ambition of three brothers, raised on a farm several miles west of Wausau, which led to a string of business successes worthy of the Wausau Group legend. When cheesemaker August Schuette was killed by a boiler explosion, his two oldest sons persuaded their mother to use their inheritance to buy them a route hauling milk to the processing plant. To supplement this income, Cliff and Earl Schuette had added pulpwood and veneer logs to the cargo by the late 1930's. The farm woodlot, economically valuable to so many during the Depression, would have even greater long-term significance for the Schuette brothers. Expanding their operations still further, they built a small sawmill to do custom-sawing for area farmers. This, in turn, directed their interest towards home building, although only on a modest scale at first, since lumber was soon diverted to national defense priorities. Once the war ended, however, the housing boom did for the home building industry what the western advance of settlement had done for the lumber industry more than a century before. Selling the milk route, the Schuette brothers joined the rush of new builders. The name of the Schuette Lumber Company was changed in 1946 to Schuette Builders Company.

Many amassed quick fortunes, only to be trampled eventually in the stampede, but the Schuettes were among the notable survivors. Over the next thirty years, Cliff and Earl, with the later assistance of their younger brother Marvin, organized a variety of companies which became an empire in the housing field. Schuette's One Stop Building Center, incorporated in 1946, became a major building materials supplier for central and northern Wisconsin. A house-moving operation, Schuette Inc., was formed in 1957; in the early 1960's, it transported an entire Michigan community to a new location. House manufacturing, however, brought the Schuette Companies the greatest national, and even worldwide, recognition. Weston Homes Inc., organized in 1968 to offer lower-priced competition to the growing county mobile home industry, shipped orders as far as South America, Africa, and the Mideast. Wausau Homes Inc., established in 1960 as the Housing Service Company, was the crown jewel of the Schuette empire. By the mid-1970's, its product was being sold by 230 dealers in thirteen Midwestern states. The firm's move at the end of 1974 to a seventy-seven acre, four million dollar plant complex in the towns of Weston and Kronenwetter provided a graphic demonstration of what creative individual efforts could accomplish in a changing postwar economy.[39]

Along with traces of old-style personal enterprise, other—less welcome—reminders of the past resurfaced. Strikes remained a source of concern. Even the usually docile Wausau Paper Mill workers walked off their jobs in 1947, following the dismissal of the firm's general manager.[40] Hopes for labor-management peace had soared briefly in the fall of 1950, when Wausau Mayor Herbert Giese appointed an unofficial nine-member mediation panel. "A Good Move" commented the *Record-Herald*. A similar committee had proved its worth in an eastern industrial city; "there [was] no reason why it couldn't . . . be highly useful here."[41] If the expectation of industrial harmony was ever realistic, it came to a decisive end on February 28, 1952 at the plant gates of Marathon Electric.

In retrospect, J. J. Wall's preference for the victorious C. I. O. affiliate in the 1937 jurisdictional struggle had brought him nothing but grief. Periodic labor troubles had haunted the company ever since. The aggressive United Electrical Workers Local 1113 had instituted work stoppages in 1941 and 1946. And trouble was brewing again early in 1952. A longstanding list of grievances, including a two cent per hour wage increase, remained unresolved. Negotiations had reached an impasse by the morning of February 28, when the union officers and stewards called for a general membership meeting at 2:00 p.m. that day. At the appointed hour, the first shift workers left the plant to attend. The consequences of this new work stoppage were not long in coming. While the unauthorized union meeting was still in progress, the second shift arrived for work, only to find the plant gates locked. A statement released by Marathon Electric the following day notified its six hundred employees that they had been discharged and "removed from the company payroll."[42] James J. Wall, the consummate bridge player, had laid down his trump card.

Battle lines were quickly drawn by the chief protagonists in the *Record-Herald*. Union president and sixth ward alderman Emil Muelver charged on March 1, that the "anti-labor corporation" had consistently violated the current union contract over the past six months. The "workers' patience" had finally reached the "saturation point." And now a "vicious 'lockout' club" was being swung over their heads. J. J. Wall's response appeared two days later: It was the workers who had violated the contract by walking off their jobs without going through the "orderly, well regulated, methodical" grievance procedure. Moreover, the company announced in the classified ads section that it was now accepting employment applications at the factory office. Picket lines went up around the plant the next day. An open letter from Wall to the newly unemployed followed on March 6. Except for union officers, stewards, and committeemen, those who wished to return to work were free to do so. But, by virtue of Local 1113's "strike," they would be without seniority and without their union, which was no longer recognized as their bargaining agent. Seniority might be restored "if later on there is orderly collective bargaining, with a union which will act in a responsible way." Plant operations were resumed on the morning of March 18, with virtually an entire new work force in place. Local 1791 of the International Brotherhood of Electrical Workers, A. F. of L., was organized and recognized by the company. Local 1113, castigating management for hiring "union busters and scabs," intensified its picketing. The longest, most bitter labor dispute in Wausau's history (and until the Kohler strike several years later, in the history of Wisconsin) was in full swing.[43]

That the "strike-lockout" would engender so much animosity was inevitable. The times were not conducive to moderation. Public fear of Communist subversion, fanned by twenty months of war in Korea

Postwar Industrial Peace At Marathon Electric

and the accusations of Wisconsin's junior senator, Joseph McCarthy, was at its height. The headline "Grandmother Tells Of Spying on Michigan Reds" highlighted the front page of the February 29 *Record-Herald,* along with news of the Marathon Electric closing. And the American labor movement was being closely scrutinized by the Communist hunters. Congressional committees were in the process of investigating Communist domination of unions. The United Electrical Workers, in particular, was under a cloud of suspicion. It had left the C.I.O. in the midst of the organization's 1949-1950 purge of Communist affiliates. *U.S. News and World Report* warned in 1951 that segments of the labor movement couldn't be trusted in an international crisis; the electrical workers were singled out for special mention in the article. Charges of a Communist conspiracy in the union leadership thus permeated the Marathon Electric dispute, adding more sparks to an already charged atmosphere.[44]

Excesses and abuses occurred on both sides. Picketers' attempts to show employees "the error of their ways" frequently involved name-calling, scuffling, and the suggesting of intriguing physical feats. The listing of "scabs" and unflattering biographical portraits in the union's newspaper, *Eye-Opener,* invited harassment.[45] Outside parties were also placed in a difficult situation. Emil Muelver explained that, as part of the union's effort to persuade workers not to enter the plant, 'We would have relatives call on relatives and by their own methods try to convince them not to do it.' A former Local 1113 official later conceded that he and the other leaders were not without fault in escalating the original disagreement beyond the point of no return. A federal circuit court of appeals, in fact, ruled in June, 1955, that Marathon Electric was within its rights in dismissing the workers.[46]

But the hands of management were far from clean. Many workers, including those on the later shifts, had not attended the unauthorized union meeting. Even if the gathering was a "breach of contract," as the company maintained, the lockout and wholesale firing punished the innocent as well as the guilty. Indeed, the intermediate report of a National Labor Relations Board examiner found Marathon Electric's dismissal of the 63 employees who had remained on the job February 28, and the group of 105 which had been laid off prior to that date, an unfair labor practice. Some of J. J. Wall's subsequent actions hardly ranked in the highest levels of industrial statesmanship. He would later recall:

> "The strikers ran a newspaper, and they said we were hiring everybody—bank robbers, thieves, mentally deficients and all. The only comment I had to make about that was they were 100 per cent correct. We hired everybody who could walk."[47]

That statement, plus the NLRB examiner's mention of additional unfair labor practices by the company, suggests that the president was something other than a victim—that he was trying once again to rid himself of a troublesome union and substitute one more to his liking. Wall's habit of driving slowly in front of the picket lines further aggravated an already explosive situation.[47]

The dissident unionists began to feel the financial pressure before the year ended. The M. E. Employees Credit Union sent out letters demanding immediate payment of outstanding loans. At least one union officer was informed that his membership had been "terminated" and his mortgage transferred to an out-of-town bank. Not all stayed, of course. Skilled and semi-skilled workers moved to Milwaukee or Minneapolis. Their leaving represented only part of Wausau's economic loss. Marathon Electric's value as a tax asset diminished, as production had to be curtailed during 1952. The consequent decline in earnings ultimately meant the city's share of state income tax dropped more than $100,000 for the year. But the company would recover. In 1959, the firm spent over $1 million to add 60,000 square feet to the Wausau plant. James Wall stepped down from the company presidency the next year, credited with making "the name of 'Marathon' . . . known among motor users throughout the country." And more growth came under successor Robert V. Jones. Plans for a five-year, $11.6 million expansion program were announced in March, 1967. To this day, however, the "strike-lockout" remains a topic Marathon Electric would prefer to forget.[49]

Attempts at dealing with another problem of industrialization—pollution—were more admirable. In 1936, Marathon Paper Mills had completed a plant for the production of vanillin, a synthetic vanilla flavoring obtained from pulp mill waste liquor. A new concern, the Salvo Chemical Company, was formed to operate the facility. A newcomer to the area headed the corporation: a young English chemical engineer named Frederick John Zimmerman. The 1942 takeover of Salvo by the Sterling Drug Company proved no hindrance to his considerable abilities, as he was chosen to supervise the firm's postwar expansion program. The Zimmerman-Sterling combination would have great significance for the advancement of pollution control. His direction of the company's research led to the invention in 1954 of a wet air oxidation process for the disposal of organic wastes. It was appropriately dubbed the "Zimmerman Process." A new Zimpro Division was created at Rothschild to develop and market the "revolutionary system," with its namesake serving as president. The first installation of a Zimmerman unit came at the Wausau Sewage Treatment Plant. Speaking at the February, 1961, dedication ceremonies, Sterling's president, Dr. J. Mark Hiebert, expressed the hope that the city's plant would be 'the first of . . . innumerable Zimmerman Process installations throughout the United States and in other lands.' By 1963, Zimpro units had been established in South Milwaukee; Chicago;

The Valley, west of Brokaw, 1976

Wheeling, West Virginia; and Rye, New York. At the time of Zimmerman's death in 1976, his technology was being used in nearly 150 cities worldwide. His work would also be beneficial to the county economy. Sterling's 1961 decision to build its Engineering Development Center at Rothschild was attributed to "Ted" Zimmerman's influence, and was seen as having "far-reaching and permanently desirable effects upon the entire community."[50]

Pride in pollution abatement was also exhibited at Brokaw. In 1959, Wausau Paper Mills became the first papermaking firm in the country to install the Magnefite pulping process for chemical recovery. Seven years later it claimed the distinction of being one of the first American operations to practice pollution control under the George Copeland system. In fact, a company spokesman told the Wausau Rotary Club in 1976 that the firm's commitment to environmental quality dated back to 1950. The first phase of its program, completed in 1972, had cost $7 million and had removed sixty-eight per cent of the solids and seventy-one per cent of the oxygen-demanding materials from the river. Phase two, having an appropriation of $6 million, was aimed at achieving even larger reductions. The air was another matter, however. Late in 1976, the mill was fined in Marathon County

Circuit Court for having discharged sulfur dioxide into the air in excess of state limits for twenty-two days that summer. Yet, in imposing a $4,400 penalty, Judge Ronald Keberle paid the company a tribute:

> I am impressed by the fact that the court did visit the plant in question and it can't be disputed that major steps have been taken by the defendant to correct its operations so that water and air pollution does not occur. You can't deny the fact that hundreds of thousands of dollars, even millions of dollars, had been spent in this area by the company, so as to categorize them [sic] as a major pollutant and someone who isn't doing things to combat pollution I don't think is correct.[51]

Even in a moment of defeat there was acclaim.

Modern Farm Scene, Town of Maine, 1976

Contradictions also characterized the farm situation. Marathon County remained an agricultural leader in the state in the postwar era. From 1940 to 1954, it maintained its top ranking among Wisconsin counties in the number of farms and amount of farm acreage. With respect to crops, it continued to hold first place in acreage devoted to tame hay, to be among the top three counties in oat acreage, to be among the top four in potato acreage, and to be among the top six in canned pea acreage. As for livestock, between 1940 and 1956, it had increased its standing from fourth place to first in the number of horses and mules. But the county remained above all a dairy center. Among the hundred leading dairy counties in the nation in 1954, Marathon ranked second in the number of milk cows and fourth in the poundage of whole milk and value of dairy products sold. By 1967, the county was claiming first place nationally in the number of dairy cows and second in the amount of milk produced. Moreover, the dairy cow's relative value to the county farmer had increased considerably. Milk had represented 57.2 per cent of gross farm income in 1931. After dropping to 51.7 per cent in 1936, it rose to 60.6 per cent in 1944, to 63.2 per cent in 1950, and to 66 per cent by 1964. As of 1973, the sale of dairy products was bringing $55 million into the county's agricultural economy, or 70 per cent of the total cash receipts.[52]

Yet behind these impressive indicators, the theme of loss lingered. In marked contrast to the total county population, the farm population had been on a general downward trend since 1934, decreasing 9 per cent between that date and 1940. The sharpest drop, however, occurred after the start of the war, when the demands of military service and defense industry work depleted the farm labor supply. Indeed, the scarcity of capable manpower was blamed for lowering the price of milk cows and for creating a "farm auction crisis" near the end of 1942. The consequent acceleration of farm mechanization accentuated the trend, once peace had returned. Attractive industrial wages, educational opportunities, and the higher capital outlays required to run a farm were additional factors in persuading many rural residents not to return to the farm after military service. From 1940 to 1950, the county's farm population declined roughly 15 per cent, compared to the approximate 6 per cent increase in the total population. Kronenwetter and Rib Mountain showed the biggest losses among the townships, with declines of 41.4 per cent and 32.6 per cent respectively. Over the next six years, all but four towns—Emmet, Easton, Cassel, and Halsey—recorded decreases. By 1955, the

Marathon County farm population had fallen 27 per cent below the 1934 figure.[53]

The number of farms had also been dropping since 1935. The 1954 total of 5,691 farms, while first in the state, was the smallest figure since 1910. C. J. McAleavy estimated that during his tenure as county agent from 1952 through 1961, farms had disappeared at the rate of a hundred per year. By 1974, the county still had the most farms in Wisconsin, but the 4,100 figure represented a smaller number than had existed at the turn of the century. Agriculture's relative importance as an employer declined accordingly. In 1940, approximately 39 per cent of the county labor force had been engaged in farming. Farming still led manufacturing, 31.7 per cent to 27.4 per cent, as of 1950. But by 1960, the agricultural percentage had plunged to 20 per cent, and to only 11 per cent by 1970. This translated into a 56 per cent decline in the agricultural labor force over a thirty-year period.[54]

As the farm population and number of farms dropped, the size of Marathon County farms was becoming larger. The rapid mechanization sparked by the war and additional technological improvements made large-scale operations more efficient. Between 1940 and 1945, the farms' average size increased from 118.4 acres to 132 acres, the biggest expansion in the county's history. In the immediate postwar years one could still find young couples clearing land north of Athens and farming much as the immigrant pioneers had done a generation or more before them. But in the older agricultural areas, consolidation was the general practice. The average size of county farms grew to 139.9 acres in 1950, to 158.2 acres in 1959, to 166.3 acres in 1964, and to 179.3 acres by 1974. In the view of one life-long Town of Rietbrock resident, this trend brought about an unwelcome change in farm life, transcending economic considerations. Along with the expanded farms, and the combines, choppers, and other mechanized aids needed to run them, came a loss of "neighborliness." The eagerness to exchange help and ideas, according to some, had been replaced by technological independence. Farming, in short, had become a big business with all the consequences.[55]

However accurate this observation, there was no denying that those who remained in farming lost one valued source of help and ideas. On June 30, 1952, William J. Rogan closed a thirty-one year career as the county's second agricultural agent. Rogan had taken over the Marathon County post (after three years of similar service in Juneau County) at a time when the three-year-old office still had to prove its value to many skeptical farmers. By the fall of 1922, the new agent had received an endorsement from the Marathon County Union of the American Society of Equity.[56] But his most important work would come during the Depression. His role in combating the grasshopper invasions has been discussed in the previous chapter. In addition, he was instrumental in securing reduced freight rates for the importation of feed, in instituting the state drought relief program, and in creating the Wausau Production Credit Association. Over $1 million was brought into the county as a result of his efforts. This 'yeoman work,' plus his consistent promotion of cooperative ventures, soil conservation, and rural electrification, drew praise from county and state officials as he neared retirement. Once out of office, Rogan's potential for serving as an agricultural elder statesman was cut short by tragedy. On the night of December 16, 1952, his car crashed into a power pole on Grand Avenue. The man recently lauded as 'the outstanding county agent in the state' died the next morning.[57]

Bill Rogan was undoubtedly missed. The postwar farming community needed innovative leaders as the cost-price squeeze tightened. While the Wisconsin farmer's gross income was rising 25 per cent between 1950 and 1964, his net income was dropping 2 per cent below the 1950 figure. Production costs, meanwhile, had climbed 41 per cent. Mechanization had made possible the efficient operation of larger farm acreage, but it also had brought additional expenses. The use of petroleum products was increased, for example; 89.3 per cent of the county's farms reported an average expenditure of $229.57 per farm in 1949. By 1954, 94.5 per cent were reporting an average expenditure of $305. The growing acceptance of commercial fertilizers and lime resulted in further financial depletion. In a predominantly dairy region with a short growing season, feed was, however, the major expense.[58] Railway shipments of dairy feed into Athens increased from fifty-eight carloads in 1941 to one hundred carloads by 1947. Ninety-two per cent of the county's farms spent an average of $804.24 for livestock and poultry feed in 1949. Five years later, 94.3 per cent were spending an average of $830. The buildings and equipment required for the care of a dairy herd were also expensive items. Better breeding practices, closer culling, and improved feeding were responsible for increasing productivity.[59] Yet the high capital outlays meant that in 1966 "the average Class A dairy farmer (authorized to market fluid milk) earned a return of only $1.08 an hour for his labor."[60]

The farmers' financial plight was reflected, in part, by the declining farm population. Those who remained increasingly sought outside work: 37 per cent of Marathon County's farmers worked off their farms in 1949, 41.4 per cent did so in 1954, nearly 50 per cent as of 1964.[61] For a distinct minority, the militancy symbolized by the Depression-era milk strikes[62] was seen as the answer. The 1955 founding of the National Farmers Organization in Iowa filled such a vacuum, with its demands for collective bargaining and for withholding production from market "to force processors to contract at prices guaranteeing a fair return."[63] Five years later, a chapter was formed in Marathon County. By the mid-1970's, an unfavorable cost-price ratio was still confronting Wisconsin farmers. Sharply rising production expenses, especially for feed, accompanied falling prices for major products such as milk and meat animals.[64] The NFO claimed the allegiance of, at most, 10 to 15 per cent of the county's farmers. But the group's ability to command public attention far surpassed the size of its membership. The NFO-sponsored public slaughter of 671 veal calves (some donated by Marathon County members) at the small Clark County community of Curtiss on October 15, 1974, received national news coverage. And it resulted in a flood of outraged letters to the *Record-Herald*. The response to the NFO's dramatic protest was not entirely negative. A Wausau businessman commented that he could understand the farmers' desperation: 'If they're getting pinched they have to do something. . . . In my business if we've got problems, we just wouldn't sell to a guy who wouldn't pay the price. But the farmers have no choice.'[65] A Town of Marathon resident summed up the rural reaction:

> How many of you non-farmers are willing to take
> a cut in wages with costs continually climbing? That's
> what we're doing. The price of everything we buy has
> gone up but what we have to sell has gone way down.
> Things just don't come out.[66]

The land had been cleared long ago, and its suitability for agriculture proven beyond question. Yet, the weekend before the calf kill, members of the Concerned Farmers Association had met with representatives of Wisconsin's political leaders at Marathon City. Their message: farmers were considering raising only enough food to feed their families and letting consumers go hungry.[67] As had been the case with the lumber industry, productivity gave no final guarantee of stability.

Many changes have taken place in Marathon County since George Stevens landed at Big Bull Falls 138 years ago. A forested wilderness was converted into a center of the American lumber industry. Organized settlements grew up with the sawmills along waterway and railroad track. First pine, then hemlock and hardwood fell, and with them the county's first major industry. This was essentially the end of the story for much of the Cutover, but not its southern rim. There, the abundance of natural and human resources led to the exploration of new economic avenues. Wausau, once the lumbering capital of the upper Wisconsin, was gradually transformed into a major business and industrial center. In this process of industrial diversification, new communities were created, and others revitalized. Meanwhile, a variety of immigrant settlers were transforming the surrounding countryside into an agricultural showcase. The expressions of farm discontent, the appearance of industrial enterprise in the countryside, and a recent proposal that villages change from agricultural service to lightweight industrial centers[68] indicate that the ideal developmental pattern for all Marathon County is still being sought. This reality, coupled with the numerous signs of growth in the Wausau area,[69] ensures that the county will remain at the center of things in more than a geographic sense for years to come.

FOOTNOTES

[1] The city purchased the old Marathon Electric plant at 125 West Washington Street, which had also served as the state's first forest products laboratory, for use as a vocational school.

One astute Edgar resident profited handsomely from the Parcherville boom. The previous spring Ben Straub had purchased twenty-six tax-delinquent lots for $1,700. By March of 1941, he had sold twenty at prices ranging from $350 to $375 apiece.

Wausau Daily Record-Herald, September 17, 1940, p. 1; March 17, 1941, p. 12.

[2] Other highlights of the war years included the election of Wausau's Helen Ohm as the first female member of the Marathon County Board (Miss Ohm had previously been the first woman to serve on the Wausau City Council from 1922 to 1924), and the U. S. Navy's decision to name one of its assault transports the "USS Marathon" in tribute to the county. See *Wausau Daily Record-Herald,* April 29, 1944, p. 1; September 12, 1944, p. 1; September 30, 1944, p. 1.

[3] The contributions of Marathon Electric and Marathon Battery to the war effort were singled out for special recognition by government and military officials. See *Wausau Daily Record-Herald,* January 10, 1944, p. 1; January 15, 1944, p. 1.

[4] *Wausau Daily Record-Herald,* January 25, 1944, p. 1.

[5] The total payroll for 1946 was expected to be fifty-eight per cent higher than in 1940, compared to a twenty-one per cent increase in employment during the same period. See *Milwaukee Journal,* January 23, 1945, p. I.

[6] Wisconsin State Chamber of Commerce, *Market Studies, Wausau and Marathon County* (Madison: 1944), pp. 1, 51, 3-6, 29, 41-49.

An interesting sidelight of the study was the determination of the county trading pattern. Wausau was shown to be most successful in attracting farm dollars for clothing, furniture, and shoes. In the categories of lumber and cement, feed, farm supplies, and groceries, there was greater dispersion among the incorporated localities.

[7] *Wausau Daily Record-Herald,* January 25, 1944, pp. 1, 10; March 10, 1944, pp. 1, 10; May 12, 1944, pp. 1, 10; October 11, 1944, pp. 1, 14; October 16, 1944. p. 3; October 31, 1944, p. 2.

[8] *Wausau Daily Record-Herald,* February 19, 1944, p. 8.

[9] *Wausau Daily Record-Herald,* March 10, 1965, p. 1; March 2, 1966, p. 1; March 7, 1967, p. 18.

[10] The Everest takeover was motivated, in part, by his fondness for vertical integration. One of the Brokaw mill's machines made paper only for Marathon Corporation's use in the manufacture of a particular kind of cup. Glenn Stevens Interview.

Once in control, Everest tried his hand at community building in Brokaw. He supervised the installation of the village's first sewer and water systems, and authorized the sale of company-owned land and houses to mill employees. One local account claims the latter reform resulted in many residents having to move out of the village when duplexes were converted into single-family units. For a depressing narrative on life in a company town, see "When: A Brief History of the Village of Brokaw." (manuscript in the Marathon County Historical Society, 1976).

[11] Karges, "David Clark Everest,' pp. 287, 293, 300-307.

"The Marathon Story," Special Wausau Number, p. 26.

"Fire, Flood, and Age," *Special Wausau Number,* p. 36.

Glenn Stevens Interview.

Milwaukee Journal, September 10, 1961, Part 4, p. 12.

Wausau Daily Record-Herald, Special Wausau Paper Mills Tabloid, September 15, 1961, p. 1; March 7, 1964, p. 3; December 28, 1967, pp. 1, 8.

[12] Everest served as president of the Wisconsin State Historical Society from 1952 to June, 1955, and was elected the first president of the Marathon County Historical Society in March, 1952. *Wausau Daily Record-Herald,* October 29, 1955, p. 11; *Centennial Edition,* June 30, 1972, p. 13.

At the end of his career Everest had no false modesty about his role at Marathon Corporation. When a friend suggested that the company should be named after him, he replied that it "was a little too much to expect;" and in any case, "most of the people who are in the paper trade or in the financial world when they think of Marathon, think of me anyway." D. C. Everest to M. M. Harrington, April 15, 1954, M. M. Harrington Papers, Archives of the State Historical Society, Madison.

[13] Karges, "David Clark Everest," pp. 309-312.

Wausau Daily Record-Herald, April 7, 1950, p. 8; October 29, 1955. p. 1; December 3, 1957, pp. 1, 4; February 28, 1967, p. 1; August 30, 1973, p. 3.

Wausau Area Chamber of Commerce, *Wausau Area News,* March, 1967, p. 1.

[14] The concept actually originated with the 1929 purchase of 4,500 acres of jack pine in northwestern Wisconsin.

[15] Moreover, declared the paper in an election year aside, the "industrial forest" project "offer[ed] . . . something that socialism, communism or 'state-ism' of the New Deal hybrid brand could not possibly offer. It offer[ed] jobs of a wealth-producing sort, in private enterprise, rather than a disguised dole financed by the taxpayers." *Wausau Daily Record-Herald,* October 25, 1944, p. 12.

[16] The Calwis firm of Green Bay made windshield cleaning chemicals and marketed chemically treated windshield towels converted by Mosinee's Bay West subsidiary. Green Bay Plastics produced plastic specialty items, including end caps used in Bay West's towel dispensing cabinets.

[17] Wausau business interests continued to have substantial representation in the company's executive leadership. Before the 1963 stockholders' meeting increased the size of the board of directors to add more Mosinee residents, Wausauites John E. Forester, Robert V. Jones, John D. Mylrea, George L. Ruder, and Ronald A. Westgate made up half of the membership. A spirited internal dispute erupted in the summer of 1971 when Board Chairman Forester and President Clarence Scholtens charged Mosinee cheese executive Francis Rondeau with an 'attempted raid' on the company through his stock purchases in order to effect 'changes in the company's management.'

Mosinee Times, Special Bi-Centennial Issue, July 1, 1976.

Wausau Daily Record-Herald, Centennial Edition, June 30, 1972, p. 6; August 30, 1963, p. 8; August 30, 1971, p. 29.

" 'Firsts' in Production," *Special Wausau Number,* p. 46.

[18] *Wausau Daily Record-Herald,* February 22, 1963, p. 1; March 10, 1965, p. 1.

Department of Business Development, *Economic Profile: Marathon County* (Madison: circa 1970).

Not that there weren't problems during the postwar period. State paper industry executives were warned at a 1946 conference in Wausau of an imminent pulpwood shortage resulting from anticipated Canadian export restrictions. *Milwaukee Sentinel,* February 13, 1946, p. 6. Construction of large wood pulp mills along the west coasts of the United States and Canada in the early 1960's was seen as presenting a competitive threat to America's Midwestern mills. And one potential solution was frowned upon by the government. In January, 1963, American Can, Mosinee Paper Mills, and Wausau Paper Mills pleaded no contest in U. S. District Court to price fixing in the purchase of pulpwood. Statements issued by the presidents of the Brokaw and Mosinee firms proclaimed innocence of the criminal charges, however. Displaying exemplary modesty, each contended that his company was a small one, and as such 'could not afford the tremendous expense of preparing for and going to trial.' *Wausau Daily Record-Herald,* September 9, 1964, p. 18; January 8, 1963, pp. 1, 7.

[19] The R. Connor Company had terminated its Stratford operation early in the Depression period. That firm ultimately fell victim to hard times, declared a special form of bankruptcy, and was taken over by the Connor Lumber and Land Company of Laona, Wisconsin.

[20] Primary responsibility for carrying out the policy changes belonged to Lawrence T. Riordan. Like his predecessor, George Silbernagel, Sr., Riordan had longstanding family ties to the woodworking business. His father, Thomas L. Riordan, a director of the Harris Brothers Company, had been involved in the lumber and building supply business for over half a century. Coming to Wausau in 1947 to carry on the family tradition, the son quickly graduated from making efficiency studies to the posts of secretary and general manager while still in his mid-twenties. In 1954, he was promoted to vice-president; three years later, to the presidency.

[21] Expansions undertaken by local industries were not confined to Marathon County. By 1974, Crestline had branch plants in Ladoga, Indiana; Corry, Pennsylvania; Petersburg, Virginia; Mechanicville, New York; Leon, Iowa; and Corning, California. *Wausau Daily Record-Herald,* March 15, 1974, p. 24. Nor was this trend limited to the paper and wood products enterprises. Marathon Electric constructed a plant in Earlville, Illinois, in 1946 and purchased the Burke Electric Company of Erie, Pennsylvania, in 1949. *Wausau Daily Record-Herald.* February 26, 1960, p. 10. By the mid-1970's, more than seventy years after the Wausau Group had first extended their operations to the southern United States, Wausau business leaders were again focusing their attention on that region. On September 9, 1975, Murray Machinery announced plans for construction of a plant in Florence, Alabama, for its newly created subsidiary, Murray Southern, Inc. Nine days later Marathon Electric announced its intention to open a new factory in West Plains, Missouri. *Wausau-Merrill Daily Herald,* September 10, 1975, p. 37; Interview with Bill Dodson, Assistant to the Chief Executive Officer, Marathon Electric Manufacturing Corporation, October 22, 1975.

[22] *Wausau Daily Record-Herald,* October 19, 1963, p. 9; May 4, 1963, p. 3; July 6, 1963, p. 3; February 1, 1964, p. 9; August 24, 1963, p. 9; March 23, 1963, p. 6; *Centennial Edition,* June 30, 1972, p. 22; July 20, 1970, p. 3; July 13, 1971, p. 14; June 29, 1964, p. 1; November 23, 1964, pp. 1, 8; March 2, 1968, p. 10.

Notes on Stevens Container Corporation, Charles Dodge Collection, Business Box.

"Pioneers Would Gasp," *Special Wausau Number,* pp. 53-56.

Milwaukee Sentinel, May 18, 1958, p. 14.

Notes on Underwood Veneer Company, Charles Dodge Collection, Lumber Business Box.

Connor, *Connor Timber,* pp. 104-107, 119-121.

[23] *Wausau Daily Record-Herald,* April 30, 1962, p. 1.

[24] *Wausau Daily Record-Herald,* April 30, 1962, pp. 1, 8; May 2, 1962, p. 6;

October 20, 1962, pp. 1, 2; February 2, 1963, p. 16.

[25] *Wausau Daily Record-Herald*, November 3, 1965, pp. 1, 8; December 17, 1965, p. 1; May 7, 1968, pp. 1, 14; August 6, 1969, p. 3; August 14, 1969, p. 23; August 26, 1969, p. 8; March 19, 1971, p. 19; July 20, 1971, p. 3.

Dun & Bradstreet Report, Marathon Battery Co., March 20, 1968.

Since approximately 75 per cent of the Wausau plant's employees were women, the shutdown aggravated an already unfavorable female employment trend in Marathon County. While 50.5 per cent of the county's 1970 population was female, women made up 29 per cent of the labor force. Nationally, 43 per cent of the labor force was female by 1970. *Wausau Daily Record-Herald*, August 7, 1971, p. 8.

[26] The reorganized Gilbert Shoe Company had been given the name Marathon Shoe Company in 1914. That, in turn, was changed to the Pied Piper Shoe Company in 1934, the brand name of the company's line of children's shoes. When the firm faced a financial crisis in 1935, the city purchased its land and buildings for $50,000. The company repurchased its property in 1944.

[27] *Wausau Daily Record-Herald*, February 25, 1965, pp. 1, 10; May 6, 1965, p. 12; March 7, 1967, p. 1; May 9, 1967, pp. 1, 10; March 15, 1973, p. 30.

[28] In 1915, Charles and Will Dodge, and George Pfeiffer acquired the H. E. McEachron Milling Company and renamed it the Cereal Mills Company. Charles Dodge left the Marathon Shoe Company around 1930 to devote full attention to his extensive milling interests. For historical background on Marathon County's once flourishing milling industry, see *Wausau Daily Record-Herald*, September 28, 1937, p. 10; February 29, 1964, p. 9; April 11, 1964, p. 9. See also Notes on Marathon County Milling Concerns, Charles Dodge Collection, Business Box. For biographical information on Charles Dodge, see *Wausau Daily Record-Herald*, May 23, 1961, p. 11; May 23, 1963, p. 1.

[29] *Wausau Daily Record-Herald*, April 6, 1968, p. 11.

Milwaukee Sentinel, September 21, 1968, Part 2, p. 9.

[30] The Mathie Brewing Company and the George Ruder Brewing Company, both organized, like the Marathon City firm, in the nineteenth century, were consolidated in 1918. The merged concern was known as the American Brewing Company until March, 1933, when the corporate name became the American Products Company. The following year it became the Mathie-Ruder Company. Operations were terminated in the 1950's. The Wausau Brewing Company was the last to be organized in March, 1913. It was acquired in 1934 by the George D. Wolf, Sr. family, owners of Wausau's Pepsi Cola Bottling Company. After the elder Wolf's death in 1960, Mrs. Wolf disposed of all local beer interests in 1961. See *Wausau Daily Record-Herald*, May 11, 1963, p. 9; December 31, 1966, p. 13; *Centennial Edition*, March 13, 1939, Historical Section, p. 16; July 20, 1963, p. 9.

[31] In reality the area concept was as old as the Wausau Group's paper mill ventures, and it had been an idea familiar to the chamber at least as early as preparation of the Bowman report.

[32] Edward A. Drott had established an automotive and crawler tractor dealership in Wausau's Eggebrecht Building in 1924. The sales and service operation was moved to Milwaukee the following year when facilities proved inadequate. However, Drott maintained a Wausau connection: his Hi-Way Service Corporation distributed snow plows made by the Wausau Iron Works. Drott's desire to be nearer his major supplier was partly responsible for the Drott Manufacturing Company's move from Milwaukee to Schofield in 1948. In December, 1967, Drott Manufacturing was purchased by the Houston-based conglomerate Tenneco Inc., and made a division of Tenneco's indirect subsidiary, J. I. Case of Racine. The Drott-Heinzen connection was renewed in August, 1971, when Edward Drott, Jr. purchased Wausau Iron Works, after having stepped down from the Drott Company presidency the previous year. *History of Drott Manufacturing Corp.*, pp. 2, 6-7; *Drott Marks 50 Years; Wausau Daily Record-Herald*, October 26, 1953, p. 3; December 22, 1967, p. 1; December 28, 1967, p. 4; August 26, 1971, p. 3.

[33] Yet, noted the *Record-Herald* in 1963, "the trend [in the Wausau area], as in the state and nation, is towards more and more service jobs for each industrial job." A survey of ninety-eight firms indicated that forty-five per cent of the employment increase between 1950 and 1968 had occurred in service industries such

234

as hospitals and schools. *Wausau Daily Record-Herald,* April 20, 1963, p. 6; October 8, 1968, p. 22.

[34] *Wausau Daily Record-Herald,* May 2, 1963, pp. 28, 30; May 19, 1965, pp. 1, 6; February 22, 1963, p. 1; March 10, 1965, p. 1.

Marathon County Economic Development Council, *Economic Profile Of Wausau, Wisconsin Area.*

[35] The D. J. Murray firm had prospered since its change of ownership and production. Annual sales increased by more than 1,000 per cent between 1921 and 1957. *Wausau Daily Record-Herald,* May 1, 1964, p. 1; *Milwaukee Sentinel,* February 17, 1957, p. 13.

[36] The Employers operation remained the Wausau Group's most successful venture. In 1923, the Employers Indemnity Corporation was organized to write auto, public liability, and other lines of casualty insurance; it was merged with the liability insurance company in 1937. The Employers Mutual Fire Insurance Company had been licensed for business in Wisconsin two years earlier. These expansions of service were grouped under the name Employers Mutuals of Wausau in 1935. By the end of 1949, the firm was licensed in all forty-eight states. In 1965, the current name of Employers Insurance was adopted; a life insurance company was also added that year. By 1970, Employers Insurance had passed Marathon Electric to become the leading business employer in Marathon County. *Wausau Daily Record-Herald,* May 15, 1964, pp. 1, 10; "Employers Mutuals," *Special Wausau Number,* p. 31; Schlueter, *The Wausau Story,* p. 15; Department of Business Development, *Economic Profile.*

[37] The Wausau Area Development Corporation was created in 1959 in response to the chamber's legal inability to raise money by issuing debentures. Another corporation project was its 1968 acquisition of the 400-acre Marathon County Industrial Airpark adjacent to the new Central Wisconsin Airport. *Wausau Daily Record-Herald,* May 2, 1963, p. 28; Wausau Area Chamber of Commerce, *Progress Through People, 1968.*

The chamber's efforts were not always successful. A major disappointment came in 1967, an otherwise banner year for Wausau area industrial development, when Zenith Radio Corporation chose Springfield, Illinois, over Wausau as the location for a 4,000 employee television assembly plant. See *Wausau Daily Record-Herald,* January 7, 1967, p. 1; March 7, 1967, p. 18.

[38] *Wausau Daily Record-Herald,* May 18, 1963, p. 3; November 30, 1963, p. 8; June 8, 1963, p. 3; February 23, 1963, p. 5.

[39] Like the Wausau Group before them, the Schuette brothers expanded their operations beyond the Wisconsin borders. A Wausau Homes plant was established in Ottumwa, Iowa; a Weston Homes facility in Newnan, Georgia. Vertical integration was advanced by the acquisition of a Marion, Wisconsin, truck body manufacturing firm.

Interview with Marvin Schuette, August 22, 1975, Marathon County Public Library Oral History Collection.

Wausau Daily Record-Herald, February 14, 1972, p. 23; September 21, 1972, p. 30; October 8, 1974, p. 18; October 5, 1963, p. 14; October 3, 1973, p. 3; June 20, 1974, p. 3.

Wausau-Merrill Daily Herald, September 29, 1975, p. 24.

[40] *Milwaukee Journal,* September 10, 1961, Part 4, p. 12.

[41] *Wausau Daily Record-Herald,* September 30, 1950, p. 10.

[42] *Wausau Daily Record-Herald,* February 29, 1952, p. 1.

Donald H. Streeter vs. Marathon Electric Manufacturing Corp., Hearing No. 15973, Industrial Commission of Wisconsin (1953).

[43] Industrial Commission of Wisconsin Hearing No. 15973.

Wausau Daily Record-Herald, March 1, 1952, p. 8; March 3, 1952, pp. 12, 16; March 6, 1952, p. 16; March 15, 1952, p. 8.

Milwaukee Journal, February 28, 1960, p. 9.

[44] David M. Oshinsky, *Senator Joseph McCarthy and the American Labor Movement* (Columbia: University of Missouri Press, 1976), pp. 98, 175-176, 88-89.

Nonetheless, U. E. Local 1113 received widespread support from A.F.L. and C.I.O. locals in the county which feared that if the Marathon Electric union was destroyed, "it would only be a matter of time before [they] and other aggressive labor organizations [would] be attacked in the same manner." The Marathon County Farmers Union pledged its "moral support" to the deposed Wausau local. *Wausau Daily Record-Herald*, March 8, 1952, p. 8; March 13, 1952, p. 12; March 11, 1952, p. 12; *Eye-Opener*, (Official Organ Local 1113 U.E.), March 5, 1953; May 13, 1953; February 26, 1953; April 2, 1953; March 12, 1953.

Ironically, the union had an important, if indirect, ally in Congressman Alvin O'Konski, one of the foremost anti-Communist stump speakers of the period. Local 1113 propaganda was broadcast over the O'Konski-owned radio station in Merrill, WLIN, thus precipitating a legal wrangle between the congressman and J. J. Wall. A Local 1113 delegation visiting Washington, D. C. in February, 1953, found Mrs. O'Konski a hospitable and sympathetic hostess. *Eye-Opener*, April 2, 1953; February 26, 1953; Transcript of Local 1113 Radio Program Broadcast Over Station WLIN, June 24, 1952, (in possession of Don Streeter); *Wausau Daily Record-Herald*, November 24, 1953, p. 1; Marathon County Circuit Court, Miscellaneous File, Alvin E. O'Konski vs. Marathon Electric Manufacturing Corporation, Case Number 19329, Clerk of Circuit Court, Marathon County Court House, Wausau, Wisconsin.

[45] The *Eye-Opener* contended, for example, that one worker changed his residence from Aniwa to across the street from the plant "so he can crawl in to do his dirty scabbing easier." The newspaper's choicest comments, however, were reserved for Marathon Electric's president. It once reported that "in Wausau a man went to jail for shouting 'Herr Hitler J. Wall! Hail!' This was slander, of course, for 'twas merely a horse trotting by with a closely cropped tail.'" *Eye-Opener*, February 19, 1953.

[46] Affidavits, Wisconsin Employment Relations Board vs. Local 1113, United Electrical, Radio and Machine Workers of America, its officers, agents and members and Emil Muelver, January 23, 1953, Marathon County Circuit Court, (in possession of Don Streeter).

Eye-Opener, February 5, 1953.

Wausau Daily Record-Herald, April 9, 1953, p. 18.

Don Streeter Interview.

Milwaukee Journal, February 28, 1960, p. 9.

[47] *Wausau-Merrill Daily Herald*, March 5, 1977, p. 12.

[48] *Wausau Daily Record-Herald*, March 6, 1953, p. 1.

WLIN Radio Program Transcript.

Don Streeter Interview.

[49] Don Streeter Interview.

Alex W. Brill to Donald Streeter, November 10, 1952; William J. Hoffman to Donald H. Streeter, September 16, 1952; William J. Hoffman to Donald H. Streeter, September 30, 1952; William J. Hoffman to Donald H. Streeter, October 20, 1952, (letters in possession of Don Streeter).

Eye-Opener, November 20, 1952; November 27, 1952.

Wausau Daily Record-Herald, February 26, 1960, pp. 1, 10; March 7, 1967, pp. 1, 18.

A new union at Marathon Electric did not preclude further labor disputes. Production was idled for three weeks in the fall of 1964, when over 700 members of Local 1791 went on strike over economic issues. For instigating intra-community divisiveness, however, Wausau would experience nothing comparable to the 1952 Marathon Electric dispute until the 1971 Wausau teachers' strike and the five-month strike at Murray Machinery in 1974. *Wausau Daily Record-Herald*, September 25, 1964, p. 1; October 17, 1964, p. 1; *Wausau-Merrill Daily Herald*, January 3, 1975, p. 1.

Emil Muelver moved on to become the director of District Council 48 of the American Federation of State, County and Municipal Employees. His name would again appear in the headlines when the Milwaukee city, county, and school employees called a strike in the early 1970's. *Wausau Daily Record-Herald*, January 5, 1973, p. 3.

[50] *Wausau Daily Record-Herald*, February 8, 1961, pp. 8, 14; February 14, 1961, p. 1; June 19, 1963, p. 10.
Wausau-Merrill Daily Herald, March 4, 1976, pp. 1, 8.
Karges, "David Clark Everest," p. 295.
Uncited clipping, Charles Dodge Collection, Business Box.

[51] Moreover, the fine of $220 per violation was relatively light. The minimum possible forfeiture was $10 per violation; the maximum, $5,000.
Glenn Stevens Interview.
Wausau Daily Record-Herald, February 8, 1961, p. 8; May 26, 1969, p. 3.
Wausau-Merrill Daily Herald, July 20, 1976, p. 3.
Marathon County Circuit Court, Miscellaneous File, State of Wisconsin vs. Wausau Paper Mills Company, Case Number 25183, Clerk of Circuit Court, Marathon County Court House, Wausau, Wisconsin.

[52] Wisconsin State Department of Agriculture, *Wisconsin Rural Resources, Marathon County*, Crop Reporting Service Bulletin (Madison: State of Wisconsin, 1956), pp. 35, 57.
Wausau Daily Record-Herald, January 7, 1967, p. 8.
Marathon County Agriculture, 1946, p. 27; 1954, p. 51.
Marathon County Resource Development Council, *Overall Economic Development Plan* (Wausau: 1966), p. 99.
Cash Receipts Data for Marathon County, (obtained from Wisconsin State Department of Agriculture).
Dairying's increasing importance within the county farm scheme was evident in the changing milling function of the Athens Cooperative Produce Company. As late as the 1940's, wheat and rye had been brought to the cooperative mill from Wausau, Merrill, Stevens Point, Chippewa Falls, and even Michigan's Upper Peninsula, to be ground into flour. In 1944, however, the cooperative donated its flour milling machinery to the scrap drive; and thereafter the preparation of dairy feeds became the company's main business. Branch feed stores were opened in Hamburg and Milan. Helgeson, "Athens, Wisconsin," pp. 69-71.

[53] *Wisconsin Rural Resources*, pp. 11, 13-14.
Marathon County Agriculture, 1954, pp. 14, 17-18.
Wausau Daily Record-Herald, October 20, 1942, p. 10.

[54] *Wisconsin Rural Resources*, pp. 17-18, 4.
Wausau Daily Record-Herald, November 4, 1961, Farm Events, p. 1.
Wisconsin Statistical Reporting Service, *1975 Wisconsin Agricultural Statistics*, p. 4.
Marathon County Economic Development Council, *Economic Profile of Athens, Wisconsin Area*.

[55] The consolidation movement provided additional business for the Schuette brothers. After buying vacated farm homes, speculators would hire the Schuettes to move the structures into the Wausau area, where they were remodeled and then sold. Marvin Schuette Interview.
Television also played a part in the loss of rural "togetherness." Improvement of local television reception after 1954 led to declining attendance at the weekly movies shown at the Marathon and Edgar village halls. These once popular Sunday outings for rural families quickly became unprofitable and were discontinued. Marzynski, "Cassel," p. 7.
Wisconsin Rural Resources, pp. 17-18.
Helgeson, "Athens, Wisconsin," pp. 75-76.
Overall Economic Development Plan, p. 95.
Interview with John Gesicki, August 30, 1975.

[56] *Marathon County Farm Journal*, June, 1921, p. 5; October, 1922, p. 7.

[57] For more on William Rogan's contributions to agriculture, see *Wausau Daily Record-Herald*, June 12, 1952, pp. 1, 10; December 17, 1952, pp. 1, 15; "Farming's Spark Plug," *Special Wausau Number*, pp. 16-17.

[58] One observer blames the present financial predicament of many farmers on their keeping larger herds than their acreage can handle, thus necessitating large feed purchases over the winter. John Gesicki Interview.

[59] Marathon County milk production:

	Producing Cows Number	Total Milk Production Pounds	Production Per Cow Pounds
1925	63,500	336,550,000	5,300
1930	68,900	399,620,000	5,800
1935	71,400	357,000,000	5,000
1940	80,000	440,000,000	5,500
1945	91,800	569,160,000	6,200
1950	83,500	567,800,000	6,800
1955	89,500	626,500,000	7,000
1965	93,300	802,380,000	8,600
1974	85,500	872,100,000	10,200

Marathon County Agriculture, 1954, p. 48.
Wisconsin Rural Resources, p. 39.
Wisconsin Statistical Reporting Service, *1967 Wisconsin Agricultural Statistics,* p. 78; *1975 Wisconsin Agricultural Statistics,* p. 78.

[60] Nesbit, *Wisconsin,* p. 509.
Marathon County Agriculture, 1954, p. 60.
Wisconsin Rural Resources, pp. 49-51.
Helgeson, "Athens, Wisconsin,' p. 78.

[61] The number working off their farms one hundred days or more grew from 17.1 per cent in 1949, to 20.5 per cent in 1954, to approximately 25 per cent by 1964.

[62] See Chapter VII.

[63] Nesbit, *Wisconsin,* p. 511.

[64] Wisconsin Statistical Reporting Service, *1975 Wisconsin Agricultural Statistics,* p. 2.

[65] *Wausau Daily Record-Herald,* October 16, 1974, p. 3.

[66] *Wausau Daily Record-Herald,* October 25, 1974, p. 4.

A Hatley farm wife replied to critics that she and her husband "do not belong to the NFO and we'll probably never join, but I do feel what they are trying to do is for the good of even you." *Wausau Daily Record-Herald,* October 22, 1974, p. 55.

[67] *Wausau Daily Record-Herald,* October 14, 1974, p. 3; For information on the Marathon County NFO, see Interview with Adolph Gruny, Jr., August 20, 1975, Marathon County Public Library Oral History Collection.

[68] Marathon County Economic Development Council, *Economic Profile of Athens.*
Marathon County Economic Development Council, *Economic Profile of Edgar, Wisconsin Area.*

[69] For how Wausau area community leaders view the future, see *Wausau-Merrill Daily Herald,* December 28, 1976, p. 3.

PART II
The Political Landscape

CHAPTER SIX

The Impact of Ethnic Heritage:
Cultural Politics, 1890-1920

The politics of Marathon County, like those of Wisconsin, are historically complex. The county which sends a young liberal like David Obey to Washington has also supported a Melvin Laird with considerable gusto, just as the state has given the nation such divergent political figures as Robert La Follette and Joseph McCarthy. Progressivism scored impressive victories in central Wisconsin during the Great Depression and again in the 1960's and 1970's; yet an underlying conservatism may be traced to the very early years of the twentieth century, when political traditionalism remained strong in an age normally regarded as the "Progressive Era."

A prominent journalist of that period, Ray Stannard Baker, only slightly exaggerated the character of politics in the Badger State:

> In Wisconsin, when two citizens meet, one instantly heaves a tough political argument at his neighbor, and the other responds by belaboring his friend with a wholly contrary idea. This continues for some time. Then one of them mentions La Follette, at which they grapple, pull hair, and roll over in the bushes. When completely exhausted they get up, shake hands, and go home feeling that it has, indeed, been a profitable meeting, and that Wisconsin is the best of all states to live in.[1]

That tradition of impassioned debate was matched by a lively tradition of political discourse in Marathon County, growing out of the historic socio-economic composition of the country's population. Intense partisanship based upon ethnic and religious identification clearly characterize the voter behavior of the county as the nineteenth century came to a close.

Like the state of Wisconsin, Marathon County retained a substantial European cultural heritage well into the new century, and this ethnic background played an important part in its political preferences, particularly before the end of the First World War. The dominant ethnic group in the county at this time was German. Situated at the western extremity of the lakeshore German settlement, Marathon was settled by peasants from the agricultural districts of northeast Germany. By 1900, these transplanted farmers and their German-born urban neighbors constituted 21 per cent of the county population, and as late as 1905, 50 per cent of Marathon County was over 70 per cent German. The heart of this settlement was to be found in the towns of Hamburg, Berlin, Maine, Stettin, Cassel, Marathon, Wien, Wausau and Rib Falls. These sometimes contained almost 100 per cent ethnic saturation.[2]

It is impossible to overestimate the significance of ethnicity in explaining the voter behavior of Wisconsinites at the turn of the century. While recent studies note that native-born old stock Americans enjoyed great political influence and the majority of participatory roles in local and regional politics, it is also clear that voter preferences were strongly influenced by religious and nationality background. In Marathon County, this meant that the strongest Democratic areas were those in which the majority of family heads or their parents had been born in Germany, Poland, or Bohemia. This trend reflected state-wide voting patterns: "the basis of voting support for the Democratic Party in all sections of the state came from both Catholic and Protestant Germans and from other predominantly Catholic and often 'new' immigrant groups."[3]

Perhaps the best illustration of the ethnic dimension of Marathon County politics is to be found in the struggle over the hated Bennett Law of 1890, which provided that no school would be regarded as a school unless was "taught therein, as part of the elementary education of children, reading, writing, arithmetic, and United States history, in the English language." This Republican-sponsored legislation raised the most bitter ethnic and religious antagonisms ever experienced in the state. German voters saw the law as an attack on their cherished parochial education system. The result was a repudiation of the Republicans in the 1890's unmatched until the Roosevelt victory of 1932. In Marathon County the Democratic challenger swamped the incumbent governor by a three to one margin, while a Wausau Democrat was elected mayor in a pattern repeated throughout the state. The ethnic impact is readily visible in two of the most heavily German townships in the state—normally Democratic Hamburg and Berlin, both over 90 per cent German. In Hamburg Democratic votes rose from 68 per cent in 1888 to 78 per cent in 1890, while Berlin voters rewarded the Democrats with an increase from 76 per cent to 97 per cent in the wake of the Bennett Law controversy.[4]

The first hint of any realignment came with the financial panic of 1893 and the ensuing depression, when the tired issues of the nineteenth century were eclipsed by the new problems of an emerging modern economy. While normal party divisions remained intact, the direction of county politics was changed by the rise of agrarian radicalism. A response to the economic crisis of the 1890's, this new vitality reflected the impact of the fledgling Populist Party in county politics. The rebels were encouraged by the mayoral victory in Wausau of a timber cruiser and political neophyte, E. J. Anderson. But the Springtime victory paled before the November realities, as Republican William McKinley grafted his stable image on a Republican party engaged in mortal combat with aroused but underfunded Democrats. Wisconsin Populists, lured by the politics of fusion, aligned themselves enthusiastically with the Democrats in support of young William Jennings Bryan in exchange for several concessions. These included the nominations for Secretary of State, one Milwaukee Congressional District, and several presidential electors. In Marathon County, fusion meant that Populists closed ranks behind the Democratic slate, which included the gubernatorial candidacy of Wausau's own W. C. Silverthorn. In the hottest election since 1876, county voters chose William McKinley as the spokesman of stability and prosperity, linking the Democrats with the Panic of 1893 and the ensuing depression. Despite the McKinley victory, the Democrats salvaged the majority of county offices, but the fusion campaign marked the beginning of the end for Populism in Marathon County.[5]

The national financial crisis of the 1890's and the uncertainties associated with Bryan's advocacy of the silver standard accelerated the political realignment under way in both state and county by 1896. This shakeup began with modest Republican gains at the county level and ended in a trend toward shared authority in county politics by the turn of the century, climaxing with the Roosevelt sweep of 1904. Along with this change, the Wisconsin Republican Party was also undergoing the first skirmishes in what was to become a dramatic conflict after 1900. The man responsible for this internal strife was gubernatorial aspirant Robert M. La Follette of Dane County, an insurgent "demanding political repentance as a means of salvation." The *Central Wisconsin* regarded the young challenger as "evidence of a mighty host which demands that Republican politics in Wisconsin shall mean more than platform announcement and subsequent manipulation, by the machine, of positions of trust that should be the gifts of the people."[6] Despite success in forcing the enactment of a reform platform, the La Follette faction lost the nomination to the incumbent governor, Edward Scofield. It was later disclosed that La Follette's subsequent failure to stump for the party candidate was the result of a serious illness, but the Democratic Wausau *Pilot* gleefully noted in 1899 that he was "altogether too healthy to suit the average machine Republicans."[7]

When the challenger announced once again for the governorship in 1900, the task before him appeared overwhelming. To the *Pilot,* La Follette's party was "past the redemption period" and "too corrupt to be headed by him or anyone else." And, echoing the conservative stalwarts who dominated the Marathon County Republican Party, the *Record* gave the reformer little encouragement in his struggle. He would only lead the Republicans into the morass already occupied by the Populist-dominated Democrats. The *Record* dismissed the idea of "imaginary political diseases" and endorsed the incumbent's record.[8]

Was the party ready for reform? The Democratic press began to predict that the "machine men" would be "laid out cold," since half the Republican party faithful were prepared to rebel. As the county caucuses approached, insurgents were reported to be actively courting Democratic support in the struggle to unhorse the stalwarts, while the *Pilot* exhorted Democrats to shun the GOP and to let them "wash their own dirty linen" since they had "lots on hand."[9]

Unwilling to relinquish power, Marathon County regulars organized for battle, while the stalwart press reiterated its own opposition to a La Follette nomination and a progressive platform. To no one's surprise, machine men, led by Frank Chesak and B. F. McMillan, controlled the Republican caucus and endorsed another term for Governor Scofield. In "a protest against the wave of sentiment that has swept over the state," Marathon County sent a solidly stalwart delegation to the state convention in opposition to the La Follette challenge.[10]

But as support for the insurgent mounted in the key caucuses and conventions, Scofield left the field. Consequently, La Follette captured his party's unanimous nomination for governor and proceeded to bring the machine into line. But a harmony campaign had its disadvantages: the 1900 election was not distinguished by sharp debate, as the nominee stressed Republican principles and the incumbent's record more than Progressive innovation. He did break fresh ground with proposals for increased railroad taxation and the direct primary election. The latter suggestion, long a La Follette favorite, was the heart of his Wausau address in October, 1900. In "the best Republican speech of the campaign," he touched upon several national issues before launching into "his pet hobby horse, the primary election law." After the candidate's peroration, an effort was made to woo Marathon County's disaffected stalwarts, as Senator Joseph Quarles "begged" for La Follette votes and party unity behind the "regular nominee" of the Republican Party.[11]

With former critics thus coming to La Follette out of expediency, the party closed ranks for a successful campaign which ended in a narrow victory in normally Democratic Marathon County. The GOP success notwithstanding, La Follette trailed the national ticket in the county; his modest margin reflected not only the depth of local Democratic strength, but also considerable footdragging by stalwart Republicans.[12]

Evidence of party regularity may be found in Marathon County's response to the major Progressive measure offered by the new governor: a direct primary election, meant to restore to the voter "the citizen's right to vote directly for the party nominee of his choice." When the governor embraced the idea again in his first inaugural address, the skeptical *Pilot* wondered aloud whether "Gov. Bob" would have "the same amount of courage to work great reforms as marked out by citizen Bob." When the primary bill was introduced, the Democratic press attacked the idea, with a reprint of criticisms from prominent Wausau Republican Louis A. Pradt, at that time serving in Washington as Assistant Attorney General of the United States. Admitting the shortcomings of the caucus system, Pradt suggested that a workable compromise might involve a primary election of all delegates to party conventions — though he maintained that the evils in the existing system would disappear if "all good citizens" attended the caucuses. Pradt found it impossible to endorse the governor's bill, which he defined as:

A bill abolishing the right of the people to meet in party conventions and to formulate their party principles in their own way, and providing for the rule of the minority in party nominations — and for other infringements upon the rights of the people.[13]

Marathon County regulars were not alone in their antipathy towards the revolutionary legislation: conservative elements in the senate, including Wausau Republican Andrew Kreutzer, succeeded in replacing the thoroughgoing primary bill with a weak substitute. To no one's surprise, La Follette vetoed the measure with a ringing indictment of the opposition, much of it directed at members of his own party. The Governor's action drew an endorsement from the *Central Wisconsin*, but the more conservative *Pilot* thought Kreutzer's action was commendable, since he "sincerely believed that he was serving his constituents better by voting in that way." In apparent agreement with this analysis, area voters returned Kreutzer to Madison, where he escalated his attack on the hated legislation.[14]

Responding to reform pressures, the Wausau senator proposed in 1903 a compromise law that allowed the voters to elect delegates to state and congressional conventions which would be responsible for the selection of candidates. This effort earned Kreutzer the enmity of reform Republicans and the La Follette press, who now viewed him as the symbol of the stalwart opposition. Despairing of party unity, the old guard succeeded in blocking the direct primary until the governor agreed to a referendum in the 1904 elections.

When the referendum was finally held, Marathon County sustained its state senator by rejecting the direct primary law by a 2 per cent margin. Several factors help to explain the county's resistance to this electoral reform, but none was more significant than the ethnic background of Marathon County voters. An analysis of statewide voting patterns reveals that predominantly German counties opposed the primary more strongly than neighboring counties, a tendency related to both the Democratic Party identification and the ingrained conservatism of many German voters. Marathon County returns were consistent with a statewide trend: pluralities against the reform were substantial in the majority of German townships and in those townships which normally gave large votes to Democratic candidates. Another force operating in Marathon County was the fact that it was generally regarded as a stronghold of conservative Republicanism, and that stalwarts naturally resisted the innovation. In its opposition to the direct primary, Marathon was unusual among the counties of the "New North;" most of these counties supported the law because it was perceived as a way to bring greater influence to outstate areas normally underrepresented by the prevailing caucus system.[15]

This last ditch resistance to Progressive innovation was symptomatic of the deep intra-party rift opened by La Follette's gubernatorial leadership. As early as 1901, Marathon County stalwarts began boosting Wausau's Walter Alexander as an alternative. While Alexander asserted his innocence of any such effort, he did allow his name to be discussed for a year before finally withdrawing in January, 1902. Much more credible was the challenge raised by State Senator John Whitehead of Janesville, who became a leader of the regular faction. Whitehead drew the early support of the *Record,* which regarded La Follette as "a factionalist and a bogus reformer," whose language and actions were "eternally at loggerheads." These reservations spilled over in a remarkable "Political Dictionary," which defined La Follette supporters in harsh terms:

> A half-breed is a Populist who trained with the Republican Party in the hope of securing office, but not succeeding now supports the governor, expecting at least to be appointed deputy game warden . . .
> A fair-minded Democrat is one who for a small consideration will attend a Republican caucus and assist the half breeds in electing their delegates . . .[16]

This brand of hostility penetrated stalwart quarters as the county convention drew near. Not surprisingly, they controlled the caucus and forced through a resolution repudiating Governor La Follette and endorsing Whitehead as his replacement. Ignoring a walkout by a La Follette minority, Marathon's delegates went to the state convention solidly pledged to the challenger. But despite grumbling over the governor's shabby treatment of fellow Republicans, the "seeds of discord" were insufficient to block his renomination.

Potentially more significant for central Wisconsin was the gubernatorial boom for Wausau Democrat Neal Brown. A man with long experience in state and local politics, including service in the state senate, Brown was highly touted as a candidate who would "not only receive the full Democratic vote but will draw from the Republican side enough votes to elect him."[17] Endorsed by the county party, Brown immediately launched a vigorous attack on the Republican record, saving his saltiest comments for "the vestal mysteries of La Folletism." The hometown favorite delighted the county caucus with a blistering assault on the proposed primary law as "radical legislation," advocating instead an innocuous electoral reform affecting local and county elections only. Thus did the local Democrats align themselves with conservative Republicanism in opposition to progressive change.

And the candidate of the north was no more successful than his party was in its doomed efforts to kill the primary. Brown's candidacy faded before the onslaught of the influential urban wing of the Democratic Party, which rammed through the nomination of Milwaukee Mayor David Rose. Although it insisted that "the convention did not act as wisely as it might have done," the *Pilot* and the defeated contender pledged full support of a man regarded by many as "the weakest candidate of the bunch." Marathon's support was ensured by a consolation prize: the nomination of local favorite Karl Mathie for State Superintendent of Education. This plum was important in healing the wounds opened by the Brown-Rose fight, which ended in the Marathon County Party's cordial endorsement of the state ticket and platform with a special pitch for Mathie's election.[18]

Democrats had long been concerned over La Follette's past appeals to the "fair minded" members of the opposition party. These fears reached fever pitch in late October when the governor's address at the opera house included "a strong appeal for Democratic votes . . . by mentioning the name of William J. Bryan." Outraged by this evidence of "political trickery," the Democratic press urged that "no Democrat be fooled by smooth words of an insincere politician, and afterwards suffer the pangs of regret for his folly." Area Republicans were no more impressed than the Democrats with the governor's performance, which failed to unify a badly split party. Powerful local stalwarts had invited La Follette to Wausau "with a will to bring about harmony in the party," but his stress on progressive taxation and the hated primary bill was not calculated to reduce prevailing "antagonism to the 'isms'" associated with his leadership.[19]

Democratic hostility and stalwart suspicion became obvious on election day, as La Follette edged Rose by 100 votes in Marathon County — a thin margin for an incumbent who swept the state by nearly 50,000 votes. The 1902 results underscore the strength of party regularity in Marathon County, where Democrats remained loyal in an election won by the governor with the support of an estimated 30,000 state Democrats. While county Democrats supported the party candidate, Republican conservatism was clearly expressed in the resounding endorsement given Senator Kreutzer, who had refused to toe the La Follette line and "exercised his right as legislator to follow his own conviction in matters not strictly party affairs." Another trend emerging was the tendency of Marathon County voters to split the assembly delegation between the parties—a pattern that was consistent during the early progressive years. And finally, the ethnic dimension of county voter preferences again appeared in massive Rose pluralities in heavily German Hamburg, Berlin, and Stettin townships.[20]

In the wake of the Progressive victory, Marathon County Republicans braced for a death struggle over control of the state party. Wausau lawyer Marvin Rosenberry, local stalwart leader and 10th District representative to the state central committee, later recalled that "both sides realized that the 1904 campaign would be decisive as to the future of the party." As regional spokesman for the regulars, Rosenberry traveled the district, "setting up an organization that would see to it that stalwart delegates were elected from each county." Thus, the 1903 legislative session was followed by an active effort by both sides to organize, instead of resting, as was normally the case. United as never before, the stalwarts were definitely preparing for a bolt; and central to these plans was the work of Marvin Rosenberry, who spoke for the stalwarts, before he led them out of the Republican convention in Madison to hold what party regulars regarded as the "legitimate" state convention. The bolters sent four delegates, including Rosenberry, to the national convention, where Senators Henry Payne and John C. Spooner maneuvered the seating of the stalwarts. This bit of chicanery, however, was less significant than the action of the Wisconsin Supreme Court, which ruled that the La Follette ticket be certified and listed as the official Republican ticket on the November ballot.[21]

In Marathon County, the conventional wisdom had the governor poised at the edge of political oblivion. The usually temperate *Central Wisconsin* chastised La Follette for using Populist methods of "arraying class against class, rich against poor and the corporations against farmers and laboring men — to gain his ends." Such behavior would mean "the political end of the man . . . as Republicans come to realize the extent of the insult he gave the party at the national convention." On a lighter note, the "sage of Wausau," Democrat Neal Brown, told a group of stalwart friends that they were "a lot of jackasses," who had "made" La Follette and lost control of their creation. Obviously enjoying the Republicans' agony, the *Pilot* reported that stalwart leaders "thought it would be better for the policies the party has been standing for to elect a Democratic governor in Wisconsin."[22]

"The Sage of Wausau," Neal Brown

Many Republican regulars acted upon this analysis, throwing their support to the conservative Democrat, ex-governor George W. Peck. Incensed by the usurpation of the party label, prominent Wausau stalwart Judge M. S. Hurley endorsed the Democratic nominee as "the strongest man the Democrats can name." And the Democratic press did all in its power to remind local citizens that La Follette's actions had "turned against him all the influential men of his own party, both in the state and outside of it." Even more obvious were the efforts of the Democratic county committee and its chief officers, John Lamont and Herbert Manson, to fish in troubled waters by emphasizing the governor's denunciation of Wisconsin's Senators and Congressmen, who returned the favor with charges that La Follette was "an imposter and a demagogue."[23]

But ironically, the crucial problem for the Democracy was not the Republican vote at all; rather, the key to the county and state election lay in keeping the party faithful in line. The *Record,* betraying an uncharacteristic concern for the strength of the Democratic ticket, had expressed reservations about Peck as a "colorless candidate," incapable of igniting enthusiasm in his own party. The journal predicted that Democrats would defect to La Follette just as they had in 1902, "when the Democratic Party made a platform, named a candidate and made a campaign to catch the stalwart Republican vote." Informed Democrats understood that the governor could not survive without a significant Democratic vote, and could find no reason to help perfect the governor's political machine, knowing full well that the incumbent would "have no more use for a Democrat than he has for a stalwart." Citing ex-governor Peck's strong, conservative business administration, the *Pilot* joined the Democratic county committee in urging their compatriots to vote the straight party ticket. When the Democratic candidate spoke at the Wausau opera house on October 7, he demonstrated his grasp of the problem, noting that the party's "young bucks" tended to stray when there was insufficient political action "to make it interesting at home." He now implored them "to come home and help chief Peck out," since a golden opportunity lay ahead if Democrats could be induced to vote their ticket.[24]

Unfortunately for the Democrats, this advice from the old war horse went unheeded, as the statewide La Follette wave created a stunning defeat for the stalwarts. The Marathon County response to La Follette again lagged behind statewide percentages, as the incumbent narrowly escaped with a 200 vote margin. Local observers noted that the governor owed his reelection to Democratic votes, as there was considerable evidence of stalwart crossover for Peck. Republicanism reached a benchmark in this election with a clean sweep of Marathon County offices that surprised both parties. A disbelieving *Pilot* remarked that the "wolf of last Tuesday was the Republican Party, and the sheep in the fold were the Democrats, and the wolf was ravenous."[25]

Its analysis correctly stressed the significance of a strong national ticket in a Republican year. Selected returns clearly indicate that Democratic margins were narrow in normally safe districts like Hamburg, Berlin, Stettin, and Rietbrock. Only in Irish Emmet, Polish Pike Lake and German Cassel were these trends resisted. In view of state and national trends, the remarkable development was not the fact of a Democratic setback, but rather the stubborn dissent of a robust minority in the face of the Progressive tide. Indeed, throughout the period of La Follette's ascendancy, the deeply-rooted Marathon County Democratic Party combined with recalcitrant stalwarts to challenge the forces of political change. In so doing, Marathon County bucked a statewide trend which ended in a new flurry of Progressive legislation, much of which found little favor among the conservative German population. Equally significant was the devastating impact of La Follette's politics of polarization on the county and state Republican Party. The *Central Wisconsin* spoke for many a county resident when it cried out against "personal abuse" by politicians and demanded a return to "a sane understanding of the political situation in this state."[26]

Beneath this harsh indictment of a reform governor was concealed a certain amount of local experimentation with Progressive political innovations. Among the new ideas emerging at the turn of the century was a new, self-conscious consumerism, like that found in countless American communities. Rooted in the rural cooperative tradition as well as in a new awareness of social change emanating from the economic crisis of the 1890's, this movement had surfaced in Wausau before the turn of the century. Viewing public education as a crucial element in any reform program, local business and professional men were instrumental in bringing extension courses in economics to the county in 1895. Another early evidence of consumer awareness surfaced in the "Wisconsin Valley Plan," which was a revolt against the Wisconsin Telephone Company's monopoly on service to Wausau, Merrill, Grand Rapids, and Marshfield. The local response to this problem took the form of a cooperative, which soon won over most of the monopoly's former subscribers. The Bell system attempted to kill the local competition by rate-cutting and even offers of free service; these efforts triggered widespread protest against this kind of corporate arrogance. Characteristic of local outrage was a letter from G. D. Jones of Wausau, indicting the company's action as "a war measure" and condemning those "who allow themselves to be cheaply boughten up." Jones counseled resistance to this attempted "destruction of our local company," insisting that the cooperative had in fact reduced rates and increased service. The *Pilot* agreed that "so plainly does the [stockholders'] report show that the trust was robbing the people of Wausau that it should be the duty of everyone to spurn its pauper service." As the struggle escalated, Mosinee interests also saw their community as "too closely identified with Wausau's, in the matter of cheap telephone service, to allow outside monopolies to come in and attempt to crowd out local or home enterprises."[27] Despite the determination of the local opposition, this struggle went on until 1903, when the Wisconsin Telephone Company finally abandoned the field to the cooperatively-owned independent.

Just as Wisconsin Valley citizens banded together to fight the trust, so rural residents united to create farmers' lines in areas too remote to command the attention of the larger telephone companies. Beginning as early as 1907 in the Town of Hull, the efforts in rural Marathon County coincided with a nationwide increase in telephone cooperative activity. And in 1908, in the Town of Holton, farmers organized the Brookerville and Holton Telephone Companies by subscribing $25 each and building lines with poles cut from their own woodlots. Serviced by the Dorchester and Abbotsford exchanges, these Progressive enterprises drew successfully on the rural cooperative tradition to bring a fuller life to county residents.[28]

Equally significant was the long struggle for cheaply-produced electrical power for street-lighting purposes. After strong support for municipal ownership in the 1899 elections, Wausau citizens found the cost of public construction prohibitive and chose to contract for the necessary service. But the issue did not die, and mayoral candidate E. C. Zimmerman pledged himself to public ownership in the 1904 election, with the full support of the local Democratic Party. Angered by an excessively high bid for service by the Wausau Electric Company, the local Democracy promised an investigation and, if warranted, the creation of a taxpayer-owned system. When the Zimmerman Administration initiated the probe, an alarmed electric company submitted a compromise plan to supply current to a publicly owned lighting system. Having secured the positive advice of Milwaukee engineer Jacob Klos, the city board of public works accepted a six year contract with Wausau Electric that retained the principle of private ownership of the power source. By stopping short of full municipal control, area citizens again demonstrated suspicions concerning Progressive innovation. This conservatism did not, however, prevent community leaders from serving the interests of local citizens, as the city-owned pole and wire line remained "a standing notice and warning to the Electric Lighting Company to furnish the current at a fair price."[29]

While the trend toward civic improvements accelerated during the ensuing administrations of Mayors Zimmerman, M. H. Duncan, and John Lamont, one reform goal remained elusive—the achievement of nonpartisan local government. Inspired by the victories of New York City reformers over Tammany Hall in the 1890's, Marathon County leaders called for the application of business values such as thrift and honesty to the political arena. Wausau reformers insisted that divisive national political issues should not be allowed to contaminate municipal elections, likening the municipality to "a business enterprise, which is purely local in its aims and business character." With the enthusiastic support of the local press, prominent local citizens spearheaded a movement toward the revision of the city charter, biennial mayoral elections, and nonpartisan nomination for high offices. The first step in the struggle required the drafting of a bipartisan "citizen's ticket" that would banish petty quarrels from the conduct of municipal affairs and bring to the fore "businessmen . . . who will look after the business interests of the city."[30]

The major deterrent to electoral reform was the partisanship spawned by long years of local political debate. Hence, it was vital to the proposed program that the offices be distributed equitably among the adherents of both political parties, lest the "party that thinks itself slighted . . . put a candidate in the field and then the jig is up."[31]

Citing successful precedents in both Green Bay and Merrill, Wausau reformers in March, 1900 created a nominations committee composed equally of Republicans and Democrats. After exhaustive deliberation, the group settled on two names, businessmen John Kiefer and Samuel Quaw, one from each party. Quaw, a Wausau lumberman, survived a drawing of lots, thus becoming the citizen's candidate for mayor. Likewise, ward committees met to approve names for ward candidates, though competitive candidates might enter the field by circulating nomination papers. All indications were that the nonpartisan drive would achieve success.

But just as the goal seemed within reach, objections from the wards clouded prospects for a nonpartisan victory. Arguing that the procedure was essentially elitist, a group led by veteran Populist C. M. Boyles emerged to threaten the citizens ticket by nominating its own slate. The Populist charges, which centered on ward candidates rather than on the mayoral race, drew the immediate fire of both the Democratic and Republican press. Typical was the sarcasm of the *Record,* whose reporter noted that the American eagle "very nearly broke a wing when he heard that his chief votary, C. B. Boyles, had been victoriously boosted into the mayoralty nomination as a rebuke"[32] to the erstwhile reformers.

Less shrill was the *Pilot's* plea for a mass community meeting to discuss the apparent impasse. After Quaw withdrew from the race, a fresh effort to rise above party was undertaken by a new citizen's committee, consisting of two Democrats, two Republicans, and one Populist. This committee solicited the cooperation of all political parties in approving a new ticket headed by Republican attorney Claire Bird, who asked for the support of all area citizens regardless of partisan affiliation. What the reformers did not count on was the dilatory tactics of the local Republican Party, which refused to endorse its own member and instead entered another candidate, accountant V. A. Alderson. It was now a question of "whether Wausau shall get in line with the other progressive cities of the Wisconsin Valley, or whether it shall remain at the tail end of the procession with Stevens Point." The Republican *Record,* long a supporter of nonpartisan local government, denounced the G.O.P. action as not merely a disappointment, but a "colossal mistake."[33] Despite support from the press, the only hope for the movement was an outpouring of independent Republicanism, which did not appear.

Thus, few surprises were to be found in the April returns, as many voters were "unable to divorce themselves from the old methods." When a strong Republican turnout for Alderson combined with a surprising Socialist Labor vote to defeat the independent ticket by a substantial margin, a dejected *Record* was forced to admit that the public pulse "did not beat in harmony with the nonpartisan movement." And, commending the Democrats for "sticking to the movement," the *Pilot* denied that it was ended. Rather, it predicted optimistically that local reformers would "be more determined than ever to see it become a reality."[34]

The *Pilot's* judgment was later confirmed, when Wausau residents approved the principle of nonpartisan local government in 1909. On the heels of this shift came a new interest in another Progressive innovation, the commission form of government. Inspired by successful experiments in a number of Wisconsin communities, area proponents of commission government took the offensive in 1911 to alter the structure of municipal government in Wausau. The movement, which enjoyed the support of many community leaders and the local press, provided another illustration of the gap between the authority structure and the electorate at large. Under the leadership of industrialist W. E. Curtis, a general committee assumed responsibility in March, 1911, for selling the program and securing the necessary referendum. Highly touted as a means of promoting economy, minimizing politics, and bringing democracy to local government, the concept of rule by elected commission was clearly consistent with the Progressive passion for efficiency and expertise in governmental affairs.[35]

The plan's supporters were fully aware of potential resistance to this attempted modernization of municipal government. Dissent surfaced in April, 1911, when a reader chided the *Record-Herald* for its propensity to reprint success stories on commission government, noting that a few years back the same local coterie had been demanding nonpartisan government. The exasperated citizen argued that they "are not fair enough to wait and see how it is going to work out . . . First nonpartisan government, then Wet or Dry, now commission form of government, and who knows what all, if the people don't stamp the root out of it all."[36]

The battle lines were more clearly drawn in late 1911, when the powerful German-American Alliance declared its opposition to the reform, due to a firm conviction that the commission system bordered on absolute government. The Alliance was a federation of Wausau German societies that retained ties with similar groups in Edgar, Marathon, and Merrill; it was an important political and social force in the county. Dedicated to the preservation of German culture in America, the organization vigorously opposed legislation it saw as undesirable: and it clearly found authoritarian potential in the prospect of local government removed from the ward level. Determined to make its views known, the Alliance launched a broad publicity campaign in December, 1911, with an open letter to the Wausau electorate, warning that promised tax reductions were unlikely under the new system, but that a significant loss of personal liberties was possible. In early 1912, the organization's key spokesman, John Ringle, was more direct in his attack:

> The commission form of government is not progres-
> sive, but on the contrary is reactionary. It restricts the
> opportunity of the people of participating and con-
> ducting their own affairs. In other words it assumes,
> that which has been disproven in every department of
> our American system of government, that the people
> are not capable of self-government.[37]

Dismissing these charges as unsubstantiated "buncombe," local reform leaders readied for battle. The opening shot came from the *Pilot,*
now insistent upon the need for commission government as the panacea
that would make Wausau "a Progressive city," with enlarged democracy
and lower taxes. Concurring in this judgment, the local citizens committee claimed that the proposed reform

> 1. "does not increase power — it increases responsibil-
>   ity."
> 2. "is not a departure from the American principle of
>   representative government."
> 3. "has proved to be a dividend paying interest."

So volatile was the issue that supporters turned in desperation to a
public meeting at the Opera House, where both sides might explore
the merits of the proposition. Although each position was represented,
Alliance spokesmen Anton Mehl and John Ringle held the upper
hand in a debate before a largely sympathetic audience. The Opera
House debate was an accurate barometer of public opinion, and even
before the election, the most committed supporters of the commission
system had conceded defeat: their analysis was verified by a resounding
repudiation at the polls.[38]

The fate of commission government raises the broader question of
Marathon County's response to the full range of Progressive issues
in the period from 1904 to 1914, years regarded as the floodtide of
Wisconsin reform. Close scrutiny reveals that county voters remained
suspicious of many ideas perceived by others as enlightened change.
The most persuasive explanation of this political and social conservatism again stresses the pervasive influence of ethnicity in the area's
voter behavior. Marathon and other predominantly German counties
continued to give a relatively low number of votes to Progressive candidates and programs in the years before 1914, in part because so many
of those reforms ran counter to socio-cultural beliefs rooted in a
European national identification. Consequently, German-Americans
were often willing to accept economic innovations such as anti-trust
action and tariff reform, but staunchly resisted those changes which

centered on what may be regarded as the "social issues."[39]

Never enthusiastic about the primary election system, Marathon County residents remained cool to what one Democratic leader contemptuously labelled "the God Democracy." In 1910, the *Marathon Times,* solidly Democratic and speaking to a largely German audience, assessed the primary as "a queer thing" that had not demonstrated any usefulness. Indeed, the editors had "not yet met a man who is perfectly satisfied with its workings, no matter whether Republican or Democrat." This coolness was rooted in frustration over the reluctance of the electorate to turn out in large numbers for primary elections, a serious problem in the early days of primary voting. Perhaps more honest was the defiance expressed to a friend by Democratic veteran Neal Brown, who refused "to fawn and cringe before our tyrant of public opinion." Brown contended that "the people are sometimes wrong, and that it don't [sic] make a law right or just because the majority of the people approve it."[40]

Less controversial but still suspect in Marathon County was the concept of progressive taxation, which was at the economic heart of the "Wisconsin idea" in government. Even the local Democratic press was unenthusiastic over "taxation for socialistic purposes only," and the more conservative *Record-Herald* later recalled with pride that it had always "condemned the Wisconsin Idea" and exposed it as "a snare and a delusion to the very classes which it professed to benefit." Although county voters gave grudging support to the proposed state income tax on a 1908 referendum, the narrow margin of victory was a far cry from the resounding endorsement it received statewide.[41]

Potentially more explosive as a "social issue" was the drive for women's suffrage, which climaxed in a struggle between Wisconsin reformers and old world influences in 1912. Put to state voters in a referendum, the proposal ignited widespread opposition, particularly in the German-American press. Equating resistance to the reform with "Germanism," opponents insisted that woman's place was in the home and forecast dire consequences for family life if mothers became politically active. Given the German-Polish heritage of many county residents, a suggestion so at variance with European concepts of home and family was doomed at the outset. Nonetheless, an occasional voice of moderation was to be heard, such as that of Neal Brown, who lent his support to suffrage not because he anticipated the millennium but because it was "a matter of justice to a large portion of our citizenship."[42] Yet the proposition suffered a crushing defeat in Marathon County. Rejecting the reform on a 6446-1924 vote, county voters administered a blow that carried heavy ethnic overtones, clearly marked by such massive negative judgments as Berlin's 146-5 verdict.[43]

On no issue was European tradition more significant, however, than the Progressive proposal to vanquish the scourge of the American housewife, "demon rum." Often a muted issue in the Progressive era, prohibition became a live threat when a proposed county option law was widely debated in the 1910 campaign. To German-Americans any form of regulation seemed a violation of personal liberty, as well as a direct attack on a long-established social practice. Consequently, the German-American press and the Alliance mobilized for a full attack on the hated legislation, urging Wisconsinites to vote Democratic because of the party's strong stand against county option. And nowhere was the question more hotly debated than in the heavily German townships of Marathon and Cassel. The columns of the *Marathon Times* were filled with articles and advertisements exploring a measure that would make the county the political unit to decide whether alcoholic beverages might be manufactured or sold within its jurisdiction.

Speaking at the Marathon Village Hall, Progressive Republican gubernatorial candidate Francis McGovern felt bound to declare his opposition to the idea and his regret that the issue had even been raised. In so doing, the aspirant marched in step with every assembly and senatorial candidate in the district, all of whom had seen the wisdom in catering to local tastes, political and otherwise. That this was the prudent course became clear three weeks later when the *Times* lashed out against county option as a policy of "hypocrisy" and "lawlessness." In a front page editorial, publisher Frank Leuschen acknowledged the necessity of eradicating the evils resulting from the excessive use of intoxicants, but insisted that

> all this can never be done by force. It must be done by a change of public opinion, by an uplifting of society to a higher moral plane.
>
> County option will never do it. The voters should therefore inform themselves where the different candidates stand on this important question before casting their ballot next Tuesday.[44]

Leuschen's blast confirmed the wisdom in McGovern's pointed reference to county option. But the Progressive candidate's efforts in Marathon, Edgar, and Athens counted for little in the general election, when the lion's share of the county vote went to Democrat A. G. Schmitz — whose party was more reliably "wet" on the great social question of the campaign.

Less than six months later, the temperance forces moved to "prohibitionize" the city of Wausau through a local option referendum. Led by an interloper from the town of Norrie, prominent congregationalist A. R. Bucknam, local "drys" drew substantial support from some of the liberal Protestant churches. But they were hardly a match for an aroused Alliance, which mobilized the German community against this assault on its cherished "principles of personal liberty." The local organization denounced the prohibitionist campaign as an attack on government economy, private property, individual rights, and the cause of true temperance through regulation. The "true believers" countered with advertising, as well as "no license" window cards and circulars, all available from several Protestant churches. In the First Methodist and First Presbyterian churches, the clergy exhorted the faithful to strike a blow against degeneracy at the ballot box.[45]

But when the votes were in, it became clear that prohibition found little favor with an aroused Wausau electorate, which defeated local option in a result termed "very damp" by an amused *Pilot*. "Damp" understated the case, as the license proposition went down to defeat by an impressive 2,725-511 margin. The turnout astonished observers, since it set a new record for spring elections in a campaign that saw no other contested offices. It is obvious that the liquor question brought out the vote, especially in the German wards of the west side, where total votes cast exceeded the record set in the presidential contest of 1908.

Curiously, both sides in the dispute professed satisfaction with the results. Most outspoken was Fred Brand, president of the Wausau Retail Liquor Dealers Association, who was convinced that the margin "demonstrated that the people are emphatically against a dry town." Openly claiming credit for the salutary outcome, Alliance President Hilmar Schmidt expressed no surprise at the vote but did admit that citizen support had exceeded expectations. Meanwhile, Bucknam, described as "one of the leading spirits" of the "dry" forces, asserted satisfaction with the open discussion of the issue promoted by the entire campaign. His compatriot, Rev. F. H. Brigham of the First Methodist Church, weakly added that "the result shows a good increase in the no-license vote."[46] Such claims notwithstanding, the verdict was clear: like many rural areas in the county, Wausau had little stomach for the prohibitionist movement.

The local option battle had again revealed the strength of European cultural tradition as well as the "softness" of Progressive sentiment in

Marathon County. Given the growth of the La Follette machine in Wisconsin, it was inevitable that a Progressive organization would develop in Marathon as well. Among the insurgent leaders were Wausau attorney A. W. Prehn and Congressman E. A. Morse, a victor in the county twice prior to the Democratic sweep of 1910. Despite this early reform attempt, local stalwarts refused to rest in peace. Weaknesses in the Republican organization appeared as early as the presidential contest of 1908, when county regulars defied favorite son Robert La Follette by sending Walter Alexander to the national convention as Wisconsin's single Taft delegate. This resistance to manipulation by the La Follette organization was symptomatic of growing factional conflict, which broke into the open when local Progressives seized control of the county party during the bitter campaign of 1910.[47]

While Democrats enjoyed modest gains throughout the state in this off-year election, Marathon County returns reveal massive defections from the Republican cause led by Progressive Francis McGovern. The most plausible explanation for Democratic success lies in Republican factionalism, which climaxed in an open bolt by disgruntled county conservatives. While special efforts were made by the Democratic candidate for State Treasurer, John Ringle, to carry his home county for the ticket, it is clear that conspicuous crossover by such prominent stalwarts as D. J. Murray and C. S. Curtis sealed the Republican fate. Both men "worked hard . . . instructing their men to vote the straight Democratic ticket," in an attempt to "beat the state ticket in this county and also to defeat all the Legislative candidates." To counter conservative footdragging, Prehn and his law partner, E. P. Gorman, made seventy speeches for the Republican ticket; but their efforts could not offset the stalwart influence in the Democratic campaign. The sting of local defeat was lessened by Prehn's conviction that "the Progressive Republican Party is now a party in existence in Marathon County" and that the reformers would "never allow the Stalwart faction again to control the party here."

Having sacrificed his law practice to battle for Progressivism, Prehn felt bold enough to urge that a county appointment be made by Governor McGovern as soon as he was established in Madison. While he vowed a fight to the finish and claimed to be "fully organized," the local reformer insisted that "an appointment will put more ginger in the movement for the future."[48] Despite Prehn's appeal, little patronage flowed north under McGovern; and it was not until after the stalwart counterrevolution of 1914 that a major plum fell to Marathon County.

In that year this brand of Republicanism was rejuvenated under the leadership of party veteran Marvin Rosenberry, who worked hard for his old friend, gubernatorial candidate Emanuel Philipp. At Rosenberry's urging, Philipp began his campaign for the nomination with an early appearance in Marathon County. The time was well spent, as the revived stalwarts carried the county for Philipp in both the primary and general elections. Rosenberry's services were rewarded in 1916, when the Wausau lawyer was appointed by the governor to fill out the term of Supreme Court Justice Barnes. Some observers saw the appointment as a political payoff, as it coincided with Andrew Kreutzer's precipitous withdrawal from the national Senatorial race in favor of a Philipp-backed candidate. While Rosenberry did discuss his intentions with his law partner, he always insisted that he had been "astonished" by the offer and made the decision to accept purely on personal grounds. In any event, he divorced himself from politics and became a respected jurist in a career which ended in his retirement from the bench in 1950.[49]

His subsequent judicial work should not, however, obscure the essentially political context of Rosenberry's elevation to the court. By his own admission, his appointment was greeted by "a roar of disapproval from the La Follette press." Continued sniping by the Progressive faction haunted him as late as 1918, when he first stood for election. Typical of this backbiting was the reaction of the Madison *Capital Times*, which regarded the justice as "a midnight appointee by Governor Philipp," who owed his position to "political deals" and "his past political record." The Progressive house organ charged that

> . . . big business operating out of Wausau pulled every string known to that kind of politics. Lumberman Heinemann worked the lumbermen. Wausau bankers worked the banks, so that cashiers of banks peddled literature throughout the county. Insurance companies of Wausau worked insurance companies all over the state. Other lines of business did the same. . . .
>
> The judicial campaign of 1918 will leave an evil trail leading into the supreme court of Wisconsin. The suspicion that a certain kind of politics have [sic] been insidiously reaching into the court to hold it for certain business interests as against the common people is not unfounded. The supreme court is in politics— the Rosenberry-Philipp politics.[50]

Allowing for the well-known proclivities of the *Capital Times*, this bitter editorial nonetheless failed to mention the equally political efforts of the La Follette machine to influence state voters with a letter

Stalwart Leader Marvin Rosenberry

of endorsement for Rosenberry's Progressive opponent, Charles Crownhart.

The Stalwart-Progressive animosity aside, the most significant political development in Marathon County after 1910 was the resurgence of the Democratic Party. Before county Republicans could mend the wounds opened by the 1910 campaign, the Progressive revolt and the disruption of the national party gave the Democrats another opportunity in the Presidential election of 1912. Although he ran on the regular Republican ticket, popular Progressive Governor Francis McGovern endorsed the Bull Mooser Theodore Roosevelt. Sulking in a corner because Progressives had passed him by for an ex-president, a sullen La Follette was conspicuously silent on the party split. Typical of this behavior was the Senator's Wausau campaign speech in favor of a unknown beneficiary. Harsh on Roosevelt and unenthusiastic about the incumbent Taft, "Fighting Bob" did battle for no one, and in the process boosted the hopes of the Democratic challenger, Woodrow Wilson. Due to the chaos on the Republican side, Wisconsin Democrats viewed the prospects for both state and federal offices optimistically. Most progressive Democrats supported the candidacy of the New Jersey insurgent, but true to form, Marathon County preferred the more conservative candidate, Champ Clark of Missouri. While Wilson won the Wisconsin primary handily, Marathon County gave its votes to Clark by a margin of 250.[51]

In the general election the county did, however, cast its lot with the victorious Wilson, although the tally reveals Republican disunity as much as Democratic resurgence. The swing to Wilson also reflected his generally positive image in the German-American press, which reminded readers that the Democratic candidate opposed prohibition and favored humane treatment for immigrants, positions that counted for much in Marathon County. Yet, despite a near sweep of state and national offices, suspicions of Progressivism ran deep in the county party. Respected leader Neal Brown, who once described La Follette as "an exception to the rule that the good die young," was equally critical of pandering reformism in his own party. Angered by progressive Democrats who made common cause with the Senator, he launched a blistering attack on the politics practiced by these reformers. In 1913 Brown reminded his compatriots that they were unable "to win Democratic victories in most of the counties in this state without the aid of all classes of Democrats." Reformers could not tell Marathon County Democrats that they were outside the party simply because they opposed direct primaries, referendum, and recall. The senior statesman was "old fashioned enough to believe that what made a man a Democrat in former times . . . up to a very recent period, will make a Democrat of him now."[52]

Brown's diatribe revealed the deep wounds of a breach of party unity in the previous campaign: internal division had fatally damaged the state ticket. A twenty-five year veteran and recent Senatorial candidate himself, the "sage" was convinced that "you can only win Democratic victories in this state by a united party," and working with "a mere faction of the party" was absolutely hopeless. While Marathon had come through for gubernatorial candidate John C. Karel, widely endorsed in the county, "fair minded Democrats" had aided in reelecting Progressive Francis Mc Govern—political behavior beyond the ken of a party war horse like Brown. Of more profound significance was a little-noted footnote to the 1912 canvass that held serious implications for future voter trends in the county. Brushed aside were the 600 votes cast for Socialist Eugene Debs, whose strong showing in Wausau's heavily German eighth ward promised further gains in the future.[53]

This link between ethnic background and a pattern of protest voting was destined to become a prominent characteristic of Wisconsin voter behavior, as wartime pressures on German-Americans escalated. Given the ethnic composition of the electorate, prejudice against the war ran deep, and the eventual American involvement was greeted with bitter opposition. Many Marathon County citizens resented "the suspicion with which they were often regarded, their enforced registration as alien enemies, and the hatred suddenly poured upon their most harmless and cherished institutions."[54]

The German-American revulsion at the thought of hostilities with the fatherland weighed heavy on the mind of Secretary of State William Jennings Bryan when he stumped for the Democratic ticket in Wausau during the campaign of 1914. Doubtless aware of the German vote in the county, the "Great Commoner" dwelt upon Wilson's commitment to a policy of strict neutrality, which would allow the United States eventually to act as mediator. He linked a vote for Democrats Paul Husting, A. C. Schmidt, and John C. Karel with loyalty to the President and all he stood for, including peace. The Secretary demonstrated unusual concern over Senatorial candidate Husting's fate:

> "I ask you to vote for Paul Husting," he said, "whom the president wants you to elect. I know this candidate and know that he has given earnest and consistent support to the reforms for which we have been contending. The president needs him at Washington to continue the work so splendidly begun."[55]

Fortunately for Husting, the campaign of 1914 coincided with heavy Progressive infighting, which ended in the elevation of the conservative Philipp to the governorship. In the senatorial contest, the La Follette legion refused to support rival Progressive Francis McGovern in November. Enjoying the tacit cooperation of "Fighting Bob," the Democratic aspirant earned a ticket to Washington and an opportunity to vindicate his President. In Marathon County Husting easily outdistanced the divided opposition in another good year for local Democrats. The victor was blissfully unaware of the complex problems he would soon face as Woodrow Wilson's supporter, when the administration's foreign policy came under attack from the county's substantial German community.[56]

And influential it was. As the European horror deepened, the German-American Alliance swung into action with a vigorous campaign opposing the extension of loans by local banks to foreign governments. After the Wilson Administration's decision to allow American loans to the belligerents, the Marathon County Bankers' Association declared its determination to avoid such transactions. The bankers, doubtless aware of the Wausau Alliance's open threat of a boycott against institutions participating in foreign loans, committed themselves to a policy of expending investment capital on home business and agriculture. On the very day that a New York banking group completed negotiations for the first major American loan to the allies, the Alliance warmly commended the county's banks for their vision in taking a stand "in accordance with our principles" and graciously described them as "entitled to public confidence and support."[57]

Evidence of the organization's influence surfaced in December, 1915, when Wausau played host to C. J. Hexamer, president of the National Alliance. At a meeting of his countrymen which filled the Opera House to capacity, Dr. Hexamer condemned "disgraceful truckling to Great Britain" in American economic and foreign policy. Denouncing as "incredible" the pro-British press that "dare[d] to question the loyalty of the German-American," he exhorted his enthusiastic audience to stand for its ideals. Both John Ringle and Judge Louis Marchetti participated in the program, the latter promoting the German Relief Fund already raising monies in the county. The Judge's comments clearly indicated the generosity of Marathon County citizens towards their homeland.[58]

So influential was the Alliance that Wilson supporter Frank Leuschen of the *Marathon Times* charged it with responsibility for the vituperative attacks on the administration in the German press.

Especially vicious after the sinking of the Lusitania, these criticisms were traced to the insidious machinations of the German National Alliance in New York. To Leuschen, one thing was certain: his "German friends . . . most bitter in their denunciations and clamor against Wilson" were members of the organization.[59]

The escalation of German-American criticism came to public attention in May, 1915, after Senator Husting published an impassioned defense of the administration's foreign policy in the *Milwaukee Journal.* The popular Democrat's statement stressed strict adherence to America's rights under international law and Wilson's impartiality in dealing with violations of neutral rights. Seizing the initiative, he charged the critics with "base and cruel slander on the President," and castigated American citizens who promoted "foreign propaganda which has for its object and end the plunging of this country into war with one side or the other." Beneath the surface lay a nagging suspicion that the country was vulnerable to subversion from within. Any suggestions that German-Americans would side with the fatherland were "base calumny upon some of our most respected citizens . . . and an insult to American citizenship." Husting warned that it was "necessary for the world to understand and know that America is united as one man," lest foreign quarters err about the patriotism of all Americans.[60]

The Senator's ideas did not go down well everywhere. Already a division of opinion on Wilson's policies was emerging in Marathon County, particularly in response to his insistence upon maximum economic freedom in the allied market. Reservations were expressed in early 1915, with a petition drive spearheaded by M. Gillmann of Marathon, in support of House Resolution 377, prohibiting the exportation of war supplies to the European belligerents. Treading a narrow line as an editor in a German community, Leuschen "cheerfully" complied with Gillmann's request that he publish the memorials in the *Times* though he personally saw little value in an embargo. Yet faced with a German readership, the Marathon journalist kept to a cautious course. While he stood firm with Wilson and neutral rights, he acknowledged that it was "foolish to talk about being neutral as far as our heart is concerned." All the same, as good American citizens his readers were obligated to "control these national feelings" and resist the temptation "to say or do anything radical in this hour of trial." But after issuing instructions in moderation, Leuschen ignored his own advice and played to his audience. Pulling out all the stops, the editor now expressed his conviction that "as for Germany, . . . rest assured that they will not be crushed in this struggle; for God will not permit this nation of thinkers and scientists, of art, culture and education to be annihilated."[61] Wilson supporters in German areas were clearly in a delicate position.

Leuschen's anxieties were temporarily relieved by Senator Husting's articulate expression of the administration's position, "an explanation of our Wilson neutrality," that the Marathon Democrat welcomed as "the best thing" he had read since the "damnable war began." He fervently hoped that all German-Americans would read it as an antidote to some of the propaganda then circulating. This concern was political in nature: the hostility of German-Americans was discouraging to the future of the President's party in Marathon County, where "at Wausau and in every other village and town," the feeling against the administration was "something terrible." In a personal communication to Husting, Leuschen confided:

> This is a time where reason and judgment are dethroned by sentiment. Too many of my German-American friends and neighbors are possessed of the idea that our administration should place an embargo upon all war supplies and food stuffs to any and all of the belligerent nations. Pretending that this should be done in the name of absolute neutrality and humanity, the only real innermost reason is the heart's desire that we should thereby assist chiefly one of the belligerents—Germany.[62]

Sympathy for Senator Husting's stand emerged in other communities such as Athens, where J. I. Scott of the *Record* endorsed it as a "rebuke to our Wisconsin 'Copperhead' patriotism that has long been needed." Nonetheless, it was the cooperation of the *Marathon Times* that intrigued the junior Senator from Wisconsin, who sensed that Leuschen was potentially a valuable political ally. His "faith in the good judgment of our American citizens" led him to encourage the widespread dissemination of Leuschen's views, and even to contemplate a campaign aimed at the suspicious German-American community. Regarding his Marathon correspondent as an expert in such matters, he appealed for counsel on an effort to get his message before the German voter. Convinced of its political value, the *Times* editor urged further distribution of the article "to show our German friends the *other* side of the question and . . . to defend our illustrious President Wilson's absolute fairness and justice." Leuschen desperately hoped that the United States could avoid involvement in "this awful war," and that his German neighbors could "be rallied back to Wilson's

banner in the next election." For his part, the local Democratic
leader pledged to do "all in my power here in my little community
to hold our Democratic friends in line," laughing off his Republican
neighbors, who "hate me heartily for it, because I am too much for
them."[63]

True to his word, Leuschen wasted little time in promoting the
Democratic cause. Picturing Wilson as trapped between conflicting
pressure groups, the *Times* extolled the President's virtues as a force
for sanity in a world gone mad. Attacked in the East for weakness and
in the Midwest for truculence, "like Lincoln [he] keeps at his post,
sawing wood for the best interests of his country." Returning from a
Wilson appearance in Milwaukee, Leuschen attacked the Republican
press for its "tirades against Wilson." Signalling the dawn of a political
year, he reminded Marathon voters that the administration had
brought widespread prosperity while preserving an honorable peace:
and "the people know it and appreciate it."[64]

But not all the people. As the presidential campaign heated up,
the disenchantment of many German-Americans became all too clear.
Sentiments typical of Marathon County's major ethnic group were
expressed at Marshfield, when the state Alliance convention issued
a harsh indictment of alleged Wilsonian partiality towards the allies.
And the ethnics were not alone: the *Record-Herald*, despite its support for Republican Charles Evans Hughes, was equally strident in
its declarations of neutralist sentiment. Though certain of the Alliance's "tactical blunder" at Marshfield, the Wausau paper and its
editor, J. L. Sturtevant, would soon reach the point of advocating an
embargo to prevent American involvement in the war. This stance
was later summarized in William T. Evjue's assessment that the *Herald*
and its editor were "responsible for much of the anti-war sentiment
in Marathon County."[65]

So meshed with foreign policy was German-American politics by
1916 that any stability in the Wisconsin German vote was shattered
in the presidential election. Sympathy for Republican Charles Evans
Hughes was connected with an unwillingness to forgive Wilson's belli-
gerence because he had avoided war. When the votes were tallied in
November, the overriding significance of ethnicity in determining the
results was striking. While Wilson narrowly lost the Badger State
by a margin of 49-42 per cent, Marathon County voters deserted the
President in droves—a dramatic turnabout from his 1912 success.
Hughes' bulge of 57-36 per cent may be directly attributed to massive
defections in Democratic wards and towns, most notably in German

areas. While Wilson had carried nineteen of twenty-five German townships in 1912, twenty-two of those towns went Republican in 1916.[66]

Contrary to the voting pattern in German strongholds, another trend emerged in townships dominated by other customarily Democratic ethnic groups. Areas dominated by recent immigrant stock (particularly the Polish and Bohemians in Mosinee, Pike Lake, and to an extent, Cassel), held firm for Wilson in accordance with traditional voter preferences. And the Irish enclave in Emmet delivered a comfortable plurality for the beleaguered President, though his 1916 margin was more modest than that recorded in 1912. Thus, ethnicity was a two-edged sword in Wilson's reelection effort, and the foreign policy issue was often a negligible factor in non-German areas. Finally, other questions sometimes entered the picture in German townships such as Green Valley, where at least one active Hughes man attributed his dislike of Wilson to the incumbent's intense partisanship.[67]

The invective hurled at the administration during the 1916 campaign was merely a hint of the trauma visited upon Wisconsin, as the United States was drawn into the European conflagration. When Congress declared war against Germany, nine of Wisconsin's congressmen, including Marathon County's Edward Browne, were among the fifty "nays" counted, while La Follette stood with five other dissenters in the Senate. Despite these reservations, however, the state's war record proved outstanding by most measures: rationing, enlistment figures, and bond subscriptions were exemplary, perhaps as a reflection of statewide ethnic self-consciousness.

Like other Wisconsin counties, Marathon early organized a "Council of Defense" to "assist in doing all things necessary to bring about the highest effectiveness within our county in the crisis now existing." Broadly representative of agricultural, business, labor, and consumer interests, the county committee (under the leadership of chairman C. B. Bird and secretary E. B. Thayer) worked with the state council in Madison to aid in the war effort—and on occasion to enforce conformity when the situation demanded it. While much of the council's workload involved such mundane matters as the promotion of farm production, bond sales, resource conservation, and heavy enlistments, the committee sometimes guided the public conscience. Such work ranged from public warnings against disloyalty to recommendations that local theaters censor unpatriotic vaudeville performances, should they become a problem. More significant were the group's exhortations to the public, demanding that any persons suspected of "maliciously spreading" rumors "to discredit our country" be promptly reported to the proper authorities. And finally, enraged by La Follette's criticism of the war, the council indicted Wisconsin's senior Senator for "causing the death of those who wear the American uniform" and "giving aid and comfort to the enemy." Carried away by a burst of patriotism, the local body dismissed any claim to free speech and urged the Senate to expel the veteran Progressive "in the interest of good citizenship, common decency and the public welfare."[68] The Senate was not heard to reply, though there was an effort to remove La Follette in 1917.

Often cited as evidence of effort on the homefront are the several bond drives, which became the focal point for local patriotic activities. In the third liberty loan drive of 1918, Marathon County exceeded its considerable past performances in such campaigns. So successful was the drive that chairman C. S. Gilbert of Wausau could announce that all townships and villages had surpassed their quotas and the county had gone "over the top" by $136,650. Yet it was not uncommon for a district chairman like Rev. Howard M. Jones of Auburndale to express frustration at his "little pro-German township," where he was forced to badger a "rabid old pro-German" into taking a $100 bond. Earlier that year it had cost a Wausau resident $500 to charge that the bonds would lose value after the war, since he dropped his remark within earshot of a local patriot.[69]

One thing is clear: an immediate casualty of the war abroad was tolerance at home—and Marathon County did not survive unscathed. Following the lead of many a nervous Wisconsin bank director, the board at the German-American Bank saw the wisdom in a change of name. President Ben Heinemann urged that the firm "show sincere loyalty to the most glorious and the most liberty-loving country on the face of the earth" by becoming the American National Bank. The directors were unanimous in their agreement. A similar change occurred in Shawano, while the directors of the German-American State Bank in Merrill paid the price for lack of foresight when a group of departing recruits decorated the building with yellow paint.[70]

Equally instructive was the debate over the fate of German language instruction in the Wausau Public Schools. Early in 1918, the Record-Herald commended the Eau Claire school system for dropping German, charging that the language was "too easy" for a credit offering and finally opposing German instruction for the duration. Behind the movement was the Wisconsin Loyalty Legion, a patriotic organization created to aid the Council of Defense in the enforcement of conformity. Spurred by exaggerated fears of internal subversion, the Loyalty Legion focused on fancied acts of treason or even footdragging on the war. Predictably, the body devoted special attention to the behavior of German-Americans, and the attempt to purge German from the public schools was intended to stamp out any trace of "slacker" sentiment in the state.[71]

As the war dragged on, the battle drove a wedge into the community, opening a rift on the school board that would be forced to render a decision. In September, 1918, on a 6-4 vote the board finally denied a petition demanding the discontinuance of German instruction. Unreconciled to the decision, board member H. J. Evans took to the columns of the *Record-Herald* with a scathing letter attacking those citizens who "through race pride and prejudice, find some difficulty in realizing they are Americans fighting Germany." The angry critic insisted that no public question could be settled without due regard to "the effect the proposed action will have on the war." Evans concluded that it had been "a racial question settled on racial lines" and that the authorities had lost their opportunity to dump German and place the public schools "out on the very forefront of Americanism." In full agreement, L. A. Pradt confidently assured the local Rotary Club that everyone who condemned the board action was "a one-hundred percent American." Taking him at his word, the organization promptly voted to request that the board reconsider its decision. Such hysteria notwithstanding, Wausau stood firm in defense of academic integrity, while some neighboring communities, such as Shawano, succumbed to the zealots' demands.[72]

The curriculum was one thing, but the public expression of dissent on the war quite another. In early 1918, Wausau hotel owner Gustave Sternberg was arraigned on charges of making "false reports and false statements with intent to interfere with the operations and successes of the military and naval forces of the United States." Unwilling to purchase a liberty bond under duress, Sternberg had charged that the war was "a rich man's war" engineered by "those Jews of Wall Street," and that "Wilson and that crowd did not know any better." After the offender had been convicted, the *Record-Herald* reported "general satisfaction at the outcome of the case," noting that "there was regret that he had not been arrested sooner."[73] Free speech fared poorly in time of national emergency.

More threatening than common sedition was the work of rumor-monger Carl Clarke, guilty of spreading the vicious report that the county's beloved Company G had been wiped out on the fields of

France. A registered German alien, Clarke was turned over to the Justice Department after throwing a considerable scare into the public with his claim of information secured at the *Record-Herald* offices. Public concern generated by this fiasco goaded the Council of Defense into repeating its earlier warning against the repetition of questionable information, along with an admonition to report offenders. In concert with the council, a chagrined *Herald* reminded its readers that the press had responsibility for the dissemination of accurate public information, and that it was unpatriotic to spread rumors that were sometimes "part of the German propaganda in this country."[74]

Sporadic arrests continued, on charges ranging from "disloyal utterances" to "leaving seditious literature between the pages of books at the Public Library." Others were held for "lurking about the city" and alleged efforts to "discourage enlistments in the service of the United States." Curiously, the suspects were generally foreign-born, often aliens, and frequently German. It is clear that the charges which most enraged the community power structure were those involving the recruitment of servicemen and attitudes toward military service. The ethnic composition of Marathon County ensured a large measure of personal and community anxiety over the demands of the draft. One widely-publicized case involved the prominent Fromm family of Hamburg, several of whom refused service when called in the summer of 1918. The actions of Henry, Walter, and John reflected their personal views, and came as a complete surprise to their family, which remained steadfastly loyal during the war. Spokesman Edward Fromm told reporters that his brothers' decision placed his family "in a very unenviable position," and that criticisms against them were "unjust," for which "we should not bear the burden."[75]

More shocking to the public was the celebrated story of Cassel resident Francis X. Schilling, whose case gained statewide notoriety. Long a pillar of the community, Schilling was the most prominent Wisconsin citizen to be convicted on charges of obstructing recruitment for the armed forces. He had "won a high place in the estimation of his neighbors" as a "man of great energy and . . . knowledge of political methods." Arraigned in Madison, the accused had allegedly "abetted and encouraged registrants . . . to enter false and misleading answers in their questionnaires to queries, with the purpose and intent of avoiding military service." Skilled in courtroom protocol, he insisted on a full reading of the indictment, whereupon he entered a defiant plea of "not guilty." Distressed by an excess of sympathy for Germany, the *Record-Herald* had harsh words for "men who ought to know better advising those of draft age to shirk their duty." Prison was the answer for German sympathizers: it might not "change their hearts," but it would clearly "make them keep their mouths shut."[76]

Given the emotional wartime atmosphere, Schilling stood little chance of acquittal. In an openly political trial, he was credited with dissuading over seventy Cassel men from enlisting and accused of boasting that he would "see to it that none of the boys from the Town of Cassel go to the war." Government witnesses from Cassel, Edgar, Marathon, Wausau, Mosinee, Athens, McMillan, and Unity recited a litany of accusations of unpatriotic actions, and defense council responded in kind. Equally damaging was the presiding judge's questionable decision to permit testimony about the defendant's record of "slacker" behavior, including food hoarding, criticism of the Red Cross and Y.M.C.A., and miserly contributions to war charities—none of which was relevant. After deliberating for scarcely two hours, an Eau Claire jury found Schilling guilty on eighteen counts of violating the espionage act: the verdict resulted in a sentence of eighteen months at Leavenworth and a $3,500 fine.[77]

A complement to such vigilance was the educational campaign carried on by a coalition of area patriots, including the press, the defense council, and the county Loyalty Legion. A common stratagem was the use of German speakers to appeal to the patriotic sentiments of their countrymen. Wausau's Karl Mathie became a traveling speaker for the Chicago-based Society of Friends of German Democracy, specializing in patriotic orations to "loyal Americans of German stock." Preferring outside talent, Frank Leuschen cooperated with the Council of Defense to bring Prof. Max Meyer of the University of Missouri into the German stronghold of Marathon City for an educational program. Meyer's castigation of German autocracy pleased the *Times* editor, who followed up the meeting with a call for "genuine, red-blooded American patriotism" and cheerful sacrifice. This appeal was entirely consonant with the long-established stance of the council: county citizens should "show to the world that we as American citizens have but one country and that one we believe in and intend to sustain and defend." Similarly, the Loyalty Legion, under the leadership of J. L. Sturtevant, led a vigorous educational campaign focusing on the war as a conflict in ideals. In February, 1918, the Legion brought its state president, Judson Rosebush, to Wausau, to lecture on German ideology and the allied alternative of a "world peopled by free democracies united in an honorable league of peace." The local patriots followed this program later in the year with an appearance by a war veteran, Private Herbert Nicholas of Rhode Island, who expounded on the alleged depth of German brutality. In a pointed reference to the local population, the gladiator denied malice towards German-Americans, though it was "up to the German here to show that he is 100% American."[78]

In the last analysis, did wartime enthusiasm banish reason? The foregoing evidence suggests that Marathon, like many Wisconsin counties, had its share of intolerance. On balance, however, the record reveals comparative moderation, as suggested by the findings of at least one recent scholar of wartime attitudes. A "tolerance scale" ranking all Wisconsin counties according to the incidence of extra-legal actions places Marathon in the category of lowest activity. Marathon County joined several heavily German counties in maintaining a degree of sanity in the face of a formidable challenge to civil rights.[79]

However, many German-Americans harbored a deep resentment against the county power structure because of the scorn heaped on them and their homeland. Nowhere was their indignation more clearly expressed than in the wartime political arena. Fed up with the state-wide loyalty campaign, German-Americans rallied to a new standard in elections during the final year of the war. Following the resignation of Republican D. S. Burnett, Marathon County voters sent Socialist Herman Marth to Madison as second district assemblyman.

The nomination of Marth, a Wausau chef and dedicated Socialist since 1911, threw panic into the traditional community leaders, who mounted a vigorous campaign against the newcomer. Vilified by the local press, his defeat seemed assured. Attacking Marth for his support of the Socialist Party platform, which called for immediate peace with Germany, the Record-Herald drew the battle lines by insisting that "the issue is strictly between loyalty and disloyalty." On election day the Herald reminded the voters that the basic question was "whether the voters want a socialist or an American to represent them in the legislature." Not to be outdone, his opponent's supporters ran a large advertisement proclaiming loyalty to be the issue and insisting that there was no middle ground: the Republican candidate, Ernest A. Dunn, was the man who would "give the soldier boys that loyal support to which they are entitled" and whose presence in Madison would "send a message of cheer to the boys at the front." The assault climaxed when the Herald's blunt election day headline said it all: "If You Haven't Voted, the Socialist May Be Elected."[80]

Indeed. When the dust cleared, Marth had routed the opposition, carrying the Wausau wards by nearly 3-1. The press was helpless to explain the outpouring of support for the cook who aspired to greater things, and both papers downplayed the results. Fulminating over the low turnout, the *Record-Herald* granted that "loyal Americans" could "stand having a socialist representative . . . if the others can." Even less enthusiastic, the *Pilot* denied "that the socialist movement has gained any strength." Yet in other quarters, an alternate analysis prevailed. The Socialist press celebrated Marth's success as evidence that workers and farmers had turned for "relief and redemption" to the only party that stood against the corporations that had "exploited" the people. The Milwaukee Socialists maintained that the Marathon County special election had horrified both Democratic and Republican legislators, who feared "that what happened in Wausau would set entire Wisconsin ablaze in the fall election of 1918." Faced by patriotic crowds and open intimidation, county voters were "unafraid . . . and determined to register their protest and sentiments."[81]

And the Socialist victory scored in Marathon County was only a

The Honorable Herman Marth

beginning; the Socialist Party burst simultaneously onto the Wisconsin political stage with a strong bid to capture the United States Senate seat of Wilson loyalist Paul Husting, a victim of a hunting accident in 1917. The contest quickly resolved itself into a struggle to determine whether Husting's successor would be a La Follette Progressive, a loyal Democrat, or outspoken Socialist Victor L. Berger of Milwaukee. Democratic efforts to preempt the loyalty issue and drive one-time La Follette Republican Irvine L. Lenroot from the race to ensure a "loyal" result ended in failure, when the Superior Progressive edged Wilson supporter Joseph Davies by a scant 15,000 votes. But in reality, the main event had been an attack on Berger, the personification of disloyalty to many people. Despite the bipartisan campaign against him, the Socialist standard bearer stunned political sages by earning 110,000 votes, nearly three times his party's previous high in Wisconsin. Close examination reveals that hard core Berger support centered in heavily German counties, including Marathon: socialism was clearly serving as a vehicle for protest against the social pressure, criticism, and harassment directed at German-Americans by enthusiastic patriots.

Marathon County returns were characteristic of trends in other German strongholds, as Berger confounded "loyalist" forces with a county victory over Lenroot and Davies. When the dust had settled, the Milwaukee Socialist had outdistanced his nearest rival, Davies, by 1,600 votes, in a remarkable display of German political strength. Just as the statewide Socialist-German correlation was substantial, so lopsided Berger majorities were recorded in the county's German heartland townships.[82] Searching the returns for a ray of sunshine, the *Record-Herald* took consolation in the city totals, where the "loyal vote was 1,773 and the disloyal vote 1,468." Moreover, it was satisfied that since the Lenroot-Davies total exceeded the "disloyal candidate's" vote, "Marathon County proved to be loyal at yesterday's election."[83] By such tortured logic, the Berger victory was not a victory.

Patriotic boosterism could not, however, erase the fact of latent sympathy for Socialist candidates in Marathon County. Although the party itself was small, its supporters were numerous and its enemies dedicated. Recounting his own candidacy for eighth ward alderman, Marshall Duranso of Wausau recalled that "on account of the war the town went crazy." Nominated for the position by his Socialist comrades, Duranso quickly learned from his foreman at Marathon Box Company, that if he was "elected on the Socialist ticket" he would "have to look for other work." Eager to avoid unemployment, he refused to campaign and declined to cast a vote in his own favor. The startling result was Duranso's defeat by a margin of 128-127: he "could have tied that with [his] vote." And Duranso was not alone. Consider, for example, the story of Socialist Alderman Gering, who reportedly discovered that his political views disqualified him for employment throughout the Wausau area.[84]

Despite the disapproval of other, "respectable" elements in the area, the county Socialist movement peaked with the November elections of 1918. Not only was the popular Marth reelected, but party member Charles Zarnke captured the assembly seat for the Marathon County First District. Even more remarkable were Socialist inroads into several important county offices from District Attorney down to Register of Deeds. These victories did not come without a struggle. Attempting to resurrect the overworked loyalty issue, the *Record-Herald* charged that any person who voted Socialist gave "aid and comfort to those indicted men, who, by their own actions, have lent aid, and comfort to the nation's enemy." Unusually non-partisan, the paper also attacked incumbent Republican Congressman Edward E. Browne for his vote against American entry into the war.[85] Though Browne trailed by 600 votes in Marathon County, patriots could find little solace in the result, since the victor was Socialist Leo Krzycki; in the final analysis, the incumbent held his position in a district where his opposition to the war was an advantage.

The dazzling Socialist success of 1918 reflected popular approval of Marth's work in the brief special session, as well as continuing resentment against the wartime loyalty campaign. Predictably, the Socialist Party of Wisconsin believed that "the farmers [had] learned their lesson," noting that "Marathon was the first rural county to break away from the clutches of big biz politicians." Seeking to perpetuate the breach, Milwaukee Socialists cited private reports that county citizens were "thoroughly satisfied" with their compatriots' administration of Marathon County, which would hopefully end in the transformation from capitalism to "a socialized system for the benefit of the masses" and a "Socialist Commonwealth."[86] Such prophecies proved illusory, and while it is true that Marth (and later Zarnke) consistently supported agrarian and labor measures, the 1918 returns reveal a good deal more about ethnic consciousness than about economic radicalism. Indeed, the election of Social Democrats in predominantly-German counties was a common phenomenon in the 1918 canvass, which was marked by Socialist gains in both Senate and Assembly.

But whether economic or cultural, their heresy was real in the eyes of those who had long exercised community leadership. Consequently, the postwar climate of reaction would bring an assault on non-conformity that would seal the fate of socialism, in the climactic election of 1920.

The Industrial Workers of the World and the Social Democratic Party drew strength from the foreign-born, including many Germans; and their anti-war stance made the transition from superpatriotism to postwar red-baiting an easy one. Not that the "Wobblies" had ever gained widespread popularity in Marathon County. Though they had undertaken organizing efforts in the county, their failures had been conspicuous. Despite the miniscule threat, the local press shared statewide concern over this "small body of the worst persons in the world who have declared a treacherous war upon everyone else." The *Record-Herald* maintained that "naturalized citizens of the I. W. W. persuasion," who had by their words and deeds repudiated the government, stood in danger of losing their citizenship for their defiant opposition to the war. And the *Pilot* added its concern over Russian-based radical agitation led by Bolshevist propagandists in America. Clearly, the combination of wartime patriotism and fear of the Russian Revolution had created an environment of irrationality as the war drew to a close.[87]

Characteristic of this new climate were the numerous editorial attacks on Bolshevism and socialism that filled the county press during the nationwide Red Scare of 1919. Often critical of the sensational press and university professors, the *Record-Herald* indicted socialist spokesmen for spreading "untruths based upon the theory that the poor are being exploited by the rich and always will be until the industrial system is done away with." The purveyors of such dogma were perhaps more to blame for the nationwide rash of bombings in 1919 than the demented souls who committed the actual crimes. The *Herald* confidently exposed what it saw as the fallacy of class consciousness, noting the failure of the Soviet experiment and the success of American business leaders "who appreciate the fact that their welfare is dependent upon the welfare of the rest of the community." Denouncing the "doctrines of a coming revolution, the doctrines of the I. W. W. and of Socialists in general," the paper recommended the "deportation of dangerous aliens and the prevention of immigration" as the first step in an anti-radical campaign. Much more succinct was the *Stratford Journal,* which denounced alien radicals as "Bullsheviki," whose political techniques were confined to "use-a da club or bomb or shoot off-a da mouth."[88]

Never was the hysteria more apparent than in April, 1919, when Wausau played host to prominent Socialist Kate Richards O'Hare, who had been convicted of obstructing the draft under the wartime espionage act. "Red Kate" delighted her attentive audience with a paean to the Bolshevik revolution and a ringing commitment to the socialist principles that would make her a strong candidate for her party's vice-presidential nomination in 1920. Pointedly condemning the "narrowness of newspaper editors," Mrs. O'Hare welcomed imprisonment "for the crime of having served the working class and defend [ed] the constitution of the United States." Not surprisingly, the *Pilot* was unimpressed by her "posing as a martyr" and the "typically socialist address."[89] The huge bunch of red carnations presented to the radical evangelist by Socialist District Attorney George Lippert no doubt seemed symbolically appropriate.

In contrast to the rhetoric of "Red Kate" O'Hare, the actions of the rapidly-growing Nonpartisan League posed a greater challenge to the forces of political stability. By 1919, the militant farm group had moved into Wisconsin with eighty paid organizers, including Otto Crouch, assigned to Marathon County. The result of this drive was a rumored 700 county farmers on the League's membership rolls by April—a "firm foothold," in the eyes of an alarmed *Pilot*. Evidence of the intense recruitment effort may be found in the report of one Town of Wausau resident who claimed that all but three of the farmers in the entire township had signed on. What concerned the *Pilot* was the Nonpartisan League program: the principle of state-owned banking, milling, insurance, and grain elevators was more than even a good Democrat could take. The *Record-Herald* found fault with the Nonpartisans' misconception that "rich folks got their money by some mysterious manipulation of the laws and all that would be necessary to do to get all the money needed would be to get control of the government and manipulate the laws themselves."[90]

As significant as the League was the hardening local attitude towards organized labor, which tended to link worker solidarity with radicalism. A clear example of this trend was the *Herald's* firm denunciation of the great steel strike of 1919, which it perceived as dangerously anticapitalist. Convinced of the steel-workers' intent to "socialize the basic industries of the United States," the paper warned local workers and capitalists alike that if the union succeeded, "the dissolute and the lazy will thrive on the industrious and saving." Part of the postwar anti-labor thrust was the open shop campaign, whose goals were more than economic. Extensive reference to "class domination," "paid labor agitators," "radical unionists," "Russian Bolshevism," "one big union," "Third Internationale," "coercion," and "slavery" in Wausau Policy advertisements suggests that the Red Scare of 1919 weighed heavy on the minds of the area industrialists behind the movement. Finally, the open shop drive meshed with fears of rural socialism in a Wausau Policy spread attacking the Nonpartisan League's textbook control system and state banking scheme. Because of "this fight between freedom and compulsion," Marathon County businessmen and manufacturers stood four square for the open shop.[91]

Conservative interest in labor and agriculture was, in fact, prophetic in terms of the sweeping political realignment under way by 1920 in both Marathon County and the state as a whole. In the summer of that year a farmer-labor-liberal coalition was born, which would carry a reinvigorated Progressive movement to major victories in the November election. The La Follette Republicans were in a position to capitalize on German-American outrage over wartime indignities, postwar suspicions of the punitive Versailles Treaty, and general anxiety over galloping inflation. Consequently, Nonpartisans, Progressives, labor unions, and even some Social Democrats moved easily into the new left-liberal alliance that would give energy to Progressive reform but end the brief moment of Socialist glory in Marathon County.

While county Socialists had long been vilified, the 1920 municipal elections provided the backdrop for a newly vigorous attack. The assault began with a broadside entitled "The Truth," published "in the interest of decency in city administration." Circulated just prior to the election, the leaflet scored Socialist county officials for allegedly hiring Minneapolis private detectives at considerable public expense to investigate gambling in Marathon County. Charging that the outsiders had been paid $1100.00 to "sleep with girls, gamble, and carouse," a local committee headed by E. C. Kretlow cited an expense account which placed the consultants in an unfavorable—and primarily amber—light. While their exploits may have been in the line of duty, the account purportedly signed by District Attorney Lippert did contain such dubious entries as: "with one of the girls at Fullers Place—$25.00," "lost in poker game at Bellis Hotel—$20.00," "Black Jack at Delmonicos—$20.00," and "Drink Around Town With the Gang—$7.50." The citizens' indictment condemned the Socialists for spending "like drunken fools," concluding with an outraged query: "Is it possible the taxpaying voters of Wausau approve such use of tax money?"[92]

Alleged "Playground" of Socialist Hirelings, Hotel Bellis

This onslaught coincided with a well-orchestrated campaign for a nonpartisan local ticket headed by AFL man Emil Flatter, who promised "business" rather than "politics" in city government. Full-page advertisements warned A.F. of L. members against Socialist efforts to woo them to the side of Assemblyman Herman Marth, who carried his party's colors in the mayoral race. Flatter warned against Socialist efforts to control the labor vote, insisting that the Socialist Party was "no friend of organized labor" and pledging that "as an old and tried union labor man," he would "represent [their] true interest." The citizens' ticket, with its emphasis on nonpartisanship, honesty, business principles, and governmental experience, recalled the nonpartisan movement of the Progressive era; although efforts to warn Wausau voters against unorthodox financial practices was novel. After all, citizens' candidate Carl Adams pledged that if elected comptroller, he "would not O.K. bills for gambling and sporting" and that a vote for him "protects the taxpayer."[93]

The citizens' ticket effort was complemented by a *Record-Herald* editorial attack on Tuetonic group instinct and government by acclamation, which took current form in "group republicanism or sovietism . . . in which the individual would count only within the group to which he belonged." In view of the forces martialed against him, Marth's loss by a scant 246 votes may be judged a creditable showing; similarly, Socialist victories in the sixth and eighth wards indicated some residual strength. To the *Herald*, however, the result was "a turning point towards better things," based upon a public recognition that "there has been a period of mistake making."[94]

Less certain that the tide had turned, the major parties kept the heat on the Socialists as the November elections drew near. Alternately worried about the Nonpartisan League's flirtation with state Progressives on one hand and latent Socialist sympathy on the other, critics launched a dual attack in the summer of 1920. And well they might, for not only had Marathon been the first rural county to send Socialists to Madison, but now the State Party chose to dramatize that broadened electoral support by brazenly scheduling its state convention in Wausau.

Attended by over two hundred delegates, the gathering demonstrated the remarkable growth of the party in response to the stimulus of wartime persecution. Among the important figures present were Victor Berger, Milwaukee Mayor Dan Hoan, and Vice-Presidential candidate Seymour Stedman, all of whom exhorted the faithful to greater efforts on behalf of the cause. When the platform endorsed national ownership of business enterprise, however, George Lippert was on his feet to qualify the meaning of the plank. Speaking for the large Marathon County delegation, the District Attorney was careful to point out that the statement "does not include the government ownership of farms" and that "there is no intention to make the program more extensive."[95] Socialism was better for some property owners than others.

His prominent role as convention chairman brought Lippert to the attention of the state committee, which reportedly considered him for the office of Attorney General. Elated by this discussion, area delegates finally contented themselves with their favorite's nomination for the Eighth District Congressional seat held by Edward Browne. As the convention neared its end, however, affection for Lippert was obvious in the warm reception he received at the Sunday picnic session. With thousands gathered at the shooting park, the rhetoric ran high; he captivated the partisan crowd with a ringing condemnation of local office holders (outside the confines of the county court house). Clearly, Lippert had built a following to match that of his comrades, Herman Marth and Charles Zarnke.

This show of political strength by the heretics jolted the Milwaukee-based Constitutional Defense League into counter-action. The League, designed to conduct an educational campaign "in behalf of Americanism and in opposition to revolutionary radicalism," carried the battle to Wausau in July by sponsoring a picnic "to answer the statements of Berger, Stedman and others made at the Socialist picnic." Central Wisconsin League representative Jack O'Brien set about to blunt the impact of the convention with a bevy of imported talent, including star attraction "Ole" Hanson, the anti-radical Seattle mayor who had stood firm to help break the general strike of 1919. While the "fighting mayor" delivered a "powerful" address, greater attention was given Montana farmer H. L. Sweet, who assured his audience that the I. W. W. and Socialists planned the confiscation of *all* property. Both warriors were supremely confident that the advance publicity had been dead right: "None Are So Blind As Those Who Will Not See."[96]

What, then, could be done to perfect the vision of Marathon County farmers before November, 1920? The *Record-Herald* lost little time in attacking county Socialist nominating procedures, which involved local caucuses of dues-paying party members and ignored the thousands of voters who had supported past tickets. All these supporters could do was "contribute their good money . . . and vote for the candidates put up by the few who pay dues regularly;" the Socialist Party was thus a "mighty fine thing—for those who are on the inside, who get the offices and the money." These benefits were of dubious value, as Herman Marth later recalled a $250.00 annual salary.[97]

But salary and benefits were not the crux of the 1920 campaign; rather, Democrats and many Republicans in Wisconsin worried over the future of free enterprise—threatened by the twin perils of Socialist and Nonpartisan radicalism. Complicating the situation was a tacit endorsement of the La Follette wing of the Republican Party, including gubernatorial candidate John J. Blaine, by the farmer-labor coalition which involved the League. The *Pilot* early understood this development, noting in September that Blaine stood "with both feet on the Nonpartisan platform." Anxious to capitalize on the new Republican departure, veteran Wausau Democrat Karl Mathie told the county Democracy that "the Nonpartisan League has laid its egg in the Republican nest," and its program was "state socialism, which ends in national socialism." Linking the "contagious disease" of Nonpartisan government with the intellectual bankruptcy of the Socialist Party, Mathie brought home his perception of imminent danger in terms aimed at the Marathon County electorate:

> Socialists don't dare to tell the truth about their farm
> attitude and nationalization projects. How are you
> going to run a country that is half free and half
> Socialist? Under Socialism farms must be socialized
> . . . So the Socialist party believes the time has now
> come for the beginning of socially-operated farms.[98]

Warning that the platform would never admit their true aims, the Wausau Democrat insisted that the Socialists would nationalize agriculture. And what were Nonpartisans but Socialists in disguise?

Rising to the challenge, Democratic gubernatorial candidate Robert McCoy of Sparta soon established himself as the anti-radical choice. Adamantly opposed to any "class law" that might be copied from "the obnoxious legislation . . . forced upon North Dakota," McCoy regarded his cause as "larger than party affiliation." Local Democrats saw him as the only candidate to offer voters a responsible choice for "orderly advancement," and many Republicans agreed that crossover voting was in order. The *Pilot* endorsement of McCoy clearly stated the position of the Democratic Party as the election neared:

> The Democratic Party in Wisconsin is pointing the
> path to constructive progress and is opposing the dou-
> ble forces of radicalism. On the one hand are the
> Socialists and on the other is the Nonpartisan League.
> The only difference is that the one runs under a name
> designating clearly what it is while the other parades
> under a title which conceals its true objects.[99]

So important was McCoy's crusade, that the Republican *Record-Herald* added its backing for the Democratic nominee, whose candidacy deserved the support of "every voter who is against socialism."[100] But county Republicans left nothing to chance. While Democrats on the hustings lashed out at Nonpartisans and Socialists, the Marathon County GOP was not idle. Determined to eradicate the Socialist blot on the county record, the Republican County Committee launched a splashy advertising campaign to discredit socialism once and for all. The opening shot was a full page ad boldly proclaiming Socialist leaders to be "against the marriage relation." Although Socialists would deny this, the party training manual allegedly endorsed free love and state-supported child-rearing. Did "good Christian women voters . . . really think the world would be better off, if marriage [were] abolished and not only all property, but children as well, made a public charge?"

If free love was insufficiently threatening, how did voters feel about "forcible revolution?" To forestall the threat of "civil war," the Republican Party urged the working people of the area to "see that no Socialists [were] elected in Marathon County." Raising the specter of Bolshevism, the blitz continued with a recitation of the evils of public ownership as practiced in the Soviet Union: "Russia tells the story." County voters were told that "every vote for a Socialist in Marathon County helps to strengthen those leaders who want to wipe out all of our present civilization."[101]

Mindful of the unique position of McCoy as the sole voice of anti-radicalism at the head of the respective tickets, local Republicans acknowledged publicly that crossover would occur and warned against local defections. On election eve the county committee reminded citizens that, in 1918, combined Republican and Democratic votes had exceeded the winning Socialist total: with this hindsight, the GOP urged that "all Anti-Socialists make their votes count by voting for the straight Republican county ticket."[102]

This vigorous political initiative coincided with a well-planned informational campaign during the final weeks of the campaign. While Pilot and Record-Herald editorials warned against the pitfalls of Russian experimentalism, the Democratic National Committee sent Mrs. Edward Bowler of Sheboygan to expose the socialistic evils of the Nonpartisan League to an audience of women voters. At the same approximate moment, Karl Mathie packed them in at Easton, Frankfort, and Marathon City, where he expounded on the "connection between the Socialists and their tool, the Nonpartisan League." On yet another front the Wausau Knights of Columbus sponsored a lecture by National Electricians' Union President Peter Collins, who told his Opera House audience that "the tenets of socialism involve atheism and plan to tear down present-day civilization."[103]

In the face of this double-barrelled assault, the Socialist county ticket was doomed. Creditable voting records on labor and agricultural issues compiled by Marth and Zarnke counted for little as long as their party stood for the end of capitalism. And Marth's performance in office paled into insignificance when his party was forced to grapple with the forces of respectability on the ground of economic interest and bogus social issues. Perhaps most significant was the transitory nature of a Socialist appeal that had found a ready audience in a resentful German-American community confronted by the white heat of wartime patriotism. Finally, the election results cannot be divorced from the political readjustments under way in Wisconsin by 1920; for a new farmer-labor coalition had brought many German votes to the

La Follette-Blaine faction of the state Republican Party.

In Marathon County, realignment meant the defeat of Marth and Zarnke by resounding margins of 1800 and 1500 votes, respectively, while the county Socialist ticket met disaster as well. The predominant interpretation of the county tally stressed a "repudiation of socialism," which "should have no appeal to a community composed largely of prosperous farmers." Seizing upon defeated congressional candidate Lippert's threat to leave the county, the *Record-Herald* gleefully implored him to remain:

> George, when I heard you'd finally decided
>   To drop that trip to Washington next year
> Although I mourned, my feelings were divided,
>   I thought, "At any rate, we'll keep you here."
> But what are these sad words that come to grieve us,
>   And fill with gloom the proletariat?
> It can't be true that you are going to leave us?
>   Good Lord, George, don't do that!
> Although the soulless capitalists flout you—
>   Such hireling knaves as Sturtevant and Pradt—
> Yet George, you know we cannot do without you,
>   You mustn't go away and leave us flat.
> Who would supply us with big-town detectives
>   To pounce upon the fiendish gambling den?
> Who'd thunder at the rich with harsh invectives?
>   Oh come, George, think again![104]

The Republican victory in Marathon County had dealt socialism a mortal blow; less celebrated but pregnant with meaning for the county's political future was the Democratic disaster of 1920. While Democratic totals shrank, reform Republicans like E. E. Browne and John J. Blaine prospered—a common pattern in heavily German counties that had formerly voted Democrat.[105] Thus, there was one last irony in the 1920 returns: local paranoia born of two years under the yoke of Socialist leadership had driven the nonconformists from the temple of government—but was the cure worse than the malady? While the Democrats lay prostrate and Socialists licked their wounds, the new county support for Progressive Republicanism promised no rest for the weary conservative who longed for stability in the house of Wisconsin government.

FOOTNOTES

[1] Karen F. Falk, "War Propaganda in Wisconsin, 1917-1918" (Master's Thesis, Dept. of History, University of Wisconsin, 1941), p. 38.

[2] Roger Wyman, "Voting Behavior in the Progressive Era: Wisconsin As a Test Case," (Ph.D. dissertation, Dept. of History, University of Wisconsin, 1970), p. 513; Harold E. Miner, et al., *History of Wausau* (Wausau: Centennial Project, 1939), p. 30. For full discussion of the source and nature of German Immigration in Wisconsin, see Kate Everest Levi, "Geographical Origins of German Immigration to Wisconsin," in *Wisconsin Historical Collections*, Vol. XIV, and Albert Bernhart Faust. *The German Element in the United States*, Vol. 1 (New York, Steuben Society, 1927). The following table summarizes the national origins of the foreign born in Marathon County at various periods in the twentieth century.

Table 1: Foreign-Born in Marathon County, 1870-1940, 1970

	German	Polish	Norwegian	Bohemian	English	Native American
1870	2239	—	73	—	49	—
1880	4387	—	367	—	123	—
1900	8712	1064	420	369	93	—
1910	8807	—	471	—	70	26
1920	5794	1673	393	414	84	45
1930	4477	1555	302	403	54	37
1940	3017	1059	206	214	43	—
1970	7725	2376	—	423	330	—

Source: United States Census, IX-XIX; 1870-1940, 1970

[3] Wyman, p. 386.

[4] *Ibid.*, pp. 70, 96; Miner & Moore, pp. 136-137.

[5] Miner & Moore, p. 139, Myman, pp. 160, 210; Louis Marchetti, *History of Marathon County and Representative Citizens* (Chicago: Richmond-Arnold Publishing Co., 1913), pp. 211. The evidence available indicates that there was a small band of Populist Party workers laboring in Marathon County as of 1896. Some fifteen names are listed in the "Journal" of Wisconsin Populist leader Robert Schilling of Milwaukee. Robert Schilling Manuscripts, Wisconsin State Historical Society, Madison, Wis.

[6] *Central Wisconsin*, March 12, 1898, p. 4.

[7] *Wausau Pilot*, April 29, 1899, p. 4.

[8] *Wausau Record*, Feb. 2, 1900, p. 2; Feb. 16, 1900, p. 2; *Pilot*, May 22, 1900, p. 4.

[9] *Pilot*, July 3, 1900, p. 4. The *Record* made cross-over political participation a major reason for its own opposition to the direct primary election. *Record*, Aug. 1, 1900, p. 2.

[10] *Record*, July 28, 1900, p. 5; July 14, 1900, p. 5.

[11] *Pilot*, Oct. 23, 1900, p. 4.

[12] Republican success in the 1900 election has been variously attributed to "technological and financial changes," the tendency of German voters to be "Presidential Republicans," and to the fact that "mills and factories in Wausau were running full time" so that "the people were satisfied with existing conditions." Marchetti, *op. cit.*, p. 212; Miner & Moore, p. 117; Wyman, p. 561.

[13] *Pilot*, Feb. 20, 1901, p. 1; Jan. 29, 1901, p. 4; Jan. 15, 1901, p. 4.

[14] *Pilot*, May 21, 1901, p. 4; see also Herbert Marguiles, *The Decline of the Progressive Movement in Wisconsin, 1890-1920* (Madison: State Historical Society of Wisconsin, 1968), pp. 51-52.

[15] This account of the battle for the direct primary is based upon Allen Lovejoy, *La Follette and the Direct Primary* (New Haven: Yale University Press, 1941), esp. pp. 79-82, 91-94. See also *Pilot*, Sept. 23, 1902, p. 1; *Wisconsin Blue Book* (Madison: 1905), pp. 334-35, 531-32.

[16] *Record*, Feb. 10, 1902, p. 2; March 4, 1902, p. 2; *Pilot*, Oct. 22, 1901, p. 4; Nov. 19, 1901, p. 4; Jan. 14, 1902, p. 4.

[17] *Pilot*, Jan. 21, 1902, p. 4; July 15, 1902, p. 4. Brown's announcement drew widespread comment in the state press, which regarded him as a formidable contender for the nomination. *Pilot*, Aug. 19, 1902, p. 4.

[18] *Pilot*, Aug. 26, 1902, p. 4; Sept. 9, 1902, p. 4; Sept. 30, 1902, p. 1.

[19] *Pilot*, Oct. 28, 1902, pp. 4, 1.

[20] Marchetti, p. 213; Wyman, pp. 553-54.

[21] Marvin Rosenberry, unpublished autobiographical manuscripts, pp. 45, 46, 50; Marvin Rosenberry Manuscripts, Madison, Wisconsin, State Historical Society; Lovejoy, *op. cit.*, p. 86; *Pilot*, Oct. 11, 1904, p. 9.

[22] *Central Wisconsin*, July 16, 1904, p. 4; July 23, 1904, p. 4; *Pilot*, May 24, 1904, p. 4; June 28, 1904, p. 4.

[23] *Pilot*, Nov. 1, 1904, p. 4; Aug. 30, 1904, p. 4; John F. Lamont and Herbert H. Manson, "To the Voters of Marathon County," in *Pilot*, Nov. 8, 1904, p. 1; see also Marguiles, *op. cit.*, pp. 75-77.

[24] *Record*, July 22, 1904, p. 2; July 29, 1904, p. 2; *Pilot*, Nov. 8, 1904, p. 1; Oct. 25, 1904, p. 4; Oct. 11, 1904, p. 4.

[25] *Central Wisconsin*, Nov. 19, 1904, p. 4; *Pilot*, p. 1; Marchetti, p. 214; Miner & Moore, p. 141. While Democratic defection is obvious in rural areas, the voting patterns in Wausau wards give less evidence of opposition support for La Follette. The three most Democratic wards in Wausau provided Peck with comfortable majorities in 1904, while Republicans deserted the governor in two of the strongest GOP wards. *Record*, April 2, 1902, p. 3; *Pilot*, Nov. 15, 1904, p. 1.

[26] *Central Wisconsin*, Nov. 19, 1904, p. 4; for evidence of continuing Democratic strength in the Progressive period, see Wyman, pp. 342, 366. See also Marguiles, pp. 79-81, especially for discussion of the stalwart defection of 1904.

[27] *Pilot*, March 29, 1898, p. 1; Feb. 8, 1898, p. 5; G. D. Jones to J. A. Gaynor, Oct. 30, 1897, in *Pilot*, Nov. 16, 1897, pp. 1-2; David Thelen, *The New Citizenship: Origins of Progressivism in Wisconsin, 1885-1900* (Columbia: University of Missouri Press, 1972), pp. 231, 242-43. The success of the "Wisconsin Valley plan" drew widespread attention throughout the state as an effective means of bringing important public services to the consumer at minimum cost with maximum efficiency. *Record*, Feb. 15, 1900, p. 2.

[28] Interview with Clarence Rankl, Town of Holton, April 13, 1976; see also William Kadonsky, "A Family History of Cooperative Development," unpublished research paper, Dec. 7, 1973, Dept. of History, University of Wisconsin, Marathon Campus; "History of Hull Township," Wausau, Marathon County Historical Society.

[29] Marchetti, *op. cit.*, p. 324; *Pilot*, March 29, 1904, p. 5; April 5, 1904, p. 5; April 26, 1904, p. 1; July 12, 1904, p. 5.

[30] *Record*, Jan. 24, 1900, p. 2; *Pilot*, Jan. 23, 1900, pp. 1, 4; Thelen, p. 141. The *Pilot* buttressed its endorsement of nonpartisan government with statements of support from numerous prominent citizens, including Mayor Joseph Reiser, John Ringle, Louis Marchetti, D. L. Plumer, V. A. Alderson, G. D. Jones, John F. Lamont, B. Heinemann, J. N. Manson, A. L. Kreutzer, Walter Alexander, E. C. Zimmerman, R. E. Parcher, F. L. Hudson, F. W. Kickbusch, Fred Genrich, Jacob Gensman, C. B. Bird, Marvin Rosenberry, W. C. Silverthorn, C. S. Curtis and H. G. Fleith.

[31] *Record*, Jan. 24, 1900, p. 2; *Pilot*, Jan. 30, 1900, p. 4.

[32] *Record*, March 20, 1900, p. 2; March 14, 1900, p. 2; March 9, 1900, p. 2; *Pilot*, March 13, 1900, p. 4; March 20, 1900, p. 4; see also Thelen, p. 152.

[33] *Record*, March 28, 1900, p. 2; *Pilot*, April 3, 1900, p. 4.

[34] *Pilot*, April 10, 1900, p. 4; *Record*, April 4, 1900, p. 2. The most significant development of the campaign was the vigorous challenge raised by Socialist Labor candidate Robert Phillip, who drew substantial support in the west side German wards. The Socialist tide was soon to crest in Marathon County as a result of the divisiveness generated by American involvement in the First World War.

[35] *Record-Herald*, March 2, 1911, p. 1; March 16, 1911, p. 4; *Pilot*, Nov. 7, 1911, p. 4. The local advocacy committee was composed of Chairman Curtis, H. M. Manson, W. R. Chellis, Henry A. Lemke, and H. F. Schulze. This group circulated the necessary petitions to ensure a local referendum, which was subsequently scheduled for February, 1912.

[36] Henry Ellenbecker to the *Record-Herald*, *Record-Herald*, April 5, 1911, p. 6.

[37] John Ringle, "Letter from Hon. John Ringle," in *Pilot*, Dec. 26, 1911, p. 1. For comment on role of the German-American Alliance in the struggle over commission government, see Marchetti, *op. cit.*, p. 330; Miner and Moore, *op. cit.*, p. 144. Full discussion of the origins, functions, and local significance of the Alliance

may be found in *Pilot,* Jan. 28, 1908, p. 5; *Record-Herald,* Jan. 4, 1908, p. 5; Jan. 27, 1908, p. 5.

[38] The referendum lost by a margin of 2009 to 738, with only two of nine wards voting for the change. *Pilot,* Feb. 27, 1912, p. 1. For full discussion of the public controversy, see *Pilot,* Nov. 7, 1911, pp. 1, 9.

[39] For development of the significance of national identity in Wisconsin political behavior, see Jorgen Weibull, "The Wisconsin Progressives, 1900-1914," *Mid-America,* Vol. 47 (July, 1965), esp. p. 208; see also Gerd Korman, "Political Loyalties, Immigrant Traditions and Reform: the Wisconsin German-American Press and Progressivism, 1909-1912," *Wisconsin Magazine of History,* 40 (Spring, 1957), p. 168. Wyman, pp. 559-61, documents the continuing tendency of Wisconsin (and Marathon County) German-Americans to vote Democratic except for presidential races. He notes the persistence of Democratic strength in such German strongholds as Stettin, Hamburg, and Berlin during the period 1904-1914; see also Weibull, *op cit.,* pp. 200-205.

[40] Brown to Henry Fetzer, Aug. 7, 1913, Brown MSS; *Marathon Times,* Sept. 2, 1910, p. 1.

[41] County opposition was entirely consistent with voting trends in heavily German counties elsewhere in the state, where traditional ethnic tendencies towards thrift and frugality remained strong. Marathon ranked among the bottom ten counties in its aproval margin, joining other areas with a similar ethnic composition. *Wisconsin Blue Book,* (Madison: 1909) p. 558; Wyman, pp. 458, 462; *Record-Herald,* Jan. 14, 1918, p. 4; *Pilot,* Jan. 7, 1908, p. 1.

[42] Brown to Fetzer, Aug. 7, 1913, Brown MSS; Korman, *op. cit.,* p. 164; Wyman, *op. cit.,* p. 337, 458.

[43] Marathon's 3-1 margin surpassed that of such predominantly European areas as Milwaukee County, where a 2-1 edge against the proposal was recorded. *Wisconsin Blue Book,* (Madison, 1913), p. 270; Wyman, pp. 458, 566.

[44] *Marathon Times,* Sept. 2, 1910, p. 1; see also Aug. 5, 1910, p. 1; Aug. 19, 1910, p. 8. For discussion of negative attitudes on local option expressed by both the statewide German press and the German-American Alliance, see Korman, p. 336, which notes that "in heavily German areas anything less than total opposition to it spelled defeat."

[45] *Record-Herald,* March 20, 1911, p. 3; March 22, 1911, p. 5; April 1, 1911, p. 8; April 3, 1911, pp. 1, 2. Bucknam was later destined to enter the political lists as Prohibitionist candidate for Congress and Governor.

[46] *Record-Herald,* April 5, 1911, p. 1; *Pilot,* April 11, 1911, p. 1.

[47] *Marathon Times,* Sept. 30, 1910, p. 1; see also Marchetti, pp. 215, 217.

[48] A. W. Prehn to Francis McGovern, Dec. 7, 1910; Nov. 10, 1910; Oscar W. Schoengarth to McGovern, Nov. 9, 1910, Francis E. McGovern Manuscripts, Madison, Wisconsin State Historical Society; see also Wyman, pp. 431, 561-62.

[49] "Autobiography," pp. 53-56; "Register," p. 1; Rosenberry MSS; *Record-Herald,* Feb. 15, 1916, p. 4, Feb. 14, 1916, p. 1; *Marathon Times,* Feb. 18, 1916, p. 1.

[50] The Judicial Election," *Capital Times,* in "Autobiography," pp. 57-58, Rosenberry MSS. The editorial alleged that Heinemann believed that "Rosenberry is necessary to the entire business structure of the State." "Autobiography," p. 58.

[51] *The Primary Election of 1910 and the Presidential Primary of 1912* (Madison: Industrial Commission of Wisconsin, 1912), pp. 20, 152-53; see also Marguiles, pp. 126-28; Marchetti, p. 218. Primary returns clearly indicate that Clark owed his Marathon County victory to a 400 vote margin amassed in the city of Wausau, where he had appeared in an allegedly "non-political" capacity in 1911. *The Primary Election of 1910 and the Presidential Primary of 1912,* pp. 152-53; *Pilot,* March 14, 1911, p. 1; *Record-Herald,* March 21, 1911, p. 1.

[52] Brown to Fetzer, Aug. 7, 1913, Brown MSS; *Pilot,* Oct. 7, 1902, p. 4; Korman, p. 166.

[53] The eighth ward was over 70 per cent German in 1912. Wyman, p. 571; Brown to Fetzer, Aug. 7, 1913, Brown MSS; *Pilot,* July 23, 1912, p. 4; Oct. 8, 1912, p. 4; Oct. 15, 1904, p. 4.

[54] Miner and Moore, p. 146; for full treatment of public opinion and war propaganda during the war, see Karen Falk, "Public Opinion in Wisconsin During World War I," *Wisconsin Magazine of History,* XXV (June, 1942), pp. 389-407; see also

Falk, "War Propaganda in Wisconsin, 1917-1918," (Master's Thesis, Dept. of History, University of Wisconsin, 1941).

[55] Over 3000 were in attendance while another 3000 were turned away from the Opera House event, which proved to be baldly partisan in character. *Pilot*, Nov. 3, 1914, p. 5.

[56] *Wisconsin Blue Book*, (Madison: 1915), p. 228; Marguiles, pp. 121-22. For discussion of the Progressive agony of 1914, see Robert C. Nesbit, *Wisconsin, A History* (Madison: the University of Wisconsin Press, 1973), pp. 430-32.

[57] *Marathon Times*, Oct. 1, 1915, p. 1.

[58] By December, 1915 over $1300 had been raised by the Wausau Alliance and forwarded to the national relief fund for use in Germany, *Record-Herald*, Dec. 6, 1915, pp. 1, 4.

[59] Frank' Leuschen to Paul Husting, May 29, 1915, Paul Husting Manuscripts, Madison, Wisconsin State Historical Society.

[60] *Milwaukee Journal*, May 16, 1915, pp. 1, 3.

[61] After this purple passage, Leuschen concluded that his readers should be "Americans first, and everything else afterwards." *Marathon Times*, Feb. 19, 1915, p. 1; Jan. 8, 1915, p. 1.

[62] Leuschen to Husting, May 24, 1915, Husting MSS.

[63] Leuschen complied with the Senator's request by publishing liberal excerpts from the *Milwaukee Journal* article. He also gave Husting detailed instructions on how to reach the local press and referred him to potentially sympathetic journalists, including E. B. Thayer of the *Pilot*, and A. Pankow of Marshfield. Leuschen to Husting, May 29, 1915; Husting to Leuschen, May 22, 1915; J. I. Scott to Husting, May 18, 1915; Husting to Leuschen, May 27, 1915, Husting MSS.

[64] *Marathon Times*, Feb. 8, 1916, p. 1; Jan. 21, 1916, p. 1.

[65] *Capital Times*, Aug. 8, 1918, *Record-Herald*, Nov. 22, 1916, both quoted in *Marathon Times*, Aug. 23, 1918, p. 8; *Record-Herald*, July 24, 1916, p. 2; July 25, 1916, p. 4.

[66] The following table dramatically illustrates the scope of defection in selected German localities:

VOTE PLURALITIES IN SELECTED GERMAN AREAS —
PRESIDENTIAL ELECTIONS OF 1912 and 1916

Unit	Plurality 1912	Plurality 1916
Hamburg	Wilson—38	Hughes—118
Berlin	Wilson—91	Hughes—108
Maine	Wilson—86	Hughes— 76
Stettin	Wilson—59	Hughes— 43
Wausau	Wilson—14	Hughes— 63
Rib Falls	Wilson—34	Hughes— 99
Wausau		
Ward 6	Wilson—44	Hughes— 43
Ward 7	Wilson—59	Hughes—123
Ward 8	Wilson—34	Hughes—103
Ward 9	Wilson— 1	Hughes— 81

Source: *Wisconsin Blue Book*, 1913, pp. 192-193; 1917, p. 216.

It should be noted that 1912 pluralities reflect the impact of the Roosevelt candidacy. However, in the townships cited, the Progressive candidate garnered only 75 votes; while in the Wausau wards, his 265 votes were largely offset by 223 cast for Socialist Eugene Debs. Further comment on the ethnic factor in both Wilson elections may be found in Marguiles, p. 189; Wyman, p. 563; and Nesbit, pp. 444-45.

[67] Reverend Howard Murray Jones of Green Valley helped carry his township for Hughes by a twenty-four vote plurality. Rev. Howard Murray Jones to Ada Alice Jones, Nov. 23, 1916, Rev. Howard Murray Jones Manuscripts, Madison, Wisconsin State Historical Society; *Wisconsin Blue Book*, 1913, pp. 192-93; 1917, p. 216. Judgments concerning the ethnic character of townships are based on D. G. Marshall, "Cultural Background of Wisconsin People (Nationality Background)" Madison, Wisconsin State Historical Society Archives.

[68] "Proceedings of the Marathon County Council of Defense," Oct. 24, 1917, Nov. 20, 1917, Aug. 14, 1917, June 26, 1917, June 12, 1917, June 7, 1917, May 3, 1917, Wausau, Marathon County Historical Society. The contribution of Wisconsin to the war effort is discussed in David A. Shannon, "The World, the War, and Wisconsin, 1914-1918," Milwaukee County Historical Society, *Historical Messenger*, XXII (March, 1967), p. 47; Falk, "Public Opinion in Wisconsin," pp. 400-403, 407.

[69] John D. Stevens, "Suppression of Dissent in Wisconsin During World War I," (unpublished Ph.D. dissertation, Dept. of Mass Communications, University of Wisconsin, 1967), p. 91; *Pilot*, May 7, 1918, p. 7; May 14, 1918, p. 10; *Marathon Times*, May 3, 1918, p. 1; Jones to Ada Jones, April 22, 1918, Jones MSS.

[70] *Pilot*, Jan. 15, 1918, p. 1; July 30, 1918, p. 1; Stevens, p. 159.

[71] *Pilot*, April 23, 1918, p. 4; Stevens, p. 163. For discussion of the Loyalty Legion, see Clifton J. Child, *The German-American in Politics, 1914-1917* (Madison: Wisconsin State Historical Society Press, 1939), pp. 26-27; Falk, *Public Opinion in Wisconsin During World War I*, pp. 403-404.

[72] *Record-Herald*, Sept. 16, 1918, p. 1; Sept. 3, 1918, p. 5; *Pilot*, Sept. 3, 1918, p. 1; Stevens, p. 163.

[73] *Pilot*, Jan. 29, 1918, p. 5; *Record-Herald*, Jan. 24, 1918, p. 1; July 23, 1918, p. 1; Stevens, p. 86.

[74] *Record-Herald*, April 13, 1918, pp. 1, 4.

[75] *Record-Herald*, July 25, 1918, p. 1; July 22, 1918, p. 1; *Pilot*, April 9, 1918, p. 7; April 30, 1918, p. 1; June 25, 1918, p. 7; Stevens, pp. 43-44.

[76] *Record-Herald*, June 15, 1918, p. 4; June 4, 1918, p. 4; June 3, 1918, p. 1; June 5, 1918, p. 1; *Marathon Times*, May 10, 1910, p. 1; Stevens, pp. 102-103.

[77] *Record-Herald*, Sept. 12, 1918, p. 1; Sept. 13, 1918, p. 1; Sept. 14, 1918, p. 1; Sept. 19, 1918, p. 1; *Pilot*, Sept. 17, 1918, p. 4; Stevens, pp. 102-103. Still walking a tightrope in a German community, Marathon's Frank Leuschen declined comment on the Schilling case, confining himself to a simple recitation of the facts of the trial. The perceptive *Times* reader could easily discern his attitude, however, from a glance at a report carried in the same issue concerning an unrelated case of draft resistance: Leuschen condemned not the "boy who deserts," — but rather "the wily agitator who induces him to desert." *Marathon Times*, Sept. 20, 1918, p. 1.

[78] *Record-Herald*, June 6, 1918, pp. 1, 2; Feb. 11, 1918, pp. 1, 2, 4; *Pilot*, April 9, 1918, p. 10; *Marathon Times*, June 14, 1918, p. 1; "Proceedings of the Marathon County Council of Defense," June 26, 1917.

[79] Another index indicates that the county stood 47th on a continuum of Wisconsin counties, with 71 ranked as the state's most tolerant. Stevens, pp. 187, 213.

[80] *Record-Herald*, Feb. 12, 1918, pp. 1, 4; Feb. 11, 1918, p. 4; Herman O. Kent, "Herman A. Marth — People's Man," reprint from *Commonwealth*, Wausau, Marathon County Historical Society. See Kent for full details on Marth's background, as well as sympathetic treatment of his legislative record.

[81] Kent; *Pilot*, Feb. 19, 1918, pp. 1, 4; *Record-Herald*, Feb. 13, 1918, p. 1; Marguiles, p. 227.

[82] The Berger majorities in Berlin, Hamburg, Rib Falls, Stettin, and Wausau were: 176-9, 160-3, 116-10, 168-11, and 129-19. Similarly, Wausau's west side wards registered a symbolic protest with large margins.
Record-Herald, April 3, 1918, p. 1; Marguiles, p. 228; Shannon, p. 53. Clifford Nelson, *German-American Political Behavior in Nebraska and Wisconsin, 1916-1920* (Lincoln: University of Nebraska Press, 1972), pp. 39, 49, 50. Nelson confirms the clear relationship between German ethnic background and Berger's statewide strength, noting that "Socialist and German percentages at the county level correlated at a new high of +.56 compared to a +.04 coefficient of correlation with Davies and a —.59 with Lenroot." Nelson, p. 39.

[83] *Record-Herald*, April 3, 1918, p. 1.

[84] Interview with Marshall Duranso, Aug. 30, 1975, Wausau, Marathon County Public Library Oral History Collection; *Record Herald*, April 3, 1918, p. 2.

[85] Socialists elected in 1918 included: Emil Tesch, Sheriff; George W. Lippert, District Attorney; Edwin Bruss, County Clerk; Frank Damrow, County Treasurer; Frank Novak, Clerk of Courts; Herman Habeck, Register of Deeds; Herman Marth, Assemblyman, 2nd District; Charles Zarnke, Assemblyman, 1st District. Kent, p. 2;

Record-Herald, Nov. 2, 1918, p. 1; Sept. 17, 1918, p. 4; *Marathon Times,* Aug. 23, 1918, p. 8.

[86] Kent, pp. 2, 3, 4.

[87] *Pilot,* Dec. 16, 1918, p. 1; *Record-Herald,* June 13, 1918, p. 4; Stevens, p. 195; Duranso Interview.

[88] *Stratford Journal,* Oct. 10, 1919, p. 1; *Record-Herald,* June 4, 1919, p. 4; June 9, 1919, p. 4; May 13, 1919, p. 4; see also Marguiles, p. 246.

[89] *Pilot,* April 8, 1919, pp. 1, 8.

[90] *Record-Herald,* April 10, 1919, p. 4; *Pilot,* June 24, 1919, p. 4; April 8, 1919, p. 8; Marguiles, pp. 250-251. The early reports of Nonpartisan League strength in Marathon County were much exaggerated, as indicated by the organization's membership lists. While 1919 totals are unavailable, the 1924 tally shows less than 25 paid League members in the county, primarily from the Mosinee and Marathon areas. Wisconsin Nonpartisan League Manuscripts, Madison, Wisconsin State Historical Society.

[91] *Pilot,* Sept. 7, 1920, p. 10; Feb. 10, 1920, p. 10; Feb. 3, 1920, p. 8; Feb. 17, 1920, p. 8; March 9, 1920, p. 8; March 16, 1920, p. 4; Oct. 28, 1919, p. 4.

[92] "The Truth," (Wausau: the Campaign Committee, April, 1920), Wausau, Marathon County Historical Society.

[93] *Record-Herald,* April 5, 1920, p. 3.

[94] *Record-Herald,* April 7, 1920, pp. 4, 1; April 6, 1920, p. 4.

[95] *Pilot,* June 22, 1920, p. 1; *Record-Herald,* June 21, 1920, p. 1.

[96] *Pilot,* July 6, 1920, p. 8; *Record-Herald,* July 9, 1920, p. 1; July 10, 1920, pp. 1, 2; Marguiles, p. 274.

[97] *Milwaukee Journal,* n.d., 1968, in files of Louis Marth, Wausau; *Record-Herald,* July 13, 1920, p. 4.

[98] *Pilot,* Sept. 21, 1920, pp. 1, 4; see also Oct. 5, 1920, p. 1.

[99] *Pilot,* Oct. 12, 1920, p. 4; Oct. 19, 1920, p. 4; Sept. 14, 1920, p. 4.

[100] *Record-Herald,* Oct. 26, 1920, p. 10.

[101] *Record-Herald,* Oct. 29, 1920, p. 10; Oct. 28, 1920, p. 10.

[102] Italics are mine. *Record-Herald,* Nov. 1, 1920, p. 8.

[103] *Record-Herald,* Oct. 30, 1920, p. 10; *Pilot,* Oct. 19, 1920, p. 4; Oct. 26, 1920, p. 4.

[104] *Record-Herald,* Nov. 4, 1920, p. 4; Feb. 10, 1968, p. 11; Kent, p. 4. For discussion of the resurgence of reform and emergence of a new Progressive coalition in the 1920 Wisconsin election, see Marguiles, Chapter VII.

[105] Marguiles, p. 278. For 1920 results, see *Wisconsin Blue Book,* 1921, pp. 186-87, 224, 231.

CHAPTER SEVEN

Between the Wars:
Progressive Ascendancy,
1920-1938

While national government settled into a pattern of complacency in the early 1920's, the politics of Marathon County and the entire Badger state were far from quiet. To the contrary, the flame of reform continued to burn among dedicated Wisconsin Progressives; their successes often contradicted the dominant trends of an era of consolidation. Dismayed by the resiliency of La Follette liberalism, frustrated party regulars groped for some means of restoring "respectable" rule to the county and the state. When the attack on "LaFollettism" sputtered, Marathon County politics finally resolved itself into a complicated, sometimes murky, struggle for the mantle of Progressivism—a label that was practically a prerequisite to success at the polls by the mid-1920's.

Such political preferences often reflected a disdain for traditional partisanship and a tendency towards independent voting patterns. But beyond this, the 1920's also saw the growth of a powerful new political coalition in Marathon County, supported by historically-Democratic and recently-Socialist rural and labor voters. And no element in the combination was more significant than the German vote, long a bellwether and still statistically significant.[1]

Just as many German-Americans had voted Socialist during World War I as a protest against the county "establishment," so their exodus from the Democratic Party became final in the 1920's, as they turned to the Progressive wing of the Republican Party in droves. Although most tended toward conservatism, they plainly preferred La Follette's interpretation of loyalty to the simple equating of German heritage with wartime disloyalty or postwar radicalism. To this coalition, past memories were more important than domestic reforms as an influence on voter behavior. Migrating from both the Socialist and Democratic Parties, the converts strengthened the forces of liberalism and dealt a severe blow to the hopes of the stalwarts. The potency of the Progressive identification after the watershed election of 1920 was obvious.

In socio-economic terms the La Follette legion was generally composed of working class troops. While stalwart Republicans tended to be drawn from what one observer termed "the noble six-hundred," business and professional people of considerable wealth and conservative philosophy, Progressive candidates were generally backed by farmers and laborers. After the postwar open shop movement, organized labor meant essentially barbers, carpenters, and railway men: by far the most disciplined were the railway brotherhoods, which sometimes provided 100 per cent support to Progessive candidates. Despite labor's relative impotence in the early 1920's, the *Record-Herald* was occasionally known to scold the movement for "the influence which syndicalists, socialists, anarchists, communists and others of the extreme breed of radicals have in a number of unions."[2]

Far more significant to the reform coalition were Marathon County farmers, who gave electoral majorities to the La Follette wing of the Republican Party. Rural voters had come a long way from 1902, when the farmer had once been dismissed as "one who does not know that there is a fight on between the stalwarts and the halfbreeds." Much more sophisticated were the county farmers of 1922 who, except for the "old line Democrats," were "Progressives almost to the man," secure in the passionately-held belief that "old Bob is our friend" and that "with all their money and men they can not beat *him*."[3] This dedication brought firm support for Progressives in farm districts, where agriculturalists were beginning to explore shared economic interests with urban workers: the trend toward coalition stands as a prevailing theme in the political story of Marathon County in the 1920's and 1930's.

While liberal Republicanism prospered, however, stalwarts fared poorly in their struggle against the La Follette organization, which they claimed crushed all dissent. Conservative frustration increased in 1922, as a result of a battle among numerous contenders for the honor of challenging the "Madison Ring" gubernatorial choice, incumbent John J. Blaine. In May, Marathon County party regulars gathered to name delegates to a stalwart conference in Milwaukee, called to determine "effective candidates to oppose La Follette Republicans at the primaries" and "present a united front." The large county delegation was composed of such prominent county conservatives as Sen. Claire Bird, J. L. Sturtevant, Walter Heinemann, Frank Chesak, Fred Genrich, Andrew Kreutzer, J. S. Alexander, L. A. Pradt, Jr., H. G. Fleith, and Walter Alexander: the group clearly spoke for what most observers regarded as the wealth and influence of the area. In view of the interests represented, there is an interesting angle to the economic concerns of the body, which decried "legislation for or against any class or faction" and opposed "the efforts of any and all organizations seeking to control any political party for its own class or special interests or policies."[4]

But hopes for stalwart unity sagged as the gubernatorial race heated up, resulting in intense competition between Attorney General William Morgan and Roy P. Wilcox of Eau Claire. Prominently mentioned as a dark horse candidate was Wausau's Andrew L. Kreutzer, who refused to campaign, but expressed a willingness to accept the endorsement of party regulars. A sympathetic *Record-Herald* fretted over the multiplicity of anti-La Follette candidates in the lists. Fully realizing that stalwart bickering in the primary would spell disaster, the paper warned that "the only hope of victory depends upon opposing La Follette men with a single candidate each." True to its own advice, it also commended the stalwarts' choice as the man "most likely to defeat his opponent," whose certain victory promised to liberate Wisconsin from "the shame of being boss-ridden and dominated by a minority faction." That "minority" managed to give Blaine a clear victory over Morgan in the September primary, including a Marathon County margin of 9,514-2,060—painful evidence of the distance separating the stalwart perception of political reality and the public pulse.[5]

The tribulations of Republican conservatives were trivial, however, compared to the floundering of a deeply-divided Democratic Party. And on no issue was the rift more clearly defined than on prohibition. Symptomatic of the Democrats' concern was the *Pilot's* effort to straddle the question by calling for a popular referendum on liquor and urging both wets and drys to enter the primary. The vexing problem simply would not disappear. Finally, it burst into the public arena at the Democratic convention in June, 1922, where the party faithful took the unusual step of endorsing two gubernatorial candidates. Those anointed were La Crosse wet A. A. Bently and Wausau's Karl Mathie, a well-known dry. The entire situation was not without a touch of irony, for the dry candidate's father had made a considerable fortune as the founder of the Mathie Brewing Company in the nineteenth century. On the campaign trail the candidate chose to stress his deep belief in majority rule on the prohibition issue, while soft pedaling his own personal list to the dry side. Devoutly hoping to shift the focus of the debate, the Marathon County favorite opened his campaign at Mosinee with a bombastic assault on the opposition party, now under the influence of "radicals." In a calculated exaggeration, Mathie claimed that "all of Wisconsin Republicanism is resting in the bed of international socialism" and that the Democratic Party "more nearly expresses the golden mean which ensures good government." Had not those "valiant sons of sovietism," Victor Berger and Robert La Follette, both been "accused of disloyalty?" Did not Progressivism translate into "progression" towards high taxes and bloated bureacracy? In this connection, the Wausau Democrat pledged to provide a "business administration" and to "work for the welfare and happiness of all our people"[6]: these views were characteristic of his party's growing conservatism during its postwar decline.

While stalwarts plotted and Democrats raised the issue of radicalism, Progressives organized. The stage was set in March, when incumbent governor John J. Blaine chose tax reform as the issue that would provide his return ticket to Madison. Calling the legislature into special session, the Governor requested repeal of the secrecy clause of the income tax law and a grant of authority for the Tax Commission to go back six years in auditing returns. While Blaine secured only the tax audit authority, the issue served him well as the election unfolded. La Follette applauded the deftness of the call to special session, which made tax reform the overriding issue in the campaign and deflected the many ancillary questions raised by the opposition; he assured Blaine that with this issue before the upcoming campaign meetings, his position would be "impregnable."[7]

The La Follette machine lost little time in preparing for the contest. In June a centralized state organization swung into action by urging its old allies in Marathon County to create a Progressive committee with a full complement of working officers. Among the "loyal friends" personally contacted by Robert M. La Follette, Jr. were Mosinee merchant Harris Hanowitz, Unity cattle dealer J. W. Salter, Marathon City physician Joseph Barber, newly-appointed Wausau Judge George J. Leicht and County Clerk Edward H. Kuhlmann. Spearheaded by the efforts of Hanowitz, this small group became the nucleus of the Marathon County La Follette-Blaine Club, the body directly responsible for coordinating the Progressive effort in the county. Once organized, the club endorsed the entire Progressive ticket, including two of its own number, Barber and Salter, for the September primary. Going along with Blaine's strategy, the group went on record in hearty support of tax reform, which struck a responsive note in the electorate. Voters from the Town of Easton, for example, were ready to "give Governor Blaine much credit to go after those tax dodgers."[8]

Early soundings revealed strong backing for the ticket, especially in rural districts. Predicting a massive La Follette victory, Assembly candidate Salter reported that he had "never witnessed a campaign in Marathon County when the enthusiasm for Progressives was so unanimous." Encouragement came from conservative strongholds, as well. Stratford railroad man F. A. Semmelbach acknowledged that his community was "a Connor town and you know what that means," but described the election as a "fifty-fifty proposition." In sum, local correspondence with the state Progressive headquarters was brimming with enthusiasm and well-founded optimism in the summer of 1922.[9]

A clear indication of Progressive popularity was the bitter factional struggle that broke out over conflicting claims to leadership of the liberal troops. The central figure in this struggle for legitimacy was the sometime Socialist, now Progressive activist, George Lippert of Wausau. The popular lawyer had come to the conclusion after the 1920 election that socialism had little future in Marathon County, due to the farmer's suspicions and unwillingness to align himself with party positions. Concerning his principles, Lippert admitted no change: he defied his critics to distinguish between his former position and "the stand of La Follette on those questions of public ownership of the great institutions." In short, he felt many people failed to recognize socialism "when Bob La Follette preaches it under the cloak of Progressive Republicanism."[10] Once he had made an opportunistic transition to the Republican Party, Lippert wasted little time in establishing himself as the wheelhorse of the organization in Marathon County.

But not without a fight. The catalyst in this situation was George Leicht's elevation to a county judgeship, which left a troublesome vacancy in the office of district attorney—a position eyed by both Lippert and one-time La Follette backer A. W. Prehn. The pressure campaign, ending in Prehn's appointment, reveals much about the struggle among county aspirants to power. Before long, it was obvious that important elements in the political "establishment" were in Prehn's corner. Among those urging Blaine to appoint the long-established local attorney were such court house politicians as the county sheriff, the register of deeds, and the county hospital superintendent. All stressed the candidate's preparation, abilities, long residence in the community, and alleged public support. More direct was Wausau lawyer Fred Genrich, who warned the governor against appointing "a man who has no use for our form of government . . . even though such people change their views and announce that they will . . . affiliate themselves with one of the leading parties of the day." Genrich insisted that it was simply "too early" for "a man of that kind to be appointed to public office" without first being "taught the true meaning of citizenship."[11] Though Lippert's name was never mentioned, he was almost certainly the target of this admonition.

And yet the neophyte Republican was not without his boosters, some of whom were important to the emerging farm-labor coalition. Most significant was Paul Prochnow, president of the Wausau Brotherhood of Railway Clerks, who reminded Blaine that Lippert had "always been a friend of labor" and was the union candidate for district attorney. Other correspondents attacked Prehn as a deserter of the Progressive cause, but the majority of practicing politicians did endorse Prehn. In acknowledging Prehn's appointment, Republican County Chairman Frank Chesak reported that 90 per cent of Marathon County Republicans approved the Governor's action, which would surely strengthen his position in the September primary.[12]

Not surprisingly, Lippert's analysis differed greatly. He flatly asserted that the appointee was "not the popular choice of the people," citing the 1918 election in which he had easily defeated Prehn in the race for district attorney. Lippert wisely pledged his full support for Blaine and La Follette, while declaring that he was "going to the people" against Prehn in the upcoming primary. As the campaign evolved, it became obvious that it was indeed Lippert who was the working Progressive. Often in touch with La Follette and Blaine, he took a leading role in organizing the county. While Prehn did make addresses on behalf of the ticket, it was clearly his opponent who had the ear of the leadership. As the campaign heated up, Lippert moved to block any endorsement by reminding the La Follette organization that Prehn had left the Senator during the bitter factional struggle of 1912-1914. And, despite his recent appointment, there was some doubt about the strength of his current commitment. The charge was put more directly by Lippert's ally, Joseph Barber, who informed "young Bob" La Follette that Prehn was "very unpopular and the Wausau stalwarts' tool."[13]

While the dispute simmered, Lippert was busy demonstrating his loyalty to the cause. Throughout his campaign, he made it clear that he had always stood with Senator La Follette—even in the dark days of the war, when "the rights of the people were being infringed upon" and "it took courage to do so." When a coalition of farm and labor organizations planned a large rally in Wausau, Lippert was at the center of action. In direct contact with the La Follettes, he strove to bring the Senator in as the major speaker. Working closely with Wausau's Edward T. Ford of the Joint Federation of Railway Labor Organizations, he orchestrated a "managed event" that brought an estimated 8,000 to Marathon Park to hear a rousing address by Governor Blaine. It was hardly coincidental that George W. Lippert was responsible for the introductions: nothing could have identified him more clearly with the Blaine-La Follette organization. And the occasion gave the Governor his chance to score some points against a recalcitrant legislature, again focusing attention on his own tax reform record.[14] All were well-satisfied: the governor with a large audience and Lippert no doubt with his personal *coup*.

The Lippert-Prehn conflict was but the tip of a larger iceberg; beneath the surface lay a bitter struggle for control of the county Progressive machinery. This factional strife finally came to public attention late in the campaign when Ralph Smith of Merrill decided to challenge established La Follette man Joseph Barber for the State Senate nomination. To most observers, Barber was the insurgents' logical choice, for his opponent's Progressive credentials were obscure at best. Consequently, there was a vague uneasiness about Smith's late entry among old line Progressives, such as J. W. Salter, who thought Smith "would not be dependable in voting for what we want."[15] Salter's comments came on the heels of the Progressive Club's decision to endorse the newcomer, thus effectively repudiating its earlier approval of Barber. Close examination reveals an internal reorganization, accompanied by the resignation of club secretary Lippert under pressure from Prehn, and his replacement by D. S. Burnett. For his part, Barber charged that a stalwart *coup* had occurred, since Burnett had once denounced La Follette as a radical and was now in contact with the Committee of Forty-four that was working to organize conservatives against the ticket. Both Lippert and Barber informed the La Follettes that Prehn and Smith were bogus Progressives, but the proof came when the Merrill candidate refused to appear on a speaker's platform with the La Follette candidate for Attorney-General, Herman Ekern.[16] In sum, a successful effort had been made by one-time Progressives and their allies to wrench the Marathon County organization from the hands of the most dedicated insurgents, who identified with the Lippert-Barber-Salter faction. It was the latter group that carried the La Follette banner in the primary, and they who would rout the interlopers at the polls.

And victorious they were. Lippert and Barber came up winners, while Salter secured the Republican nomination without opposition. On the wider scene, the La Follette-Blaine combination swept Marathon County by a five to one margin. But the most profound development of the primary campaign was the precipitous decline of the Democratic Party, both in the county and the state. Fearful of disaster, the *Pilot* had implored Democrats to vote in their own primary. When the tally was in, the results were stunning: favorite son Karl Mathie had polled only 412 votes in his home county, while statewide, the Democratic Party failed to receive 10 per cent of the total cast.[17] Because the party had failed to gain the statutory minimum for major party status, Democrats suffered the humiliation of running as independents in the general election.

Since nomination as a Republican was tantamount to election, it was all over but the shouting. Smith would offer a futile challenge to Barber as an independent along with Independent Democrat A. J. Plowman, and the Governor would face a token campaign from Independent Democrat A. A. Bently, who had vanquished Mathie in a struggle between also-rans. But the futility of the Democratic position was confirmed by a La Follette-Blaine landslide in November. And Marathon County proved a bellwether in this trend: while Blaine was reelected with 76 per cent of the statewide vote, Marathon gave him a smashing 84 per cent! So low had the Democrats sunk that Bently failed to poll 9 per cent of the county total.

How had it come to this? The 1922 results reflect the completion of the postwar realignment that had first surfaced in 1920. Henceforth, the Democrats would be "insignificant" in county politics, and Republican party identification (later Progressive) would be the ticket to success. Primary post-mortems stressed one fact above all: ten German counties, the backbone of the Democratic Party, had given their votes to the La Follette-Blaine ticket and wiped the Democrats off the November ballot. The *Pilot* was absolutely convinced that German voters "voiced their protest against America's participation in the World War by leaving their party" for the unlikely haven of radicalism. Insisting that they were "with rather than of the radicals," the Democratic paper went on to express its hope that these German voters would return to their natural home "once the prejudices of war have disappeared."[18]

The massive nature of the La Follette-Blaine victory makes it difficult to test the *Pilot's* interpretation of the election result. As we examine the returns, it is possible to record Progressive landslides in such German strongholds as Berlin, Hamburg, Maine, and Stettin, where Blaine obliterated the combined opposition 196-6; 121-10; 174-31; and 207-31, respectively. Strong support. But it is equally possible to find other traditionally Democratic townships with alternate ethnic identities displaying similar voter behavior. While victory margins were not as staggering, Blaine outdistanced his foes in Emmet, Cassel, Mosinee, and Reitbrock by comfortable totals: 103-42; 121-37; 69-22 and 113-19. One plausible explanation would lie in Blaine's unabashed espousal of the "wet" cause, as rural Marathon County was never fond of the "noble experiment." Even more suggestive is the disparity between urban and rural tallies. While the incumbent governor was never in trouble in Wausau, he polled 68 per cent of the total votes cast in the city, substantially below his 81 per cent performance in rural, small-town areas. In sum, rural support may have been more potent a force than ethnicity in explaining Blaine's conquest of Marathon County in the 1922 primary.[19]

The governor's formidable position notwithstanding, area stalwarts looked forward to the 1924 canvass with eager anticipation. The central figure in conservative speculation was the perennial candidate, Wausau's Andrew L. Kreutzer. As early as January, 1924, members of the influential Wisconsin County Boards Association began to consider Kreutzer a prime candidate for the Republican gubernatorial nomination; and in March an association delegation urged him to seek the office. Led by Marathon County Board Chairman M. J. Berres, the county leaders emphasized the statewide support the Wausau Republican might expect because of his commitment to cost-cutting, tax reduction, and an intelligent revamping of state aids programs. Predictably, the *Record-Herald* responded enthusiastically to the local favorite's candidacy: not only was he well-qualified by his experience in business, banking and legal affairs, but he had not sought the office. Critical of the "professional politicians and their hangers on," the local paper saw Kreutzer as a refreshing alternative to "the self-seeking self-aggrandizing crowd which has been running things in Wisconsin."[20]

Before long other endorsements began to pour in. The Marathon and Lincoln County Boards, the Democratic *Wausau Pilot,* and the statewide Republican press: all offered hope to stalwarts longing for a return to conservative government. The early optimism only accentuated the disappointment when Kreutzer was forced to abandon the race due to ill health, thus extinguishing "the one ray of light in Wisconsin Republicanism."[21] And with the Kreutzer boom at an end, local attentions soon turned to the more volatile arena of national politics, in a pivotal year for the Progressive movement.

By early 1924, labor unions, farm organizations, and Socialists had turned to third-party action in hopes of realigning American politics on more clearly ideological lines. United by a common desire to oust conservative Republicans from national office, most Progressives understood that La Follette was the one reform politician with sufficient stature to offer hope of victory in a Presidential election; they also realized that the Senator had long eschewed the third party approach. Yet by March, he was sending out signals that 1924 might be a year of personal decision. Not that the Wausau press was enthused about a possible Republican defector. The *Record-Herald,* for example, urged La Follette to make a break and to do it quickly, since he "hasn't been a Republican for some time." Like other Coolidge backers, the *Herald* thought it unfair for La Follette to masquerade as a Republican before the April primary and run La Follette delegates, maintaining the "pretense that he is a good Republican . . . though an effective member of the third party now in the process of forming."[22] But by late spring, the local press thought a third party campaign of any consequence unlikely. Secure in the belief that La Follette was never "fond of forlorn hopes" without "speedy and worthwhile political advantage to himself," the *Herald* saw no significant challenge on the horizon. All the more disconcerting, therefore, was the Senator's defiant announcement of candidacy in July. While the press was unenthusiastic, others saw the Progressive bolt as the beginning of a new era in American politics. Remnants of the Wisconsin Nonpartisan League had been girding for battle since February, in hopes of reaching the elusive goal—a farmer-labor party.[23] Equally dedicated were members of the A.F. of L. and the railroad brotherhoods, although the Marathon County labor movement was only in its infancy.

Local labor leaders involved in the national campaign included the militant Wausau trainman, Bert Rasmussen, and young Fred Kannenberg of Texas, who headed Progressive organizational activities for the quarry workers' union in several midwestern states. Others active were Joseph Barber and the assistant district attorney, Gerald Boileau. But none could match the dedication of the popular George Lippert, who came to the rescue when the Marathon County effort seemed to falter. Not only did the district attorney engage in a vigorous speech-making program throughout central Wisconsin, but under pressure from the La Follette organization, he became financial chairman for the Eighth Congressional District. Despite a heavy workload, Lippert was "so bent on assisting Mr. La Follette" that he pledged to "work over time to bring results." And it was he who supplied the state coordinator with that precious political currency—the names of one-hundred key Progressives in Marathon County—from his personal files.[24]

Even so, not all insurgents were thrilled by the Lippert faction's assumption of local authority. An unidentified Progressive veteran wrote Bob, Jr. that he was "greatly disappointed" by the confidence placed in Lippert by the state organization. He was especially perturbed by the local leader's inexplicable endorsement of A. W. Prehn in the September primary against the venerable Edward Browne, a steadfast Progressive. Lippert's surprise endorsement should have been no surprise at all, for as an outspoken "wet" he made repeal of prohibition a prime goal, one that justified the removal of a dry congressman. The unsuccessful effort to unseat Browne by the Lippert forces would not be the last, and it did little damage to the district attorney's rising stature in the county Progressive movement. As the general election approached, he remained the dominant force in the county La Follette effort, ably assisted by a promising young lawyer from his own office, Gerald Boileau,[25] who dared to stand openly for the senior senator and his program.

Any La Follette success in the presidential race would certainly be achieved in spite of rather than because of the local press. Having endorsed Coolidge, the *Record-Herald* did all in its power to "educate" voters to the dangers inherent in "La Follettism." Insisting that no Republican should feel any obligation to the state platform rammed through by the Progressives in September, the *Herald* again raised the spectre of radicalism: the state meeting was, in its view, "no more Republican in principle than a national convention of the I.W.W." In short, the only safe vote for Americans was a Coolidge vote: advice taken in thirty-five states nationwide, Wisconsin standing as one bold exception, with its thirteen electoral votes for its favorite son. Intense loyalty was to be found in Marathon County, where voters gave La Follette a comfortable two-to-one edge, while supporting other Progressive Republicans with similarly generous margins.[26]

By the mid-1920's, then, the insurgents had captured the Republican Party in Marathon County and were entrenched in all significant county offices. Led by an immensely popular and sometimes flamboyant district attorney, they had created a smoothly-functioning political organization destined to dominate county politics for more than a decade to come. The aggressive Lippert, linchpin of the Progressive structure, was instrumental in inspiring many young liberals to become politically active; and the leadership brought together at this time, including persons like Roland Kannenberg, Walter Graunke, Gerald Boileau, Joseph Barber, Mildred Barber, and Henry Ellenbecker, would chart the course of the county Progressive movement as it crested in the 1930's.

As the leader of a liberal faction on the ascendant in 1925, Lippert could hardly have foreseen the personal disaster that would alter the

George Lippert — Progressive Martyr?

course of his own career a year later. By May of 1926, he stood accused of conspiracy to violate the unpopular prohibition law he had long disagreed with. The district attorney had allegedly extorted a bribe from Schofield bartender Reuben Wendorf in exchange for immunity from prosecution under the prohibition law, a charge Lippert consistently denied throughout the deliberations on his case. And there were many persons who agreed with his contention that he had been "framed" by his political opponents. State Senator Barber, for example, told Governor Blaine that the stalwarts had "crippled one of the greatest Progressives in Marathon County" in a "political game . . . to keep him from running for Congress." Always a bit paranoid, the Marathon County veteran was convinced that dark figures from the conservative establishment had "set numerous traps" for himself as well, hoping to "make the field clear for a stalwart senator."[27]

Faced with a federal indictment, Lippert had little choice but to step down while his case remained in litigation; and his formal suspension touched off a lively contest for the position of provisional district attorney. This struggle brought to the fore a new political personality in the person of Gerald Boileau, who would be the next bright star in the area's liberal movement. Far and away the popular choice by most accounts, Boileau received support from many county political figures, including county board members, town officials, and Progressive activists like Joseph Barber, Mildred Barber, Henry Ellenbecker, and John King. King, a lonely man as a banker for La Follette, maintained that Boileau was "the only true-blue Progressive among the lawyers of Marathon County," an assessment concurred with by the Barbers. Mildred laid it on the line, citing Boileau as the "only lawyer, outside of Lippert, who ever came before the people of this county as a Progressive," adding that outstate loyalists could not keep the faith if Madison chose to "appoint rank and rotten stalwarts who *never did* nor *never will* do anything for our cause." Last came the confidential endorsement of Lippert himself, who told Blaine that Boileau was a man of Progressive convictions, "and not afraid to assert it." He confirmed the suggestion that Boileau and he were indeed "the only two lawyers who made any speeches for the movement in 1924 and 1925," a fact that certainly strengthened Boileau's position as the rightful heir to the throne. Finally, the breadth of Boileau's popularity was driven home by the warm endorsement he received from labor groups, particularly the various trainmen's unions, which saw him as "a man with a big political following in Wausau." One trainman put it quite succinctly: "labor likes Boileau . . . and the appointment of Boileau would be popular with labor."[28]

Confronted by such formidable opposition, the other contenders for the position were never really in the race. However, men like Robert W. Monk of Mosinee and A. H. Eberlein of Wausau did claim Progressive credentials and therefore presented a ticklish problem for Blaine, who dearly wished to avoid a choice between rival supporters. With welcome advice from Wausau Judge George Leicht, a trusted Progressive, the governor managed to extricate himself from this situation by appointing Earl Plantz of Langlade County temporary district attorney for Marathon County, pending the disposition of the Lippert case. Since the potential county appointees were all candidates for the position in the September primary, Blaine piously claimed that the public interest would not be served by a local appointment. His decision also allowed him to avoid an unwanted choice. While the governor skillfully skirted the factional dispute, his solution to the problem was not met with universal acceptance. The Plantz appointment resulted in considerable grumbling over the partisan concerns which had prevented some qualified county resident from assuming the position. In short, the "selection of a stranger" seemed "an insult to Marathon County."[29] in some quarters. In any event, the final decision was left to county voters, whose ultimate response would launch yet another political career.

But what of the fallen star? Despite his protestation of innocence, Lippert was convicted in a September trial that drew wide publicity because of the involvement of an important public official. While he insisted that he had been "conspired against," he accepted his fate because he had been found guilty by "an American institution" in which he firmly believed—a jury of twelve men. After serving a year of his eighteen month term at Fort Leavenworth, the Progressive-in-exile won a parole, after which his odyssey took him to a new business career in Oregon and finally back to Marshfield, Wisconsin.[30] Disbarred and forgotten, the aging firebrand was only a shadow of his earlier self when he cropped up briefly in county politics in the late 1930's, ironically as an opponent of a new Progressive establishment led by Wausau attorney Walter Graunke.

While Lippert sank into oblivion, his successor moved quickly to fill the void created by the popular prosecutor's departure. Emerging victorious from a five-man primary race, Gerald Boileau was in an unbeatable position as Republican candidate for district attorney.

Any plans on the part of runnerup Robert Monk to mount an independent candidacy were squelched by Governor Blaine's decision to appoint Boileau immediately. Not only was the interim arrangement resented in Marathon County, but also provisional prosecutor Plantz was anxious to return to Antigo full-time; and as a strong Blaine man with the support of the county Blaine club, Boileau was the logical choice. Equally significant to the governor's decision was the strong endorsement given the primary victor by his beleaguered predecessor. Lippert told Blaine that Boileau had openly supported him, that he was the voters' choice, and that he saw no way of making "a more popular selection—either for the cause, the people, or yourself—than by picking Boileau."[31] Through his success at the polls as well as his steadfast support for the Progressive movement, the young attorney had earned the position that soon projected him onto the national scene.

Thus, a key political change had stemmed from George Lippert's miseries; and no development could have revealed more clearly the link between politics and the most disruptive social issue of the day: prohibition. Never popular in Marathon County when milder forms of restriction had been under discussion, the reform encountered open hostility when total abstinence seemed about to become the law of the land. An accurate barometer of county opinion was Frank Leuschen of the *Marathon Times,* who was convinced that "prohibition was wrong and that a man had as much right to enjoy . . . moderate use of wine, beer, or any other drink, as he has to satisfy his natural instincts and desires for any other beverage." Denying the possibility of making "a perfect moral man by means of the law," the rural editor did his best to defend "the American saloon" from unwarranted attacks. But all to no avail: in a burst of anti-German and anti-Bolshevik fervor, Wisconsin became the thirty-sixth state to ratify the Eighteenth Amendment in January, 1919. The prohibition amendment was less than welcome, however, in many quarters. Not only was brewing the state's fifth largest industry and barley an important cash crop, but, more significantly, many Wisconsinites viewed the "noble experiment" as a blow against personal liberty and cultural preferences. A prime example was Athens realtor, Frank Chesak, stalwart chairman of the county Republican Committee and himself an abstainer. His own position aside, Chesak vowed he would "never support any dry candidate" because of his belief in "freedom and personal liberty and not slavery."[32]

A large sector of the consuming public agreed that precious personal liberties were to be preserved, regardless of the social cost. But most accounts agree that Marathon County citizens did not suffer greatly during the long thirst of the 1920's. The home and commercial production of moonshine was common-place throughout the county, where according to one estimate in 1926, there were "about 100 road-houses, blind pigs, and places where intoxicating liquor could be purchased." Gerald Boileau later recalled that "there wasn't an intelligent person in the city of Wausau who couldn't have written down the names of twenty-five people that were violating the pro-hibition law." In sum, with an abundance of bootleggers and moon-shiners at hand, it was a dull man indeed who seriously believed that the county's numerous "soft drink parlors" trafficked in root beer alone.[33]

The traffic in illicit liquor was not without its negative effect. In Athens, for example, high school principal W. T. Phillips dropped a "bombshell" on the rural community with a charge that the "moon-shine menace" was "eating its way into the lives and futures of the young people." The high school, in particular, was "feeling the effect of continued debauchery," as it prepared for the expulsion or dropout of several students laid low by the "devilish menace" that threatened them "from nearly every business block in the city." But the market was hardly confined to adolescent boys. Indeed, the Chief Wausau Brewing Company, ostensibly engaged in the manufacture of "near beer," was at one point charged with making shipments of fully alcoholic lager to the lucrative Chicago market area. Another brewery in Marathon City was more unlucky, as its "near beer" was adjudged too close for comfort, resulting in the firm's untimely closing.[34]

The diligence of the federal agents led to some bizarre incidents, such as the discovery of four hundred gallons of illegal liquor in the yard of Anton Jaegler of Weston, who professed surprise at learning of the cache but prudently entered a plea of guilty on charges of posses-sion. Or perhaps the case that found a dedicated prohibition agent commandeering a civilian vehicle in Wausau while in hot pursuit of a suspected bootlegger, only to have his citizen-driver halt the chase. Informed of the nature of his mission, the draftee commented: "Nothing doing. I'm a tombstone salesman, not a chaser of beer runners." The life of a government man was anything but smooth. Characteristic was the predicament of three prohibition agents who raided the home of Mrs. Vincent Chruscicki in Kronenwetter without a proper search warrant. As a result of a tussle over a jar of mysterious brown liquid, the officers were faced with a successful lawsuit, charg-

310

"The Noble Experiment" in Marathon County
Left to Right: District Attorney A. W. Prehn, Sheriff Fred E. Schroeder,
County Judge George J. Leicht, Unidentified Enforcer, Clerk of Court
Henry A. Beilke

ing that the innocent housewife had suffered mental and physical injuries as she defended her home by attempting to destroy the celebrated jar.[35] All in the line of duty.

Such misadventures should not obscure the fact that there was a certain amount of support for prohibition in Marathon County. From the outset the *Record-Herald* lent its endorsement to the measure, which would curb "the most unscrupulous organization ever known in American politics"—the liquor interests. By 1922, the *Herald* was satisfied that men were showing up for work on Monday mornings and women and children were no longer observed waiting outside saloons hoping to "get a few dollars before the saloon keeper got it all:" prohibition was pronounced "a decided success." But another three years of hard experience tempered the early enthusiasm. All too familiar by 1925 with the weakness of the county flesh, "drys" turned to bitter criticism of violators who wrongly assumed "that people are entitled to exercise a bit of discretion about which laws they shall obey." In a rare introspective moment the *Herald* scolded local patrons, noting that the way to halt the moonshiners and bootleggers was to starve them out; in short, upstanding citizens should "refuse to patronize the prohibition law violators . . . and insist upon Wausau being truly law-abiding."[36]

An improbable ally was to be found in the Marathon County Guernsey Breeders Association, an organization alive to the vested interest dairymen had in retaining the prohibition law. Reporting the results of a membership poll in 1926, association secretary R. R. Runke noted that 87 per cent of the large producers opposed repeal in hope of consolidating "their industry's gains made through the operating of the Volstead Law." Hence, economic interest superseded personal preferences when the chips were down. Women's Christian Temperance Union state president Anne W. Warren agreed with the dairymen, asserting that consumers had undergone an attitudinal shift that by 1928 had led to greater purchases of food, milk, and meat in preference to alcoholic beverages. But paradoxically, she felt constrained to warn her Wausau audience to stop buying so that "there will be no bootlegging."[37]

Her concern was well-founded. As early as 1926 Badger state "wets" conceived the idea of petitioning Congress for a modification of the Volstead Act to permit the manufacture and sale of beer. Apprehensive "dry" forces warned that "wets" should not build their hopes on an expression of one state's wishes, adding that few "drys" were likely to participate in any referendum on the question. While the *Herald* minimized the significance of the outcome, it did acknowledge that the referendum would "provide an interesting expression of public opinion in Wisconsin." And the voters spoke clearly: 66 per cent of the statewide electorate favored the reinstatement of beer, while the margin reached a robust 75 per cent in Marathon County. Unique distinction came to the village of Marathon, where a unanimous (128-0) vote was cast in favor of beer. But the political significance of prohibition in the 1926 election reached far beyond the referendum results. Returns in the all-important primary demonstrated the awesome power of the "wets" in Wisconsin. After a bitterly-contested campaign, incumbent Senator Irvine Lenroot succumbed to a spirited challenge from Governor Blaine, an avowed "wet." Likewise, Secretary of State Fred R. Zimmerman, a supporter of the beer referendum, vanquished Attorney General Herman Ekern in the gubernatorial race. While many issues were involved, both losers were found guilty of having blurred their positions on the liquor question. Predictably, both went down to defeat in Marathon County.[38]

Although the referendum had been worded to secure federal modification of the Volstead Act, the outcome was viewed by "wets" in the Wisconsin legislature as a mandate for a change in state liquor laws. Their offensive took the form of an assault on the Severson Act, which provided the government machinery for state enforcement of the prohibition law. When a referendum was placed on the April ballot in 1929, "dry" leaders recognized it as a moral crisis. The temperance forces, led by such persons as the Rev. Howard Murray Jones, a part-time resident of Green Valley, moved to "save our beloved Badger state from the guilt and shame of nullification, repudiation and uncontrolled liquor" by getting "drys" to the polls. Jones, working out of Madison, persuaded several "prominent" citizens to go on record against repeal of the Severson Act, but in a candid moment admitted that he "expected to lose this fight when I went into it, but I went in just the same."[39]

His pessimism was borne out by the referendum results, which provided ample evidence of statewide hostility towards prohibition. By a vote of 350,337 to 196,402, Wisconsinites called for the repeal of the hated enforcement law, and the margin of five to one in Marathan County left no doubt concerning the popular will. What did the verdict mean? The *Pilot,* long critical of the liquor law, regarded it as a clear message to Washington politicians, who tended to ignore the wishes of their constituents. Action was needed because of the wholesale violation of the law, a problem that would be further complicated without a state enforcement law. County court records substantiated the charge: during the year ending April 29, 1929, the court's greatest revenue source was liquor law fines, which accounted for $9,300 of $13,323 collected. It came as no shock, therefore, when a *Literary Digest* poll found Wausau "overwhelmingly wet." In sum, Wausau, Marathon County, and the state of Wisconsin remained restive under the yoke imposed by proponents of the great reform; and on few issues was the line between cultural tradition and social conduct more clear.

A second important social development of the 1920's was the rejuvenation of the Ku Klux Klan, which fed on the popular prejudices of the day—hostility to Catholics, Jews, blacks, and foreigners. At first glance, Marathon County seems an unlikely seedbed for the growth of such sentiments, and it is true that the Klan did not enjoy wide popularity in the area; but it is also clear that a local effort did materialize during the organization's brief period of statewide success between 1923 and 1927.

The membership drive began in 1924, when state leader William Wieseman of Milwaukee put Kleagle Willis Dean to work in Marathon County. His labor did not go unnoticed. On February 1, a public meeting at the Talbot Montgomery American Legion Post resulted in the formation of a local committee to visit the intruder at the Hotel Bellis with orders to leave town. And none too soon, as an ugly mob was forming outside. The threat of mob violence provided sufficient motivation for Dean to make an escape on the next train out, but not before threatening that though he was forced to leave, "two more will come in my place."[41]

Angered by the fleeing Kleagle's final words, a group broke off to form the Wausau Anti-KKK Association under temporary president Major Frank Gottschalk and secretary Frank Barden. The following Sunday saw the establishment of a permanent organization to "act if the Klan tried to perform such acts as it is credited with doing in other cities." George Borowitz recommended that the American Legion continue the work it had begun in exposing the evil influence, while Gottschalk blistered the Klan as un-Christian, "as Christ had never taught hate and violence." The meeting ended with the establishment of a local watchdog organization, to be widely representative of community religious groups. It was now a matter for all citizens of Wausau to "protect the people from the influence of the Klan propaganda."[42]

Was all the furor justified? The very secretive nature of the KKK precludes a definite answer. Before he beat a hasty retreat, the Klan organizer told a *Record-Herald* reporter that the group was growing rapidly in Wausau and contained some of the "most intelligent and best citizens of the city." Unquestionably, anti-Klan leaders were convinced that there were many members in the area and that secret meetings were being held in "unknown places." The state organization flatly claimed more than one hundred Klansmen in the Wausau vicinity, and it is reasonable to assume that a portion of the $1 million taken out of Wisconsin by the KKK originated in Marathon County. Convinced of its existence, the new anti-Klan association was determined to "ferret out the members" of the Invisible Empire and "make them come into the light."[43]

But all of this was mere conjecture. Local concerns took on new urgency with the fiery reality of a twelve foot cross that illuminated Wausau's south side in early April. Adding to the mystery, a stranger peddling Klan propaganda appeared the following week at the *Herald* offices to claim credit for the cross-burning, which allegedly signified the signing of 1500 members in the area. This assertion of strength contrasted with prior estimates of Wausau membership which was thought to range from 400 to 1200. While local police suspected vandalism, the unofficial journal of Wisconsin's Invisible Empire quickly exploited the incident by proclaiming that with this action "Wausau joins [the] ranks of [the] Klan." The *Badger-American's* enthusiasm was matched by the Wausau Anti-KKK Association's alarm: in the belief that the Klan's membership goals had been met, the local enforcers scheduled an emergency meeting at the armory. Ultimately, the gathering turned into a harmless anti-Klan rally, as its organizers persuaded the audience that the authorities could handle the situation.[44] This was a wise decision, for the organization was already entering a period of decline in Wisconsin that would see the Empire crumble in record time. While a massive ten-day meeting would be held as late as 1926 in Marshfield, the Klansman's brief moment in the county had passed. If Wisconsin had been infertile ground for Klan-style Americanism, Marathon County proved barren; even during the great "kluxing" days of 1924, Wausau enjoyed some distinction as one of two central Wisconsin communities in which citizens combined to run enterprising kleagles out of town.[45]

On one other social frontier of the 1920's, Marathon County was counted among the more progressive in the state—the opening of opportunities to newly-liberated women. While female suffrage had not been popular in the county, the Nineteenth Amendment did shake some long-held social and political prejudices. An early harbinger of change was Rothschild's decision to make Mrs. Esther Janacek village justice in 1922, which the *Pilot* viewed approvingly as evidence that women were "gaining their initial experiences in public offices in Marathon County." The Democratic paper was even more enthusiastic over La Follette's opponent in the 1922 Senatorial race, Mrs. Ben Hooper, whose influence was destined to "have a cleansing effect upon Wisconsin politics." After her visit to Wausau in October, the paper waxed eloquent over the candidate's "love of womanhood," "unselfish service," and "approval of everything that is progressive;"[46] it is difficult, however, to escape the conclusion that her Democratic credentials meant more to the *Pilot* than her qualifications.

Profoundly more significant was the landmark 1924 assembly campaign of Marathon's Mildred Barber, a firebrand Progressive. After a hard-fought primary, Barber ousted the incumbent, old-time La Follette man J. W. Salter of Unity. And running unopposed in the general election, she joined Helen Brooks of Green Lake and Helen Thompson of Price County as one of the first three women elected to the Wisconsin legislature. Her tough primary campaign was evidence of her considerable political skills, but there persisted an element of condescension in the insistence that her "crusade" was not "for the day's political issues," but rather for those "cherished" by supporters of the Nineteenth Amendment. It came as a shock to the *Pilot*, therefore, when she proved to be a fighting politician. Controversy swirled around her bill to remove criminal jurisdiction from the justices of the peace in favor of the municipal court, a measure designed to promote economy in the administration of justice. Facing opposition from a conservative county bar association, the neophyte was far from docile. Her response was to go public with an open letter attacking the bar association as serving the self-interest of a few members in a manner contrary to the public interest. Challenging the legal establishment to debate the issue, Barber sought taxpayer support in raising standards and saving public money in the county courts. Strong words for a young legislator—so strong, in fact, that it destroyed the *Pilot's* faith in her: it expressed disappointment in her comment, which "might have been given by any politician making grist for the political mill."[47]

Thus, in the final analysis, a separate standard was held up for a woman politician, who was not expected to fight for her principles in the traditional way. Small wonder that Mrs. Fred Becker could later report to the Wausau W.C.T.U. that Wisconsin dragged its feet on opening political opportunity to women. Despite legal adjustments, strong resistance to female assertiveness remained a firmly held local attitude. It is probable that the *Record-Herald* uttered a widely-held view when it declared in 1928 that women were "best fitted for rearing and training children and caring for the home." In full agreement with presidential candidate Herbert Hoover, the *Herald* counseled caution before adopting any "policy calculated to further lead women from the place for which they are designed by nature."[48] Clearly, Progressive Mildred Barber had failed to get the message. If anything, her brief political career was more consistent with the image of the new woman that was emerging nationwide in the 1920's.

Progressive successes in Marathon County could not suppress the modest conservative revival under way by mid-decade. Convinced that the Progressives had forfeited their Republican credentials as a result of the La Follette Presidential candidacy, long-frustrated stalwarts moved in 1925 to impose discipline on party regulars. Under the leadership of Oshkosh businessman William Campbell, they organized a central body that emerged as the Republican voluntary committee in 1926. As early as August, 1925, the group concluded that the key to future stalwart success was unity; such a result could only be achieved by skirting the primary law through the endorsement of favored candidates. Although the early voluntary committee was dominated by southeastern Wisconsin Republicans, Marathon County was represented at both the Oshkosh organizational meeting and on the first executive committee by Anne M. Wendt of Wausau. Regarded with suspicion by business interests and county Republicans, the voluntary committee was less than successful in 1925, though it would be instrumental in the gubernatorial campaign of Walter J. Kohler in 1928.[49]

The conservative choice for governor in 1926 was Charles Perry, endorsed by the growing voluntary organization at its Milwaukee convention. While a full Marathon County delegation attended that gathering, local stalwarts were unable to deliver for Perry in the September primary; in Marathon County the race was strictly a Progressive show, with Fred Zimmerman challenging the anointed successor, La Follette man Herman Ekern. Tagged as the candidate of the "Madison ring," Ekern was no competition for a gregarious political chameleon like Zimmerman, despite his own support from respected Progressives like Gerald Boileau. And disregarding a Perry endorsement from prominent conservative Andrew Kreutzer, county stalwarts gave their votes to Zimmerman in hope of defeating the La Follette candidate. Once successful in dumping Ekern, some conservatives refused to back Perry's misguided candidacy as an Independent Republican, completely ignoring Zimmerman's early career as a Progressive. Striking evidence of this trend was stalwart Walter B. Heinemann's decision to give Zimmerman's campaign a $5,000 boost, much to the dismay of the "Oshkosh group."[50] Thus, in the county and in the state, stalwarts deserted Perry to strike a blow at the "Madison crowd" through Zimmerman votes; and as a consequence, the voluntary committee's endorsement strategy lay in shambles, waiting to be resurrected at a more opportune moment.

But Marathon County regulars did not come away empty handed. Many had been gunning for Senator Barber, considered by conservatives to be a "renegade Progressive"—a term of opprobrium reserved for only the most radical La Follette supporters. The conservative choice to unhorse the good doctor was businessman Otto Mueller of Wausau, a respected local figure who drew immediate support from the stalwart and Democratic press in his battle against "the administration candidate." Nonetheless, the challenger scattered literature calling himself a "Progressive Republican" around the district, in the knowledge that a declared stalwart was unelectable. This infuriated Barber, who charged his opponent with lobbying against tax reform in the previous session and pointed out that "the stalwart newspapers are not campaigning for me."[51]

When the votes were in, however, Mueller had captured the Republican nomination by a comfortable margin. How may we account for this conservative island in a Progressive sea? The endorsements, Barber's link with the "Madison ring," and confusion concerning ideology were all factors; but were they sufficiently damaging to explain the defeat of a man with a strong farmer-labor voting record? The key lies in Progressive defection from Barber, probably related to a political error by the Senator himself. After signing Senator Lenroot's nomination papers, he traveled with the Blaine campaign, thus causing some Progressives to condemn his "wishy-washy attitude." Some argued that "for the sake of Progressive principles that man should be defeated."[52] In short, internal division within the insurgent movement made the incumbent's position untenable in the face of a stiff challenge. The result was a stalwart triumph.

As the 1928 presidential contest neared, the stalwart unity drive gained momentum. Fully aware of lingering Marathon County opposition to the voluntary movement, the "Oshkosh group" scheduled a peace conference for Wausau in September, 1927, with an eye to the election of "real Republicans" as delegates to the national convention the following year. While harmonious sentiments filled the air at the Hotel Wausau, tension bristled beneath the surface, with "the wicked Republicans who did not attend the Oshkosh conference two years ago . . . quite conspicuous by their absence." All assembled deplored any dissension among conservatives, but outstate resentment against William Campbell and the Oshkosh group was manifest. A closed caucus was held to allow for a full airing of dissident views, but as the meeting drew to a close, skepticism on the likelihood of conservative unity prevailed. While many Wausau Republicans attended, the *Record-Herald* dragged its feet, with a malevolent report that "Campbell's G.O.P. met here today" but that the meeting was poorly attended. Racine's Senator Walter S. Goodland provided further evidence of the latent tension with a tirade against the *Herald* for its charge that he had been a "La Follette shouter" who opposed the lumbermen who "robbed northern Wisconsin of its natural resources." The latter remark may have been a barb aimed at prominent Wausau Republican Walter Heinemann, who claimed that the Racine Senator, as an ally of the Oshkosh group, carried on a personal vendetta against him. Heinemann was adamant in his refusal "to go along with any organization in which Mr. Campbell is a dominant factor."[53] In any event, Goodland's words did not go down well in Wausau.

The constant bickering within the Republican ranks did not bode well for the local party in the upcoming campaign, one in which the voluntary committee was to reach the promised land with conservative Walter Kohler at the helm. But early in the year, the action was to be found in the Presidential race. Here the stalwart choice was Commerce Secretary Herbert Hoover, while Progressives generally threw their support to Nebraska Senator George W. Norris. At the national convention, the split Wisconsin delegation caused the victor some embarrassment, as the Progressives stubbornly refused to compromise principles. The Wisconsin Progressives, including Wausau's Gerald Boileau, voted for Norris on the final ballot in a firm refusal to swallow the party pill. The campaign back home was equally tense. Boileau, "one of those who refused to go along with Hoover," would not speak for the party standard-bearer when he stumped for other county candidates. On one vote-gathering expedition to Little Chicago, he shared a platform with an imported party man from St. Louis who made a thinly-veiled reference to Democratic Presidential candidate Al Smith's Catholicism. Appalled at the intruder's approach, Boileau refused to be seen with him on the campaign trail; and in short order the offender was removed from the Marathon County team.[54]

Despite liberal foot-dragging Hoover did generate some excitement in Marathon County, where he carried the enthusiastic endorsement of the stalwart press. One of his earliest Wisconsin backers, the *Record-Herald* was hot for Hoover. Conservatives were no doubt optimistic, therefore, when word arrived that President Calvin Coolidge would honor Wausau with a visit in August while enroute to his northern Wisconsin fishing vacation. Was not this the perfect chance to say a word for his party's candidate? The President had other ideas. Greeted by long-time booster Walter B. Heinemann and his wife, the Coolidges first endured a long parade to Marathon Park. Here, the President's prepared remarks were more tailored for the Wisconsin American Legion Convention then in progress than for the throng of 30,000 area well-wishers who swelled the Wausau population for the occasion. In a bland address, he spoke to the question of keeping the peace through adequate defense and international conciliation. His words seemed "common sense," to the *Herald* but even it was forced to admit that Coolidge had "no desire to attain a reputation as an orator."[55] His reception was warm, but Hoover partisans could not have failed to notice that "silent Cal" was true to his image as far as politics were concerned.

As the Presidential battle moved into its final months, Republican leaders were unsure of their prospects, yet encouraged by stalwart gains in the September primary. Beyond this, the campaign was haunted by a peculiar "anti-election apathy" that troubled stalwarts mightily. Their anxieties were somewhat relieved by a vigorous political address from Congressman Joseph Hooper, imported from Michigan for the occasion. A large and attentive crowd at the Grand Theater provided assurance that Marathon County could be "relied upon to give a larger vote for Hoover than . . . even ardent Republicans may have expected."[56]

Optimists in the GOP camp were ignoring some significant local political developments, not the least of which was a 58 per cent increase in county voter registration. Increased registration was a good omen for a reviving Democratic Party, which had been almost moribund since 1920: many local observers accurately predicted that the party's postwar impotence was at an end. Smith partisan Patrick Stone told his comrades that their first planning session was "one of the most enthusiastic meetings since the days when the county was known as a Democratic stronghold." Not only did Smith chairman Otto Muenchow have adequate finances and numerous volunteers, but more significant was the "number of Progressive Republicans who this year have aligned themselves with the Democrats." By October, the *Record-Herald* was worried over efforts to link Hoover with the Republican Party's entire record, which resulted in brickbats in their candidates direction.[57] There is a touch of irony in this concern for clean campaigning in a year when Al Smith's religion would be the great unspoken issue in the election.

Muted though they were, religious questions and the "Happy Warrior's" entire urban-wet-immigrant image played a role in his defeat. For illustration, we need only turn to the correspondence of Auburndale's Reverend Howard Murray Jones. Highly critical of "loud-shouters," the cleric remained confident that "America is too dry and too Protestant, and Hoover is too big a man internationally, for a Ballyhoo put on by Irish Roman Catholic wets to beat." It was views such as these that the *Pilot* sought to combat with its sweeping endorsement of the New Yorker on the eve of the election. After defending him on the "social issues," the voice of the county Democracy stung the Republicans on the political scandals of the early 1920's by insisting that a Smith voter "purges himself and his country of a stigma attached to Washington since Harding."[58]

The election returns demonstrated that Marathon County was relatively unresponsive to the politics of the racial-ethnic slur in 1928. Indeed, as was true in many localities throughout the country, the race was a critical election in an important reorientation of voter loyalties. The returns reflect a movement of two sorts: first, the clear tendency of Progressives to be "Presidential Democrats" and second, the return of many Democrats to their traditional party home. But while Smith brought some traditional Democrats back into the fold, it would be an error to overemphasize this trend, since his votes also came from frustrated Progressives who had nowhere else to go. Smith's 50 per cent of the Marathon County total was a modest 6 per cent higher than his percentage of the statewide vote. Thus, the Democratic Party took at least a small step back towards major party status with the 1928 campaign.[59]

As noted earlier, however, it was not only the Democrats who bounced back in 1928. For this was also the year of a victory long awaited by anxious Wisconsin conservatives. The voluntary committee finally hit pay dirt with gubernatorial candidate Walter J. Kohler, who ran a conservative campaign while Progressives split between incumbent Fred Zimmermann and La Follette choice Joseph D. Beck. Although stalwarts were heartened by Kohler's landslide win over lackluster Democrat Albert Schmedeman in the general election, Marathon County party regulars could not have been overjoyed at the dead heat run between the two in the county. Yet many professed a belief that the Kohler victory had broken the back of the infamous "Madison ring" Progressives. Typical was the enthusiasm of Howard Murray Jones, who saw the victory as the beginning of a "new era in Wisconsin politics" that would be free from the "evil spirit of La Follettism."[60]

A new era, yes. Optimism, yes. But no observer of the county scene could possibly have foreseen the economic dislocations that were destined to shape the politics of an unborn era—the age of the Great Depression. In the aftermath of the stock market crash in October 1929, the reflex action of the county press was to accept Hoover Administration assurances that the economy was fundamentally sound. While the *Pilot* did "expect greater accomplishments than words," it remained convinced that the local economy was "intact." And as late as January 2, 1930, Wausau Mayor A. V. Gearhart was able to describe 1929 in his New Year's proclamation as "successful and prosperous." This brand of boosterism was combined with a renewed emphasis on personal and governmental conservatism, industry, and honesty. But frugality and positive mental attitude could not alter the economic facts: times were hard and unemployment a stark reality. By April, 1930, the Wausau Federated Charities confirmed the widely-held belief that the unemployment rate was the greatest ever experienced in the community.[61]

The collapse of the American Dream in the wake of an unprecedented economic crisis was to result in a reaffirmation of the liberal voting trends of the mid-1920's. Shaken by the apparent failure of the system, many county voters turned to political figures who seemed to grasp the problems besetting society in this desperate hour. In most county elections, this sentiment translated into Progressive victories at the polls. And as one local Progressive recalled, "the issue was economic—bread and butter." Rising to exploit this popular concern was a new generation of liberal politicians, headed by such militants as youthful labor lawyer Walter A. Graunke, veteran Progressive Joseph Barber, and rising public figures Gerald Boileau and Roland Kannenberg. With the exception of Boileau they were often thought of as the "renegade" or "radical" Progressives of Marathon County, but all enjoyed success at the polls. United by a determination to seek "a fair share for all" and impressed by "what could be done with laws,"[62] the new fraternity of leadership hitched itself to the La Follette star again on the rise in Badger state politics.

Fought against the backdrop of deepening depression, the 1930 campaign saw the rebound of the La Follette organization, under the leadership of "Old Bob's" younger son Phil. In spite of his tender years, he ran away with the Republican nomination, stunning incumbent Walter Kohler by a 3-2 margin. True to its Progressive tradition, Marathon County gave the La Follette heir a handsome 2-1 vote and, with the notable exception of Senator Mueller, came through for the new liberals in several other races. Significant were the victories of Walter Graunke for District Attorney and Congressional aspirant Gerald Boileau. With these results, the former solidified his position in the county hierarchy, while the latter took an important step towards revitalizing the national Progressive movement. While Roland Kannenberg was turned back in his quest for Henry Ellenbecker's assembly seat, the fact that both men claimed Progressive credentials illustrates the depth of liberal strength in the county.[63]

Similarly, the Congressional race had pitted two Progressives against one another: young Gerald Boileau and the venerable La Follette man, Ed Browne of Waupaca. The 1930 campaign was the last in a series of efforts by Marathon County liberals to shift the balance of power in the Eighth District northward by knocking off the aging incumbent. Mindful of the "great economic questions" before the nation, the Marathon County District Attorney pledged to support measures to "remedy conditions among the farmers and laborers," such as a protective tariff and spreading the work. No babe in the woods, he made prohibition the key issue, in the knowledge that Browne's dry stand was his fatal weakness. The aspirant thus defined prohibition as "one of the most important issues before the American people" and came out foursquare for legal wine and beer. Boileau later recalled that it became "the principal issue in the campaign."[64] As the campaign progressed, it certainly drew the greatest attention. When the candidate opened his campaign with a blast at the Volstead Act as a "national calamity," he drew mild criticism from the *Record-Herald* for treading "on ticklish ground." Yet the voice of the stalwarts was quick to acknowledge his "fair presentation of the wet side of the argument." He did enjoy some support from the *Pilot*; it thought that Boileau would "prove to be a thoroughly competent and conscientious representative of the people" if elected. The flavor of the campaign had not changed by the eve of the primary, when Boileau replied to Browne's assertion that he was the candidate of liquor interests. Rejecting the charges, Boileau turned the tables by suggesting that contrary to earlier claims, his opponent had the active support of the Anti-Saloon League. And the campaign got even rougher when the incumbent's friends reminded voters of Boileau's earlier ties to a District Attorney who later took up residence at Ft. Leavenworth. In response, the *Pilot* sprang to his defense by citing his "honesty and ability" and condemning Browne's "henchmen" for "using smart but rotten tactics that are misguiding and unclean."[65]

When the dust had settled, the Wausau Progressive had unhorsed an eighteen year incumbent with a liberal voting record and a La Follette endorsement, if only by 775 votes. How had this feat been accomplished? One thing is certain: Boileau piled up a lead in his home county which proved to be insurmountable. Browne had never been a popular favorite in the county, and many Wausau voters thought the largest city in the district "should have a Congressman." The Boileau candidacy offered, in Judge Marchetti's words, "the best opportunity we have had in over twenty years to send one of our own number" to Washington. And the prohibition question was crucial.

It explains why Senator Blaine, a notorious wet, quietly "passed the word among some of his influential friends" that Boileau was the right man for the job.[66]

With Boileau in Congress, La Follette in the Statehouse, Ben Lang and Henry Ellenbecker in the assembly, and Graunke holding forth in the Court House, Progressives seemed poised on the threshhold of action in the interest of the average man. And the need for change was becoming acute. Earlier in the year a cynical *Pilot* remarked that a "good motto" for the Republican Administration in Washington was "an empty pocketbook rather than the full dinner pail." Despite the new hope brought by a New Year, the *Herald* optimism was tempered by *Pilot* rumblings in support of "the right of every man to earn a livelihood." Nonetheless, Wausau Alderman Walter Mueller could proudly announce in February, 1931, that 80 per cent of the needy were being cared for by the council's poor committee. The 20 per cent were not heard from. But Phil La Follette was. A state-sponsored unemployment conference in September attracted several county officials, including Mayor Otto Muenchow, County Board Chairman Paul Luedtke, County Clerk Edward Kuhlmann, and Hans J. Hagge. They returned confirmed supporters of the Governor's plan to explore the long-range need for public works employment, to which they gave full support. Many, however, were less enthusiastic over the administration's public works program. Although Phil always rejected outright relief payments, his emergency relief bill was scuttled by Senate conservatives like Otto Mueller. Mueller's action was undoubtedly popular with some area residents, like the *Record-Herald* reader who denounced the relief bill as a "steal,"[67] but others were enraged.

The stalwart Senator not only opposed the relief bill, but also refused to commit himself to a mortgage moratorium bill very popular with many farmers and laborers. His conservatism finally prompted the more radical Progressives to launch an effort to force a recall election in 1932. Orchestrated from Madison, where Governor La Follette urged in a radio address that Marathon County citizens recall Mueller, the campaign was carried out by the most dedicated and radical Progressives under the leadership of the fiery Walter Graunke. Aided and abetted by Joseph Barber, Roland Kannenberg, and a group of Lincoln County dissidents, the District Attorney coordinated the effort from his office. In the last analysis, however, it appears that the Lincoln County group instigated the local plot. Although Graunke was at first "very much in favor of the move," he lost interest and dropped out in the later phases of the movement. It was also the Merrill delegation that ventured into a quarry in the Town of Texas to draft Roland Kannenberg for the job of defeating the Wausau conservative. Kannenberg was described by "Doc" Barber as "the only man who can beat Mueller."[68]

Amidst charge and countercharge a hotly-contested battle unfolded in 1932. The Governor was seen behind the move, yet Marathon and Lincoln County Progressive Clubs were either neutral or hostile toward the effort. Kannenberg was castigated as the "evil genius" behind the plot, yet he claimed to have been approached by others. Fearful of an insurgent upset, the Republicans trained the "big guns" on the 25th Senatorial District. Senatorial candidate John B. Chapple denounced La Follette's "racketeering tactics," while gubernatorial candidate Walter Kohler portrayed the governor as "attempting to set up a dictatorship." Area residents were invited to hear Speaker of the Assembly Charles B. Perry tell the "truth about the recall." Beyond this, the incumbent enjoyed the complete support of the local press. Under the circumstances, Kannenberg's defeat was no surprise. While the young liberal "lost that fight," he "was pretty burned up about it;" so disturbed that on election night he "decided to start a two year campaign" against Senator Mueller.[69] And youth's day would soon come.

Other stalwarts were less fortunate than Mueller in 1932. While Kohler and Chapple would survive the primary, neither won in Marathon County. More significantly, conservatives were to fall on hard times in the general election, which saw the completion of a trend first observed in 1928. The 1932 results would demonstrate clearly that the liberalism of county voters was not confined to support for Progressive Republicans. County interest in Franklin D. Roosevelt had surfaced in the April presidential primary when the New York governor outpolled even Progressive choice George Norris, and Wausau attorney Patrick Stone was sent to the Democratic convention as a Roosevelt delegate. Equally promising was the large Democratic vote cast in the September primary. Of greatest importance was the decision of many Progressives, including Graunke and Boileau, to abandon Hoover as a symbol of the tired politics of the past. At the Republican national convention, Graunke had served as chairman of the Progressive delegation and himself tried to nominate Senator Blaine for President. In his words, "Blaine came in second—President Hoover received 1154 votes and Blaine 11." He wrote off the convention as a "disgraceful, boss-ridden exhibition which a true American should be ashamed of," and proudly told home audiences that the Progressives had "refused to arise for candidate Hoover even though a cheap trick of prostituting the flag had to be brought in to try to arouse false enthusiasm."[70] Such defiance did not bode well for Republican presidential hopes, thin as they were.

As the campaign drew to a close, the press divided on the presidential candidates. While the *Herald* concluded that Hoover's experience was a known quantity and thus qualified him for office, the *Pilot* stood with FDR, its favorite since January. Endorsements, however, counted far less than a depressed economy; even so, few predicted as sweeping a change as occurred in Marathon County. When the Republican roof caved in, it came down with a crash. Stunned Democrats had a near sweep, though the popular Gerald Boileau escaped disaster. The 78 per cent Roosevelt landslide in the county carried in a pair of Democratic assemblymen in a show of strength that ignored the Progressive label. Albert Schmedeman, a 63 per cent county choice, became the state's first Democratic governor since the nineteenth century. It appeared that the party of Jefferson had gained a new lease on life.[71]

Certainly, the new President enjoyed the good will of Marathon County citizens as he entered office in 1933. The Democratic press exuded confidence in Roosevelt, and the *Record-Herald* pointedly remarked that "Democrats and Republicans alike are anxious to see the new administration make good." Indeed, the paper demonstrated a grasp of the emergency by supporting a law to give the President the authority to rearrange national bureaus and commissions, in the full knowledge that it would mean "a virtual dictatorship." By the late 1930's, this tolerance was to be considerably diminished.[72]

A man of the hour, Roosevelt moved to exploit his mandate. One idea that gained early acceptance was the concept of industrial stabilization through government-supervised price-fixing and market-sharing. A variety of this concept was discussed at the state level by the La Follette Administration, and it certainly bore some similarity to the efforts of Wisconsin lumbermen to control their business environment in the early depression years. The national expression of this principle was the National Recovery Administration, which provided for industrial autonomy in wage-setting, price-fixing, and market control. This agency, which legitimized industrial self-government, became the core of the early New Deal. And once understood by the public, it was well-received in Marathon County. Its goal, according to the head of the local N.R.A. committee, Gerald Boileau, was to reduce hours, increase payrolls, and put people to work. Once local businesses were in compliance with their industry code, they were entitled to display the Blue Eagle as a symbol of their cooperation in fighting the depression. By September, 1933, Boileau could report that area employment had risen by 700 and payrolls by $900,000, since Marathon County N.R.A. activities had begun.[73]

Another New Deal stimulus to the county economy was direct relief expenditures. Perhaps the major source of federal largesse in the early 1930's was the Civil Works Administration, which poured government funds into public construction projects. By early 1934, 1400 county residents were employed by C.W.A. While many area residents had been slow to accept the principle of state and federal work relief, it is noteworthy that when C.W.A. programs were threatened with termination in 1934, the Marathon County Board dispatched an urgent plea to federal administrator Harry Hopkins asking that the program be extended "until such time as economic conditions improve and men are able to care for themselves once more." And in later years, it was the Wausau Chamber of Commerce that worked to persuade the Works Progress Administration to construct a major recreational facility in the Eau Pleine reservoir basin. Aside from the self-respect and sustenance provided by federal dollars, other monuments to a creative national government remain: the Athletic Park in Wausau, the classroom addition at Wausau Senior High School, the Rib Mountain Shelter House, the Marathon Park Youth Building, the Eau Pleine and Eau Claire Dells recreational facilities, and numerous street and highway improvements. The federal government came to stay in the 1930's, and its hand touched the lives of many Marathon County citizens in a profound way.[74]

No group of residents were more vital to the overall economic health of the county than the farm population. By early 1933 the mood of many farmers was gloomy and, in some cases, ugly. On occasion, they would join in attempting to prevent foreclosures on farm mortgages. Sometimes violence occurred, as on the Jake Wasniewski farm in Knowlton, where two Stevens Point men were badly beaten while unsuccessfully trying to foreclose a chattel mortgage. The price paid by Wasniewski for defending his home was sixty days in jail. Equally alarming was the group of four hundred farmers on the August Borkenhagen farm in Rib Mountain who gathered to prevent the sale of cattle for similar reasons. In this case, numerous bids of five and ten cents were ignored by attorney A. W. Prehn, who was conducting the sale. One farmer was heard to cry: "Shoot us. We'd just as soon die now as any time." Ultimately the sale was stopped, and a settlement arranged to Borkenhagen's satisfaction.[75]

These rumblings were minor in comparison with the cresting milk strike movement of 1933. Wisconsin dairymen, suffering from sharply depressed milk prices, organized into a variety of rival pressure groups. When one of them, the Wisconsin Milk Pool, called a strike in February, local concern mounted. While one report indicated that sixty-eight farmers had signed withholding agreements in the Town of Easton alone, spokesmen for Wausau dairies did not expect any interruption of production. With few Milk Pool farmers in the county, the strike was ineffective. But when a second holding action was called in May, greater participation was anticipated by county authorities. At a mass rally attended by 1500 people in Marathon City, "Doc" Barber called for united action. The farmer-politician argued that unless dairymen organized, "they will take your homes from you." When a straw vote was taken, as many as three hundred farmers agreed to support the strike; and a noticeable decline in county milk deliveries was recorded the next day, though Wausau dairies seemed unaffected.[76]

By comparison with other state counties, support for the action was minimal in Marathon. When, on the eve of the May strike, Governor Schmedeman embargoed all milk deliveries in Wisconsin until farmers in each county could decide on their position, the vast majority of Marathon County farmers voted to ignore the strike. Hence, Marathon was among the fifty-two counties in which the embargo had been lifted when the action began. And, while two men were killed elsewhere in the state, only one serious act of violence occurred locally: a milk truck was fired upon near the intersection of highway F and 29. The driver, Walter Kemps of Marathon, escaped injury and completed his delivery to the Bowman Dairy. While the local press was generally critical of the strike, each of the major papers had a kind word for the dairymen. Noting that highway blockades and searches were illegal, the *Herald* supported Schmedeman's embargo and called for an early end to the holding action; but when cooler heads had prevailed, the stalwart paper commended Marathon County farmers for their orderly conduct and resistance to agitators. A more perceptive *Pilot* looked to the future. Regretting the disorder that had occurred, it likened the rural experience to that of organized labor in its formative years. True to the collectivistic trend of the 1930's, it saw the "turbulent demonstrations" as the advance agent of collective bargaining: "it will be to everybody's advantage if the farmer has finally realized that he cannot work independently."[77]

Taking this advice, farm militants kept the pot boiling over the summer. Sharing a platform in Edgar with Congressman Boileau, Walter Singler of the Milk Pool exhorted his audience of six hundred to united and constructive action. By October, the activists were ready to move. The Farm Holiday Association called a strike, which soon gained the support of the Milk Pool. In marked contrast to the earlier disturbances, Marathon County was a key location in this struggle. Determined pickets temporarily closed the Federated Cheese warehouse and the Kraft-Phenix plant in Wausau, the Lemke Cheese factory in Berlin, and the Kraft-Phenix plant in Milan. While Marathon County Farm Holiday Chairman William Klemme of McMillan discouraged violence, plants were occupied, vats of milk dumped, and roads closed by the strikers. On November 2, some sixty men were arrested on charges of unlawful assembly, which led bands of farmers to descend on the court house. Their attitude was described as quiet; but "underneath outward appearances" there was "noticeable resentment at the turn developments [had] taken." Unlike the earlier fizzles, the fall action was effective; so much that for several days Wausau was "faced with a milk famine," and the "canned cow" had "come into evidence in many homes for the first time."[78] However, despite strong support from Milk Pool members who vowed to fight to the end, the strike "petered out" in mid-November. But not before Marathon County citizens had become acutely aware of rural frustration in what was for many a time of desperation.

Was there a better way to handle rural anxieties? The Roosevelt Administration's farm relief program, centered in the Agricultural Adjustment Administration, offered new hope to American farmers. The legislation won the qualified support of the *Record-Herald,* which knew that "if the farm relief bill can raise prices to the 1909-1914 level it would be a good thing for the whole country." The county Farmers Union firmly supported such programs as the AAA, land bank, soil conservation service, and government debt adjustment schemes. Indeed, most farm organizations came to support the basic agricultural policies of the administration through their leaders. Even so radical a strike leader as William Klemme became a firm advocate of price supports as treasurer of the Marathon County Soil Conseravtion Association. Klemme's involvement stands as symbolic evidence of the extent to which Roosevelt's programs succeeded in dulling the edge of radicalism in a potentially dangerous period.[79]

Popular as the President was in Marathon County, a new wind was blowing by 1934. Dedicated liberals realized that Phil La Follette's defeat at the hands of Kohler in the 1932 primary had loosened the La Follette hold on the Republican Party, and that, given the party's current unpopularity, nomination on its ticket was not terribly valuable in any case. Equally significant was the escalating pressure from radical farm and labor groups, as well as ideologically-minded persons, all of whom looked towards a clear conservative-liberal division in American politics. Finally, most observers agreed that Phil was becoming the moving force in Badger state Progressivism; and he was interested in a fundamental reorientation in political alignments. At this time, Marathon County was known to have one of the most vital Progressive clubs in the state—one of a handful that actually held regular monthly meetings year after year. The moving spirit in the group was the ideologue Walter Graunke, whose sympathy for the laboring classes led him to choose a lonely path in the 1930's as a "people's lawyer." It was Graunke, more than any other political leader, who charted the course of the county Progressive organization, moving his troops in tandem with an army of militants commanded by Phil La Follette.[80] So the Wausau lawyer stood in the vanguard of the movement that ended in the establishment of the Wisconsin Progressive Party in 1934.

Ably supported by his county lieutenants, Graunke played a key role in the Madison conference of March 3, 1934, which set the scenario for the public meeting where a "decision" on the new party was to be made. An invitational meeting called by the "party chiefs," the first gathering drew several Marathon County liberals—Walter Graunke, Roland Kannenberg, Ed Radant, "Doc" Barber, and railroad man H. R. Johnson. Of the county's contingent, Graunke and Kannenberg were most vigorous in demanding a new party. They were not to be disappointed, as the Madison conference laid the groundwork for a revolutionary change in the Wisconsin party system, pending a state Supreme Court decision on procedures for getting on the ballot. Once the legal issues were resolved, the Marathon County Progressive Club, three hundred strong with representatives from every precinct, met to select a county delegation to the Fond du Lac meeting that would break with the Republican Party. County delegates included: Walter Graunke, Roland Kannenberg, Mr. & Mrs. H. R. Johnson, farm protest leader William Klemme of McMillan, and durable Cassel politician Francis X. Schilling—a group that could be trusted to fight for a new party.[81]

As spokesman for the Marathon County Progressives, Graunke was eloquent in his demand for an independent political force. In a bold attack on backsliding Progressive Republicans, he insisted on "our own party column," to prevent "all these weak sisters sliding in on the shirttails of our reputation." And once the inevitable decision for a third party had been made, the county's delegation sided with the radical forces in urging the convention to christen its creation the "Farmer-Labor Party." Graunke sensibly argued that Minnesota liberals had "paved the way" by using that phrase and that it would be wise to avoid a "crazy-quilt" pattern from state to state. Moreover, he insisted, if that name were adopted, "you can't have a candidate . . . on both sides of the fence at the same time. They have to take sides." The Wausau orator concluded with a flourish, asserting that since all present were "in the general classification" farmers or laborers, they should "call [them] selves what [they were] and put it over with a bang."[82] When the verbal fireworks were over, the assemblage proceeded to ignore such advice and name the fledgling organization the Wisconsin Progressive Party.

The new party entered the lists under the leadership of gubernatorial candidate Phil La Follette, the man behind the new organization. Others, like Bob, Jr. and Gerald Boileau were less than enthusiastic, but went along with the idea once the initial step had been taken. A pragmatic liberal, the Wausau Congressman understood that both his political allies and a supportive constituency were in the Progressive camp. He also knew that his own political principles were much more attuned to the ideas of the bolters than to those of conservative Republicans or Democrats. So successful was the new departure that some liberals thought of creating a national liberal party, a prospect feared by the Roosevelt Administration.[83]

Concerns over a rising tide on the left were evident at the major county political event of 1934—the state Democratic Convention in Wausau. State Chairman Joe Martin of Green Bay opened the gathering with a plea for Progressives to join the Democrats for the coming election. Later in the meeting, Senator F. Ryan Duffy insisted that the party was the "great liberal, progressive party," without the "insanity fringe on its liberalism." Finally, the muse of history must have blushed when conservative Governor Albert Schmedeman baldly claimed that his party had always been a liberal party, but that unlike the "professional liberals," Democrats opposed "building on distress and unrest."[84]

Perhaps not entirely by coincidence, Wisconsin Socialists gathered in Wausau for a farmer-labor conference and rally on the same date as the Democratic convention. Characteristically optimistic, the Milwaukee-oriented group forecast a rebirth of the party based on broader participation by rural as well as urban labor. Special guests were Abbotsford's Charles Goldamer of the Farm Holiday Association and Walter Singler of the Milk Pool, men whose day in the limelight had already passed. More pathetic were the almost unnoticed Marathon County Republicans, whose county convention harangued the Roosevelt Administration with shrill denunciations of a "dictator" and an administration "intoxicated by over-indulgence in brain trust stimulants." Stalwart frustration was aptly summarized in the *Record-Herald's* plaintive comment:

> Wisconsin Democrats, Socialists and Progressives are all competing for the radical or liberal vote in Wisconsin this year, and even the Republicans are talking about a "liberal" platform and "liberal" candidates. Doesn't anybody care about the conservative vote? Or aren't there supposed to be any conservatively-minded voters in the state any more?[85]

The question was legitimate. All appearances were that the electorate distrusted traditional conservatives, whether Democrats or Republicans. One of the prime beneficiaries of this skepticism, young Roland Kannenberg, later recalled that "the people were ready to follow leadership that would give them a fair share of the wealth." Kannenberg, who had come to prominence during the milk strike as a spokesman for Walter Singler and the Milk Pool, drew significant rural support as he upset veteran stalwart Otto Mueller in the 25th Senatorial District. Although never so radical a Progressive as "the boy Senator," Boileau, too, went to the voters with an economic appeal. Winding up his campaign at Mosinee, he endorsed the idea of spreading the work and returning purchasing power to the hands of the consumer. Farmers were to have liberal government credit and the cost of production plus a reasonable profit. Likewise, Bob, Jr., made the rounds to Wausau, Athens, Edgar and beyond with Kannenberg, Graunke, Boileau and Barber at his side. The message was simple: aid to Roosevelt where they agreed; more advanced programs where they parted company—on issues like old age and survivors pensions, taxation of the wealthy, and a more equitable distribution of weath.[86]

On election day county voters confounded the pundits and party professionals by handing the new party an important victory in the state and national races. While the national electorate endorsed the New Deal in the midterm elections, Wisconsin and Marathon County voters poured out their affection for the La Follettes and their allies.

While Progressives and Democrats divided the less ideological county offices, only Democratic Assembly candidate Rudolph Meissner survived the liberal onslaught in 1934. Locally, the "one-time powerful and unapproachable Republican Party was relatively unimportant" in the contest. Conservatives were crushed, as even so prominent a figure as Otto Mueller, "veteran and competent State Senator . . . went down to defeat before the youthful Roland Kannenberg."[87] The stage was set for dramatic change.

How had the chemistry of local politics been altered to provide the Progressives with such a mandate? Colorful as it may have been, the oratory of Kannenberg, Graunke, Boileau, Barber, and the La Follettes was insufficient to turn the tide against the Democrats who had come in on Roosevelt's coattails. In fact, vital to Progressive successes was the farmer-labor coalition that was coming to fruition by the mid-1930's. Efforts to forge this link were rooted in the 1920's, and accelerated under the pressure of adverse economic conditions after 1929. The Farmers Union, Farm Holiday, and Milk Pool organizations formed the core of Progressive support, and were carefully cultivated by party wheelhorse Walter Graunke, as well as his aides Kannenberg and Barber. In the early 1930's, leaders in a restive union movement began to explore common concerns through tentative farmer-labor meetings in Wausau. Equally significant was the feeble attempt by the Socialists to extend a hand to rural voters at the 1934 Wausau conference. By 1934, county laborers showed signs of militancy, as in the letter to Phil La Follette from a dozen Wausau area workers, who were "glad to hear that the farm and labor movement has been started" and ready to "back the new party 100 per cent at the polls."[88]

By 1935, these halting efforts had taken organizational form with the creation of the Wisconsin Farmer-Labor Progressive Federation, a political action arm of rural and urban worker groups. The Federation was an important but never dominant force in the third party movement. In Marathon County, Walter Graunke, no political neophyte, took control of the Federation machinery to prevent Socialists or urban interests from swallowing the newborn Progressive Party. His strategy was uncomplicated: simply organize the county Progressive Club as the county Federation with identical officers in identical slots. By thus establishing a paper organization, county liberals were able to resist any outside attempts to control the political movement. Always suspect in central Wisconsin because of its labor and Socialist overtones, the FLPF was also a thorn in the side of Walter Graunke. By early 1936 the Marathon County leader was embroiled in a feud with state FLPF secretary Henry Rutz over the county's unwillingness to endorse favored candidates in local races. The battle ended in the state Federation's decision to "discipline" the Marathon County leader, which only led to the "permanent dissolution of that once dynamic local." In short, Rutz made a serious tactical blunder in suspending the "outstanding Progressive leader in the county," thus alienating his "large and loyal following."[89] The broader problem limiting the success of FLPF in central Wisconsin lay in the considerable tensions besetting any effort to get urban and rural interests to ride in double harness.

By early 1936, however, the most advanced Progressives had their minds on other matters. As persons of social vision, they saw in the moderate reforms of the New Deal only the opening act in a hoped-for transformation of American society. Certainly "clear-eyed men of destiny" were not in short supply in depression America. Not the least of the visionaries was California's Doctor Francis Townsend, who promised to end poverty among the elderly with a generous pension program funded by a tax on business transactions.

Despite his skewed economics, the kindly doctor attracted a large following in Marathon County. The Wausau area organization, under the leadership of John B. Coleman, claimed eight hundred members by 1936 and was busy developing groups in Marathon, Halder, and elsewhere in the county. While Graunke and Kannenberg favored the scheme, Gerald Boileau was the man on the spot. His strong liberal credentials notwithstanding, the Wausau Congressman boldly refused to support a plan that was funded by such an unjust mechanism as the transaction tax. In this position, he drew support from an unusual source when the *Record-Herald* agreed that the plan was "impracticable" except to those "who regard Uncle Sam as a Santa Claus."[90]

Criticism rolled off the backs of "true believers," however; and it was undeniably a seductive idea that could bring seven hundred people to the Wausau Theater in below zero weather to hear the Rev. Daniel Woodward expound on the virtues of the Townsend Program. Six months after the Roosevelt Social Security Act had apparently defused the movement, the doctor's troops remained steadfast. In fact, the long-range solution brought no short-run benefits: as a result, by 1936 county leaders began to feel that "unless old political parties accept Townsendism, the third party idea will grow."[91]

And there were men to nurture the thought. The radio priest, Father Charles E. Coughlin, was becoming increasingly vitriolic in his attack on FDR for his failure to drive the money changers from the temple of government. Of greater potential significance was the "King-fish," Senator Huey P. Long of Louisiana, in 1935 riding a wave of popularity with his "Share Our Wealth" program for a guaranteed annual income funded by near-confiscatory taxation. An unabashed Populist, Long drew backing from the most extreme Progressives in the Marathon County organization, Walter Graunke and Roland Kannenberg. In agreement with the Kingfish's pledge to "take every-thing over $5 million dollars in income earned through war profits," Kannenberg was an early supporter of his presidential ambitions.[92]

Yet when the Union Party emerged as the midwestern Progressive alternative to the major parties, the Graunke-Kannenberg-Barber group closed rank with its presidential choice, the uninspiring Congressman William Lemke of North Dakota. Theoretically uniting the Town-send-Coughlin-Long chorus of dissidence, the new party was thought to have the potential for realigning the American political system on liberal-conservative lines. While never underestimating their appeal, the *Record-Herald* had long believed that by 1940, the "radical agitators" would be "pretty well 'talked out' without seeing many of their pet panaceas tried out."[93] Some county liberals had other ideas.

Quick to seize the initiative, Graunke tried to turn the tables on the FLPF by pushing for a statewide Lemke endorsement at the or-ganization's 1936 convention. Although the Federation refused to act, the third party issue would not die. The Lemke boom among rural Federationists actually picked up steam as the largest upstate units in Marathon and Vilas Counties gave their full endorsement to Lemke. In a grandstand gesture, the Marathon County local offered the presidential hopeful a "lifetime honorary membership" in the county FLPF, a gift of dubious value. Always the North Dakotan's major local booster, Graunke signed on as his Wisconsin campaign manager. Never hesitant to use his own considerable influence, the Progressive leader engineered a much-disputed endorsement from the Marathon County Progressive Club. On one occasion, the chairman's account of unanimous club support for Lemke was challenged by several mem-bers. Graunke's advice to the most persistent critic was to "keep his nose out of the conversation."[94] Even dedicated liberals sometimes closed debate.

As the campaign heated up, Graunke moved to spark enthusiasm for his candidate. Lemke made a major appearance in September before an estimated four thousand at Marathon Park, where he prom-ised his audience to "kick the brainless trust out of Washington." Flaying the bankers, industrialists, and major parties alike, he pledged monetary reform. And, to the delight of his receptive audience, he promised that Father Coughlin, Dr. Townsend, and former Long associate Gerald L. K. Smith would be welcome guests in the Lemke White House.[95]

More significant than the Union Party rally was another gathering of liberals held one week later in Chicago to organize Progressive support of the Roosevelt Administration. Breaking with the "radical" wing of the county movement, Boileau joined the La Follettes, eastern liberals, southern Democrats and western Progressives to launch a national alliance as a first step in a projected political realignment. The new organization, headed by Senator La Follette, avoided the use of party names but made its support of FDR "on a non-partisan basis" clear. Boileau's position was perfectly consistent with his frequent support of New Deal legislation, and demonstrated that he was closer to the mainstream of American liberalism than some of his Marathon County compatriots. And at heart, the left wing knew it. In a reflective moment Kannenberg recalled that "in the main we realized that Roosevelt would be the winner."[96]

While the liberal leadership sparred over presidential politics, preparations were under way for the all important state and local races, as well. Graunke reported to Phil La Follette in August that Progressives would have a full slate in the general election, with multiple candidates for most offices. Confident that the organization had been strengthened since the 1934 campaign, he predicted a "specially great inroad and progress" in Wausau. Labor lawyer that he was, he proudly announced that with 2,500 union men in Wausau alone, the local organization would "bolster up the Progressive vote in our city materially." Or, as another Wausau liberal put it, Phil need not inquire as to the Wausau vote, since he could "go on a vacation and win." This sense of confidence did not prevent local Progressives from waging a spirited campaign, and by mid-August, the untiring Walter Graunke was on the stump nightly speaking for the Governor. When Phil brought his traveling show to Marathon County on the eve of the election, he was enthusiastically received at Wausau, Stratford, and Mosinee. Appearing with Graunke and Boileau, he asked for a Progressive legislature to help him redeem his program; it was generally conceded that the popular Boileau and the Governor would "keep many voters within the Progressive ranks for their entire ticket."[97]

Meanwhile Democrats fretted over the state and local condition of their party, heavily dependent as it was upon the accomplishments and reputation of FDR. At a county conference, speakers such as

R. E. Puchner, Frank P. Regner, and John Ringle, Jr. preached the virtues of organization and the practicality of identification with Roosevelt's image to the party faithful. The Democrats' dilemma was vividly illustrated in August when gubernatorial candidate Arthur Lueck was forced to prove to a Wausau audience that he was a "better" Roosevelt man than Phil La Follette. Desperately grasping for the President's coattails, Lueck told his small crowd that La Follette's support for FDR was a masquerade and that he was the "Roosevelt Democrat." To make matters worse, conservative Democrats agonized over their party's liberal pledges to use federal power to meet national problems in labor and agriculture. The *Pilot's* editor wondered "how far the party will be led into radical fields in the light of the 1936 Democratic platform."[98]

The voters displayed no such reservations in handing Roosevelt an overwhelming 66 per cent of the vote, and even the exhortations of an inspired Walter Graunke could deliver only 6 per cent of the total to the agrarian radical, William Lemke. In short, Marathon County shared in the national outpouring of support for FDR that left Republican Alf Landon firmly in control of Maine and Vermont. Yet the President's coattails were short in Wisconsin, where he enjoyed an unspoken agreement with the La Follettes. Only incumbent Democratic Assemblyman Rudolph Meissner was able to withstand the liberal trend that saw Phil outdistance his nearest competition by a two to one margin in Marathon County. In large measure, the county was still Progressive territory and played a role in giving the Governor his first control of the full legislature in 1937 and 1938.[99] Few understood in the hour of triumph that the county Progressives were enjoying their last great victory and that the end of liberal hegemony was near.

In retrospect, it is clear that depression-era Progressivism entered a golden era in the period 1934-1938, peaking in the wake of the 1936 victories. What were the legislative results? Roland Kannenberg, whose Senate term coincided with those years, recalled with pride the establishment of aid to dependent children programs, expansion of university extension opportunities, the passage of the Mortgage Moratorium Bill sought by the farm organizations, the implementation of a state unemployment compensation program provided for in the 1931-1932 session, the creation of the Wisconsin Development Authority in imitation of the federal TVA power project, and enactment of the Labor Disputes Bill that granted labor unions in Wisconsin treatment similar to that provided in the federal law. A supporter of all these, Kannenberg was a prime mover in the areas of farm mortgages, extension, and the WDA. His Senate record offered a vivid contrast with that of his conservative predecessor, Otto Mueller, and the moderate area Democrats in the Assembly. For example, his 1937 voting record on key issues was ranked .897 per cent "in the public interest" by the liberal *Capital Times,* while Mueller had scored a less spectacular .130 per cent for the 1933 session.[100]

As a young and often eager legislator, Kannenberg was sometimes the subject of good-natured ribbing from his colleagues, as in the response to his first press conference concerning a perfect attendance record. The *Milwaukee Journal* caustically noted that the "young Wausau solon, who is often seen sucking lollypops," was in line for a "gold star" attendance award. Such jibes notwithstanding, few regarded the "boy Senator" as shy and retiring. A case in point was a running battle with the *Capital Times* over his attempt to secure state funding for a university campus at Wausau. Failing to win approval in 1935, Kannenberg revived the proposal in 1937, to the dismay of the liberal *Times.* The proposal, which had the endorsement of the Wausau city council, drew fire from the Madison press as contrary to the state constitution. At one point in the debate the *Capital Times* printed a picture of the capitol atop Rib Mountain, with the argument that the state government would have to move to Wausau before the facility could be built. On another occasion the Wausau Progressive stood accused of logrolling when he threatened to vote against university funding and to halt action on the Labor Disputes Bill unless he got action on the extension proposal. He lost that battle, but the struggle demonstrated his determination to "increase educational opportunity to the boys and girls of northern Wisconsin."[101]

Another measure especially desired by Wausau's "boy Senator" was the creation of a Wisconsin Development Authority modeled after the New Deal's Tennessee Valley Authority. Convinced that the bill was "aimed at private business initiative," the *Record-Herald* bitterly opposed the concept of public power development: it might lead to too great an expansion of the powers of state government. The heart of conservative opposition centered around "the prospect of having the state of Wisconsin engage in business in competition with private enterprise." Such reservations aside, Kannenberg worked closely with the Governor to ram the legislation through in the controversial special session of 1937, but the state Supreme Court invalidated the plan before it could get under way. [102]

In sum, the vitriolic debate of the 1937 session dealt with state measures that rounded the edges of the New Deal. Although The Progressives had been returned to Madison in greater numbers, the initiative had largely passed to Washington, and Wisconsin liberals found themselves mired in discussions of how to imitate and implement federal programs. While it may be argued that Badger state programs and proposals had inspired much New Deal legislation, the center of action had clearly shifted to the banks of the Potomac by 1937.

That shift was obvious to Marathon County conservatives. Displaying his usual political acumen, Auburndale's Rev. Howard Murray Jones wrote from Madison that Roosevelt would certainly not "have it all his own way" in the 1936 election. Closer to reality was prominent Wausau Republican Charles F. Smith, who told the 1936 Republican convention that it would be a tough battle. As keynote speaker, Smith attacked the Roosevelt Administration's supposed trend toward socialism and "appeal to class strife." Yet an unmistakable sign of the times was the Wausau man's description of his own group as "the liberal new Republican Party."[103] It was necessary to join the enemy to beat him!

This theme persisted during Alf Landon's ill-fated presidential campaign. Billing their candidate as a "poor man's Coolidge," Republicans were forced to argue that it was quite possible for a person to be a liberal without being a big spender. As state director of the Landon-Knox clubs, Smith became a leading figure in the Republican effort. Hence, when the campaign rolled into Wisconsin, Wausau got an opportunity to hear "frugal Alf" expound on his personal brand of liberalism, similar to that preached by the Wausau Republican at the convention. No doubt aware of Marathon County's reputation as a Progressive stronghold, Landon praised Badger state conservation measures without stressing the role of the La Follette organization in promoting them. Appearing with the challenger's party was A. W. Prehn, Republican congressional aspirant, whose candidacy presumably strengthened the ticket because of his early link with Progressivism. One party wheelhorse was confident that Landon's short visit meant 1000 extra votes in the county; unfortunately, Alf pulled up 10,000 short in November. In the wake of the Roosevelt landslide, the *Record-Herald* thoughtfully expressed the dilemma of the conservative when it counseled GOP legislators to provide responsible opposition that would "place the Republican Party of Wisconsin upon record as soundly Progressive."[104] The conservative path remained rocky and fraught with contradiction.

Alf Comes Calling, 1936

If Marathon County was a hotbed of Progressivism, how do we explain the party's precipitous decline two years later? The explanations
are many. Many studies have noted that strong local organization is
instrumental in the perpetuation of political power. Assuming this
to be true, Democratic inroads at the county level take on significance.
One development of the 1930's was the trend toward "voting the
man rather than the party." That tendency, combined with a strong
Democratic national ticket, had resulted in the Progressives' loss of
many county offices by 1938, when only Sheriff Oscar Brandt and
County Clerk Edward H. Kuhlmann remained.

Equally significant would be the debilitating influence of tight control by a select group of leaders. Few would deny that Marathon
County Progressivism had fallen into the hands of a clique headed
by the ubiquitous Walter A. Graunke. As early as 1936, the Marathon
County FLPF local was reportedly disintegrating. Dissension surfaced
over Graunke's open and active work for Lemke, as well as allega-

tions that he backed non-Federation candidates for state offices. In October, Socialist, Farmers Union, and labor leaders on the county executive board "filed charges" against their chairman, indicting him for his use of "dictatorial methods." These pressures from the Marathon County unit finally led the state FLPF board to "suspend Graunke pending an investigation."[105] While the farmer-labor federation was not an especially effective political force, this internal friction was symptomatic of growing tension among county Progressives over the dominance of the Graunke-Kannenberg-Barber axis.

Dissent against the Graunke group's sometimes heavy-handed tactics was not confined to the local Federation. Kronenwetter politician Casimir Orzechowski learned early in his career that the Progressive Party was often manipulated like other party organizations. As an active Progressive, he was privy to planning conferences for the 1935 Progressive Convention in Fond du Lac; those sessions made clear the La Follette inner circle's intention to control the meeting. Even more instructive was Orzechowski's attempt to introduce Republican Robert Monk at a 1937 Progressive rally at Peplin Hall. The Polish leader's memoir describes an enraged Graunke's response: "Casimir, some day you might run for Assemblyman. You think party [sic] will support you?"[106] Graunke's determination to chart the course of Marathon County Progressivism was as lengendary as the loyalty he inspired among many farmers and laborers.

Part of the Progressive malaise was rooted in the growing impracticality of the farm-labor coalition itself. As the state FLPF efforts veered more towards organizational action in the trade union movement, the rural Federationists kicked over the traces. Sensing this trend, the *Record-Herald* fueled the fires of discontent by chiding the state Federation as a "Socialist tail . . . determined to wag the Progressive dog." Meanwhile, such "renegade Progressives" as Barber began to wonder when "organized labor was going to stop asking for things from this legislature." Assessing the labor disputes bill, demands for state group insurance, and plans for aiding relief clients, the grizzled veteran remarked that there were "plenty of Progressive leaders who don't favor this kind of junk." Ultimately, he dismissed the Socialist and labor programs as "Communistic all the way through."[107] Clearly, the farmer-labor alliance was fraying at the edges.

Equally significant was the erosion of the Progressive coalition from the Democratic side. The midterm elections of 1938 witnessed a "liberal split between the Progressives and the followers of Roosevelt," resulting in significant Republican gains in that year. Despite Governor La Follette's vision of a national liberal party, he had always found it expedient to identify with the New Deal in presidential years. It has been argued that this ambivalence toward FDR "confused and weakened the whole liberal movement in Wisconsin." To Boileau, the liberal split between Democrats and Progressives seemed decisive because "the stalwarts had it all by themselves on the Republican ticket."[108]

An important development in the 1938 campaign involved an effort by Democratic and Republican conservatives to combine against the Progressive ticket. Victorious in the Democratic gubernatorial primary after running on both tickets, coalition candidate Robert K. Henry withdrew in favor of Milwaukee Republican Julius P. Heil to give him a clear shot at La Follette. While Democrats did offer nominal opposition, Heil went on to retire the governor in the November election. At a Wausau campaign appearance, Phil blistered the coalition as "an insult to the integrity and intelligence of the people of Wisconsin." Counting on liberals to repudiate this "sordid example of horsetrading," he indicted the Democratic conspirators as betrayers of Roosevelt's liberalism. The Governor concluded that the choice was "between Hoover reaction and orderly progress." Coalitionist intrigue at the state level was matched by the machinations of Marathon County Democrats in at least one race. Perhaps taking a cue from the coalition, Wausau Democrat R. A. Meissner's surprise withdrawal from the Senatorial race left Republican veteran Otto Mueller face-to-face with Progressive incumbent Roland Kannenberg. While Meissner cited "business reasons" for his eleventh hour decision, he also came out against a "three party election which generally results in a minority electing a man to represent the majority."[109]

The fusion of conservatives was not necessarily fatal for liberals. Congressman Boileau later recalled that he "could have overcome that." But there were other impediments to a Progressive victory that proved decisive in the Boileau race and probably had a certain amount of "negative fallout" for the entire ticket. Foremost among Boileau's problems was the intense opposition generated by the Townsend Clubs, which retained their vitality long after social security legislation was enacted. Gunning for Boileau, Dr. Townsend made a personal appearance at Marathon Park to promote his pension plan as a stimulus to economic recovery. The doctor took the occasion to urge the election of friendly Congressional candidates, while demanding Boileau's ouster for allegedly "betraying Townsend supporters." Later in the campaign, the national vice-president of the movement came to Wausau for an endorsement of Republican challenger Reid F. Murray of Waupaca over the incumbent. While Murray was perceived as an ally, Boileau had been a "chronic aginner." Local Townsend president Reno Zahn followed with a plea for Murray's election.[110]

Of course, other reasons for the liberal collapse of 1938 have been advanced. Roland Kannenberg was convinced that the Progressive Party's most serious problem was financial. While the Farmers Union and the Milk Pool had been able to help in 1934, they did not contribute as generously four years later. Consequently, the "boy Senator," who had made a name for himself in liberal circles, was unable to speak and to "reach the voters." In contrast, the opposition was well funded. In part because of his leading role in the creation of WDA, Kannenberg knew that "anyone who ran against [him] would have money." Few Progressives ran well-financed in the 1938 campaign. But while Kannenberg faced economic hurdles, Boileau was forced to deal with a subtle and perhaps more influential force: the Roman Catholic hierarchy. As a strong liberal, he had taken a position favor-

Progressive Compatriots, 1938
Congressman Gerald J. Boileau (left) with Governor Philip F. La Follette

ing the loyalist, democratic government in Spain against the fascist challenge led by Francisco Franco. Boileau was one of several Progressives who signed a telegram expressing support for the loyalists. He was fully aware of the Church's sympathy for Franco, but he regarded the question as a matter of principle. In the face of considerable clerical criticism, the Congressman stood his ground; but the political price was high.[111]

Beyond these transitory problems, the 1938 campaign was the occasion for Phil La Follette's ill-fated decision to launch a national third party: the National Progressives of America. Like many liberals Phil devoutly believed it possible to revive the nation's confidence and its economy with a disciplined political movement that would reverberate with a new sense of purpose. Contemporary critics and modern scholars have been quick to note the NPA's similarity to European fascism, from the staged rallies to the party's symbolic flag—a cross in a circle, sometimes reviled as the "devil's swastika." Such analogies have limited value, for Phil's goals of full employment and moral revival were a far cry from militarism; but the impact of the doomed crusade was to muddy the water further in an already confused political sea.[112]

Not so confused, however, that Marathon County Republicans failed to see their opportunity. As early as April, Charles F. Smith released an open letter to the state Republican committee decrying the "Roosevelt-made recession" of 1937-1938 and calling the GOP to arms in a holy war against executive dictatorship. Not long after, county Republicans met to plot an aggressive campaign for all offices. The gathering was exceptional in two respects: an usually large rural representation and the apparent competition for positions on the ticket. Conservative hopes soared when the primary returns revealed a decided shift from the Democratic to the Republican column, as voters gave the GOP its highest total since "the Republican years." While Marathon County Progressives held their own, their statewide vote declined significantly; this development led the *Record-Herald* to insist that "the 'swing' is there" and that "voters are looking for a change."[113]

There was indeed an unusual blend of anticipation and uncertainty among the politicians as election day drew near. Republicans and Progressives were described as "romping through the Badger state with lots of vim and vigor," while the hapless Democrats followed "as though years of New Dealism had wearied them a little." The county campaign was hot and heavy, with nightly meetings the rule among

Republicans and Progressives. Sensing their opportunity, the GOP brought in the first team with gubernatorial aspirant Julius Heil and coalitionist dropout Robert Henry speaking against La Follette at a Grand Theater rally. Meanwhile, the fading Progressives were, characteristically, embroiled in a family feud which pitted the ascendant Graunke faction against a group of challengers who charged the party leadership with irregularities in the selection of the Progressive county chairman. Most vocal in dissent was a voice from the past: vanquished warrior George W. Lippert, attempting to enter the lists as the minority candidate for party treasurer. So vigorous was Lippert's challenge that it earned him an untimely ejection from the hall at the hands of the sergeant at arms. Forcing a new election through court action, the dissidents fared no better the second time around, as the opposition slate was again defeated by Graunke's more disciplined troops.[114]

While Progressives enjoyed the luxury of an internal skirmish, Democrats were busy convincing themselves and the public that they had not been wiped out by what District Attorney Clayton Crooks accurately perceived as "an aggressive organization" on the Republican side. Thus, when Senator F. Ryan Duffy's campaign manager attempted to arouse Marathon County precinct committeemen, he was forced to counter "propaganda to the effect that the Democratic Party was disintegrating and flopping over to the Republicans." The Duffy man denounced such reports as "falsehood," maintaining that "on the contrary, the Democratic Party was very much alive."[115] But when the cheerleaders left, the voters took over; and the result was an electrifying political victory for Republicans and fusionists. The Progressives would never fully recover from the blow.

When the votes were in, the county's vaunted Progressive organization lay in shambles at the feet of the victorious GOP. "Apparently desiring a change of administration all down the line," county voters deserted both Progressives and Democrats and "gave old guard candidates decisive majorities." The landslide victory, which "left even avid Republicans gasping," marks a watershed in the political history of Marathon County. Gone were such sturdy liberals as Gerald Boileau, Roland Kannenberg, Joseph Barber, and Phil La Follette: all went down to defeat in a county long regarded as a Progressive stronghold. The only Progressive survivors were unopposed incumbents county clerk Ed Kuhlmann and Surveyor Calvin Cook, as well as Assemblyman John Dittbrender of Ringle, victor by a razor thin margin of eight votes. The rout of the Progressive state and national ticket coincided with losses for New Deal Democrats. The most prominent loser to go down "under the avalanche" was Senator Duffy, who lost badly to victor Alexander Wiley in Marathon County. The "about-face" was interpreted locally as a "repudiation" of the New Deal and the government interventionism it represented.[116]

And so it was. In keeping with a state and national trend toward 'retrenchment, "the issue everywhere, even in Wisconsin was New Dealism." Long an arch-enemy of the La Follettes, the *Record-Herald* took pleasure in the Republican "slam" as an "exhilarating restorative to belief in Democratic institutions." With the specter of "a one-party system" dispelled, it was possible to turn attention to setting straight the "complicated muddle of Progressive state government." The future would find Governor Julius Heil, a man viewed by one student of Wisconsin politics as a "gregarious, irrepressible bungler," equal to the challenge. He was destined to preside over the dismantling of the Progressive legacy of the La Follette Administration. And with conservatives, led by Senator Otto Mueller, in the local driver's seat, Marathon County liberalism was doomed to collapse. Before another election was held the Progressive Party had "practically disintegrated."[117] The future belonged to others.

FOOTNOTES

[1] The 1920 census recorded Marathon County in the category "15-25 Per Cent Foreign-born," placing it in the same group with such heterogeneous counties as Milwaukee. While Polish voters comprised an increasingly significant percentage of the foreign-born, Germans remained the dominant ethnic group in the county. U.S., Bureau of the Census, *Fourteenth Census of the United States: 1930. Population*, III, p. 697.

[2] *Record-Herald*, July 24, 1922, p. 6. The nature of the emerging Progressive coalition in Wisconsin is discussed in Nesbit, pp. 462-63, 468 and Karl E. Meyer, "The Politics of Loyalty From La Follette to McCarthy in Wisconsin, 1918-1952," (unpublished Ph.D. dissertation, Dept. of Politics, Princeton University, 1956), pp. 66-67. Also very instructive concerning the movements of Socialist voters were personal interviews with former Congressman Gerald J. Boileau, Wausau, August 25, 1975 (Marathon County Public Library Oral History Collection), June 17, 1976; and Roland Kannenberg, Mercer, June 27, 1976. See also Alfred W. Gerhard to Blaine, May 27, 1926, Blaine MMS.

[3] D. S. Burnett to Robert M. La Follette, Jr., June 1, 1922, Phillip F. La Follette Manuscripts, Madison, Wisconsin State Historical Society; Wyman, p. 807; the Kannenberg and Boileau interviews confirm the strong rural support given Progressives in the interwar period.

[4] *Record-Herald*, May 11, 1922, p. 1; May 4, 1922, p. 1.

[5] *Wisconsin Blue Book*, 1923, pp. 461-64; *Record-Herald*, June 3, 1922, p. 6; May 31, 1922, p. 6; *Pilot*, June 1, 1922, p. 1. Kreutzer, the Wausau dark horse, barely emerged from the stable, running third to Morgan and Wilcox in the battle for conservative endorsement. *Capital Times*, June 2, 1922, p. 1; June 1, 1922, pp. 1, 4.

[6] *Pilot*, Aug. 10, 1922, pp. 1, 5; July 6, 1922, p. 1; June 22, 1922, p. 4; *Record-Herald*, Aug. 11, 1922, p. 1, 10; *Milwaukee Sentinel*, June 28, 1922, p. 1, 4; *Capital Times*, June 28, 1922, p. 1. Not surprisingly, Mathie won the enthusiastic endorsement of

346

the Democratic *Pilot*, which lauded his commitments to state government consolidation, economy, and honesty. *Pilot*, Aug. 31, 1922, p. 4.

[7] Robert La Follette, Sr. to Blaine, March 18, 1922, Blaine MSS. The secrecy
clause prohibited the Tax Commission from publicizing the name of any corporation or individual who filed an erroneous or fraudulent return. Blaine later
established that there were 3,000 corporations in the state whose tax reports were
incorrect, resulting in substantial losses in tax revenues due the state. "Announcement of Governor John J. Blaine As a Candidate for Reelection," May 31, 1922,
Blaine MSS.

[8] A. E. Bessert to Robert M. La Follette, Jr., June 8, 1922; Robert M. La
Follette, Jr. to Harris Hanowitz, June 14, 1922; Hanowitz to Robert La Follette,
Jr., June 15, 1922; June 24, 1922; July 8, 1922; Philip F. La Follette MSS. The
charter officers of the La Follette-Blaine Club were Edward T. Ford, Wausau;
J. W. Salter, Unity; John G. Waef, Wausau; George W. Lippert, Wausau; Hugo
Richter, Ringle; W. F. Lemke, Berlin; Harris Hanowitz, Mosinee; and Francis X.
Schilling, Cassel. For report of organizational activities and endorsements, see
Pilot, July 13, 1922, p. 2.

[9] F. A. Semmelbach to Robert M. La Follette, Jr., May 29, 1922; August Wiesman
to Robert M. La Follette, Jr., June 3, 1922; Bessert to Robert M. La Follette, Jr.,
June 8, 1922; A. C. Wagner to Robert M. La Follette, Jr., Aug. 19, 1922; George W.
Lippert to Robert M. La Follette, Sr., Aug. 1, 12, 1922; J. W. Salter to Robert M.
La Follette, Jr., Aug. 21, 1922, Philip F. La Follette MSS.

[10] *Record-Herald*, July 27, 1922, p. 1. Many observers acknowledged Lippert's
political rise in the Socialist Party, though some doubted the depth of his commitment to socialism. Boileau Interview, June 17, 1976.

[11] Fred W. Genrich to Blaine, May 27, 1922; Fred E. Schroeder to Blaine, May
25, 1922; George A. Runkel to Blaine, May 25, 1922; John D. Christie to Blaine;
May 25, 1922, Blaine MSS.

[12] Frank Chesak to Blaine, June 4, 1922; Paul R. Prochnow to Blaine, May 25,
1922; Blaine to Mrs. Joseph Barber, June 1, 1922; Joseph Lemmer to Blaine, May,
1922; Blaine MSS.

[13] Joseph Barber to Robert M. La Follette, Jr., July 10, 1922; George W. Lippert
to Robert M. La Follette, Jr., July 18, 1922; Aug. 4, 1922, Philip F. La Follette
MSS; Lippert to Blaine, June 2, 1922, Blaine MSS.

[14] *Pilot*, Aug. 3, 1922, p. 1; July 20, 1922, p. 6; July 6, 1922, p. 2. For evidence
of Lippert's pivotal role in the planning stages, see Lippert to Robert M. La
Follette, Sr., April 25, 1922; May 29, 1922; June 9, 1922; June 26, 1922; Aug. 1,
1922, Philip F. La Follette MSS.

[15] Salter to Robert M. La Follette, Jr., Sept. 2, 1922, Philip F. La Follette MSS.

[16] Robert M. La Follette, Jr., to Salter, Sept., 1922; Barber to Robert M. La
Follette, Jr., Aug. 23, 1922; Sept. 11, 1922; Barber to Robert M. La Follette, Sr.,
Aug. 24, 1922; Lippert to Robert M. La Follette, Jr., Aug. 5, 1922; "Political
Advertisement," La Follette-Blaine Progressive Republican Club of Marathon County, Aug. 22, 1922, Philip F. La Follette MSS. Prehn was not widely regarded as a
dependable Progressive, while Barber and Lippert were generally thought of as
faithful La Follette supporters. The litmus test would come in 1934 when Prehn
ignored the new Progressive Party and Barber followed Phil La Follette into
the third party. Boileau Interview, June 17, 1976; Kannenberg Interview.

[17] *Wisconsin Blue Book*, 1923, p. 462; *Pilot*, Aug. 31, 1922, p. 4.

[18] "From the *Milwaukee Journal*," *Pilot*, Sept. 28, 1922, p. 4; Sept. 14, 1922, p. 4;
for an account of the frustrations of the county's independent Democrats, Socialists,
and Republicans, see *Pilot*, Oct. 26, 1922, p. 1; primary returns may be found in
Wisconsin Blue Book, 1923, p. 462. For comments on the Democratic weakness
and Progressive Republican strength of the 1920's see Boileau Interview, Aug. 25,
1975. Nesbit argues that "the war so jarred society in Wisconsin as to generate
new issues, new alignments . . . a new mood of anger and bitterness." Nesbit, p. 467.

[19] Raw figures are drawn from *Wisconsin Blue Book*, 1923, pp. 460-462.

[20] *Record-Herald*, March 31, 1924, p. 6; March 29, 1924, p. 1; *Pilot*, April 3, 1924,
pp. 1, 9.

[21] *Pilot*, June 26, 1924, pp. 4, 1; April 3, 1924, p. 4; *Record-Herald*, April 23, 1924,
p. 4; May 5, 1924, p. 1; April 4, 1924, p. 10; April 2, 1924, p. 6.

[22] *Record-Herald,* March 25, 1924, p. 6; March 18, 1924, p. 6; April 3, 1924, p. 8. For summary treatment of the 1924 Progressive campaign, see James H. Shideler, "The La Follette Progressive Campaign of 1924," *Wisconsin Magazine of History,* Vol. XXXIII (June, 1950), pp. 444-57; David Thelen, *Robert M. La Follette and the Insurgent Spirit* (Boston: Little, Brown & Co., 1976), pp. 181-192.

[23] *Record-Herald,* Feb. 9, 1924, p. 3; May 10, 1924, p. 6. While the Nonpartisans were involved in the La Follette effort, they focused much of their Wisconsin attention on the effort to elect their spokesman, George F. Comings, to the governorship. In any event, they represented a declining force in state politics by 1924. Nesbit, p. 465.

[24] Lippert to C. M. Dow, Aug. 14, 1924; Sept. 6, 1924; Sept. 12, 1924; Dow to Lippert, Sept. 10, 1924; Sept. 13, 1924; Dow to Barber, Sept. 17, 1924, Philip F. La Follette MSS. The Progressive list was composed of persons from all areas in Marathon County, though residents of eastern districts were apparently less involved in the movement. Activists were to be found in Abbotsford, Dancy, Naugart, Athens, Hatley, Unity, Brokaw, Wausau, Edgar, Marathon, Colby, Auburndale, Stratford, Eland, Mosinee, Fenwood, Marshfield, Birnamwood, Hamburg, Elderon, Spencer, Milan, Knowlton, Dorchester, Merrill, and Rothschild. "Marathon County," 1924, encl. in Lippert to Dow, Aug. 14, 1924, Philip F. La Follette MSS.

[25] *Pilot,* Oct. 30, 1924, p. 1; Alfred W. Gerhard to Blaine, May 27, 1926, Blaine MSS; anonymous correspondent to Robert M. La Follette, Jr., Sept., 1924, Philip F. La Follette MSS.

[26] *Pilot,* Nov. 6, 1924, p. 1; *Record-Herald,* Sept. 18, 1924, p. 8; Sept. 19, 1924, p. 8; Sept. 30, 1924, p. 9.

[27] Barber to Blaine, May 26, 1926, Blaine MSS; *Pilot,* June 24, 1926, p. 1; April 8, 1926, p. 1. Gerald Boileau, who worked in the district attorney's office at the time, expressed some uncertainty concerning Lippert's guilt or innocence. He "never did believe it in the beginning" and is still uncertain as to "whether it was true or not." Boileau Interview, June 17, 1976.

[28] Theo Gandman to Blaine, May 28, 1926; Oscar Larson to Blaine, May 28, 1926; D. F. Praedel to Blaine, May 27, 1926; Lippert to Blaine, May 25, 1926; John King to Blaine, May 28, 1926; Mildred Barber to Blaine, May 24, 1926; Henry Ellenbecker to Blaine, May 28, 1926; Joseph Barber to Blaine, May 26, 1926; county board members and town officials to Blaine, May 28-June 1, 1926, Blaine MSS. Given the circumstances surrounding Lippert's suspension, it was perhaps unavoidable that the liquor question should be raised in the appointment of any successor. Boileau was known as a "wet," certainly not a liability in Marathón County. In this connection the comment of Mrs. Helena McNeight expressed the view of many concerned citizens: "I know Mr. Boileau himself is a little inclined to be moist. I also think that he is willing and anxious to enforce the law as it stands." Helena McNeight to Blaine, May 26, 1926, Blaine MSS.

[29] *Pilot,* June 3, 1926, p. 4; "Announcement," June 2, 1926; George J. Leicht to Blaine, May 28, 1926; Blaine MSS; Boileau Interview, June 17, 1976.

[30] Boileau Interview, June 17, 1976; *Pilot,* Oct. 26, 1927, p. 1; Oct. 21, 1926, p. 1; Oct. 7, 1926, p. 1; Lippert to Blaine, Oct. 2, 1926, Blaine MSS.

[31] Lippert to Blaine, Oct. 2, 1926; Leicht to Blaine, Sept. 21, 1926; Earl Plantz to Blaine, Oct. 2, 1926; Hugo Richter to Blaine, Oct. 8, 1926, Blaine MSS; *Pilot,* Oct. 14, 1926, p. 1.

[32] Chesak to Blaine, June 4, 1922, Blaine MSS; *Marathon Times,* April 27, 1917, p. 1. For discussion of the link between anti-foreignism and prohibitionist support, see Jeffrey Lucker, "The Politics of Prohibition in Wisconsin, 1917-1933," (unpublished Master's thesis, Dept. of History, University of Wisconsin, 1968), p. 14, 18; Nesbit, p. 462.

[33] Boileau Interview, June 17, 1976; Aug. 21, 1975; *Record-Herald,* Sept. 28, 1926, p. 6; A. G. Straub, *History of Marathon, Wisconsin, 1857 to 1957,* p. 28. One La Follette fund raiser from Ringle complained that the only people with money were the bootleggers, "of which there are plenty here about." A spot check of local newspapers reveals arrests, indictments, prosecutions, and conviction of county violators in such widely-dispersed locations as Athens, Fenwood, Frankfort, Green Valley, Harrison, Hewitt, Holton, Hull, Kronenwetter, Maine, Marathon, Mosinee,

Norrie, Ringle, Schofield, Stettin, Texas, Weston, and Wausau. Clearly, no county area held a monopoly on sin.

[34] Straub, p. 28; *Pilot*, Feb. 25, 1925, p. 3.

[35] *Pilot*, Dec. 8, 1927, p. 1; Dec. 1, 1927, p. 1; July 11, 1929, p. 1; July 23, 1925, p. 2; May 13, 1926, p. 1; Sept. 23, 1926, p. 1; Oct. 14, 1926, p. 1.

[36] *Record-Herald*, March 12, 1925, p. 13; Oct. 3, 1922, p. 6; May 25, 1922, p. 6.

[37] *Pilot*, June 21, 1928, p. 2; March 18, 1926, p. 1. While dry charges that repeal would hurt the milk business were frequently heard, it is also true that as soon as New York state's enforcement law was repealed, Wisconsin farmers began to feel competition from New York dairymen seeking compensatory markets. Lucker, p. 119.

[38] Lucker, p. 99; *Pilot*, Sept. 16, 1926, p. 3; Nov. 4, 1926, p. 1; *Wisconsin Blue Book*, 1927, p. 593; *Record-Herald*, Sept. 28, 1926, p. 8. For evidence of Lenroot's desperate attempt to camouflage his past weakness on the prohibition question, see his full-page ad in the local papers, claiming that he could do more for beer than any "brewery Senator" like Blaine. *Record-Herald*, Sept. 4, 1926, p. 3.

[39] Jones to Ada Jones, March 21, 1929; March 29, 1929, Jones MSS; *Pilot*, March 28, 1929, p. 1; Lucker, p. 99.

[40] The survey recorded 619 for repeal, 365 for modification, and a mere 167 in favor of enforcement. Since it merely confirmed previous soundings, "few Wausau residents evidenced much surprise over the results." *Pilot*, May 15, 1930, p. 1; April 4, 1929, p. 4; May 2, 1929, p. 1; *Wisconsin Blue Book*, 1929, pp. 872-73.

[41] *Badger American*, Vol. 1, (Feb., 1924), p. 5; *Record-Herald*, Feb. 2, 1924, p. 1. The Klan effort in outstate Wisconsin is described in Norman Frederic Weaver, "The Knights of the Ku Klux Klan in Wisconsin, Indiana, Ohio, and Illinois," (unpublished Ph.D. dissertation, Dept. of History, University of Wisconsin, 1954), p. 59; see also *Milwaukee Journal*, Oct. 13, 1946, p. 12; Nesbit, p. 466.

[42] *Pilot*, Feb. 4, 1924, p. 1.

[43] *Record-Herald*, Feb. 2, 1924, p. 1; Feb. 1, 1924, p. 1; *Badger American*, Vol. I, (Feb., 1924), p. 5.

[44] *Record-Herald*, April 7, 1924, p. 1; April 8, 1924, p. 1; April 10, 1924, p. 1; *Badger-American*, Vol. II (April, 1924), p. 8; Vol. II, (May, 1924), p. 6.

[45] *Milwaukee Journal*, Oct. 13, 1946, p. 12; April 8, 1928, pp. 1, 4; E. H. Coulasz to Blaine, July 26, 1926, Blaine MSS.

[46] *Pilot*, Oct. 19, 1922, p. 4; April 13, 1922, p. 1.

[47] *Pilot*, Feb. 12, 1925, p. 4; Feb. 5, 1925, p. 1. Mildred Barber lost her reelection bid to fellow Progressive Matt Berres by 150 votes. *Pilot*, Sept. 16, 1926, p. 3.

[48] *Record-Herald*, Sept. 14, 1928, p. 8; *Pilot*, March 16, 1922, p. 1.

[49] William J. Campbell, *History of the Republican Party of Wisconsin Under the Convention Plan, 1924-1940* (Oshkosh: privately published, 1942), p. 4; Nesbit, p. 469; William J. Campbell to Albert D. Bolens, Nov. 22, 1926, Albert D. Bolens Manuscripts, Madison, Wisconsin, Wisconsin State Historical Society.

[50] Even more disconcerting to Heinemann was the Zimmerman committee's forgetfulness in not reporting the contribution (as reported in the *Capital Times*). Heinemann denied the story, but refused to enter a public controversy with the Progressive newspaper. *Capital Times*, June 7, 1927, pp. 1, 20; Heinemann to Bolens, June 9, 1927; Campbell to Bolens, Sept. 20, 1926, Bolens MSS; *Record-Herald*, Sept. 2, 1926, p. 1; Sept. 9, 1926, p. 6; Boileau to F. M. Wylie, July 22, 1926, Blaine MSS; Ernest Kannenberg, Jr. to Ira Lorenz, June 11, 1926, Philip F. La Follette MSS; Campbell, p. 11; Nesbit, p. 468.

[51] Otto Mueller Clippings Book, Wausau, Marathon County Historical Society; *Pilot*, Aug. 12, 1926, p. 4.

[52] C. J. Randall to Frank Kuehl, July 19, 1926, Blaine MSS; Mueller Clippings Book.

[53] Heinemann to Bolens, Sept. 28, 1927, Bolens MSS; *Record-Herald*, Sept. 9, 1927, p. 1; Sept. 8, 1927, pp. 1, 9; Sept. 7, 1927, p. 1; Campbell, p. 13; *Pilot*, Sept. 8, 1927, p. 8.

[54] Boileau Interviews, Aug 21, 1975; June 17, 1976.

[55] *Record-Herald*, Aug. 16, 1928, p. 10; Aug. 15, 1928, p. 4; *Pilot*, Aug. 16, 1928, pp. 1, 10.

[56] *Record-Herald*, Oct. 19, 1928, p. 8; Sept. 13, 1928, p. 10; June 15, 1928, p. 10.

[57] *Record-Herald,* Oct. 12, 1928, p. 8; *Pilot,* Oct. 4, 1928, p. 1; Nov. 1, 1928, p. 1.

[58] *Pilot,* Nov. 1, 1928, p. 4; Oct. 18, 1928, p. 4; Jones to Ada Jones, May 5, 1928, Jones MSS.

[59] *Pilot,* Nov. 8, 1928, pp. 1, 4; Nesbit, p. 546. Gerald Boileau noted that in 1928, Al Smith began a trend, which accelerated in 1932, towards the revival of the county Democratic Party, and that a substantial number of Progressives returned to the Democracy in the process. Boileau Interview, Aug. 21, 1975. Al Smith garnered 10,675 Marathon County votes, while the victorious Hoover nearly matched him with 10,127. Meanwhile the Republican candidate handily defeated his opponent by a margin of 93,946 statewide. These totals gave new hope to county Democrats who saw success just over the horizon for a party back in the political game. *Wisconsin Blue Book,* 1929, p. 815.

[60] Jones to Ada Jones, Jan. 8, 1929, Jones MSS. In contrast to the statewide Kohler bulge of 153,000 votes, the conservative hope bested his Democratic foe by a mere 250 in Marathon County. A cursory examination of the results reveals a strong Democratic comeback, especially in those rural areas historically identified with the party (and more recently with Progressive Republicanism). Democrats had reason for optimism coming out of the 1928 campaign. *Wisconsin Blue Book,* 1929, p. 845; Nesbit, p. 542.

[61] For evidence of early optimism coupled with an insistence on retrenchment, see David Bernhardt, "A Wausau Area Viewpoint: Early Depression Years, 1929-1932," May 2, 1973, research paper, University of Wisconsin-Marathon campus, in the hands of the author, pp. 10, 15-16; see also *Pilot,* March 6, 1930, p. 4; Jan. 2, 1930, p. 4; Dec. 26, 1929, p. 4; Nov. 21, 1929, p. 4.

[62] Kannenberg Interview, Boileau Interview, June 17, 1976. Others active in the Progressive movement of the 1930's were John Dittbrender, Frank Theil, Bert Rasmussen, and the other Kannenbergs, Fred and Ernest. Important centers for the Wausau movement were Socialist Herman Marth's Midget Cafe in the 1920's and Theil's Barber Shop, where the Progressive Club met in later years. The Midget was the scene of continuous political discourse between regular patrons like George Lippert, the Kannenbergs, and owner Herman Marth. Roland Kannenberg recalls meeting many political figures there, including county board members. While employed at the Midget, he "got a background of the problems of the rural and the poor." Kannenberg Interview; see also Gail Hoeppner, "Senator Roland E. Kannenberg," July 11, 1972, research paper, University of Wisconsin-Eau Claire, on file at University of Wisconsin-Eau Claire Library, p. 5. The only local party regular strong enough to withstand the Progressives tide in 1930 was stalwart Otto Mueller, firmly entrenched in the State Senate where conservatives often held sway. And even he was destined to fall before the Progressive onslaught in 1934.

[63] Though the incumbent identified himself as a Progressive, Kannenberg insisted that "Ellenbecker called himself a Progressive, but he really wasn't." There was, in fact, some disagreement in the liberal camp on this question. Boileau, for example, saw Ellenbecker as a bona fide Progressive.

In the senatorial race, Mueller nipped his Progressive challenger, Barber, by less than 400 votes out of 14,500 cast. The narrowness of the margin would come back to haunt the incumbent, when Progressives later eyed his seat in a recall campaign. Hoeppner, p. 8; Boileau Interview, June 17, 1976; *Pilot,* Sept. 18, 1930, pp. 1, 4. For discussion of Phil's 1930 comeback, see Nesbit, pp. 484-85.

[64] *Pilot,* April 10, 1930, p. 1; Boileau Interview, June 17, 1976. Boileau noted that "I was wet and he was dry . . . Most people in Wisconsin were wet, certainly in this area." On other issues, county Progressives "wanted to place the tax burden on the shoulders of those best able to pay . . . and favored old age pensions . . . Generally, the Progressive-stalwart split was like the modern liberal-conservative split." Boileau Interview, June 17, 1976.

[65] *Pilot,* Sept. 4, 1930, p. 6; Aug. 7, 1930, p. 1; April 10, 1930, p. 4; Sept. 18, 1930, p. 2; *Record-Herald,* Aug. 5, 1930, p. 4; Aug. 6, 1930, p. 8.

[66] Boileau Interview. June 17, 1976; *Pilot,* Sept. 4, 1930, p. 6; Sept. 18, 1930, p. 2. It was standing practice for the La Follette organization to back incumbents with Progressive voting records. Browne thus qualified for team support and even drew the backing of some Marathon County Progressives, such as Bert Rasmussen. But

once elected, the new Congressman was welcomed into the La Follette group because of his own liberal record.

The Wausau Progressive edged the incumbent 24,701 to 23,926 and thereby became the first Wausau man to serve in Congress since Alexander Stewart's service in Washington. Nomination as a Republican was normally tantamount to election, and in the 1930 general election Boileau ran unopposed. Boileau Interview, June 17, 1976; *Pilot*, Sept. 18, 1930, pp. 1, 4.

[67] "The Redistribution of Wealth," Mueller Clippings Book; *Pilot*, Feb. 5, 1931, p. 1; Sept. 24, 1931, p. 1; April 2, 1931, p. 4; June 5, 1930, p. 4; Bernhardt, p. 17; Nesbit, p. 487. Despite local suspicions, the *Pilot* urged the City of Wausau to abandon the "demoralizing dole and to substitute a logical system of work and pay which will maintain a creditable morale and produce a spirit of optimism." To minimize public expense, it recommended a work relief program that involved payment in scrip redeemable at accredited stores. So that the unemployed could contribute "services to the community" a "program of work for what is given" was needed "without delay." *Pilot*, Sept. 24, 1931, p. 4; Oct. 8, 1931, p. 4.

[68] Hoeppner, p. 10; "District Attorney Drafted Petition to Recall Senator," "Black Jack Weapon Used By Governor in Mueller Recall," Mueller Clippings Book.

[69] Hoeppner, p. 10. During the course of the 1932 campaign, the "radicals" were charged with having illegally secured names on the recall petitions. One later critic insisted that when Kannenberg "couldn't get enough names," he "wrote their names in for them" and "took names off the tombstones in the cemetery." The allegation remains unsubstantiated.

In addition, there were reports that many signers of the recall petition did so "without knowing what they were signing" and that some "thought they were signing nomination papers." Prehn Interview; *Pilot*, Aug. 11, 1932, p. 1. For ample evidence of Mueller support in the Marathon and Lincoln County press, see Mueller Clippings File.

[70] At one point, the convention officials had played the national anthem in a vain effort to force the Wisconsin dissidents to rise in a standing ovation for Hoover. *Pilot*, June 23, 1932, p. 1; April 7, 1932, p. 1; Boileau Interview, June 17, 1976; "A Memorial of Marathon County Bar Association for Walter A. Graunke," Nov. 19, 1973, courtesy Philip Graunke, Wausau.

[71] The most impressive totals were Roosevelt's 17,744 to Hoover 6,210 and Schmedeman's 15,426 to Kohler's 8,850. Even the incumbent Boileau was in jeopardy, though his bulge in Marathon County gave him a 2,585 edge over unknown Democrat Frank Chapman of Berlin. *Wisconsin Blue Book*, 1933, pp. 512, 533, 553, 628. For sample of editorial opinion in 1932, see Bernhardt, pp. 20-21; *Pilot*, Jan. 21, 1932, p. 4; July 7, 1932, p. 4; Sept. 15, 1932, p. 4; Sept. 22, 1932, p. 4.

[72] The *Record-Herald* believed that "Roosevelt may show what can be done by one not afraid of office holders . . . who will place the public good ahead of the personal greed of any one man." *Record-Herald*, Feb. 23, 1933, p. 6; see also March 1, 1933, p. 8; *Pilot*, July 20, 1933, p. 4.

[73] *Pilot*, Sept. 28, 1933, p. 1; Aug. 10, 1933, p. 1. Boileau indicated that 100 per cent compliance was achieved in Marathon County and that the N.R.A. "was not criticized too much once you explained it. It was just an attempt to lick the depression." Boileau Interview, Aug. 21, 1975. Wausau Mayor Otto Muenchow endorsed the agency and pledged the community's full cooperation with the Roosevelt Administration. *Pilot*, July 27, 1933, p. 1. While the local press was generally receptive, the *Pilot* urged that the "administration write the codes." The *Herald* disagreed, fearing that national standards on working hours would not benefit all workers in all states. *Pilot*, Sept. 21, 1933, p. 4; *Record-Herald*, April 7, 1933, p. 6. For evidence of early Wisconsin attempts to bring order to a chaotic lumber industry, see chapter 1; for general discussion of the state level proposal, see Nesbit, p. 487.

[74] Based on government figures, the *Pilot* estimated in September 1938 that $13,613,128.86 in federal dollars had been expended in Marathon County since 1932. *Pilot*, Sept. 8, 1938, p. 4. For evidence of Chamber of Commerce and County Board concern for creative use of federal work relief funds, see *Pilot*, April 8, 1937, p. 8; Jan. 18, 1934, p. 1; Feb. 15, 1934, p. 1; *Record-Herald*, Jan. 30, 1937, p. 1.

[75] *Pilot*, March 30, 1933, p. 1; April 27, 1933, p. 1.

[76] *Pilot*, May 18, 1933, pp. 1, 4; Feb. 16, 1933, p. 1. The May action caused greater apprehension than the first effort, which had been poorly-organized. Determined to curb violence, Sheriff H. M. Kronenwetter swore in three hundred deputies when Shawano County militants were rumored to be on the way to assist their Marathon County comrades. In fact, picketing remained non-violent and was confined to Marathon City, Stratford, and Abbotsford, pockets of sympathy for the strike. *Pilot*, May 18, 1933, p. 8.

[77] *Pilot*, May 4, 1933, p. 4; May 25, 1933, pp. 1, 8; *Record-Herald*, May 11, 1933, p. 10; May 18, 1933, p. 12; May 19, 1933, p. 8. The official tabulation of strike support in May revealed that 90 per cent of Marathon County farmers opposed the holding action. J. D. Beck to Phil La Follette (encl.) Aug. 22, 1936, Philip F. La Follette MSS.

[78] Reports throughout the state indicated that picketing centered in Marathon, Clark, and Wood Counties. The *Pilot* noted that "private cars, trucks, and all vehicles are being stopped and in many cases searched by bands of pickets." *Pilot*, Nov. 2, 1933, p. 1; Oct. 26, 1933, pp. 1. 5. Later in the month, after quiet had apparently returned to the county, Wausau was treated to a parade and demonstration of strength by cooperating farmers. As many as six hundred angry men milled about the court house, where a delegation was sent to complain about "heavy county governmental expense." But the strike was clearly at its fag end by this time. *Pilot*, Nov. 16, 1933, p. 8. For full treatment of the 1933 action in rural Wisconsin, see Herbert Jacobs, "The Wisconsin Milk Strikes," *Wisconsin Magazine of History*, Vol. IIIV (Autumn, 1951), pp. 30-35; Nesbit, p. 489.

[79] Gerald Boileau recalled that at first the concept of parity was not widely understood, although the leadership of the farm organizations grasped the policy and gave it their support. They understood the meaning of acreage restriction very well, as county farmers supported Boileau in a successful drive to prevent lands taken out of cotton and tobacco production from being used to raise dairy feeds. Taking land out of production was acceptable in Marathon County, only so long as it did not lead to competition for dairy farmers. Boileau Interview, June 17, 1976; *Record-Herald*, Dec. 3, 1937, pp. 1, 2; Dec. 11, 1937, p. 1; Jan. 7, 1938, p. 1; June 1, 1938, pp. 1, 2; April 21, 1933, p. 8. For evidence of Farmers Union backing for Roosevelt's programs, see Interview with Clarence Mielke, Aug. 22, 1975, Wausau, Marathon County Public Library Oral History Collection. By 1938, the *Herald* had retreated from its early, more tolerant position and launched an attack on AAA, particularly on the principle of a guaranteed salary for rural producers through government purchases of surplus commodities. There was, in the *Herald's* view, "something so completely screwy about it that it seems very likely to be tried" for "the screwier the proposal the more attractive it appears to be to the New Deal's so called planners of the more abundant life." *Record-Herald*, Oct. 7, 1938, p. 8.

[80] For comment on the primary role of Graunke in the third party movement, see Charles H. Backstrom, "The Progressive Party in Wisconsin, 1934-1946," (unpublished Ph.D. Dissertation, Department of Political Science, University of Wisconsin, 1956), pp. 53, 72; Boileau Interview, June 17, 1976; Kannenberg Interview. For discussion of the organization of the Progressive Party, see Backstrom, p. 46; Meyer, pp. 117-118; Donald Young, ed., *Adventures in Politics: the Memoirs of Philip La Follette* (New York: Holt, Rinehart & Winston, 1970), pp. 208-209; Nesbit, p. 490.

[81] Actually, the third party question was all but settled and the Fond du Lac meeting would be a ritualistic act of faith. The initial Madison conference involved a "picked group" of Marathon County personalities who were expected to favor the new departure. For Kannenberg, for example, there was never any serious doubt. He "thought it was a good decision," and believed that they "should have remained a third party" after 1946 when the Progressives broke up. Kannenberg Interview; Graunke to Philip F. La Follette, May 12, 1934; "Minutes of Statewide Conference of Progressive Leaders," March 3, 1934, Philip F. La Follette MSS; Young, pp. 209-210.

[82] Graunke was implying that in north-central Wisconsin, half-hearted Progressives had a habit of presenting themselves to the electorate as the real article. By adopting the Farmer-Labor Party label, all doubt concerning an aspirant's Pro-

gressive credentials would be eliminated. The six members of the Marathon County delegation were unanimous in their support of the third party, the establishment of which was never seriously in doubt, but found themselves on the losing side when the convention chose to call the new organization the Progressive Party. "Minutes of the Fond du Lac Progressive Conference," May 19, 1934, pp. 33, 54, 57, 76, 80-81; in the Philip F. La Follette MSS. Isen La Follette described the efforts of the left-wing group, which included the Marathon County delegation, as motivated by a desire to "emphasize the Marxian idea of the class struggle." To be sure, Graunke had insisted that "we have been ruled by the international bankers of Wall Street," but one must conclude that his was a native American radicalism rooted more in the soil than in exotic European social or political theory. Young, p. 210; "Minutes of the Fond du Lac Progressive Conference," p. 76.

[83] Meyer, p. 117; Boileau Interview, June 17, 1976. Boileau's decision to file as a Progressive was reportedly influenced by the threat of opposition by former Congressman Ed Browne if he remained within the Republican Party. Backstrom, p. 226. Boileau's announcement stressed consistency in principle. *Pilot*, June 28, 1934, p. 1.

[84] Wisconsin Democrats had been unsuccessful in consolidating their positions after the unanticipated victories of 1932. Schmedeman, whose background was in a conservative party of opposition, fumed as he observed Roosevelt court the La Follettes and their liberal backers in Wisconsin. Nesbit, p. 489; *Pilot*, June 14, 1934, pp. 1, 4; *Record-Herald*, June 9, 1934, pp. 1, 4.

[85] *Record-Herald*, June 11, 1934, p. 6; June 9, 1934, pp. 1, 3, 4.

[86] La Follette, in particular, "defended the new Progressive alignment, emphasizing the importance of its independence of the ideas and limitations of the two old parties." Late in the campaign, former Wittenberg resident Senator Gerald P. Nye of North Dakota came to endorse the new party for all "who hold that opposing parties should really stand for different things." *Pilot*, Oct. 25, 1934, p. 2; Oct. 4, 1934, p. 2; Nov. 1, 1934, p. 6. For material on the Kannenberg campaign, see Hoeppner, pp. 9-11; Kannenberg Interview. For a brief discussion of the first Progressive campaign, see Nesbit, p. 491.

[87] The *Herald* recognized that there was little to cheer Republicans, but also noted that while "Democrats nationally are rejoicing the country's endorsement of the New Deal, Wisconsin Democrats are feeling a bit chastened. They never thought Brother Phil would slip into the executive office, carrying all other Progressive candidates with him, under the shadow of Brother Bob's wing." *Record-Herald*, Nov. 7, 1934, p. 8; *Pilot*, Nov. 8, 1934, p. 4; Miner and Moore, p. 148.

[88] John J. Kimball, et al., to Philip La Follette, Dec. 10, 1933; see also Wisconsin Legislative Board, Brotherhood of Railroad Trainmen (H. R. Johnson, Sec.) to Philip La Follette, Aug. 30, 1934, Philip F. La Follette MSS. See also *Pilot*, Nov. 1, 1934, p. 1; June 9, 1932, p. 2; June 12, 1930, p. 7; Sept. 8, 1932, p. 1.

[89] A continuing problem for the FLPF was the uneven level of interest in rural areas. During its "active" period the Marathon County unit was one of a very few that maintained regular meetings and activities. But once Graunke had been "disciplined," he took Marathon County liberals out of the Federation to the dismay of many county activists. State Secretary Rutz did invite Marathon County members to reorganize under his tutelage. Predictably, the request from Wausau never came. Lester Schmidt, "The Farmer-Labor Progressive Federation: the Study of A 'United Front' Movement Among Wisconsin Liberals, 1934-1941," (unpublished Ph.D. dissertation, Dept. of History, University of Wisconsin, 1954), pp. 132-33; 156, 191. For comment on Phil La Follette's successful struggle with FLPF to maintain control of the burgeoning third party movement, see Nesbit, pp. 490-91.

[90] Boileau later recalled that it seemed unjust to hand one essentially non-producing group in the population as much as $400 per month when their working children were unable to earn anything near that figure. Boileau Interview, June 17, 1976. For opposition in the press, see *Record-Herald*, March 21, 1935, p. 10; Jan. 18, 1935, p. 8. Boileau's position was clearly stated in his "newsletter" of January, 1936, in *Pilot*, Jan. 23, 1936, p. 1; see also Jan. 9, 1936, p. 1 for discussion of Townsend Club organizational activity in the county.

[91] *Pilot,* Dec. 19, 1935, p. 5; March 14, 1935, p. 4; Feb. 6, 1936, p. 1.

[92] Kannenberg supported Long in part because he believed that World War I had required unequal sacrifice. He felt that "the real bottom of the trouble is a lifetime of war . . . the rich made great profits out of the war . . . they didn't want to share the wealth . . . The only reason war is won is for wealth." Hoeppner, pp. 30-31; Kannenberg Interview.

[93] Likening the demagogues of 1935 to the Populist radicals of the 1890's, the *Record-Herald* had earlier stated that when the national emergency had been explained "fairly and in an understandable manner, old-fashioned American common sense will rally about sane leadership once again." Yet there was always the possibility of "a new division between the major parties, based upon conservatism and liberalism, rather than the principles which have separated Republicans and Democrats for the past seventy-five years." *Record-Herald,* April 26, 1935, p. 10; March 19, 1935, p. 6.

[94] The incident occurred following a meeting at which Graunke had just refused assembly candidate A. H. Eberlein permission to address the Progressive Club. The chairman had urged members to back only "genuine Progressive candidates," adding that a "former secretary of the stalwart party was present." *Record-Herald,* n.d., Roland Kannenberg Clippings File, in possession of Mrs. Natalie Tackett, Maryville, Mo.; for discussion of Graunke's fight with the FLPF, see Schmidt, pp. 142, 161, 164-65. The Federation Secretary finally had to tell Graunke to halt his efforts to secure FLPF backing or face disciplinary action from the state board. Not surprisingly, Graunke ignored his advice. Schmidt, p. 165.

[95] *Pilot,* Sept. 10, 1936, p. 1. Kannenberg later explained his own backing for the Union Party in Populist terms. Lemke and the agrarian radicals were worthy of support because "they all tried to get a greater share of the wealth for the people." Kannenberg Interview.

[96] Kannenberg Interview; *Pilot,* Aug. 13, 1936, p. 1; Sept. 17, 1936, p. 4.

[97] *Pilot,* Oct. 29, 1936, pp. 1, 4; Graunke to Dow, Aug. 18, 1936; Graunke to Philip F. La Follette, Philip F. La Follette MSS. It was obvious from correspondence between the Governor's office and an impatient Walter Graunke that Phil was confident of a substantial Marathon County victory. He was in no rush to arrange his county appearance. Dow to Graunke, Aug. 19, 1936, Philip F. La Follette MSS.

[98] *Pilot,* Aug. 6, 1936, p. 4; Aug. 27, 1936, p. 1; March 19, 1936, pp. 1, 4.

[99] *Wisconsin Blue Book,* 1937, pp. 390-91, 432; Nesbit, p. 491.

[100] Mueller was not alone. Marathon County Democrats Frank E. Bachhuber and Frank J. Shortner joined him with ratings of .217 and .391, respectively. *Capital Times,* n.d., 1933, in Philip F. La Follette MSS; Kannenberg Clippings File. In later years Kannenberg asserted that "Phil considered me his heaviest hitter in the Senate." Kannenberg Interview.

[101] In 1959, a variety of the Kannenberg proposal was implemented when Marathon County erected the first extension campus with county funds after local officials had gained legislative clearance. For an account of Kannenberg's fight for a extension building in Wausau, see Hoeppner, pp. 21-23; Kannenberg Clippings File; Kannenberg Interview. For the *Milwaukee Journal's* wry criticism of Kannenberg on the "attendance" question, see *Pilot,* July 18, 1935, p. 1.

[102] The WDA, "fathered by Senator Roland E. Kannenberg," would have permitted the indirect state purchase and operation of utility plants, as well as assisted municipalities in utility acquisition. *Record-Herald,* Jan. 11, 1938, p. 1; see also April 1, 1937, p. 10; April 27, 1937, p. 6; Nesbit, pp. 487, 492.

[103] *Pilot,* July 9, 1936, p. 1; Rev. Howard Murray Jones to Ada Jones, March 2, 1934, Jones MSS. It is interesting to note that among the delegates to the Republican Convention were A. W. Prehn and R. W. Monk, who had often claimed Progressive credentials in past years. *Pilot,* July 2, 1936, p. 4.

[104] *Record-Herald,* Jan. 14, 1937, p. 12; *Pilot,* Sept. 24, 1936, p. 4; Aug. 6, 1936, p. 4. For a summary feature story on Landon's visit, see Win Freund, "Depression and Election-1936," *Wausau-Merrill Daily Herald,* Focus Section, Feb. 20, 1976, p. 15.

[105] Schmidt, pp. 186-87.

[106] In affronting Orzechowski, Graunke quarreled with no mean adversary. A man with a strong local following in the Polish community, he claimed to have

been "king" in town politics, capable of electing any local officer in Kronen-wetter with an endorsement. The proverbial bridesmaid when it came to state office, he failed in several bids for the state Assembly. Casimir Orzechowski, fragmentary personal memoir, Orzechowski Collection.

[107] Barber's suspicions did not prevent him from soliciting and receiving the FLPF endorsement in his unsuccessful reelection bid of 1938. Barber to Rutz, Sept. 9, 1938; Rutz to Barber, Sept. 13, 1938, Farmer-Labor Progressive Federation Papers, Milwaukee, Milwaukee County Historical Society (hereafter referred to as FLPF Papers); Schmidt, pp. 190, 227; *Record-Herald*, Jan. 15, 1938, p. 6. FLPF efforts to mollify the rural Federationists were fruitless. State Secretary Rutz's persistent attempts to "reorganize" the "once-powerful" Marathon County local ended in "an abysmal failure." Schmidt, p. 281.

[108] Boileau Interview, Aug. 21, 1975; June 17, 1976; Schmidt, p. 401.

[109] *Pilot*, Oct. 20, 1938, p. 1; Oct. 10, 1938, p. 2; for discussion of the coalition effort, see Nesbit, pp. 493-94; Leon Epstein, *Politics in Wisconsin* (Madison: University of Wisconsin Press, 1958), p. 43.

[110] *Record-Herald*, Nov. 4, 1938, p. 1; *Pilot*, July 28, 1938, p. 2. Boileau believes that the organized opposition of the Townsend movement was the key factor in his defeat. He recalls that Reid Murray's "principal campaign support was the Townsend Clubs." Although the Waupaca Republican was more conservative than Boileau, he signed a petition to have the Townsend idea brought to the floor of the House of Representatives. Boileau remains convinced that had the bill come up, Murray "would have been the last man in Congress to vote for it." Boileau Interview, August 21, 1975; June 17, 1976.

[111] The Church, opposed to the communist-backed Loyalists, asked that Boileau remove his name from a letter congratulating the Spanish legislature for meeting in the midst of civil war. Boileau, firm in his support of the democratic forces in the Spanish conflict, refused to comply with the request from Father Kennedy of the Milwaukee Catholic *Herald-Citizen*. As a consequence, Kennedy and the paper came out against him, asserting that signers of the letter were in favor of the communists. This allegation was reprinted in the La Crosse diocesan newspaper, setting off a flood of letters and calls from clergy and friends urging that he renounce his position. As a "believer in democracy," Boileau refused to budge. Boileau Interview, June 17, 1976; see also Backstrom, p. 181. For Kannenberg's comments on Progressive financial woes, see Kannenberg Interview.

[112] For discussion of the NPA, see Nesbit, pp. 493-94; Young, pp. 254-55.

[113] *Record-Herald*, Sept. 21, 1938, pp. 1, 2, 8; *Pilot*, April 7, 1938, p. 1; June 2, 1938, pp. 1, 4.

[114] There is circumstantial evidence that the FLPF had a hand in the rebellion. Earlier in the year "Doc" Barber had met Lippert on the West Coast and discussed county politics with him. Barber enrolled the itinerant liberal on the spot and encouraged a Lippert-Rutz meeting, subsequently sought by the FLPF leader himself. Seven months later Lippert turned up as a central figure in the revolt against the Graunke organization. Barber to C. C. Handley, Feb. 28, 1938; Lorayn Fox (Secretary to Henry Rutz) to Lippert, Feb. 28, 1938, FLPF Papers; *Pilot*, Oct. 6, 1938, p. 2; Oct. 13, 1938, p. 4; Oct. 20, 1938, p. 1; Oct. 27, 1938, p. 1; *Record-Herald*, Nov. 4, 1938, pp. 1-2.

[115] *Pilot*, Oct. 13, 1938, p. 4.

[116] *Record-Herald*, Nov. 9, 1938, pp. 1-3.

[117] Boileau Interview, June 17, 1976; Nesbit, p. 494; *Record-Herald*, Nov. 9, 1938, p. 10.

CHAPTER EIGHT

Beyond Progressivism: From Republican Dominance to Mainstream Liberalism, 1939-Present

Stunned by their defeat in 1938, Marathon County Progressives hoped to regroup for the crucial presidential contest of 1940. But they failed to see that the traditional alliance of leftist economics and isolationism in foreign policy was fraying at the edges. As the clouds of war gathered, Wisconsin Progressives divided into rival camps—one loyal to an increasingly interventionist Roosevelt and the other siding with the isolationist La Follettes. Phil La Follette's decision to launch the ill-fated National Progressives of America during the 1938 campaign had accelerated the decline of the liberal-isolationist alliance in Wisconsin politics.

But in heavily German Marathon County, the isolationist course of the new party was welcome. Not surprisingly, over one hundred county residents were listed as charter members of the Marathon County NPA, which was headed by La Follette operative Walter Graunke. Equally predictable was the fact that the officers were identical to those of the county Progressive Club of 1938:[1] Graunke was up to his old tricks again, using the same strategy as he had in controlling the local Farmer-Labor Progressive Federation at an earlier date.

Perceiving war as incompatible with domestic reform, Progressives spoke for a foreign policy of strict neutrality. Thus they endorsed views widely held in Marathon County before 1941. In part, the noninterventionist line may be traced to the bitter memories of the German-American experience during World War I. Equally significant was the revulsion against war that resulted from postwar disillusionment. As early as 1938 these feelings brought footdragging on rearmament because of concern "lest our country be stampeded into war." The *Record-Herald's* view, expressed in 1939, was that "nobody is going to attack us or has any reason to if our government will keep its eyes in the boat and quit meddling abroad." *Herald* Managing Editor Mark Byers reaffirmed these sentiments when he told the Wausau Jaycees that America had no right to interfere in the clash between fascism and democracy in Europe "either to preserve free government abroad or in this country."[2]

Given such views, it is not surprising that foreign policy loomed large as an issue in the 1940 presidential race. Nor is it a shock to learn that Roosevelt was attacked as a "war lord" who had gotten the country "half way or better into the war, and quite obviously intended to take us all the way in." The litany of administration sins was extensive: violating the third term taboo, coddling the shiftless, destroying rugged individualism, and increasing the tax burden. But these charges paled into insignificance in comparison to charges that the "Roosevelt war scare" would embroil the United States in the European holocaust. Speaking before the Marathon County Republican Women, Mrs. Robert A. Taft, wife of the Ohio Senator, after listing general New Deal failures, concluded that the election offered a clear choice between the "road to war" or Republican challenger Wendell Willkie's pledge that "no American boy will fight on foreign soil."[3]

So dominant were national issues that county voters were treated to what one observer termed the "dullest campaign in many a year." As the primary drew near, "campaign guns and political generals" were silent. While a few speeches had been made, "not one big political rally had been held in Marathon County." With the Progressives only a shadow of their former selves and Democrats showing little interest, the GOP was the only party to field a complete slate of candidates for county and assembly posts. The greatest excitement generated by the campaign came in October; several thousand Wausau citizens turned out to hear Willkie deliver a whistle-stop address denouncing the "third term" as a "policy that tends to take us down the road to dictatorship."[4] And despite the obligatory visits of Senator La Follette and Governor Heil, the unusual formality displayed suggested a sense of the imminent challenge that would soon transcend the arena of state and local politics.

When the last vote had been counted, the new configuration of county politics was clear—the Republican success of 1938 had been no fluke. Consistent in their support of GOP incumbent Heil, county voters also sent Republicans Orville Fehlhaber and Martin Lueck to Madison to support the gubernatorial choice. But the real bombshell came in the presidential race, where the electorate turned against Roosevelt and the New Deal. While the 1500 vote Willkie margin was modest, it was a far cry from the President's 10,000 vote landslide four years earlier. And while partisan realignment, disenchantment with the New Deal, and third term concerns were all important, the ethnic factor again emerged as a vital force in county politics, as the German-American preference for neutrality in foreign policy was expressed in a strong Willkie vote. As Democratic Chairman Clayton Crooks later recalled, foreign policy was a troublesome issue and Roosevelt loyalists encountered stiff resistance when they embraced Roosevelt's internationalism.[5]

As the Republican star rose in Marathon County, the Progressive Party went into precipitous decline. Assemblyman Dittbrender went down, Boileau failed to recapture his seat, and even the durable Senator La Follette saw his margin shrink dramatically, despite his isolationism. And once the war broke out, Progressives suffered from a marked leadership vacuum. Clayton Crooks observed that with Phil overseas and Bob, Jr. in Washington, the Progressives were cast adrift. While Walter Graunke carried on the fight, Republican successes gradually brought Progressive fortunes to a standstill. While La Follette backers maintained a complete slate of county committeemen, it became increasingly difficult to persuade quality candidates to carry the Progressive colors, as the party's vote-getting potential evaporated. Although Marathon County Progressives eked out one last victory when Orland Loomis edged Governor Heil in 1942, the win was clearly a swan song. Republicans had swept the remaining state offices. And if the Progressives had reached the end of the road, Democrats had been left in the ditch. Running a poor third, the county party again found itself in the role of the loyal and distant opposition.[6]

At the heart of liberal problems was their inability to reconstruct the fractured farm-labor coalition that had served Progressivism so well in the 1930's. Fumbling efforts to revive the old Farmer-Labor Progressive Federation following Graunke's suspension ended in abject failure. After Gerald Boileau's 1938 defeat, Wisconsin FLPF Secretary Harry Miller solicited the ex-Congressman's aid in reorganizing the Marathon County unit in 1939. The body's membership rolls did climb to 150 in that year, but the old combination was unable to put Boileau over in his comeback bid. Equally unproductive were wartime attempts to patch up the alliance. At the 1942 State Farmers Union Convention in Wausau, Graunke's plea for renewed political unity fell on deaf ears. Indeed, the bipartisan nature of the meeting itself spoke volumes about the futility of any bid to resuscitate the worker coalition of the desperate 1930's.[7] Such a development was not destined to appear on the county political scene until a reorganized Democratic party asserted its claim to farmer-labor support in the late 1950's.

Rather, the political story of Marathon County in the 1940's is one of Republican consolidation; for it was the GOP that became the most energetic party after the Progressive collapse. A number of factors contributed to this resurgence, including the salutary effect of the Heil and Goodland governorships on party strength. Control of the statehouse coupled with the leadership vacuum among Progressives was a strong boost to local Republican organizers. Even more significant was the emergence of strong local leaders such as District Attorneys Elmer Hohman in 1938 and Frank Loeffler in 1942. If local and county organization was the key to political prosperity, the office of District Attorney was the nerve center of any successful party operation; both Hohman and Loeffler fulfilled their responsibilities as partisan leaders with consummate skill.[8]

The potency of the new Republicanism was verified by a massive county victory in 1942, which sent Martin Lueck, Paul Luedtke, and William McNeight to Madison. Resisting this trend was the lone Progressive winner, successful gubernatorial candidate Orland Loomis, who edged the incumbent by a scant 1200 votes in Marathon County. Meanwhile, Democratic frustrations increased: while Everett J. Freeman captured the office of County Treasurer, he was lonely in victory. The sad state of the Democracy was laid bare by the fate of Attorney General hopeful James A. Fitzpatrick of Wausau, who ran a humiliating third in his home county.[9] As the election of 1944 drew near, therefore, there was little cause for optimism on the part of local Roosevelt supporters. The presidential race would confirm their darkest fears.

The anemic state of the President's party in Marathon County did not, however, prevent Wisconsin Democrats from holding their 1944 state convention in Wausau. The major development at the lackluster gathering was an attempt to reconstitute the farm-labor coalition that had served Wisconsin Progressivism so well. The effort took the form of party endorsements for two important and frankly symbolic candidates: Farmers Union President Kenneth Hones for Governor and A. F. of L. leader Marshall Whaling for Lieutenant Governor. Labor and farm leaders responded by pledging their support for the Democratic ticket and berating the long-suffering Herbert Hoover. Bitter memories surfaced as union leaders insisted that labor was not forgetting the "Hoovervilles of the early 30's." Equal treatment went to farm supporters who were cautioned against a "return to Hooverism, when no farmer could make ends meet." These incantations were followed by a pointed jab at Republican presidential candidate Tom Dewey, derided as "the mustached dandy from the city of New York"—hardly "the one and only farmers' friend."[10] The mysteries of populism included the need for a clear villain.

The Republicans themselves supplied the other important question to emerge at the Democratic love feast. For a few days earlier Wausau party leader Charles F. Smith had told his GOP comrades at their state convention that Roosevelt had "bungled" the war effort, and that the allies were winning "in spite of your FDR." Not only was the Republican Party dissatisfied with the conduct of the war, but it saw internal and foreign policies "on a toboggan due to the 'pinks' and 'punks'" Roosevelt had brought in. Smith's words were obviously standard campaign rhetoric, but "a strong undercurrent of resentment over the remarks" swept the Wausau Convention. Asserting that Wausau was a "city where everything is lovely and where man only is vile," former Senator Henry Bolens suggested that Smith "go to Berlin and give a speech." Likewise, Senatorial candidate Howard McMurray attacked the Wausau Republican as a "carping critic" and spokesman for "the diehard reactionaries who would rather beat Roosevelt than win the war." McMurray went on to exceed Smith's hyperbole with his own verbal overkill by describing the GOP as "covered with shame ever since the shrieking voice of Smith joined that of Goebbels in denunciation of President Roosevelt."[11] If nothing else, the momentary outbreak of excitement breathed life into a drab party function.

Far surpassing the Democratic parley in public appeal, however, was Vice-President Henry A. Wallace's Wausau campaign stop in October. Following a late afternoon campaign meeting at Mosinee and a public reception at the Hotel Wausau, the Vice-President addressed a rally described by Democratic Party Chairman Clayton Crooks as "the largest in Wausau's history." Partisan exaggeration aside, Wallace provoked an audience response "such as [had] seldom been witnessed here in campaign addresses." Capturing the crowd with his patented smile, he warmed to the occasion with welcome pledges of just peace and full employment in the postwar era. Well aware of the county's economic character, the Vice-President railed against the GOP farm record, charging that Republicans "had listened to dictation from Wall and La Salle Streets and the big millers for its farm program."[12] Under the Wallace spell, Democratic loyalists readily accepted his prediction of a Roosevelt victory.

A worthy adversary was the Republicans' major stump speaker of the 1944 campaign, Congressman Everett Dirksen of Illinois, who brought his own traveling show to the Grand Theater in the same month. Rejecting Democratic warnings against a change in wartime leadership, the GOP spokesman maintained that "the one indispensable man in history was Adam." The Illinois spellbinder arraigned the administration for excessive secrecy, unwise foreign commitments, and bankrupt domestic policies that held no promise of postwar stability. And if Dirksen was a skeptic, the county Republicans were non-believers. Their more strident attack linked the New Deal with "the road to Communism" under the aegis of American Communist Earl Browder and the CIO's Sidney Hillman. In taking that advanced position, the local party agreed with the *Record-Herald's* earlier reference to Browder's support of the President. The local paper thought it "plain to see who stands behind FDR . . . old Uncle Joe himself, boss of the Kremlin."[13]

In retrospect, it is obvious that Republican anxieties were unwarranted. An indicator of their growing strength was the very breadth of the county campaign waged in 1944. So energetic had the local party become, that its adherents boldly launched a Dewey organizing drive in the CIO and A. F. of L. under the leadership of J. F. Allard of Wausau and Kenneth Hoard of Mosinee. Their bid for a broadened Republican electoral base exposed a weakness in the Democratic armor that the GOP would exploit successfully until the late 1950's. And the hard organizational work of Hohman, Loeffler, and Smith resulted in a sweep that sent the Republican Party into the postwar era unchallenged as the dominant political force in Marathon County. Except for the Truman upset of 1948, the party would cling to that position until a fundamental Democratic Party reorganization would open the way for yet another shift in local political preferences after 1958, the ramifications of which are still being felt. Flush with the county Dewey victory, the *Herald* issued a timely reminder that "a strong minority of the nation stands opposed" to Roosevelt, whose victory was "a decision not to change horses crossing the turbulent stream of war—not a signal for social revolution."[14] Marathon County, like the Badger state, was clearly turning away from 1930's liberalism.

But some liberals could not accept the reality of the new order. Many Wisconsin Progressives devoutly believed that if only the party could ride out the war years, its domestic program would again arouse enthusiasm as the public turned away from foreign policy problems. Since 1938, however, the Progressives had experienced widespread defection to the ranks of the ascendant Republicans; this movement accelerated after the 1944 election revealed serious liberal weakness at the polls. In Marathon County this seepage had become a massive hemorrhage by the end of the war, so severe that the best that Progressives could hope for was the retention of Robert La Follette, Jr.'s precarious hold on his Senate seat. By 1946 the major question for the Senator had become the choice of a party vehicle to ensure the La Follette succession; and for all but the diehards, the drift was clearly in the direction of the Republican home of the early Progressives.

For all but the diehards. And Marathon County was the home base of the truest of the true believers—the irrepressible Walt Graunke. So it was that when the Wisconsin Progressives assembled for their own funeral ceremony at Portage, the Wausau firebrand led the charge in favor of preserving a separate liberal party identity. "A real power in those days," Graunke "went down swinging in his effort to retain the party's identity." His rhetoric sharp as ever, the old warhorse insisted that no Progressive worthy of the name should be willing "to crawl under the same blanket as Tom Coleman and President Truman."[15]

In fact, support for maintaining an independent Progressive party ran deep. One farm delegate characterized the event as a strange funeral "because we're having trouble getting the corpse into the grave." So strong was third party sentiment that Senator La Follette was forced to take the floor for a declaration of his own intent to return to the Republican fold. Until that point the third party forces had held

Veteran Progressive Firebrand Walter A. Graunke

their own, but La Follette's words changed the character of the meeting. Graunke later recalled that "we had a chance until the Senator spoke, but after that we lost ground fast." When the vote was tallied, Marathon County's eight votes were on the losing side, as the last of the Midwestern third parties was pronounced dead on March 17, 1946.[16]

While Graunke and his Marathon County colleagues had gone down swinging, they loyally pledged their support to La Follette in his bid for the Republican senatorial nomination. Predicting an early ideological split within the GOP ranks, Graunke confidently promised that "the Progressives will be found on the liberal side." Painfully aware of the truth in his words, the *Record-Herald* was less than enthusiastic over La Follette's homecoming. A biting editorial reminded readers of the Senator's earlier rejection of "a political maneuver that merely promotes my own or any one else's candidacy" and posed the rhetorical question: "How does that go again, Bob?" This skepticism was not shared by the county electorate, which gave Bob a 500 vote victory in his losing primary race. However, once the magic of the La Follette name was out of the picture, voters returned to their now-established pattern of Republicanism by giving a handsome 2700 vote margin to the man of the hour—Joseph R. McCarthy.[17]

In certain respects the Senator-elect was not an unknown in Marathon County. Having done legal work in the county during his years on the bench, McCarthy was respected by many members of the county bar. He is often remembered as a hard-drinking, card-playing, back-slapping visitor with a rather engaging personality. His character and energy aside, it is also true that he ran well in the rural German-American areas that had been important to the old La Follette coalition. More significantly, however, McCarthy benefited from the new Republicanism, which made the county a virtual GOP preserve from 1946 to 1958.[18]

In these "golden years" of county Republicanism, the party in power provided steady, if somewhat colorless, representation in the halls of government. So comfortable were county voters with Republican leadership that, in the memory of one observer, "you had to walk a mile to find a Democrat." One reason for the continuing GOP strength was the emergence of Melvin R. Laird as Reid Murray's successor in Congress in 1952. Always a consummate politician, Laird served the district effectively and worked assiduously to solidify his own political position. In the knowledge that Marathon and Wood Counties were the key to the Seventh District, he always gave particular attention to his Marathon County constituents. After riding in on the Eisenhower landslide of 1952, Laird combined workmanlike service with the power of the incumbency to build an impregnable position that would ultimately enable him to withstand the Democratic trend of the 1960.'s.[19]

But in contrast to responsible Republicanism, a new kind of politics had come to stalk the land by 1950, in the form of militant anti-Communism. Not that such concerns were new in the 1950's. Indeed, fears and suspicions of the Soviet Union may be traced back to the late war years when the *Record-Herald* chose to "honor" Bob La Follette, Jr. for speaking out against the European policies of Russia. These concerns were linked with the rise of militant labor by speaker A. A. Nicholson of New York, who warned Wausau Kiwanians of a communist future, already suggested by the power of the CIO's Sidney Hillman. In the immediate postwar years, anti-communism escalated to the point at which the *Record-Herald* equated red-baiting with "honor and patriotism." A strong editorial in 1946 asserted the need to "drive these weasels out into the open," on the theory that "a Communist exposed to the light of day is a Communist dehorned and harmless." Given such sentiment it is not surprising that in his 1946 senatorial campaign Joseph McCarthy stressed the Communist issue by running an ad charging some Democratic candidates with "communist backgrounds and thinking" and reminding voters that he was "100 per cent American in thought and deed."[20] In the aspirant's tough rhetoric there was a prophetic hint of things to come.

And come they did. As a result of Soviet expansionism in Eastern Europe, as well as a series of sensational espionage cases within the United States, the public was receptive to the arguments of men with easy answers to complicated foreign and domestic policy questions. And no simplifier proved more successful in the early 1950's than the junior Senator from Wisconsin.

The paranoia over the communist threat to internal security reached its zenith in Marathon County with the nationally-publicized "day under Communism" staged in Mosinee on May 1, 1950. Under the auspices of the Wisconsin American Legion and an enthusiastic local committee, Mosinee was converted into an American vision of a community under Communist control. Legion officials selected Mosinee as the site of the mock coup "because it is a typical American community, far removed from the scenes where Communists normally are active." Local citizens, "whose Americanism could never be questioned," voluntarily surrendered their freedom as an object lesson to all Americans.[21]

Mosinee Mayor Ralph Kronenwetter (left) Imprisoned by the "New Regime," May Day, 1950

On the eve of the "takeover," Communist "party cells" held an improbable rendezvous at the local American Legion clubhouse to "plot the overthrow of the city." But local patriots were not alone in their awareness of Mosinee's impending disaster. Equally alert was the Communist Party of Wisconsin, which blanketed the city with propaganda leaflets attacking the "boss," the "American Legion big shots," and "stool pigeons;" all of whom were accused of distorting the truth about life under Communism. Confronted with such unanticipated opposition, the authorities tightened security and "announced they were ready to combat any subversive incidents." One account suggested that "sleep was fitful Sunday night for residents of Mosinee, nervously aware that the rise of Monday's sun will bring with it Communism."[22]

At daybreak the wheels began to turn with the arrest of Mayor Ralph Kronenwetter and the liquidation of police chief Carl Gewiss. Their replacements were Joseph Kornfeder of Detroit and Benjamin Gitlow of New York, both ex-Communists imported for the occasion. The presence of penitent Communists lent an air of chilling reality to the proceedings and provided a measure of authenticity to the steps taken by the conspirators. Under their leadership Mosinee was treated to a day of confiscation, censorship, atheism, executions, and book-burning, with black bread and soup as the only available provisions. Replacing the *Mosinee Times, The Red Star* (appropriately printed on pink newsprint) announced the annihilation of the American Legion, whose members were regarded as "enemies of the people" to be arrested and tried forthwith. The publication also revealed the "purge" of "Pig Schweinler," whose "filthy capitalist sheet" (the *Times*) had been "guilty of printing insults and infamous lies regarding the Soviet way of life." Finally, the Council of Peoples Commissars proclaimed the people's triumph over capitalist rule and bourgeois government and the establishment of the United Soviet States of America.[22] All in a day's work.

While Mosinee's May Day brought national television, newsreel and press attention, there were other less noticeable evidences of the escalating concern over the threat of Communism, real or imagined. In September, 1950, for example, the Wausau Advertising Pool felt compelled to sponsor a prominent spread extolling the virtues of the American capitalist system. Disturbed by "those who say the communistic system of government provides more for the average man," the Pool asserted that the American worker makes more, has more, and enjoys more than any other citizen under any other system." Recognizing that capitalism had its flaws, such as periodic unemployment and depression, the advertisers still thought it good sense "to correct the faults rather than talk about changing the system." Equally committed were the central Wisconsin bankers, who in October heard Dr. Paul Kiniery of the Loyola University graduate school warn of advancing Communism. Holding forth at the Wausau Club, the Chicago educator told financial leaders that if the Communist element took over they would "simply be starved to death." Apart from that, they had "little to fear from Communism." Evidence of bone-deep concern over Communism was the capitulation of veteran liberal Walter Graunke, who reminded a Labor Day union audience of their "sacred obligation and solemn duty to do everything within their power to stop the onward march of Communism and monopoly." Rejecting both rightist and leftist dictatorship, the aging labor favorite thundered against both the "march of monopoly" and the "ruthless encroachment"[24] of its opposite number. Thus did liberalism succumb to the temper of the times.

Given such a milieu, the rise of the McCarthy star was predictable. Already popular in Marathon County, the junior Senator took Wausau by storm in October, 1950, when he filled the Elks Club with a call for the support of those who "hate Communists and love America." Buoyed by the intense enthusiasm of the overflow crowd he berated the Democrats and observed that something was "radically wrong with the nation." There was something of the snake oil salesman in his flashy presentation, which featured reproductions of "secret files" on "Chinese Reds" linked with suspect scholar Owen Lattimore and files allegedly belonging to such a well known "leftist" as Secretary of State George C. Marshall. A partisan response was heard in the resounding ovation that echoed throughout the hall at the conclusion of his performance.[25]

Without a doubt, McCarthy's appeal at the time was real. Republican chairman Richard P. Tinkham, who presided over the festivities, declared that the Senator had earned "recognition in the hearts of every one of us throughout the land." The county Republican Party was so taken with his message that it made Communism the lead issue on a major advertisement in the 1950 campaign: Democrats were linked with Alger Hiss, Judith Coplon, the loss of atomic secrets, and numerous communist associations. Clearly, 100 per cent Americanism was a powerful attribute in 1950. Observers of county politics often recall the tremendous pull of McCarthy in the early 1950's and the devastating effect of charges made against Democratic organizers. One worker for Thomas Fairchild against McCarthy in 1952, for example, later recalled being told by his neighbors in the Marshfield-Spencer area that he "ought to go back to Russia."[26]

The activities of Fairchild backers reveal that despite the climate of hysteria, there were those who stood against the tide. Close examination of the 1952 returns further indicates that Marathon County was somewhat less subject to the virus of militant anti-Communism than many neighboring areas. While McCarthy won in Marathon, his 55 per cent margin was lower than the 61 to 78 per cent he ran up in adjoining counties.[27] Even more remarkable was the personal action of one Wausau Republican and former McCarthy backer, who publicly expressed her profound dissatisfaction with the Senator before a group of Democratic women at the 1952 party convention. Prompted by the urgings of a Madison friend, Mrs. Mathew Gjetson leveled a broadside at the junior Senator, stressing his record on the bench, in the military, as a citizen, and as a public servant. Expressing a sense of "weariness," "shame," and "deep sorrow" over the man's "abuse of public trust," she indicted him as a "full blown demagogue." Her message was clear: "any voter who takes his conscience to the polls

Senator Joseph R. McCarthy Chats With D. C. Everest Aboard the Eisenhower "Look Ahead" Special Train, October, 1952

Courtesy of The Post-Crescent, Appleton, Wisconsin

cannot cast his ballot for McCarthy."[28] In a predictable footnote to this story of one person's personal testimony, the combination of the McCarthy phenomenon and the appeal of the liberal Adlai Stevenson brought a new convert to the Democratic cause in Marathon County.

And by this time, a quiet revolution was well under way in the Democratic ranks. For a variety of reasons, the county party was in serious trouble during the postwar years. Liberalism had been cast adrift with the collapse of the Progressive Party, while the regular Democratic organization was unable to field a full ticket in many local races. The momentum of Republican successes discouraged aspirants for office from running as Democrats; in short, "if you wanted to go places, it was easier to do it with the Republican Party." Postwar Democratic Chairman Clayton Crooks remembers clearly the futility of attempting to attract strong candidates to the party standard: the support was simply not forthcoming and the politically sophisticated knew it.[29]

While Democrats searched for help, the remnants of Progressivism fragmented. Many Progressives followed Senator La Follette into the GOP, where they remained after their leader's defeat. Others, like Walter Graunke, floundered aimlessly. Repelled by Republican ideology, the veteran liberal was equally cool to the Democratic Party he had long denounced as an engine of conservatism. It is also true that after long years as a Progressive leader, the role of supporting player held little appeal for the dynamic Graunke. Walt had trouble facing the reality that his cherished political organization had leaders but no followers. Thus, the liberal cause had reached a low point by 1946, when Democratic futility came into clear relief with the outbreak of an internal squabble that found challenger Archie Spatz ousting veteran Clayton Crooks with the aid of the politically-conscious C.I.O.[30] At the time, the clash seemed a battle to mount a dead horse.

And yet the aged mare lived to run again. In view of the Democrats' miseries, the Truman victory in the 1948 Presidential race was a decided jolt to local political observers. Never a Truman paper, the *Record-Herald* mechanically recorded the pre-election polling results with the observation that the campaign seemed lacking in excitement. Almost bewildered by predictions of a Republican landslide, the *Herald* in a moment of doubt posed a prophetic question: "could the polls be wrong?" It hardly seemed possible. With Henry Wallace sniping at the President from the left, the loss of liberal support seemed certain. His People's Progressive Party generated little support in Marathon County, although Wallace backers Emil Muelver of the CIO and Ben Riehle of Halsey did appear to represent important farm-labor constituencies. But when the chips were down, the only farm-labor coalition in evidence was firmly in the President's camp, as Truman outdistanced Dewey by 4400 votes in Marathon County.[31]

A trifle embarrassed, the *Record-Herald* explained the upset in terms of Republican overconfidence, labor's organizational work, and heavy government spending in the farm states. But even the Republican press gave Truman his due. In the *Herald's* opinion, "no nervier fight for the Presidency was ever made." Adding a curiously modern flavor to its analysis, it also chided the already red-faced pollsters for contributing to GOP apathy. Confronted with the charge that the polls had "created" Republican overconfidence, "Messrs. Gallup, Crossley, and Roper" were challenged to "explain themselves." Not a little surprised were Truman backers, as well, for the President's team had been composed basically of the established Democratic organization that had compiled a lackluster record in recent years. Such party veterans as Truman delegate Clayton Crooks, Ray Maguire, Kurt Bayreis, and John Ringle hardly represented new blood.[32] With such a tired organization, how did Truman pull it off?

A variety of factors explain the upset, and none was more significant than the temporary revival of the farmer-labor alliance that had historically been the key to Marathon County political success. Hard work with labor paid off, as Truman won in normally-Republican Wausau despite some Wallace sympathy in the CIO. Far more significant, however, was the rural vote for the President. Farm support for the incumbent and his program of price supports was manifest in the 4,000 vote majority stacked up outside Wausau. It was clear to the *Record-Herald* that "farmers liked things as they are, and didn't want to risk a change."[33]

By the same token, there was little movement away from the familiar pattern of Republican dominance in state and local politics in 1948. So tight was the GOP grip that Martin Lueck was returned to the Assembly by an awesome 6700-228 vote, while his colleague Paul Luedtke ran unopposed. There could be no doubt about the meaning of those returns. Perusing such comforting figures, few Republicans were concerned over the revolutionary forces simmering within the Democratic Party of Wisconsin at mid-century. Yet the *Record-Herald* was aware of the change under way. Although Carl Thompson's gubernatorial race ultimately proved unsuccessful, it had been evident since the primary that a band of "Young Turks" had captured the party and that "the Democratic old guard [had] been defeated."[34]

The realignment had begun with former Socialist Dan Hoan's movement into the Democratic Party to run for governor in both 1944 and 1946. Though never a victor, the Milwaukean made a vital contribution to the reconstruction of the party by bringing with him the lakeshore urban-industrial counties. In 1946 he carried the battle to Wausau with a speech denouncing "the Republican reactionaries" and urging that the "liberals again band together" to give the farmer and the common man "a voice in government." His bid to rebuild the old Progressive coalition in Marathon County was unsuccessful, though he was able to narrow the GOP margin over him in the 1946 race. In so doing, he helped bring many Progressive voters into the Democratic camp, once the new party came into being with the establishment of the Democratic Organizing Committee in 1948.[35]

It was this event that was to dramatically alter county politics by the late 1950's. The first step and the main hurdle for the DOC leaders throughout the state was the task of organizing Democratic units in as many Wisconsin counties as possible. The earliest Marathon County efforts came in 1949, when a group of state DOC workers persuaded Weston Democrat Archie Spatz to organize a meeting, with the intent of revitalizing a weak county party. The Spatz coup, engineered without the knowledge of county chairman Clayton Crooks, had all the earmarks of a palace revolution. In elevating Spatz to the chairmanship, the DOC had found it expedient to work with old line Democrats, because the young firebrands were nowhere to be found. Perhaps for this reason, the rebellion produced few tangible gains in the short run. One indication of this weakness was the failure of county Democrats to subscribe to the DOC monthly publication. Based on previous Democratic voting patterns, Marathon County's subscription quota was set at 281. By December, 1949, a grand total of 8 lonely persons were receiving the *New Wisconsin Democrat*; hardly an auspicious beginning.[36]

More promising was the election of a full slate of new officers in March, 1950. Inspired by the exhortations of Madison-based organizer Warren Sawall, a small band of traditional Democrats took a small step forward by selecting Mosinee mayor Ralph Kronenwetter as their leader. Less than a year later, another Mosinee resident, Rudolf Melaun, took over the county organizing committee after the mayor's untimely death. In this period progress was measured in inches, as reflected by the anemic 63 paid up members recorded in September, 1950.[37]

Despite the sobering statistics, some Democrats perceived a turn for the better. It was this optimism that brought the DOC to Wausau in October, 1951 for its annual convention. The "Young Turks" clearly hoped to reestablish a beachhead on what had once been liberal turf. Mindful of the organization's purposes, the *Record-Herald* welcomed the visitors and encouraged them in their drive to make the "party in Wisconsin stronger—but, mind you, not too strong."[38] Despite the diligent efforts of Melaun and his fellow-Democrats, however, the *Herald* had little cause for alarm on the local scene.

While the first, tentative steps on the road back to respectability had been taken, the party was still floundering in 1951 when young Robert Dean established his law practice in Wausau. Dean, who became an energetic organizer in the 1950's, later recalled that a normal turnout at a Democratic meeting in his early years of activity was a less-than-robust five or six persons. Convinced that "a two party system was necessary," the newcomer participated in a county organizational meeting with DOC operative Patrick J. Lucey in 1952. And a sparse group it was: Dean, Ray Maguire, George Cashulett, and a few more hardy souls became the nucleus of the new Democratic Party of Marathon County, such as it was. Under Dean's leadership, the party moved to rebuild itself on liberal-progressive lines. By most accounts, it was Dean who "kept the local troops together in times when there wasn't much to keep together." In short, he "*was* the Democratic Party in Marathon County in the 1950's."[39]

How was the feat accomplished? One thing is certain—all support was welcome. DOC organizers worked tirelessly with both New Deal Democrats and dissident ex-Progressives. While older Progressives had gone Republican, their younger comrades often found their way into the revitalized Democratic Party. In addition, some Progressive warhorses, like Walter Graunke, were disenchanted with La Follette's loss to McCarthy in 1946 and the growing conservatism within the Wisconsin GOP. The Marathon County DOC found that antipathy to McCarthy combined with the appeal of the urbane Adlai Stevenson "attracted a number of new Democrats to the party." They reported that in 1953 over half their members were people not previously active in Democratic politics. A diligent local membership committee, including Mrs. Gjetson, Henry Wachtl, and N. K. Nielsen was "largely responsible for the good result."[40]

In economic terms, the "new" Democrats succeeded in reassembling the old coalition of the 1930's. While labor gradually became more assertive, county farmers were dissatisfied with Eisenhower's Secretary of Agriculture, Ezra Taft Benson. The linkage of an unpopular Republican Secretary of Agriculture and decreasing farm prosperity afforded county and state Democrats a golden opportunity, upon which they capitalized. Out of this discontent, the farm-labor alliance was reborn. One student of Marathon County politics explained this resurgence as the result of a change in statewide AFL-CIO leadership. While noting that many rural areas began going Democratic long before any coalition was in place, Wausau liberal Jerry Madison viewed the influence of A. F. of L. President John Schmitt as crucial to long run success. Since Schmitt's predecessor had been a Republican, efforts toward farmer-labor cooperation had lain dormant. It was also true that the bedrock of Marathon County Democratic support was rural, and that the first hint of a crack in the Republican armor came in agricultural precincts. Particularly significant to farm voters were the Eisenhower policies, the tradition of New Deal-Fair Deal programs (REA, high parity levels, etc.), and the collapse of the milk market in 1954. In short, "the farmers were up against it, and they voted that way."[41]

"Voting that way" in 1954 meant a Democratic breakthrough with the election of Ben Riehle of Halsey to the Assembly. Symbolizing the coalition struggling to be born was the near miss of labor candidate James Sorenson of Wausau in the same year. Important to the Democratic revival was the increased militancy of agricultural interest groups. While the Farmers Union had long been identified with the Democratic Party, the organization found new strength in the 1950's in opposing the free market agricultural policies of Ezra Taft Benson. Likewise, many members of the REA cooperatives came to believe that the Eisenhower farm program had not encouraged strong price levels. Later, in the 1960's, the National Farmers Organization would add its muscle to what became an impressive vote-getting juggernaut. Most important of all, however, was the return of Marathon County farmers to their historic Progressive voting pattern. Once they began to hear traditional Progressive ideas from Democrats, they found it possible to pull the Democratic lever.[42]

But one victory did not a party make. The 1950's were Republican years in Marathon County, as evidenced by the strong Eisenhower showings of 1952 and 1956, as well as Melvin Laird's hold on Reid Murray's Congressional seat. Conversely, the county supported Democratic gubernatorial candidates from 1954 through 1958, in what seems a contrary trend. It is apparent that the county was undergoing the rebirth of a two-party system that had been weak since World War I.

In this trend, Marathon County mirrored voter behavior throughout Wisconsin, which was itself becoming a politically competitive state.[43] And while the GOP clung to Paul Luedtke's Assembly seat and sent Hugh Jones to the State Senate, the salad days were coming to an end. Crucial to this Democratic resurgence was the personal commitment of Robert Dean, who became the sparkplug of the new party organization in Marathon County. Dean's work as a labor lawyer enabled him to establish important ties with Marathon County workers that paid future dividends at the ballot box. The end result, after a near miss in 1954, was the young lawyer's landmark election to the State Senate in 1958, which brought to an end the Republican lock on the Marathon-Shawano County seat. When labor "came out" for the 1958 race, the final link in the chain of a resurgent liberal coalition was forged. While Dean clearly benefited from the widely acknowledged state Democratic breakthrough of 1958, the key to his victory lay in hard organizational work, particularly in the often-neglected Republican areas of Shawano County. Intensive canvassing was important in reassembling the Progressive coalition;[44] once that tie was renewed, Republican fortunes took a turn for the worse, the results of which are evident in modern Marathon County politics.

The impact of the 1958 election was electric; Dean's win, coupled with the gubernatorial success of Gaylord Nelson made the Democrats a "party of good standing." It was this campaign that moved the Democratic Party away from "opposition party status" and firmly planted the two party system in Marathon County soil. One local Democrat recalled that victory brought respectability, as voters gradually realized that the party was not out to "Sovietize Wisconsin." Finally, the 1958 race was significant in one more way. It helped lay the groundwork for John Kennedy's successful fight for the presidential nomination two years later, when most county party regulars worked for the young Massachusetts Senator.[45]

The Kennedy organization was based upon an effective Wausau-Mosinee axis forged by Senator Dean and Francis Rondeau, a prominent businessman. By February, Dean headed a twenty-six person Kennedy committee in Marathon County. His major opponent, Hubert Humphrey, found some support in labor, but it was loosely organized. Syndicated columnist Joseph Alsop quoted Humphrey leader Hal Verhoven of Wausau as declaring: "Sure I'm for Humphrey, but nobody ever told me I was county chairman of anything." Alsop noted that Marathon County was the key to the critical Seventh Congressional District, which was widely believed to be "the

The 1960 Presidential Primary Brings A Touch of Glamour to Marathon County Politics, Left to Right: unidentified well-wisher, State Senator Robert W. Dean, John F. Kennedy, Jacqueline Kennedy

swing district in Wisconsin's make-or-break Democratic Presidential Primary." And finally, after consulting twenty-three County Board members, he concluded that Kennedy was the Marathon County favorite.[46]

Despite a heavy Catholic Republican crossover vote, Humphrey managed to squeeze out a close county victory over the Massachusetts Senator in the April primary. And, while the Seventh District went for Kennedy in the primary, the crossover vanished in November as Richard Nixon was victorious. Many observers believed that the religious issue played a role in the Marathon County race. While Catholic Republicans returned to their traditional voting patterns to support Nixon, Kennedy trailed the rest of the Democratic ticket by 15-20 per cent in predominantly Protestant townships. And Kennedy chairman Robert Dean recalled that he had "spent a lot of time explaining that Catholicism was not a political issue."[47]

Dean's vigorous support of Kennedy may have been a factor in his unscheduled retirement from the State Senate two years later, for it was heavily Lutheran (and Republican) Shawano County that cost him reelection. The result was a surprise to many county Democrats, who had watched their man's meteoric rise in state politics. Elected minority leader of the Senate in his first term, Dean seemed in a strong position as the election drew near. Proud possessor of near-perfect farm and labor records (as defined by the AFL-CIO and Farmers Union), he was ready to run on his performance in office. Governor Gaylord Nelson gave the Wausau Democrat high marks on leadership ability. At a Schofield rally, the Governor cited Dean's "statesmanship" in representing the state as well as his district and voting "as his conscience and his reason told him." Particularly significant were his role in pushing through the $50 million resource development bill and a student loan law that had "proven an example for other states to follow."[48]

But these words were the obligatory partisan endorsements. There were other views expressed with equal vigor. While acknowledging Senator Dean's "personal abilities," the *Record-Herald* made a case for Republican challenger Charles F. Smith, Jr. as an "equally capable" man. Convinced that Wisconsin needed a Republican governor and a "Republican-controlled legislature," the Wausau paper supported not only Smith but also incumbent Paul Luedtke and newcomer Rupert Kurtzweil for the two county Assembly seats. Especially enthusiastic about Smith, the *Herald* was certain he would "vote in favor of tax and economy measures which will serve the best interests of every citizen." Meanwhile, Luedtke's opponent, David R. Obey, was dismissed as a talented "young man who has done well in the classroom but has had practically no experience in the school of hard knocks." Certainly the neophyte stood little chance against a "successful Wausau businessman" who had "served in government for nearly 50 years."[49]

In defining tax policy as a primary issue, the *Record-Herald* had selected a battleground on which Democrats would stand and fight. As the campaign developed, the GOP became closely identified with the general sales tax, which Dean, Obey, and other Democrats rejected as regressive. Dean told a Stettin audience in October that the Republican revenue policy meant "a tax on everything." A week later in Marathon he thanked the GOP for embracing the sales tax; in so doing, they had transformed the election into a "referendum in disguise." Clearly, the issue loomed large and Democrats felt close to the public pulse on this question. Meanwhile, the GOP, skittish over the implications of a general sales tax, advanced an exemption scheme to minimize the regressive features of the proposal. While he embraced the party position on tax policy, Smith tried to make government spending the primary issue in his campaign.[50]

By so doing, the Wausau lawyer was able to eke out a narrow win over Dean, thus successfully getting what Republican chairman Claude Jasper called the "tax monkey" off his back. No one was more surprised than Smith, who retired on election night thinking he had lost. Even in victory, Smith was unable to carry his home county; the Senator-elect definitely owed his success to Republican Shawano County. In Marathon, the old Progressive coalition remained intact, as the incumbent amassed a 1400 vote plurality. Just as Democrats had been surprised by Dean's 1958 upset victory, so his defeat in 1962 came as a considerable shock. Equally surprising was the emergence of David R. Obey as Paul Luedtke's successor in the Second Assembly District. If anything, the results confirmed the variegated voting patterns that marked Marathon County politics in the early 1960's. While Democrats had "held their own," Republicans were firmly entrenched in the state Senate and in some county courthouse positions. And although the *Record-Herald* was "particularly pleased" with Smith's victory, it expressed "grave doubts about how favorable will be the statewide results on Wisconsin's future." Fearful of a "fiscal fiasco," the *Herald* viewed the election of Democratic Governor John W. Reynolds as a vote "in opposition to reasonable tax reform."[51]

The mixed results of 1962 paved the way for a struggle two years later, when an important watershed in Marathon County politics would be reached. It has often been observed that the key to political power was dominance of the county courthouse. As early as 1958, Democratic State Chairman Patrick Lucey had declared that "the courthouses of Wisconsin constitute the real bases of political strength." Always the hard pragmatist, Lucey reduced the matter to a simple formula: a single uncontested county office "will cost state and congressional candidates at least 100 votes." In this belief, the Democratic chairman launched an intensive effort to control Wisconsin courthouse posts. Accepting the validity of Lucey's principle, Marathon County Democrats laid plans to capture the Republican courthouse stronghold. Their recruitment of a young and strong slate of candidates signalled a bid to make the 1964 race a highly competitive battle.[52]

High hopes notwithstanding, few would have predicted the result. The Democratic tide swept through county government, leaving in its wake only Treasurer Damon Reynolds and Surveyor Archie Becher to carry the local Republican standard. Among the victors were many who were to become permanent fixtures in county government, including District Attorney Daniel La Rocque, County Clerk Raymond Ott, and Register of Deeds Robert Gernetzke. The victory was consistent with a trend toward significant Democratic gains in upstate counties, the largest in Marathon County and the Tenth District. In the gloating words of the partisan *New Wisconsin Democrat,* Marathon County "took honors for the state by replacing four Republicans in the Court House with Democrats."[53] The "revolution of 1964" reflected not only Democratic prudence in candidate selection but also the coattail impact of the landslide for President Lyndon B. Johnson. Fears generated by the conservative candidacy of Barry Goldwater were important in an electoral disaster from which county Republicanism has never fully recovered. And while labor's Committee on Political Education worked hard for Democratic candidates, the returns confirmed the fact that the rural vote was the key to the courthouse door. This voting pattern remains an axiom of modern Marathon County politics.[54]

Thus, by the mid-1960's, the outlines of modern Marathon County politics were becoming clear. Democratic dominance in county office holding had been established, and Assembly seats would also remain in Democratic hands. Yet Republicans clung tenaciously to the Senate seat, first occupied by Smith and later by Walter John Chilsen. In one sense, therefore, county politics had come full circle, for the pattern of Senate conservatism as an island in a liberal sea had deep historical roots. It was, in fact, a modern adaptation of the political trends that had once ensured the positions of State Senators Claire Bird and Otto Mueller against first Socialist and then Progressive adventurism. The other GOP holdout was the durable Melvin Laird, whose congressional seat was assured by his careful attention to the district. In this instance, service was more significant than a political philosophy that increasingly diverged from the views of the county constituency. While the *Record-Herald* applauded the Marshfield Republican's "valuable insight and foresight," as well as his refusal to be a "rubber stamp Congressman," a slight decline in his Marathon County support had begun to occur by 1968. This slippage became wholesale defection when Senator Chilsen confronted young David Obey without the advantage of the incumbency in the 1969 special election after Laird's appointment as Secretary of Defense.[55]

Since the Obey victory of 1969, Chilsen has been the standard-bearer for the Marathon County GOP, with Sheriff Louis Gianoli and Treasurer Damon Reynolds occupying marginally political positions. What has been the key to Chilsen's longevity in office? Most observers agree that one important consideration has been the moderate image projected by Chilsen, who has bucked the conservative trend in his own party. This middle-of-the-road tendency accelerated following Chilsen's near loss to challenger Edward McClain in 1970, which underscored the gradual movement of the district towards mainstream liberalism. Equally significant to Chilsen was the ample publicity he had received as a television personality prior to his first term. He was, in the words of one commentator, a "known household face" by 1966; and since that time experience and the incumbency have also worked in his favor. In recent years, moreover, he has emerged as a man with both considerable political skill and a modicum of leadership potential in a party whose ranks have been thinning statewide. Finally, not to be dismissed lightly is the fact of overwhelming Republican strength in Shawano County, the historic power base of successful GOP Senators as far back as 1954.[56] Walter John Chilsen's success in an increasingly Democratic area stands as evidence of the modern reality of Marathon County politics: traditional conservatism is no longer viable currency in the area's political marketplace.

But even the Senator's middle-of-the-road image could not save him in the showdown Congressional race of 1969. That struggle confirmed Marathon County as Democratic turf, as upstart David R. Obey surprised observers with an upset victory. Many factors contributed to that result, including Republican overconfidence, dedicated Democratic organization, and a bruising Republican primary. Even more significant was a state issue—the much publicized "revenue gap" which surfaced in the wake of the 1968 Republican gubernatorial victory. With only one race to concentrate on, Democrats were successful at "underdog" psychology, as they linked Chilsen with Governor Warren P. Knowles and his increasingly suspect "no tax increase" campaign.[57] With Obey's reelection in 1970 the die was cast. The young Congressman had brought the district and the county back to a mainstream liberalism rooted in the area's Progressive tradition.

Yet even the vaunted Democratic organization could not escape the forces of history. By 1968, cresting opposition to the war in Vietnam had created serious fissures in the national Democratic Party organization, fissures that had dramatic impact in Wisconsin. In Marathon County, as elsewhere, the revolt against incumbent President Lyndon B. Johnson had modest beginnings. A January organizational meeting at the Wausau Labor Temple brought together a small band of politically obscure activists from peace groups, student groups, and the professional community. Forming a county organization under the leadership of local attorney Roy Traynor, the dissidents began the task of reaching the voters. While President Johnson began his drive in Wisconsin with the endorsement of most party functionaries and state legislators, Eugene McCarthy started with nothing but a disparate collection of alienated citizens—and an increasingly unpopular war as an issue.

By early March, the state organization was able to convene a major leadership conference in Wausau. The Wausau meeting provided an early stimulus for the campaign, after which "new McCarthy chapters began to spring up overnight" around the state. Since the Minnesota Senator spent much of the early campaign engaged in the vital New Hampshire battle, the Wisconsin and Marathon County efforts were in local hands until the final two weeks.[58] Outside personalities visiting Wausau to assist the local effort included Arnold Serwer of *Progressive* magazine, Allard Lowenstein of the Americans for Democratic Action, and actor Paul Newman.

While the McCarthy forces expanded at the "grass roots" level, the Democratic Party leadership was not totally inactive. National Committeeman David Carley confidently predicted that Johnson would "clobber" McCarthy in the state. Locally, Assemblyman Obey gave public support to the President, while privately encouraging a bombing halt in Vietnam. But for all practical purposes, McCarthy was the only organized candidate in the county. When Johnson coordinator Clement Zablocki contacted City Attorney Anthony Earl to arrange an organizational effort for LBJ workers, Earl's response was: "Do you want both of them there?" With that kind of Johnson support, and without Robert Kennedy or George Romney in the Wisconsin race, the Minnesotan won the election going away.[59]

On the Republican side, the stage belonged to Richard M. Nixon, then in the midst of his 1968 comeback campaign. His Wausau speech to the American Farm Bureau was enthusiastically received by an overflow crowd at the Holiday Inn. Their warm response was matched by a strong county vote in the primary, though the weakness of the opposition was a factor in Nixon's success. And despite a vigorous campaign, his victory was upstaged by the more dramatic events occurring in the Democratic race.

By most accounts, McCarthy's Marathon County victory could not have been attributed to his campaign appearance in Wausau. After local workers had assembled a crowd of well over 1000 at the Marathon Park Youth Building, the candidate underwhelmed his audience with a scholarly address obviously directed at the county's large rural population. Although McCarthy was introduced by local National Farmers Organization leader Adolph Gruny, Jr. of rural Marathon, the farm contingent at the gathering was minimal. And by downplaying his trump card, the war issue, McCarthy left his audience without an opportunity to express their obviously warm support. While the Senator's admiring troops waited to be thrilled, he responded with milk prices. The one spark of enthusiasm was ignited by a casual closing remark on the war and the significance of the election as a referendum on the future role of government in America.[60] Hardly the stuff of which crusades are made.

Yet when Lyndon Johnson made his historic speech announcing his retirement, the McCarthy volunteers in the crowded Third Street headquarters exploded with enthusiasm. And in that moment, it was possible to glimpse what one Wisconsin writer described as "the real story" of the campaign—the "way in which the McCarthy campaign closed the 'generational gap.'" Students, teachers, professionals, workers, and housewives stood united in a spontaneous expression of faith in a political system that appeared to have worked.[61]

Many of the "new faces" in Democratic politics had come to stay; four years later these same workers made up the shock troops of George McGovern's volunteer army in Marathon County. Indeed, the local significance of the McCarthy effort was that it brought a new group of activists into the county Democratic Party, many of whom remain involved today. In the short run, their presence led to some factionalism; but they have probably changed the complexion of the local party as they have been slowly integrated into the party structure. The most influential of the McCarthy group have been those willing to adopt the mainstream liberalism exemplified by the Obey leadership. A prime example is Representative Edward McClain, who has moved from the leftward fringes of the local party through a stint as county chairman to his present position as successor to liberal Anthony S. Earl in the Assembly. While the passage of time has tempered the spirit of left-liberalism, it may be successfully argued that "the party is still the domain of the activists—and it all stems from that campaign of 1968."[62]

As early as 1972, these "new Democrats" used their political experience to chart the course of the local party in the ultimately disastrous presidential race. In retrospect, supporters of heavily-favored Maine Senator Edmund Muskie recognize that the neophytes simply out-organized their adversaries. Still driven by opposition to continuing American presence in Vietnam, a group of hard-core liberals had established a Marathon County McGovern Committee by April, 1971. Not only did the McGovern forces lock up a majority of liberal activists, but they also took pains to develop a balance of socioeconomic groups on the working committee.[63] From the summer of 1971 on, the local McGovern forces held monthly meetings to plan a campaign and reinforce their commitment, at a time when their candidate was showing an unimpressive 3-5 per cent in national polls. While feverish activity was the by-word in the McGovern camp, the confident Muskie campaign chose to rely upon endorsements from influential state and local party leaders, including Congressman Obey and Marathon County Assemblymen Anthony Earl and Laurence J. Day. Local Muskie leader Tony Earl later noted that he had trouble generating volunteer support, and that those who did work were "the same old faces:" faithful Democrats, but not the types who got out to "beat the streets" for a candidate. Meanwhile, the McGovern legion was staffed with willing workers short on experience but long on enthusiasm. Their efforts enabled the organization to sustain an image of perpetual activity that was lacking in the Muskie camp until late in the campaign.[64]

Each candidate made appearances in Marathon County, and in each case, the response was impressive. While McGovern's December address at Wausau's Holy Name Catholic Church provided both the impetus and the cash for the remaining three months of the battle, Muskie's impressive visit to Marathon City in February created an illusion of momentum that allowed the favorite's supporters to dismiss the significance of McGovern's more active local organization. In fact, the Muskie fiasco of the final weekend was more characteristic of the Maine Senator's flawed campaign. On that occasion, a crowd of Muskie partisans at the Midway Motor Lodge were disappointed to learn that their candidate had passed up a Seventh District appearance and taping session for a Sunday at the Milwaukee Zoo without press coverage. For all practical purposes he had conceded. To some, Tuesday's results were an anticlimax. Looking back, Muskie worker Jerry Madison could conclude that the McGovern people "knew how to get the vote out" and that at the organizational level it was "no contest."[65]

The same might have been said of George McGovern's race against President Richard M. Nixon in the fall. The challenger's early white collar-independent support was insufficient to carry the day in November. In Marathon County as elsewhere, McGovern's errors and his identification with the "social issues" led to a blue collar desertion unparalleled in recent Democratic politics. A Republican drive stressing the incumbency (and featuring a Wausau visit by Tricia Nixon) was more than enough to turn back the advocate of "new politics" and make realists of many McGovern supporters. The President's 3,000 vote bulge marked the first GOP presidential victory in Marathon County since a younger Nixon had defeated John Kennedy twelve years earlier.[66]

But the McGovern debacle failed to alter the fundamental political character of Marathon County. So entrenched had the modern Democratic Party become that Wausau Republicans were unable to field a candidate against popular Assemblyman Anthony Earl; and Congressman Obey and Assemblyman Laurence Day easily outdistanced their opponents in an impressive show of strength running counter to the Nixon trend. Retaining their courthouse base, the Democrats have solidified their position as the dominant political force in a county rich in Progressive tradition. Indeed, with success has come a new set of troubles. Not only does overconfidence loom as a problem, but without the stimulus of underdog status it becomes more and more difficult to motivate "door-knocking canvassers." Thus, at the peak of success, the new majority party began to stumble in 1974; Edward McClain won by only a razor-thin edge over political unknown Frank Savino in the Eighty-Fifth Assembly District. And the traditional diversity of county politics was maintained with incumbent Walter John Chilsen's easy victory in the Senatorial race.[67] These results indicate a residual unpredictability in the county electorate, despite an increasing acceptance of mainstream liberalism.

The prosperity that has come to the Democratic Party may be attributed to a number of developments. First, the overwhelming Democratic dominance of Wisconsin politics since 1974 suggests that Marathon County has undergone a transformation shared by many Wisconsin voters in recent years. At the county level both Republicans and Democrats recognize the significance of the courthouse successes since 1964. As the modern Democrats became the prevailing political force at the county level, they were more successful in attracting young, aggressive political candidates. And certainly the impact of the "new Democrats" lent vigor to an already impressive Democratic organization. Symbolic of their significance was the extent to which the activists of the 1960's became integrated into the presidential campaign of Obey favorite Morris Udall in 1976. While not all McGovern operatives found their way to the Udall camp, their substantial presence was evidence of their growing pragmatism.[68]

Finally, and most significantly, political trends since 1958 mark a return to first principles for county voters who had supported militant liberalism in the generation after World War I. In this historic sense, the mainsteam liberalism of the 1970's cannot be viewed as an entirely new departure in county politics. Quite to the contrary, area citizens have again embraced the Progressivism that constitutes their modern political heritage. The third party activist at Portage had been right in 1946: in the last analysis, the Progressive spirit remained a living force in Marathon County.

FOOTNOTES

[1] "Officers of the Marathon County Chapter of the National Progressives of America," Nov., 1940; "Officers of the Marathon County Progressive Club," Nov., 1938, Philip F. La Follette MSS. For comment on the shattering impact of foreign policy issues on the Progressive coalition between 1938 and 1941, see Richard Carlton Haney, "A History of the Democratic Party of Wisconsin Since World War II," (unpublished Ph.D. dissertation, Dept. of History, University of Wisconsin, 1970), p. 16; Samuel Lubell, *The Future of American Politics* (New York: Harper and Brothers, 1952), p. 140.

[2] *Record-Herald*, Feb. 8, 1939, p. 5; Feb. 22, 1939, p. 8. Jones to Ada Jones, Feb. 26, 1938, Jones MSS. Aware of such opinion at home, Congressman Boileau had felt comfortable as a booster of the Ludlow amendment to require a national referendum before any declaration of war. Paul W. Glad, *The Dissonance of Change, 1929 - Present* (New York: Random House, 1970), p. 107.

[3] *Record-Herald*, Oct. 16, 1940, p. 1; Sept. 16, 1940, p. 6; Sept. 11, 1940, p. 8; Sept. 26, 1940, p. 14. So close was war, in the *Herald's* view, that it "could already smell the smoke" in a situation "all too reminiscent of 1916." *Record-Herald*, Oct. 26, 1940, p. 6.

[4] *Record-Herald*, Oct. 21, 1940, pp. 1, 4; Nov. 1, 1940, p. 1; Sept. 11, 1940, p. 1.

[5] In nine selected German-American townships, Willkie outpolled Roosevelt by a 2-1 margin in 1940; the same towns had given Roosevelt a 4-1 bulge four years earlier. The results included lopsided Republican margins of 301-26 and 311-54 in the bellwether German strongholds of Berlin and Hamburg. *Wisconsin Blue Book*, 1937, pp. 390-91; 1941, pp. 623-24. This voter behavior was common to many heavily-German counties nationwide, in which Roosevelt experienced heavy losses. Lubell, p. 132. Interview with Clayton Crooks, Sept. 15, 1976, Wausau.

[6] The Progressives' last hope vanished when Loomis died before his inauguration, thus elevating Republican moderate Walter Goodland to the governor's chair. Frances J. Sorauf, Jr., "The Voluntary Committee System in Wisconsin: An Effort to Achieve Party Responsibility," (unpublished Ph.D. dissertation, Dept. of Political Science, University of Wisconsin, 1953), p. 33; Meyer, p. 144; Crooks Interview; *Record-Herald*, Sept. 8, 1942, p. 13.

[7] *Record-Herald*, Oct. 21, 1942, pp. 1, 16; Harry Miller to Boileau, Aug. 31, 1939; "Marathon County Unit," 1939, FLPF MSS.

[8] In retrospect, Democratic Party veteran Clayton Crooks recalled the superb organizational abilities of the two Republicans. Hohman, in particular, enjoyed the support of a wide spectrum of voters. His success was crucial in building a county following for his party. Crooks Interview. The county thrust was paralleled by a statewide organizational drive spurred by Republican State Chairman Tom Coleman in the 1940's. Sorauf, p. 115.

[9] *Record-Herald*, Nov. 4, 1942, pp. 1, 9.

[10] *Record-Herald*, May 8, 1944, pp. 1, 10.

[11] *Record-Herald*, May 8, 1944, pp. 1. 10; May 6, 1944, pp. 1, 12; May 4, 1944, p. 1. The November returns suggest that Smith had some listeners in Marathon County, where Dewey outpolled the President by 2,500 votes. *Wisconsin Blue Book*, 1945, p. 633.

[12] *Record-Herald*, Oct. 25, 1944, p. 1.

[13] *Record-Herald*, Oct. 2, 1944, p. 8; Nov. 1, 1944, p. 2; Oct. 24, 1944, p. 1.

[14] *Record-Herald*, Nov. 8, 1944, pp. 5, 8; Sept. 14, 1944, p. 8.

[15] Graunke argued that all true liberals should recognize the issue as a matter of "expediency versus principle," and stand for the latter. *Record-Herald*, March 18, 1946, p. 1. See also Interview with Jerry Madison, Wausau, Sept. 29, 1976, in Marathon County Public Library Oral History Collection. Detailed discussion of the Portage Convention may be found in Roger T. Johnson, *Robert M. La Follette, Jr. and the Decline of the Progressive Party in Wisconsin* (Madison: State Historical Society of Wisconsin, 1964), pp. 113-117.

[16] The final tally was 284-77 in favor of a return to the Republican Party, with 51 favoring the Democrats and 3 the Socialists. The Marathon County dissenters were: Graunke, Peter Bisbecos, Henry Stanton, George Bliss, Art Weiland, all of Wausau; Charles Frayer, Schofield; John Dittbrender, Ringle; and Ben Riehle, Town of Halsey. *Record-Herald*, March 18, 1946, p. 1. For detailed comment on the Portage deliberations, see Johnson, pp. 113-117; Meyer, pp. 129-130.

[17] *Record-Herald*, Nov. 6, 1946, p. 8; Aug. 28, 1946, p. 14; March 20, 1946, p. 18; March 18, 1946, p. 1.

[18] James Donoghue has shown that Marathon County was clearly dominated by the Republican Party in the immediate postwar era. County voters cast their votes for Republican candidates 63 per cent of the time in the 8 elections from 1946 to 1960. Moreover, average Republican percentages of the major party vote for minor state offices in those years ranged from 53 per cent to 60 per cent. The figures are more striking when corrected to screen out Democratic gubernatorial victories in 1958 and 1960. James R. Donoghue, *How Wisconsin Voted, 1848-1960* (Madison: University of Wisconsin Extension Division, 1962), pp. 27, 39. For discussion of McCarthy strength among rural German-Americans, see Meyer, pp. 137, 205; Michael Paul Rogin, *The Intellectuals and McCarthy: the Radical Specter* (Cambridge: M. I. T. Press, 1967), p. 99. Rogin acknowledges German support for McCarthy, while denying a link between McCarthyism and Progressivism. This account of McCarthy's early contacts is based in part on Crooks Interview.

[19] Laird became such an awesome figure that the Democratic Party was often hard-pressed to recruit candidates to oppose him. As realists, most Democrats simply refused to believe they could unseat such a powerful incumbent. Madison Interview.

[20] McCarthy's simplistic attack concluded with the assertion that "this is America" and an admonition to "keep Americans in the government." The flavor of the full advertisement foreshadowed the "Twenty Years of Treason" thesis the Senator would later develop in a brutal attack on the New Deal-Fair Deal regimes. Meyer, p. 147. See also *Record-Herald*, Sept. 28, 1946, p. 6; Oct. 31, 1944, p. 9; June 14, 1945, p. 14.

[21] Members of the local planning committee were: Francis F. Schweinler, E. C. Klug, Henry Decker, N. S. Stone, Henry Steffes, William Mayer, Howard Dessert, Earl Bachman, E. P. Wenstadt, Al Moldenhaver, C. M. Green, E. J. Oleson. The prime purpose of the program was "teaching Americanism," according to Schweinler, who was named local chairman of the event. *Mosinee Times*, Aug. 8, 1957, p. 17.

[22] *Milwaukee Sentinel*, May 1, 1950, pp. 1-2; for evidence of Communist propaganda activity to counter the Legion's demonstration project, see "Mosinee — Mock Communist Takeover," Clippings File, Wausau, Marathon County Historical Society. Not only did the Communists attack the mill owners and their allies, but they also publicized their own May 1 peace rally in Milwaukee. In addition, they called upon Mosinee citizens to write their congressman in opposition to then-pending Communist control legislation.

[23] The propaganda sheet was filled with the writings and careers of Stalin and Marx, as well as news of the changes resulting from the coup. Workers were told that "only in a Communist society is it possible to increase production, reduce wages, and at the same time enrich each and every individual." The mill workers

386

were "informed" that paper was first made by Russian chemist Nocolai Chrono-
plotski, whose discovery was now affording them the necessities of life. They had
merely "been duped into the belief that the Ancient Chinese and Egyptians were
the originators of papermaking." The Young Communist League was instructed
on "the fallacies of the imperialist capitalist rule," while area automobile owners,
who had obtained cars "by shackling the workers," learned that "their former privileges no longer exist[ed]." *The Red Star*, "Mosinee-Mock Communist Takeover,"
Clippings File; see also *Mosinee Times*, Aug. 8, 1957, pp. 17, 51; *Record-Herald*,
May 1, 1950, p. 1. In a tragic footnote to Mosinee's big day, Mayor Ralph Kronenwetter, himself a grudging participant, suffered a heart attack on his way to an
evening Americanism rally and died one week later. *Mosinee Times*, Aug. 8, 1957,
p. 56.

[24] *Record-Herald*, Sept. 5, 1950, pp. 1, 14; Oct. 21, 1950, pp. 1-2; Sept. 6, 1950, p. 19.

[25] Clearly, McCarthy's presence was deemed an asset, for he was surrounded by
a literal court of attendants, including gubernatorial candidate Walter J. Kohler,
Jr., Congressman Alvin O'Konski, Assemblymen Martin Lueck and Paul Luedtke,
Clerk of Court Neal Jones, District Attorney Robert Altman, County Clerk Lucile
Zielsdorf, Sheriff Carl Mueller, Register of Deeds Andrew Miller, and Senator
Clifford Krueger. *Record-Herald*, Oct. 6, 1950, p. 1.

Merrill attorney Leonard Schmitt, who challenged McCarthy in the 1952 primary,
clearly recalls widespread backing for the incumbent among Marathon County
"regular" Republicans. Although many disliked the Senator, few were willing to
repudiate a Republican in office. Consequently, Schmitt received no support from
the Marathon County party or its leaders in his unsuccessful bid to unseat McCarthy. He at least had the personal satisfaction of exposing the incumbent's excesses.
In Schmitt's words, "I knew what he was and I called him on it." Telephone Interview with Leonard Schmitt, Merrill, Nov. 17, 1976. Mrs. Mathew Gjetson of
Wausau, Chairman of Independents for Reuss of Marathon County, noted that she
"was a good friend of Schmitt, but was already committed to the candidacy of
Milwaukee's Henry Reuss." And a voice from the past, Roland Kannenberg of
Mercer, agreed: he refused to support Schmitt in the belief that only Reuss had
a realistic chance of defeating McCarthy. *Capital Times*, June 28, 1952, pp. 1-2.

[26] It is also true that the linkage between the Democrats and alleged sympathy
for Communism, once forged in the public mind, remained a factor in county
politics until the late 1950's. Madison Interview. For coverage of the McCarthy
visit in 1950, see *Record-Herald*, Oct. 6, 1950, pp. 1, 8; the 1950 advertising spread
may be found in *Record-Herald*, Nov. 3, 1950, p. 22.

As the irrationality escalated, a note of caution was heard from the editorial
columns of the *Record-Herald*, which sounded an alarm over the lengths to which
the search for Communists had gone. While endorsing the need for concern, the
Herald rightly noted a new "hysteria" that was overstepping the bounds of reason.
Urging that the "government take over," the paper sought "no witch hunts."
Record-Herald, Sept. 19, 1950, p. 18. In the final analysis, however, the acceptance
of wide government authority was itself a danger to the "innocent persons," whose
interests the *Herald* wished to safeguard.

[27] The single exception was Portage County, where his 54 per cent edge approximated his Marathon County performance. Donoghue, p. 97. See also Madison
Interview.

[28] Mrs. Gjetson's "fiery speech" describing McCarthy's "conduct as a Senator" as
"truly scandalous," was cheered by the fifty listeners at the Democratic women's
meeting. *Milwaukee Journal*, June 28, 1952, pp. 1, 3; *Record-Herald*, June 28, 1952,
p. 10; "The McCarthy Record," 1952, in the possession of Mrs. Mathew Gjetson,
Wausau.

[29] Crooks Interview; Madison Interview. These perceptions were painfully accurate. County Democratic losses in Presidential contests between 1936 and 1944
had been dramatic, a pattern quite common in German-American counties. The
Democrats experienced a 23.5 per cent decline in Marathon County. In many Wisconsin areas, "war—particularly war with Germany—was associated with bitter
memories . . . the fact that once more a Democratic Administration became the
harbinger of World War added force to older grudges." Meyer, p. 142. In the
postwar era, wartime voting patterns were strengthened.

[30] *Record-Herald,* Sept. 5, 1946, p. 1; Crooks Interview; Madison Interview. While Graunke would attend Democratic functions, his heart was with the old Progressive Party. Madison Interview.

[31] *Wisconsin Blue Book,* 1950, pp. 701-702; *Record-Herald,* Oct. 20, 1948, p. 20. For evidence of long-standing antipathy towards Truman in the local press, see *Record-Herald,* Nov. 4, 1944, p. 10.

[32] *Record-Herald,* Nov. 3, 1948, p. 18; Crooks Interview.

[33] *Record-Herald,* Nov. 3, 1948, p. 18; Madison Interview; Crooks Interview. Other factors also played a role. The Wallace candidacy "took the left-leaning image away from Truman" and aided the President in finding the middle road. In addition, it may be argued that "Dewey was not a candidate'for central Wisconsin Republicans," whose first choices had been Harold Stassen and Douglas MacArthur in the presidential primary. And finally, Republican overconfidence and Democratic organizational efforts were important factors in determining the ultimate outcome. Madison Interview. It should also be noted that some scholars argue that a German-American swing to the Democrats was crucial to the Truman victory. Samuel Lubell asserted that the 1948 election demonstrated that "many voters may not even be consciously aware of how ethnic feelings influence their voting." He notes that while exceptions occurred, "Truman's greatest gains generally came in the same German-American counties where Roosevelt suffered his heaviest losses in 1940." Lubell, pp. 133-34. Ethnic considerations aside, the economic factor seems to have been a more powerful political force in Marathon County.

[34] In the general election, the upstart ran surprisingly well in Marathon County, trailing Gov. Oscar Rennebohm by less than 1000 votes out of 28,000 cast. *Wisconsin Blue Book,* 1950, p. 702; see also p. 760.

[35] While 1948 witnessed the organization of the modern Democratic Party in Wisconsin, Dan Hoan's 41 per cent of the three party vote as early as 1944 "marked the emergence of the Democrats as a New Dealish party and as the major opposition, instead of the Progressives." Epstein, p. 49; see also Nesbit, p. 528. Hoan's Wausau appeal in 1946 was tailored to a labor audience with an eye to the agricultural hinterlands as well. *Record-Herald,* Sept. 29, 1946, pp. 1, 16. With the Progressive Party off the ballot, the Democrat was able to cut the 1944 deficit of 5200 votes to 2700. While the turnout was considerably below that of the presidential year, it is likely that some of the county's 2900 Progressive votes of 1944 moved to the Democratic side of the ledger two years later. *Wisconsin Blue Book,* 1946, p. 633; 1948, p. 642.

[36] *The New Wisconsin Democrat,* December, 1949, p. 2. For comments on the Spatz takeover, see Crooks Interview. One active central Wisconsin DOC operative recalled that organizational work was certainly under way before 1951, since the voluntary organization staged its 1951 convention in Wausau. Local workers were essential to any such undertaking. Telephone Interview, Milton Schneider, Wisconsin Rapids, Nov. 6, 1976. Other local Democrats agreed that organizational efforts took place prior to the 1950's revival. Telephone Interview, Francis Bachhuber, Wausau, Nov. 6, 1976.

[37] *The New Wisconsin Democrat,* Sept., 1950, p. 7. Other officers in 1950 were N. K. Nielsen, Leo Fahl, and Rose Kryshak of Wausau.

[38] *Record-Herald,* Oct. 19, 1951, p. 4. The Wausau convention is more fully discussed in Haney, pp. 152-154. For treatment of the DOC and its organizing tactics, see Haney, p. 112; Sorauf, pp. 49, 123; and Epstein, p. 51.

[39] Madison Interview; comments on the plight of the Democratic Party of Marathon County in the early 1950's and on DOC efforts to reverse the situation are based, in part, on an interview with Robert Dean, Sept. 8, 1976.

[40] *The New Wisconsin Democrat,* Oct., 1953, pp. 5-6. By 1952, Roland Kannenberg had joined his liberal colleague Walter Graunke as a convert to the "new" Democratic Party. Regarded by some Democrats as an "unwelcome addition" to the party, Kannenberg surfaced at the 1952 convention as a candidate for Alvin O'Konski's Congressional seat with a proposal for a soldier's bonus to World War II veterans. *Milwaukee Journal,* June 27, 1952, pp. 1, 21; *Capital Times,* June 28, 1952, p. 1.

The movement of Progressives into the Democratic Party is discussed in both the Madison and Crooks Interviews. This trend is confirmed by modern scholarship, which illustrates that "old Progressive counties became new Democratic power bases." Haney, p. 87.

[41] Madison Interview; see also Haney, p. 222.

[42] In this sense, there was "nothing new" about the coalition other than the Democratic label. Madison Interview.

[43] Donoghue, pp. 1, 86-87; Angela Burger, *Benchmarks in Wisconsin Politics, 1956 and 1972* (Madison: University of Wisconsin Extension, 1975), p. 1.

[44] The Democratic Party of Wisconsin had "suddenly come of age" in 1958, and in the words of Patrick Lucey, "temporarily" become "the majority party." Theodore White, in *Making of the President 1960*, described Wisconsin Democrats in 1958 as "fashionable, full of vigor, victorious." Haney, p. 396. Marathon County, then, was sharing in a trend which swept the state in 1958 and seemed pregnant with meaning for the political future. Comments on the 1958 county race are based upon Madison Interview and Dean Interview. Areas of staunch Democratic support were found in a band of townships stretching from Reid, Bevent, Mosinee, and Kronenwetter in the southeast through Schofield and Weston to Marathon, Cassel, and Rietbrock in the northwest. While rural areas tended to cast Democratic ballots, Wausau and the villages remained strongly Republican.

[45] Madison Interview.

[46] Joseph Alsop, "Kennedy and Mink Lead in Wisconsin," *Miami Herald*, Feb. 17, 1960, p. 6A; Dean Interview. For comment on the significance of the Seventh District in the 1960 primary, see Haney, p. 411; Madison Interview. Kennedy worked the Seventh District very hard. As early as the fall of 1959, a major state organizational meeting was held in Wausau. Attended by 100 state Kennedy leaders, this conference was the scene of intensive planning for the state effort. The Massachusetts Senator made campaign appearances in both Wausau and Marshfield during the primary battle, while Dean labored successfully to line up Marathon County party "regulars." He also traveled the Seventh District promoting the Kennedy cause. Dean Interview; *Record-Herald*, Nov. 13, 1959, pp. 1, 7; Madison Interview.

[47] Dean encountered especially stiff opposition in the heavily Lutheran areas of Shawano County. Dean Interview. In Marathon County, the religious dimension of the campaign was evidenced by the results in German Lutheran areas. In Hamburg, Berlin, Texas, Maine, and Stettin, for example, Kennedy trailed gubernatorial candidate Gaylord Nelson by substantial margins. *Wisconsin Blue Book*, 1962, pp. 826-27; see also Madison Interview; Haney, pp. 443-44.

[48] "Election News," Nov., 1962, pp. 1-2, Clippings Book, 1962 campaign, in possession of Robert W. Dean, Wausau. The Dean record promised to seal the farmer-labor alliance once again, as he scored 20 out of 20 and 19 out of 20 on key farm and labor bills, respectively. *Ibid.*

[49] The local paper was convinced that "to insure full and fair consideration of its interests," Marathon County needed a "good Republican delegation." *Record-Herald*, Nov. 2, 1962, in Dean Clippings Book.

[50] The challenger viewed legislative reapportionment as another significant question in 1962. He also felt that his own ties with town chairmen and County Board members were helpful to the cause. Many observers credited his victory in part to a vigorous personal campaign, particularly in areas of traditional Republican strength such as Wausau and the rural precincts to the northwest. Finally, the significance of his father's name and the assistance of Melvin Laird played a role in the outcome. Interview with Charles F. Smith, Jr., Wausau, Nov. 16, 1976; Interview with Bradley Nielsen, Wausau, Dec., 1976; *Record-Herald*, Oct. 9, 1962; Oct. 25, 1962; Oct. 26, 1962; Oct. 30, 1962; Smith Campaign Leaflet, in Dean Clippings Book.

[51] *Record-Herald*, Nov. 7, 8, 1962, Dean Clippings Book; see also Madison Interview. There was an element of validity in the *Record-Herald's* concern, for the closeness of the race set the stage for a fierce struggle over the 1963 budget that ended in a virtual deadlock, finally broken by Reynold's decision to accept the sales tax.

Smith's pre-election estimate of his own prospects is drawn from telephone interview wi h Ben Powell, Wausau, Dec. 2, 1976.

[52] Haney, pp. 347-48; Madison Interview. The Lucey effort had increased Democratic courthouse seats from 104 in 1958 to 125 in 1960. In 1964, the figure jumped

to 152. Haney, pp. 347-48. An important Marathon County breakthrough was Patrick Crooks' election as District Attorney in 1962, which put a chink in the Republican armor. These inroads in county offices had a substantial impact upon Democratic fortunes from 1964 on. Smith Interview; Powell Interview.

[53] *The New Wisconsin Democrat*, Nov., 1964, p. 3; Haney, p. 348; Madison Interview. One former Republican also noted that the conservatism of the county GOP organization hampered their own candidate selection process. Powell Interview.

[54] Madison Interview; Nielsen Interview.

[55] By 1968, Laird's percentage of the total vote had declined from a record 63 per cent in 1960 to a more modest 56 per cent in 1968. Chilsen could capture only 43 per cent of the county total. William Smiley, III, "Voting Trends in Rural Marathon County," research paper, Dept. of Political Science, University of Wisconsin Center, Marathon County, 1973 (in possession of the author), p. 5; data sheets attached; *Record-Herald*, Nov. 1, 1962, Dean Clippings File.

[56] Madison Interview; Smith Interview; Nielsen Interview; Powell Interview. Even his Democratic adversaries acknowledge that Chilsen is more moderate in his views than many rank and file Republicans. He has compiled a middle-of-the-road labor and farm record that has enabled him to survive in a district that is receptive to his "folksy" personality. Madison Interview.

The importance of mainstream political views to success at the polls was underscored by Republican Ben Powell's strong challenge to Assemblyman Ben Riehle in 1966. Though Powell's liberal Republicanism had considerable voter appeal he failed to dislodge the incumbent. His progressive political views subsequently drew him into the Democratic Party.

[57] Madison Interview.

[58] Arnold Serwer, "Gene McCarthy's Winning of Wisconsin," *Progressive*, XXXII (June, 1968), p. 25.

[59] Madison Interview; *Wisconsin Blue Book*, 1970, p. 822. The McCarthy margin of 5,000 votes in the primary shrank to a Humphrey edge of only 1,300 over Richard Nixon in the general election. These totals reflected both Republican crossover in April and the candidacy of George Wallace in November.

[60] In addition to Gruny, the Senator shared the platform with Abbotsford attorney Jack Nikolay and Wayne Bassett of the Wausau Public Library, a long time McCarthy supporter. Press accounts described a "somewhat unresponsive" audience and a speech which "failed to spark significant applause, except upon his entrance and when approaching and leaving the podium." *Record-Herald*, March 27, 1968, pp. 1-2.

[61] For comment on the McCarthy campaign in Wisconsin by a key participant, with particular reference to the closure of the "generational gap" and the role of the "grass roots" organization, see Serwer, pp. 25-26.

[62] Madison Interview; the assimilation of McClain into the party mainstream was perfectly consistent with his past political behavior. Unlike many of the rebels of 1968, McClain's opposition to the war was more the product of his belief that it was senseless public policy than a conviction that it was immoral. Hence, his movement towards pragmatism represented no change in his basic political views. McClain's support of Edmund Muskie in 1972 was a logical extension of his political realism.

[63] While the original Steering Committee was dominated by professionals and educators, it also included both labor and farm representatives as well as persons identified with the local party organization in low-level positions. This careful attention to interest group balance on the committee was evidence of the political experience gained by the activists since 1968. "News Release," April 14, 1971, in files of McGovern Co-Chairman James J. Lorence, Wausau; see also Howard R. Klueter, "The End of the New Beginning: the Muskie Campaign in Wisconsin, With Special Emphasis on the Seventh Congressional District," research paper (fall, 1972), University of Wisconsin, Dept. of Political Science, in hands of author, p. 4; see also Madison Interview.

[64] Klueter, "The End of the New Beginning," pp. 12-13.

[65] Madison Interview. Klueter notes that the last minute debacle at the Midway Motor Lodge was only the last of many incidents during the Muskie campaign in which indecision and organizational weakness were evident. One early break-

down occurred when Muskie showed up an hour and one-half late for a crucial meeting with a farm-labor-activist group at the Wausau Labor Temple. After his tardy entrance, the Senator "gave a short, easily forgotten speech in which he called Dave Obey 'Bill' twice." The end result was a less-than-favorable first impression made on Seventh District Democrats. Klueter, pp. 7-8; 15-16; 19-21.

More impressive, and of great concern to many local Democrats, was the arrival of the George Wallace road show in Wausau. Complete with country-western music by Billy Grammer and George C. Wallace, Jr., the Alabama governor exhorted a capacity crowd at Wausau East High School to "send them a message." While the Wallace faithful gathered within, the AFL-CIO Committee on Political Education spread its own message outside the door; its anti-Wallace literature reflected escalating Democratic anxieties over the Governor's appeal.

[66] A casual look at the returns suggests that the McGovern candidacy alienated blue collar voters normally found in the Democratic column. Ward after ward in working class districts went to Nixon, as the neutrality of organized labor was felt in a dramatic way. While the Wausau west side wards were going Republican, the traditional Democratic rural areas failed to provide sufficient margins to offset wholesale blue collar defection. Only in the most solid Democratic towns, such as Bevent, Cassel, Emmet, and Reid was McGovern able to exceed the 1968 Humphrey margin. In only 28 of 87 precincts reporting, was the Democratic candidate able to match or exceed the Humphrey totals; and of these, 19 could be classified as rural. General Election Computer Printout Returns, Nov. 7, 1972, in Lorence File; for further evidence of blue collar defection from the Democratic Presidential column, see Madison Interview.

[67] Madison Interview; *Wisconsin Blue Book*, 1973, p. 828; 1975, pp. 827-831.

[68] Madison Interview; Smith Interview; Powell Interview. Jimmy Carter's successes in the Seventh District stand as solid evidence that endorsements are declining in significance as a force in modern Wisconsin politics. While Udall edged Carter in Marathon County, he lost the district. Thus the district's Democratic voters had again chosen a presidential candidate who lacked the support of local organizational leaders. And not to be forgotten were the 3,600 votes cast in Marathon County for another political "outsider," Alabama Governor George C. Wallace. Thus, the county electorate has retained a healthy independence in recent times. Computer printout of 1976 election returns, in files of Howard R. Klueter, Wausau.

Selected Bibliography

I. PRIMARY SOURCES

   A. MANUSCRIPT COLLECTIONS

John J. Blaine Papers, Wisconsin State Historical Society, Madison, Wisconsin.

Albert D. Bolens Papers, Wisconsin State Historical Society, Madison, Wisconsin.

Neal Brown Papers, Area Research Center, Stevens Point, Wisconsin.

William Campbell Papers, Wisconsin State Historical Society, Madison, Wisconsin.

Charles Dodge Collection, Wisconsin State Historical Society, Madison, Wisconsin.

Employers Mutuals Papers, Area Research Center, Stevens Point, Wisconsin.

Farmer-Labor Progressive Federation Papers, Milwaukee County Historical Society, Milwaukee, Wisconsin.

Michael M. Harrington Papers, Wisconsin State Historical Society, Madison, Wisconsin.

Paul Husting Papers, Wisconsin Historical Society, Madison, Wisconsin.

Reverend Howard Murray Jones Papers, Wisconsin State Historical Society, Madison, Wisconsin.

Philip F. La Follette Papers, Wisconsin State Historical Society, Madison, Wisconsin.

Francis McGovern Papers, Wisconsin State Historical Society, Madison, Wisconsin.

John D. Mylrea Journals, Marathon County Historical Society, Wausau, Wisconsin.

Casimir Orzechowski Collection, Marathon County Historical Society, Wausau, Wisconsin.

Marvin Rosenberry Papers, Wisconsin State Historical Society, Madison, Wisconsin.

Robert Schilling Papers, Wisconsin State Historical Society, Madison, Wisconsin.

Socialist Party Papers, Marathon County Historical Society, Wausau, Wisconsin.

Don Streeter Collection, in possession of Don Streeter, Wausau, Wisconsin.

Wisconsin Nonpartisan League Papers, Wisconsin State Historical Society, Madison, Wisconsin.

B. PROCEEDINGS AND MINUTES OF BUSINESS AND CIVIC ORGANIZATIONS

Cook, Calvin, comp. "Summary of Marathon County Board Proceedings, November 14, 1911 - April 24, 1912." Marathon County Historical Society, Wausau, Wisconsin.

International Brotherhood of Teamsters, Local 446. "International Brotherhood of Teamsters, Local 446 Minute Book, March 16, 1937 - October 4, 1939." Area Research Center, Stevens Point, Wisconsin.

Marathon County Council of Defense. "Proceedings of the Marathon County Council of Defense, May 3, 1917 - February 20, 1918." Marathon County Historical Society, Wausau, Wisconsin.

Northern Hemlock and Hardwood Manufacturers' Association. *Some Lumber Problems, Minutes of the Sixth Annual Meeting.* Wausau, Wisconsin: Secretary's Office, 1915.

Wausau Boom Company. "Minute Book, Wausau Boom Company, 1871-1905." Marathon County Historical Society, Wausau, Wisconsin.

C. NEWSPAPERS AND JOURNALS

American Lumberman. 1899-1906, 1910, 1927.

The American Sheep Breeder, 1916-1917.

Athens Record. 1904-1945.

The Badger American. 1923-1924.

The Breeder's Gazette. 1916, 1918.

Capital Times. 1916, 1922, 1927, 1933.

Central Wisconsin. 1857-1910.

The Country Gentleman. 1918.

Eye-Opener. 1952-1953.

Facts About Your Government. 1959-1967.

Good People. 1976.

Green Bay Press-Gazette. 1946.

Lakeland Times. 1958.

Marathon County Farm Journal. 1919-1930.

Marathon Times. 1909-1930.

Marshfield Herald. 1912.

Miami Herald. 1960.

Milwaukee Journal. 1931, 1939, 1945, 1946, 1961, 1975, 1976.

Milwaukee Sentinel. 1890, 1895, 1898, 1900, 1946, 1950, 1955-1958.

Mosinee Times. 1898-1907, 1957, 1975.

The New Wisconsin Democrat. 1949-1966.

Sheboygan Press. 1946.

Stratford Journal. 1919-1921, 1923-1924.

Wall Street Journal. 1975.

Wausau Daily Record. 1897-1907.

Wausau Daily Record-Herald. 1907-1974.

Wausau-Merrill Daily Herald. 1975-1977.

Wausau Pilot. 1890-1940.

West Plains (Mo.) *Daily Quill.* 1975.

Wisconsin State Journal. 1930, 1950.

D. GOVERNMENT PUBLICATIONS AND RECORDS

Commons, John R. *An Economic Survey of Wisconsin.* Madson: Prepared at the Request of Governor Philip La Follette, December, 1931.

Davis, M. G., comp. *A History of Wisconsin Highway Development 1835-1945.* Madison, State Highway Commission of Wisconsin, 1947.

Industrial Commission of Wisconsin. *The Primary Election of 1910 and the Presidential Primary of 1912.* Madison, 1912.

Marathon County Circuit Court. Miscellaneous File, State of Wisconsin vs. Wausau Paper Mills Company, Case Number 25183. Clerk of Circuit Court, Marathon County Court House, Wausau, Wisconsin

Marathon County Circuit Court, Miscellaneous File, Alvin E. O'Konski vs. Marathon Electric Manufacturing Corporation, Case Number 19329. Clerk of Circuit Court, Marathon County Court House, Wausau, Wisconsin.

Marathon County Resource Development Council. *Overall Economic Development Plan.* Wausau: 1966.

Roth, Filbert. *Forestry Conditions of Northern Wisconsin, Wisconsin Geological and Natural History Survey,* Bulletin No. 1, Economic Series No. 1. Madison, State of Wisconsin, 1898.

U.S. Department of Commerce, Bureau of the Census. *County and City Data Book.* 1949.

U.S. Department of Commerce, Bureau of the Census. *County Data Book.* 1947.

U.S. Department of Commerce, Bureau of the Census. *Census of Manufactures.* 1900, 1910, 1920, 1930, 1933, 1940.

U.S. Department of Commerce, Bureau of the Census. *Census of Population.* 1870-1970.

U.S. Department of Commerce, Bureau of the Census. *Census of Retail Trade.* 1933, 1935, 1940, 1972.

U.S. Department of Commerce, Bureau of the Census. *Census of Wholesale Trade.* 1935, 1940, 1972.

Wisconsin Blue Book. 1901-1970.

Wisconsin Committee on Land Use and Forestry. *Forest Land Use in Wisconsin.* Madison, Executive Office, 1932.

Wisconsin Historical Records Survey Project. *Inventory Of*

The County Archives of Wisconsin, Number 37, Marathon County. Madison, Wisconsin Historical Records Survey Project, 1940.

Wisconsin State Board of Health. *Stream Pollution In Wisconsin,* A Joint Report of the Conservation Commission and State Board of Health of Wisconsin Concerning Activities in the Control of Stream Pollution, From July 1, 1925 to December, 1926. Madison, State of Wisconsin, 1927.

Wisconsin State Department of Agriculture. *Marathon County Agriculture,* Wisconsin Crop Reporting Service Bulletin. Madison, State of Wisconsin, 1940, 1946, 1954.

Wisconsin State Department of Agriculture. *Wisconsin Livestock, Dairy, and Poultry,* Special Bulletin No. 78. Madison, State of Wisconsin, 1961.

Wisconsin State Department of Agriculture. *Wisconsin Livestock, Dairy, and Poultry,* Supplement to Special Bulletin No. 78. Madison, State of Wisconsin, 1963.

Wisconsin State Department of Agriculture. *Wisconsin Crops,* Wisconsin Crop and Livestock Reporting Service, Special Bulletin No. 80. Madison, State of Wisconsin, 1962.

Wisconsin State Department of Agriculture. *Wisconsin 1962 Crop Summary,* Supplement to Wisconsin Crop and Livestock Reporting Service Special Bulletin No. 80. Madison, State of Wisconsin, 1963.

Wisconsin State Department of Agriculture. *Wisconsin Rural Resources, Marathon County,* Crop Reporting Service Bulletin. Madison, State of Wisconsin, 1956.

Wisconsin State Department of Agriculture. *Wisconsin Rural Resources, Marathon County, 1958 Supplement.* Madison, State of Wisconsin, 1958.

Wisconsin Statistical Reporting Service. *Wisconsin Agricultural Statistics.* 1966-1968, 1971, 1973, 1974, 1975.

E. INTERVIEWS

1. MARATHON COUNTY PUBLIC LIBRARY ORAL
    HISTORY COLLECTION

Boileau, Gerald J.
Corey, Irwin
Duranso, Marshall
Fehlhaber, Orville
Forester, Alice
Forester, John E.
Geurink, Wilhelmina
Gruny, Adolph, Jr.
Hagge, Daniel
Karlen, Louis
Karlen, Mrs. Louis
Kuechle, Benno E.
Loeffler, Frank
Madison, Jerry
Mielke, Clarence
Olson, Carter
Prehn, Mr. and Mrs. Delos
Schuette, Marvin
Stevens, Glenn
Streeter, Don
Stueber, Leona
VanDouser, A. M.

2. INTERVIEWS BY THE AUTHORS

Bachhuber, Francis E. Wausau, November 6, 1976 (tele-
    phone).
Boileau Gerald J. Wausau, June 17, 1976.
Crooks, Clayton J. Wausau, September 15, 1976.
Dean, Robert W. Wausau, September 8, 1976.
Dessert, Margaret. Mosinee, June 21, 1976 (telephone).
Dodson, Bill. Wausau, October 22, 1975.
Gesicki, John. Poniatowski, August 30, 1975.
Kannenberg, Roland. Mercer, June 27, 1976.
Landon, George C. Wausau, June 30, 1976.
Nielsen, Bradley. Wausau, December, 1976 (mail).
Powell, Ben. Wausau, December 2, 1976 (telephone).

Rankl, Clarence. Town of Holton, August 4, 1975.

Rankl, Clarence. Town of Holton, April 13, 1976 (telephone).

Schmitt, Leonard. Merrill, November 17, 1976 (telephone).

Schneider, Milton. Wisconsin Rapids, November 6, 1976 (telephone).

Smith, Charles F., Jr. Wausau, November 16, 1976.

Sitko, Mrs. Conrad. Town of Kronenwetter, August 15, 1970.

Former Athens area resident (anonymous at his request) Wausau, April, 1976.

F. MISCELLANEOUS PRIMARY SOURCES

"Building in Basics." Tenneco film.

Bowman, Francis F., Jr. "An Analysis of the Wausau Industrial Area." Wausau Area Chamber of Commerce, 1939.

Campbell, William J. *History of the Republican Party of Wisconsin Under the Convention Plan, 1924 to 1940.* Oshkosh: Privately Published, 1942.

Carter Campaign File. In possession of Howard R. Klueter, Wausau, 1976.

Clippings Book, Election of 1962. In Files of Robert W. Dean. Wausau.

Clippings Book, Otto Mueller Senatorial Career. Marathon County Historical Society, Wausau.

Drott Marks 50 Years. Company broadside.

Everest, Kate Asaphine. "How Wisconsin Came By Its Large German Element." *Collections of the State Historical Society of Wisconsin,* Volume 12. Madison: Democrat Printing Company, 1892.

Fitch, Edwin M. and Curtiss, Ruth L. *Industrial Trends in Wisconsin.* Bulletin of the University of Wisconsin, Madison, 1933.

League of Women Voters, Wausau, Wisconsin. "Foreign Trade and Manufacturing in Marathon County (Seventh Congressional District)." June, 1956.

Levi, Kate Everest. "Geographical Origins of German Immigration to Wisconsin." *Collections of the State Historical Society of Wisconsin,* Volume 14. Madison: Democrat Printing Company, 1898.

Marathon County Economic Development Council. *Manufacturers & Processors Directory of Marathon County.* Wausau: Wausau Area Chamber of Commerce, 1975.

Marshall, D. G. "Cultural Background of Wisconsin People (Nationality Background)." State Historical Society, Madison.

Martin, George Alfred, comp. "Wausau in 1900."

"The McCarthy Story." Speech by Mrs. Mathew Gjetson, Democratic State Convention, 1952.

Mc Govern Campaign File. In possession of James J. Lorence, Wausau, 1972.

"Mosinee — Mock Communist Takeover." Clippings File, Marathon County Historical Society, Wausau, May, 1950.

National Land Colonizing Company. *How You Can Get A Wisconsin Farm.* Bulletin 1, Madison, n.d.

National Land Colonizing Company. *Letters From Farmers On Ready-To-Start Farms.* Bulletin 3, Madison, n.d.

National Land Colonizing Company. *Marathon County, Wisconsin, Home of Ready-To-Start Farms.* Bulletin 4, Madison, n.d.

"Otto Schoepke's Autobiography." Marathon County Historical Society.

Sanford, Albert Hart. "The Polish People of Portage County." *Proceedings, Wisconsin State Historical Society,* 1907, pp. 259-288.

Serwer, Arnold. "Gene McCarthy's Winning of Wisconsin." *Progressive,* Volume XXXII (June, 1968), pp. 24-27.

The Wausau Advancement Association. *Farming in Marathon County, Wisconsin.*

Wausau Chamber of Commerce Annual Reports. 1934-1975.

Wisconsin State Chamber of Commerce. *Market Studies, Wausau and Marathon County.* Madison, 1944.

II. SECONDARY SOURCES

A. BOOKS

A Case History. Racine: J. I. Case Company (privately published), n.d.

Allen, Frederick Lewis. *The Big Change, America Transforms Itself, 1900-1950.* New York: Perennial Library, 1969.

Bopf, Della. *Rib Mountaineer, The Mountain and a Township.*

Bowman, Francis. *Paper In Wisconsin, Ninety-Two Years Industrial Progress.* Rothschild, Wis.: privately published, 1940.

Burger, Angela. *Benchmarks in Wisconsin Politics: 1956 and 1976.* Madison: University of Wisconsin Extension, 1975.

Burnett, Etta., et al. *Spencer, Wisconsin, 1874-1974.*

Carstensen, Vernon. *Farms or Forests, Evolution of a State Land Policy for Northern Wisconsin, 1850-1932.* Madison: University of Wisconsin Press, 1958.

Child, Clifton James. *The German-American in Politics, 1914-1917.* Madison: University of Wisconsin Press, 1939.

Colby, Wisconsin Centennial, 1873-1973.

Connor, Mary Roddis. *A Century With Connor Timber, Connor Forest Industries, 1872-1972.* Stevens Point: Worzalla Publishing Company, 1972.

Donoghue, James R. *How Wisconsin Voted, 1848-1960.* Madison: University of Wisconsin Extension Division, 1962.

Epstein, Leon. *Politics in Wisconsin.* Madison: University of Wisconsin Press, 1958.

Faust, Albert Bernhardt. *The German Element in the United States, Volume 1.* New York: The Steuben Society of America, 1927.

Fiftieth Anniversary Of Workmen's Compensation In America, Fiftieth Anniversary Of Employers Mutuals of Wausau. Wausau: Employers Insurance of Wausau (privately published), 1961.

Fries, Robert F. *Empire In Pine, The Story of Lumbering in Wisconsin, 1830-1900.* Madison: The State Historical Society of Wisconsin, 1951.

Fuchs, Lawrence H. *American Ethnic Politics.* New York: Harper Torchbooks, 1968.

Glaab, Charles N. and Larsen, Lawrence H. *Factories in the Valley: Neenah-Menasha, 1870-1915.* Madison: The State Historical Society of Wisconsin, 1969.

Glad, Paul W., ed. *The Dissonance of Change, 1929 - Present.* New York: Random House, 1970.

Goldman, Eric F. *Rendezvous With Destiny.* New York: Vintage Books, 1955.

Gregory, John G., ed., *West Central Wisconsin: A History,* Volume 2. Indianapolis: S. J. Clarke Publishing Company, Ind., 1933.

Helgeson, Arlan. *Farms In The Cutover: Agricultural Settlement in Northern Wisconsin.* Madison: The State Historical Society of Wisconsin, 1962.

Hidy, Ralph, Hill, Frank, and Nevins, Allen. *Timber and Men: The Weyerhaeuser Story.* New York: The MacMillan Company, 1963.

Holton's Heritage.

Johnson, Roger T. *Robert M. La Follette, Jr. and the Decline of the Progressive Party in Wisconsin.* Madison: The State Historical Society of Wisconsin, 1964.

Lampard, Eric E. *The Rise of the Dairy Industry in Wisconsin: A Study in Agricultural Change, 1820-1920.* Madison: The State Historical Society of Wisconsin, 1963.

Leuchtenberg, William E. *The Perils of Prosperity, 1914-1932.* Chicago: University of Chicago Press, 1958.

Lovejoy, Allen F. *La Follette and the Establishment of the Direct Primary in Wisconsin, 1890-1904.* New Haven: Yale University Press, 1941.

Lubell, Samuel. *The Future of American Politics.* New York: Harper and Brothers, 1952.

Maine Mirrors, 1866-1976.

Marchetti, Louis. *History of Marathon County And Representative Citizens.* Chicago: Richmond-Arnold Co., 1913.

Marguiles, Herbert F. *The Decline of the Progressive Movement in Wisconsin.* Madison: The State Historical Society of Wisconsin, 1968.

Miner, Harold E., and Moore, Hugh T. *History of Wausau.* Wausau: Centennial Project, 1939.

Morlan, Robert L. *Political Prairie Fire: The Nonpartisan League, 1915-1922.* Minneapolis: University of Minnesota Press, 1955.

Mosinee Centennial, 1857-1957.

Nelson, Clifford. *German-American Political Behavior in Nebraska and Wisconsin, 1916-1920.* Lincoln: University of Nebraska Press, 1972.

Nesbit, Robert C. *Wisconsin: A History.* Madison: University of Wisconsin Press, 1973.

Olszyk, Edmund G. *The Polish Press In America.* Milwaukee: Marquette University Press, 1940.

One Hundred Years — Abbotsford, Wisconsin.

Rector, William G. *Log Transportation in the Lake States Lumber Industry.* Glendale: The Arthur H. Clark Company, 1953.

Rogin, Michael Paul. *The Intellectuals and McCarthy: The Radical Specter.* Cambridge: M.I.T. Press, 1967.

Schlueter, Clyde F. *The Wausau Story of Employers Insurance of Wausau.* New York: Newcomen Society in North America, 1974.

Stare, Fred A. *The Story of Wisconsin's Great Canning Industry.* Madison: The Wisconsin Canners Association, 1949.

Straub, A. G. *The History of Marathon, Wisconsin 1857 to 1957.* Marathon: *Marathon Times,* 1957.

Thelen, David. *The New Citizenship: Origins of Progressivism in Wisconsin, 1885-1900.* Columbia: University Missouri Press, 1972.

The Town of Texas, 1856-1976.

Wisconsin Valley Improvement Company. *The Wisconsin River — Namesake of a State.* Wausau: (privately published) n.d.

Zamzow, DuWayne, ed. *Berlin's Memories In 1976.*

B.   BIOGRAPHIES

Kearns, Doris. *Lyndon Johnson and the American Dream.* New York: Harper and Row, 1976.

Pinkerton, Katherine. *Bright With Silver.* New York: William Sloane Associates, 1953.

Thelen, David. *Robert M. La Follette and the Insurgent Spirit.* Boston: Little, Brown and Co., 1976.

Young, Donald, ed. *Adventures in Politics: the Memoirs Philip La Follette.* New York: Holt, Rinehart, and Winston, 1970.

C. ARTICLES

Alexander, J. H. "A Short Industrial History of Wisconsin," *The Wisconsin Blue Book,* 1929.

Asher, Robert. "The 1911 Workmen's Compensation Law: A Study in Conservative Labor Reform," *Wisconsin Magazine of History,* 57 (Winter, 1973-1974).

Delgado, Jeanne Hunnicutt, ed. "Nellie Kedzie Jones's Advice to Farm Women: Letters from Wisconsin, 1912-1916," *Wisconsin Magazine of History,* 57 (Autumn, 1973).

Dorner, Peter. "Farming Changes in Wisconsin, 1940-1960," *Wisconsin Agricultural Experiment Station Bulletin 561,* January, 1963.

Ebling, Walter H. "A Century of Agriculture in Wisconsin," *The Wisconsin Blue Book,* 1940.

Falk, Karen. "Public Opinion in Wisconsin During World War I," *Wisconsin Magazine of History,* 25 (June, 1942), pp. 389-407.

Fromm, Alma. "Sellin Sawmill Was Thriving Pioneer Enterprise," *Wausau Daily Record-Herald,* November 25, 1967.

Jacobs, Herbert. "The Wisconsin Milk Strikes," *Wisconsin Magazine of History,* 35 (Autumn, 1951), pp. 30-35.

Korman, Gerd. "Political Loyalties, Immigrant Traditions and Reform: The Wisconsin German-American Press and Progressivism, 1909-1912," *Wisconsin Magazine of History,* 41 (Spring, 1957), pp. 161-168.

Rector, William G. "From Woods to Sawmill, Transportation Problems in Logging," *Southern Lumberman,* July 15, 1949.

Shannon, David. "The World, the War, and Wisconsin, 1914-1918," *Historical Messenger,* 22 (March, 1966), pp. 43-56.

Special Wausau Number Wisconsin Magazine, 1952.

Twining, Charles E. "Plunder and Progress: The Lumber Industry In Perspective," *Wisconsin Magazine of History,* 47 (Winter, 1963-1964).

Weibull, Jorgen. "The Wisconsin Progressives, 1900-1914," *Mid-America,* 47 (July, 1965), pp. 191-221.

D. UNPUBLISHED STUDIES

"Ethnic Groups, Bohemians," written observations by Loddie Loskot. Marathon County Historical Society.

"History of Drott Manufacturing Corp." Marathon County Public Library.

"History of Hull Township." Marathon County Historical Society.

"History of Milan." In possession of Alfred Schmidt, Milan.

"History of the Town of Emmet." Marathon County Historical Society.

Marzynski, Dolores. "Cassel." Marathon County Historical Society.

Newhouse, John, et al. "History of Wausau." State Historical Society of Wisconsin.

Prahl, Ruth. "History of the Town of Wausau." Marathon County Historical Society.

"Rings In The Woods, A History of Township of Frankfort." Marathon County Historical Society.

Salsieder, Michael. *Employers Insurance—Meeting the Needs of the Policyholders,* Employers Insurance of Wausau.

Thayer, E. B. "A Tale Before The Daughters American Revolution, March 8, 1929." Manuscript in the Marathon County Historical Society, 1929.

Thayer, E. B. "Observations on the History of Marathon County." Manuscript in Marathon County Historical Society, 1939.

Thorpe, Elsie, comp. "History of the Township of Easton." Marathon County Historical Society.

E.   THESES, DISSERTATIONS, AND RESEARCH PAPERS

Backstrom, Charles H. "The Progressive Party in Wisconsin, 1934-1946," Ph.D. Dissertation, University of Wisconsin, 1956.

Bernhardt, David. "A Wausau Area Viewpoint: Early Depression Years, 1929-1932," Unpublished Research Paper, Department of History, University of Wisconsin Center - Marathon County, May, 1973. In possession of David Bernhardt, Wausau, Wisconsin.

Branch, Maurice L. "The Paper Industry In The Lake States, 1834-1947," Ph.D. Dissertation, University of Wisconsin, 1947.

Falk, Karen F. "War Propaganda in Wisconsin, 1917-1918," MA Thesis, University of Wisconsin, 1941.

Fries, Robert F. "A History of the Lumber Industry in Wisconsin," Ph.D. Dissertation, University of Wisconsin, 1939.

Frost, Reuel B. "The Geography of the Distribution of Sheep in Wisconsin," MA Thesis, University of Wisconsin, 1928.

Haney, Richard Carlton. "A History of the Democratic Party of Wisconsin Since World War II," Ph.D. Dissertation, University of Wisconsin, 1970.

Helgeson, Arlan C. "Athens, Wisconsin, A Study of the Economic Development of a Northern Village," MA Thesis, University of Wisconsin, 1948.

Hoeppner, Gail. "Senator Roland E. Kannenberg," Unpublished Research Paper, Library, University of Wisconsin - Eau Claire, July 11, 1972.

Karges, Steven Burton. "David Clark Everest and Marathon Paper Mills Company: A Study of a Wisconsin Entrepreneur — 1909-1931," Ph.D. Dissertation, University of Wisconsin, 1968.

Klueter, Howard R. "The End of the New Beginning: the Muskie Campaign in Wisconsin, with Special Emphasis on the Seventh Congressional District," Unpublished Research Paper, Department of Political Science, University of Wisconsin, 1972. In possession of author.

Lampard, Eric E. "The Rise of the Dairy Industry in Wisconsin: A Study of Agricultural Change in the Midwest, 1820-1920," Ph.D. Dissertation, University of Wisconsin, 1955.

Lucker, Jeffrey. "The Politics of Prohibition in Wisconsin, 1917-1933," MA Thesis, University of Wisconsin, 1968.

"Thomas Mesalk, Depression Interview," Department of. History, University of Wisconsin Center — Marathon County, December 1975. In possession of James Lorence.

Meyer, Karl Ernest. "The Politics of Loyalty, from La Follette to McCarthy in Wisconsin, 1918-1952," Ph.D. Dissertation, Princeton University, 1956.

Schmidt, Lester F. "The Farmer-Labor Progressive Federation: The Study of a 'United Front' Movement Among Wisconsin Liberals, 1934-1941," Ph.D. Dissertation, University of Wisconsin, 1954.

Seitz, Kerlin M. "Part-Time Farming In Northern Wisconsin," Ph.D. Dissertation, University of Wisconsin, 1954.

Slatin, Alfred. "Wisconsin Progressivism in Transition: A Study of Progressive Concepts, 1918-1930," MS Thesis, University of Wisconsin, 1952.

Smiley, William, III, "Voting Trends in Rural Marathon County," Research paper, Department of Political Science, University of Wisconsin — Marathon County, 1973. In possession of author.

Smith, James Bruce. "Lumbertowns in the Cutover: A Comparative Study of the Stage Hypothesis of Urban Growth," Ph.D. Dissertation, University of Wisconsin, 1973.

Sorauf, Francis Joseph, Jr. "The Voluntary Committee System in Wisconsin: An Effort to Achieve Party Responsibility," Ph.D. Dissertation, University of Wisconsin, 1953.

Stevens, John D. "Suppression of Dissent in Wisconsin During World War I," Ph.D. Dissertation, University of Wisconsin, 1967.

Voight, Wilbur Robert. "A Survey of Manufacturing in Wisconsin," MA Thesis, University of Wisconsin, 1938.

Weaver, Norman Frederic. "The Knights of the Ku Klux Klan in Wisconsin, Indiana, Ohio, and Illinois," Ph.D. Dissertation, University of Wisconsin, 1954.

Wyman, Roger Edwards. "Voting Behavior in the Progressive Era: Wisconsin as a Test Case," Ph.D. Dissertation, University of Wisconsin, 1970.

INDEX

414